how they matter to the practice of the church. She refuses both the dumbed-down casualness of domesticated faith and reductionist confessionalism that is easy and safe. Her book is a welcome witness for confident faith that has no interest in accommodation to the whims of the day. Her book will have a durable life in the company of the great thinkers of the church; it will also give courage in a time when the gospel is so urgently required and so easily distorted. Much thanks to her!"

—Walter Brueggemann, Columbia Seminary

"In this study of the triune God, Sonderegger speaks a word of hope to we who have lost a sense of wonder: God can be known, and this God is beautiful, holy, and righteous. We must step to the side, Sonderegger insists, and live no longer according to our own certainties or our own confusions. In developing her understanding of the Trinity, Sonderegger draws deeply from the 'Scriptures of Israel,' arguing that they have a 'double identity'—one for Jews and another for Christians. Sonderegger's 'strange' and unique approach may well be a game-changer for how Christian theologians work with Old Testament texts."

—Cynthia Rigby, Austin Theological Seminary

"This second volume of Sonderegger's *Systematic Theology* is a marvel. Refusing the soteriological tethers of much recent Trinitarian theology, Sonderegger continues to provide readers a profound schooling in both the piety of thought and the practice of unabashedly metaphysical theology. Her study invites us to contemplate the thrice holy God of Israel anew and aright from a place firmly rooted in the witness of Scripture. The result is a truly incomparable, creative, and contrarian contribution to contemporary Trinitarian theology."

—Philip G. Ziegler, Aberdeen University

"In the rather tired Trinitarian revival, it is rare to find a contribution that is truly fresh and that requires us to think again. Katherine Sonderegger is immersed in Scripture and tradition; she is a deeply learned, sympathetic, and illuminating commentator on classical and modern theology; and at the same time, she is a profoundly independent thinker. It is an extraordinary combination."

—Karen Kilby, Durham University

"Katherine Sonderegger continues to surprise us—and to compel us really to think. No ordinary back cover comment will do for such a stunning and rich rethinking of Trinitarian dogmatic profession. The mind staggers to keep up with her as she refuses the 'standard' paths while demonstrating her mastery of them and as she underscores that the Triune God is the most powerfully interesting reality while recognizing that few people seem interested in it. Does her Temple-shaped account of the richly processional unity of God, with its Relatio or Doubling, succeed in grounding a Trinity rather than a wondrously fertile Unity? This extraordinary book should awaken us all from our Trinitarian slumbers, especially those of us who thought we hadn't dozed off."

—Matthew Levering, Mundelein Seminary

"Katherine Sonderegger is one of the freshest and most distinctive voices in contemporary systematic theology, bringing together Scripture and Trinitarian dogmatics in unpredictable ways. She is learned, robust, lyrical, challenging. Her writing not only stimulates the mind, it also stirs the spirit and touches the heart."

—Walter Moberly, Durham University

"In this second volume of her systematic theology, Katherine Sonderegger continues her theological meditation on the one God whose transcendent aseity is ever mysteriously present to the creaturely world. This book boldly offers biblically grounded speculation on the inner life of God as Trinity and does so by refusing to follow the typically modern strategy of reducing the doctrine of the Trinity to soteriology. Instead, Sonderegger's faith-filled, canonical reading of Scripture offers readers a reflective path to the God whose Trinitarian life fully manifests the divine unity that she makes central to her theology. Sonderegger's proposal for rethinking traditional Trinitarian categories is remarkably creative and will shape theological discussion for many years to come."

—John Thiel, Fairfield University

"Katherine Sonderegger's hymn of praise to the Holy Trinity is an exhilarating read. It is poetic and provocative, controversial and gracious. Its forthright statements—and there are many—are surrounded by a delicate tracery of connections and acknowledgments. Sonderegger's path takes her deep into the Christian theological tradition, which she explores with unusual independence—but her journey is powered above all by a delighted, creative, and at times astonishing rereading of the Scriptures. This is a book that invites generous and extended engagement. There isn't a page that I don't want to argue about—but there isn't a page that I don't also want to reread and savor. It is a feast."

—Michael Higton, Durham University

Systematic Theology

Systematic Theology

Volume 2, The Doctrine of the Holy Trinity:
Processions and Persons

Katherine Sonderegger

Fortress Press
Minneapolis

SYSTEMATIC THEOLOGY

Volume 2, The Doctrine of the Holy Trinity: Processions and Persons

Cover image: Margaret Adams Parker, "Ignis Sanctus," Woodcut print, 2019 (margaretadamsparker.com)

Cover design: Joe Reinke

Library of Congress Cataloging-in-Publication Data

Print ISBN: 978-1-4514-8285-0

eBook ISBN: 978-1-5064-6418-3

Contents

Acknowledgments

Here the sublime, perfect Oneness of Almighty God turns toward home. This volume, the first of two on the Mystery of the Holy Trinity, takes up the surpassing Concreteness of the One God of Israel, the Trifold Unicity of the Holy God. Here I hope to make good on at least some of my promises, grandly laid out in volume 1: that Unicity would govern all other predicates and properties of God; that Trinity would be seen to be a form of monotheism; and that the Scriptures of Israel would not fall silent or cease to instruct when Christian doctrine turns toward home. As far as light has been given to me, I have attempted to fulfill these ambitious goals, but others will judge this far fairer than will I. That this will be an unusual dogma of Trinity will surprise no one, I suppose. My hope is that it might spark fresh conversation in the church and beyond about Israel's temple cultus, its sacrificial rites and liturgies, and the place of them all in Christian reflection on the Triune Mystery who is God. Much has been said of late about the centrality of the whole canon of Scripture to Christian theology; now is the time to test our mettle.

Many hands have made light work. I read sections of this manuscript in draft form to audiences in Bristol, Durham, Cambridge, and Edinburgh in the UK (at least for now!); at the

New Haven Theological Discussion Group; and in Heidelberg, Germany, and I am deeply grateful for the attention, careful questioning, and continued conversations I have had with faculty, graduate students, and clergy since those papers were read, several years ago now. I owe a special debt to two groups of readers who read and carefully commented on the whole: John Thiel, in Connecticut, and on the far coast, Matt Jenson, Ryan Peterson, Fred Sanders, and Adam Johnson. They could not endorse the whole, of course, but they did save me from major calamities in order, sources, argument, and doctrine. My editor at Fortress Press, Ryan Hemmer, has proved himself a formidable theologian in his own right and a constant source of instruction on current schools of Thomism and on the conceptual architecture of Bernard Lonergan. No theologian can work for a moment without friends, colleagues, and critics like these; they are a providential gift from the Good God. Caleb Hendrickson, a doctoral student at the University of Virginia, was an invaluable ally, discussing fine points of the manuscript, supplying citations where I left only the most obscure squib in draft, and preparing the long draft files for their new home at Fortress. My own seminary, Virginia Theological Seminary, has supported my work in every way: by sabbatical leaves, by collegial exchange and conversation, and by daily worship with faculty and students, the real wellspring of any dogmatic work.

I also have dearest memories of conversations overlooking Lake Champlain with dear friend Karen King, who shared my excitement for this project, for St. Bonaventure, and who gave me rich insights into the mysterious "relation of identity" that is doubling. Every scholar should have an intellectual companion of such integrity, spiritual passion, and conceptual clarity as Karen; I am blessed. I also have the rare good fortune of sharing what we call "the late work" with my dear friend Peggy Parker, who executed the woodcuts for the covers of this *Systematic Theology* and whose own achievements in printmaking and sculpture, all in service of the church, fill me with wonder and an utterly undeserved reflected glory.

But the last word must go to my dear friend the philosopher Lynne Rudder Baker, whom the world lost at the end of 2017. I was privileged to call her friend since our teaching days at Middlebury College, some thirty years ago now, and at every step of my long way, she encouraged, she taught, she relished and enjoyed, and she prodded and demanded my best thought. Our "theological-philosophical walks," as we called them, taken each day we visited each other, were a school of mind and soul and opened a door into the luminous realm where the intellect enacts what it was created to be. Lynne lived to see this first volume, and I grieve she can see this second only from Another Shore and in a Greater Light. I dedicate this volume to her—to her shining memory.

Katherine Sonderegger
Feast of St. Joseph, 2020

Introduction

This is a book on the inner Life of God. As such, it is a strange book, a disorienting one, and, some would say, an impossible one. I want to pause a moment on this little word, *impossible*. It is a strong word, even a daring one, but a term that has been used with full seriousness by Christian theologians in many seasons of the church's life, but especially now, in the modern era. In ancient times, it was held to be a special mark of piety to acknowledge the transcendent Mystery who is God and to confess our proper ignorance of this Unique, Eternal Being. Dionysius the Areopagite has been widely recognized as the epitome, perhaps the source, of this tradition of "apophatic" or "negative theology" in the patristic era. Of course, one thinks of the pagan parallels and influences here as well: Plotinus and varying schools of Platonism. Students of ancient Christian texts will advert to the lovely evocation of "dogmatic unknowing" in the *Orations* of St. Gregory Nazianzus or the desire-filled longing of St. Augustine for the Beloved Mystery, at once "so Ancient and so New." But even so sturdy a traveler in the speculative domains as St. Thomas can speak of Christian theology as an intellectual relation as if to One unknown. In every season of the church's life, some theologians and many spiritual adepts have sounded the note of reserve, even nescience, before the transcendent, inner Life of

God. Indeed, it has been taken as a kind of dogmatic axiom that Almighty God, as Immense, Eternal, Holy, and Infinite, cannot be comprehended by the particular, bounded, and sin-bound creature.

Yet it is the modern era that has made the impossibility of creaturely knowledge of the inner Life of God nearly canonical. Of course, one reverts immediately to Immanuel Kant, the giant of modern Protestant dogmatics, as if "adverting to the best explanation." True it is that Kant aimed to awaken us all from our dogmatic slumbers and to cauterize that longing, fatal and false, to penetrate phenomena to the "things in themselves," most especially the Divine Being. Kant taught a generation of Protestant and Catholic academic theologians to repudiate a direct knowledge of God in Himself and to seek God rather in His Self-Disclosure, in the economy of salvation, recorded in Holy Scripture. These are epistemic worries, principally, with metaphysical correlates in train. But Kantianism is not the engine of metaphysical reserve, not by a good measure.

The greater resistance to any direct attempts to investigate the inner Life of God has come from those movements in theology, usually but not always Protestant, that have styled themselves "antispeculative," "antimetaphysical," or, more positively, "biblical." The great name of Karl Barth must be mentioned here, but in truth, most descendants of the magisterial Reformers can be counted in this school. The aim here is to focus intently and exclusively on the events and teachings of Holy Scripture in such a way that all alien elements, especially those thought to be "philosophical" or, in the modern idiom, "Hellenistic," are to be shunned and denied as aides to a proper doctrine of God. *Revelation* rather than *speculation*; *biblical* rather than *rationalistic*; *faith* rather than *reason*; *narrative* over against *system*: these are the watchwords of modern, post-Kantian dogmatics.

The doctrine of Trinity that emerges from such severe compression is a Triune Lord set forth and anchored solely to the "economy," the biblical account of our salvation, achieved in Jesus Christ. We know God in His Economy, it is often said, or not at all. Indeed, some have advanced the claim that God can be known only *as* Trinity. *Bare monotheism* is taken to be a shame phrase. All this makes a book on the inner Life of God, the "Immanent Trinity," to be odd, impossible, and dogmatically unlicensed.

This is not the whole story, of course. The renewed interest in the doctrine of Trinity in the West, after the rationalizing shocks of the eighteenth century, has come to be known as the "Trinitarian revival" and closely associated with the work of Karl Barth and Karl Rahner. In them, an axiom has come to the fore that carries profound strictures for Trinitarian construction: "The 'economic' Trinity is the 'immanent' Trinity, and the 'immanent' Trinity is the 'economic' Trinity" in Rahner's lapidary phrase.[1] These theologians and their descendants do not shun altogether the inner Life of God or simply refuse to discuss—"speculate"—about it. Rather, Barth and Rahner *identify* the Immanent Trinity with the economic so that the God encountered in Holy Writ just *is* the Eternal, Holy, and Living God. The Triune Lord is the God of our salvation. Now Barth and Rahner are not the same kind of theologian, and I do not wish to suggest that their Trinitarian doctrines are grounded or governed by the same sort of biblical and dogmatic aims. Each deserves his due in the history of this doctrine. But the commonality is telling: the Royal Road into the inner Life of God, they say, in through the life and Passion of Jesus Christ, the God with us.

Immanence in God will bear a Christoform face: those who behold Christ will have beheld the Father. In just these ways, Trinity becomes a type of *Christology*. In Rahner's words: Trinity is soteriology, the event of our saving encounter with God. With the furniture arranged such, it is a small, perhaps natural step to consider "obedience," exemplified perfectly by the Incarnate Son, to be ingredient in the Eternal Persons, the Father eternally commanding, the Son, in all Eternity, freely obeying. This is an Immanent Trinity commandeered by Christology and conformed to it. Knowledge of the True God, Barth would solemnly warn, is impossible without it.[2]

Trinity as a subaltern of Christology has neatly mirrored the current historiography of the development of Nicene orthodoxy. In this school of opinion, the problematic that issued in Trinity emerged from the early worship of Christ "as of a God." In some way, to be forged in the molten ore of polemic and exile, the adoration of the Savior was to be reconciled with the One God of Israel. The early debates turned on the Eternity and Equality of the Divine Son: Arianism became the primal heresy of the early Christian confession of the Son of God. The history of the developing Nicene position, and its confused cries of alarm about Arianism, is wonderfully complex. I do not pretend to do it justice here. Rather, my aim here is to note the intimate ties between Christology and Trinity in the ante-Nicene era, and the ordo cognoscendi it implies. Together they suggest that Trinity is, first and principally, a dogma of the *Divine Persons*.[3]

As with the little word *impossible*, so we might pause here a moment to consider this term *persons* and this concentration on the Triune Persons as the centerpiece of the Trinitarian Mystery. For many Christians, as for many skeptics, the dogma of the Trinity just *is* a doctrine about three Divine Persons, Each of whom and All of whom is God. The Mystery of the entire doctrine of God is taken to be the confession that the One God is comprised or comprehends or depends on three Eternal and Co-Equal Persons, in Nicene idiom and name: Father, Son, and Holy Spirit. To be sure, many distinctions and refinements entered in: the Relations among these Persons; the Identity of Properties of these Persons; the form of Unity and Distinction They possess; and the Relation between these Persons and the Divine Nature, a relation of order (*taxis*) and of Procession, Generation, and Spiration. The matter of the taxis among the Persons became church dividing—or was taken to be so—such that the Latin Church's confession that the Holy Spirit proceeded from the Father *and the Son* (in Latin, *filioque*) was repudiated by the Greek Church as contrary to the Nicene Symbol and its ecumenical authority. All these are sophisticated theologoumena of Trinitarian doctrine and cannot be dismissed from any proper ecclesial systematics. As I intend this work to be a theology of and for the church, the Divine Persons, and Their complex and beautiful Relations, One with Another, and One in Another, will receive Their due here, too.

But They will receive it in Their proper order and place. The doctrine of the Holy Trinity, I say, is not a teaching, first and principally, about three Eternal Persons. Despite the Gospel and Pauline attestation to the Triad of Persons—Father, Son, and Spirit—the Mystery of the Triune God, I argue, is not properly denoted by the phrase "three Persons in One Nature" or in its Greek antecedents, three Hypostases and one Ousia. Trinity is not at its fundament a Mystery about Persons. Nor is it basically and at ground a form of Christology. The Trinity, in its full and primal form, does not conform to the history of its articulation and definition; Trinity, as metaphysical Truth, does not mirror the rise and polemic of the early church. It is not a subspecies of anything else: Christology, soteriology, liturgy, or late antiquity. Trinity is the Mystery of the Holy God; as such it is properly basic and rests on nothing else and belongs to no other school. It simply is the *Holy Life* of the One God, the Movement and Perfection of the

Good God. Not Persons but rather *Processions* are the foundation of the dogma of Trinity.

Trinity, I say, is ethical monotheism, the Holy Self-Offering and Self-Sanctification of Almighty God. To explore and confess the Holy Trinity is to stand before the Thrice Holy God, to adore His Sacrifice which is His own Fiery Nature and Life, to intellectually contemplate the Procession of Wisdom and Goodness that just is the Eternal and Consummate Existence and Return of the Living God. The dogma of the Holy Trinity unfolds, on bended knee, the permanent Mystery of the inner Life of God.

So, it seems that we must undertake the impossible here: to set forth the "Immanent Trinity" as the inner Life of God. This entire book, more properly, should be described as a doctrine of the Holy Processions, concluding in the Persons. The scholastic distinction between Processions and Missions, that is, should be preferred over the modernist nomenclature of Immanent and economic Trinity.[4] The life of God, it seems to me, has not been given its proper attention in the dogma of Trinity; few have followed St. Bonaventure in his profound meditations on the Fecundity of the Living Nature of God. Yet we may say with some confidence that Holy Scripture testifies, time and again, to Almighty God as *Living*—Dynamic, Generative, Glorious, Holy. This God sets Himself apart from all that is dead, inert, hollow, or merely formal. He is the God of the living, not the dead; He is Source, Light and Life, and Consuming Fire. To the primal generations in Israel, to Moses and all prophets, to His enemies and scoffers, to His Incarnate Son and all apostles, the Lord manifests Himself as Active: speaking, moving, harkening, and defending; riding the wings of the wind; tearing the clouds; and coming down. The celebrated bargaining exchanges with Abraham and Moses testify to this same inner Dynamism. In the vivid idiom of Holy Writ, this is the affirmation of the Holy God as Living and Fecund. (This distinction, quietly endorsed, between subject matter and genre or idiom, will preoccupy us in our reflections on Holy Scripture.) Above all, Holy Scripture exhibits the Lord God as *Holy*, the One who originates, maintains, and renews the altar sacrifice of Israel, demonstrating His own Holy Life, its own inner Movement and Goal, sanctifying Himself even as He demands and gives Holiness to Israel. Just this holy sacrifice is consummated in the Perfect Self-Offering that is the Passion of the Incarnate Son and His ascending in the Spirit of Exaltation to the Highest Heaven. And just this is the table sacrifice of the Christian altar, the Divine Life broken and given for the Life of the world, the Bread from Heaven. Both Testaments are joined in their rich testimony to God as Living and as Holy—and this is a confession of the Processional Life of God. It is the Fecund Source of Trinity.

Christians capture this testimony to the Holy Life of God in the doctrine of the Divine Processions. Nicene tradition speaks of two: Generation and Spiration, or Donation, as it speaks, from Them, of two Persons, Son and Holy Spirit, proceeding from the personal Source of the Father. (This account of the Trinity will also follow the Augustinian, Latin position in affirming that the Spirit also proceeds from the Son: the church-dividing "filioque clause" of the Nicene Creed.) Significant to the entire confession of these Processions is that they are also *One*, One Life, One Holiness, One God. The Movements of Holiness, a generative descent and a donative ascent, are profoundly at One—a Unity in Distinction I shall call a "doubled Unity." Following the lead of Bonaventure and the wonderfully generative insights of the present-day Thomist Gilles Emery, I will develop this mystical Unity of the Divine Processions as a form of "redoublement," a category of the Relation of Identity. The two Processions of Holiness are not "count nouns." They are not two "Things" or "Substances" or "Individuals" any more than they are "parts" in the One, Unique, Spiritual God. Rather, the Fiery Glory of God lives as a "doubled Unity," the Heat and Light, the Wisdom and Benevolence, the *Ratio et Bonum* that is the Dynamic Holiness who is God.

Now, readers of Trinitarian theology will note how the terms I have just used for the Processions will echo the ecclesial synonyms used for the Persons, especially Wisdom and Goodness or Gift. That usage is designed to show the intimate relation between the Processional Life of God and the Triune Persons. The modern worry over the technical term *person*, its history and etymology, seems to me outsized in proportion to the proper place of the Hypostases in the Mystery of the Trinity altogether.[5] My aim, at any rate, is to re-moor the concept of *person* to that of *processions*, such that the Persons can be seen as the Holy Life of God, taken as a whole. Indeed, I believe that the patristic debate, ante- and post-Nicene, can be seen as an extended reflection on the Dynamism, Emanation, and Generation of the One God. Certainly, the stature of the Person of the Son is central! But it does not seem to me that the documents support the notion that the Nicene position was sparked and governed principally by the concepts *hypostasis* and *ousia*. Indeed, the casual mention of these terms as synonyms in the Nicene Symbol lends confidence to this view. Better, it seems to me, is to say that the Divine Life-Acts of creating and proceeding, setting forth, are the framework in which the equality or subordination of the Logos is forged. In my view, Arianism posed such a lively and long-lived threat to Nicene Trinitarianism (is it really overcome?) just because it joined the Act of Creation—the emanation of all things from God—with Generation, the coming forth of the Son and Word from the High God. To find the proper expression of God's fecundity, within Himself, and ad extra, toward the world, was the work of the fourth century, and I believe, guides a present-day Trinitarian monotheism of Processional Life, consummated in the Persons.

Of course, as Living, God is Personal! There is no random, dispersed, or mechanical movement in God; rather All is Agential, Intelligible, Intelligent. But the Triune Persons will express and praise the Living God in His Perfection, His Infinite Entirety, as Primal Origin, as Rational, as God. It is the whole God we name in this way, and as the Processions indwell One Another, so the Persons mutually entail and include One Another—in Each and All, One Holiness, One Perfect Peace. (As a rational aid, we will suggest some parallels here to modern set theory, especially that of Georg Cantor's Transfinite Sets.) Together, this Dynamic Unity of Nature, Fiery Procession, and Consummate Persons just is Trinity, the Eternal Structure of the Living God.

Along the way of setting out this scriptural vision of the Holy Trinity, I have mentioned some secular parallels to the Mystery. These I take to be *vestigia Trinitatis*, traces of Trinity in the world the Lord God has made. I affirm and develop this Augustinian theme, borrowing in part from Ludwig Wittgenstein's later notions of "seeing as" and, more enigmatically, as the "dawning of an aspect." These traces of the Holy God can be seen in ancient and modern attempts to consider Being as such, attempts I have labeled a "problem in the neighborhood." I have taken these incursions into a modified apologetics as an endeavor, out of the rationality of the faith, to underscore the intellectual dignity and legitimacy of the dogma—a legitimacy I see as sorely tried in the modern era. The heightened preoccupation with revelation as shield to the dogma of Trinity has led this doctrine, as I see it, into narrow ecclesial confines that have not served it well. A greater confidence in the cultural plausibility and intelligibility of the doctrine of the Trinity could be better demonstrated, I say, in small-scale analogies of the conceptual structures of the dogma in the intellectual preoccupations of our day. Metaphysical and epistemic realism is the nearest ally, I say, to Trinity.

Now, all this talk about the inner workings, structure, and intelligibility of the doctrine of Trinity must give many readers pause. Where does this theologian get all this? Can she in truth pry the inner Life of God from the economy as she claims? Has some door into the Third Heaven opened up for her? Or, on the other hand, has this dogma become so rationalized, even explained, and conceptually ordered that the Holy Mystery of the Trinity has been explained away and faith critiqued to make room for reason? Just how, some readers may ask, have we preserved a dogma ex fide? How have we honored its proper stature as Supernatural Mystery? Indeed, if any teaching of the faith deserves the title *supernatural*—if the term can be so used—Trinity surely is chief. Yet here, speculative metaphysics seems released to run free, unconstrained, it seems, from the tethers of the economy. How is this not a crude univocity of concept and of Being in the most sacred preserve of Christian dogmatics? These are central questions in the dogma of Trinity, and touch on the scope, the authority, and the internal coherence of the doctrine.

In these pages I attempt to address each in turn, defending Trinitarian teaching as scriptural; its confession as a matter of grace and of faith; its content, profoundly luminous; its pursuit, the consummate Christian joy. But above all, I seek to conform my answers to what I take to be a central deliverance of the medieval, Latin Church, the Canons of Lateran IV. There, in the midst of a welter of other teachings, condemnations, rules, and definitions, Lateran IV makes a determination on technical matters of Divine Unicity and the Processions, ignited by the fiery abbot Joachim of Fiore against the rising star Peter Lombard. The scholastic distinctions on exhibit there will be relied on to guide Trinitarian Unity in Distinction and to assess some modern proposals in what has come to be called "social Trinitarianism." More generative still is the famous recalibration of the doctrine of analogy as a likeness between God and creature that is governed by an Ever-Greater Unlikeness. Just this Movement, from likeness to unlikeness, is I believe the scholastic expression of Divine Holiness, the Lordly Act of setting Himself apart. This is the Eternal *Mystery* of God, and It is the Life and Work of the Divine Processional Holiness, descending in any creaturely image to encircle, elevate, and exalt such image and symbol up into the inner Reserves of Light, the Mystery whom no creature approaches and is guarded, maintained, and hallowed by the Living God Himself. In this sense, this book, too, acknowledges the impossibility of a grasp of the inner Life of God by frail creature and ever frailer theology. Trinity is the Self-Sanctified Preserve and Mystery who is God.

This, I believe, Holy Scripture teaches about the Holy Trinity. In this book far less is said about the New Testament, the Gospels and Epistles, than is commonly encountered in Trinitarian theology. Set pieces—such as the baptism of our Lord in the Jordan River or the Baptismal Name, given in the Great Commission at the close of Matthew's Gospel; the great Supper Discourses in John; the *Carmen Christi* in Philippians; or the profound reflection on the deep things of God in Romans 8—are mentioned in passing or not at all. This, I may say, is another reason why readers may find this book disorienting and strange (I promise patient readers that they will find all these New Testament texts and more in the next volume, which will concentrate all its powers, as granted me, on the Divine Economy—on Christology and Pneumatology). In their stead, I offer extended theological exegesis of Isaiah 53, a patristic Megiddo over the Generation of the Son, and of Leviticus, focusing on the sacrificial cultus and the ordinances and narratives surrounding that Divine Act. These texts bear the imprint of the Holiness School and I believe they ground, teach, and guide the doctrine of the Divine Processions, and, under their own idiom, of the Divine Persons. Trinity, I say, is a deliverance of the Old Testament.

Now, in one sense, there is nothing especially new in all this. The Christian act of reading the Old Testament "Christologically"— seeing, that is the presence of the Divine Son in the teachings, doings, and figures of ancient Israel, either in foreshadowing or in manifestation (a "theophany")—is one of the oldest forms of Christian canonical exegesis. This reading in *figura* and prophecy made the Christian Bible one book in two testaments, and broke open a new form of realism, so memorably described by Erich Auerbach in his wonderful wartime book, *Mimesis*.[6] Preserving the canon of Scripture against the dismembering born of anti-Judaism, early and late, and more tragically, of a form of philo-Judaism, ingredient in our pluralistic spirit, is of principal importance for Christian theology. To this end I believe it vital to return the Old Testament to its traditional seat as *magistra* in matters of Christian doctrine. The confidence shown by our ancestors in the faith in their wide-ranging, speculative, and dogmatic exegeses of the First Testament is the lodestar and ideal. Just this expresses the proper confidence in the God of Israel as the Almighty Lord Christians may also, by grace and pardon, bow down and worship; it demonstrates the confession that the church is built on the Law and the Prophets: Jesus Christ, born of a woman, born under the Law, the Pioneer, Head, and Defender of this assembly. For such a church, the Old Testament cannot simply serve as *preparatio* or shadow of truths to be revealed and made perfect in the New. No, something stronger must arise. Like Augustine, like almost any premodern Christian exegete, theologians must seek instruction from Israel's Scripture for the principal truths of doctrine; high truths and mysteries. As Augustine's *De Trinitate* boldly demonstrates, the Old Testament itself can guide and ground the doctrine of the Divine Processions and the full equality of the Persons. This doctrine of the Immanent Trinity is an attempt, as I am given it, to live out this creed.

But we do not live in Augustine's world, but in our own blood-soaked era, the geography established and defiled by the "war against the Jews," in Lucy Dawidowicz's haunting phrase.[7] In such a world, the Christian use of the Old Testament can never be innocent or "once-born." It is not that Christians could never propose a distinctive *interpretation* or *lens* through which these ancient texts could be read: of course, in our pluralistic academy, such polyvocal and polyvalent readings are expected, often courted. But this theology is proposing something stronger, something more boldly realist, in its reliance on the Old Testament. It is rather muscular to claim that subject matter can be separated from genre; more incursive still is to say that the Old Testament *itself*, in its own idiom, teaches the Triune Processions and Persons of the One Holy God. I would hazard that no people or culture wishes to see its own literature appropriated or "colonized" by another, especially by a people hostile and imperial to those it rules. In the old Christendom, Jews had their sacred scriptures appropriated—expropriated—by Christian prelates, theological masters, exegetes, and missionaries from the time of Justin Martyr to Ernst Troeltsch. They, of all peoples in Christian lands, have reason to assert their title and ownership over these holy texts. And I, too, want to recognize that right!

In this volume, my aim is to develop, and expand at some length, the view that the doctrine of the Trinity should be conceived as a form of the qua relation in which one reality is, and is seen to be, *as* another, all the while remaining the same. A woman, *as* a wife, does not become a third reality or thing; she remains whole and entire, a female human being. Yet the categories, properties, idioms, and perhaps causal powers vary, each to each; they are distinct yet one. Now such qua relations have a tangled history all their own in Trinitarian dogma: Sabellian modalism may be seen as a species of "as relation," or in more modern parlance, a dogmatic example of relative identity. But my aim in evoking this philosophical notion is not to locate Trinity within any of its Christian confrères, but rather to offer it as a vade mecum for proper Christian instruction in the riches of Israel's Scriptures. In a more theological idiom, I would say that the Scriptures of Israel *as* the Old Testament is an instance, the prime literary instance, of *redoublement*, a doubled identity. The Holiness School teaches us about the Glory of the Holy God, its Fiery *Dunamis* that resides in Cloudy Reserve and explodes from its own Sanctum to burn, cleanse, consume, and hallow. It is Most Holy. In its Doubled Form, this Majestic and Living Fire is the Processional Life of God, the Giver and the Gift, the Spirit of Holiness ascending into the Heights. The *Names* of these Processions and the Persons who are Their Entirety are given in the New Testament and the church councils that gave a rule for their interpretation. But the Divine *Structure*, if I may style it so, the concrete Living Movement who is God, is taught, in sacrificial idiom, in the Law and the Prophets, and forms the fundament, as it were, some brilliant sapphire, stretched out as the very length and breadth of the Holy Trinity. Christians and Jews *share* this confession of the Living God, I dare to say, and express in our worship, our varying doctrines and practices, our mystical literature and hymns, the wonder that Holy Fire should touch our earth and that still we should live. The idioms and resonances, the florilegia of doctrine, dogma and statute, the Mysteries of God in their bold or more apophatic voice—all these belong to church or synagogue, and they retain their distinctions.

Doubled Unity does not erase difference or even set aside Franz Rosenzweig's "fraternal enmity" between Christians and Jews.[8] But it does mean that the Old Testament teaches a "Processional Trinity," the Movement and Structure of the Living God, and this is the Thrice Holy God of prophets and of apostles. I do not believe such a confession to teach doctrinal supersessionism or scriptural colonization; this book is written in this hope and trust. But it is a doctrine of the Holy Trinity written by a gentile called in the One Lord's service, a sinner in need of Christ's own redeeming, and engrafted into the Living Root who is Israel, the Beloved. The book is a grateful confession of this Triune Lord, whose Name is Holy and is One as Father, Son, and Holy Spirit, whose ways are Truth and Righteousness, and whose Path, in all Eternity, is Peace.

Such are the contours of an unfamiliar, perhaps odd book on the Holy Trinity. I invite you into the Land of Unlikeness.

"I am the Alpha and the Omega, says the Lord God, who is and who was and who is to come, the Almighty." (Rev 1:8)

"Fear not, I am the First and the Last, the Living One." (Rev 1:17)

Notes

1. Karl Rahner, *The Trinity*, trans. Joseph Donceel (New York: Herder and Herder, 1970), 22.

2. Karl Barth, *Church Dogmatics*, IV.1, The Doctrine of Reconciliation, ed. G. W. Bromiley and T. F. Torrence (Edinburgh: T & T Clark, 1956), §59.

3. Aloys Grillmeier, *Christ in Christian Tradition: From the Apostolic Age to Chalcedon* (London: Westminster John Knox Press, 1965); R. P. C. Hanson, *The Search for the Christian Doctrine of God : The Arian Controversy 318–381* (Edinburgh: T & T Clark, 1988); Peter Brown, *The Rise of Western Christendom: Triumph and Diversity, A.D. 200–100* (Oxford: Blackwell, 1996); Lewis Ayres, *Nicaea and Its Legacy: An Approach to Fourth-Century Trinitarian Theology* (Oxford: Oxford University Press, 2004); Khaled

Anatolios, *Retrieving Nicaea: The Development and Meaning of Trinitarian Doctrine* (Grand Rapids: Baker, 2011); Robert Louis Wilken, *The First Thousand Years: A Global History of Christianity* (New Haven: Yale University Press, 2012).

4. Fred Sanders, *The Triune God* (Grand Rapids: Zondervan, 2016); Ralf Stolina, "Ökonomische und immanente Trinität? Zur Problematik einer trinitätstheologischen Denkfigur," *Zeitschrift für Theologie und Kirche* 105 (2008): 170–94.

5. See Rahner's proposals regarding persons in *Trinity*, 43–44, 68–73. Barth opts for "ways of being" (*Seinsweisen*) over "persons" in *Church Dogmatics*, I.1.

6. Erich Auerbach, *Mimesis: The Representation of Reality in Western Literature*, trans. Willard R. Trask (Princeton, NJ: Princeton University Press, 1953).

7. Lucy S. Dawidowicz, *The War against the Jews, 1933–1945* (New York: Holt, Rinehart and Winston, 1975).

8. Franz Rosenzweig, *The Star of Redemption*, trans. William Hallo (New York: Holt, Rinehart and Winston, 1971), 415.

§ 1. Holiness as Triune Mystery

"The Lord is in His Holy Temple; let all the earth keep silence before Him!" (Hab 2:20)

The pilgrimage to the Mystery of the Holy Trinity begins in the temple. There we encounter the One Lord, present to His sanctuary as can be no idol, plated be they in silver or gold. This is the True Lord, the Sovereign of heaven and earth, the Living One who spoke in fire and glory, from the thorn bush, from the mountaintop, from the cloud above the altar and people on the march, from a river near the wilderness, and from a hillside where disciples trembled from the Glory covering them all. This is the Lord God of Israel who is the Triune Lord; He is present in His Holy Temple. He is against all idols, all that is dead, inert, powerless, and profane. He alone is Hidden, He alone Present as the Unseen. He marks Himself off from all that is manufactured and made. He alone is not set apart; He sets Himself apart, sanctifies Himself, declares and defines and guards zealously His Holiness. His Holiness is Mystery, Incommunicate, Utter Reserve; He is Unlike, without contrast or comparison. Yet in just these ways, He is Present. In just this way, in just this mode, He is Trinity.

To encounter this holy place where the Glory of the Lord dwells is to be undone, made anew. In the temple, filled with smoke and with glory, the priest and the prophet Isaiah can only cry out in awe: "Woe is me!" It is not first the creature's undoing and then the Holy Presence, but first the Holiness and then the terror of sin exposed and owned, seared, and burned away. Just so the Deity of the One Lord, Jesus Christ, fills the disciples with awe as the roaring waves fall into stillness, and Peter, the fish spilling out of the nets and breaking them into pieces, breaks apart in fear and confession: "Depart from me for I am a sinner." Holiness is *contagion*, overspilling the holy precincts, the furniture, the vestments, the altar; It annihilates, reduces to ash. The Most Holy cannot be seen. He is the High and Lofty One, dwelling with the lowly, and the Humble One, dwelling invisible in His own creation. Holiness is hidden between the wings of gold, elevated high beyond the savory and sweet offerings, rising in smoky incense and fire. Holiness is Power, *Dunamis*; It is Mystery. It is the Spirit of Holiness, the Fire and Glory that illumines every dark corner; convicts, renews, lifts up the Son of Man and reveals the vision; lifts up the people from the parched places and the grave; and raises up the Final Son of Man and makes life the end of all things. The Spirit of Holiness drives newfound preachers from village to village, making witnesses of these Holy Things, freeing and giving stout hearts, until the whole earth is filled with the knowledge of the Lord as the waters cover the sea.

The Presence of the Holy One discloses sin and blessing, but even more, the searing Fire of Holiness teaches the silence in which every mouth is stopped. Holy Wisdom bestows the fear of the Lord that stills any presumption, any rash speech. Silence, we might say, is the music of the temple. The free will offerings, the cereal and sin and well-being offerings, the whole pungent and blood-soaked work of sacrifice are made in silence; the inner courtyard is bathed in blood and in silence. The Lord's Presence, His smoke-filled Glory, consumes any voice but the heavenly beings who can but cry, "Holy!" The whole earth is reduced to silence when the Lord descends to His temple. It is the very first praise and reverence of creatures before their God; the wordless worship of the greater and lesser lights, the stars in their courses; the silence, rest, and blessing of Sabbath; the silence of the prophets before the One who calls; the silence Aaron must keep when fire burns away rebellion; the silence that envelops the boy Samuel in the haunted darkness of the temple; the sheer silence of the Lord as He passes by; the stillness in heaven after the Lamb, alone the Worthy One, breaks open the seventh seal and the mighty choruses and tumult are stopped; and at the end, when all have drawn their last breath, the primal silence that breaks out for seven days, the holy consummation and peace, the final Sabbath, the Serene Glory that stood at the beginning of all things. The whole earth, the whole human race, the whole creaturely realm—not just the chosen people—keep this silence. But to Israel is given this prophecy and gift, to them the temple, the sacrifice, the presence, the holy law, and they endure forever. And always the holy blessing is more. Israel is the light to the nations; it is representative, universal existence. The Divine Light overspreads, succeeds, presses down, and spills over so that the whole earth falls into the Silence who is the Holy God. Silence is the Presence and the sign of Presence of the Holy Triunity, the Majesty of the One God.

Holiness is Trinity. That is the central claim of Christian Triune monotheism. We do not seek first and principally the Triune Names—Father, Son, Spirit—when we speak of Trinity. We do not begin with the Divine Persons. Nor do we focus entirely on the Processions, the generative and self-giving Life of the One God, when we begin the encounter with the Triune Lord. Rather, we begin with Holiness. We stand before the Holy One, in life and in intellect: Holiness commands all. These terms of art in the dogma of Trinity—*hypostasis* and *ousia*; *begetting* and *procession*; *relation* and *origin*—these must be encountered in the Mystery of Holiness or not at all. Trinity is, without a doubt, a full-fledged metaphysical doctrine. It comprises an army of argument, of speculative reason, and of delicate, complex teaching. It is *not* simple, and I do not believe we make proper progress in the dogma by hoping or promising that it is so. But I believe there is *one* element of simplicity in Trinity, and that is its divine foundation in the One Lord's Holiness.

The dangerous Christian philosopher G. W. F. Hegel shows us just how Holiness can serve as the principle metaphysical Divine Mode. In the celebrated preface to *Phenomenology of Spirit*, Hegel argues that the Absolute Idea or Spirit must be "self-generating," not constructed from without or elaborated through relations Hegel called "external"—those that were brought to a freestanding object by another power, adding and connecting the object to others. No, the proper relations of Spirit must be "internal," essential, not received but rather moved and generated from within. Though we will not take the time now to comment and identify Hegel's baroque vocabulary, it is worth tasting his remarkable fare directly:

> The living Substance is being which is in truth Subject, or, what is the same, is in truth actual only in so far as it is the movement of positing itself, or is the mediation of its self-othering with itself. . . . Only this self-restoring sameness, or this reflection in otherness within itself—not an original or immediate unity as such,—is the True. It is the process of its own becoming, the circle that presupposes its end as its goal, having its end also as its beginning; and only by being worked out to its end, it is actual.[1]

Hegel did not rest content with his early experiments in the conceptual, self-moving Idea, but developed them historically, religiously, and doctrinally in a late series of lectures now published as *Lectures on the Philosophy of Religion.* In the last section, fittingly titled "The Consummate Religion," Hegel directs his earlier conceptual work toward the doctrinal but once again underscores the internal, self-generating force of the Idea itself:

> If we assign predicates to God in such a way as to make them particular, then we are immediately at pains to resolve their contraction. This is an external action, a product of our reflection, and the fact that it is external and falls to us, and is not the content of the divine idea, implies that the contradictions cannot in fact be posited by it. Its proper content, its determination, is to posit this distinction and then absolutely to sublate it; this is the vitality of the idea itself. . . . Specifically, the eternal idea is expressed in terms of the holy Trinity: it is God himself, eternally triune. Spirit is this process, movement, life. This life is self-differentiation, self-determination, and the first differentiation is that spirit is as this universal idea itself.[2]

Now we will have more leisure to inspect this fertile notion of Divine Life when we consider the Divine Processions in full, but here we may say that Hegel captures the sole magnificence of Divine Holiness: It is self-moving Idea and Spirit. In one way we might say that Hegel's entire philosophical program, from logic to jurisprudence to philosophy proper, is a reflection on the Idea of God. It is a full and robust account of the structures of reason itself, a structure that is Spirit, Triune Spirit. It would be blind to portray this as orthodox Trinitarianism; we cannot follow Hegel along many of his pathways. But he sees further than many traditionalists, for he knows and unfolds the radiant truth that Trinity must be the final harbor in the journey into the very idea of God: to think the One God through to the very end is to think Spirit. God is Self-Moving Thought in just this sense: Triune Subject. From Hegel we learn how to reflect on Holiness. For Holiness is the Transcendental Mode of the One God, the Living Triunity.

§1.1. Holy Trinity and Israel

The Trinity is the One God, Present and Mighty in Blessing to Israel: One God, Thrice Holy. The dogma of Trinity, we have said, teaches monotheism. And Christian monotheism is Trinity. Now, for Christians, such confessions seem altogether natural. As the Holy God is Triune, in and for Himself, so He is Trifold Eternally; never was there the One God who was not Triune. But what is natural for the church, essential to doctrine and to the metaphysics of God, is alien to present-day Israel, to Jews of the Second Temple and of today. How can this be? How can the confession of the One God, the fundamental affirmation of Israel, from the days of Moses until now, not include the confession of the Holy Trinity, as it also is the very Mode and Reality of Israel's God? The disciples of Jesus Christ share with Israel the Shema, the confession of God's Radical Oneness, His Unicity; it is the Lord Christ's own teaching. And we, Jews and Christians, share the reverence for Moses, the friend of God, who records and discloses the first commandment, that the Lord God is beyond all form, all image, all likeness, that He is Utterly Unique, Wholly One. How can congregations called together by the One God, chastened and directed by the same ten words, called to task by the same fiery word in prophets and seers, drawn to the same lovely earth, from Judean hill towns to Jerusalem, from shrines at Bethel and oases on a wilderness route to the Jordan River and to the Great Sea—how can congregations called and shaped and blessed by all these biblical treasures stand so very far apart in the one thing needful, the doctrine of God? How can Holy Scripture teach such different lessons to such similar peoples? Karl Barth was fond of saying that the great ecumenical question for Christians centered on the anguished relation of church to synagogue, not the broken tie of church to church,[3] and it is just here, before the Presence of the Holy One, that this saying takes on its full measure. Anyone who has wrestled with Romans 9–11 and burned with the zeal that scarred the apostle Paul shares the very deep puzzlement, mystery, and sorrow of this fundamental question in the dogma of Trinity.

We have begun our intellectual worship of Trinity with a collation of Holiness texts from Israel's Scriptures; they will be our steady companion throughout this doctrine. But it is a signal truth that present-day Israel does not read its Scriptures thus and, in more polemical moments, considers the Triune faith of the church a vulgar polytheism, a paganism in the heart of the church. In such Judaic polemics, the Christian faith is *apostasy*, a pagan rebellion directly prosecuted in the face of the One God, even as the people liberated from Egypt sat down to eat and drink, to rise up and play, in the very moment when the saving Torah blazed forth in word and fire to Moses on Sinai. In this sense, Israel says, Trinity is not new and is to be rejected for that reason, pulled from the thin air of Platonism. No! Christian teaching of the Triune God is, in such diagnoses, an old, old sin, a rebellion against the God of Sinai, a lawless and wayward and idolatrous heart. Medieval Talmudists scoffed at the attempts to make a rational defense of Trinity or at the Christian assurance that this dogma is taught in Holy Scripture; an Incarnate God can only be idolatry, flat paganism. In the modern era, Franz Rosenzweig speaks for many when he diagnoses the Christian as "striving with the hidden pagan" in the Christian heart.[4] And this Christian reader, at least, must say that *The Star of Redemption* is not a misunderstanding but a shrewd, deep, and sympathetic understanding of the Christian faith—that empathy drove Rosenzweig to such sharp rebukes. So, too, Leo Baeck, another student of the high academic tradition in modern Christian theology, discovers a repellant paganism, a "Romantic religion," in the fundamental categories of the Christian faith, a drawing near to God only in order to flee and disobey.[5] To anchor Trinity in the temple, its sacrificial cultus, its holiness, and its Holy God is to expose, right from the first step, the painful legacy of Christians and Jews, together before God, at enmity about God.

Thus begins the long, ugly history of warfare over one another's Scriptures. Who interprets, understands, "owns title" to Israel's Scriptures? Is the apostle Paul the first Christian traitor, the first Pharisaic thief and apostate who declares the Torah the possession of the church? Justin Martyr quarrels with Trypho over just these questions; Chrysostom denounces Christians who bow before "Jewish law"; Athanasius draws his great essay on the Incarnation to a fiery close by denouncing Jews who read their own Scriptures with a "veil over their minds." These are ancient debates, certainly, but the modern era of theology is not bereft of such polemics. No one who has read Martin Luther's late, bitter treatises can imagine that anti-Judaism belongs only to the early, persecuted church. That Luther, a doctor of the church and a master of Holy Scripture, can advocate the penalties against Jews he names there and mock the Jewish fidelity to and observance of the Torah can only fill one with remorse. The legacy of debate over Israel's Scripture turns dark there indeed. And though we must postpone a proper exposition of his remarkable legacy to the doctrine of the church, the great name of Karl Barth must be mentioned here. His was a "discovery of Israel for theology,"[6] to cite an early commendation, but at a cost. Jews were not "faithful to their election" but were rather "disobedient to their own covenant," unable to read their own Scriptures that testify to the One, elected for rejection, the Savior of Jews first but also of gentiles.[7] The Scriptures remain a battleground here, teaching a history of calling and promise, yes, but also of rebellion, self-justification, and blindness. All Israel will be saved but only because the Son of God dies a saving death for the ungodly, His enemies. There is no easy summary of a theological mind as vast and rich as Barth's, but we cannot allow ourselves the comfortable thought that anti-Judaism lies only in the distant past. (Modern anti-Semitism, I say, is another terrible story altogether, one that Christians must also face squarely and make proper contrition.)

So far, we have spoken in sweeping terms of the church catholic, the faith of Greeks and Latins. And polemics over common texts do mark the legacy of the church, both East and West, but it is in the West, the Latin Church, that this neuralgia breaks out as a fever. To the doctrines of providence and election belong the hard work of shining a relentless light on the Latin Church's heritage of anti-Judaism: its hardness of heart and cruelty toward Jews and Judaism, its shabby exploitations and self-justifications, its vulgar credulity for "teachings of contempt," its quickness to harass and exile, its halfhearted and self-serving condemnations of pogroms— always late, never enough. There will be, must be, time for this. And though we cannot here rehearse a proper history of the tangled thread binding Jews and Christians within medieval and modern Europe, we must at least bring out of the shadows the medieval debates over the Scriptures of Israel.

Long centuries had passed since Jews were a prominent cultural force in Roman civic affairs; long eclipsed was the dominance of a widely respected and feared Judaism over a ragtag, unappealing Christianity of the late empire. In medieval Christendom, Jews were now "resident aliens" in their own homelands, and their faithfulness was a sign to Christians of "Jewish stubbornness and obduracy." In such a world, with crown and altar wary but close allies, the Old Testament became the text that Christians alone truly understood, possessed, and controlled. In medieval France and Spain, the public disputations began. Rabbis and scribes were summoned to debate Christian scholars—many converts—over the true and proper exegesis of the Law and the Prophets. The transcripts of these debates make somber reading. The courage and tenacity of these Jewish exegetes can be scarcely imagined: real arguments were advanced, real debating points defended, and an air of sturdy scholastic inquiry attended the whole. But there could be no doubt about the conclusion: Jews could not win or triumph in such a debate. The *purpose* of these disputations was to affirm and underscore the Christian reading of the Old Testament, to strike at the heart of early medieval philo-Judaism, to defend the Christological interpretation of the whole, and to show how the church supersedes the synagogue.

Now it is cheap fare to diagnose errors in the past and pretend they lodge only there. Of course, the medieval history of Jews in Europe is complex. It is real history, real particularity and ambiguity. We could say, after all, that such public trials reveal a hidden but forceful respect for the art of argument, for the immense learning on both sides, and for detailed knowledge of Scripture in its many modes. The outcome may have been determined, but the means by which it was achieved remained intellectual, rational, deeply moral, scholarly. This is a grudging respect—grudging and filled, no doubt, with ill will but respect, all the same.

But the Christian claim to the Scriptures of Israel takes on public and concrete shape here; it becomes visible to the public eye as the private debates of the schools never do. These disputations declare: "The Holy Scriptures of the Old and New Testaments have one theological meaning, one doctrinal constitution, and that is Christian." Now, the question for us, the deeply moral and existential and religious question, is this: Can a doctrine of Trinity be lodged in, and instructed by, the Holiness Code and remain philo-Judaic? Will the Scriptures of Israel become the Old Testament *in this sense*—that Christians alone know what they truly teach? Can a difference as profound as this one, over the very Reality of God, be grounded, *each tradition*, in the same Scriptures, the same Law and the Prophets? Do Habakkuk and Leviticus teach the Trinity? Could the chosen people in fact and in truth be wrong about these books? The Bible itself demands we ask these things.

In fact, and in truth, we must say that Israel and the Christian faith, synagogue, and church *agree* in the doctrine of God and in the teaching of Torah. That is the simple and firm truth before God. But it is no simple matter to say how this is so. As with any deep truth, the explanation takes our best effort and demands a full measure of time. This entire volume is an attempt to show this vital agreement. But we can begin with a direct disavowal. Such an agreement about God and before God cannot mean that one party to the agreement simply gives way. We cannot mean here that church and synagogue agree in this trivial and empty sense— that in the end there is really only one side standing; the synagogue is wrong, silenced, and cannot disagree. That is the legacy of the medieval disputations, of early modern polemics, of a radical and untempered "mission to the Jews," and of Christian anti-Judaism, vulgar and sophisticated, in both crude broadsides and also refined Protestant diatribes against "Pharisaism" and "petty legalism."[8] We simply renounce these; that way is now closed. But neither do we say that the church is wrong; Nicene Christianity does not simply end; the dogma of Trinity does not fall silent and vanish.

We seek a dogmatic solution in which both sides to this debate remain standing, affirmed, and proper repentance is brought to the altar. As Christians we must make a proper beginning to our repentance by renouncing the claim that the church owns or controls the Scriptures of Israel. This volume on the Holy Trinity is not and must not be a quiet—or noisy—attempt to colonize the Law and the Prophets for our own good or the good of the Christian imperium. This doctrine of the Holy Trinity is not, and must not be, a sustained attempt to show, however politely or respectfully, that Jews are *wrong* in their reading of the Bible or, worse, that their doctrine of God is false or mistaken. No! The church is built on the Law and the Prophets and cannot live without this living root.

Yet we cannot and must not say that the dogma of the Holy Trinity is false or simply a Christian metaphor or façon de parler. The dogma of the Trinity outlines the Immanent Life of God. It is true and metaphysically Real. Even less do we attempt to resolve this painful dilemma by simply passing over the Scriptures of Israel in silence, as if they had no word of instruction for us Christians or no teaching we must heed on the inner Life of God. No, the Law and Prophets are *Scripture* for Christians, the very Word of God in its fullness. The Old Testament belongs to the Christian canon with full membership rights: we find the Living God there. As with John Calvin, we affirm that ancient Israel possessed the sacraments and the covenant; with the early church fathers, we affirm that we may be guided and corrected by the Old Testament in our investigation of the Holy Trinity. Indeed, it is our claim that the Old Testament itself *grounds* the dogma of the Holy Trinity: it is our starting point and lodestar. So, a dogmatic and moral resolution to the Christian and Jewish debate over the Holy Scriptures demands full realism, full canonicity, and full repudiation of Scriptural supersessionism. How can such a peace be won?

I say that this dogmatic resolution is found in a species of the qua relation, the conceptual notion that one reality can be seen *as* something else and that both descriptions of that one reality are true and truly present. Later we shall develop Ludwig Wittgenstein's fertile suggestion about the qua problem in his analysis of the famous duck-rabbit image, a problem he dubbed the "Dawning of an Aspect." We will put that in service of the doctrine of the *vestigium Trinitatis*. But here we want to say something rather stronger than Wittgenstein—more robustly realist in character, less linguistic or intently epistemic. It will follow more closely the notion of redoublement, as proposed by Gilles Emery, or a "primal doubling" as found in the Trinitarianism of St. Bonaventure. In sum, we seek a doctrine of Holy Scripture that acknowledges a subject matter that can be addressed in its native genre and idiom but is *also* distinct and separated from them. The *same* subject and subject matter can be addressed *as* Christian doctrine, first in its original idiom and then *as* a dogmatic locus—and this *because* these descriptions belong properly and really to the inner Life of God.

The doctrine of the Holy Trinity, that is, is a dogma about the *inner Life of God*. It is not first and principally a teaching about God's ways with us—not a dogma concerned primarily with what has become known as the economy or, in more modern times, as the economic Trinity.[9] No, Trinity teaches us, first and principally, what God is *in Himself*, in His Holy Aseity and Mystery, in His own Transcendent and inner Life. This, I say, exists *as* a Movement and a Structure that is both Unicity and Distinction, both monotheism and Trinity; Unicity *as* Distinction, monotheism *as* Trinity. The Living Structure who is God is the One Reality manifested and depicted in Holy Scripture; this Eternal Life is properly confessed *as* Lord and *as* Trinity. These doctrines of God are the idiom of ancient Israel *and* the church, one expressed *as* and *in* the idiom of the other. This book on the Blessed Trinity will develop and confess the conviction that the One God is *Holy* and is *Living*: these two Predicates and their Relations are the structure of Almighty God, expressed by Christians *as* Trinity. The event—the Movement—that manifests this truth is the sacrifice of the altar in ancient Israel; the books, especially Leviticus, that teach it are the Holiness School. My confession and prayer is that *Holiness* grounds and structures this entire doctrine of God: it is the Royal Road.

Now, such a defense of the Christian reading of the Old Testament may raise what we might call—following the example of the great German systematician Karl Rahner—the Rahner problem in Christian teaching about God. Have I suggested, in this qua relation, a form of the Rahnerian notion of the Anonymous Christian[10]—that Jews are silent and unwitting Trinitarianists? Am I denying supersessionism by quietly dissolving Judaism into Christianity? Such a result could be hardly called a resolution; it could not deserve the dignity of a theological confession in the face of the reality and the covenant of Israel. It would fail the original desideratum that both church and synagogue remain standing in and after the dogmatic resolution, and each in their mother tongues. Nor can we revert to a resolution that softens the dilemma by making Christian and Jewish doctrines of God separate, though friendly, traveling companions, each in its own carriage, running on parallel rails. No, the qua resolution must instead affirm that any full intellectual investigation of the doctrine of God that rests on Holy Scripture will arrive at a conceptual structure and set of problematics that in biblical idiom will be entailed by the affirmation of Holiness and Life; in postbiblical Judaism will be expressed in the idiom of sacrifice, in Christianity, in Trinity. My prayer is that this volume in Christian dogmatics will not make Jews Trinitarians—though of course the Holy Spirit calls witnesses from both Jew and gentile—but rather that they see something familiar, a beloved dwelling place that is expressed in another language and belongs to another culture. But it is familiar, respectable, as an intellectual endeavor that seeks to be faithful to the One God of Israel.

Now, to be sure, some forms of postbiblical Judaism have put to one side such metaphysically speculative tasks as a direct doctrine of God and investigations of the Divine Nature. In their stead, the Law and its observance take center stage. For this reason, some scholars of Judaism take the central emblem of the tradition to be practice, not theology or doctrine. Yet those Judaic thinkers who undertake a conceptual investigation of the creaturely status of Torah, or of the prophetic encounter with Almighty God, of sacrifice and atonement, or the eternal election of Israel, will find, I believe, some of the biblical and intellectual building blocks that find their way into a wholly different structure. (I take Franz Rosenzweig to develop a position akin to this in the celebrated part III of the *Star of Redemption*.) This, I say, is Divine Holiness *as* Eternal, Living Truth. The genre and idiom of the Old Testament determines the original, native tongue and is never silenced or lost. But the church's idiom of Nature and Procession and, finally, of Person will be its new language, the mother tongue of Christians. One *as* the Other: this is our aim.

In short, we will not follow the path laid out, on the Christian side, by Rosemary Ruether in her early, courageous indictment of Christian anti-Judaism. *Faith and Fratricide* was an epoch-making book; it seared any Christian reader of conscience when it appeared soon after *Nostra Aetate*, the Vatican's *Declaration on the Relation of the Church to Non-Christian Religions*.[11] In a moving expression of Christian self-sacrifice, Ruether counseled the end of "fully realized eschatology": Christianity in repentance for its ancient fratricide would recognize in Jesus only the "paradigm and prolepsis" of the end times, when the full redemption of the suffering and evil age will be ushered in in power; with rabbinic Jews, Christians would wait in hope for that Messianic deliverance. Christians wait "in Jesus's name"; they share in his longing for the kingdom, but they no longer claim that "history has been fulfilled" in Jesus's Passion and Rising. With Jews, Christians eagerly await a time that lies beyond the times when promise at long last turns over into fulfillment.[12] A bold proposal, then and now! And though Jesus Himself taught us to lose our lives for the Reign of God, not find or guard or save it, we cannot in truth lay down the Nicene faith in an act of self-immolation, a whole burnt offering, on the altar of our most proper remorse. For the Christian faith is true, and its teachings will endure and abide when all else goes down to dust. We cannot solve the riddle of scriptural teaching by declaring ourselves impeached. Rather, we say that both scriptural bodies of faith perdure; we say instead that they agree, they join forces, they teach the one thing needful. I mean this in quite a strong sense. Such strength can be measured by examining a few alternatives not taken; they will clarify the road ahead.

Let me begin with a widely admired proposal, an attractive one, tame-seeming, that we may well believe stands behind Ruether's radical program: the progressive revelation and development of doctrine. Now the development of doctrine belongs by rights to the doctrine of providence, as does Barth's complex proposal, too, but it is right to touch on this great theme here, as a doctrine of Scripture lies embedded in its high, vaulted spaces. We might summarize it briefly this way: the dogma of Trinity is the deliverance of the early church. This seems such an ordinary, a rather commonsense, remark that it is hard to see its breathtaking reach. The claim undergirding the whole is that the Mystery of Trinity is not taught *in the Bible* but is rather the achievement of bishops gathered in Holy Synod, putting down heresy, advancing the gospel. Note here that this doctrine does not deny the scriptural element of Trinity; rather, it affirms it. But the claim is a careful one. The Mystery of a Three-Personed God is consonant with Holy Scripture; it draws on biblical texts, Old and New; it reflects warring exegeses of the Gospels from the ancient Christian sees. After Nicaea—or, perhaps better, after Chalcedon—Trinity becomes the Christian way of reading, understanding, and narrating the Bible itself. But the doctrine *itself* arises from the postbiblical era, in the conflict of the schools, and directs the Christian to the proper, settled, reading of the church's book. The Trinity is *defined* in the fourth century. We need not develop a causal theory here and can remain neutral on emergent, or top-down, accounts of the relation of Scripture to dogma. Defenders of development say that Trinity takes shape there, in the era of the church, under the guidance of the providential Spirit; before that, in the time of revelation, it is indefinite, implicit, a treasure buried in the field.

Now, there are variants within this wide family, and I do not mean they all teach with one voice on these matters. But Cardinal John Henry Newman, in his remarkable *Essay on the Development of Doctrine*, opened up fertile ground for an ecclesial account of Holy Trinity.[13] Newman's celebrated imagery—and lovely prose!—deserves to speak directly:

> It is indeed some times said that the stream is clearest near the spring. Whatever use may fairly be made of this image, it does not apply to the history of a philosophy or belief, which on the contrary is more equable, and purer, and stronger, when its bed has become deep, and broad, and full. It necessarily rises out of an existing state of things, and for a time savours of the soil. Its vital element needs disengaging from what is foreign and temporary, and is employed in efforts after freedom which become more vigorous and hopeful as its years increase. Its beginnings are no measure of its capabilities, nor of its scope. At first no one knows what it is, or what it is worth. It remains perhaps for a time quiescent; it tries, as it were, its limbs, and proves the ground under it, and feels its way. From time to time it makes essays which fail, and are in consequence abandoned. It seems in suspense which way to go; it wavers, and at length strikes out in one

definite direction. In time it enters upon strange territory; points of controversy alter their bearing; parties rise and fall around it; dangers and hopes appear in new relations; and old principles reappear under new forms. It changes with them in order to remain the same. In a higher world it is otherwise, but here below to live is to change, and to be perfect is to have changed often.[14]

Under Newman's shadow, we could say, for example, that the dogma of Trinity is a pilgrimage, a long one, that begins at the Resurrection of Christ. Robert Wilkin's recent work on Trinity traces just this arc, as does Paul Hinlicky's.[15] Or we might take recent work on Arius or Augustine—think of Rowan Williams or Lewis Ayres—as the starting point for Trinitarian thought form and development.[16] John Zizioulas famously anchors the Triune Life in the pioneering work of the Cappadocian fathers, and many, such as Catherine LaCugna, have found themselves drawn to themes they see first and most powerfully expressed in the Greek-speaking Christian world of the fourth and fifth centuries.[17]

The early church, in short, is *generative*—that is the heart of the development of doctrine. Development not only shows us how we might properly read the Bible but also forges the architecture, the conceptuality, and the argument for a Triune God. Now this is an attractive proposal, certainly! We no longer need a little attested verse such as the long-elided Johannine comma to warrant Trinity, nor do we seek to scour the Scriptures for terms of art such as *hypostasis* or *procession* to ground the dogma. We need not press the Pauline triads, found scattered in his letters, to serve as Trinitarian prooftexts, nor nervously collate Gospel events that comprise three Names—Father, Son, and Spirit. Fra Angelico could artlessly portray the Christ Child teaching St. Augustine the Triune dogma, but we embarrassed moderns consider this an awkward and unhistorical feat. Trinity is not contained in Scripture, most moderns say;

It is not taught there *explicitly*. Rather, with the dogma in hand, the Bible tells a Trinitarian tale. The notion of development is a *historical* one; the Constantinian era brings into being a form of argument—a thought-world, idiom, and semantic range—that earlier eras could not and did not produce. Development is at once material, political, and intellectual history, the rich polyphony that drives a dynamic culture and gives it shape. From these elements arises the doctrine of Trinity, articulated, sturdy, made orthodox. The Bible may *compose* the doctrine of Trinity, but it does so in the way that elements receive their definition from the finished work they constitute. The whole makes the parts. All this has become second nature to us in the modern era. Indeed, so natural is this ecclesial reading of Trinity's origin that sixteenth-century radicals, in the birth of the modern, declared the dogma of Trinity unscriptural and, in just this way, unnecessary or unwanted in the Christian faith, *semper reformanda*.[18]

A sacramental parallel is instructive. Consider the reigning doctrine of sacramental theology, born under the impress of liturgical renewal in the interwar years. The church, under the guidance of the Holy Spirit, has developed a sacramental system to mediate an ecclesial and corporeal Presence of Christ to His faithful. Here, too, we expect development out of scriptural elements! But no longer are we forced to ground confirmation or unction or marriage in a direct commandment of Christ; no longer will penance or ordination be discovered in an unlikely and unattractive reading of a New Testament text. No, we say that the mind of the church, under its Gracious Lord, searches further, receives a deeper truth, looks once again and more searchingly into the well of Scripture, and sees reflected there a fresh image for the church. Holy Scripture remains the perpetual food of the saints, the sacred page for theology, but now only as revealed, interpreted, and set forth under the providential instruction of the church. Just so we might read Holy Scripture under the impress, instruction, and wisdom of the ecumenical councils of the church of Jesus Christ. The Trinity, we would say in this vein, cannot be the source of conflict between Jews and Christians, for this dogmatic Mystery emerges only in the postbiblical era, the era of the Spirit, the era of the church.

Now, I have focused here on a doctrine of development that locates dogmatic definition in the post-Constantinian era. But could Holy Scripture itself develop? We might come closer to the notion of Christian and Jewish agreement—and disagreement—over Holy Scripture by viewing the canon of the Bible itself as a product and record of historical and conceptual development. Robert Jenson offered a tantalizing account of canonical development in a slim volume devoted to Lutheran maxims and rules of thumb, *Lutheran Slogans: Use and Abuse*.[19] With such a pithy title, the work might lead us to expect some unmuzzled dicta on Lutheran theology and practice, and we would not be disappointed. But Jenson is a sophisticated theologian of the post-Holocaust world, and in the footnotes to this informal and bustling text, he offers a dense, fruitful, and wonderfully suggestive proposal for Christian and Judaic reading of the Bible. In a concluding chapter, "Tethering," Jenson summarizes his narrative doctrine of Trinity—laid out in technical form in his *Systematic Theology*[20]—in a compressed form: "For that is how Christians identify their God, as the Lord of an eschatologically universal history: as whoever rescued Israel from Egypt and set her on the way to being a universal and concluding blessing, and rescued Jesus the Christ of Israel from the tomb to be that blessing in person."[21] Note how our problem is closed up in the little room of this one sentence. Jenson considers all this doctrinal talk to express in conceptual idiom a fundamental *narrative*: the

Bible is story, the historical story of God. (Of course, this sounds Hegelian, but he means it in a denatured form.)

Now it is no secret that many parts of the Bible are not story, not narrative in form at all. We could scarcely open the Pentateuch were we to expect narrative on every page. Jews especially might chafe under the yoke of story: Is Leviticus really an unfolding narrative? The Psalms? Proverbs? If we believe that overarching structures for biblical reading—scriptural theory and method—must be exemplified in and characterize biblical examples, then we might well pause before we agree to narrative as our reigning interpretive schema. (Much postliberal defense of narrative as theological method attempt to handle this complex problem.)[22] But Jenson is fully alive to this secret! Indeed, he offers a solution that incorporates his own deep study of rabbinics with a sophisticated account of New Testament development.

After noting how the Bible's Wisdom literature is neither narrative in the main nor likely to give rise to a story-shaped church, Jenson defends the category as fundamental: "It was and is the gift of a small second volume, attached to the first Scripture, that determined how Scripture would shape the Christian movement. For that volume comprises the Gospels' story of what happened with Jesus, and in various forms the claim that this story is the climax of Israel's Scripture. Thus, the church was constrained to read Israel's Scripture as the sort of discourse that can have a climax, that is, as narrative, and then to read the two testaments together as one great meganarrative of God's works with his people."[23] Now this is a rich passage! Much method and precision are packed tight in these few lines, and we could not hope to examine the whole. But Jenson appends a footnote to this text that belongs in the center of our reflection on Trinity and Holy Scripture among Christians and Jews. He writes: "The rabbinic movement that became the

Judaism we know was also blessed with a second volume, the *Mishnah*. This is a collection of legal commentary, applying sacral law to daily life. As the New Testament constrains the church (it is *tethered*) to read the Old Testament as narrative, with theological and moral commentary, so the *Mishnah—with equal legitimacy—*constrains Judaism to read the Old Testament as Torah, with narrative context."[24] Note the sophisticated turn to the theory of development Jenson makes here.

Jenson acknowledges from the start that we might not arrive at narrative as our winning genre were we to tote up instances within Scripture itself. There are strong alternative candidates, and we do not, cannot, make a determination with the "first Scriptures" themselves. Indeed, on coherentist grounds, we might find an alternate reading—Law, for example—equally compelling. Note how radical a claim this is! We have something like a literary parallel to the systems of non-Euclidean geometry: each in its own way consistent, each by its own definitions and axioms self-validating, each plausible, intellectually attractive. What settles the choice is a determinate lying outside the system itself, a physical referent, perhaps, or a practical application—or, in our case, a second, concluding text. Jenson is alive to the historian's proposal that Christianity and Judaism arrive on the world stage at roughly the same time, shaped by early Messianic communities scattered around the Mediterranean basin or by Pharisaic schools established in Roman Palestine or Iraq.[25] Something like the branch theory of evolutionary biology, Jenson's doctrine of narrative development, if we may term it so, proposes a single Scripture for both Jews and Christians, capped by a second volume, the New Testament or the Talmud. It is this second volume that becomes an external determinate: law as overarching category for Jews, narrative for Christians. Note that neither Jew nor Christian need defend the notion that law or narrative is *empirically* or *numerically* the predominate genre. We need not search the Scriptures *in that sense.* Israel's Scripture is indeterminate, plastic, susceptible to either definition. Jenson's is a fully coherentist schema in this way, though one we might term neofoundationalist in character, following Alvin Plantinga's usage. We learn through the rival concluding texts to regard the ancient Scriptures as one kind of book or another, and our allegiance is shaped—determined, really— by the religious communities that stand behind the Gospels and Mishnah and claim us as members. Either the New Testament or the Talmud is "properly basic."[26] The call for decision, so vital to modern Lutheran theology, plays a central role here. Under the Spirit of the Living God, we decide in faith for rabbinic Judaism or for Christianity. And if Christian, we identify our Lord as the One who *both* liberated Israel from Egypt *and* raised Israel's Messiah from the dead. Now this powerful proposal casts some odd shadows on the question before us.

Jenson prefers the term *Identity* for the Divine Persons, the Hypostases of the Triune God: the Bible narrates the Three Triune Identities of the God of Israel. Note how the shaping works here. We cling to the Gospels of the New Testament church; we discover narrative there as the overarching theme and structure of the Bible. This arc traces the Life of God from Creation to Consummation, yielding an Identity that is the Father of Israel, calling into being the chosen and beloved son, the people Israel, who will hold surety, be the preexistence of the Divine Son, the Second Identity of the One God, raised in the Spirit, the Third Identity, poured out on all flesh at Pentecost, Israel's harvest festival. These are the narrative structures of Israel's God, disclosed in the Scriptures sculpted by the story of Jesus of Nazareth, the Son called out of Egypt in the last days. The Identities are distinct; they play different roles, exhibit distinct character, in the drama of our salvation, yet they are the One God. This is not the "naked or unbaptized" God, Jenson reminds us, because from the very beginning of the story, the Identity of God is named and disclosed by the actions taken with and for Israel: the covenant people give rise to the church, the community that defines Trinity, as the outworking of narrative in the doctrine of God. Now we will have to say much more about this handling of the dogma of Trinity when we examine the relation of Processions to Missions, Immanence to economy, in the architecture of Triunity. But here we must reflect on the odd shape Jenson's proposal impresses on the reading of Holy Scripture as source of Trinitarian dogma.

In Jenson's hands, Trinity is a dogma of the New Testament, of the Gospels themselves. I think the proposal is that strong. It is not that the Old Testament plays no role in Trinitarian teaching— on the contrary! The history of Israel—its covenant, law, exile, and return—form a central Originary Identity in the Triune God. Israel worships, follows, and teaches the Father. In just this way, the chosen people are the protohistory of the Eternal Son. But this daring use of Israel's covenant history does not in truth *begin* there. It begins rather with the Gospels, the story of this One Jew, born under the law, His exile and death outside Zion's walls, His restoration and consecration as Life-Giving Spirit. The impress of the Gospels as *this* story allows the entire Bible to be read as an integrated whole, a coherent drama, that leads from Sinai to the heavenly Jerusalem. Now, famously, Jenson shares with Wolfhart Pannenberg and Jürgen Moltmann the conviction that the future— the eschaton—gives rise to the present and in another way to the past; we *receive* our reality from there, thence, and must raise our eyes in hope, not cast them backward toward a remote and lifeless past. Jenson even dares to say with Pannenberg that Almighty God receives His Being from His own Future, the eschatological Spirit of Liberty. So, it will come as no surprise to those who know these German-inspired theologians that a Second Testament, coming after the First, could determine—no, *originate!*—the First. But this will mean that the Old Testament does not teach Trinity in itself, nor would non-Christians discover it there. Instead we are taught to affirm, in a Kurt Gödel–like turn, that the principles for proper Christian reading lie outside the system itself, in the Second Testament, appended to and completing the First.

In our earlier discussion we asked: Is the dogma of Trinity a deliverance of the development of doctrine? And now we must press the interrogation further: Is the dogma, instead, the deliverance of the New Testament? By joining narrative to Divine Identity, Jenson shows us how we might take the Gospels and Epistles to teach and develop the Mystery of God's Triunity. This, too, is a deeply attractive, almost natural, affirmation for a Christian to make. It allows us to say that Jews read the Bible as Torah, teaching, and discover there the commandments, ordinances, and decrees of a Unique and Utterly Unitive God. We Christians, on the other hand, read a larger Scripture, in which a Truth is taught and developed that illumines the whole but is contained only in the New. The Trinity, we might say in this vein, is an extended reflection on the Begotten One, the Origin, Passion, and Risen Life of the Son of God. This is the Christological concentration in the dogma of Trinity, and it marks out the new and revelatory in the Gospels of Jesus Christ.

Of course, there are continuities in the Testaments. The struggle over Marcion's principle of parsimony—that the Christian Bible should contain only the radically novel, the unanticipated Word from above—could not in the end persuade the church to abandon the Scriptures of Israel. Instead the Word and Spirit were discovered afresh in the Law and Prophets; those Scriptures become the Old Testament of the church. But they became old in a second sense as well: the Triune Reality of God was revealed in the New. Indeed, this was the very purpose of the New, to reveal through the Son, a fresh Word, the Mystery of the Trinity. The life of Jesus Christ is, to be sure, a journey of salvation. We do not have in the New Testament doctrinal revelation only; it is not propositional *in that sense*. Rather the saving Person and Work of Christ encompasses both the Truth of Trinity and the Gospel of salvation. But the great Truth of the Three-Personed God could be disclosed only in the fullness of time, when the Son is manifest on a dark night, to a sin-sick world. *This* is the *oecomene*, the economy of our salvation. The Trinity is disclosed in the New Testament because it is the record, the very good news, of our deliverance in the Eternal Son, raised in the Holy Radiance of the Divine Spirit. So far, we might say, speaks the inner logic of Trinity as the narrative unfolding of the Incarnate Savior.

Now we ask, is this right? Is the New Testament the sole revelation and determinant of the Christian doctrine of God? I believe we must quietly, but firmly, answer no. The New Testament is not the birth of Trinity, not the source of this teaching, not the era that determines and discloses the Truth of Divine Triunity. I want to be firm about this but careful too. There *is* fresh teaching in the New, truths we learn and gifts we receive. But the saving Work and Person of the Redeemer is not the origin of the doctrine. The economy of our salvation is not the revelation of the Triune Mystery: that is the thesis I am to unfurl here. A proper reading of Holy Scripture, I believe, distinguishes the doctrine of salvation from the doctrine of Trinity; a doctrine of soteriology must not be allowed to do all the heavy lifting in Christian dogmatics. Nor is Christology the ground and spring of Trinitarian teaching, however central it may be to the ordo cognoscendi. The Mystery of Trinity belongs to the Divine Aseity, I say, in a strong sense. It is a fully speculative dogma. The doctrine is not grounded in the economy, and it is not principally or exhaustively a deliverance of our Lord's Saving Work. The Holy Mystery of Triune monotheism belongs principally and originally to Divine Holiness: Trinity is a deliverance of God's Utter Holiness. The Holiness of God, received and thought through to the end, is Triunity. Or, we might say, Trinity is the conceptual unfolding of the Superabundant Holiness of God. Holiness just is the Mystery, the Immanence and Sovereign Aseity of God; It is the Hidden and Infinite Majesty of the One Lord. The doctrine of Trinity begins with this Aseity, this Transcendent Dignity and Life. The Triune Lord draws near in His temple, and in this searing Nearness, He is Lord, High and Lofty, Utterly Hidden and Sovereign, Incommunicate and Royal. The whole earth falls silent before Him, the Primal, Omnipotent, Unoriginate God. For this reason, the task of theology, the privilege of this human service, is to reflect, worship, and obey this Holy Lord, the Triune God, present and remote from His creation and creature, searing the earth at His altar and throne. The Old Testament teaches and worships the One, Triune God. *That* Mystery we must explore and set forth with great care—and with great joy.

§1.2. Trinity, Christology, Soteriology

Just so we must return to the anguished question of Jewish and Christian fidelity to the One Book of Israel, the Law, the Prophets, and the Writings. In what way are we to say that Christians discover there the surpassing Mystery of Triune Holiness? How does the Old Testament teach Trinity? Now it may be clearer to begin with a negative, counterfactual version of this question: Were the Eternal Son never to have become Incarnate, *per impossibile*, would the dogma of Trinity be known, worshipped, and adored on the earth? We are not asking a metaphysical question here about the Eternity of the Trinity; if true, most certainly, the Trinity always was. We ask, rather, a question about the doctrine and the source of that doctrine. Were the Divine Missions never given, would Trinity be known, taught, laid on the inner chambers of the heart? It is no easy matter to answer this question. We have become accustomed, through long exposure to the history of doctrine, to the notion that the Mystery of Trinity is a moment in the history of Christology. We assume, as Christians, that the dogma enunciated at Nicaea is forged in the white-hot fury of debate about the Son of God: Whose Son is He; and what is His stature before the Lord God, the Creator of heaven and earth? Thus has formed the doctrinal conviction summed up forcefully by Catherine LaCugna. She writes, "Christology, then, provides an analogy for the project of this book, which is to substantiate the thesis that the Doctrine of the Trinity, when it is formulated on the basis of the economy of salvation, has radical implications for the Christian life."[27] The anchor for Trinitarian doctrine and the engine of its development, she says, is the doctrine of the Son. This, we say, is a tight summary of the conflicting exegeses of Scripture animating and dividing the early Christian church.

Now I think the historical record is extensive and persuasive: the ordo cognoscendi of the dogma of Trinity is the third- and fourth-century controversy over the life and Gospel record of Jesus of Nazareth. But is this the ordo essendi? Do we teach this dogma *because* the aim of the Incarnation is realized in this way, that the Mystery of Trinity is now revealed? It seems to me that the scholastic distinction between the two orders has been honored in the breach but not been put to work, in fact, in the Trinitarian dogma. It has been quietly assumed, on the contrary, that the cognoscendi just *is* the essendi and that the very reality of Trinity—Its Structure, Aim, and Healing Purpose—is to reveal the Eternal Begetting of the Son. It wonderfully extends to include us, unworthy and unheeding, into the great Mercy of the Son's Self-Offering, sinners sealed and married to Him in the Spirit. Though I do not believe that Christian theologians have made explicit this assimilation of metaphysics to epistemology, it seems evident from the rise of modern Trinitarianism that Trinity apart from the Incarnation appears unthinkable, certainly unappealing.

Let me take as cardinal instance the path-breaking work of Karl Rahner, a chief influence on LaCugna. In his remarkable essay "The Trinity," Rahner catches up this assimilation of Trinity to Incarnation with great precision. He writes there, "The isolation of the treatise of the Trinity *has* to be wrong. There *must* be a connection between Trinity and man. The Trinity is a mystery of *salvation*, otherwise it would never have been revealed."[28] Now it seems to me that this pithy opening to Rahner's famous subsection, "The Axiomatic Unity of the 'Economic' and 'Immanent' Trinity," deserves as much attention as his more well-known "maxim," "The Economic Trinity is the Immanent Trinity, and the Immanent Trinity is the Economic Trinity."[29] These opening lines belong, certainly, as one element within, or reexpression of, Rahner's maxim, but as introductory remarks, they do their own work. They show us the religious impetus, the *drive*, of the whole. Rahner is not preoccupied, by and large, by the formal problems related to economic and Immanent "Trinities," though, to be sure, he carefully picks his way through them throughout the treatise. Rather, Rahner seeks a grounding of Trinity in soteriology: the Mystery of Trinity is a conceptualization of God's Saving Self-Communication. Nothing is revealed that is not for our benefit—I believe Rahner would go this far. Here is the striking conclusion to the essay as a whole:

As is evident from our basic axiom, Christology and the doctrine of grace *are*, strictly speaking, the doctrine of the Trinity. They are its two chapters about either divine procession or mission ("immanent" and "economic.") [NB, as comment on the maxim] Hence what we have already present here is and intends to be nothing more than a certain formal anticipation of Christology and pneumatology (doctrine of grace) which are to follow. In order to understand them, we must emphasize in Christology the dogma that "only" the Logos became man and that this manifests him *as such*. We must emphasize the insight that this was obviously not due to a random "decree" of God, who might also have decided the incarnation of another divine person. Further, in pneumatology, we must construct a doctrine of grace which possesses a trinitarian structure. When all this happens, then the real doctrine of the Trinity is presented in Christology and in pneumatology.[30]

When we understand and receive the benefit of the Incarnation and the outpouring of the Spirit, we understand Trinity: that, I believe, is Rahner's fundamental conviction. Of course, there is much more in Rahner's essay that we might consider, learn from, and, in part, set to one side, but here we must encounter the spiritual depth of Rahner's vision.

The dogma of Trinity, he tells us, is ultimate Mystery *because* it is our salvation, the Self-Giving of God. This is the very purpose of theology, to redescribe and set forth the marvelous word of our deliverance, to pronounce, in conceptual idiom, the news that God is Mighty to save. The dry margins of doctrine, the speculative dainties of scriveners, cannot in truth capture us anymore. We might not even find grudging admiration for their architectonic subtlety; instead, for us moderns, they "remain kerygmatically rather sterile."[31] Of course no one is more subtle than Rahner! His theology is a matchless gift to the church for this reason, too: he is a consummate systematician. Rahner does not mean to denigrate scholastic learning; he is in his own way an heir of the schoolmen. But he envisions another world, another country in which theology properly dwells. In modern dogmatics, Rahner counsels, we are to receive and examine the astonishing gift of salvation, that God has drawn near—no, has *given* Himself to us. There really is nothing to compare with this, and nothing deserves our attention so much as this one thing needful. We are made captive to it, and our dogmatic work unfolds this vital center of creaturely life, enveloped in the Mystery of the Triune Creator. "To know Christ is to know His benefits"; this is another famous maxim, from Philip Melanchthon, and while he lived to regret its staying power (did Rahner, too, we wonder?), he aptly summarizes Rahner's spirit and tone. There must be benefits to the central Christian dogmas; they are Mysteries for just that reason. The Holy Trinity must find a purchase on us; It is revealed to just that end. It is not so much saving Truth—though, to be sure, it *is* that—as It is saving benefit.

The ignorance of this identity, Trinity and soteriology, gives rise to an arid, technical, and otiose manual Trinitariansim that I believe to be Rahner's fundamental, spiritual conviction. Rahner's essay is famous for suggesting that Christians are nominal Trinitarians; functional Unitarians. The gears of Triune Reality never engage, he charges; the wheel spins free, touching and driving nothing more than a lovely display case of scholastic puzzles, wordplays, and fine-drawn distinctions. At most, we might occupy an unseeing modalism—a "bare God" descends from highest heaven to rest in manger straw. And Rahner is by no means alone in this conviction. Students such as LaCugna echo this analysis, but so, too, do major Protestant voices: Colin Gunton, Robert Jenson, and Paul Hinlicky.[32] Preachers and seminarians give ample testimony to the spirit, at least, of Rahner's diagnosis. No one seeks to preach on Trinity Sunday, so the story goes; to the curate, the visiting pastor, the seminarian falls this unwanted duty. Trinity is technical, explanations run afoul of careful distinctions right out of the gate, analogies court heresy at first use, and no one is the wiser when the sermon limps to the end. These are widespread assumptions, almost proverbial in the church these days. Now I think the history of doctrine confirms without hesitation the technical character of Trinity; one can go wrong here at almost every turn. And I would hazard that few of us have heard sermons on Trinity that strike us as powerful, illuminating, or unforgettable, which is all too true. But I think we have reason to hesitate before Rahner's *explanation* of this melancholy fact.

As natural, as forceful as is Rahner's diagnosis, we might well pause before we hold that the Dogma of Trinity is better conceived as a Mystery of our salvation. The cure of a pallid Trinitarianism, I say, should not lie in a vigorous soteriology. The exceeding Brilliance of the One Lord's Triune Reality does not find Its stride by displaying Its healing power among us. The burden of this book is to justify this claim. But we should not underestimate the headwind in our face. Rahner is simply the strongest, purest, and freshest breeze in this prevailing system. Rahner holds that the Triune God offers Himself to us in Truth and Love, and just that is our salvation. We are ultimately concerned with such a Mystery. We cannot but long to hear word of it. Such an existential bent to Christian doctrine has proved deeply attractive in Western theology, and not just in Germanophones such as Rahner and Paul Tillich.

Against the position I advocate here, the Western tradition has spoken—not with one voice—but forcefully tying doctrine closely to salvation. That the Mysteries of our faith are kerygma, saving truths *pro me, pro nobis*, belongs to the broad heritage of Latin Christendom. We could not hope to latch on to the maelstrom that is Luther without this tool in our hands. Calvin strikes the same chord with his evocation of piety at every turn: nothing abstract, nothing frigid or remote for him! Friedrich Schleiermacher does not innovate but rather conserves when he discovers in the Christian faith a religion of the teleological or ethical sort, tying all things within that faith to the "redemption achieved in Jesus of Nazareth" (GL §11). Barth's Christological concentration heightens the soteriological zest of dogmatic theology, broadening and universalizing the salvation history promoted by postwar biblical and liberation theologians. Religion, we might say in shorthand of this prevailing temper, just *is* salvation, the incomparable good news of our deliverance. All dogma, all liturgy, all teaching and preaching and exegesis are to set forth this signal truth. Such is the broad consensus in modern Trinitarianism, in modern theology as a whole. And it is just here that I think we must set our bold counterstroke: for all is not soteriology!

Excursus: Soteriology in Dogmatics

Part 1. Distinction between Theology and Soteriology

I want to linger on this vital point, that not all is soteriology. It is deep, and it runs all the way down. Just what are we about when we enter into the strait gate that is religion? When we speak of Christianity and of its central teachings—Trinity, Christology, Creation, Consummation—what do we address, what is our *scopus*, our telos? When we invite others to come and see, to taste and know the Lord, to awaken to His Might and Goodness, to bow down before His Exceeding Holiness, what in truth and in the end do we aim to offer? Just what is the praise of Israel, the song of the church? For long centuries, the answer has been: we seek, we praise, we proclaim *our salvation*. The Gospel of Jesus Christ is the Word of our redemption. Or to phrase this in the language of the history of religions school: Christianity is a "salvation religion." Its central categories are sin and divine redemption. Now, this traditional answer cannot be simply *ruled out* or *ruled wrong*: of course, the One

Triune Lord is the God of our salvation! It would be a stony heart without compare that considered our deliverance from the prison of our own making too light a thing to praise or meditate on. No, eternity is too short to properly praise the One who comes down under our roof and drives death to flight!

But we must say here that the traditional answer—Christianity is a salvation religion—is severely narrowed and distinctly incomplete. It has mistaken part for whole, the Divine Compassion for the entire Goodness of God, the Incarnation for the Infinite Triune Mystery of God, the sinner for the creature, tout court. The Holy Scriptures *contain* all things necessary for our salvation, yes. But they are not *exhausted* in it, nor are the other elements of Scripture mere stage-setting or *preparatio* to the drama of our redemption. Our misery and our sweet relief from every trouble cannot occupy the whole of Christian knowledge or piety. Rather we sinners must be moved, quietly but firmly, out of the living center of the Christian religion. Only God stands there.

Only God stands there: this is a shocking and relentless claim, and it transforms everything it touches. Just this is what we mean by monotheism, Christian Triune monotheism, in theology: God brooks no rival. St. Thomas expresses this axiom when he defines the center of sacred science as "God and all things in relation to Him."[33] Now, if this is so, it must be possible for the human creature to speak of God and His own Royal Aseity *objectively*; that is, without direct referent to the creature or sinner who speaks of Him. Such a conviction cuts to the very bones of realism in theology. And everything in theology rests on realism. Indeed, I would hold that it marks off the sturdy metaphysical confidence of the early church from its tormented and unrelenting self-critical dogmaticians of the modern era. When we open the expansive first pages of any early Christian text, we find bold and unrepentant sayings about the very Being and Reality of God. Of course, that does not rule out a steady plea for conversion, for holiness in the student of Divine Things! But the patristic boldness stands as the proper antechamber to the scholastic treatise on the doctrine of God. First, we speak of Almighty God; then, only then, of our language and Names for this Unique One. In this way, premodern theology shares the confidence of the great classical metaphysicians of the Hellenistic world. Aristotle, no more than Plato, ignores the human knower. Indeed, one could hardly open the *Metaphysics* of Aristotle without encountering the probing reflections on human inquiry and the search for wisdom. But the Fifth Book of the *Metaphysics* speaks frankly and unapologetically of Being qua Being, the famous expanse of reality arching over the whole of Western thought.[34] It is, Bonaventure teaches us, the "first object" of the intellect.[35] We have to be startled, then, by these twin guardians who stand watch over the gate to Latin theology—the plain, direct metaphysical reality and, its partner at the gate, the plain, direct seeker after wisdom. The unembarrassed and unconflicted presence of these two should call us moderns to an abrupt halt. But rarely have we diverted from our steady course.

Since the birth of the modern, we have been inclined to consider the realism of the Greek and medieval West to be precritical—to be wrapped, that is, in the arms of dogmatic slumber. Now, I do not want to make light of a particular kind of development of dogma, the further reflection and conquest of complex rational thought. We *can* see further from time to time, morally and cognitively, and there is, in truth, progress over the past, in the humanities as in the sciences. But it is not quite the Whiggish affair that we imagine. The doctors of the church speak confidently of the Reality of God, of Being Itself, as the first matter of Christian confession: It proceeds, It holds the center, It commands the whole. The human knower—the sinner—*follows*. This, I say, comes close to being the first axiom of Christian realism. (Almighty God, His Glorious Reality, is the first axiom; He demands unique pride of place.) We must think carefully here, though, how the Being of God, His own Surpassing Objectivity, can dominate theology and drive all before Him. Yet we creatures remain. How can we think such thoughts?

Hic Rhodus! Hic salta! The proper speech and exposition of the Holy Triunity begins at this crossroad. When we say, "God Exists," everything changes. The Divine Reality is Radical and Commandeering in just this sense: nothing remains the same, not one block and stone on another. The metaphysical Reality of God— His Sheer Objective Life—displaces, overturns, breaks through every certainty, every creaturely form. *That* is the Infinite Reach of the One beyond form, beyond image and idol. God does not simply set aside our epistemic conventions or rules; that hardly plumbs the proper depths. In one sense, after all, every object, every organism or concept, every kind and school, demands a particular form of knowledge; just this is the rise of disciplinarity in modern academic thought. Something Greater is here. If God is Real, nothing is as before. For there is a Mystery that *Lives*, that is—Who is!—the Source of Reality and is Reality Itself. The One Lord God *manifests* Himself, communicates and radiates the Light He is, His own Unique Subjectivity as Object. He sets aside and remakes our categories, our forms of thought. This is not to say He is *irrational*, no. The Reality of God is supremely Rational: He is Logos, Utter Sheer Truth, and Reason. But Almighty God just *is there*.

This may seem like an odd expression for a Formless, Utterly Unique, and Transcendent God, the One who is Holy Spirit, but in truth, it cannot be avoided. Holy Scripture speaks of Almighty God as *Place*, as the One who is *there*. We need not settle here the quarrels over Divine Name theology; it is enough here to say that when the prophet Habbakuk confesses that the Lord is in His Holy Temple, he expresses and relies on the Bounded Infinity, the Weight of Glory, the *Kabod*, who is God. He is Refuge and Rock, Crag and Stronghold; He is Cloud and Fire; He is Hypostatic Reality. It is not enough to say that He is the *Given*, though, of course, that is true. He rather is *Concrete*—just this is what we must say when we confess that God has Place, has Thereness, is Hypostatic Being. Or to say this more plainly, God simply *is*. We must speak of the Holy Lord's metaphysical Reality first and confidently because such Obdurate Mystery *intrudes* Itself. It demands a hearing; It explodes into human thought. Just as Truth, the One God is *compulsive*; we are broken on Him.

Now, of course, the Reality of God can be denied. Human history is the overweening proof of that fact. But the denial rests on the Superabundant Humility of God, who will lay Himself down, be *there* in His world, just as the truth and hard reality of a heedless and colorless secular age. But when reality turns the reins of our willful ways and manifests itself as Reality, as Concrete, Living Being, nothing else matters. Or better, everything now can in truth matter at all. God manifests His Being, and we receive this thought as the gentle dew from Heaven; we cannot live without it. To explore the Reality of God is much closer to stumbling over a Barrier, a Rock, a *Skandalon* than it is to quietly entertain an idea and comfortably consider the path by which this concept became ours. We run after It; we gaze at Its Contours; we fall silent. This, too, is the Sovereignty of God.

Now the Triune Lord's Objectivity is not properly or basically a deliverance of the doctrine of revelation. To say this is to extend and explicate the conviction that Christianity is not principally or exhaustively a salvation religion. Not all is soteriology! Not all is revelation! We confront just here what it *means*, what the cost and significance are of the claim that God is just *there*. We have a delicate task before us, and we should not hurry it. We must account for the *force* of Divine Concreteness, His Reality as Objective and Place that cannot be known without a shattering, a strike against and across all that we know and assume and store quietly away as ours. Yet all this must be affirmed without moving the doctrines of salvation and revelation into the center of theology. Only God is there! We must see and acknowledge and give thanks for God's Speech in Holy Writ; we must not overlook or pass by on the other side the event of God's Self-Disclosure in Scripture. God speaks there! Yet we must carry out these tasks of proper dogmatics, of proper worship, without assimilating the whole of Christian reflection to the gift of Divine Revelation and human healing. How can we perform such delicate surgery? Who will guide us in these narrow pathways? No better place can be found than that of Holy Scripture itself.

Just so, we ask here: Is Holy Scripture the record and effect of God's Saving Ways toward us? Is that its proper identity and character? Now it appears to be nearly overwhelmingly true that the Bible is the record of God's salvation to a lost world. I do not think that is too strong an expression. It is not simply the Gideons who find the Bible a solace and guide in the hour of need. We might think—just to narrow our task to a bearable measure—of the Letter to the Hebrews.[36] Many and varied the speech of Almighty God to ages past, the letter begins, and now God speaks through and by a Son. And what is this Son but the High and Humble Priest who intercedes for us, the New and Living Way? And how are we to live in such a world, perforated and commandeered by such a Word, and to be faithful, not to backslide, not to yield, not to forget or doubt the promise? The great encomium to faith and the faithful in Hebrews 11 and 12 might serve us a summary of the Saving Acts of

God, the witnesses and martyrs to God's Revealing Will toward us. Time would fail us to expand on all the heroes of the faith recorded there—of Abel and Enoch; of Rahab and Abraham and Jacob, leaning down in worship over his staff; of Joseph, longing for his homeland; of Moses, who feared not kings nor kings' commands; of Gideon and Samson and David; and of the martyrs slain even in the present day, showing in their own blood the unworthiness of the world to possess them. The Exodus, the covenant, the temple cult and its sacrifices, the stopping of lions' mouths, the overthrowing of empire and kingdom, the daring and scandalous hope that the dead will rise in a better resurrection and that these numberless witnesses shall not be saved without us: all these are ringing memorials to the God who saves and the people who are created, preserved, and delivered by the Living God. Here it seems is the very heart of the matter. Here God reveals His own Will, His own Son; here God delivers; here God seeks and gives faith; here we receive a kingdom that cannot be moved so we can by grace serve God with reverence and godly fear, for our God is a Consuming Fire. With the Letter to the Hebrews as frame, we could readily identify the Bible as a whole as the Book of the Revelation of Salvation. And not just Hebrews! Consider Paul's magisterial Letter to the Romans.

Surely the striking verses that open Paul's great Letter to the Romans underscore the tight unity of revelation and salvation to Holy Scripture itself: Paul, a servant of Jesus Christ, called to be an apostle, set apart for the gospel of God, the gospel concerning his Son, descended from David, declared Son of God with power, from whom we have received grace and apostleship to bring about the obedience of faith. Even in these staccato phrases, we hear the long line of Scripture itself—that it is the good news of salvation, of deliverance, of light overspreading this weary, darkened world. So liberation theologians have heard God's Living Voice in

Scripture: the chains of slavery are broken and the oppressed set free. So Luther heard the mighty Word of Grace, shattering the prison of a righteousness of our own, standing us on the Rock of God's own Righteousness, the revelation of the Son, the Humble Savior. So countless Christians have picked up and read: the sinner is encountered and overthrown and renewed—no, raised up!—by the gospel of the Son, the revelation promised beforehand through the prophets, in whom we have found, at long last, grace and peace. This is the very notion of gospel, a disclosure of salvation. So tight is this linkage that the very foundation of our knowledge of Jesus Christ is called the Gospel, the good news, *evangelium*, narrated according to the traditions and confessions of the four Evangelists.

The unity of the scriptural canon, then, turns on the anticipation and expression of this Gospel: the relation of promise to realization, or expectation to reception, or prophecy to fulfillment, or type to antitype, or, in another key, law to gospel, old covenant to new. We cannot grasp the radicality of the Triune Lord's Objectivity, His decentering and laying claim to the whole, without plunging into the rich loam that is the Bible as Saving Revelation, Saving Faith. How can we give expression to a counterstroke as radical as this?

We say: the Bible is about God, not about salvation, principally or exhaustively. We can begin there. In time we must set out a doctrine of Holy Scripture, its unity and address, that takes up this claim and proffers, in exchange for traditional preoccupations of this doctrine, an exposition of the Bible as mode of Divine Presence—but that time has not yet come. We here bear down on the central dogmatic claims in the doctrine of Trinity that moves firmly to one side the centerpiece of soteriology and its disclosure to sinners. Perhaps in shorthand we might say that we set—or, perhaps better, contain—the dialectic of law and gospel to a place, but only *one* place, in the larger confession of the Christian faith.

How can such things be? It is worth asking that troublesome question—repeating it, in truth—because the bold claim previously asserted, that the Bible is about God, not about salvation principally, seems impossible to state without the redemption of the speaker. Note that this is the very heart of the modern preoccupation with the doctrine of revelation: the knower herself must come in for the initial, cauterizing scrutiny so that the Object may be discerned, set forth, praised. Is this not, after all, the very pattern of the prophetic call in Isaiah 6? I saw, I confessed, the burning coal was brought to my lips, I was sent forth, and the terrible words of not-knowing were laid upon me. Mutatis mutandis, we have here the pattern of every epistemology since René Descartes: first the knower, the subject, and then the move, however tortuous, from inner to outer, from subject to object, from self to world. Distinctive to modern Christian epistemologies (Christian doctrines of revelation) is the conviction that judgment and chastening and gracious renewal must make knowledge possible and confirm it—and not just for religious readers. The pattern must sound deep, familiar chords in any student of the modern era in the West: from the knower to the known; from knowledge to being; from conditions of possibility to experience of the real. However we might trim the complex of Christianity to the modern or secular world, we must be struck by the profound intermingling and resonance between the spirit of self-critical knowledge and the scriptural disclosure of saving faith. How can such intimate ties be broken open? On what ground, after all, could such a divorce be proclaimed?

Already in volume 1 we have encountered, and bypassed, this neuralgic question. We have set aside any prolegomena in the doctrine of God and rather have simply begun. We began with the

One God—His Reality, His Superabundant Unicity, His Glory—and we did not look back. This was a quiet and implicit break, a rupture, with modern dogmatics in just this sense: it began with metaphysics—the Reality of the One God—and not with the knowledge of God or with the knower. Proper theology need not begin with the modern innovation in dogmatics I assumed there, with no introductory prolegomena, no sources and methods of self-critical knowledge. Rather, I enacted the confidence that theology may simply begin where Holy Scripture itself begins: the Lord and His Glory. Now is the time to say why, to render explicit what has remained implicit, to speak directly rather than to demonstrate, to enact the metaphysical move. But how shall that be done?

It seems that such a move ignores the central truth of the Gospel, that God is Holy. As we have begun with this Mode and Perfection of Almighty God, it seems that we now stand trapped between high walls of our own making. You shall be holy as the Lord your God is Holy: this is the burden of the Holiness School in Holy Scripture. Does not this theme join together in closest intimacy holiness and salvation? Does it not tie the Reality of God to His Self-Disclosure, His Revelation, as the Holy One? And is not the knowledge of the Holy Lord wedded most closely to the chastening, judging, and renewing of the sinner, caught up in the Holy God's mighty ways on this earth? Just so Calvin entwined knowledge of God and knowledge of self in the well-known opening paragraphs of the *Institutes of Christian Religion*. So, too, Søren Kierkegaard famously ridiculed the lofty Hegelian who could not quite remember that "he remained a man," a frail human being, a concrete life that could not be escaped nor should be, in all the vast palaces of philosophy.[37] Is not a metaphysics of Divine Holiness a folly, too, if it imagines it can be set forth apart from revelation, apart from sin and redemption?

Just who, we might ask, is writing such a doctrine? And just where is the famed "self-involving" character of Christian confession? Here we stand plainly before the crossroads that is the modern in Christian theology.

I do not enter this crossroad lightly. I could not take the next step, could not lay down or defend the central claim that God alone possesses the center of theology, without kneeling at the altar rail, without confessing my need of prayer, without bending down before the Sole Majesty of God. The aim of this dogmatics—to recover a full-throated metaphysics in the doctrine of God—cannot be had by a bloodless coup, as if a revolution of this sort were won by calculators or dry algorithms, calmly and coldly setting out a new table of contents. No, a sinner of the Lord's own redeeming: that is who writes these words. I would find it an easy conviction at my own tribunal were I to write a doctrine of Trinity that excluded a confession of my own failure, inadequacy, and faithlessness in undertaking and setting forth such Majesty. No one could be more keenly aware than I—or so it seems to me—that a sinner has set her hands to this dogmatic task, seeking to praise the Triune Lord, the One who is Holy. There is a temper in modern theology that finds the doctrine of Sin to be overwrought and altogether too dominant in Christian teaching: more of created goodness, more of joy and reconciliation achieved, it pleads, less of sin and sorrow and sighing—let it pass away! But I am not of this temper, nor do I possess the life that might tempt me to peer beyond the doctrines of sin and the cause of grace. This attempt to move soteriology and revelation out from the center of dogmatics, out most cleanly from the doctrine of the Holy Triunity, is not a *compensation* or a rearrangement and reweighting of cardinal truths. No, I stand too far within the enclosure of Latin Augustinianism to consider sin and grace elements that deserve quiet demotion, nor do I find my own existential lot somehow reserved or removed from their arresting grasp.

I am deeply grateful that I have been permitted the great grace of faith, in whatever measure it be accorded me, and that the light of the Gospel, its saving power, is revealed in this darkling plain and overspread in this one small life can but fill me with wonder and thankfulness. I do not believe that theology can be properly written apart from worship; it is an enactment of the intellect at prayer. All this makes theology an act and not simply a teaching, a confession of faith that is properly existential and self-involving, a breaking and a breaking open. Schleiermacher is quite right here: the dicta of the faith are anchored in the life kindled by awe. But if all this is so, how could we pretend to decenter soteriology and the Self-Disclosure of the Redeemer? Is *pretend* in truth strong enough a word? We will not break the riddle of relationalism in theology—the mediating theology of nineteenth-century academic theology[38]—by simply placing our hands on the scale of the Objective and weighing it down until the scale of the human subject lifts out of view. This is the vain hope that we can speak of God rather than the human by simply "looking at the moon rather than the finger which points at it," to adapt this Zen maxim for my own ends here. The intimacy between Object and subject, the Divine Holiness and the human sinner, cannot be ruptured by simply refusing to speak the sinner's name. How can this riddle be unraveled so that the Sole Truth of the Triune God can be set forth, His Power, His Sovereign Glory?

Theology is not liturgy: that is our next small step forward. Schleiermacher made such a distinction axiomatic in his work, and the place of theology within the modern university—the high calling of his *Brief Outline on the Study of Theology*—trades on such a distinction.[39] Here is Schleiermacher building the delicate dialectical architectonic between liturgical and scientific speech that shapes the whole *Glaubenslehre*: "§15 Christian doctrines are accounts of the Christian religious affections set forth in speech" and "§16 Dogmatic propositions are doctrines of the descriptively didactic type, in which the highest possible degree of definiteness is aimed at." Now between these two methodological propositions lies Schleiermacher's account of the "poetic" and "rhetorical" forms of Christian speech, each distinct from the "didactic," each caught up and defined in the "logical perfection" of scientific dogmatics. Note how all forms of Christian speech are "doctrine" in Schleiermacher's technical idiom—they all set forth Christian piety in speech. He does not aim to *divorce* preaching or devotional reflection from theology proper; rather, he seeks to ground all religious expression in the original piety awakened by the Redeemer and His pure dependence on God. Yet the more direct and emotive forms of doctrine—worship and hymnody, prayer and prophecy, proclamation—exist in dialectical relation to one another: "the poetic expression is always based originally upon a moment of exaltation which has come purely from within . . . the rhetorical upon a moment whose exaltation has come from without, a moment of stimulated interest which issues in a particular definite result."[40] We can detect here the subtle analysis of human awareness that undergirds the whole, the agency and receptivity, the beyond and within that characterize human being in the world. And in parallel with that sweeping motion which constitutes finite consciousness, Schleiermacher lays down speech, *communication*, as the making present and explicit what lies within and beneath. "This [religious] communication is something different from piety itself, though the latter cannot, any more than anything else which is human, be conceived entirely separated from all communication."[41]

For that reason, the three distinct forms of Christian utterance, poetry, rhetoric, and dogmatic proposition, coinhere: they all and each aim to set forth Christian piety in speech. They plant a stake down deep into the soil of religious affection, the sorrow and joy that come from dependence on the One, the Source of all, the Source of all blessing. Yet scientific dogmatics does something more, something exclusive for the pious community: it orders and renders clear and definite the *communicative* power that resides in the whole. In Schleiermacher's rather baroque idiom:

> Let us conceive of the comprehension and appropriation of what is given in a direct way in these two forms [the poetic and rhetorical], as being now wedded to language and thereby made communicable: then this cannot again take the poetic form, nor yet the rhetorical [one wonders just why; fears of infinite regress?]; but being independent of that which was the important element in those two forms, and expressing as it does a consciousness which remains self-identical, it becomes, less as preaching than as confession (*homologia*), precisely that third form—the didactic—which, with its descriptive instruction, remains distinct from the two others, and is made up of the two put together, as a derivative and secondary form.[42]

The two primal, direct forms of Christian doctrine yield up a teaching, a didactic expression, that can be isolated from both, rendered autonomous and self-contained: scientific dogmatics is distilled piety, language itself.

And as if these technical fireworks were not sufficient, Schleiermacher launches a Christological display to illumine and ground the whole. We will not follow him here, but that's a point that can be registered later on. Jesus Christ, Schleiermacher says, is *Self-Proclamation*; He just is the Communicative Word. To be sure, He speaks in poetic utterance—parables and vivid scene painting— and shows Himself a master of rhetoric, exhorting and chastising and consoling the crowds and elders and apostles and rulers who come into His Luminous Presence. But in exact conformity—no, they to Him—the communicative element, the Word, is the living center of His Self-Giving, His Life as Speech. In this way we might say that Jesus Christ just is scientific dogma for Schleiermacher. Yet the Lord Christ as "scientific proposition" is a way unique to Him: His is the unsurpassed depth of perfect repose in God. Even His poetry does not *express* his Conscious Depths but, strictly speaking, only *reflects* them, an effortless and unhurried full tide of Blessed Perfection. Just so, Christ's own Pious Dependence, the communication of His own Pure Receptivity of God—which, wonderfully, just *is* His Activity—cannot be the direct material of scientific dogmatics; rather, they undergird it. He is Redeemer in just this way, *communicating* His own Perfection and Blessing to those attracted to Him.

Schleiermacher shows us in all these ways how we might best consider the proper distinction between theology and liturgy. It is the proper place and weighting of *distinction* in theology that we seek to pursue here. Note that the *Christian faith* sets out a pair of ordered distinctions: affective doctrines turning over and distinct from scientific ones and Christ's own potent Self-Communication distinct from the didactive speech of the community He founded. Neither is reduced, one to the other—no distinction is lost or ranking upended—yet each is anchored in the primal reality, which is God in Christ, the Redeeming Word. Now, to be sure, there will be marked differences between a Christian dogmatics understood as *Glaubenslehre* and one that seeks to set out a full-throated metaphysical doctrine of the Triune, Holy God; I do not mean to minimize these. But Schleiermacher as a prince of the church does not simply teach material doctrines or even formal, methodological principles. He also shows us how to properly and elegantly *distinguish*: he has a supremely delicate touch in dogmatic theology. What he teaches and exemplifies here is the differentiated whole, the organic unity that retains ordered domains and concepts.

All this he dares to do even in Christology, the Living Center and Form of every theology! Just so, I say, we must learn at this school how to properly distinguish worship from the task and realm of dogmatic theology; how to distinguish Trinity from soteriology.

Consider for a moment the poetic and rhetorical dimensions of Christian worship. Here, in the church's liturgy, are combined the art of preaching, with the symbolic poetics of gesture and rite, of voices raised in song and speech, of sacramental acts and reception, of contrition and confession and praise—the whole communicative expression of Christian people in the Presence of their Lord. Liturgy joins the Triune Names with the doctrine of salvation; in worship, we offer thanks and praise to the Father, through the Son, in the Holy Spirit, for the great mercy of our redemption. Of course, not all preaching makes explicit the doctrine of salvation, nor do all prayer and confession overtly state the doctrine of revelation! We do not lay claim here to the whole *material content* of Christian worship; rather, we say that the people gathered together before Almighty God "render thanks for the great benefits received at His hands," as the Book of Common Prayer has it. Rahner is right to see the doctrine of Trinity as the doctrine of salvation, were we to speak of nothing but the church's liturgy. We see and receive and hear Christ as Redeemer there; we rehearse the *Magnalia Dei*, the Mighty Acts of God, in season and out; we follow our Lord from humble birth to defilement and death, a cold death in the cold ground, and rise up with Him in His Victory, His Triumph that is the distant reveille of our freedom, just over the ridge of our death. We would see Jesus, the Greeks tell Philip, and that might sum up what we lost ones would do when we open the sanctuary doors. Holy Scripture, read in the people's nave, reveals the Self-Communication of the Lord, the Redeemer, and all this in the Spirit who leads to the Father. The rich banquet of the Lord's own

Supper, giving Himself to us, by His own Hand: this is the shape of Christian deliverance while on long pilgrimage to the Jordan. No one could be formed by the worship of the church, the astonishing breadth of liturgical rite, and not feel the weight of the church's tradition, the hands of the Blessed, pressed down on every head, around every heart that is drawn to prayer and thanksgiving, sacrament and song, the overspilling grace that is worship of Almighty God. Just here is where the complex legacy of modern theology receives its historical grounding: revelation, salvation, and Trinity are the proper Mysteries of all Christian liturgy.

But now, we distinguish! Theology is not liturgy. By this we mean that dogmatics serve a distinct role in the Christian life, to render explicit the teachings of the church as embedded in Holy Scripture and to set forth their articulated and ordered whole. Now this is not "second-order" work! Schleiermacher is especially powerful as instructor in just this way: he will not accord to theology some separate domain that is immune or sealed off from religious life. Not for him any notion of grammar or logical structure; no, each domain in theology is a form of Christian doctrine and remains tethered to the grace of sheer dependence on God. Theology is *piety* in just this sense. And I believe Schleiermacher is just right on these points. We do not seek to pry the Mystery of Trinity out from the religious life of the theologian, nor of the covenant people and church that gave it intellectual expression. Rather, we say, with Schleiermacher, that theology develops in clear and articulated fashion an element common to the life of the faithful: the Objectivity of God. We have spoken of God as *Being there*, having a Blessed Resistance and Persistence that is the Glory of God's own Reality. Theology speaks explicitly and directly of this Sovereign Beauty. Always the community of the faithful rely on the Objective Reality of God; always the Christian at prayer and feast and confession assume, rightly, that God stands over against them, in lofty and inaccessible Light, Uncreated, Independent, High, and Lifted Up. That is the quiet assumption of all relational and mediating theologies, after all; the quiet assumption of all doctrines of prayer and rite. God is *encountered*; He is utterly Prior, the First. This is why all theories of projection strike at the heart of worship, the heart of the Christian life. The Unrepentant Reality of God beckons us to turn aside and see this Great Wonder; it is not of our own making. Only idols are that.

Note then that we need not follow Schleiermacher's *linguistic theory* to learn his art of distinction. Remember that *The Christian Faith* made quiet but ambitious claims about the linguistic and communicative dimensions of human being: to be human, he said—almost in passing—is to express inwardness in speech; we are essentially a linguistic animal. Scientific theology for Schleiermacher is the highest art because it makes this ordered discourse the very centerpiece of its task: dogmatics is the human-forming discipline. Theology is ordered speech, and human beings are linguistic creatures. Theology, for Schleiermacher, is the lingua franca of the human. Now this makes Schleiermacher a distinctly *modern* dogmatician. His anthropology is governed by the human interior working its way outward in gesture, symbol, and, above all, in language. Shaped as we are these days by a stronger linguistic turn, we moderns often reverse the tide of Schleiermacher's anthropology: for us the inward might well be the child of the outward, language opening up and deepening the interior cavern we call inwardness. But we see commonality all the same here: experience, speech, praxis, all interwoven to make the human being, the linguistic animal. We might even say, to borrow a leaf from Barth, a "well roared, lion!" But it is just here that we return to our original point: we need not follow this linguistic turn to learn from his art of distinction. We may recognize that dogmatics is not liturgy, even apart from a full-blown account of the communicative moment, the "religious affections set forth in speech." Not everything is soteriology! That is the force of Schleiermacher's distinction for a proper, realistic dogmatics.

But here I think I hear my reader saying what must have sprung to mind some pages back: Is it really all that easy? Can a distinction, even a scholastic one, in truth perform such wonderful surgery? Perhaps one might say, this is all too wonderful, too tidy and well dressed, to be true. And how could we not bow before such a rebuke? Does not all this admiration for careful distinction smack of the artificial, the convenient—worse, the cheap? Sigmund Freud famously ridiculed a similar host of well-meaning distinctions by religious believers with the snort, "It would be very nice if there were a God who created the world and was a benevolent providence, and if there were a moral order in the universe and an afterlife; but it is a very striking fact that all this is exactly as we are bound to wish it to be."[43] The deep things of God cannot be had through intellectual architectonic; we cannot rearrange the bits on the theologian's desk so that all works out neatly and well. The peril here is that the distinction between liturgy and dogmatics is just such an artifice, a feeble paper dam erected against the roaring Flood who is God. Have we committed such a folly here?

Now I think there is every reason to fear that a human system of thought, even more, a whole human life, will seek to flee from the God who is Redeemer and Judge. The claim that Almighty God lays on the creature is met, time and again, by worshipful lips and a deceitful heart. Theology can offer idolatry in just this way: to make distinctions where there is no difference; to elaborately unfurl a grammatical and formal concept that never penetrates to the *Sache*, never obeys, that quietly sweeps into the corner the very tinder that should set the whole ablaze—that is the sophisticated disbelief of systematics. Do we diagnose that here? Should we?

I think not. But the reason for this decision is not easy to state. We must begin, I would say, at a perhaps surprising place, by a careful reflection on the place of the temple in the life and the land of the people Israel. Where Schleiermacher grounds his art of distinction in Christology, we do so in the people Israel. The distinction Schleiermacher has set out with conceptual flourish for us must be anchored in the covenant people, or not at all. Just how are we to understand the temple cultus, the place of sacrifice, in the elect people of God? Just this is the subtlety and sublimity of the Holiness Code and its living, fiery center in the temple, its courts, its altars, its ark of the covenant, its prophet, priests, and Levites. It is Zion, in midst of Judah; it is the proper love of her very rubble. As we will develop in time, this Holy City, with its temple and altar and inner sanctum, is the molten core of Israel, the fundament of this people and its holiness. Yet in the face of all this, it is patent that holy Zion is not the whole of Israel, the temple—even the numinous ark—not the totality of the covenant people, its history, its kingship and prophecy, its law and Torah. Leviticus does not comprise the whole of the books of Moses; it is not even their center. Indeed, the early history of the covenant people unfolds without a temple or a temple mount, not even a settled hill shrine or precinct. And though early on in the palmy days of the United Monarchy, King David wished to build the Lord a House, it was rather the Lord who built David, His royal son, a house, a lineage, a spacious realm and sea of descendants. Even the worldly-wise King Solomon, who was granted, at last, the liberty to build the Divine House, knew that the temple could not contain the Majesty of God; He did not dwell there as idols in their banquet halls. The whole of Israel escapes the temple grounds, swells out beyond the precincts, spills into the borderlands of Moab and Egypt and Phoenicia, climbs up onto the world's lampstand and illumines all nations on earth. The Torah sweeps into its nets every practice and living kind of Israel, the high and low together, the weekday and Sabbath; it is a generous whole, a universe in which the temple, its purity, rites, sacrifices, and offerings, constitute but one part, though, to be sure, a holy one, a Divine Fire. Israel, we must say, is not "a religion," though it has one. It is a people, a history, a nation—a concrete reality in the midst of the realia of the ancient Near East.

This bears reflection. We again explore a distinction, put to work in systematic theology. Israel does not name or stand for a cultus only, a sacrificial system, an ascetical practice and training ground without remainder. Israel is not *religious* in that sense. Consider, after all, what the people, history, and land of Israel would resemble were it a religious cultus and liturgical system alone. When we opened the Holy Bible, we would be entering an esoteric and ritualized realm. Its pages would be devoted to a temple customary: rules for vestment and preferment in office; regulations for filling and maintaining the Great Sea; articulated design for the temple veil, its appointment and cleaning; proper manufacture of temple lights, the tallow and taper and oil stands that are fitting for such sacred work; the technique for proper slaughter of holy animals, and the manner of selecting, preparing, and washing the basins for sacred blood; the clothing for arms and hands in offering up grain or turtledoves or incense; the proper manner for placing the tables of the Law in their resting place, for their maintenance and care, and a rite for their inspection, contemplation, and devotion. The Old Testament would be a collection of ritualized practices and rules of this sort—a library of religious manuals and not just this. Were Israel to be exclusively a religion in the form of a temple practice and cult, the Holy Scriptures would teach the pious exercises and the ancient forms of training in religious devotion. We would read in Holy Writ the proper state of mindfulness, the art of deepening contemplation of the Holy One, the proper regard for sacred hours, and postures, and preparation, the pattern of true faithfulness, of error and distraction, of turning aside to other gods and other cults. We would find between the covers of Scripture a rich compendium of prayers and the skill of fostering prayer, a viaticum for those who have lost their way, a praise of those whose lives have become transparent to the Holy Light of Eternity, a preparation for death and dressing of the soul for its quietus, a mortification of conscience before the Holy Judge, a quickening of repentance, a path for true offering of goods for sacrifice. The people Israel as a *religious* body would be guardians and heirs of the temple, and their identity and purpose would be caught up solely in the traditions, orders, and prayerful states of those who long to serve Almighty God in just these ways of the elders, to become adepts.

Now I do not intend to ignore the elements of all these rituals and religious states that can be found in Holy Scripture; indeed, I confess that much of the Holiness Code concerns itself with proper order and purity of sacred things. And I would suppose that most Christians have uncovered religious manuals of the kind I imagine for a purely religious Israel: manuals of spiritual direction, rubrics in missal and altar book, directions to altar guilds and sacristans, and devotional books of many kinds. These are important texts for the faithful of many traditions! We need not make light of ascetic discipline or practice or pretend that counsel of this sort is not longed for by those who seek after God, by those who wish to see beyond earthly time and possession. There *is* religion in Israel; there are prayers and proverbs and hymns; there is Talmud and halakah and kabbalah; there is a form of pietism and askesis; above all, there is sacrifice. We may treasure the set prayers that have been laid down deep in our marrow by spiritual guides, by mothers and fathers in Israel; we may cherish the means for searching Scripture aright, for finding the quiet, still point in a world passing away, for making true confession and amendment of life. We may long to be *religious* in just this way. And theology would be altogether poorer—stony-hearted!—if it were to cast aside such helps to pilgrims. But we consider here whether such pieties form in truth the whole of the eternal people of God. For Israel is not, in its entirety, temple, nor is its people religion.

Now we apply the distinction: doctrine, then, even the doctrine of Trinity, is not entirely and exhaustively, liturgy, salvation religion. We have to see rather a distinction, a delimitation, that orders dogmatics even in the doctrine of God. Now, note how fine-grained this is—a fine-grained subtlety Schleiermacher has taught us to see right from the start in the *Glaubenslehre*. For we are noting the distinction between liturgy and theology wholly *from within* the Holiness Code. We are standing *within* the temple precincts and finding *there* the conviction that not all is soteriology! We are discovering from within the temple courts the Israel who spills out beyond those walls, however precious, and we are hearing another note and theme sounded within the very worship of Israel. Just such insight is uncovered for us in the remarkable worldliness of the prophet Habbakuk: The Lord is in His Holy Temple; just this we would expect of a liturgical nation—let the *whole earth* stand in awe of Him—but not this! Now we are seeing drawn up to the Exceeding Holiness of God the entire cosmos, the whole of the created order; nothing escapes. Just this knitting together of temple and cosmos impels a deeper grasp of the particular and the concrete in the work of theology. As Most Real Being, God's concrete existence overspills any delimitation: the Spirit is Liberty. Israel is the Light to the nations, the overspilling of the banks of the Jordan, and the ringing summons to the whole round earth, just because it is *this very one*, this singular, definite, and concrete people. From within its own temple, the call goes forth to the nations. Now this must mean that the liturgical life, the round of festival and sacrifice and pilgrimage, must itself—*from within*—generate a distinction that overspills the temple walls and comes to life in the people Israel, their everyday world, and even more startling, in the nations of the earth, their stubborn and godless ways, their quiet service of the Unknown God. The people Israel, in its obdurate reality and historical concreteness, shadow forth for systematic doctrine, how Trinity is to be related to soteriology. As temple and law and sacrifice stand at the heart of the covenant people, yet do not exhaust or comprehend it, so the doctrine of salvation cannot contain, define, or exhaust the whole of Trinity. The metaphysical Reality, the Unsurpassed Richness and Infinity of the Holy God overspills any of our local concerns, even the burning matter of our own redemption. Trinity is no more an existential, anthropological doctrine than Israel is a compendium of temple practices and sacrificial lore. The Reality of both is much more. Indeed, the Reality who is God will superabundantly exceed even this analogy, indeed, all analogies. Just this is the Greater Unlikeness, amid all likenesses, which I will call the Triune Processions.

Just so we must assume that from within Holy Scripture as a narrative of redemption, the bold and relentless Objectivity of God is demarcated; from within the revealed word, the doctrine beyond revelation and beyond salvation is announced. For this reason, the very notion of transcendence must be reconceived. What it means for Almighty God to be Beyond, to be Superabundant and Free must not mean that the Lord is *contrary* to the world. It means precisely not that. We are thinking now of the principle definitions and notions of any theology: they must not be conceived as pairs of opposition. The Transcendence of God over the world He has made, His Being as the Beyond, does not entail, cannot entail, that He is *not-creature*. His Eternity does not, cannot, mean He is *not-temporal*. His Sublime Majesty is more and other than lowliness— but not opposed to it. And His deep Mystery as Trinity does and cannot annul or stand over against His Supreme Unicity. Just this is the exacting lesson of transcendence. We might say that it is an extension of the broader lesson on proper distinction in theology, the lesson Schleiermacher would teach us at every turn.

Here, for example, is the master on this very point: "§51 The Absolute Causality to which the feeling of absolute dependence points back can only be described in such a way that, on the one hand, it is distinguished from the content of the natural order and thus contrasted with it, and, on the other hand, equated with it in comprehension."[44] Note here that Schleiermacher sets out the primary Divine Attribute—Absolute Causality—as a form of distinction from creatures and, *therefore*, a contrast. He is careful not to phrase this as an *opposition* but rather as difference or delimitation.

Here Schleiermacher teaches us that distinction in theology is not a matter of opposition or, worse, contradiction. We might think properly here of the difference or contrast between the colors red and yellow: a genuine difference, a clear demarcation, but not an opposition. Red and yellow are members of a set, true; they constitute a pair of primary colors, also true; and they are not to be confused or reduced, one to the other. Yet their distinctiveness rests not in their reality set one against the other but rather in the line of contrast that runs down between them, color patches on the artist's pallet. There is more. These two colors are not simply beads on a string or elements in a table. They are not standing side by side in a mere "external relation," as idealists put this point, as though lined out by some random order maker. No, these colors belong together, under a genus, but as *contrasting* members. They are elemental, primary. Unlike other hues or tones on a color wheel, these two are not composed of other colors but rather compose them. The building blocks of color structure the whole of sight—offering what Thomas called the "formal object of sight"—by way of distinguishing, marking, and ordering the whole, opened to our eyes. We might say that they are related to one another, siblings, each rubbing up against the other, having a territory and task between them, a common load. Yet they remain distinct in just that way; yoked and contrasted, side by side.

Just this fine-grained contrast we see in the divine works ad extra, the Presence and Transcendence of the Creator to His creation. Distinction—contrast—structures a proper doctrine of God. The days of creation, marked out and made distinct by evening and morning, each day, do not make the days opposed to one another, nor does the divine act of creation halt or break off between each solemn blessing and completion of that day's work. The days of creation form a series, an unfolding string of distinct acts that are *both* fresh each morning *and* continuous. Note for example that in the Genesis prologue, we see the Creator act in this distinctive fashion: He does not create one compound reality, one super-dense—to borrow a term from physics—creature, that then is unfolded, or unfolds itself under the direction or impulse of its Lord. No, Moses tells us that there is a distinct act for each day, a word, a delimitation, and, for some, a blessing, a radiant goodness beheld and confirmed. Each day is a particular, and it stands in contrast to the rest. Yet this just *is* creation! One act, one work ad extra, one singular bringing forth of all reality. Just so we see the Sabbath Day, a hallowing and blessing of this work, but also a day of the Divine Rest, the great Divine Peace that breaks out over the whole. It is a day; it stands in the series; it contrasts with them; yet it is the confirmation, the consummation, the sublime unity of the whole that makes this a *world*, not a random collection of things.

We might express this delicate relation of contrast to opposition in a second way as well. Genesis tells us of the very idea of the *Day*, the divine day, the character and formal expression of the *Creatio ex nihilo*. Toward us, the Lord God acts as the One He is, and all his works are one—and this is expressed by the distinction of "the Day." Unity and distinction are not opposed, that is, but rather compatible, joined together in one *opus ad extra*. The Day of creation, that is, is a *perfect work*. It stands for the whole, the complete, the ideal. The Day, Genesis tells us, consists of an evening and a morning, the twilight and night hours leading the way, the sunrise and daylight hours rounding out the whole: One Day. The distinctions belong to a perfect work; they demarcate it. They make a strong contrast with one another, but a contrast that is placed in rhythm and motion, much as are seedtime and harvest, summer and winter, cold and heat that set forth the Noachide Covenant. There are six of these days in the work of creation, and we might think of them as the biblical expression of the universal or general concept. Each day gives rise, under the Divine Command, to fresh life, of kinds and exemplars, of whole swarms of living things, of lone particulars, a greater and a lesser light: each day, particular, unique. Yet they belong to the kind and category day of creation.

They follow the rhythm of rest and renewal, night and day, the movement and turning that lies under the Divine Hand. They are *the generations*, the vast, untiring, unstinting fertility and making of a world. In just this way, we see the generations of the whole human family, the distinctiveness *and* the representative nature of those first human lives, unfolded in the generations until Abraham and Sarah follow the long pathway from Ur of the Chaldees, and human history, the history of the generations of Israel, explodes. The history of Israel and the history of creation mirror one another, each a story of seasons and of days, of generation and waxing strong, flourishing under the sun the Lord God hung in the dome of the sky, but fading, too, as the breath of the Lord blows across it, returning to the dust and to the night, a Day, One Day in the great workings of the God of Israel.

These Days are gathered together. They do not simply stand, solitary, in a series, one next to another. They are not unrelated, not bare items in a set. Rather, this ideal type, the Day, moves in its stately motion, to a *telos*, an end that is the Lord's own. The end of creation is a Day, also. It is the Perfect Day, the Sabbath Rest, the Lord God's own Rest. Here the generation, the movement and the rhythm, draw to its completion, its perfection. Each Day is not *annulled*, neither surpassed nor violated, but rather the generations of the heavens and the earth, even as the generations of Israel, are gathered together in their completion: they *enter in* to their Rest, their Blessing, their Promised Land. Nothing is lost; but the fragments are gathered up, basket upon basket. People who speak this way, we should say, show that they belong to Another Country, that is, a Heavenly One: the end of all history, of all time and flourishing, of up-rising and down-sitting, of weal and woe, is that Last Day, the Perfect One, when God is All and in all. In just this way, Holy Scripture shows us that the Day, its distinction and its unity, its movement and its Perfect Rest, are signs and markers, too, of the One God Himself, His Perfect Unicity, His Perfect Generation and Distinction. The Day, in Scripture's instruction, is, at the end and fundament, *Holiness*, the Holy One. God hallows that Day, the Sabbath, as the Day of days, the Terminus and Perfect Peace of all Holiness. It shadows forth what the Divine Holiness must be—though in Mystery and Superabundance: it must partake of Distinction and of Life, and gather them up as One, One Perfect Holy Rest.

For this reason, the categories and kinds that inhabit theology do not function quite as they do in pure conceptual work: they are not the elements of a philosophy but of a dogmatics and, in just this way, gather together and elevate the strict codes of reason. But this is a *contrast*, not an opposition! The universals and kinds, the particulars and singulars, the temporal markers and ordering, the immanence and transcendence: these belong, too, to theology, but under the Command and Mystery of God. They super-exceed their place within rational argument, always beyond, always more. Just so we can see the distinctions in kind and category that troubled Schleiermacher and many of his heirs put to work in fresh ways in Holy Scripture and in dogmatics. Even Schleiermacher, that is, could have made greater use of his fine-grained doctrine of distinction than he did. Consider the relation of creation and preservation, a distinction, Schleiermacher feared, without a difference.[45] He reasoned that the doctrine of creation clearly contained the elements assigned by custom to preservation: the holding in being and directing of all creatures to their ends, a providential ordering. For this reason, dogmatics is better served, he thought, by showing the unity of the Divine Working in collapsing the distinction between the two, and laying out, in their place, a doctrine of continuous creation. Freed from anxious worry over beginnings, the *Glaubenslehre* could serenely chart the unshadowed power of God's Causal Act, finding in the parts and in the whole, the freedom and the reception, the complete *Naturzusammenhang*, the proper effect of a Single Absolute, Transcendent Creator. And Schleiermacher does not stand alone here. So, too, Augustine, reasoning along these lines, proposed an initial creation, an intellectual whole, perfect, unsullied, utterly potent and generative, obedient, and suffused with the elixir of desire for God: this one intellectual creature must contain in some way the whole that unfolds in the *Hexameron*. And consider, too, the pressure some Reformation theologies placed on the work of the Cross and the work of the Empty Tomb: Must we choose the atoning moment? Must they be identified? So, too, we might think of the more modern worry about the categories of revelation and the development of doctrine or the church's magisterial teaching: How do the categories and kinds function here? Are these, too, distinctions without difference? Or must they be ranked, opposed, winnowed in proper dogmatics?

The Perfect Work of the Day gives us guidance in discerning unity and distinction, contrast and opposition. Here we see a category, a class or kind, being at once exemplified *and* gathered together in Perfect Unity. There is One Work ad extra even as there is One God, One Sublime Reality beyond all kind and category and seeming. Yet just what does it mean in Holy Scripture for there to be a singular opus ad extra? How is it that the Bible relates the unity that flows from the Giver of every good and perfect gift? It tells us of six days of creation that just are the One Work; the days that simply are also One Day, One Rest. We are being shown here something odd, something majestic, about Divine Working, Divine Eternity: this Work can be unfolded in distinct elements, and they are One. Just this marks them as Perfect. Creation and preservation can be identified in just this way. They can share the elements Schleiermacher and Tillich discover in their definitions; they can show forth a Creative Power or Ground that is common and vital to both, that can serve the same End. Yet they remain distinct! So, too, we say that Passion and Resurrection form One Work of Redemption, One Whole, One Marvelous Light and Deliverance. They are the Perfect Work where the Almighty and Holy God stoops as the Humble One to His wayward and lost creature: they break every lordless power and turn evening winding sheet over into morning. They are ordered, even as are the days of creation; they are singular, marvelous. And they are *One*, One Perfect Work.

The Day, then, is no ordinary category or creature. Of course, this is no discovery of today! From Philo and Basil and Augustine forward, Christians and Jews have felt the magnetic power of the Genesis account and have puzzled, wide-eyed, at these six elemental and mysterious Days. Modern naturalists have made it their lifework, in desperate hope or in contempt, to show how these Days range against the cosmology of present-day science. Certainly, they do not measure up well. It does not take *Essays and Reviews* to tell us that the ancient paleography does not accord exactly—perhaps not at all—with the movement and distinction of the six days of creation in Genesis.[46] It is the subject of some modern scorn to note that the first days are marked before the sun and moon are fashioned and hung like lanterns in the spacious heavens—but this, too, was known from long ago. On all sides, early and late, the day of creation is taken as luminous (or scandalous) mystery. It is composed of evening and morning, yet its name is Day, not night, and like the light itself, the luminous Day is found good, hallowed, and blessed. What should we make of this remarkable creature, the Day? How should we hear Scripture speaking here?

The days of creation are, I should say, the creaturely echo of the Divine Processions, or to borrow that haunting phrase of Plato's, they are the "moving image of Eternity." This is the scriptural realization of distinction as a matter of the doctrine of God. We are seeing something here in Holy Scripture that will be taken up, refined and rekindled in the creation of humankind: the Image and Likeness of God. The Day is that first *Imago*, that first *Similitudo*, disclosed and made freely from the great Abyss of Divine Life. It is a creature that belongs to the Primal Days, the First Haunting, when the Origin was young. Like Israel itself, we will move in stages, from this Primal Day to the exile that marks all our earthly days, to the blood spilled over the first sacrifice, to that worldly day when we built the tower that would climb back to Eden to the Primal Days, to the heavens above, and finally, descent upon descent, day upon day, distinction and separation, one piled upon the other, we come to our days, we children of Eve, children of Abraham and Sarah, children of the earth. Not just the Garden but those Imago Days are sealed off from us by the flaming sword, by the angels standing at the end of our pathways and ambitions. We long for them and catch the faint echo of their majesty when we raise our eyes to Holy Writ. But they are barred to us, their perfection, their distinct wholeness and holiness. *Our* days pass away like smoke; but *they* endure forever. They taste Eternity. They move, one into the other, distinct in their work, yet conjoined, always present. They are simply Day, the Evening and Morning, all alike, all one definition, one motion, One. The Seventh Day, the Sabbath, shows us this. It perfects the series; it consummates it. It is the Stillness who just is the Origin, the Unfathomable One. Yet it is simply Day, Evening and Morning. All Days are this; and the Sabbath, the Holy Day, is just what Evening and Morning are made for. *This* is the Full Image of God, the Triune Lord.

Just so our Lord Christ rested on His final Sabbath Day, closed up in the earth. Just so He took death with Him into that dark night, into the friendless tomb, the creature in all its frailty and pride and suffering, down with Him into the Absolute Rest, into the Stillness that is the Seventh Day. Barred from that Primacy once again, large boulders blocking our way, angels in dazzling robes parting us from the Day when it turns over into Life, we glimpse only the contours of that Primal Age, the Likeness that conforms to its Maker. Just this, we may say here, is what it means for the Sabbath to be made for humankind, not humankind for the Sabbath: for the Son of Man is Lord of the Sabbath. He, the Incarnate Word, the Primal Light, comes to His end, His perfection, in His entrance into the Sabbath Rest. This is His Day, His consummation, His final hallowing and holiness. And just so we must say that this Sabbath, this Terminus, is set apart from the Lord's Day, the First Day of the Week; yet it is One with it. The Life that just is the Superabundant God pours forth on that Day, the Primal Light escaping from the prison house, the whole Seven Days caught up in this One, the First, the Origin. The universe rings with the joy of this Day, this goodness, this deliverance; everywhere it is the greening of this old earth. It is a Perfect Work, each act distinct, costly, yet continuous and in the strongest sense, a unity. The church honors this primal distinction and unity in its Passiontide, the Triduum. Three days in the tomb, three days from Cross to Resurrection, yet one service, one "extended simple,"[47] without dismissal or benediction, from Good Friday to Easter Sunday, from death to life: and there was evening and there was morning, One Day.

We have spoken here of Perfect, Primal Days as an echo or shadow of the Divine Life, Its Perfect Unicity, Its Perfect Distinction. And we have suggested that these Days exhibit a kinship with Eternity, an Eternity in motion; an Image and Likeness. These are resonances of transcendence, of the Mysterious and Sovereign relation of Creator and creature, a demarcation of contrast, not opposition, a distinction that in all its proper and stately indefiniteness, makes a far more radical determination between God and cosmos than any remoteness or distance could capture. Now, it may be all too clear by now that this is an exceedingly odd and angular way to read the opening chapters of Genesis. It will belong to the doctrine of creation proper to indicate how such angular readings can guide and instruct the account of God's making of all that is. And it will fall to the full doctrine of Holy Scripture to say just how the Bible can receive, even encourage, such speculative, spiritual exegesis. But before we begin a careful examination of Scripture and its relation to soteriology, we pause to pull threads together. We began this excursus with the conviction that "not all is soteriology!" We found Schleiermacher a fine guide in making a careful distinction between liturgy and theology, but an even finer guide was discovered in Scripture itself. First the concrete and rich existence of Israel, a people rather than a religion; then the temple itself, a molten center of Israel's cultus, yet pointing beyond itself to the Sole Sovereignty of God; and finally the days of creation, successive, distinct, yet one: all these demonstrated a fine-grained form of distinction that serves theology well. The Objective Reality of God can be distinguished from the sinner's teaching and deliverance in just these ways—a careful contrast and articulation that points always beyond to the Mystery who is God. That the days of creation can speak in the biblical idiom of the Divine Processions is cardinal instance of the whole. Even in the primal history, God commands center stage; in the midst of His creation, He the Triune One testifies to Himself; He alone stands there.

Part 2. Holy Scripture and Soteriology

Here we must indicate, even briefly, the *force* of such readings for the reverent upbuilding of the dogma of Trinity. We must indicate, in swift strokes, why a full-throated *metaphysical* reading of the kind practiced here might be welcome in the courts of present-day theology. We are assuming here, in a rather flat-footed way, that God is the Author of Holy Scripture. Now I mean this in a strong sense—strong, but not literal. The proper notion of Almighty God as Author, I would say, does not bring in its wake the famous troubles early modern interpreters spotted in this doctrine: anxious attention to divine dictation, to "autograph" manuscripts, to extensive protection of the solemnity and dignity of the very words of Scripture, their inerrancy, their plenary inspiration. Divine Authorship, I would say too, does not tie us down to the irritating family quarrels over human agency, historical limitation and context, and forms of human fallibility, sinful or no. It, too, is no categorical system of opposition! (Indeed, theological compatibilism is a far greater ally in this family dispute than is any system of opposition or control.) Rather, Divine Authorship of Holy Scripture points to the Lord's Transcendent Presence, His Holy Nearness, to creatures in the Sacred Writings of Israel and church. We should say, as a fuller description, that as Author, God is Source.

To have a Divine Source of the Bible would hold, I would say, for any doctrine of inspiration, of text, of Evangelist, of reader. But I believe we should consider the notion of Source against a particular background: Holy Scripture has a Divine Source, and that claim is clarified over against the notion of Scripture as produced by a Divine Revealer. God does not *primarily* reveal the Bible, I say, nor reveal what is within its covers—not principally, not exclusively. We are not thinking, first and exhaustively, of God as Speaker within Holy Writ, who discloses and teaches and determines the content of Israel's belief or practice. God is not first or exhaustively a Revealer. For this reason we must say again, "Not all is Revelation!" He is not the Bearer of Divine information. Nor is He a Character, even a Transcendent and Holy Character, within the long covenant history of Israel and the in-grafting of the nations. The Bible is not *about* God, not in that sense! The Bible has God as its Source not principally in the Acts of Lawgiving or Teaching or Judgment, though, to be sure, He acts in all these ways. We do not first look within this book, however reverently, to find out His Ruling on this matter or that. The Bible is not an instruction manual in that sense! It is not the Perfect Example of the Guide to Religion or Conduct. To expect such things of the Bible is to secularize it, I say, and to place it firmly though piously on the shelf with all other wise and useful and edifying tomes. God as Divine Source stands in contrast—not opposition!—to all that.

God is More, always More. He is more than the Lawgiver and Judge, more than the Voice and the Thunder and the Searing Holiness out of the darkness of Mt. Horeb, more than the Outstretched Arm, more than the Blessing of the Beloved Son, more than the Voice of Many Waters in the Last Days. God cannot be reduced to a Part, a Particular, within some earthly realm. He will be *this*; He will come under our roof, but He cannot be *reduced*—never exhaustively defined or confined but always Free, always Strange and Glorious, always Beyond. Just so, in Holy Scripture, God as Source will enter into the pages and events of Israel and church—He the Holy One will humble Himself this far!— but He cannot be reduced, captured, exhausted by this Nearness to His lonely world. There is no domestication of the Holy One of Israel! Just so, God as the Bible's Source stands in strict parallel to the temple in the larger life of the covenant people: dwelling there, honored, prominent, central, revered, but not the whole, not the entirety, not the purpose and main event of election history.

As Source, that is, God can be Near to and Sovereign over the whole of the Bible. He is *Holy Presence*, the Transcendent Origin, the One in the entire compass of this Inspired Book. Every word in Holy Writ bears His Impress; it *echoes* Him. It is suffused with His Melody; it is distillate of His Being. The Bible is *creature*, certainly. Indeed, I believe it is a fallible—at times, painfully fallible— text. But it stands in the rank upon rank of creatures as unique, strongly unique. It is not head or supreme or invulnerable among creatures: the Bible is not protected from creaturehood in that sense. Rather it has been elected out of the nations of the earth, though small and of no account, to serve this end, that the whole world should have a creaturely echo, a resonance, a pattern of the Divine Life, held in its hands, sweet in its ears. The Lord God has laid Himself down in this cradle, illumining the whole, calling and making these human words the *imago Dei*, the Hidden, Indirect, yet Real Likeness of the Incomparable God. It is sacrament of the Divine Presence, yet much more and other than that, too. It is sacrifice and fragrant offering, yet far beyond and other than these gifts of cultus and rite. It is prayer, contemplation, consolation, but more earthy and other than these spiritual acts as well. The Bible has its Source in God, and the Divine and Provident Author radiates its reality with the Ocean of Reality, the Light of Eternity. Holy Scripture, in unrivaled excellence, is the *vestigium Trinitatis*. Nothing else does this in this way or is hallowed for this end.

For this reason, the Bible may and ought to be read under its own distinct idiom. It should be read as the Book whose Source is God. In *this* sense, the Bible *is concerned with* God! In its pages we are to read about, to encounter, the Being of God, just that. This is not to say that the Bible is not about, does not refer to, many creatures and events and things, to worldly signs and things; we cannot set these two against one another. But the central and essential property of Holy Scripture, though hidden to many eyes, is its being bearer of the Divine Likeness. We look for God in His Aseity, as He is, there, in this book. When we read the Bible, then, we are being shown the Fabric and Contour of the Divine Transcendence. The Bible is not a story, first and primarily, about the Divine Missions or the divine economy with us. Holy Scripture, rather, is the creaturely mirror of the Divine Immanence, the inner Triune Life of God.

To read Scripture, on the other hand, as the narrative of the economic Trinity is such a commonsense, intuitive, and near instinctive reading for Christians that it is worth our while to linger a moment over this point. We have not climbed to the dizzying heights of God's Authorship of Holy Writ when we see in the Bible only the trace of His decision to dwell with us. To be sure, the Bible *is* this, and it tells that story. But the *force*, the exceeding wonder of the Bible is not that it could utter such things. No! It has been called to far greater heights, to see greater wonders than these, to be swept along to the Heaven of the Heavens, to be brought into the divine throne room. To say that God is the Source of the Bible is to affirm that the Immanent Being of God is redoubled, manifested, impressed in each part and all parts of this unique work.

Now this may seem impossible, overreaching, or blasphemous. And I do think it a dangerous doctrine indeed. I want to observe great care in this doctrine of inspiration because we stand now on the Holy Edge of the camp, where the Fire burns and the Cloud descends. It is a Strange Work, a Perfect One, that we meditate on here, and we must be willing to turn aside a while to encounter It. Under the rubric of Holy Scripture, we are reflecting once again on the nature of the Divine Reality, *and* Its Holy Presence in our midst. The notion of God as Source of Scripture retraces the entire Mystery of God's Aseity, His Transcendent Being, in our mouths and minds, our lives and rites, our works and ways. It is the struggle for realism, a proper and vibrant realism in theology, touching down, searing the edge of Scripture's page. We must be able to affirm that Holy Scripture teaches—but more, *manifests*—the Aseity of the True, Holy, and Triune God, or we have no Divine Source at all. It is that strong.

Now it may seem that here I am riding roughshod over delicate terrain. Have we not a broad catena of patristic and scholastic theologians who draw a rather daring line between the Mystery or Essence or Transcendence of God and His Revelation and Acts and Energies toward us? Is that not indeed the origin, the faithful origin, of all distinctions, fine or broad, between God in Himself and God for us? Is this not the reverent teaching of the *Theological Orations*, of the *Life of Moses*, of the *Prima Pars* of the *Summa*, and, in different idiom, of Calvin's stern counsel against the idle and the speculative in the doctrine of God? And this list is but a sample—powerful but hardly the full scope of those who counsel a humble devotion to God's Economy, the place and words where He is pleased to dwell, the sights He is content to grant to us. It is the temper of some ancient theology to acknowledge a stark contrast between Creator and creature, the Aseity of God and His Economy and Ways with us. The ruling of Lateran IV on analogy—"every similarity to God is embraced and governed by an ever-greater dissimilarity"—conforms to that temper. It is a holy reserve before the Holy Mystery of God. And such reserve must not be lost! But our point here is to insist that that reserve must be carried through the hazards of the modern era unscathed. For the modern era in dogmatics has calcified and salted that ancient reserve; it now carries special dangers for a proper doctrine of Holy Scripture. The modern preoccupation with critical method in dogmatics has made the smooth movement from Scripture to doctrine, practiced so confidently by the ancient church, an angular and painful affair today: we seem anchored in the Acts of God and cannot move one step beyond. To break that iron grasp, strong solvents need be applied.

In the modern era, the doctrine of revelation appears to be the medicine we need. In that remedy, the Bible can be honored as a source of knowledge—the knowledge of the matters God wishes Himself to reveal to us. Good. But that beachhead comes at a cost!

The conviction that Holy Scripture reveals God's ways to us—and only that!—drives modern theology to the far reaches of theological epistemology. At those radical limits, the skeptical problem rises up to the Heavens. Could we possibly know anything about the High God at all? Are we not rooted to, bound up with, the *phenomena* of God, the appearance that just is Holy Scripture? Once this divide springs up before our eyes, we cannot look away. It seems, then, that the very doctrine of inspiration that extolled Divine Revelation has now made revelation itself impossible. Nothing, it seems, can be truly *revealed* at all. Just this we may think drove Immanuel Kant's blind affirmation of the noumenon: appearance, he said, almost in passing, loses its meaning without *something*—the Thing in Itself, we assume—to appear. It did not take long for the ruthless tides of skepticism to shear off that noumenon and open wide the philosophical world to a thoroughgoing phenomenalism.

Note how delicate this problem truly is. The very notion of revelation assumes at its core that something of the hidden Reserve, something of the True but Unknown God, *can* be handed over, can be discerned and received by the faithful seeker. Revelation, especially in its apocalyptic vein, rests on the (sometimes suppressed) confidence that a Secret exists, and that it can be unveiled. When we speak of Holy Scripture as Revelation, we quietly assume that the One who resides in the heavens can be known through His own Act: He can tear the heavens and come down; He can rain down His Word like showers upon His prophets and scribes; He can speak and a word can be heard, received, honored. This assumption had been given the name *economy* in the Greek fathers, and it lay behind the very notion of revelation as a solution to the modern dilemma of proper knowledge of God. But note how near the doctrine of revelation lies to the skeptical terrain we know well. We might say that the very idea of revelation *generates* the crisis of proper theological knowledge. Students of modern European philosophy will recognize this dilemma immediately: it is the Cartesian problem in philosophical realism. We can descend to inner certainty, say, but how to escape once again to outer reality? Of course, we can assume the appearance is itself real and possesses real causal powers, but does our assumption in truth purchase the reality we prize? The sign that this neuralgia has infected the whole is the broad concession we have heard others rehearsing throughout this excursus: that we know in Holy Scripture "only what appears to us," "only what we receive in the Economy," "only what accords with the limits of human language, history, and intellect." Such a universe closed up in that small word: *only*!

Now, Karl Rahner proposed a daring counterstroke to that entire edifice of the theological economy: revelation would be rescued and regrounded in a transcendental Christology. The Aseity of the Son would be revealed, truly disclosed and *known*, in the economy, narrated in Holy Scripture. We can know One Truth, the one thing needful, and that will ground all else in theology. We know the Son; better, we know the Eternal Son. He alone is, but truly is, as He appears. The "is of identity" makes its way forward right here, in the Christological joinery between Immanence and economy, heaven and earth. In just this way, the economic and Immanent Trinity are unified, identified, and revelation secured. Now it is easy to see the cost of such rescue work, even in our admiration for its daring ambition and reach. Far more cautious than his descendants, Rahner hoped to shore up the Transcendence and Freedom of Almighty God against the erosion of Divine Immanence by the economy. But this is difficult, uphill work! The solvent will cut deep into the very treasure it prizes. It seems that revelation demands making the economy *necessary* to God, and this cost must be paid to the voracious appetite of skepticism in the modern doctrine of God.

Now, much more can be said here, and we have hardly broken the surface of this very deep and still ocean. But the central task here, in this excursus, is to show that the modern preoccupation with the doctrines of revelation and of soteriology rest on a profound anxiety about the place of the doctrine of God within a doctrine of Holy Scripture.

How God acts toward and with us—the economy in a broad register—has deflected and thinned under the strong downward pressure of modern skepticism and secularism; it has become the chronicle of divine appearance or, in the stern medicine of modern parlance, of "religious construction." For this reason, though not this reason alone, Holy Scripture in modern dress no longer *manifests* the Lofty Immanence of God. It is not Source in this proud sense. Now, I believe that we cannot properly reflect on the very idea of a Divine Source of Holy Scripture without encountering dangerous, rocky shoals. Indeed, we might say that the whole of a systematic theology is simply the repeated and neuralgic meditation on these very questions. They are not so much solved as *cauterized*; they are the record of our standing, with all the covenant people, at the door of our tents while the Cloud and Fire descend outside the camp. So, we will not say all that can or should be said here, but we must begin.

What we say here is that the Bible carries the Impress of God's Being; it is a Divine Seal. In this sense it is Likeness and Mirror and Image: the Bearer. Now, Almighty God can be with us as He is in Himself: this is the central axiom of theological compatibilism. But this is something quite different from Rahner's maxim and quite different again from the full-blown doctrine of analogy that undergirds scholastic knowledge of the Being of God. It differs strongly from Rahner's maxim in all the ways anticipated already in this analysis of revelation and soteriology: Holy Scripture as Bearer of the Triune Image does not begin with or assume the primacy of Scripture as economic; it does not countenance a distinction between "Trinities"; it does not rely on a Christological "moment of identity" to anchor the Divine Immanence or disclose the Divine Transcendence; it is not principally a doctrine of salvation at all. We have said less about the crown of scholastic method, analogy, than about Rahner, yet there, too, we might spot some familiar markers in place. We will in the doctrine of faith take up analogy with direct attention, and there accord it the respect such a sophisticated notion deserves. But even here we can affirm that our starting point and our knowledge is not principally from sense impression or from the economy, as a broad record of human experience; we are not here in search of a method or formal ratio by which knowledge from below is purified, elevated, and directed to the heavens above; we do not rest our large-scale pattern in dogmatics on a well-worked notion of cause, even the radically renovated notion of equivocal or universal cause. The God-world relation is not causal; rather, it is unique! A world of theological difference is bound up in those few words, and we will aim to lay that out, patiently and in course; but here we give our promissory note.

And finally, we should say that the doctrine of Scripture as Holy Likeness is *totaliter aliter* from Colin Gunton's brash endorsement of univocal predication of God.[48] The Bible is unique, strictly unique. Such a claim is so strong as to resemble a first principle, given, not justified. It is indeed "properly basic," as Alvin Plantinga would put this and, in this sense, can be only unfolded and enacted, not demonstrated or defended. But Scripture as Unique Gift of God the Source can be put at some distance, in a secondary fashion, from these aforementioned rivals. To say that Scripture is the Divine Seal is not to affirm that we know in a straightforward and familiar way the Being and Mystery of God. Scriptural language and image are not *univocal* to the Reality of God. This is because God is Present, in Scripture and in world, as *Holy*; He is Holy Mystery, Inescapably Invisible, Lofty, Infinite. To be sure, the Infinite is Incomprehensible; this might be taken as an essential property or even a definition. But Divine Infinity and Holiness means something far greater, far more dangerous than this. When the Holy One descends into His temple, the pivots on the threshold tremble; the world passes away. The priest cannot speak; cannot endure this Presence; the cries of the angelic hosts consume the living, and the mortal turns to ash. Isaiah the priest is *cauterized*, not burned away, even as the Lord's own Fire does not consume but radiates the thornbush. But the world of unprotected creatures cannot abide Holiness; it is the End of the living. This is the Searing Truth of Transcendence. Its Nearness is the One, True Radical Reality; it cannot belong among things that are passing away. It is not *against* them—precisely not that! It is *Other*, *the* Contrast, the Infinite Undoing that is God. It is so Far, so Omnipotent; it can be only Near, Intimate, the Humble One.

Now language here is taking on strange properties. It appears—contrary to all sallies against Gunton—that I am in truth endorsing his daring view. Few qualifications hedge the statements I have made, no "as it were," beloved of the fathers, no paradox or oxymoron reveled in by the ancient Syrians. No, it seems that I can rather boldly, though dramatically, describe God as Holy and mean just that. It seems, then, that I am univocally setting forth a Unique, a Strongly Unique, Reality that can inhabit, at some cost, the ordinary landscape of our world. It may well be, that is, that God in His Unfathomable Being remains the Different or even the Equivocal Reality in the world of persons and things, but the statements used to express that fact seem rather commonplace, familiar, and well defined. Could not ordinary language address, identify, and describe an altogether Unique Reality? This, I think, is Gunton's point, shorn of some of the Christological and epistemological breastworks. So, it will be significant for our proper reading of Holy Scripture to see just why this more refined account of Gunton's thesis should not hold. Mutatis mutandis, we ask whether Holy Scripture can indeed be a unique, radically unique creature, a Singular Imago of the Divine Mystery. Can it, in truth and in concept, carry a metaphysical impress that utterly transcends its idiom and tongue, and in just this way, resides deep and indirectly within?

What we mean is that the proper answer, the proper doctrine of Holy Scripture, can rest in the end only on a proper doctrine of God. God Himself, Alone, can account for a Bible that exposes, manifests, enacts the Being of the High God. Just this is what we mean when we say that God is Source of Holy Scripture. We mean that God in His very Being, His Searing Reality, can be also *Concrete*. He is Trifold. He does not cease being Universal, Abstract, Transcendent, and Free, no, He remains this, indeed *demonstrates* and verifies this, by His Being as Concrete. *He* can be *there*. We might transpose all this into the key of creaturely language by affirming that God can *conform* our little ways and words to His Mighty Being; He Alone can do this. I do not want to make light of such resource or look away from the rich, expressive, and dynamic elements Karl Barth brought, with his own magical powers, to such a notion, and the actualistic doctrine of Scripture it conjures. There will be time and place to honor all that. But here it is much more vital to affirm that the solution—if we can call doctrine by such a dry and utilitarian name—to the dilemma of realism in theology and Scripture is simply, majestically, the Holy, Triune God Himself. *This* is what we mean when we say, in the doctrine of inspiration, that God is Triune. Just that!

God Himself is the Pattern, the Living Pattern of the Concrete and the Abstract, the One Universal and the Particular, the Blessed Life, Unimaginably Free and Remote and Sweet, and the Goal, the Finality, the Rest at the End. God Himself *is* this. And He is Concrete *in* this very Pattern. He can be the One God beyond genus and form and likeness; Utterly, Starkly Beyond. And He can be the God of Israel, the Holy God in His Temple, the Fire of every prophet and of every age, the Spirit burning at the heart of all creation, the Lord of life and of death. He can be Concrete in this way, also. Holy Scripture is the Impress, the Seal of this very Pattern; the Bearer of this Triune Holiness. The Bible cannot be the *direct*, the univocal expression of such Majesty, this Living Mystery of the Universal and the Concrete. Nothing creaturely, even the strongly unique creature that is Scripture, can be utterly beyond form and genus and kind, even if it is graciously allowed to echo these. Nothing creaturely, even the lonely creaturehood of the Bible, can be in itself the One and the Many, the Omnipresent and the Indwelling, the Searing Holiness and the Humble One, laid down in Love. Scripture is the creature created by the Triune God who elects to make present this Unimaginable Goodness, this Triune Pattern. He wishes to be Present as the Transcendent in this fashion and mode; this is the Bible and all that we intend by saying that the Bible has God as its Source.

But the Lord is not simply Source of Holy Scripture; He is also Author. An important distinction is ushered in with this term, and it brings us closer to the contrasts we have pushed aside so far. Author brings in its trail the Agency and Intelligence vital to any proper doctrine of the True God. God is not Source as is a fountain of the water pool; He is not Source as is axiom for conclusion or less of material for product. He is the Living God, and He pours forth life and Presence in a wholly Spiritual, Vital, and Intelligent mode.

He is Lord. For this reason, it is fruitful still to speak of the Bible as the Sacred Book from the Sacred Author. Here at some reserve we greet the notion of revelation, after its risks and travails in our era. We do not endorse *wholesale* the doctrine of revelation, nor can we embrace its particular, modern role in theological epistemology. But we *can* admit a small-scale and chastened form of this once-mighty doctrine, after all. The *metaphysical* elements we have underscored in the very idea of Source—God's Nearness; His Echo and Pattern, laid down there—does not crowd out altogether the vital fact that revelation, too, stems from God's action toward this book. God is Author of the Bible in this more limited sense, too, that He elects and determines, He teaches and judges, His Omniscient Being is Present as truth and Law, and in earthly truth and God-given Law. Out of His storehouses, He brings forth treasures, both the old and the new. To this notion belongs the deeply familiar and rightly prized convictions that to read Holy Scripture is to discover the Divine Will, or to learn His plans for us, or to study His fear and favor, to stand in His Truth. The Bible is *concrete* in this way, too. It has within its covers the elements of Divine Instruction, revealed in its prophecies, its religious rites and cultus, its law and Holiness Codes, its rulers and alien-sojourners, its treaties and warfare and defeats under the angry press of empire and of time. We can read the Bible in this way, too, because God as Author encompasses a Luminous, Living Source, who also and in great, generous grace, will teach his rude and untaught creatures about His Works and Ways. In this chastened idiom, the Bible can be read as Revelation, can be Source of knowledge, can inform and guide and constrain Christian doctrine.

But always this is a second step, a second reading, a second moment in the proper encounter with Holy Scripture. Because God is not principally, exhaustively Revealer but rather Source of

Being, the One Who Is, the Bible as the unique creature of this Real God contains the seal and bears the impress of the Divine Life. It manifests; it shows.

Spiritual reading of Holy Scripture honors this metaphysical and epistemic gift. It honors the artifact that has received the Divine Pattern, and such reading dares to stride into the Divine Being in proper fear but in proper confidence, too. It will see in the Bible the Aseity and Transcendence of God and build a proper doctrine of the Divine Trinity out of its pages. It will do so in a mode and manner proper to this unique creature. It will honor and guard zealously the wholeness, the unity of the Bible; it will recognize in that prize possession the Radical Unicity of the One God. And it will honor and marvel at the distinctiveness and angularity and character this work possesses against all the worldly creatures that surround it. And in just this way it will recognize the Concrete Being, the Subsistence and Distinction that is also the True and Living God. Holy Scripture will manifest both Substance and Subsistence, both Unicity and Distinction, both Living Procession and Perfect End. It will relate the doings and sufferings of creatures, yes—and of the covenant people in particular, certainly—but it will do so as Image not of the economy *only*, not of Immanence *alone*, but rather as Image and Likeness of the Very God, the High and Lofty One, whose Being is Beyond all opposition, all contradiction. Holy Scripture manifests the dogma of Holy Trinity, the inner Life of God.

Now after some considerable detour we can return to Schleiermacher and his instruction about the proper relation and difference between God and the world. We recall that our insistence that Trinity is not soteriology led us to seek a Transcendence of God over the creature and her needs. But such a lofty Freedom is not easy to define or conceptually secure. Schleiermacher shows us how delicate an operation this truly is. Consider, once again, how such a notion of a unique God-world relation might illuminate—but occlude, too—the contrast Schleiermacher draws for us between Creator and creature. Schleiermacher is as jealous to preserve the Creator-creature distinction as any in the tradition. Indeed, we might say that he makes such a jealousy the hallmark of true Christian fidelity. His entire notion of Absolute Causality turns on the utter, uncontested, and sovereign Causal Power of God, the unbrooked Omnipotence of the Creator, over the doings and sufferings of the creature. This, we might say, is utterly elemental, primary. But the question that agitates Schleiermacher—and any theologian alive to the troubling genius of Baruch Spinoza—is the delicate one of *securing* such a primary distinction. Over and again Schleiermacher diagnoses a Divine Transcendence in the work of the tradition that is little more than a conceptual blind. The categories used to affirm the Freedom and Aseity of God over His cosmos, time and again, unwittingly affirmed that, despite all protests, God is enmeshed in, and structured by, the fabric and being of the world. An example:

> The interrelationship of partial causality and passivity makes the natural order a sphere of reciprocal action, and thus of change as such, in that all change and all alteration can be traced back to this antithesis. It is therefore just in the relationship in which the natural causality is set over against the divine, that the essence of the former is to be temporal; and consequently, so far as eternal is the opposite of the temporal, the eternity of God will also be the expression of that antithesis.[49]

The central axiom of Schleiermacher's constructive system is that *antithesis*, opposition, constitutes the creature. I do not think any conceptual conviction lies as deep as does this one in the *Glaubenslehre*. Indeed, we could consider the whole complex, heuristic structure of the introduction to turn on a patient unfolding of the dialectical pairs that define and animate the whole creaturely realm. In this passage, Schleiermacher rests his gaze on the world of reciprocal action, of change, that just is the opposition of agency and passion. But this is time, the measure of change. (Schleiermacher has read his ancients well!) So, to define eternity as *opposed* to time is to subject the Divine to antithesis, to make Him a creature.

Now this is a fundamental and oft-repeated lesson of Schleiermacher's whole work as a dogmatician; I say nothing new here. But the extraordinary truth of this widespread lesson is that it is exceedingly difficult to follow! And not just the generation of Schleiermacher's teachers; most all of us must sit in the principal's office after school to learn this lesson aright. The demanding character of Schleiermacher's axiom is its thoroughgoing radicality. Nothing after the searing heat of Thomas's maxim, *Deus non est in genera*, has exacted such a price as does Schleiermacher's lesson on transcendence. It is an easy, perhaps cheap, thing to say that we should not think in binaries or that a theologian should deconstruct or overturn or destabilize the same, but the point is to change it. In truth I think Schleiermacher's contemporaries felt the sting and burden of this task more acutely than do we. They *fought* with him, charged him with pantheism, with Spinozism, or, as with the ever-upright Charles Hodge, with the first fateful step toward atheism. Like Barth, some generations on, these nineteenth-century critics took the measure of this radical platform and could not but struggle against it and admire it, too. But in our day, I fear we consider Schleiermacher a lesson learned and tidily stored away. But how to think away the fundamental antithesis of all creaturehood! That is the demand here, and it is relentless.

We must consider conceptual categories, Schleiermacher warns, that *preserve* the Creator-creature distinction, without fail and without exception, and that, all the same, *overcome* opposition and contraries. To perform one of these, yes, of course. But both! That is the radicality of the *Glaubenslehre*. The altogether homespun example of color contrast falls to the ground before such a demand. It can only speak of distinction within a kind, after all—and just this is what is denied by one horn of the dilemma.

Now famously, Schleiermacher performed this radical feat through an iron reduction of all dogmatics to Absolute Cause. And we can see the correlate in our thesis statement: Absolute Causality is contrasted with the natural order, so that and just because, it is *equated* with it in its range and extent. In exact parallel—and this drove Charles Hodge to pious fury—the Omnipotence of God is fully exhausted by and identical to the world and its happenings. What is, God willed; what God willed, is. Or, in Barth's idiom, God's Omnipotence is identified with His Omnicausality.[50] This radical cauterizing of the divine possibility or freedom of Divine Will shocked Hodge and woke him to the relentless purity of Schleiermacher's demands. What Hodge saw is that the traditional language of the church, the very notion, embedded deep in the sinews of Christian piety, that God is Personal in a direct, realist sense, cannot be vindicated before Schleiermacher's tribunal of transcendence. Perhaps we hold, as do students of Barth everywhere, that Holy Scripture and its mother tongue cannot be held captive to abstract schemas and worldly philosophies but rather only to the royal throne room of Christ. I, too, want to praise and acknowledge the sovereign dignity of Holy Scripture. But we ignore Schleiermacher's maxim at our peril! We cannot wave the wand of anti-Hellenism over this problem and expect it to politely disappear. What emerges instead is a conceptual structure that reduces the Lord God to a creature with a system of nature, all the while assuring us, through some biblical elixir, that we do not have to think that way. Now, not everything can be rationalized! And the exceeding Mystery who is God cannot be exhaustively *explained*.

But I mean here that the very notion of transcendence by which we conceive the Mystery of God, and seek out its relation to the world, ought not to be set out in such a fashion that Divine Transcendence is simply unthinkable.

We seek, then, a notion of transcendence and of objectivity that draws on *contrast* and *compatibility*. Indeed, if we read Schleiermacher right, compatibility must give rise to contrast; contrast to be an ingredient in compatibility. There must be a form of Divine Nearness, of Immanence, that is *also* a Contrast, a Lofty Transcendence. We hear echoes here of the notion of difference that has preoccupied several postmodern theorists; and it belongs by right, and in its own form, to doctrine, too. It must be that Almighty God, in His Presence, His irreducible Goodness to the creature, is His own Distinction, His own sovereign Loftiness and Freedom over the creature. The God–world relation is *unique*.

Now, here we take our final step. The Mystery of the Holy Trinity just *is* the Sole, Sovereign Objectivity of God, His Impenetrable Concreteness beyond all creaturely need and knowing, beyond all creature, altogether. When we consider the riddles we have been patiently and painstakingly rehearsing, we, in another idiom, speak of the Divine Triunity of God. Trinity Itself is the answer to the question we have posed. He, the Triune Lord, is the Metaphysical One who stands apart, before, beyond all knowledge, all speech, all *relatio*; He is their Ground. When dogmatic theology claims to speak of and praise a God who rides the winds of the air, Unique, High, and Lifted Up beyond all creaturehood, beyond all desire, it simply says and shows Trinity. We stand in His Domain. He, the Triune One, is *there*; He crowds us out; He is Lord. This is what we mean when we say that Holiness is the conceptual name of the Triune Mystery. The Holy One is in His temple; the whole earth stands in silence before Him.

Now, this is to affirm that God's relation to the world is unique, *strongly unique*. We might better say: God is Sovereign over and in His own Relatio to the creature. In His Objectivity He remains the Lord; He does not enter into our epistemological frameworks or our puzzles about proper, true, and verified belief. He makes possible our knowledge of Him. But that is not strong enough, not by a good measure. Every object in its own kind makes possible our knowledge of it; just that is what we intend when we speak of knowledge of the world, or of realism. (Of course, this is our intention, but the science of epistemology, its long labors, are proof enough that achievement and intention are not the same.) But when we speak of the Holy One as Sovereign Lord, even in our speech, knowledge, and need of Him, we mean something about His very Being, His Concrete Reality, the Near God who also Hides Himself. We mean Triunity Itself.

The Mystery of Trinity teaches that Almighty God is not exhausted in Dunamis, in raw Omnipotence. God is not simply and utterly Power, though, to be sure, He *is* this. When we say Trinity, we affirm that Almighty God is not exhausted in *Extension*; God is not simply and utter Omnipresence—though, to be sure, He *is* this. God is Being Itself, not simply Source, though, again, He *is* that. But He is Plentitude of Being, Fullness, Rich and Richly Unique Sea of Being. Yet Being Itself, the Most Real Being, though the Transcendental Reality of all our little ways and truths and realities, is not exhausted and utterly expended in that most general of concepts, Being. Beyond all kinds and forms and genera, God as Being, as Life, Superabundant, Radiant Life, is not undifferentiated Vitality; though there is no life apart from Him. No, Almighty God is *Concrete*, an Infinite Boundedness. For the Lord is Good, His Mercy is Everlasting, and His Truth endures, from generation to generation. When we confess Triunity, we affirm as rational truth—no, rational mystery—that Definiteness belongs to the Unique and Limitless God. In such a way, and beyond all thought, Almighty God has *Endurance, Permanence* as His Bounded Life; He is Eternal. His very Nature is Infinite, an Infinity that is "positive," to speak in scholastic idiom: not indefinite, not negative—the lack of completion or ending—not simply rule-bound, as integers following in sequence and pattern, not this. But rather an Infinity that is Perfect, Definite, Complete. God is Holy. The dogma of Trinity, which shall be our life and joy throughout this volume, expresses in dignity and delight this Infinite Boundedness; it expounds and consists in this Rational Mystery.

So, in this excursus we affirm that Divine Triune Holiness exceeds Infinitely the doctrines of salvation and of revelation. To be sure, the Triune God *encompasses* those gifts, Perfectly, Completely. But He exceeds, superlatively exceeds them. Now, this is so because Concreteness is God's own Life, not ours. It is commonplace to say that God is not an Object as are others; indeed, for many theologians, not an Object at all. But this does not capture properly, we say, the sturdy and Eternal Reality that is God, the One who can be Objective, can be Object in His Holy Subjectivity. But He is *Infinite* Object; this is what we mean in part by His Triunity. He is Immeasurably, Obdurately Definite; that, too, is Triune Mystery. I, the Lord, am Holy: that is the Triune God's Self-Declaration; He defines and differentiates Himself. He is not *our* conceptual object; we do not discover and define and limit His Objectivity. He Eternally Generates His own Definitiveness. He *sanctifies* Himself. In this way, He is Omnipresence, He is Omnipotent, He is the Being of all beings, the Life of all the living, the Truth of all our small truths. He, this very One! I drew on Augustine's remarkable doctrine of Illumination in my first volume, and we learn from him again here: God is the Means by which we know, the Means by which we exist and make our pilgrim way. He is the Way and the Agent of the Way. He, this very One!

Wolfhart Pannenberg has made Self-Differentiation a hallmark of the doctrine of Trinity, and we will have occasion to explore more fully this notion of Divine Person and Procession. But here we may say, even in staccato, that God as Object of our thought and longing remains Agent, the One who delimits His very Being, defines His own Holiness. *He* gathers to a Greatness. We do not speak of *revelation* here; this is not a disclosure of Being or Nature or Act. It is not strong enough to say that God is Self-Disclosing, though, to be sure, He *is* that, too. The Humble One lays Himself down in our finite world, our dust. He spreads Himself like morning dew across our small world, Ingredient in our life and ways and works. This is Infinite Being, Reality Itself. In this Lowliness He defines Himself, delimits and bounds His own Infinite Life, so that His Objectivity is His own Subjectivity, His Triune Differentiated Being. We can think this thought because He is the Source and Reality of this Concreteness, His own Mighty Working. When we say that the Triune Lord is beyond soteriology, beyond revelation, beyond liturgy and worship and praise, we trace, in this beyond, the Mark of the Lord's own Self-Definition. It is His Stamp, His Concrete Die, His Lofty Sovereignty. He, this very One!

Let us sum up. We began this excursus with a puzzle, a deeply *religious* puzzle, over the place of soteriology and revelation in the dogma of Trinity. It seemed that the entire Mystery of Trinity, properly conceived and animated, led to an affirmation of this dogma as the Conceptual Clarification of our salvation; it was disclosed as such. Thus, it seemed that the central riddle of modern, Western philosophy has a dogmatic analogue: subjectivity and Objectivity belong together, like horse and carriage, love and marriage. But this was not an epistemic problem alone! We also noted the deep mystery of sinners before the Holy God: How could the doctrine of God, the Holy Triunity, be thought apart from judgment, pardon, renewal? The doctrine of revelation, the methodological center of modern theology, carries a broad moral and ascetic character. Our knowledge of God is *saving*, it seems, in just this sense—that we are killed and made alive by this Truth. Now the proper path out of this thicket, I proposed, had two branches. We are to distinguish dogmatics proper from liturgy, doctrinal theology from worship. Schleiermacher came to our aid here in offering a deft demarcation of the whole field, ranging from poetry through preaching to didactic and conceptual precision, all and each wonderfully grounded in the experience of radical dependence on the Cause of all. I am to think and set forth with proper Objectivity what in other realms I can only adore. Schleiermacher's radical notion of communication, bred into the very notion of the human, made revelation, on the other hand, too commandeering on the whole. And the second branch led out into the broad field that is this volume as a whole: the Holiness of God as the Infinite, Concrete, and Bounded One, who manifests Himself, indwells His temple. To think Trinity is to think the sacrifice, the death, but also the radical renewal, of the marriage of heaven and earth, the Creator and creature. Holy Scripture itself has this Triune Lord as its Source and Author, and that in a very strong sense. The Bible, we have said, is Seal and Impress, Bearer and Likeness of this Triune God, the creature made and set apart for this work. In just this way, the Bible is not restricted to the Ways of God us-ward; it is not primarily revelation; it is not principally economy. Rather Holy Scripture bears the mark of the One who is its Source, the Holy One, who is Universal and Concrete, Beyond and Near, Abstract and Personal. The Bible is His creature. Apart from the Triune Mystery there is no issue from the riddle of knowledge, the riddle of sin and ignorance, the riddle and sorrow of our earthly, earthbound lot. Trinity is not soteriology, nor is It revelation; It cannot be reduced to or contained by these other loci. The One Holy God rather is Lord, the Center and Sovereign of all thought, all being, all theology.

Note the force of this claim. Our second branch, in truth, can only be the first, the lone sovereign, the One. The Reality of God is properly basic; God is the Absolute Primitive. Now that means that God grounds and commands doctrine both formally and materially. There is no procession back behind this very One, no standpoint beyond or outside the Holy God that permits a conceptual grasp of God and world together as a neutral, coordinated pair. To borrow Rahner's idiom for a moment: there is no horizon against which God and the creature stand out together, as objects, even in opposition. The claim of this volume is that the dogma of the Holy Trinity just *is* materially and formally *this* problematic. The Tri-Personed God is the conceptual expression of the very notion that God can be known and can be present to the creature, known and present as the One He is, always Beyond. Triunity is the form of the creaturely knowledge that God is One. But materially, the Triune God is more radical still. Holiness is Its own Ground. It is impossible for the creature to win through to a neutral conception of the conditions for the possibility of knowledge of or encounter with God. This is not a rejection of Divine Objectivity or the Givenness of God: it is precisely not that! God is the Shattering Object, the Uncontained and Unconstrained Reality, the One Who Is There. God is not coordinated with our salvation or our hunger to know Him because He is Beyond, always Beyond such pairing. Just this is the meaning of *contrast* rather than *opposition* in the doctrine of God. The Lord bursts into the cosmos as His own Fire: the first temple sacrifice is lit from His Beyond. This is what we mean, what we stammer toward, when we say God is Free;

God is Liberty Itself. The Triune One is the Ground of His own Relatio to the world in just this sense, that it is impossible for God to be known, revealed, worshipped without the creature; yet God is known not in appearance, not as Savior only, not as *Revelatio* but as the One He is, Beyond, Infinite, Free. He is the Holy One. *This* is the force of our saying that God is the material ground of all theology. Just that.

Note that we, mere creature, cannot properly say this. In the end this demand and impossibility, this impossible demand is the only self-referential problem worth its salt. We cannot explain or express this Shattering Objectivity, this Explosive Concreteness who is God. This is the radical edge of the broad claim that God is not known as are common objects in our realm. The impossibility, the conceptual defeat of our organizing schemas—all our schematizations of the Infinite—are caught up in the Absolute Primitive who is God. Of course, we must *gesture* toward this Sovereignty: we say that God is more than our salvation; He is more than our images and explanations, however sublime; He is Subject in and over every Objective portrait, worshipped, revealed, obeyed. Such statements *enact* the Divine Primacy: He cannot come under our roof. These are not univocal statements, nor are they analogies as the scholastics know them. They are *negativa*, to be sure, in some measure. But at heart and base these statements are *affirmations*: the Triune God is Positively Infinite. Modern atheism shadows this impossibility, but only at a domestic reserve. It is the Searing Holiness of God that radicalizes every doubt, every objection, every conceptual impossibility in Divine knowledge or Presence. Of course, we could overcome such worries through a frank Doctrine of Projection or a more delicate notion of accommodation, where the Holy One appears in the guise and idiom of our tribe. We would expect then a robust doctrine of development, a refined and ennobled *visio Dei* bursting forth from early, incomplete allusions. But this is not in truth what Holy Scripture teaches or what the church or synagogue confesses. Rather the True God is known, worshipped, and obeyed as the Free and Holy One, in His own Aseity, as the One who shatters every idol, digs down every false altar. This cannot be yet is. Just this we intend when we affirm theological compatibilism, when we point to the Transcendental Perfections, poured out into our realms and hearts, when we confess that God creates *ex nihilo*, when we confess He is Trinity, the Divine Contrast to all creaturehood. Trinity is Annihilating Concreteness. Just so is God the Holy One.

Finally, it is the dogma of Trinity itself that tells us why this Mystery is not primarily nor principally a doctrine of our salvation. It, this One Mystery, expounds why it is not principally nor primarily a doctrine of revelation. It is the task of thinking through this dogma to the very end that teaches us these two vital, unmistakable lessons. It will take us the entire volume to set forth just how we are to understand and follow this Triune lesson. But here we must say that Trinity is much too large to be confined to such human-scale tasks. Trinity is a Mystery of the Holiness of God; it concerns God's own Perfect Being as the Holy One, Complete, Infinite, Set Apart. It does not stem principally or finally or, much less, causally from the Incarnation: not all is Christology! The very structure of the Divine Life forbids us this familiar route of self-absorption. What the scholastic tradition has called the Missions cannot absorb, exhaust, or delimit the Processions. They are the Eternal Life of the Holy One. When the Holy God manifests Himself in scorching Fire on the earth, He demonstrates and enacts His *Life*: He is the Living One. As the Living One, He sets Himself apart, He *contrasts* Himself with all that is, all the frailty and finitude and defilement we creatures are and love, these long days, east of Eden. He *shows* this, enacts and lives it; He does not *reveal* it. What He shows is a Land set apart, a Holy Land, a Living Majesty, a Sabbath Day that is defended and defined and guarded by God Himself, for it is His own Being. We look up at this. We see it in the Darkness and Cloud, the Fire that rises up Beyond the cosmos. In Holy Scripture we watch as this Lord displays His Concrete and Distant Life, in temple and Beyond. We look up at it. We look up, through the words and events and persons of Holy Writ, up into the Dark Reserve, the Luminous Mystery that is the Pattern of the Divine Life. It is the Distant Thunder, the Far Shore and Perfect Day, the Last Music that steals on the ear from Beyond—that is what we catch sight of in the spiritual depth of Scripture. This visio Dei simply traces the Pattern of Divine Life Itself, the Nearness that is at once and also the Beyond. The Triune God Himself makes such thoughts possible, impresses them on our minds. It is searing, hallowing to think such thoughts; it changes the intellect that encounters it. But it is not itself the thought of the Hidden revealed, nor of the creature, perishing, now saved. It is the thought of the Holy, the Set Apart, the Sanctified One who distinguishes Himself from all that is profane. It is thinking the thought of the One who draws near in order to set the Limit, in order to hallow—that is, to prohibit and demark all that is not God. This is the Contrast, the Transcendence that is the Immanence of God. All this we intend when we say that God is Holy.

Now of course an excursus of this kind could never conclude without acknowledging the astonishing and humbling gifts of divine revelation and, even more, of salvation. The final word in any dogmatics must be gratitude, and this is perhaps especially so in an excursus designed to distinguish Trinity from other doctrines, however vital. Schleiermacher has a lesson to teach here, too, about proper distinction in theology. There will be time in this dogmatics for a full-throated praise of the Work of Christ and the sanctifying gifts of the Spirit, time for the theological epistemology that will gain life and direction from revelation. The aim of a proper, biblical dogmatics is to allow generous room for the pluralism, the rich polyphony that is Christian theology. God is One, the Holy One; the creature is many. Though it has a center—the Living God!— theology cannot serve its Lord through reducing all loci into locus, however vital. No praise will be too high for the teaching about Christ's Deliverance of sinners, bought at a price. No hymn will be too glorious for the truths disclosed to ignorant and wayward creatures, a revelation out of the Third Heaven. But the fundamental work of theology is to see the Perfection of God, a Perfection that is echoed in the world by an inexhaustible richness, a distinction upon distinction, work upon work, each complete, each integral and whole, yet continuous, extended, unified: Perfect. It is the majesty, the joy of theology to revel in this richness, the marrow and the fatness; follow these distinct pathways; watch these unexpected, odd events and persons and acts, the astonishing byways that await every visit to Holy Scripture, these wonders; and discover there the world the Lord God has made, an order and a wholeness that is entirely of the Lord's own making, glorious and free. *This* is concreteness in theology, an echo in our own creaturely idiom, of the One God who is Perfectly, Gloriously Universal and Concrete, the Triune, Holy Lord.

§1.3. Holy Trinity and Its Justification

Let us now draw a bit nearer to the problem that has ignited our whole search in the Mystery of Trinity: Just what element, divine or human, generated the entire dogma and mystery of the Triune God in the first place? We have considered the candidates offered by modern Trinitarian reflection, and not so modern. The very idea of Trinity can be birthed from cardinal texts in the New Testament, we have said, from the Gospels to the pregnant imagery and blessings of the apostle Paul or, in more modern dress, from the great, fertile contemplation and teaching of Mother Church. Trinity can be the Mystery sparked by the conflict of empires and emperors, of great prelates and controversialists, from Hellenists of all sorts. It might be the fruit of heresy, the gift showered on the faithful even by their enemies (for all things must work for good for those who love the Lord). Trinity, that is, can be generated from Holy Scripture; from the womb of the church; from the nations, their philosophers, and speculative religionists; or from heresiarchs, noble or base. Trinity appears to be a doctrine launched by a thousand ships; who knows its compass? For our part, we have begun the careful advocacy of the Old Testament as proper home for the dogma of Trinity, and we aim in the end to unfold the very idea of Holiness as birth and source and secure ground of Divine Triunity. But we will need to sharpen the whole edge of this endeavor in order to make progress here: Just what does it mean, we ask, to *generate* a Mystery of the faith? And perhaps more pointedly: Why must we ask this question at all?

Think for a moment of the central Mysteries of the Christian religion. We might list those associated with the church's creeds: doctrines of creation; Divine Attributes and Powers; election and providential care; the great festivals of Incarnation, Passiontide, and Easter Light; the Mysteries enfolded in the church and its saints, sacraments, Scriptures, and great hope; Justification before the Final Judge and Judgment. All these and of course many more might compose a catalogue of Christian teachings, the faith once delivered to the saints, or the faith disclosed to pilgrims along the long way home. Theologians and pastors may well disagree on this list; we need not assume there is one only. But our main conviction seems to be this: teachings along these lines, covering these general areas, touching on these cardinal points will not need to be generated but rather only refined, deepened, purified. There is, so to say, a certain *self-evident* quality to these Christian dogmas. We need not *derive* them, though to be sure, we can; we rarely feel constrained to *justify* them, though of course we might do so to their opponents; we may not even feel bound to *explain* them but rather can take them up, burnish and prune them, love them more deeply, honor them properly, and, in those ways, hand these dogmas on to the next generation of the faithful. Of course, we need a doctrine of creation, we may say; of course, we need a Christology! But of what school and kind, springing from which texts and tradents, worrying over which objection, modern or ancient? These are the theologians' tasks—and for most doctrines, they are troubles sufficient unto the day.

But not so with the dogma and Mystery of the Holy Trinity! Here we enter another landscape altogether, and we are handed fresh tasks, well beyond those already named. In the dogma of Trinity, theologians are asked to *justify* the doctrine; to discover this realm, once more and altogether; to carry, for the whole church, the inescapable burden of advocating, simplifying, motivating, and accounting for this Mystery, as if it were a trip necessary but unpleasant and unbidden. For this dogma especially we hear said, often in plaintive tones: Why do Christians teach such a doctrine at all? What brought on such an elaborate, technical, and, to speak frankly, broadly implausible doctrine as this as candidate for our belief? This is the question outsiders have raised, early and late, about Trinity, and it is a mark of the modern in theology that insiders, too, have felt constrained by such queries, wounded by them. The dogma of Trinity, unlike the doctrines of creation or the sacraments, say, is itself a *problem*, awaiting—no, demanding— explanation. It is *itself* a puzzle case, the grand puzzle case of the tradition. "Where did the church get all this?" the critic may well ask. That is the demand the world dares to pose—the modern world, inside and outside the church dares to pose—and more astonishingly still, theologians feel constrained to answer. Why do theologians oblige their critics? The answer lies in the rise of the modern, so we must turn once again to the architect of the modern, Friedrich Schleiermacher, and learn from him the weight and force of such odd, compulsive, and neuralgic self-analysis.

As is well known, the *Christian Faith* concludes with a brief section dedicated to the doctrine of the Trinity. In three crisp, numbered paragraphs, Schleiermacher lays out what the modern temper finds puzzling about this doctrine, what skeptics, ancient and modern, find implausible about the teaching, and what radical surgery must or might be performed on the whole to make the remnant viable, even comely. All this in three brief sections, a scant thirteen pages in the old English edition of the *Glaubenslehre*! Such brevity made Schleiermacher's many critics consider the entire treatment an "appendix" (so the early Barth and Emil Brunner), and this was hardly laudatory. Of course, the flaws in Schleiermacher's distilled treatment are open to the eye: an unvarnished Sabellianism, a frosty disregard for scholastic developments, a lordly dismissal of the early patristic exegesis and formulation (so early in the day, so tarnished with heathenism!), an easy conscience about wholesale recasting of an entire tradition. These may not make for warm recommendations of the whole section. But Schleiermacher in truth has a deeper and more urgent task at hand than the broad reworking of a dogma, however marred. Always radical, Schleiermacher goes to the root of the matter. In historical vein, Schleiermacher diagnoses two conditions at the core of the entire Trinitarian enterprise: the unsteady *status* of the dogma of Trinity within Christian theology and the underlying *problem* it seeks to address. At one stroke, he exposes the *source* of the dogma *and* the reason for its incredibility in the modern era. We might think of this section, in truth, as a brilliant facet rather than flaw: it has the density and clarity of a proper gem.

Consider first the matter of Trinity's status in the faith. In Schleiermacher's analysis, the Mystery suffers from what we have learned to call a lack of "cultural plausibility."[51] The Holy Trinity is not of self-evident importance, that is, but rather must be explained, warranted, justified. Just this is to be rendered implausible in contemporary culture. To express this positively: those elements with a full-throated plausibility structure behind them simply *must* be taken seriously, taken into account, taken as vis-à-vis, taken for granted. Famously, Peter Berger considered science to enjoy plenipotentiary plausibility: no serious intellectual can ignore or gainsay it; no government program discount it (not for long, at any rate); no schoolchild prefer to learn nothing about it; no theologian pretend it is a passing fashion or obsolete worldview. No, the exact sciences just *are*; they are the given. Mutatis mutandis, we might say that Creation or Christology just *are* in Christian theology; these are the currency of the realm, and everyone trades in them. But not so Trinity! The very notion of a Trinitarian Revival, much lionized in present-day dogmatics, underscores the cultural implausibility: the legitimate do not pass out of fashion. The genius of Schleiermacher's brief Trinitarianism is his accounting for that impermanence and implausibility. It is not taste in dogmatics! Schleiermacher says this: "§170: All that is essential in this Second Aspect of the Second Part of our exposition is also posited in what is essential in the doctrine of the Trinity; but this doctrine itself, as ecclesiastically framed, is not an immediate utterance concerning the Christian self-consciousness, but only a combination of several such utterances."[52]

Under this dry summary, Schleiermacher plants an explosion. His point, note, is built on the anodyne notion of an "ecclesial framing." To "frame" a doctrine is to express or convey religious content in the manner and mode of the church's creedal definitions: they *present* it in suitable speech. They are court dress; they are made to be put on and off. The "essentials," the flesh and blood, *just are* the "second Aspect of the Second Part" of the *Christian Faith*. That is, the essentials of Trinity are constituted by the "Explication of the Consciousness of Grace," itself in turn a refinement of the whole, longer second half of the work, denoted by an "Explication of the Facts of the Religious Self Consciousness as they are determined by the Antithesis of Sin and Grace."

Now, in the final paragraphs of the *Glaubenslehre*, Schleiermacher sums up these Facts as the "union of the Divine Essence with *human nature*" [NB!] and that in two parallel forms: the "personality of Christ and the common Spirit of the Church."[53] Everything turns on this, Schleiermacher assures us. "Unless the being of God in Christ is assumed, the idea of redemption could not be thus concentrated in His Person. And unless there were a union also in the common Spirit of the Church, the Church could not thus be the Bearer and Perpetuator of the redemption through Christ."[54] So, the essentials of the Trinity bear down on two cardinal points, the Incarnation (understood in Schleiermacher's own distinctive idiom) and the donation of the Spirit to and in the church. Now, this is a remarkable and subtle doctrine of Trinity! Entirely New Testament in origin, the doctrine shows itself as strongly and unsurprisingly Christological, Person rather than Procession centered, and sharply, polemically ordered around the Divine Essence. We are drawn to Schleiermacher's remarkable doctrinal treatments, his concise and canny summaries of dogmatic development, his analytic rigor, the clarity that emerges under this reductive glare: all wonderfully instructive! These elements of Schleiermacher's treatment we will take up in time, but here we want to tie these essentials to the *facts* of the system, the antithesis of sin and grace, the leitmotif of the Second Part, and the consciousness of grace, the luminous center of the concluding sections. They are the *determinates* of the whole. They stamp, they define, they drive the whole of the *Christian Faith*.

Schleiermacher, in truth, does not have doctrinal realism or objectivity in view, however much he knows and deftly handles it. Rather, he is preoccupied by a conception of the human, its order, structure, and springs. That is why the Divine Essence is joined not to the world but to humankind. Schleiermacher holds that the human world is cleft through by a dialectic, an antithesis, one that defines and animates the whole of human history and will end only when the dialectic turns over into peaceful unity, the final victory of grace. This is a dynamic vision of culture and of the human, rent and driven by the war of Spirit and flesh, but always and to the end, a victory song, for the grace of Christ will conquer and unify all things, in heaven and on earth. *This* is what it will mean for there to be one flock, One Shepherd. So, we must see Christian dogmatics as a record of this dynamism and this struggle, a journal of the Christian, caught by and caught up in the polarity of sin and Grace. All Scripture will be the expression of this polarity, itself in its realism and objective referents, an enactment of the Union of the Divine Essence with human nature, its purpose and its goal.

Now that means that theology has a Source and a Limit, and these are to be strictly observed. We are to see the content of religious teaching, the essentials and deep structure, in the human rhythm of inner and outer, temporality and extension, agency and reception, autonomy and dependence: the *Christian Faith* is critical realism in just this technical sense. The ecclesial frame of this living antithesis is Trinity. In its essentials, the central experience of a sensitive human life is its ceaseless struggle with conscience, a worldly God-forgetfulness. Moments of deliverance invade that struggle, relieve and release it, and every moment of that freed life is bathed with a fresh and unfamiliar Light. A solemn joy then animates and spills over the events of the everyday: all is gift. This is the experience of grace, the victory over sin that comes to us from Beyond. It is *struggle* because the relation between worldliness and piety is *conflict*, opposition, not contrast or distinction. Once again we see the subtle work contrast or distinction undertakes in the *Glaubenslehre*: the human world of sin and suffering lies under the constraint of opposition; the divine world, in union with the human under the blessing of contrast or simple distinction. In Schleiermacher's hands even the architectonic serves the Gospel. The human world is torn straight through, and we can do nothing but live within its civil war. Romans 7 is the cardinal text for the *Glaubenslehre*. But we receive in its midst an amnesty and a deliverance; Another fights for us. Our experience is of a reprieve from that inner war. We are astonished it is so, that such ceasefire could steal over such bitter terrain, and it appears without prior warning, like life out of death. When we report such victories, we are told of the Redeemer: Jesus Christ is the One who fights for us. The church just is the gathered assembly of the war-torn, at rest under the banner of Peace. The experience of partial victory, of a ceasefire that holds, a bit more firmly each day, just is the life of faith; it is what the Christian receives and cannot achieve. Now, this life of faith, of war and deliverance, just is Trinity. Or, to express this in the method of the *Christian Faith*: this experience is set forth in the speech of the church as the dogma of Trinity. But the essentials are this inner narrative—the Union of the Divine with our nature, taught and communicated by those who, too, have tasted this Victory and this Rest. *This* is the Spirit of Christ, the Realm of Grace.

The dogma of Trinity cannot, then, be a direct deliverance of the pious self-consciousness. Trinity is neither self-evident nor immediate; it is rather the upper-level expression and framework of this original antithesis, yielding to the Unity of God with us. Such an account allows us to see why in the modern era the Mystery of Trinity has little cultural plausibility. Trinity does not have the tang of the human world; it does not taste of our inner life. Trinity is not self-evident in just this sense: it does not emerge out of our everyday encounter, our sorrow and joy, with the world we have made and receive. We can live without such a dogma. We can elaborate an account of our moral struggles that does not yield its categories or terms; our small victories do not lead us on a search for its structure, Persons, or Relations. For just this reason, secular reason has not developed a theory of the Trinity, and non-Christian religions have not taught it as essential to the doctrine of God. Rather, we discover Trinity through an intellectual history. In the church, we are taught the account of the early patristic debates, coming to a conceptual resolution over the early struggle about Jesus Christ. It is ecclesial: the experience of grace overcoming sin is explained and given meaning by an intellectual and historical institution. Trinity is tradition, the sum and resolution of a tradition. It is also framework: the inner world of joy and resolution and peace needs outward expression in a language learned from others. Others teach us Trinitarian idiom and show us the organizing concepts that order our expression: Trinity is no individual affair. But what is *given*, what is ineluctable and all-too-familiar is the antithesis, the unshakeable conflict at the base of every human life. We cannot avoid or overlook it; it is the structure of everyday awareness. And we cannot help loving, looking eagerly for, praising the release from such burdens; *that* story must be told. But Trinity, in itself and by itself, does not.

All this is quite modern. To be sure, there are traditional notes here that Schleiermacher is sure to have laid to his account. St. Thomas, for example, held that the dogma of Trinity was the prime instance of a Revealed Truth, a doctrine of the church that belonged to the realm not of reason but of faith. His appeal to a use of number in Trinity that was neither additive nor extensive—the so-called transcendental number—announced a doctrine that could only be Permanent Mystery. It was commonly held that Trinity was Mystery that exceeded all human knowing; the Cappadocian literature is filled with apophatic comments of just this kind. Augustine never tired of underscoring the inadequacy of all his human analogies. Indeed, he was far more cautious in their use than his later admirers. Lateran IV taught that Trinity could not be rationally explained or derived, a Mystery that stood always beyond our cognition, surrounded by an ever-greater dissimilarity in the midst of any likeness, analogy, or similarity.[55] Even St. Anselm, whose brio in the *Proslogion* appeared to make direct knowledge of God a sturdy deliverance of reason, guarded against any hubris of this kind by denoting God as the Limit and the Beyond of which nothing greater can be conceived. The dogma of Trinity, in fact, seems the strongest candidate in the tradition for apophatic restraint. So perhaps we should consider Schleiermacher a traditionalist here, and nothing more.

I say: True, a tradition stands behind Schleiermacher here, but he innovates, all the same. In his characteristic pattern, Schleiermacher evokes a traditional theme only to remake it wholly from within. In the *Christian Faith*, we do not treat Trinity as an intellectual Object on its own terms, so to say. In a dogmatics dedicated to

Glaubenslehre, we take up Trinity as a second-order doctrine, a frame built up around a deeply religious portrait. Now, this very notion of the "second order," so familiar in contemporary methodologies, exhibits the characteristic architecture of the modern. We might think of philosophical analogues: John Locke's primary and secondary qualities, Descartes's cogito and the outer world of extension, Kant's towering structure of the noumenon and phenomenon, all ordered dualisms that remake metaphysics. The superstructure is erected upon a primary level, perhaps intuitive, perhaps immediate, which is then captured, elevated, clarified, and ordered by analysis, category, speech, and argument. The upper-level structure simply lays bare the impulse and weight of the lower; it frames it in the clothing of concept. Now we need not here sort through or adjudicate the relation of language to inwardness, nor the thicket produced by the very idea of immediate and irrefragable content of experience. Of course, all these are contested. Here, rather, we focus on the broader schema Schleiermacher offers on view: that Christian theology has a two-level object in its teaching and proclamation. This is distinctly new.

The *object* of Christian theology, the referent of Christian statements, is now twofold, double and ordered. We are not now expecting that Christian dogma principally, even less exhaustively, aims at conceptual and analytic teaching; Christian Mysteries are not doctrines, in the first place, at all. The point of Christian dogmatics, rather, is to make explicit the fit and persuasiveness of a linguistic expression to a primal and primitive experience of dependence and change. The ordering here is vital. The real content, the working material and engine, of all dogmatics—its urgency, color, and mastery—is the human world of inner struggle and repose, of suffering and deliverance, of intermittent sorrow and inexpressible joy. *This* is piety, and Christian theology feeds hungrily on it.

Christian dogmatics, then, builds into its self-expression an upper and lower division, with the pride of place belonging to the lower. The upper must give way to the lower or inner conviction; it supervenes upon it and must see itself as malleable, historical, and, in a broad sense, conventional. Schleiermacher was once accused with some regularity of being ahistorical, individualistic, rationalistic. Not a bit of it! Instead, Schleiermacher gives us the portrait of a modern intellectual whose worldview is entirely communal, historical, and subject to analytic transformation. The point of ecclesial history is its communal development. Christianity is an ethos, a culture and movement, and it has developed its own distinctive vocabulary, self-understandings, and pioneers. Indeed, Schleiermacher organizes the *Christian Faith* around the creeds and confessions of the magisterial Reformation: they provide the distinctive notes that are to be recalled, clarified, and purified by a Protestant dogmatics. Like the early nation-state, a birth Schleiermacher witnessed and furthered, Christianity seeks its own proper character, defends its own proper ideals, and advances its cause. To belong there is to know the past, to *integrate* it, and, in just that way, to carry it into the future. But being a citizen of such a nation does not rest principally or primarily on the knowledge of its laws, customs, and heroes, nor is it at heart a participation in cultural events or pastimes: citizenship is not essentially a knowing or a doing. This is why citizens can be accused of being unpatriotic in the midst of lawful, even wholly laudable, activities. Proper membership in a nation-state, rather, is the experience, the inner recognition of an ethos, an élan, an esprit de corps. This is the modern parallel we see strikingly developed in the *Christian Faith*. The first order, immediate content of Christian doctrine is a particular form of inwardness, deeply human and humane, a matter of conscience and gratitude. *This* is immediately realized, communicated, blessed by Christ, the great Teacher and

Redeemer. The second order belongs to the culture of the church, its practitioners and scholars, a living, vital history that names the sorrows and blessings of human life.

Now in such a structure, Trinity can never hold center stage. It cannot command our full attention or first loyalty because it is in itself an epiphenomenon, the second-order conception of an inner deliverance. It will seem implausible, perhaps incredible—even when endorsed by Christian adepts—because it belongs by definition to the linguistic and historical realm of concept, argument, and development. It does not demand our assent because the ineluctable in human life lies far deeper than all that; ecclesial framing may give voice to what I undergo, perhaps even eloquently, but it is the afterglow of the human fire. As Schleiermacher expresses it: "It is important to make the point that the main pivots of the ecclesiastical doctrine—the being of God in Christ and in the Christian Church—are independent of the doctrine of the Trinity."[56] So, religion in this sense cannot be like science. It cannot hold cultural legitimacy by concept and theory and empirical trial alone. Religion enters the modern world, as do all great historical actors, laden with custom and past glory but driven by inner desire and hope, an experience that animates a whole world. Trinity is in the train of that great movement.

We might wonder, then, why Trinity occupied the Christian imagination and intellect for so many generations. Why quarrel, as Gibbon famously jibed, over a diphthong? Wonderfully, Schleiermacher can tell us that, too. The *Christian Faith* quietly teaches a historical lesson about the development of dogma, one that gives back to the doctrine of Trinity with one hand a seriousness robbed by the other. Schleiermacher holds that there is a perduring experience and dilemma that drives the upper-level articulation of doctrine. It is built out of the fundamental elements of the Christian life and rests on them, so in an indirect fashion it, too, is inescapable. And these elements are in restless dialectic with one another, so the nagging dilemma is never dull, never complete, never consigned to the museum shelf. This analysis makes Trinity a *puzzle* or, perhaps better, a *task* and project that ever erupts into Christian consciousness, and each generation must encounter it anew, wrestling each time for clarity and better mastery of the inner riddle. Schleiermacher expresses it this way:

> We shall have to put up with the fact that the problem [of distinguishing the peculiar being of God in Christ as an individual, and in the Christian Church as a historical whole, from the omnipotent presence of God in the world in general] can only be solved approximately, and that formulae which has antagonistic points of departure must always remain opposed in tendency; for interest in the problem is bound always to spring up afresh.[57]

There are ancillary arguments at work here, but the central claim follows directly on Schleiermacher's ground rules: the proper expression of the union of the Divine Essence with human nature will be driven by an inner tension, irresolvable and eternally present. On one hand, the redemption achieved by Jesus of Nazareth can only be properly honored by the confession of the Being of God in Him. And on the other, the blessing and peace received through membership in the church can only be confirmed and explained by the Being of God in the Assembly of the Faithful. We have a twofold Agency of the Divine on human nature, yet they seem to the believer ineluctably One and altogether Divine, the uniform action of God on the world. It is one faith, one deliverance, one victory over sin, yet Christ is the Redeemer, without question or peer, and the church the bearer of redemption, necessary and unrivaled by any other society. Now, how can these things be? *This* is the question that cannot be answered or dismissed.

The history of the church shows that Christians have attempted to ease this tension by letting loose of one hold or another, though never fully successfully. In the history of dogma, some Christians have sought to diminish the full Being of God in the individual, Jesus of Nazareth. Some have considered Him a mere prophet or dignified creature; in more modern times, they have honored Him as Teacher or Sage, One among many, though perhaps the best, the very best, of religious leaders. From such diminishments spring the schools of Arianism, Socinianism, and some kinds of religious or spiritual pluralism. These Schleiermacher considers a religious response to the riddle of Divine Presence to an *individual*—the problem the twentieth century taught us to call the "scandal of particularity." Here some Christians show a readiness to trace their redemption to Jesus of Nazareth, but perhaps not everyone's and all. It may be that this Jesus is God's Instrument, His Advocate and Exemplar, but God may design redemption through other channels, other lords. This forms one whole school of second-order reflection on the Union of God with human nature.

But we can see opposition rising up against such a release of tension in the Christian problematic. For in what way can we attest to Christ's redeeming work at all should God not be truly present there? Could sinners in truth rest secure on their deliverance from God-forgetfulness and cruelty to their neighbors if Jesus were but one teacher among many, one sage and helper—an aid, certainly, a blessing, yes, and consoler, but are there not others? Could we not—should we not—wait for Another? Would an instrument of God, even a noble and powerful one, in reality *redeem*? Is that not divine work?

These Athanasian questions struck Schleiermacher, too, as central to any full Christology. But true to his era, Schleiermacher also asked questions not on Athanasius's lips: Is religion not a matter of the pious heart, an inner compulsion and movement, not an idea or teaching or doctrine in the first place at all? And is not that Christian experience of the heart one of being delivered by no one else but Jesus of Nazareth? Is redemption not ineluctably bound to Him, that very One? When we examine our escape from the antithesis that haunts life in the flesh, do we not turn on each side into the arms of this Jesus? Grace, Schleiermacher holds, just is the Name of Jesus Christ. We may receive many blessings throughout a day and season, many divine prompts or leanings, a certain elevation of feeling, and joy in our companionship through life—but Grace, Deliverance, Redemption has but one Face, One Name. We are sinners of His own Redeeming: that is Schleiermacher's fundamental conviction about the life of faith. That this is the enduring heart of Christian piety Schleiermacher thinks confirmed by the common confession of Jesus's Lordship—His Christian cultural plausibility—even by those who hold no other doctrines in common, even the Mystery of Trinity. In his words: "It is natural that people who cannot reconcile themselves to the difficulties and imperfections that cling to the formulae current in Trinitarian doctrine should say that they repudiate everything connected with it, whereas in point of fact their piety is by no means lacking in the specifically Christian stamp."[58] Unitarian societies in England and America along with a few anti-Trinitarians in Germany still find their redemption tied intimately and essentially to Jesus; they are recognizable, then, as Christians. True to his method, Schleiermacher adduces no argument here; these are first-order expressions, discovered, not defended. A little introspection, he famously assures us, will tell us all this. The inner antithesis between a "high" and "low" Christology—if these terms be used at all—drives one pole of Trinitarian doctrine, the Union of God with an individual, a Redeemer.

But we might see the opposing school form as well. Here the inner experience of the Christian finds the mainspring of its Higher Life in the Presence of the Spirit. For these Christians a great and wide, an "ugly ditch" has opened up between their present-day religious life and the Redeemer who walked our earth so long ago. We might recognize, they say, the Being of God in Him; we might even elevate His stature to Incarnate Son, Sole Lord. But He, too, had His season and a day. He lived and suffered once; taught once, long ago; belonged to His people and land; was hanged on a Roman cross; and entered into the past by the wide door that opens for us all, a final suffering and death, His own Passion and mortality. Such Christians may also recognize an Easter Life, a resurrection that is Christ's own, His flesh glorified, and His obedience honored by a place at the Father's Right Hand. These may all be ecclesial frameworks recognized and endorsed by these believers. They may teach and rejoice in such speculative elements of the faith. But these doctrines cannot override the central puzzle: that this One Lord lived long ago, in another culture and land, ineluctably particular and historical, and it is by no means clear that such an event, such a life, can be the direct redemption of a sinner in our time, defined by and enmeshed in our experience. How does "then" become "now"?

For such believers, the church may be the answer. The riddle of the past become present could be resolved by a Union of God with the communal life of humanity, an Assembly under the Aegis of the Living God. Note here that the inner experience and movement of these Christians uncover and rest on a second, distinct Act of God in the world—the Union of the Spirit with the faithful. Christology alone cannot account for their inner life and deliverance; that pole must be diminished in order that the Spirit can be given its full, true measure. (This is one pole of the antithesis that governs the doctrine of the Spirit in the history of dogma. There is also the diminishment of the Spirit, even a denial, so that Christ may be Sole Presence of God on earth.) The doctrine of the Trinity is born not simply from the redemption achieved by Jesus of Nazareth; it arises from proper reflection on the church as Communion in the Spirit. The Fellowship in the Spirit brings us Christ—we cannot know and love and rest upon Him, such Christians say, without being brought into His Presence through the church. Christology, that is, comes through Pneumatology. The sacraments as Spiritual Act of the church, for example, might hold the key to the transformation of time, from Christ, past, to Christian, present: in the Eucharist, say, the Passion of Christ is made present, represented, such that this rite shows forth His death until He comes. So, too, the assembly's proclamation of Christ, the Word announced through human words, could signal the event of Christ drawing near; the *Christus praesens* in the ecclesial act of preaching.

There is, in such second-order reflections, an *indirect* but vital Christology: the church *mediates* the living Presence of Christ. Something *bestows* Christ on the seeker. She comes to learn about Him, to read and hear His words, to recite His prayer, to seek after His wisdom and His mercy. The Redemption achieved in Jesus of Nazareth is announced but, even more, is made effective in the Assembly of the Faithful. It is in the church that he comes to know the Lord. In the idiom of first-and second-order analysis, we have here an explication of the Latin Filioque. The church becomes the bearer of God; it is that strong. (Is that a Marian note in the resolutely Protestant *Christian Faith?*) Here Schleiermacher in his uncanny genius takes the historical element of the Christian faith and turns it to doctrinal use: that Jesus redeemed humanity in a single historical moment is sign and instance of a historical mediation of Divine Union with the creature. We should expect a collective, particular expression and communication of a singular, particular Life. That is one entire school of Christian teaching about redemption. And it is itself an *enactment*, a living generation of the dogma of Trinity.

To examine the contrapuntal movements between Christology and ecclesiology is to trace out the dynamic of Trinitarian debate. In Schleiermacher's view, Christian history is the dialectic, the antithesis between a religious experience of the sole, sovereign working of Jesus Christ, and the experience of that Redemption offered, mediated, by the Assembly of the faithful. We honor one pole of that twofold experience, elevate and perfect it, in one season, and then in another, honor the other. We hold all captive to Christ; and we do not quench the Spirit. We recognize that the One God acts in the world. We experience our utter dependence on Another who is Source of our life, of all life. That is the Divine Causality, we say, at work in our lives, the still point at the center of a noisy life. All these are dimensions of our inner life, our Deliverance, our Communion, our sheer Dependence and Peace. They are utterly One. Now the task of finding language for such a remarkable manifold, at once complex *and* simple, is the problem that cannot be solved, cannot be put to rest, without some upper-level expression in speech, some doctrine. Trinity is the speculative Name we give to the restless movement of our pious hearts, the approximate summary of a dynamic experience.

Now, Schleiermacher thinks we cannot rest content with the classical ecclesial frame of this Mystery but must press on to reformulate the doctrine in light of the living faith of the Protestant church. He offers his concluding reflections as tentative steps in this direction—or, if we read him closely, a rather firm and brisk movement toward an economic Trinity, fully Monarchian, fully receptive of the Living Spirit of Christ. We need not examine this proposal in detail now. Rather, we learn from Schleiermacher here the lessons taught by the modern: that Trinity appears speculative, technical, and abstract because it cannot make direct appeal to religious experience, yet we cannot let it go because our Christian life necessarily moves between intimacy with Christ and intimacy in the Spirit, redemption in One, redemption among the many. At a deeper level, our introspection tells us that the awareness of utter, absolute dependence comes to us only in the dialectical force of a knowing and a doing, a knowing that impels a doing, a doing that cannot be alienated from our knowing the object and the deed. These are the psychological roots of our God-consciousness in Christ, and our love of the good in the Spirit. They are, we might say, an Augustinianism in the idiom of modern subjectivity. Our immediate experience of encounter with God, then, necessarily assumes these two Forms, two Dynamisms, a Union of the One God with human nature that is at once a Being in Christ and a Being in the church. Because of Schleiermacher's intense relationalism, such Divine Agency can be only economic: there is no (human) concept of God that is not the thought of creature thinking Creator, of the Creator uniting Himself with creature. But if we allow this thoroughgoing epistemic and metaphysical restraint, we discover in the *Christian Faith* a dogma of Trinity that is inescapable, dynamic, and forever elusive of the Framework imposed on it. A remarkable achievement for a few dense pages!

But what lesson might we draw from all this, sharing, as we do, so few of the methodological restraints, so little of the dogmatic and Christological architectonic? Of course we have named some in passing (without endorsing them all): the historical interplay of Spirit-saturated and Christ-saturated pieties; the disdain for the speculative and abstract, a stern legacy for much of modern Protestantism; the implausibility and illegitimacy of technical doctrines, removed from direct and immediate expression of religious devotion; the rich appeal of experience that can undergird but also undermine and make relative the creedal achievements of earlier eras; the wholesale recasting of the dogma as an expression of the God-world relation, the only real content of a *Glaubenslehre*. But there is a more complex, more lasting lesson to learn as well.

Christian theology needs in each generation to discover and set forth the irresistible *problematic* that generates the dogma of Trinity. Theology needs to *legitimate* the dogma in just this sense. In our day, that is, the dogma of the Holy Trinity needs justification, an intellectual defense and warrant. Even as Divine Omnipotence needed careful explication and defense in the doctrine of Divine Attributes, so the dogma of Trinity needs intellectual warrant in the doctrine of God. We hasten to add that such legitimating should be severely limited in scope: Christian theology does not require a psychological foundation for the Mystery or a rational explication and reduction of a complex teaching. Neither psychologism nor rationalism should be courted by a proper Trinitarianism. But there is, all the same, a plausibility that should be uncovered and defended by Christian teaching, an intellectual seriousness that springs from a recognition of an intellectual problem that needs to be recognized, honored, and addressed. Like Hegel, Schleiermacher recognized this need and supplied his own distinctive answer. In his idiom, the history of Christian dogma is intelligible only if a polarity is assumed in Christian experience, one that rests on a deeper unity— the attempt to express that restless oscillation is Trinity, and that just is the history of Christian thought.

Note in Schleiermacher's answer that we have moved a full step beyond description. This is not, strictly speaking, a species of the development of doctrine, as aired earlier. We are not now seeking to legitimate the dogma of Trinity by examining the history of the worship of Christ in a monotheistic religion. Nor are we rooting out the intellectual sources—Hellenism, Second Temple

Judaism, "mystery religions"—to provide historical backdrop and cogency to a doctrinal movement. Rather, Schleiermacher provides an *analysis*: the very structure of Christian experience demands a manifold *and* strongly unified doctrine of God. *This* is the pattern of legitimacy Christian theology should seek and defend. We are to seek some conceptual problem, some perduring structure of the faith, some broad enigma of human thought, that echoes the dogma of Trinity. Cultural plausibility stems from the conviction that a lasting dilemma of human or natural life is investigated, diagnosed, and treated through such a religious teaching. And we can be loftier still. In our dogma of Trinity, we seek legitimacy by examining a full, metaphysical puzzle, a lasting question about the very structure of reality, that cannot be fully resolved in such a way that it could slip into the past, or appear only as a philosophical riddle now answered and quietly shelved away. The dogma of Trinity, if it is to be understood as a proper doctrine of God, a proper metaphysical teaching, must investigate and set forth an intellectual problem about reality itself—that is our quest. Not Trinity Itself but its echo, its problematic, its logical form, is what here we seek: *we are after the perennial philosophy, the question of Being.*

Note that we do not seek to legitimate the Mystery by appeal to self-defined *Christian* experience: this is not an attempt to set forth the mystery of redemption or sanctification or Christian teaching about creation, say, or Last Things *as* an expression of Divine Triunity. We break decisively with Schleiermacher and his legacy here. Already we have argued that Trinity is not a "Mystery of Salvation," parting ways with Rahner's maxim in *that* sense. The kind of plausibility we seek does not rest on an analysis of inwardness, though to be sure it will include it, nor is it looking for a broad cultural and religious movement that can be caught up and expressed in Threefold form, though it may comprehend this, too. A proper intellectual motivation for the dogma of Trinity will be found not in Christian sources, first and exclusively, either individual or collective, but rather in the broadest, most comprehensive reflection on reality itself. It will be fearlessly abstract and unrepentantly conceptual. It will dare to be universal in a fully intellectualist and logical sense. It will be metaphysical in the oldest and grandest sense. Intellectual legitimacy will spring from an analysis of Being Itself. The lesson we draw from Schleiermacher, then, is this: there must be a *problematic*, an irresoluble disturbance in our account of reality that prompts investigation into a living, differentiated structure of Being Itself.

We begin this quest with a reflection on conceptual analysis itself, its status and place in the intellectual architecture of theology. We do not seek a traditional *apologetics* here. A traditional apologia of the Trinity would seek a direct argument for a Triune God in the resources of natural or secular reason. Such an argument would assume, implicitly if not explicitly, that Trinity is a deliverance of reason, a fully rational doctrine. I do not seek such a warrant, nor do I consider it a *desideratum* of the faith. The doctrine of the Holy Trinity is a dogma, *the* dogma of the Christian faith. It just *is* the Supernatural. What I seek here is an *analysis* of the dogma that discloses its intellectual rigor and reach. There are rich and deep problems in the very notion of Being, I say, that emerge whenever realism is investigated or taken to heart. These are *structural problems*, if I may style it so, and they demand a hearing in any serious account of reality, created or Increate. Even secular philosophers must wrestle with these structures, I will argue, and propose ways to integrate and harmonize the problems ingredient in realism. To recognize this structural problem is not to become a Trinitarian, however, or even to become a Trinitarian manqué. It is rather to realize what Christians might be talking about in Trinitarian dogma, to recognize an intriguing or ambitious attempt to resolve or honor it and to *respect* it.

These parallel structures of intellectual work I will call "problems in the neighborhood." We are not all talking about the same thing; we are not seeking the same idea even covertly; but we recognize a neighboring intellectual pattern and acknowledge the kinship. To do this, in our day, is to defend the intellectual dignity of the dogma, to take it seriously as a theological proposal about Absolute Reality and to invite others to see it in that light. All this I intend in a low-flying, rough-and-ready sense: this is not a *technical* proposal or method. Rather, I suggest that intellectual problems have a kind of recognizable shape, and those who work in such areas spot them and sense kinship: "so *you* have to worry about such things, too!" These are "family resemblances," as Wittgenstein famously styled this, and we will discuss all this further as the argument progresses. To do all this, I say, is to receive what Schleiermacher bequeathed to the church in his brief but trenchant analysis of Trinity. I aim to follow his lead. So, we are not attempting a natural theology of the later Thomistic school or according to the programmatic teaching of Vatican I. Legitimating the doctrine of Trinity sets out a different and distinctive agenda from either of these traditional movements of Christian thought into secular culture. It is a delicate task to explain how they differ, one from another, so it is worth our while to linger a moment over this point. In the next section, I will set out the alternatives as I see them.

Notes

1. Georg Wilhelm Friedrich Hegel, *Phenomenology of Spirit*, §18, trans. A.V. Miller (Oxford: Clarendon Press, 1977), 10.

2. G. W. F. Hegel, *Lectures on the Philosophy of Religion: One-Volume Edition: The Lectures of 1827*, ed. Peter C. Hodgson, trans. R. F. Brown, Peter C. Hodgson, and J. M. Stewart (Berkeley: University of California Press, 1988), 420, 418.

3. Karl Barth, *Ad Limina Apostolorum: An Appraisal of Vatican II*, trans. Keith R. Crim (Edinburgh: St. Andrew Press, 1969), 30, 36.

4. Rosenzweig, *Star*, 350.

5. Leo Baeck, "Romantic Religion," in *Judaism and Christianity*, trans. Walter Kaufmann (Philadelphia, PA: Jewish Publication Society of America, 1958), 189–292.

6. Friedrich-Wilhelm Marquardt, *Die Entdeckung des Judentums für die christliche Theologie: Israel im Denken Karl Barths* (Munich: Kaiser, 1983).

7. Barth, *Church Dogmatics*, II.2, The Doctrine of God, ed. G. W. Bromiley and T. F. Torrence (Edinburgh: T & T Clark, 1957), §34.4.

8. E. P. Sanders, *Paul and Palestinian Judaism: A Comparison of Patterns of Religion* (Philadelphia: Fortress Press, 1977).

9. Stolina, "Ökonomische und immanente."

10. Karl Rahner, "Anonymous Christians," *Theological Investigations*, trans. David Bourke (New York: Seabury Press, 1974), 6:390–98.

11. Walter M. Abbott, ed., *The Documents of Vatican II* (Chicago: Association Press, 1966).

12. Rosemary Radford Ruether, *Faith and Fratricide: The Theological Roots of Anti-Semitism* (New York: Seabury Press, 1974).

13. J. H. Newman, *An Essay on the Development of Christian Doctrine* (London, 1845).

14. J. H. Newman, *An Essay on the Development of Christian Doctrine*, 38–39.

15. Robert Louis Wilken, *The First Thousand Years: A Global History of Christianity* (New Haven: Yale University Press, 2012); Paul R. Hinlicky, *Beloved Community: Critical Dogmatics after Christendom* (Grand Rapids: Eerdmans, 2015).

16. Rowan Williams, *On Augustine* (London: Bloomsbury, 2016); Lewis Ayres, *Nicaea and Its Legacy : An Approach to Fourth-Century Trinitarian Theology* (Oxford: Oxford University Press, 2004).

17. John D. Zizioulas, *Being as Communion: Studies in Personhood and the Church* (Crestwood, NY: St. Vladimir's Seminary Press, 1985); Catherine Mowry LaCugna, *God for Us : The Trinity and Christian Life* (San Francisco: Harper, 1991).

18. On the radical reformation and its reformers see Stefan Zweig, *The Right to Heresy: Castellio against Calvin*, trans. Eden and Cedar Paul (New York:

Viking Press, 1936); Roland Bainton, *Hunted Heretic: The Life and Death of Michael Servetus 1511–1553* (Boston: Beacon, 1953); G. H. Williams *The Radical Reformation* (Philadelphia: Westminster, 1962); David C. Steinmetz, *Reformers in the Wings: From Geiler von Kayserberg to Theodore Beza* (Philadelphia: Fortress, 1971).

19. Robert W. Jenson, *Lutheran Slogans: Use and Abuse* (Delhi, NY: American Lutheran Publicity Bureau, 2011).

20. Robert W. Jenson, *Systematic Theology*, vol. 1 of *The Triune God* (Oxford: Oxford University Press, 2001).

21. Jenson, *Lutheran Slogans*, 76–77.

22. For a sense of narrative, postliberal theology see George Stroup, *The Promise of Narrative Theology: Recovering the Gospel in the Church* (Atlanta: John Knox, 1981); Ronald Thiemann, *Revelation and Theology* (South Bend, IN: Notre Dame, 1985); William Placher, *Narratives of a Vulnerable God* (Louisville: Westminster John Knox, 1994); and Paul de Hart, *Trial of Witnesses: The Rise and Fall of Postliberal Theology* (Hoboken, NJ: Wiley-Blackwell, 2006).

23. Jenson, *Lutheran Slogans*, 79.

24. Jenson, *Lutheran Slogans*, 79n106. Emphasis added.

25. Peter Brown, *Late Antiquity* (Cambridge, MA: Belknap Press, 1998).

26. On "properly basic belief" in Alvin Plantinga's reformed epistemology see *Warranted Christian Belief* (Oxford: Oxford, 2000) and *God, Freedom, and Evil* (Grand Rapids: Eerdmans, 1989).

27. LaCugna, *God for Us*, 7.

28. Rahner, *The Trinity*, 21.

29. Rahner, *The Trinity*, 22.

30. Rahner, *The Trinity*, 120.

31. Rahner, *The Trinity*, 120.

32. Colin Gunton, *The Triune Creator: A Historical and Systematic Study* (Grand Rapids: Eerdmans, 1998); Jenson, *Systematic Theology*; Paul Hinlicky, *Beloved Community*.

33. Thomas Aquinas, *ST* I. Q14, a. 7.

34. Aristotle, *Metaphysics*, Greek text with English commentary, ed. W. D. Ross, 2 vols., (Oxford: Clarendon, 1924), book 5 (Δ) and book 7 (Z).

35. Bonaventure, *Itinerarium in mentis Deum* (*Journey of the Mind to God*), trans. P. Boehner, ed. S. Brown (Indianapolis: Hackett Books, 1993), Chapter 5.

36. John Webster, "One Who Is Son: Theological Reflections on the Exordium to the Epistle to the Hebrews," in *The Epistle to the Hebrews and Christian Theology*, ed. Richard Bauckham et al. (Grand Rapids: Eerdmans, 2009), 69–94.

37. Søren Kierkegaard, *Fear and Trembling*, trans. Edna Hong and Howard Hong (Princeton, NJ: Princeton University Press, 1983), especially the preface by Johannes de Silentio; Søren Kierkegaard, *Concluding Unscientific Postscript to* Philosophical Fragments, trans. Edna Hong and Howard Hong (Princeton, NJ: Princeton University Press, 1992), part 1, chapter 3, "The Speculative Point of View," and part 2, chapter 1, especially p. 130.

38. Hans Wilhelm Frei, "The Doctrine of Revelation in the Thought of Karl Barth, 1909–1922: The Nature of Barth's Break with Liberalism" (PhD dissertation, Yale University, 1956).

39. Friedrich Schleiermacher, *Brief Outline on the Study of Theology*, trans. Terrence N. Tice (Richmond: John Knox Press, 1970).

40. Friedrich Schleiermacher, *The Christian Faith*, §16.1, ed. H. R. Mackintosh and J. S. Stewart, trans. of the 2nd German ed. (1928; reprint, Philadelphia: Fortress Press, 1976), 78–79.

41. Schleiermacher, *Christian Faith*, §15.2, 78.

42. Schleiermacher, *Christian Faith*, §16.1, 79.

43. Sigmund Freud, *The Future of an Illusion*, trans. James Strachey (New York: Norton, 1961), 33.

44. Schleiermacher, *Christian Faith*, §51, 200.

45. Schleiermacher, *Christian Faith*, §164.

46. John W. Parker, ed., *Essays and Reviews* (London: John E. Parker, 1860).

47. Martin Pickup, "The Trinity and Extended Simples," *Faith and Philosophy: Journal of the Society of Christian Philosophers* 33, no. 4 (2016): 414–40.

48. Colin Gunton, *Act and Being: Towards a Theology of the Divine Attributes* (London: SCM, 2002), see especially chapters 5 and 6.

49. Schleiermacher, *Christian Faith*, §51.1, 201.

50. On Barth's view of Schleiermacher see *Church Dogmatics*, III.3 §§48 and 49, esp. 49.2 and 49.3.

51. Peter Berger, *The Sacred Canopy* (New York: Anchor, 1967), 127–75.

52. Schleiermacher, *Christian Faith*, §170, 738.

53. Schleiermacher, *Christian Faith*, §170, 738.

54. Schleiermacher, *Christian Faith*, §170, 738.

55. See H. J. Schroeder, *Disciplinary Decrees of the General Councils: Text, Translation and Commentary* (St. Louis: B. Herder, 1937), 236–96.

56. Schleiermacher, *Christian Faith*, §170.3, 741.

57. Schleiermacher, *Christian Faith*, §172, 748.

58. Schleiermacher, *Christian Faith*, §172.2, 749.

§ 2. The Intellectual Legitimacy
of the Trinity

The first alternative: the Mystery of the Trinity can be set out as a regional dogma. Its legitimacy and probity stem from the intellectual and cultural seriousness of Christianity itself. God's Triunity, that is, could be understood as a distinctive *Christian* teaching that sets forth how Christians see and worship and unfold their *visio* Dei. Now, this could be done in a particularly sophisticated and deft manner. Indeed, in the history of Christian thought, we should say that this is the most honored, the most elevated, and the most developed of all the alternatives in Christian exposition of the dogma of Trinity. In less skilled hands, this alternative can simply display Trinity to the reader as a *choice*, a religious flavor, enjoyed by Christians and offered to the world. "Others see the Divine Being in some such way; we Christians, on the other hand, see Triunity." This is a regionalism of a bold and unvarnished sort. It is in its own way a refusal to seek intellectual legitimacy at all—at least of the public or secular sort. It gives the negative coloration we often find in the term *fideism*. We might say, following the tagline, that there is no accounting for taste, but I think it is perhaps closer to say that theological doctrine as choice or style spring from reasons of the heart. This unvarnished version simply offers the guest a sample of the Christian fare. Like Jonathan Edwards's famous example of the taste of honey, such offerings must be encountered, tried on, lived into—as words fail before the experience.[1] (Of course, Edwards as a theologian cannot be counted a member of this raw choice school at all!) A particular regional teaching, in this line of thought, simply expresses preference, and we choose it for perhaps psychological reasons, as William James argued, or perhaps family and historical ones, as many religious pluralists say. The legitimacy of regional preferences, if such there be, rests in this case on the respect or toleration we extend to religious forms of life: this is how Christians see things; Hindus in another. But this is not the strongest or most persuasive form of the regional dogma. At its best, this alternative does not exhibit such a straightforward, discretionary, and arbitrary style.

Rather, it seems to me that a proper and careful notion of Trinity as a regional dogma will envision the doctrine as the Name and Structure and Essential Ingredient of the entire Christian Mystery. It will be impossible to enter deeply into the school of Christ without confessing Trinity; it will arise necessarily from deep conversion to the Mystery of God in Christ. Here we have something of a *trajectory* in the Christian life, a movement from catechumen to communicant, that recognizes in Trinity the sum of the whole journey under the Cross of Christ. It is, in this sense, the *explicatio* of the whole, the God who stands at the end of all our thought and devotion, the Mystery that is finally uttered when all Christian speech falls silent. It is an ethos, of course, and a style in religious discourse—but these are pale shadows of the true weight and dynamism of this school. In this deeper form, we express in this alternative a conviction that the dogma of Trinity is the final, the ultimate Mystery to be disclosed to the pilgrim: the Treasure hidden in the field. To be sure, it can be taught to seekers, catalogued in the creeds and catechisms, developed at the head of many systematics, listed as a distinctive—perhaps *the* distinctive—Christian teaching in a world religion survey. But the true mettle of this alternative is proved in its status as proper Christian Mystery: it is just what we mean by the Deep Things of God.

§2.1. The Regional Alternative: St. Thomas and Karl Barth

Now, such a view will entail that the dogma of Trinity gains its theological seriousness, its intellectual legitimacy, from its stature as the Deep Structure of the Christian faith. I will call on Thomas Aquinas and Karl Barth as witnesses for this school. Here is Aquinas on such a notion: "Although by the revelation of grace in this life we cannot know of God *what He is*, and thus are united to Him as to One unknown; still we know Him more fully according as many and more excellent of His effects are demonstrated to us, and according as we attribute to Him some things known by divine revelation, to which natural reason cannot reach, as, for instance, that God is Three and One."[2] In this celebrated section from the even more celebrated twelfth quaestio of the *Summa*, Thomas draws a distinction between those truths known by natural reason and those known by the "revelation of grace." In this earthly life we can know truths about God through reflection on His action on us—the "many and more excellent effects"—that disclose to us how grace can heal, elevate, and guide our lives toward our supernatural end. In our terms, we might think of these as elements and structures of the Christian life: the sacraments, the life of service and self-giving, the confession of wrong, the defense of the right, the allegiance to the common good, the loyalty to the church and reform of its ways. Note that these are modes of the knowledge of *God*, and not simply the Christian life or its teachings. These graces showered on the pilgrim raise her up even in this mortal life to a better, truer, and sounder knowledge of God—though, in that haunting phrase, it is a union as to One Unknown. Thomas adds to such knowledge springing from the workings of grace the deliverances of divine revelation—that is, the "science of the blessed and of Holy Scripture." God's Triunity is the cardinal instance of such knowledge, disclosed earlier and apart from natural reason.

Here we are shown an intellectual structure built on two levels, a natural and supernatural, a realm of nature and of grace, of those truths discovered by unaided reason and those revealed by the shimmering light of God, the region of earthly science and the glorious and superabundant region of the science of the blessed, the Light of Glory. In Thomas's famous maxim, these levels are not in opposition to one another but rather grace elevates and perfects nature. Like Friedrich Schleiermacher, Thomas envisions a divine world of contrast, of Self-Distinction, not of contradiction or destruction. Nothing is lost but all is gathered up: that is the expansive medicine of grace. Now the dogma of Trinity belongs to this glorious, transcendent, and perfecting realm. It is not a paradox, not an irrational doctrine that must be defiantly endorsed in its absurdity, nor one of the six impossible things to be believed before breakfast. The entire structure of intellectual thought militates against the notion that a truth of revelation would *destroy* reason in such an anarchistic fashion. This is a vital point to underscore in the examination of this alternative because its near cousin, the school of intuitive preference or raw experience, might suggest an underlying irrationality and irrealism to the cognitive structure of this whole endeavor. But not so! Thomas shows us that rationality is a roomy structure, a large and generous region in which some elements rise above others and some truths are proud against the surface of ordinary thought. The dogma of Trinity is a Supernatural Truth in just this sense: a glorious and rational Light that must be received by an intellect healed, elevated, and strengthened to withstand Its Beauty.

Now in such a view, the Mystery of the Trinity will receive its plausibility, its intellectual dignity and rigor, by its place within the whole compass of Christian teaching. It is not a second-order teaching; not an epiphenomenon of some lower, controlling insight; not an amalgam of other central elements, an ecclesial shorthand for the whole lived mystery of the Christian life. No, Thomas here shows us how the intellectual furniture of the Christian world is built up out of variegated materials, some carved out of the ordinary discourse and knowledge of the everyday world, others—the most sturdy, the lightest, the best—of a reason that can only be given, that belongs to Realms of Light, that resides in this world as a Crown, a Perfection, a Majesty. It is "above reason," as John Locke would have it, but in an entirely or, we should say, preeminently rational manner. It sanctifies the thinker to think this Triune Thought because, bathed in this Gracious Light, the human intellect becomes Deiform. These Augustinian notes in St. Thomas are not the only ones, of course, and a fuller exposition of the well-worked furrows of quaestiones 12 and 13 of the *Summa* would allow us to distinguish from, as well as assimilate Thomas to, his teachers in the faith. But we can say even in this brief comment that Thomas drinks deeply of Augustinian wisdom here just because they both stand committed to the idea that Christian theology, from stem to stern, from everyday practice to sublime Mystery, is wholly, deeply, gloriously rational. Christian teaching is *Truth*, ascending and descending on a ladder raised up on the earth. The dogma of Trinity stands as Summit of Christian Truth, its legitimacy stemming from the architecture of the whole Christian system of thought and from the lives made holy, broken and broken open, by meditation on its Keystone.

Trinity, however, is not self-evident; indeed, such Revealed Grace could never be so. It is not to be discovered through lifelong, disciplined, and faithful reflection on the very Idea of God; it does not lie *at the bottom* of anything, or even of all things. The dogma of the Trinity is a church teaching in just this sense—it cannot be prized out of the earth by any earthly tool; it must be received from Above. The community of the blessed must donate this Glory to the church and from the church to the world. It bears the dignity of a gift, the Royal Gift that enriches the whole immiserated earth.

Now in many ways Thomas Aquinas and Karl Barth make a good pair. Thomas's careful endorsement of Trinity as Revealed Grace might be twinned with the doctrine of Trinity as Revealed in the first volume of Barth's *Church Dogmatics*. In Barth we have another radiant example of the conviction that the dogma of Trinity belongs to the Christian faith as capstone to its whole teaching, treasure of its whole distinct, and distinctive, intellectual capital. These two, however, are not identical twins. Barth does not share the Thomistic conceptual structure of a natural realm, crowned by that of grace; or of nature and *supernature*, should such a term even be hazarded; or even less of a world of reason perfected and elevated by a crown of faith. But Barth *does* share with Thomas two elements that make them a particularly suitable pair of advocates for this alternative vision of doctrinal legitimacy. Like Thomas, Barth considers Divine Revelation a Source, *the* Source, of Trinitarian dogma; like Thomas, Barth holds that God's Triunity cannot be a deliverance of natural reason or self-evident to the rational structures of human thought. Thomistic, yes, but Barth takes these Thomistic themes into new lands and reshapes them there. For Barth there can be no *vestigium Trinitatis* in scholastic terms. Trinity is the Invasion from Another world, the Rupture, the Evangelium shattering the clouds and coming down to the earth. Revelation is the Divine Incursion into the world of sinners. It is "Veiling and Unveiling," an Apocalyptic event, *the* Apocalyptic event of all Scripture. Here is how Barth expresses these motifs in two numbered *Stichworte*: first, the celebrated §8: "God's Word is God Himself in His revelation. For God reveals Himself as the Lord and according to Scripture this signifies for the concept of revelation that God Himself in unimpaired unity yet also in unimpaired distinction is Revealer, Revelation, and Revealedness."[3] Then the less well-known, but vital, §9: "The God who reveals Himself according to Scripture is One in three distinctive modes of being subsisting in their mutual relations: Father, Son and Holy Spirit. It is thus that He is the Lord, i.e., the Thou who meets man's I and unites Himself to this I as the indissoluble Subject and thereby and therein reveals Himself to him as his God."[4] In these two propositions Barth deftly catches up the traditional idiom of Procession—the event of revelation—and of Person: "modes of being" subsisting in relation. The interrelation of these two *Themen* structure and constitute Barth's dogma of Trinity, a rich, influential, and highly charged doctrine, a gift to the whole church.

This is Christian speech, grounded in its own sources and norms: "The Doctrine of Trinity is what basically distinguishes the Christian doctrine of God as Christian, and therefore what already distinguishes the Christian concept of revelation as Christian, in contrast to all other possible doctrines of God or concepts of revelation."[5] In this way, and in just this way, God's Triunity can be understood as an expression of the biblical statement—Barth is insistent on that location!—*Deus dixit*, God speaks. "Logically [questions about Trinity] are quite simply questions about the subject, predicate and object of the short statement, 'God speaks,'

Deus dixit.[6] With ruffled feathers Barth responds abruptly to a critic of this short thesis when it first appeared in the earlier version of this volume: "The serious or mocking charge has been brought against me that here is a grammatical and rationalistic proof of the Trinity, so that I am doing the very thing I attack elsewhere, namely, deriving the mysteries of revelation from the data of a generally discernible truth. . . . Naturally it was not my thought then, nor is it now, that the truth of the dogma of the Trinity can be derived from the general truth of such a formula."[7] No apologetics for Barth, either! Rather, Barth insists that "God speaks" exhibits a logical structure that he has now come to call Revealer, Revealed, and Revealedness, and answers, in staccato, three central questions from Scripture and Scripture alone: Who is God in His revelation? What is He doing? What does He effect? Now, in these three questions, Barth draws the entire dogma into intimate relation with the creature—a dangerous liaison! Barth dares to say this:

> In the Bible revelation is always a history between God and certain men. Here one man is separated and led out into a foreign country like Abraham, there another is called and anointed to be a prophet, a priest, or a king. Here a whole nation is chosen, led, ruled, blessed, disciplined, rejected and adopted again. There faith and obedience are aroused, or there is complete hardening. There a Church is gathered in the light of this whole occurrence, and the kerygma and sacraments are instituted as signs of recollection and expectation, because man is now 'in Christ,' a future has been won, and along with it a present between the times. . . . The man who asks about the God who reveals Himself according to the witness of the Bible must also pay heed to the self-revealing as such and to the men to whom this self-revealing applies.[8]

Barth sums up his logical positioning of the dogma this way:

> When we ask: Who is the self-revealing God? the Bible answers in such a way that we have to reflect on the triunity of God. The two

other questions: What does this God do and what does He effect? are also answered primarily by new answers to the first question; Who is He? The problem of the three answers to these questions—answers which are like and yet different, different and yet like—is the problem of the Trinity.[9]

Note, once again, what Barth has learned from Schleiermacher! And then, in firm tones: "In the first instance the problem of revelation stands or falls with this problem."[10] This is not the place, however, to develop Barth's entire doctrine of Trinity—there will be time for that—but ingredient in the very notion of intellectual legitimacy in the modern era is the expectation of an examination of the roots of Barth's doctrine, and the long but definite shadow Immanuel Kant casts over the entire landscape of Barth's Triune Revelation.

Notice, for example, that in this whole catena of citations from *Church Dogmatics*, I.1, Barth aims to anchor Trinity in Christian discourse and biblical speech. He seeks there to generate Trinity out of a Divine encounter with creatures, especially with Israel and the church; he considers Divine Self-Disclosure a repetition of the answer to the primary question, Who is God? And he holds that this Triune Event is principally a Demonstration, an Agency, of Lordship. The central problematic of Trinity is the Identity of God—*Who* not *What* He is—and it can be answered only in faith, the obedience to the Master who calls and commands. This is an appeal to Divine Revelation that brings Barth in the neighborhood of Thomas's teaching about the realm of grace, but in the neighborhood only. This volume of the *Church Dogmatics* shows us what is transformed when doctrines of revelation move out of the schoolmen's intellectual framework into the world shaped by the modern, especially the architecture of knowledge built by René Descartes and even more by Immanuel Kant. These two philosophers are the alchemists behind the modern notion of revelation, and Barth, too, even in his rebellion, serves his apprenticeship at their workshop.

Consider, for example, the force Barth gives to the very word *revelation* in §8: "We may sum all this up in the statement that God reveals Himself as the Lord." So far, as we expect. Then, the alchemy: "This statement is to be regarded as an analytical judgment." Barth will then "actualize" this Kantian dictum in a characteristic event-centered fashion: "The distinction between form and content cannot be applied to the biblical concept of revelation. When revelation is an event according to the Bible, there is no second question as to what its content might be. Nor could its content be equally well manifested in another event than this." Then Barth's threefold analysis of the event: "To be Lord means being what God is in His revelation to man." (An amazing statement!) "To act as Lord means to act as God in His revelation acts on man. To acquire a Lord is to acquire what man does in God when he receives His revelation—revelation always understood here in the unconditional sense in which it encounters us in the witness of Scripture."[11] This is a modern theological epistemology in full technical dress; its claim on our intellectual assent follows suit, or loses its hold, just in line with its strictures. The very notion of legitimacy has been swept along by the modern engine of thought.

Think for a moment what it might mean for the statement—no, the confession—that "God reveals Himself as Lord" to be an "analytic judgment." We remember that in the first *Critique*, Kant suggested that in an analytic judgment the predicate "adds nothing" to the subject of the proposition. Though maddeningly elusive, Kant's distinction between analytic and synthetic judgments seem somehow transparent and intuitive—at least on first meeting. We might consider the statement "a wife is a married woman" to be an analytic judgment, almost by definition, so to say. When we understand wife, we see "contained within it"—another celebrated and elusive suggestion of Kant's—"married woman." But now consider the statement "a wife ceases bearing children late in adulthood." Here Kant says we cannot find, however long we search, the predicate, "ceases bearing children" or, more broadly, "childbearing age," *within* the very concept, wife. It "adds" something new; it must be discovered, or invented, or taught. It is, in Kant's idiom, a "synthetic judgment." Famously, for Kant, arithmetic sums are synthetic judgments (the integers 5 and 7, when analyzed fully do not contain within their concepts, 12, Kant says), as are any statements derived from the scientific laboratory (the atomic weight of hydrogen is 1), any empirical proposition or finding (this boulder weighs twelve pounds), and any historical or social fact (Kant lived in Königsberg).

Fundamental to the analytic-synthetic distinction, then, is the very idea of analysis. We are asked to imagine a complex—perhaps a definition or an essence—that can be broken into constituents, "analyzed," or reduced down to the essential elements of its very nature. In an analytic judgment, Kant says, we cannot think the idea or substance of a grammatical subject without "containing"— entailing, perhaps, or assuming, at times unwittingly—the very property that becomes this subject's predicate. Now Barth crossed the theological threshold during the great ascendency of Kantianism. The wildly heretical thought of questioning the analytic-synthetic distinction still stood many years off. The entire first volume of the *Church Dogmatics* would be clothed in this distinction, and the whole development of the doctrine of revelation would bear its contours. God reveals Himself as Lord: think of this now as an analytic judgment.

We are to analyze revelation into these essential components, Barth says: the Divine Subject, God, "contains" within Himself the predicate "Lord," or perhaps better, "Lordship." We cannot actually *think* the idea of God without discovering or assuming Lordship: to be God is to be Lord. (We can see here a worry about the entire intellectual furniture: Is this in truth an identity statement, x = x? If so, is it not empty, true but trivial, as philosophers say? Or two distinct terms, genuinely distinct, such that they could be related *as* one or the other? A qua relation, perhaps, so that x = y as *z*? If so, is not something added? Could it be a "synthetic a priori judgment," the golden prize of the *Critique of Pure Reason*? We might well suspect that Barth, were he working today, would push aside the whole distinction as too compromised to bear this heavy doctrinal load. But more of that in what follows.) Note that Barth claims, under the strong impress of this idea, that the form-content distinction must fall away in the idea of revelation. We do not in truth have a large-scale, a "formal" notion of Deity that is then "filled out" with the biblical content Lordship. There is no general category God, known universally or naturally, that is now elevated, or purified, or determined by scriptural content: God is Lord. No, the proper methodological distinction in the doctrine of God is analytic-synthetic, not form-content; everything, Barth claims, rests on this claim. In just this way, Barth breaks with Thomas, with scholastic natural theology, and with what Barth here calls Protestant modernism. Revelation is Christian speech in this strong sense: there is no universal category filled out, filled up with scriptural or doctrinal determination; rather, there is only an analytic judgment to be made, in which God Lord, Lord God, is received, endorsed, confessed. In just this way we set aside all speculation about Godhood, *Deitas*, for the general notion Deity has been ruled out of court. Thus, God's Identity, the Sole God, makes Himself known, and that is as Lord.

Now, notice how this Kantian stamp transforms, too, the way this very idea of Divine Revelation is received by the knower.

Remember that Thomas time and again in *Summa Theologica* 1, quaestio 12, affirms that "what is known is known according to the mode of the knower." It is this very distinction that allows him to separate natural from supernatural, assisted knowledge and to mark off the realm of nature from that of grace. In just this way Thomas protects the exclusive and exclusively Christian account of the Holy Trinity. It is not so for Barth. Something else explodes into view here. God just is Lord; just so is He known by the creature as the One who seizes him, the Revealer who is her Sovereign in the very act of being known. There is no neutral act of knowledge with this Subject, only obedience. Our attention is being drawn now not to the intellect of the knower which in the light of grace is being slowly illumined, made Deiform, the weak eyes strengthened to bear the Glorious Light. No, rather our attention is drawn to the Revealer, He, the Lord, who declares Himself, intrudes Himself into our world, commandeers and commands, such that the knower simply recognizes—confirms what is the case!—that he or she has a Master. Just this is the Unveiling of God.

Now here Barth trades heavily on his Kantian training: his elaboration of the analytic-synthetic distinction organizes a Trinitarian analysis of the whole. Remember that Barth takes Divine Self-Disclosure to follow or, perhaps, "contain" three forms: Revealer, Revelation, and Revealedness. These are event-terms; they explode into our world. They are *relational*: God is Unveiled *to the creature*. But Barth insists that this does not entail the dangerous implication such relationalism brings quickly to mind: God does not need the creature in order to be revealed as the Three-Personed God. Now, we may well wonder, Why not? Have we not thrown all our eggs into this basket, revelation? Lordship? And do these terms, when analyzed, not *entail* the God-world relation? It seems that strong! Surely, we might object, God does not reveal Himself as Lord to Himself! The Father would not be Lord of the Son and Spirit, would He? Such anxieties seem only heightened by Barth's ready embrace of the analytic relation in the doctrine of revelation. Yet Barth here is fearless. Surely, he knew as well as any, better than most, that relationalism in theology carried grave risks. But still he confidently appeals to Kantian analysis as the intellectual form of Christian Trinitarianism. It seems that academic and dogmatic legitimacy remained, all the same, in Kantian hands.

Perhaps Barth thought along these lines. Holy Scripture, he might say, is *essentially* Revelation. Here Barth may have reflected the early modern distinction between positive and general or rational revelation, drawing the line between categorical and historical religion and the rational or universal, as do Schleiermacher and Kant, though they clash on which side of the divide to honor. Barth honors positive revelation but in a heightened form. There is but one revelation, strongly concrete, historical, and positive, and that is Almighty God's disclosure to Israel and the church. That is the primal event of human history, the primal event of creation. And there is something like a record, or a trace, or an "empty crater," to borrow Barth's early war-inflected term, that shows the place and force of this primal event: that is Holy Scripture. In these early volumes, Barth is eager to draw a distinction between the event of revelation, the divine unveiling, and the scriptural witness to that event. Of course, this has to do in part with Barth's own doctrine of inspiration and his training in modern historical exegesis. But even more, I think, it reflects Barth's early doctrine of God, his encounter with the dogma of Trinity. He knows, and follows, Schleiermacher's claim that Trinity is an ecclesial framing; Barth in this first volume considers Trinity an "interpretation" of the event and record of revelation. Trinity, he says there, is not "in Scripture" in a straightforward and direct fashion. We need not seek out particular passages—either celebrated ones in the history of premodern exegesis or the unlikely, unanticipated modern ones—to warrant and authorize the dogma. The doctrine of Trinity is not a "direct Christian utterance," he says in echo of the cardinal teaching of the *Glaubenslehre*. Rather Trinitarian Processions and Persons—modes of being—are second-order reflections and expressions of the primary text, that is, of God's own Self-Disclosure, His Speech as Lord. *This* is positive revelation; God's own Being just *is* Revelation.

Here we see the force of the analytic judgment: God does not reveal something; He does not communicate or disclose a truth or even a central truth; rather, He lifts the Veil that covers every nation, showing and demonstrating *Himself*, His own Unveiled Face. (Barth trades quietly here on a distinctive reading of the Sinai traditions in Exodus and 2 Corinthians.) Barth moves from there to claim a remarkable reweighting of the dogma of Trinity. In the sequence—Revealer, Revelation, and Revealedness—the palm is given to *Revelation*: who God is can be answered principally as "Revelation." Now this follows directly from Barth's reliance on the analytic-synthetic distinction: the Revealer just is Revelation; they are the Relata of an analytic judgment. The three questions Barth raises as the framing of his whole treatment—Who is God? What does He do? What is His effect?—can be reduced, *analyzed*, as repetitions of the first. They state, analytically, who God is. But they do so in this remarkable way. The center of gravity in this series has, in Barth's hands, shifted from who God is to what He does—that is, from Father to Son, from Revealer to Revelation Itself.

The traditional teaching of taxis, ordering in Trinity, undergoes subtle changes here. We see the ancient ordering in the grammatical or logical character of Barth's treatment: the Subject of the Triune Revelation is clearly the Father, the Speaker of the Word. But in the exegetical sections of this volume, Barth is eager to insist that the Bible just is revelation, Word, and we have no other proper source for Christian instruction. *Sola Scriptura* in this region means: Holy Scripture is revelation, Word of God; Jesus Christ is Incarnate Word, Revelation Itself. The Second Person of the Trinity, then, anchors or grounds the doctrine of Trinity in a manner at once exegetical, historical, and conceptual. We begin with Christology, yes, but even more, we Christians begin with Positive Revelation, the Very God who is Very Word. This is what it means to have a Lord, to cry *Kyrios Christos*. So, Barth's celebrated Christological concentration begins early: it is itself the root of the dogma of Trinity.

All rich and wonderful and daring! But are we not here even deeper in the thickets we spotted earlier, at some distance away? Is this not now a relationalism deepened and compounded by a strong, forceful Christology? Even the very taxis of the tradition seems impelled to serve the created order. It is as though Schleiermacher's insistence on the divine economy exacts its price even from his most bitter opponent. Can a Kantian distinction serve Barth faithfully here, or have we only welcomed in a friend who lifts up the heel against us? We do well to consider carefully this question here, because the very notion of legitimacy, of the intellectual rigor of what I have called the regional alternative, rests on our reply. Can we claim that the dogma of the Trinity is Christian speech, Christian speech alone, yet ward off, firmly and properly, the lingering suspicion that the creation itself, or perhaps this one treasured slice of it, is made necessary, in this very defense, to the God of Revelation?

Here we might return to our earlier query about the analytic-synthetic distinction: What does it mean to say something again in other words? Is this translation or transposition a grammatical form of the analytic judgment? Is it a scriptural expression of a Trinity grounded in revelation? We now step back into the subtle questions raised earlier about the analytic-synthetic distinction itself. Just what kind of relation between the subject and predicate should we understand when analysis is applied to the doctrine of Trinity? Is this an identity statement, and if so, just what sort of identity is it—should identity, in fact, come in sorts? To answer these questions is to answer the worry about the Sovereignty, Aseity, and Freedom of the Triune God. It explains—at least to Barth's satisfaction—why the Revealed God does not need or entail the creature. It is the vital move in the first volume of the *Church Dogmatics*, the essential first step beyond Schleiermacher and beyond modalism. He reasons like this.

In an analytic judgment, two terms or names are brought into relation by the knower, x is y. Now, this copula, *is*, has the force of *sameness*, not predication: x = y. Yet, x is not identical to y, for the entire premise of the original judgment is that *two* terms are brought into relation, not one, repeated. Students of Duns Scotus will recognize this territory: it is the rich reflection on the "formal distinction," the notion that the Divine Attributes can be One yet in some way, and at the same time, distinct. Perhaps something of Scotus's legacy burnished Barth's appeal to "unimpaired unity in unimpaired distinction." So, too, we might think of the grammatical notion of the synonym, familiar to and favored by Aristotle in the *Categories*, disputed and exiled by W. V. Quine.[12] In a synonym, we use terms in the same manner, toward the same referent, that mean roughly the same thing. In Aristotelian dictum: univocal predication. But key is "roughly the same thing." That is the very question under examination here. Wife and married woman are synonymous, the same; are they identical? We might think that they have different etymologies, different language groups and histories; their distinction, one from the other, could be adventitious. But it might be that, however coined, these terms capture something subtly distinctive in the state of marriage that a woman may enter. We speak often of connotation in such settings: wife connotes something distinctive from married woman, though the referential power we call denotation might remain the same for both. Note how this discussion brings us quickly into the realm of discourse, grammar, speech; does it also bring us into the realm of metaphysics? (We might think of Saul Kripke's celebrated essay, *Naming and Necessity*, here.)[13] Just this is *the* question of revelation. Can this Divine Word speak itself? And can it do so "in a second way"? Can it disclose or exhibit something more than a linguistic relation, something beyond grammar? Or, perhaps more radically, is there something beyond grammar in God? Barth claims God and Speech to be an analytic relation *and* a metaphysical one. Sign and Referent are One.

God can repeat Himself in a distinctive and related way: that is the force of Deus dixit as an analytic judgment. He says Himself in Distinction and Unity, genuine Sameness, and genuine Difference. But note the worries that cannot seem to be quieted. In truth, does not Revelation seem to "add" something to Revealer? Is this not in the end a form of synthetic judgment after all? Is that not just what we mean by something "new"? Is that not in fact the stubborn quality of the synonym, that it adds fresh connotation to an underlying sameness? Or, on the other hand, can we affirm that we "discover" Revelation in the very notion of Revealer; is it "contained" there, as definition or constituent? Should we not say, rather, that Speech is a *Predicate*, though it be a Divine One? Does the analytic relation in the end serve Barth well? Barth meets these crucial questions with an apocalyptic flair. He writes:

> Revelation in the Bible means the self-unveiling, imparted to men, of the God who by nature cannot be unveiled to men. . . . It is not impossible nor is it too petty a thing for Him to be His own *alter ego*

in His revelation, His *alter ego* to the extent that His self-unveiling, His taking form, obviously cannot be taken for granted but is an event and an event that cannot be explained by or derived from either will or act of man or the course of the world at large; to the extent that He Himself must take a step towards this event; to the extent that this step obviously means something new in God, a self-distinction of God from Himself, a being of God in a mode of being that is different from though not subordinate to His first and hidden mode of being as God, in a mode of being, of course, in which He can also exist for us. The God who reveals Himself here can reveal Himself. The Lordship discernible in the biblical revelation consists in the freedom of God to differentiate Himself from Himself, to become unlike Himself and yet to remain the same, to be indeed the One God like Himself and to exist as the one sole God in the fact that in this way that is so inconceivably profound He differentiates Himself from Himself, being not only God the Father but also—in this direction that is the comprehensive meaning of the whole of the biblical witness—God the Son. This Sonship is God's Lordship in His revelation.[14]

Now here we have Barth taking the risks he repeatedly affirmed as necessary to a faithful dogmatics. In astonishingly daring language, Barth speaks of a God who exists in a Mode that is "for Himself" but also "for us," a Revelation, that is differentiated yet the same, unlike—even something new in God!—yet also identical, the Father but also the Son, Unveiled yet Veiled, and all this as the Lord. In just this way the One God in His Revelation as Lord is Triune. Note now how Barth holds that analyticity serves his aims—even if it proves to be a rather unreliable servant in our eyes. The Revealer repeats *Himself*, not an idea or a teaching or a dogma. With the liberal party of many generations, Barth affirms that Revelation is not "propositional." The central intuition here is of the same Subject reiterated as a Second, a Second who is *reflexive*—God Himself—and therefore distinctive. The repetition has a relative autonomy; it is not a "bare identity" or empty tautology. But it is the very subject in a different way, a Divine Synonym. This, Barth says, is analytic: the Same God in a Different Way.

Father, Son, and Spirit are something like terms of an analytic judgment, each exhibiting the status of distinctive or independent terms. Yet these terms are "contained" in One Another; they are "mutual relations." But, it seems, not of opposition—for that, it seems, is not "contained" in analyticity. The Revealed God cannot be exhausted in the economy, Barth says, for this very same reason. Were God to be only "Phenomenal," the appearance of God only, without disclosing the Noumenon, the True God, we would not have the kind of sameness analyticity demands. Were God to reveal only teachings or miracles or extraordinary gifts—an economic, propositional, or synthetic disclosure—we would not have the kind of necessity the analytic relation requires. Instead in revelation itself we encounter the Subject in Act, the True God, the Immanent and Majestic Lord, who repeats, determines, distinguishes His very Self in another Term and Another, Distinct yet One. In this way Barth takes the traditional notion of Procession, the Divine Life or Act, and derives from that Divine Event the Revelation that is Son, the Revealedness that is Spirit of the Father, the Revealer. Now none of this, though necessary to this Divine Reflexivity, can be understood as necessary toward us, Barth says. The Unveiling will remain impossible for creatures: God will remain Subject, Veiled, even in this Act, this Procession, of Unveiling. This, Barth says, is just because it is analytic: God Himself is the Revelation—He Himself is Lord—so we encounter the majesty, the sovereign freedom of God in this Unveiled Lord. The *Deus revelatus*, Barth says, remains the *Deus absconditus*. The Same God in a Different Way: that is the doctrine of Trinity born out of a complex, actualized account of Kantian analysis.

We might say, then, that the intellectual legitimacy Barth extends to the dogma of Trinity belongs to Christian revelation alone—but one explicated in a Kantian mode, flavor, and transposition. Our task now is to assess this Kantian flavor: Has it imparted to Barth's Christian confession an intellectual rigor that exacts our respect? Has Kant allowed Barth to speak in legitimate discourse to his intellectual peers? Has it lent an air of academic dignity to a Dogma held to be incredible in the modern era? It is not easy to say, for the entire relation of philosophy to theology, of reason to faith, or rationality to dogma, is caught up in these several, vexed, and many-sided questions. After many turns, it appears that we have touched down once again at our beginning: Is all this analysis of Revelation a kind of natural theology in disguise, a rational exposition of a Mystery? Just what kind of alchemist is Kant in Barth's workshop? He clearly stands behind Barth's workbench, but exactly what kind of work does he do there?

On one hand, we should surely say that Barth uses Kant lightly; not too much rests on anything Barth receives from Kant's hand. In a famous quip, Barth replied to a dense methodological query about the place of philosophy in theology by saying simply: "I use it."[15] Throughout the *Dogmatics*, Barth seems genuinely free of philosophical strictures. He moves confidently—unmatched confidence!—through mazes of intellectual knots and puzzles, never hemmed in, tentative, or skittish but always ready to take whatever helps his cause and to leave the rest behind, let over the side with a royal dismissal. It is lovely to inhabit a realm as free as Barth's, to join him there and breathe that mountain air. We might say in this vein that Barth picks up the Kantian tool of analyticity, wields it for a time, and lets it drop when he is done. Not the tool but the work accomplished by it: that should be our focus! Now such a free and unimpaired relation of dogma to philosophy or rational argument would make Barth a full member of our first alternative: legitimacy for Christian doctrine would stem from Christian confession alone, stubbornly alone. Barth's early defiance of natural theology, Protestant modernism, and the *Analogia Entis* would all seem to point us to this happy country. But there is something of a "sameness amid difference" here, a stubborn "on the other hand," that, try as we will, will not fall silent. And perhaps this draws Barth closer to Thomas than we might first imagine.

Consider this: it seems that Barth holds that Kant has laid bare a basic logical structure, a relation that belongs to reason itself— perhaps better, Reason Itself. Remember that in reply to his early critic, Carl Siegfried, Barth likened his summary statement, Deus dixit, to a "formula": "It is from the truth of the dogma of the Trinity that the truth of such a formula can perhaps be derived in this specific application, that is, in the Doctrine of the Trinity." Barth explains the little word, perhaps, in the direction of his earlier freedom: "the truth of the dogma of the Trinity does not stand or fall with such a formula." But he also says this: "All dogmatic formulations are rational, and every dogmatic procedure is rational to the degree that in it use is made of general concepts, i.e. human *ratio*."[16] Barth shows the proper weighting to be observed between the ratio and the dogma: "It can be called rationalistic"—not a compliment!—"only when we can show that the use is controlled not by the question of dogma, i.e. subordinated to Scripture, but by something else, most probably some kind of philosophy." There we have the standard Barthian reply to the place of reason in the realm and defense of the faith.[17] But Barth is careful here. He returns to his conviction that Scripture demands an analysis of this kind, a reasoned reflection by a human ratio, that "opens up" into the dogma of Trinity. For Kant, reason itself "contains" a logical structure that inhabits and defines and structures "pure reason," thought itself. That is the force of Kant placing the categories and the judgments made of them in the realm of the understanding. It seems that the very act of thinking, the act of reason itself, requires and is guided by the form of pure judgment—the division of all predication into analytic and synthetic relations, those "contained in" and those "added to" the subject. Now were we to apply this dictum of reason to speculative dogmatics, we would say that in God there is no division between language and referent, no proper distinction between discourse and metaphysics, so that we have a grammatical structure that is also a structure of reality, of Reality Itself.

Now, to be sure, this is the kind of speculative thesis Kant abhors; indeed, he presses every lever in the *Critique of Pure Reason* to lift it out of sight. But Barth? How does such rational speculation stand in the world of the *Church Dogmatics*? Barth's pivotal book on Anselm's *Proslogion: Fides Quaerens Intellectum* renders this question especially acute. There he wrestles Anselm to the ground in a full dogmatic manner but with a deep respect for the metaphysical élan shown there. In the first volume of the *Church Dogmatics*, he reports with his customary wry delight that he is now being suspected of being a "Catholic metaphysician," a sign perhaps that others have wondered about the question we worry over here.[18] What should we say about the analytic ratio in Barth's doctrine of Trinity? Is Scripture indeed the controlling and grounding element here?

Perhaps Barth's view, in truth, offers a Thomism that has journeyed through the Reformation, a scholastic ratio that has tasted Geneva. Barth could be closer, that is, to the Protestant Orthodoxy he studied in those years through Heppe and Schmidt than it often appears—closer, it seems, than he himself supposed. Perhaps we see in Barth here, especially in this early volume on the Trinity, a full *metaphysical* account of revelation, an elevation of categories of theological epistemology into the realm of Divine Being, into Rational Being Itself. This could be an unembarrassed realism about God the Word, the Discourse who is God, the God who Speaks in the structure of Reason Itself. Now such a reading of Barth's theological program would place Scripture in the logical position occupied by grace in the scholastic system. We would not have a gift given to the natural intellect, here, a divine medicine dispensed, to aid, strengthen, elevate, and heal the intellect; no, the road through Geneva would quell this remedy. We still remain, then, in the "domain of the Word" (the phrase is John Webster's). But we would have in Holy Scripture a proper starting point, a healthy guide and gateway, a safe conduct that would open up for us, for the first time, a full, true, and obedient rationality, a created intellect at last equipped for thinking the thought of God. If we begin where Scripture places us, the intellect will be liberated and armed for full speculative reason. This might be one way to understand Barth's appeal to "control": Scripture could "control" theological reason by serving as its starting gate: we begin in the Bible, we apply our ratio on its signs and things, we think the thought of revelation, and we return to it, time and again, to renew our minds and set our thoughts on the heavenly country. Perhaps Barth might say that we become philosophers, true philosophers, only when biblical revelation gives us the concepts, events, and material that will guide or fill out the work of reason. In that case, Kant's critical philosophy would properly *begin*—we would realize the Kantian task—when we take up revelation as the entrance and form and event to which any Kantian procedure will properly apply. "Reason within the limits of religion alone": that might be the Kantianism proposed here. If that is so, we might say that analyticity reaches its full measure and is exercised fully and truly only in the scriptural realm, where it explicates and unfolds the rich metaphysical reality of revelation. Trinity in this vein would serve as a kind of transcendental deduction of the Idea of God within the category of revelation.

Well, this could hardly serve as a full portrait of Barth's position on reason and revelation; it is a sketch only, and one devoted to an early volume, and an early account of the doctrine of God. But this sketch, and the Kantian adventures leading up to it, help us see the *kind* of legitimacy Christian dogma holds in the Barthian world. This first alternative we have surveyed here, from Thomas to Barth, has located intellectual plausibility in the Christian thought-world itself: doctrine is Christian speech, resting on Christian experience, or Scripture, or Revealed Grace; it funds its own schools and raises up its own teachers; it looks within. Now such a position has been termed *fideism*, and it has not garnered praise in the broader academy. It has been contrasted to public theology and has been thought to resist larger intellectual scrutiny, the light of public inquiry and its searching arguments, and to abandon Christian responsibility for civic debate and civic policy. Fideism has been charged with refusing the intellectual gifts of the age and turning a cold shoulder to the academic tasks others must carry. Little wonder that Christian doctrine appears so implausible to such critics! What kind of conversation can be held with those who talk only with themselves! But is this in truth the position Thomas and Barth hold? Is it the form of intellectual legitimacy they propose or seek?

I think we have reason to say no. This first alternative, the regional doctrine, is not fideism—or perhaps better, fideism is not the solipsistic adventurer its critics assume. We have to think carefully here about what these theologians intend when they offer an exposition of the doctrine of the Trinity. What does it mean, they ask, for human intellect to explore the Mystery of God's Triunity? Just what kind of intellectual or rational task is it? Now this is an interesting question, a provocative and rich one! This is a question about the very notion of intellectual legitimacy; it touches on the fundamental idea of rational dignity itself. In their own ways and idioms, Schleiermacher, Barth, and Thomas consider the dogma of the Trinity *the* intellectual task of rational human beings. It is that strong, that deep! So, we might ask here, with them: What does it mean for human ratio to think the thought of Trinity? Or perhaps it is better expressed, for this tradition and these theologians: Is it possible to think the thought of Trinity? Is analyticity, for Barth, a means of thinking the very idea of Trinity?

Perhaps we should consider Barth here to make use of a solid scholastic notion—that of exemplarism. In several places within the *Church Dogmatics*, Barth seems to reach for such an intellectual tradition. The general notion of person, say, rests on God who is the Proper, True Person, the Exemplary Person. Barth will dare to say this about language itself: God is the True Word, or Christ Himself is the True Human; he moves in the same formal territory when he makes the concrete instance—Israel or Saul or Judas—the source of the universal or general, election, bourgeois rebellion, elected rejection. Revelation could be the exemplar, the source and pattern and norm of all analyticity. In exemplarism, we think the thought of God *indirectly*: God is Goodness Itself, and the Good of every created good; the Life of all who live; the Truth in all our little truths—the Goodness of God, but not in the same way, not in the same measure, not in the same definition! God remains Veiled in His Unveiling! But in the event of revelation—Barth, we might say, "actualizes" exemplarism—God discloses what true analyticity is, the Revelation, Revealed from the Revealer; all other analytic judgments are parasitic on this Threefold One. We must know *who* God is—that is Barth's fundamental conviction—but the answer to that question is surprisingly *formal*: God is the One who Reveals Himself, who Speaks. Because He is True Speaker, the Lord, He exceeds and is ground of all speech; He is Sovereign over all creaturely thought. But He is known in this relation, this analytic judgment!

Now I think this is not quite Dionysian; we are not joined to God as to One Unknown. Indeed, I believe that the philosophical rationality in Barth's doctrine of Trinity offers far greater insight into the Reality of God than Thomas would dare—even in the long speculative quaestiones of the *Prima Pars*. But the Deus absconditus remains in this Analyticity, Barth claims; He remains Hidden, Veiled. But in all this Remoteness, God remains True, Exemplary Lord: it is true to affirm of Him, in an analytic judgment, that God is Lord. Famously, Thomas is willing to say that we know "that God is" (*an sit Deus*) not "what God is" (*quid sit Deus*) by reason, unaided by grace and Divine Revelation. The "essence of God"—this might stand surety for Barth's who God is—cannot be known in this life, Thomas teaches, unless supernatural gifts were given, as were bestowed on Moses and Paul, the great friends of God. But Barth ventures further. We know who God is; we know His Being from that Identity, the Triune Lord; we know the structure of His Act-in-Being, the Analytic Synonymy; we know He is Revealer and Being Revealed, contained in Revelation Itself. We can think these thoughts, follow their structure, recognize their intellectual cogency; stand in their Rational Light. Indeed, to think "analyticity" or "revelation" in the abstract or highly formal state of philosophical concept, just is "to be joined to God as to One Hidden yet Known." That, I believe, is the rational dignity of the doctrine of revelation Barth proposes as Christian speech. It is its own world; it speaks out of its own sources; but it is King, King over the whole earth.

So, Barth and Thomas join hands in this sense. Each holds that Trinity is known only in and by faith. Each considers Trinitarian dogma to be taught—revealed—by Scripture. Both make use of philosophy to explore and order what has been revealed about

Almighty God. But Barth makes revelation an event, an explosion of the God who is Lord. This igniting of Majesty is the Exemplum of all authority, of all Lordship, of all analyticity. For Barth, to think Trinity is to think through to the end the inescapable truth that I have a Lord. This entwining of Economy and Immanence divides Thomas from Barth, for all their similarities, and makes the doctrine of revelation a dangerous ally in a full and proper doctrine of God.

So, we close our discussion of this first alternative, the regional alternative, as an investigation of the intellectual integrity and legitimacy of Trinity as a form of Christian speech. It is a proud tradition, and it shows the range, the sophistication, and the cogency of such self-grounding intellectual work. Schleiermacher, Thomas, and Barth, widely differing theologians, can speak in this idiom; they can draw from its deep springs. The dogma of Trinity seems especially apt as an instance of this bold, inner speech, for it, above all else, appears to rise up out of the fire of Christian life, a doctrine and mystery that appears in no pagan treatise, a conception of God that belongs to none but the Christian. It would be especially tempting to treat this dogma in particular as a "preference," a refined and delicate taste in theology, for here Christians seem to fly their own colors, plant their own stake in the good earth. But our theologians do not yield to temptation; they stoutly defend the coherence, probity, and analytic power of this dogma. They dare to extend a certain rationality to the whole. We have taken the measure of this ratio, and its surprising claim to universal suasion and license. It seems that these theologians believe that in a certain, broad sense, the dogma of Trinity *can* be argued for, can be explained, can be enrolled in the academy, at least as those that borrow its books, study its manners and ways. The intellectual rigor of this alternative, in the end, seems to spring from the conceptual seriousness of the theologian and of the tradition she or he represents: How well does he or she think through the problems raised by their own tradition, their own texts and rulings? In this way we might think of this alternative, the regional alternative, as sharing the disciplinarity of the modern academy. In one sense—a sense Schleiermacher himself might favor—an academic discipline just is a regional study, built up out of its own materials, forged through its own distinctive and self-critical methods. Theology, even in this alternative, could be called "scientific"—a "science of the blessed and of the Church," in Thomas's idiom. Barth favored the idea that theology was truest to its own dignity and its own scientific character when it studied its own Object with the tools fashioned for this very task. Regionalism might simply be the name for any modern discipline in any modern university; the canons of rationality might well belong to segments along a line, distinct even when joined in one direction, one plane. Perhaps "proper basicality," as Alvin Plantinga fashions it, belongs to intellectual work, per se, each discipline grounded in its own axioms, its own first principles.

Now, I have argued against this conclusion, most especially for the dogma and Mystery of Trinity. I have said that this dogma in particular and as best must receive an intellectual legitimacy that exceeds the regional and the disciplinary—exceeds, does not compete or dismiss but decidedly moves beyond the interior speech of the church. I want to be careful in this move of excess, however; there are pitfalls scattered all along this path, and we cannot rush in.

So, we have lingered over this first alternative, the legitimacy that springs from Christian elements alone. And it is right that we have done so, for it is the path well traveled and well honored in Christian doctrine. Giants have walked here. Nothing else in what we develop will quite compare. But there are smaller paths to be followed here all the same, quieter voices, a smaller entourage, but honored in their day and faithful. We have enjoyed the sun of these broad paths—so well illuminated! so well marked!—but there are theological tasks that must draw us into a deeper shade, a narrower way. Now, another alternative we might consider among the minority traditions is what is customarily called apologetics; perhaps in our spatial idiom we might consider it a common alternative. In such broad, common, and general rationality, we would seek intellectual legitimacy from a wide-ranging appeal to common norms, common structures of belief, common arguments, common places. This alternative is largely conventional, though hardly trite or blind. Rather it seeks a ground we all stand on, an assumption we all share, a burden we all shoulder. It looks for the larger room where we stand together; we recognize this place, its customs and rules; we argue with the same terms; we dispute over the same prizes. This theological alternative is common in all these senses.

§2.2. The Common Alternative: Paul Tillich

It is fitting to explore this common alternative through the work of Paul Tillich, as he is the great apologist of the modern era. The material and the dogmaticians we have examined in the regional alternative shaped Tillich directly and deeply, and he shared with them many of the doctrines and ideals of a complete, Christian world. For a time, Tillich was thought, too, to be a giant on the earth. His name was inevitably linked with Barth's as an early ally and later critic; in those years, he dominated North American Protestant faculties of divinity; his *Systematics* was required reading for any serious student of theology, Protestant and Catholic alike. But it is instructive for us to consider the sea change that has washed over those shores. Unlike Barth, Thomas, and Schleiermacher, Tillich has lost standing in the theological realm; his is not a name that commands wide attention in scholarship—nothing to rival

Thomas or Barth—nor does it dominate graduate departments; unlike a generation ago, seminaries no longer feel under obligation to appoint a Tillichian or to further his theological program through dissertations or large-scale conferences. He has lost cultural legitimacy.

In this section, we have aimed to set forth varying accounts of intellectual and cultural legitimacy, the plausibility structures that drive some ideas, some figures and movements, to the head of academic study and to the attention of a larger public while others quietly fall away. Tillich himself is a study in this odd, potent, and often tragic development in the human arts. For Tillich and his work have become a "specialty," a focused and self-chosen research area, and we might liken Tillich's stature now to that of Alfred North Whitehead's—an academic well worth study, an important historical figure, but a serious philosophy department need not hire a Whiteheadian in order to have a complete and respectable doctoral faculty. Tillich for a season and a day made his branch of apologetics—in his technical idiom, the "method of correlation"—a vital, dynamic, and expansive school of theology. He lent his name to an entire Protestant revival of philosophical theology and to dogmaticians immersed in the study of human culture, fine arts, and psychodynamic accounts of the person. Tillich, in a nearly singlehanded fashion, made human experience a salient category once again in Christian theology after a generation of relentless, sometimes savage, criticism of Schleiermacher and his school. Tillich brought to the American shores a European breadth, an air of the great Germanophone tradition in the arts, and a liberalism that caught the spirit of the postwar age: expansive, creative, and wonderfully dynamic. Much that falls under the heading of constructive theology and many of the early feminist schools sprang up under his broad canopy. It is easy, when an era has passed, to think a once-dominant figure in truth had little authentic power and now is shown to have few features worth close study. But such easy devaluation is rarely right, and in the church, where all are alive to God, it is never right. Tillich is a cardinal instance.

Here we have someone who put the neo-Kantian training of the Marburg school into service of dogmatic theology; his *Systematics* is the fruit and outworking of Protestant academic theology under the impress and shock of two world wars. *This* is what the German idealist and historicist tradition looks like, most especially the speculative idealism of Schelling, how it functions and orders the dogmatic whole, when the idiom of existentialism enters the lists. We should not assume too quickly, that is, that *apologetics* is the source of Tillich's ready ascent and sharp descent among academic theologians, nor has the category experience lost its lure for the theological imagination. It is hard to say, in truth, what has caused Tillich's sharp decline in cultural legitimacy. Of course, there *is* fashion in dogmatics, and, like Tillich, Schleiermacher and Barth may lose cachet suddenly, like an old-style suit of clothes. Nothing seems quite as alien and stale as a style that has faded away. And then there are the undefinable and arbitrary facts of ecclesial and university culture; what could be more contingent and happenstance in intellectual life than the rise and fall of intellectual elites? Tillich himself considered symbols an art form that must spring up from the earth, we know not how; they cannot be created but must rather be discovered, given to us; perhaps symbols are the contingent, often arbitrary *Denkformen* of Tillich's own dogmatics. Perhaps. But I think what we see here—between Barth and Tillich and, more instructively, between Schleiermacher and Tillich—is something more complex, more demanding than any of these more ready and rather cheap explanations. I will hazard an account here—and acknowledge that it may be found even cheaper than all the rest!

Tillich, we might say, has lost his hold on broad, academic theology not for his weaknesses, whether personal or dogmatic, I say, but rather for his strengths. In his apologetic theology, Tillich pressed to the fore the central question of *ontology*, the sweeping study of metaphysics, as *the* compelling question in divine and human reality. He did this under the structure and vocabulary of European existentialism—a world that has been swept away by the conventionality and attenuation of a global consumer society. But such older vocabulary would not, in itself, debar scholarly interest and legitimacy; indeed, for scholars of Barth and Thomas, such historical and linguistic analyses serve often as entrées into the academic field. Rather, we should wonder whether Tillich's bold insistence that a hunger for Being Itself—the "ultimate concern" or "Ultimate"—is not too self-involving, too direct and honest and earnest, too metaphysically demanding to be tolerated in our deflationary age. (The subtle interplay between "ultimate concern" and "concern for the Ultimate," or as we might style this now, subjectivity and objectivity, is one of the key thematics in Tillich's work, and a source of anxiety always for Barth and all Barthians.) Ours is a commodified world, materially and intellectually: flattened out, hollowed out, enamored of skepticism and cynicism, as if they were weapons against the exceeding dark, and all too ready to plume itself on its small scale and antispeculative endeavors, as if "questions of meaning" were the hobby of a rather embarrassing old classmate. If this sad diagnosis is correct, we can never under its rule revive the cultural legitimacy of Tillich's apologetics; they could never be taken seriously by a culture where the notion of "ontological depth" cannot itself be given serious airing. Perhaps this is so; another age than ours will hand down the verdict. But on the strength of this intuition we might venture to explore a topic altogether transgressive of the present age: How does Tillich's quest for ultimate meaning offer an alternative to regional Christian legitimacy in dogmatics? How would the doctrine of Trinity be given cultural cogency were metaphysics of the existential sort to arise and take hold of our dogmatic endeavors?

We might begin by asking first what it might mean for us to view human life as a "question" or a "quest." Like Karl Rahner, Tillich dares to think of human beings as life-forms that are *by nature* unfinished, incompletable. Rowan Williams's recent Gifford lectures might be taken as a contemporary example of this thesis, rendered in linguistic idiom.[19] A human life, lived "authentically," is a struggle, a search for purpose, for direction, for self-knowledge and self-mastery; its limits urge one on, to explore, to understand, to experience; its failures prompt renewed struggle with the aim, the goal of human living, the place of the human race under the sun. A human life is the one reality we are never through with, though to live it aright, we face always the end of life in death. Yet we are never exhausted by the task of a human life because it is "the question we are," the open-ended search that constitutes us as human. We can catch the echoes of Martin Heidegger here, the common legacy of prewar phenomenology Tillich shared with Rahner. But Tillich has made this theme his own by giving this ontology a moral and individual urgency.

For Tillich this categorical, unending task is properly named the "ultimate concern," the *Sorge*, the worry and burden and care that consumes one's life, just because it *is* that life, the unanswered quest. It is ultimate because it cannot be put down, stilled, replaced; it seizes a life, and all intermediate ends must serve it. An ultimate concern can be recognized by the life that is sacrificed to it: human nature that is possessed by something ultimate can be laid down before the ultimate just because it is made a salient life, a meaningful life, when it is given away. These are "existential questions" because they are "lived, forced and momentous," to borrow from William James for a moment; they give shape to an entire existence. We are defenseless before our ultimate concerns; we consume them as they consume us daily. In just this way these matters of ultimacy both constitute and transcend morality: they are the good we will do anything to possess. They are a matter of life and death; they shimmer with the dark "threat of non-being." As we become this overriding question, we enter the realm defined by the "ontological elements," Tillich's existential metaphysics. Existential questions pose and are structured by the unfinished polarities of lived experience: of individualization and participation, of freedom and destiny, dynamics and form. We seek the courage to risk everything, as we must choose among these dialectical pairs, live them out; we seek creatively to discover the life that is charged by these elements, to receive it, to incorporate it into our life's task. For everything is hazarded here.

The "power of being" is in such a question—the immersion in the real that fills one's life with meaning—but also the danger of the "demonic," the fiery destruction that splits apart the very forms of experience, fragments, empties and divides. The demonic stalks the ultimate. In every task that demands a whole life, the idolatry of a false ultimacy stands in its shadow. Destruction and the love of death mimic the eros that leads to life and the good. The transcendent that leads to ecstatic meaning beyond earthly bounds can turn over to irrationality and formless power. Ultimacy is the religious, as New Being, as Courage, but also as the demonic, the intolerant and the cruel. It is the climax to a life that seeks the treasure hidden in the field, the one who sells everything, who loses one's life in order to possess it.

Now this is a sketch of a common account of human life as a self-involving, self-expending, dynamic, and unfinished quest. It is a sketch, Tillich proposes to us, of a life lived with eyes wide open to the ambiguities and hazards serious human life presents. It is not childish or sentimental; it is exposed to the criticisms of the age; it recognizes that folly and futility will be admixed in the task. But it is assumed; it is taken on as one's own. Now I think a culture that could imagine the human as significant could find its way into Tillich's description.

We do not now, I think, live in such an age, but we can remember it, a nearby, though distant, cousin. Of course, we in the West often speak of our time as the Anthropocene, and we entertain and condemn the human race as the dominant specimen on the earth. And in a developed nation such as the United States, human beings indeed inhabit their niche as the voracious that can never be satisfied, a demonic echo, we might say, of an ultimate concern. But we remain, in these early decades of our century, immune to the *human* as a distinct task, reality, and way of being. We are workers; we are specialized mammals; we are bodies; we are the possessors of things; we are collections of information; we are brain states (worse, "wet ware"); we are death, destroyers of worlds. These are not *human* much less humane forms of *ontos* but rather definitions of successful biological beings, perhaps too few in number, perhaps too many, a mighty army, underfed, misused. To house, to feed, to preserve from predators and enemies, to reproduce and raise the young, to train and put to work: these are our tasks, too, but hardly a realm set apart. Human beings in our world are expensive—everything must be used up to serve us—but cheap, too; some can even be thrown away. Of course, to develop fully a rich doctrine of the human—the Image and Likeness of Almighty God—requires a dogmatic exposition all its own. But even here we can say that Tillich urges on us the brave notion that human beings are not these kinds and types and members but rather unique forms of being: we are the ones who seek. To awaken to this brave notion would be to consider apologetics of an existential sort possible once again. Once again, we would see a common ground opening up before us, and we would embrace the task of occupying and defining it, holding it against others but with them, for them, too. We would seek the eternal weight of glory that is the human question, lived out and lived to the end.

Now in such a rediscovered world, religion would receive fresh legitimacy. In Tillich's hands, the doctrine of God is an expression of the "search for depth," the Ground of Being. We might say, in this vein, that Tillich considers the human quest an open encounter with the hope or fear that reality itself, all being and each, has a *Ground*, that the cosmos itself and all things and forces within it do not exhaust Reality but rather open out onto It. This is *depth*: physical being is not self-evident, not self-generated. To think such thoughts, to dread or embrace them, is to encounter God. Let us, then, turn our full attention to Tillich's revised form of apologetics, an approach to theology I deem the common alternative.

This is how apologetics finds a fresh start in Tillich's existential ontology. Tillich, remember, considers his form of apologetics a "method of correlation." In such a method, the question and the answer do not fit together in either a deductive or algorithmic or mirror-like manner. We do not "discover" the answer in the question—it is not an analytic judgment! Nor, Tillich says, do we use the question to guide or limit the answer. We are not "talking to ourselves." Rather, the answer, Tillich tells us, must be "spoken to us," a fresh reply that answers truly, but "synthetically," a novel and revolutionary summons over the past. Tillich puts it this way:

> The following system is an attempt to use the method of correlation as a way of uniting message and situation. It tries to correlate the questions implied in the situation with the answers implied in the message. It does not derive the answers from the questions as a self-

defying apologetic theology does. Nor does it elaborate answers without relating them to the questions as a self-defying kergymatic theology does. It correlates questions and answers, situation and message, human existence and divine manifestation. Obviously such a method is not a tool to be handled at will. It is neither a trick nor a mechanical device. It is itself a theological assertion, and like all theological assertions, it is made with passion and risk; and ultimately it is not different from the system which is built upon it. System and method belong to each other and are to be judged with each another.[20]

Notice now that Tillich has expressed in fresh idiom the Kantian thought-world that Barth inhabited throughout his early career. Like Barth, Tillich explores the form of judgment, the task of predication, and its relation to the subject of a statement. And like Barth again, Tillich foregrounds the notion of revelation or divine speech: these are grammatical subjects and predicates cast in the form of discourse—questions and answers. Tillich shares with Barth the struggle to define the proper *relation* of subject to predicate or, in Tillich's idiom, whether the answer is "derived from the question" or should be. The idea of "correlation" offers a bow to Tillich's neo-Kantian teachers, Hermann Cohen prince among them. But in closer alliance to the early Barth, Tillich understands correlation to break the pattern Schleiermacher laid down over dogmatics as a whole. As Tillich hints in compressed fashion above, proper apologetics will not endorse the ready assimilation of the doctrinal answer, the "message" or kerygma, to the question, the existential situation or experience. Echoing the early dialectical theology. Tillich affirms that we must "be told" the answer: it must be *revealed*. We might say, then, that Tillich's method here is dialectical. (Barth and Tillich moved in each other's shadows in those early years!)[21] We move between question and reply, but the reply, the predicate, is synthetic to the subject, the seeker; the human and divine subjects are not given together to experience but, rather, are related as the "ungiven," the Divine Subject interrupting, commanding, *addressing* the human, never given over to the creature, never inert but always Dynamic, Alive.

Compare the method of correlation, then, with Schleiermacher's account of pious experience. It is from Schleiermacher, and from their common ancestry in Kant and Schelling, that grammar or discourse came to command the field. Schleiermacher, we remember, discovers in human awareness an inwardness that must be given utterance: piety rendered in speech. So Christian theology will be a particular form of discourse, an upper-level, ordered grammar that sends roots down into the contemplative, wordless center where God is the Other, present to and in all reception and feeling. Such an architecture allows Schleiermacher to present dogmatics as "forms of Christian speech." Pious awareness is the "primary" or "basic form," but it does not exhaust theological form! Rather, the *Glaubenslehre* demonstrates that religious experience can be inverted, or reweighted; it is a complex whole, its parts entwined and implicated, one in the other. Just this is the *force* of Schleiermacher's oft-cited dictum, that God is the "Whence of pious experience." In the idiom of *The Christian Faith*, we could say that the parts of a Christian dogmatics are arbitrary in order; convenience and convention govern the sequence. So, Schleiermacher's dogmatics presents the first form always, the piety, structured by dialectical pairs, followed by the Christian doctrines devoted to the Being of God and the nature of the world. This is the threefold structure of human experience: the self into which is given God and the world, the Others of devout awareness. We can say, then, that the doctrines of God, the church, and the world are *included* in the reality of human piety. We speak first of our faith; then of the Divine Implicature—the Whence—of that faith; then the world which must be creature of that Divine Cause. We analyze experience; its constituents yield God and nature. Of course, Schleiermacher is not confused about the *causal* sequence or power of these three poles; he, too, knows that he "has a Lord." But the speech that just is theology simply lays out before our eyes the rounded wholeness that is the blessing and mindfulness of religion: in our devotion everything is truly already there.

Now Tillich drinks deeply here. He knows this threefold ordering of piety; he, too, considers reality structured by self, God and world. He, too, knows a pious experience that can precede and order doctrine; he recognizes an "abyssmal" dependence that can rise up in speech that will never exhaust its depth or power. But for Tillich the primary form cannot "contain" the other two structures; God cannot be *implicated* or already given in existence. Were we to misunderstand this point, Tillich tells us, we would relapse into old-style apologetics, some schools of which were "disgusting" or intellectually contemptible. (Tillich reserves some of his harshest words for the "Teaching of Ignorance," the *argumentum ex ignorantia* pattern of theology we have learned these days to call the "God of the gaps.") Bourgeois Liberalism domesticates God, Tillich says; it learns nothing new from listening to its own sleek contentment, uttered in soothing, elevated speech. But apologetics properly ordered considers nothing *implicated*, nothing contained in the existential situation. We learn nothing of what we long to hear by examining within. Just that is the point of insisting that human being is the unfinished *ontos*, the incomplete being: *the* question. There is no first form that turns over into the second or third form of Christian speech. There is only the poverty of human struggle and need, and the Answer that comes from Beyond. All this, it seems, could be said by the brash young author of *Word of God and Word of Man*.

But Tillich is not Barth. He shares with Barth—or believes he does—the conviction that the Word Preached, the Kerygma, is the Divine Predicate that can never be contained or given in the human subject. But Tillich echoes a long line of critics of Barth when he says—wrongly, I believe—that kerygmatic theologians such as Barth consider the Word of God to be "hurtled from Beyond" like an alien stone, unknown, unrecognized, unintelligible to the human hearer. The "method of correlation" claims that real work, real dogmatic and structural work, must be done by the human subject, by the Hearer of the Word, as Rahner would cast this point. Here Tillich lays claim to a distinction that echoes across the methodological struggles of Barth's first volume of the *Church Dogmatics*: form and content. "Form and content can be distinguished but not separated," Tillich writes. "Form and content do not function as the basis of a deductive system; but they are the methodological guardians at the boundary line of theology."[22] Tillich then applies the distinction:

The Christian message provides the answers to the questions implied in human existence. These answers are revelatory events on which Christianity is based and are taken by systematic theology from the sources, through the medium, under the norm. Their content cannot be derived from the questions, that is, from an analysis of human existence. They are "spoken" to human existence from beyond it. Otherwise they would not be answers, for the question is human existence itself. But the relation is more involved than this, since it is correlation. There is a mutual dependence between question and answer. [Just what, we may wonder, is the relationship between "non-derivation" and "mutual dependence?"] In respect to content the Christian answers are dependent on the revelatory events in which they appear; in respect to form they are dependent on the structure of the questions which they answer. God is the answer to the question implied in human finitude. This answer cannot be derived from the analysis of existence. However, if the notion of God appears in systematic theology in correlation with the threat of nonbeing which is implied in existence, God must be called the infinite power of being which resists the threat of nonbeing. In classical theology this is being-itself. If anxiety is defined as the awareness of being finite, God must be called the infinite ground of courage. In classical theology this is universal providence. If the notion of the Kingdom of God appears in correlation with the riddle of our historical existence, it must be called the meaning, fulfilment, and unity of history. In this way an interpretation of the traditional symbols of Christianity is achieved which preserves the power and which opens them to the questions elaborated by our present analysis of human existence.[23]

Tillich here demonstrates the power of correlation, and its danger. Both the power and the danger must be vivid to us when we turn to our own plea for cultural legitimacy, the problem in the neighborhood. He drives a sharp wedge between form and content, and he assigns to form the existential dimensions or norms he developed earlier: that religious material expresses as ultimate concern, that it touches on life and death. To this extent, and in this realm, the question shapes the answer, for answer and question belong together; they are caught in a relation of "mutual dependence." Now we might wonder how this would work—and Tillich supplies us with examples. The "symbols" of the kerygma will follow, respond to, and fit closely the existential struggles of an age: anxiety, meaninglessness, death. Theology must speak our language; we must hear the Gospel in our own mother tongue. It must address our deepest longings, in the idiom and frame of those desires. Like Rahner, Tillich holds that the lock must fit the key; the key must be sized to enter—and turn!—the lock.

Tillich has brought us into the intellectual realm of subject and object, the Divine Object sized to enter and turn the human subject, imprisoned in estrangement. This is theological relationalism, the indwelling and mutual conditioning of subject and object, the knower and the known; it is the world Schleiermacher built, the world Protestant liberalism enjoyed, inhabited, and refined.

The cultural plausibility and cogency of the Christian message rests in the descriptive power of the form, its ability to capture the anxiety and suffering of an age. When done well, Tillich says, the Christian kerygma will indeed be, and be seen to be, an answer. Perhaps it will not answer all questions, perhaps it will not persuade all questioners, but it will be greeted as an answer, a plausible, respectable, recognizable solution, one solution to the riddle that is human existence. The form of the existential question will change; indeed, Tillich built an impressive historical repertory on the changing face of past cultures, the changing shape of past religious answers. But the claim here is that the *religious content* does not change, is not exhausted in its form, and will outlive and outstrip any transitory expression of its Reality. *Rex mortuus est; vivat Rex.*

Now we may well wonder whether such a tidy scenario can perform in the fashion acclaimed for it, whether the distinctions so prominently displayed can ward off the bad and conserve the good in quite the confident manner promised. Do we in truth find a content that underlies form and survives—even thrives!—when form is stripped away? Can this be so in Divine Things? Barth considered it transparently false: Protestant modernism showed to his satisfaction the collapse of content into form, the hollowing out of an Answer unexpected and sovereign over the human questioner. Here Barth brought forward the little word *control*: the philosophical conceptuality, he charged, controlled the Word spoken and heard. Objectivity in theology, he said, could never be found by examining more closely the subject and the structures of the knower. These were closed circles, self-reinforced and self-validating, however much the "novelty" of the answer is trumpeted or the "theological circle" proclaimed open and obedient to the Word. Everything becomes old in such a circular universe, answer and questioner, form and content go down into oblivion together.

That is Barth's verdict, and there is much to commend it. There is an air of relativism that sweeps over Tillich's work, despite the urgent reminders that Divine Content remains the same. But what would count as "sameness" in such kerygma? And, of course, it is a profound methodological worry of all mediating theology that the religious object, given to experience, is in truth and in disguise to the knower, just an echo of our own desires and ideals. Under what criteria do we separate the wheat from the chaff here? Tillich gives us norms and criteria and formal elements—a formidable armature—but it seems alarmingly easy to imagine, all the same, that we are soothing ourselves from our own most vivid nightmares.[24]

But all this is so much methodological warfare from another age, is it not? So much noise from a now distant generation! Can theological method, even in a white-hot dispute, be revived and fought out once again—in life and death—as a matter ultimate for us and our culture? Frankly, what is staler than such debates? Should we not turn, rather, to doctrine, the prize in every fight? For it is in Christian teaching itself that we come to know another theological vision, another path to intellectual seriousness. So, we might once again and more closely examine Tillich's answering theology to test his alternative to a plausible and intelligible Christian doctrine: How might the dogma of Trinity express the question that is our own life? Here form and content do their work; here question and answer speak a Final Word. In this dogma, Tillich is at his full strength; he becomes a living cultural theologian here.

Tillich begins boldly. Trinity, he says in *Systematic Theology*, volume 1, can be divided in two parts: a full doctrinal exposition, laid out in volume 3, and a "conceptual" and "preparatory" doctrine, briefly sketched in the opening chapters. Trinity, that is, can be viewed in its *principles*, its "presuppositions," and these will be primarily spiritual. The Trinity, as Concept, is *Spirit*. Hegel is the clear authority of these early sections, the clear legitimator of the ultimate theological task. To think Trinity, Tillich says here, is to think Spirit; it is to examine the Ground of Being in its very Structure and Life. Spirit is Actual Life, the Realization and Confirmation of everything possible or notional. It is the Whole, the Complete. Tillich puts it this way:

> As the actualization of the other two principles, the Spirit is the third principle. Both power and meaning are contained in it and united in it. It makes them creative. The third principle is in a way the whole (God is Spirit), and in a way it is a special principle (God has the Spirit as he has the logos). It is the Spirit in whom God "goes out from" himself, the Spirit proceeds from the divine ground. He gives actuality to that which is potential in the divine ground and "outspoken" in the divine logos. Through the Spirit the divine fulness is posited in the divine life as something definite, and at the same time it is reunited in the divine ground.[25]

Here we see Tillich speaking in the broad and allusive fashion that the notion of "symbol" underwrites. He can countenance a God who is not "actualized," not "creative," not "whole," but made so in the Spirit. The Triune God, in principle, can be Reality that develops, as Hegel also dared to propose. It can move through contradiction, through "polarity," to be fully itself, to become Absolute. Spirit in this sense just *is* God, the Telos, the Consummate God, standing as Holy Unity at journey's end.

But Tillich does not think only in Hegelian terms here. He casts his thought back to the architecture of being in its most general and abstract form. Like Thomas in the *Prima Pars*, Tillich can speak of reality in fully universal concepts. Not the Aristotelian abstractions of possibility and necessity, potency and act, change and motion and effect, but abstractions all the same. In Tillich's idiom, these are ontological elements, and they *structure* being. But they do so in the *Denkform* of the modern: as movement and as pairs, dialectical pairs in motion. Being is event. It is the "moment"—Tillich is free with his Hegelianisms here—of dynamic and form, of individuation and participation, of freedom and destiny. Now note that in principle God as Triune will express and exhibit and be defined by these dialectical pairs. Indeed, Tillich holds that the symbolic realm, the content, just *is* dialectics, the living movement from origin to consummation. Our human being follows these patterns, too: we also participate in being, under our own conditions. But we do so as those "estranged" from true Being; the dialectics for us are opposed, contrary, alienated. But in God these Principles are Alive. God is the Living God; He is Spirit. The dialectical pairs will be found in God, then, as Procession and Person. They will express both Power and Meaning. The Power of God is the "Divine Abyss," the Lordship and Majesty of God, the Father. The Ground of Being must be Infinite Depth, awesome, numinous. But this Dark Ground must yield to Light, to Logos, to Meaning. It must issue forth from the Absolute Origin, it must clothe the Naked God, it must give Rationality to Ultimate Reality. What is Formless will be given Form; what is Singular, Relationality; what is Utterly Free and Boundless, the Bad Infinite, Concreteness, and Destiny. All this is a Dynamic Unity in the Spirit, who makes the Principle of Being, Real and Living.

Now this is Trinity as a conceptual system. It is not "nonsense about the number 3 and 1," as Tillich dares later to write. "The statement that three is one and one is three was (and in many places still is) the worst distortion of the mystery of Trinity. If this is meant as a numerical identity, it is a trick or simply nonsense," Tillich writes with a flair in volume 3.[26] Trinity, rather, is the structure of reality, Being in its most general state, and it emerges, Tillich suggests, from a deep encounter with Being and the threats to it. Trinity as Ground, Form, and Act—another summary of these ontological structures—must contain within itself the finite, the concrete, the risk of non-Being, so that it can be Absolute, a Living Infinity, Divine Life that overcomes separation and death. Such analysis will prepare the seeker for the Christian symbol of Trinity, the Mystery of the One God, Father, Son, and Holy Spirit. Such a content-rich symbol will emerge only out of Christology, not Pneumatology, and it will incorporate the sacrifice, suffering, and death that new Being must undergo in order to point truly and inescapably to the Transcendent God. Tillich will develop this Christological dogma throughout volume 3, and we will return to Tillich's Triune Christology when we turn to the Mystery of the Incarnation. But here we ask about Tillich's final claim: that without these principles of being, the presuppositions of Trinity as Ground, we would teach a doctrine of Trinity that was reduced to a hopeless and irrational myth, a tritheism, an obscurantist riddle. Legitimacy lies in the principles of being.

Is he right? We ask now, and in a final way, about the method of correlation and its role in the origin, coherence, and probity of the doctrine of Trinity. Can the existential form accompany the doctrine of Trinity in such a way that the Triune God Himself is known, worshipped, and obeyed? I think we must answer, in a mild tone, not quite. Tillich's apologetic theology gives us Trinity, in principle and in dogmatic history; it speaks directly of God; it does not pretend we know Him already or that we "contain all worlds." But the architectonic that orders Tillich's thought takes the Lutheran *pro me* into a fully systematic realm where it does work that Luther never imagined in all his deeply personal, highly colored dogmatic confessions. The novelty and danger of Tillich's thought-world, as I see it, is the strong sense of *correlation* that governs the whole. Here the lesson for a proper "problem in the neighborhood" must be truly laid to heart. It is not simply that question and answer are "mutually dependent," or that in some fashion the answer conforms to and meets the question, or even that the form of theological speech must borrow the reigning idiom of the day. A vigorous dogmatics can absorb such blows, I say—the powerful Lutheran theologies of the twentieth century, European and North American, are proof sufficient.

What makes a present-day systematician answer with a modest "not quite" is Tillich's seeming insistence that the existential form must "accompany" each dogmatic content and reply, the "I think" that structures each theological experience. *This*, it seems to me, shows the problem of "control" that agitated Barth in his early work and not some broader anxiety about the dialectical shape of query and reply—or should not have been. Human experience in this broad sense should never have been identified as villain of the piece; it is inescapable as generations of Barth's critics have noted, time and again. But I do not think Barth in truth made such a sweeping embargo of human experience his platform; he of all people knew that one cannot leap over one's own shadow. Like Tillich, in fact, Barth wrote expansively and polemically, and his celebrated war against natural theology brought Barth from time to time dangerously close to such sweeping generalizations. But properly, when tempers cool, Barth said (or should have said) that the worry about the existential form is its *persistence*, its claim to correlate with each and all theological statements. This, I think, is what "control by philosophical conceptuality" amounts to.

As I see it, Tillich turns the method of correlation into a *grounding* mechanism, where each doctrinal utterance is directly and individually tied back to a human question or experience. This has the effect of making all doctrine a religious expression. As all Israel is not religion, not temple, so all Christian doctrine is not existential, soteriological. Famously, Schleiermacher performs just this surgery on proper dogmatic statements: they must each and every one be rooted, grounded, directly in pious awareness. Now such individual grounding in experience severely limits the expanse, the range, and the task of Christian theology. It does not destroy or riddle it—nothing that fatal! But a steady correlation of Tillich's sort limits doctrinal development, and ties it back, again and again, each after each, to a human struggle that must have answers from Beyond. For dogmatics this means that Christian doctrine can only carry a human face: it exists only where human being has uncovered ultimacy and must hear a Word to still that cry. For Tillich, theological discussion cannot exceed ultimacy. We do not develop a dogma in areas, historical, exegetical, or conceptual, that have no existential bearing; Christian teaching cannot soar free of its firm anchor in human need. We see that restriction in Tillich's treatment of Divine Triunity.

A bold structuring in Being Itself, good! A movement among dialectical pairs that unfolds a Living God, good! A treatment of Trinity first as Spiritual Reality, then as Christological confession, also good! But note that these dogmatic treatments are spare, severely so for a full systematics: some five scant pages in the first volume (admittedly only on "principles") and a bare fourteen pages in volume 3, the Christological exposition of the dogma. To be sure, Schleiermacher performed miracles in a small room—his Trinitarian discussion is yet more compact than Tillich's—so we should not place too much stock in page count. But it points to a deeper worry, I believe. It seems that Tillich has exhausted what can be said about Trinity—from his special point of view!—in these brief treatments. Certainly, there is no speculative unfurling such as we find in Thomas's *Prima Pars*; no extensive exegetical discussion as we see in the first volume of the *Church Dogmatics*; no long account of historical debates about Trinity, early and late; no rich exposition of the dogma's technical and conceptual legacies: we cannot seem to enter these larger rooms. No Christian theologian, I believe, would want to deny the place, perhaps the place of honor, of human longing and hope in Christian teaching. God is not a Reality to be known in a state of indifference or encountered only in thought. No! God is Holy, and He enters into our lives, our mind and our world, as Commanding Mystery, as Holy Beauty, as Remote Nearness before whom we bow and confess. The existential dimension of the Christian life and Christian thought should never come under doubt; of course, God is Ultimate and Ultimate Concern! But we can see the price exacted by the conviction that such existentialism should inform each Christian dogma: for there is no direct correspondence, in truth, point to point, between the Infinite, Holy God and human need. We do not have an ultimate concern about Relations of Origin or Mutual Relations; about distinctions between the Processions; about the history of dogmatic development of the Homoousion; about the relation between Divine Notions and the Divine Nature; about magisterial teaching on Triunity; about traditional exegesis in support of the dogma. They "do no real work," William James complained, and Rahner and Tillich alike, though for different reasons, might consider such unpragmatic truths "dry as dust." But these teachings are just what we mean by *objectivity* or, better, *realism* in theology!

Christian doctrine must break free of its touchstone in human experience, human concern, human preoccupation; it must serve Another Lord. In truth, we would better say, under grace we are *freed* to serve this Lord, to enter His Holy Realm, to think the thought of God, the Pure, Sovereign, and Utterly Free Reality of God. Just this, we might say, is the "supernatural elevation" that Thomas teaches us about, to think about a Truth beyond and apart from our everyday need, a Reality who is not us. To dwell *there*, to linger at that altar and throne room, to explore that Heavenly City, to glimpse a Reality that transcends the creature, who just is, yes, Wholly Other—that is the Divine Gift, the beauty and majesty of Christian theology. To say this is to affirm that systematics may begin with a human question; perhaps in some settings, it must. But it must also leave that behind; think a history, a text, an Event that is Sovereign, Set Apart, Capacious, Infinitely so, Absorbing, Luminous. It sets Its own Boundaries, enlarges Its own Kingdom, determines Its own Structure and Elements. It invites us *there*. Like a mathematical realm that takes its origin in a familiar discipline (Euclidean geometry, say) and discovers an entirely fresh, self-contained realm of axioms, lemmas, and proofs (of the non-Euclidean sort, say) Christian dogmatics may begin with human struggle, with human culture and development, but it should not linger there. Theology enters a world where the Holy God declares Himself.

Now, if this is so, we might well wonder about the cultural legitimacy of such an apologetic realm, however dazzling, however luminous. I am not prepared to say, with Barth, that all *systematic* apologetics merely confirms the truth it quietly slipped into the initial axiom when it began, nor do I find apologetics always springing a trap on the unsuspecting secular interlocutor. But I do worry that a method of correlation—or any schema that regularly joins creature to Creator at every point and in every locus—does not allow the intellectual dignity necessary to theology as an autonomous form of human study. The significant element in cultural legitimacy is its quiet authority to command attention *in its own right*, to draw the eyes away from other objects to its own shores and enclose the knower in the world it has made and not another. I do not mean by this something like the invulnerability or infallibility that Karl Popper diagnosed and derided a generation ago.[27] I do not believe that Christian theology would gain cultural salience were it regarded as previously given or impervious to criticism and falsification. Even as bold a proposal as Plantinga's "proper basicality" recognizes the weakness of a conceptual system that cannot be defeated—the "great pumpkin problem," as Plantinga terms this objection, with his customary élan.[28] Plantinga meets this objection with elements of the common alternative, drawing from church history and the lives of the saints as counterweights to a system of thought that appears grounded only in its own stubborn soil. Properly defended, Christian thought establishes a realm that does not extend far into foreign lands: theology cannot persuade if it hands itself over to the culture in which it lives, but it cannot persuade, either, if it refuses any conformity to the rationality a culture follows and obeys.

There is no general solution to these twin extremes, however. Little is gained in dogmatics, I say, by abstract and structural schemas about theological method. We can sense, in Tillich's work, that "correlation" makes doctrine dog the steps of human existence; and we can sense the worry, in "unvarnished regionalism," that doctrine joins the list of irrelevant hobbies in a culture of uprooted seekers. But these are intuitions only—at best a shaking of the head at something caught out of the corner of one's eyes. What is demanded here, instead, is a proposal that is straightforwardly *doctrinal* in subject matter and in character. The intellectual dignity we seek here is tied to the dogma of Trinity, concretely and in particular. We aim for a form of theological argument and presentation that unfolds the dogma of Trinity as a matter of cultural importance, of rational dignity. It does not do so because the Mystery of Trinity answers human needs. Not everything is soteriology! Nor does it do so because Christian theology simply commands the field, and all bow before it. Rather, the Mystery of Trinity should be set forth in such a manner that its own intellectual coherence and power are *demonstrated*, enacted, without defensiveness or timidity, *and* that this demonstration, in Spirit and in power, will show the rational probity of this task for any ultimate and searching reflection upon Being Itself.

§2.3. The Problem in the Neighborhood

Although I have mentioned this in passing before, I now want to address and defend directly the "problem in the neighborhood." I want to be careful here. There are many ways of expressing a problem in the neighborhood that would undermine the dignity and autonomy of Christian doctrine, and many more that would undermine the freedom, diversity, and particularity of other traditions. We are not seeking a reductive account, nor one that "supersedes" the teaching of the people of Israel! The aim, rather, is to motivate a dogma of the Trinity that points to and unfolds a conceptual problem that commands attention in any proper speculative metaphysic. Note that the "problem in the neighborhood" does not intend to teach that every proper cosmology or metaphysical system is in truth or at bottom a dogma of Trinity. Nor does it aim to disclose, in apocalyptic fashion, the secret that has been veiled for long centuries by the philosophical systems of the nations. It is rather taking a leaf from Tillich's bold Trinitarianism by suggesting that there are conceptual problems— "principles" in Tillich's idiom—that are ingredient in all fully developed metaphysics of Being and that these problems are expressed and integrated in their own fashion in the Mystery of the Holy Trinity.

This is a doctrinal alternative that holds that a rational investigation of Reality Itself will encounter structural elements that must be investigated and incorporated, and these will have an *echo*, a parallel, in the dogma of Trinity. It is a program of indirectness. As a form of the common alternative, the problem in the neighborhood will seek to unfold and investigate the enduring conceptual problems in the notion of the real. My axiom is that any serious probing of reality itself—what an earlier generation called Being Itself—will encounter certain dilemmas, puzzles, and questions that will lead to sophisticated formal and conceptual explanations. It is my view, for example, that the problem of individuation—what makes a singular object an *individual*, not a clone or duplicate?—will emerge in any serious account of biological lifeforms, or general ontology. This problematic will not be expressed in the same idiom; indeed, I believe the qua relation, mentioned earlier—something *as* something else—lies at the heart of the problem in the neighborhood. Rather, I hold that intellectual work on the real will exhibit common structures and worries— individuation is one—and each practitioner in the field will be able to recognize such common efforts. The problems are not *identical*; they are not sited on the same block, so to say, even less, at the same address. But they *are* in the neighborhood. As will be evident later on, I am claiming Ludwig Wittgenstein as an ally here. (Yes, I read him as a realist.) And I hope to lean hard on his more pragmatic, rule-of-thumb procedure than any well-structured architectonic and method.

In the problem in the neighborhood, an investigator reads another account of reality and says: I would not put it this way; I do not like those concepts or thought-forms, but I see what they are driving at. They are concerned with my problem, but in their own way and in their own speech. Such analysis will allow some generous distance between form and content, subject matter and genre, and give license to intellectual translation, from field to field. I do not have in mind an algorithm that governs this conceptual recognition, nor do I think it rests on any technical account of analogy. Rather I hold that investigations into realism exhibit common patterns and formal preoccupations that can be recognized by those who work in allied fields.

It may help here to say what I do *not* mean. The problem in the neighborhood is not a pragmatic or breezy way of saying, "Everyone is at base saying the same thing." It is not a cover for reductionism. Nor is it a folksy way of defending the idea that all realists are theists (or theists manqué). Even less is it a Christian campaign to make all religions Trinitarians. I want to be especially firm about this with rabbinic Judaism and Talmudic readings of Holy Scripture. The problem in the neighborhood is an invitation to intellectual kinship, not a colonial adventure! There will be structural problems of universality and concreteness, of individual identity and presence, of act and persistence, that will attend any close investigation of Reality Itself. I can recognize these in Buddhism or Islam without becoming a devotee, and I believe the same may be said of Jews or Hindus, examining the problematics and proposals of Christian Trinitarianism. Just this exchange, this interest and recognition, is what I mean by intellectual legitimacy, and I seek it for all followers of realism. It is an urgent task in Trinitarianism, I believe, and I hope a particular form of plausibility or cogency can be uncovered through such a proposal. It may seem an odd or dangerous venture; I can but try.

Let me give an example. We might say that the notion or doctrine of the soul points to a problem in the neighborhood that lends it surprising cultural moment in our materialistic society. Think for example of the practical, moral, and legal questions raised by the treatment of the human corpse as it is prepared for burial or dispersion. Medical students are frequently trained to observe proper protocols in the handling of a cadaver or in the treatment of a corpse during autopsy. Such training reflects the respect—but the ambivalence, too, we might think—that living human beings experience at the sight of a body at once human and no longer so. The desire to reify a corpse, to reduce it to a thing through ridicule or indifference, we often term *desecration*, in a revealing turn of phrase. Such ambivalence is powerful and nearly universal: consider the ancient, and modern, practice of vandalizing graves or the even more ancient practice—even in Christian eras, or especially then— of avoiding them and considering them accursed. The mark of war on soldiers—the making of corpses—carries over into the civilian population when bodies of enemies are displayed in city streets as mutilated and deformed, an act that at once honors and fears the human corpse. Mass graves can still offend in our shallow and pitiless age, still we avert our eyes at traumatic injury or cannot pull them away, and we can never have enough pulp film and fiction on the "living dead," the embalmed, the corpse that walks. On the other hand, we can nearly circle the globe by studying burial practices in diverse cultures; bodies are honored, not discarded, by ritual and cult. We might say that ritual in its most elemental form just *is* the honoring of the body in death. In our post-Christian era, still we decorate coffins, open them at funerals, and dress the corpse. So lifelike, we exclaim! Even secular events become ritual when brought near death. Those who have attended another's death, in hospital or home, know the numinous moment when the body of the beloved becomes a corpse, dead flesh and bones, when the head and limbs are slipped into a carrier and someone—an official, a friend, a chaplain—can bear to close it shut over sightless eyes. In all these ways, human cultures enact and express the explosive power of the human body in life and especially in death.

We might think, too, of the complex legacy the human, body and mind, has left in modern academic discourse. It is no easy matter for contemporary secular thought to weigh the proper attitude toward human life, nor its status in the world of living things. It seems that human beings are animals with odd properties; or perhaps they, we, are *animals,* tout court, flourishing in our niche, or quietly destroying it. Perhaps the world is entirely biological—naturalistic, we now say—and human beings take their place within the evolutionary forces and structures of organic life. Or perhaps, as one present-day theology would have it, we are simply *bodies*, one kind and family within a vast expanse of bodies, organic but inorganic, too, visible certainly, but only as a single thread within a cosmic fabric.[29] Yet we remain in search for human rights, an inherent dignity and claim to just treatment, that belongs to human beings just because we are human, members of this kind. In a secular academic age, it is no easy task to adjudicate or ground such rights, yet the torture, neglect, and cruelty toward human beings, often the most vulnerable among us, outrages the conscience still and cries out for redress. Against such rights, or perhaps in line with them, we hear appeals to broaden the horizon of rights, to extend their defense of the voiceless to (other) animals, to vegetation, to the planet Earth. Can nonhuman beings have rights? Can they have duties, obligations, faults? Is there a cultural failing and blindness we rightly call speciesism? Can human beings wrongly elevate our own kind; can we accord dignity to our species and prefer, defend, and cultivate it in ways that are morally corrupt and bigoted? Or is such a preference simply another marker of our membership in an evolutionary kin group, looking to flourish in our landscape, perhaps at others' expense, and to reproduce our kind? Can such a biological "instinct," if such there be, be held morally liable? This is our larger question about the human body, reframed in an evolutionary idiom.

Or think, finally, of the quest for the natural in the midst of the mind-dependent and the social. Here we in modern Western culture exhibit the complex ambivalence about the character and stature of the human within a larger world. An older generation considered the human being to be set over against nature or, better, Nature. The artifice, the linguistic and ideal thought-world, the realm of custom and habit: these were the human legacies in a natural world; they set us apart and above. The very notion of the artifact, as old as Aristotle, told us about ourselves as those who lived at the borderlands of the natural, who crossed and remade them. It would not be possible to enter very far into Marx's thought were the idea of the "new need"—and the *homo faber*—to be abandoned for a wholly materialistic or naturalistic universe. Yet it is the recurrent fascination for Nature and the natural that marks modern, Western culture. Romanticism, certainly, is unthinkable without it, but so, too, are the humble practices of gardening and sightseeing and camping under the starry heavens. We seek time and again the natural in our gestures, our conversations, our ways of life. And we moderns, so absorbed in our technology, so impressed and fearful of it, long to use technique and artifact to heighten and conserve the natural. We might consider here the single example of the medical artifact, the prosthetic limb, the cataract lens, the heart valve or pacemaker, the cochlear implant: technology designed to become natural, to become human. Yet these are bodies, limbs and members and parts of bodies! We consider them possessions, additions or corrections or aids to our own bodies, and we embrace or fear them as elements in our embodied life.

But it is the singular hallmark of modern medical artifice that we, the bearers, do not *identify* ourselves with these technologies but rather own them, incorporate them, welcome them, or refuse them. The large-scale calamity that is dementia in developed societies reveals the terror, just under our skin, that we and the ones we love may no longer master our bodies, no longer live in and move them but rather collapse into them, be truly one with them. We need not settle—at least not here!—the long, tangled philosophical debate about the human "self" and the status of this deeply held belief by modern people that "we" are not disease but rather "have" it, that "we" are not our "broken knee" but "fix" it. Human beings continue to exhibit a sense of distinction or mastery over the natural, including their own bodies, and more stubbornly still, they continue to identify themselves not with the flesh but with the spirit, the inwardmost part. The study of inwardness in the modern, secular university, however, can take place only under the aegis of the natural, the scientific: neurobiology, cognitive science, consciousness studies. We cannot let our own selves go it seems, yet the categories we have left in academic circles for such obsession can be only those of nature. Perhaps it is a counterstrike to all such naturalistic reductionism that computer scientists and philosophers have also devoted themselves to the development of artificial intelligence—or perhaps it is a radical extension of naturalism. The proposal that computers could "think" or "make judgments" independent of and in opposition to human knowers appears to collapse intellect into the artifact, or perhaps on the other hand, to make the artifact the living, natural being, the one we have made. It does not take Mary Shelley to name the fears that accompany all such investigations. These are intellectual expressions of the complex and ambivalent stature of the human in our cultural moment, the sense of identity and dignity tied up in it, and the loss that threatens it on every side.

All this is what I would call a problem in the neighborhood of the doctrine of the soul. Note that the term *soul*, or even a modern simulacrum, need not appear in the neighborhood. The claim here is not that historians and scientists and philosophers and doctors and their patients are all discussing "human souls" avant la lettre.

We are not supposing here that Christian ideas lie embedded in human culture, especially former Christian lands, in such a way that their structure and thought-form guide even the blind. No, we do not envision a *decoding* project here or a prophetic unveiling. This may even fail the lower bar of *transposition*, a change in key or mode. The point we have in mind here is not to discover the Christian doctrine *directly* or *implicitly* within secular ideas and practices, a hidden civic norm; it is not *common* property in that sense. Rather we look for a discussion within the larger public realm that turns on similar axes, that takes up common problems, that echoes familiar themes. In our example we would note the way in which human dignity is an unsettled good in public, intellectual debate. We would note, too, the ambivalence with which human bodies, corpses, remains are held, honored, disguised, displayed. The academic debates over philosophy of mind, evolutionary biology, environmental and international law, and computer science raise questions that find a resonance or correspondence in Christian doctrine. We might make explicit here the geometric analogy: these are similar *structural* shapes, parallel constructions—not identical, not matched halves, but *corresponding* wholes. To discuss whether human beings have rights in virtue of membership in humankind is to investigate a topic that mirrors Christian affirmation of a special dignity in virtue of the Gracious Creator and His graces bestowed on the human creature. To ask whether (other) animals have rights is to raise a question that finds resonance in the Christian reflection on human stewardship of a creation made good—blessed and declared, altogether, very good. To find a culture convulsed by the destruction of bodies, in war, in disease, in cruel indifference and neglect, is to listen to a culture reflecting, in its own idiom and genre, moral loci that in Christian tongues would be given over to the embodied soul and its destiny. The cultural legitimacy of the doctrine of the soul, then, rests in its own integrity and self-determination, but it mirrors, learns from, and instructs the deep wrestling modern Western culture exhibits as it thinks about its own humankind.

I have used geometric and musical analogies here—but I want to be quick to add that these thought-forms lend an air of *system* and *regularity* to the comparison that I hope to ward off. We should be seeking here something much closer to a rule of thumb, a commonsense recognition and practice, than anything abstract, ordered, and deductive. We should be imaging a familiar human happening, something like recognizing an old neighborhood, or perhaps one that reminds us of home. Many of us will have had the experience of traveling on foot or by car through a new city, a new warren of streets, only to feel stealing over one the sense that we have "been there before" or "know where we are" or that this place "reminds us" of another, beloved or feared. Perhaps we point to a particular store or house—"see, this is the one that I think used to have a grocery in it," the "house where the organist lived"; but, of course, I might be wrong! We turn to our traveling companion: "I think we could turn left here and find the main street or the bus station—I think that's how it goes." These are echoes, signs, odd and innumerable indications of a familiar landscape, and we use a rule of thumb to guide us through it. It is constitutionally "vague"; there is no exact number of matching and corresponding signs that designate it as familiar. Nor is it always the same pattern that allows the sense of recognition to steal over us. It is not always houses, not always stores, not always a meeting of the two on a particular kind of corner. No, it just looks right, looks familiar, looks like a place I once knew well. Of course, it is fallible! Not only is this recognition of a neighborhood indeterminate, it also can be in the end shown to be mistaken. No, I cannot actually find the train station that way; no, I do not really know that yard or hotel lobby; no, I suppose that in truth it's actually far different in tone and layout and character from the place I remember so long ago. These signs of fallibility, too, are commonsense, ordinary realism. There is no structured failure here, no conceptual bar that has been found too high, no interior angle that is not replicated in the new. Rather, we try out a route and see how it turns out, where we land. We look around us in the shop we enter; we walk on a bit to see how it appears at the end of the block. This is everyday experiment and trial, and we learn it, it seems, by living long enough: traveling new places, remembering the old, finding ourselves lost, finding our way out, our way home.

Readers of the later Wittgenstein will recognize the kind of pattern I suggest here, the "family resemblance." I do not want to endorse everything about Wittgenstein in this analogy: this is not a philosophical program even of the Wittgensteinian sort! But I do want to borrow his evocation of recognition and similarity: to be "like" something is not simply one kind of relation; to belong to a kind is not one form of membership. It may indeed fall under the elusive and wonderfully evocative category Wittgenstein called "seeing as" or "the dawning of an aspect." The nineteenth-century example of the duck-rabbit is of course well known and well used, deservedly so. Surely it, too, has Trinitarian resonances! But I find myself drawn more closely to the cardinal role recognition plays in Wittgenstein's account. We might look for a long time, perhaps in concentration and focus, without seeing what another is showing us. This, too, is commonsense practice. How many of us have gone to the picture gallery with artist friends and cannot see what they would teach us! Look at those brush strokes, the play of light, the use of negative space, they exhort—but we see nothing, only the familiar landscape we have passed by, sightless, countless times. We remember the day it dawns; we see it! This is the ready experience

Wittgenstein calls on here: very common, very familiar, and on reflection, remarkable, compelling, odd. Here is Wittgenstein on these themes.

In the first, more structured part I of the *Philosophical Investigations*, Wittgenstein adduces the famous example of the game:

> 66. Consider for example the proceedings that we call "games." I mean board-games, card-games, ball-games, Olympic games, and so on. What is common to them all?—Don't say: "there *must* be something common, or they would not be called 'games'"—but *look and see* whether there is anything common to all.—For if you look at them you will not see something that is common to *all*, but similarities, relationships, and a whole series of them at that. To repeat: don't think, but look! [Here follows a marvelous stretch of Wittgenstein's fertile and unsettling examples. Then:] And the result of this examination is: we see a complicated network of similarities overlapping and criss-crossing: sometimes over all similarities, sometimes similarities of detail.[30]

After that rich exposition, alive with the startling urgency that made him a philosophical and sometimes personal explosion, Wittgenstein draws a famous conclusion:

> 67. I can think of no better expression to characterize these similarities than "family resemblances;" for the various resemblances between members of a family: build, features, colour of eyes, gait, temperament, etc. etc., overlap and criss-cross in the same way.—and I shall say: "games" form a family. [Here follows a complex allusion to number. Then:]
>
> But if someone wished to say: "There is something common to all these constructions—namely the disjunction of all their common properties"—I should reply: Now you are only playing with words."[31]

The charge that careful conceptual or philosophical analysis is "only playing with words" has a long history in the study and interpretation of Wittgenstein. It is clear from the *Investigations* that Wittgenstein held to this view firmly, but just how we are to understand it, follow or overturn it, carries us deep into Wittgenstein's intellectual project as a whole. In our setting we might rather use Wittgenstein's caustic remark as a sign of the commonsensical and the ordinary observation of regularity and membership. Wittgenstein seems to have elaborated on this whole notion of irregular and "crisscrossed" likeness in the less ordered and unfinished part II of the *Investigations*. In the midst of the famous example of the duck-rabbit, we find also, and I think more significantly, some logia on Aspects.

> Here is a game played by children: they say that a chest, for example, is a house; and thereupon it is interpreted as a house in every detail. A piece of fancy is worked into it.
> And does the child now *see* the chest as a house?
> "He quite forgets that it is a chest; for him it actually is a house." (There are definite tokens of this.) Then would it not also be correct to say he *sees* it as a house?
> And if you knew how to play this game, and, given a particular situation, you exclaimed with special expression "Now it's a house!"— you would be giving expression to the dawning of an aspect.
> If I heard someone talking about the duck-rabbit, and *now* he spoke in a certain way about the special expression of the rabbit's face I should say, now he's seeing the picture as a rabbit.[32]

Proper interpretation of these sections is itself a demanding enterprise, but for our theological use here, I think we might focus on the very common experience of suddenly seeing a connection, an example, a resemblance, an identity. We are not to imagine that the child playing house sees the chest of drawers, decorated perhaps or pulled over on its side, and says, let us pretend it is a house. Rather we are asked to *enter* into the game as it unfolds: now it is a house, and we see it as such. Look and see! Perhaps as visitors we stumble across this game, and we watch the child with his favorite piece of furniture. In time, and with imagination,

Wittgenstein proposes, we "tumble" to the answer: he is playing house! Wittgenstein proposes the use of the exclamation as sign that we suddenly *see*: the aspect has awakened, or "dawned," for us. It is not that we see the chest of drawers and the house or the furniture and tell ourselves the child imagines it's a house. Rather our eyes are opened: we recognize the house; we stand already inside the charmed circle of the game. We cannot control this awakening as we can control our gaze. It comes over us. "Their eyes were opened, and they recognized Him." It is a truth that compels, a vision that now occupies our whole experience. Wittgenstein himself reported that he had trouble seeing the duck-rabbit as both aspects (no duck for him!), and he asks us to consider the common experience of attempting to "see as" or "to see an aspect" and failing despite our struggle, our concentration, our reliance on direction from others. The pattern remains dormant for us, and who knows what elixir is needed to awaken it from slumber? So far, Wittgenstein.

Now for Christian doctrine as it examines the "problem in the neighborhood." Students of Wittgenstein will notice that I have quietly conflated two different schemas in the *Investigations*: in one, I have explored the "family resemblance" among several different, distinct objects; in the other, the "dawning of distinct 'aspects'" of a single object. These are not the same problematic, not by a good measure! But in the problem in the neighborhood, I propose to borrow a theme by which they "resemble" one another. Here I suggest that the varying aspects and worlds—"ways of life"—that appear in the investigation of reality share the polyglot and "crisscrossed" relation of a family. The problems in the neighborhood share family resemblances that must be "received"—"awakened"—such that their similarity can be acknowledged and worked through. They are *many*, but they share a neighborhood.

The doctrine of God, per se, is another matter. Here we do not speak of a neighborhood but of a single house, one household. Here the qua relation among the Aspects of the One God must hold sway. Still, the Aspects must "dawn upon us"; we must look and then, perhaps, see. We are given and do not deduce their resemblance or the way in which they capture and portray the whole. But it is a gift of faith to see this, to have our eyes opened, and to find ourselves children of the One God, kindred, one of another. These complex relations of faith will govern our exegesis of Israel's Scriptures and of the Triune Holiness I see dawning there. That will hold our attention in time. But here, let's dive into the family resemblance among many objects, fields of thought, and worlds of life.

We might borrow, in an informal and light-handed way, the sense of parallel systems of thought, each sharing a family resemblance—belonging, in their own way, to a family of numbers or games. We "look and see" the likeness amid many differences; we do not expect a strong match or correspondence; we do not see the one cluster of ideas coordinated completely and regularly with the other. We are awakened to this likeness; we suddenly see it. The legitimacy that Christian doctrine seeks in broad cultural themes is one in which the elements of rational debate, the worries raised and defeated, the candidates brought forward as solutions, the interminable or insoluble all can be seen as "familiar" conversations, as nearby neighborhoods, as kindred tongues. We do not colonize that territory; we do not surrender to it. Rather, we *recognize* it. Mutatis mutandis Christians investigate just these avenues, explore just these paths. The cultural legitimacy and rational dignity such recognition wins for Christian dogma is the awareness of a common endeavor, the sense of belonging to common tasks, the taking on of common struggles in the intellectual and material world we all inhabit and receive—not more than that! These are not "theological sources" or "norms" or any of the elaborate architectonics Schleiermacher or Tillich proposed for modern Christian theology. It is a prize, I say, something won from a culture now some distance removed from its Christian past, but a modest one. Yet it is a prize worth pursuing—for the doctrine of the Holy Trinity is the Mystery and Glory and Consummation of all human intellect, all human and humane culture, all Scripture, all Perfections of the One God. Should the secular world suddenly awaken to the resemblance it, too, would win a prize—no! receive the Gift—that doctrine would extend to our secular neighbors, the Pearl of Great Price.

But now I think I hear someone eager to interrupt all this philosophical chatter. Students of the tradition have been waiting, perhaps impatiently, for me to admit what they long ago have already suspected: that all this reflection about the problem in the neighborhood is a modern form, a modest one, too, of the ancient, dignified notion of a *vestigium Trinitatis*. Now, true, I have bent this form rather severely, but even in its battered state, it can be recognized, I know, as a member of this school. The problem in the neighborhood honors the Divine *Persons* in just this way. It seeks traces of Them in the world the Lord God has made. In time I will argue for the priority of Procession over Persons in the construction of Trinity, but here, in the prolegomena of the common alternative, I honor the Persons and give Them pride of place. Think, for example, of the original evocation of this theme in Augustine's *De Trinitate* and the classic elaboration of it in Thomas Aquinas. Both rely on Wisdom 11.20, "You have arranged all things by measure and number and weight" and, perhaps even more expressly, Wisdom 8.1, "Wisdom reacheth from one end to another mightily;

and sweetly doth she order all things," as the translators would have it. This sweetness envelops Augustine:

> That inexpressible embrace, so to say, of the Father and the image is not without enjoyment, without charity, without happiness. So this love, delight, felicity, or blessedness (if any human word can be found that is good enough to express it) he [Hilary] calls very briefly "use," and it is the Holy Spirit in the triad, not begotten, but the sweetness of begetter and begotten pervading all creatures according to their capacity with its vast generosity and fruitfulness, that they might all keep their right order and rest in their right places.[33]

Here creation shows forth the Love and Peace and Delight that just is Trinity through the creature's orderliness and stability. Such coordinated bliss Augustine terms a "trace," vestigium:

> All things around us that the divine art has made reveal in themselves a certain unity and form and order. Any one of them you like is both some one thing, like the various kinds of bodies and temperaments of souls; and it is fashioned in some form, like the shapes and qualities of bodies and the sciences or skills of souls; and it seeks or maintains some order, like the weights or proper places of bodies, and the loves or pleasures of souls. So then as we direct our gaze at the creator by "understanding the things that are made," we should understand him as triad, whose traces appear in creation in a way that is fitting. In that supreme triad is the source of all things, and the most perfect beauty, and wholly blissful delight.[34]

Thomas has thought through these evocative remarks with his customary skill and rendered them systematic under the concept of cause:

> *I answer that:* Every effect in some ways represents its cause, but diversely. For some effects represent only the causality of the cause but not its form; as smoke represents fire. Such a representation is called a *trace,* for a trace shows that someone has passed by not who it is. . . . [Then follows an influential *differentia* between trace and image; to

be treated in the *Imago Dei.* Thomas continues, drawing upon the Doctrine of the Persons:] In all creatures there is found the trace of the Trinity, inasmuch as in every creature are found some things which are necessarily reduced to the divine Persons as to their being, and has a form, whereby it is determined to a species, and has relation to something else. Therefore as it is a created substance, it represents the cause and principle; and so in that manner it shows the Person of the Father, Who is the *principle from no principle.* According as it has a form and species, it represents the Word as the form of the thing made by art is from the conception of the craftsman. According as it has relation of order, it represents the Holy Ghost, inasmuch as He is love, because the order of the effect to something else is from the will of the Creator. . . . For a thing exists by its substance, is distinct by its form, and agrees by its order.[35]

Now in this quaestio, Thomas testifies to the benefit he has received from scholastic debate about the conceptual relation of creature to Creator, and the specialized doctrine of knowledge that has emerged from these medieval schools. He more clearly draws on Aristotelian categories than does Augustine, who reaches customarily for Platonic modes of thought, but Thomas's main preoccupation turns to the degree to which the creature can speak and mirror the Triune Creator. It is in this scholastic form that we brush up against the commonsense notion I have called the problem in the neighborhood, and it raises the most profound and delicate questions for the intellectual warrant I have proposed for the dogma of Triunity.

Note that Thomas relies on the doctrine of the Divine Person here in the idea of the creaturely *trace* of God. (The Divine Processions are more properly considered the *type* of creatures as they pour forth from the hand of God; Q 45, art 6.) Thomas is careful to place the idea of vestigium alongside the doctrine of Appropriations, for he, too, is anxious over the place of the creature and its powers in the dogma of Trinity. He seeks to constrain this idea, to place it in a rather remote storeroom and not allow the Mystery of Trinity to devolve into a human-scale hobby of trefoils and three leaf clovers. But the *vestigium* resides clearly and plainly in Augustine's magisterial works, and Thomas recognizes the nub of the thing (it dawns on him!): the dogma of Trinity and of Creation must not be entirely walled off from one another. Though the *opera Dei ad extra unum sint*, and the "causality of the creature belongs to the [Divine] common nature,"[36] nevertheless a trace of the Triune Persons, All and Each, must be found in creaturely substances, because the taxis of the Divine Relations sweetly orders the gift of creation. So, Thomas directs the idea of trace to the concept of substance in its primary sense: the freestanding individual, the subject of all predication, the continuity amid all change; this man, that horse. To be an object, a creature and thing, is to have being, to participate in it, and as an individual, to belong to a kind—a natural kind, genus and species—and to have a place in an environment and under natural laws, to be ordered. Worried about an infinite regress, Thomas refuses to consider properties as traces of Trinity; vestigia belong properly and exclusively to *things*. Each created substance, then, bears the mark of the Triune Persons *under a creaturely category*. They simply are a substance; they simply can be identified as a member of a kind; they simply follow the ends and laws of their kith and kin. Creatures are not small gods; they do not mirror or exhibit Deity directly. God remains Hidden here, Transcendent and Majestic, not seen explicitly or known by *visio* in this life but rather reasoned toward, received by faith. We know in this way that Some One passes, but not who that One is. *As finite creatures*, objects possess traits that can be traced back, smoke to Fire, to the Triune Cause. They are His.

So modest, so restrained! So little handed over to the creature; so much Divine Mystery preserved! What could be worrisome about all this? Thomas himself supplies an answer, and Karl Barth drives the worry home. The worry is this: perhaps the notion of a *vestigium Trinitatis* offers the possibility that a creature could know the Mystery of Trinity through reason alone or, perhaps in more polemical tones, that the dogma of Trinity could be a deliverance of natural theology. Now this is just the question that is raised by the entire program of *legitimating*, rationally and culturally, the doctrine of Trinity. (A question I should be especially alert to!) This may be done in subtle fashion—we need not suppose that the natural theology proposed is by way of explicit advertising: here is the creature that spells out Three-in-One is God. We are not supposing that the trace of Trinity in the secular cosmos is *propositional*, such that the teachings of Person and Relation, taxis and order, are stated, *engraved* in the ratio of the human intelligence, the substance or reality of the natural realm. Strictly speaking, this would not fall under the category trace at all; it is too bold, too concrete and specific. It may be doubted that any serious theologian of the Tradition has taught a rational knowledge of Trinity in such a straightforward and implausible fashion. But in a more subtle and plausible way? Is this just what a problem in the neighborhood or a list of conceptual "principles of Being" amounts to? A Hegelianism with a junior membership? Is the price of cultural legitimacy a doctrine that is no longer Mystery, no longer the proper province of the church and its teachings, no longer a matter of faith but rather a deliverance of reason? A birthright for a mess of pottage? Can a proper and faithful doctrine of Trinity countenance such a risk? Or conversely, is it a risk at all? We should not hurry over our reply.

We might examine first, and with care, the stakes at risk in this entire debate. Just why have Christians taught that Trinity must be revealed? Why have they—not one and all, but most, and the most prominent—thought that the dogma of Trinity is not a deliverance of unaided reason? Is this a worry we should share? Thomas sums up the medieval answer this way:

> Whoever tries to prove the trinity of persons by natural reason derogates from faith in two ways. Firstly as regards the dignity of faith itself, which consists in its being concerned with invisible things, that exceed human reason; wherefore the Apostle says that "faith is of things that appear not; and the same Apostle says also, "We speak wisdom among the perfect but not the wisdom of this world, nor of the princes of this world; but we speak the wisdom of God in a mystery which is hidden." Secondly, as regards the utility of drawing others to the faith. For when anyone in the endeavor to prove the faith brings forward reason which are not cogent, he falls under the ridicule of the unbelievers: since they suppose that we stand upon such reasons, and that we believe on such grounds.[37]

We grasp the nettle here. Thomas thinks that the arguments offered by natural reason—problems discussed, we might say, in the neighborhood—will be so implausible and unpersuasive that secular intellectuals will assume we Christians are fools and that we believe on nothing more than strawmen and elaborate fallacies. This second position seems in truth to underlie the first, as it would be manifestly question-begging to assume Trinity exceeds human reason as the answer to the question of whether the Trinity of the Divine Persons can be known by natural reason. It appears that Thomas has never met a rationalistic argument for Trinity that did anything more than embarrass him. This might surprise at first glance, as Thomas himself appears to offer a full slate of rational arguments for the Triune Processions and Persons in the *Prima Pars*. Indeed, he is often chided in the modern period for his speculative Trinitarianism and his seeming boldness to enter the Inner Courts of the Divine Being. But Thomas, we may think, sees this otherwise. Not independent arguments, he would say, underlie the treatise *De Deo Trino*, but rather the careful unfolding and explaining of truths held, de fide. (More on this follows.)

In quaestio 32, Thomas cites some examples of rational arguments for Trinity—or taken to be such—in the initial objections to the first article, from worthies such as Aristotle and Trismegistus, but also from doctors of the church, Augustine, Richard St. Victor, the patristic glossers. These did not satisfy. The ancients did not in truth speak about Trinity, Thomas claims, but rather divine appropriations; Augustine did not speak univocally of divine and human persons, as a rationalist must assume; the Victorines have not shown a created effect caused necessarily by an Infinite Goodness and Self-Giving. In short, Thomas argues that human reason can merely *confirm* or elaborate on an article of faith, or it can rebut or defang objections. But an article of faith—the Trinity of Divine Persons—is *believed* in virtue of *authority*, the authority of the church and the Divine Science. We think such thoughts, if at all, by the elevation of grace, so that, by little and by little, our intellects are made Deiform, healed and directed and brought to their Fulfillment. So, if we followed Thomas here, we would say at most that the Dogma of Trinity could be confirmed or given a secondary warrant by the logical and conceptual elements in secular metaphysics, or given conceptual redescription, as we find in the *Prima Pars*, and nothing more.

Barth strongly agrees. (For this reason alone, both theologians belong in the "Regional Alternative.") As we have seen, Barth agrees with Thomas on many elements of Trinitarian theology, however much Barth repudiated the analogy of Being and other dangers he found ingredient in Thomism. The dogma of Trinity is revealed; it is held de fide; the doctrine is a creature of grace, as we are brought, by the Triune God Himself, into His Lordly Presence, and made His knowing subject. As in the *Summa*, the doctrine of Trinity is not given rational argument or grounding in the *Church Dogmatics*—both works belong to the initial regional alternative—but rather Trinity is generated, revealed, by a Commanding Voice: God is Lord. "In trying to analyse the biblical concept of revelation, we have arrived at the thesis that this analysis reduced to its simplest form, the threefold yet single lordship of God as Father, Son and Spirit, is the root of the doctrine of the Trinity. In other words, the biblical concept of revelation is itself the root of the doctrine of the Trinity. The doctrine of the Trinity is simply a development of the knowledge that Jesus is the Christ or the Lord."[38] So we might think of Barth's exposition of Trinity in the first volume of the *Church Dogmatics* as an exegetical and conceptual unfolding of an Article of Faith, where reason, Kantian reason, has entered the lists as confirmation and explanation. But not justification or warrant! Barth is firm about this. The Sovereign Freedom of God hangs in the balance here, not of course on the Divine Side, the *Jenseits*, but on ours, in our small intellects and systems. God is not *given* to the world in such a way that we can "look and see," or think the thought of God, unaided, undirected; God is not Objective or Neutral Being *in that sense*. He is not the Other of pious awareness so that we could place Him in waiting until the "second form of doctrine" could be unveiled and pressed into service. Here is Barth on this point:

> The question is whether these *vestigia Trinitatis*, in virtue of the conclusions that are to be drawn from their acknowledgement even if only in the form of the list of questions mentioned, do not compel us to pass over first to the easy double track of "revelation" and "primal revelation" (P Althaus) [but could we not also add P Tillich?] and then very quickly from this half-measure to the genuine Roman Catholic theology of the *analogia entis*. And then would they not bring to our attention at the right moment the fact that theology would do well to

desist from the impossible attempt to understand itself as theology and to acquiesce in being the only thing it can be at root, namely, part of man's understanding of the world and himself, in the development of which the concept, "God," like a superfluous x in the numerator and denominator, should now be cancelled out to simplify the counting on both sides, since with or without the concept the only real concern is man, or, in this case, man's own triunity.[39]

Barth returns time and again in this short discussion to the central structural point about the proper "root" of the dogma. Trinity is a deliverance of *revelation*, of God's Lordship, and the *vestigia* exist like a serpent in Eden: crafty, though good, ready to tempt even when given only a modest speaking role in the drama. Barth acknowledges the way creatures might well exhibit something of the Triune Creator, should the Lord grant it. These would be *vestigia creaturae in trinitate*, even when presented as more robust vestigia Trinitatis. (We might well see seeds of the justly famous *Lichtelehre* in *Church Dogmatics* IV.3 here.) But they remain temptations! There is much "slippery slope" argument cascading through the section. For we are drawn, Barth warns, to discover other "roots," other sources of the doctrine, just because we do not wish to have a Lord. As rebels we find much, much to like in our own world, in our own kind and our doings and aims, and much to flee and repudiate in the Good Gifts of the Good God. Indeed, Barth confesses, in a second-order fashion, that his own trifold account of revelation could be a trace of the rebellious sort, another Trinitarian root, though he verbally and firmly rejects such a path.

Barth aims to *interpret*, not to *illustrate*, he notes, in a revealing methodological aside. To interpret, he tells us, is to "say *the same thing* in other words"; to illustrate, "to say the same thing *in other words*."[40] It is a matter of emphasis. The statement is the same in both, but in the second, Barth says, the "other words" threaten to steal the thunder, to demand our attention, and to take on a life of their own. We claim to be interpreting; we utter the same sentence; we reach only for a *trace*, a sign, an aid in our search for the Same Thing. But in truth we have begun to be our own Lord, to investigate our own reality, and to turn to the creature as our own final end. We have said the same thing *in other words*. For Trinity to be *revealed*, on the other hand, is for God *alone* to justify, ground, and command the dogma: just this is what Lordship means in the intellectual structure of theology. We simply say the Same Thing; we have not been disobedient to the Heavenly Vision. In all this Barth issues stern warnings! What should we make of them?

We must answer with our own quiet but firm confidence that the Divine Trinity is recognized, indirectly, in the world of creaturely reason. We stand on the side of St. Thomas here. The Mystery of the Holy Trinity is the Eschatological Consummation of all our human thought; It is the Fullness, the Perfection, of all our intellectual longings, the End of all knowledge. In just this way, the dogma of Trinity is inaugurated in the metaphysical searches of humankind; it leaves its traces there. Now, the Triune God is the most Generous Giver, and He does not leave our kind with only traces and hints and starting points; He leaves also an Image. He plants among us the holy temple, and He dwells there in His Glory; and He dwells Beyond. The temple—its cult and its holiness, that is—is a stronger, more direct, more concrete expression of the Holy Trinity and, in just this way, a stronger, more direct, more concrete *metaphysics*. The Triune One *communicates* Himself as Holy, a Concrete and Infinite Being, who in His Incommunicable Mystery expresses and gives and communicates His Life, His Perfect Wisdom. He will not withhold even His Triunity: His is a Superabundant, Perfect Goodness. It is the End of all and every creature, the Consummation of the cosmos, the Sweet Savor of every sacrifice. It is Perfect Gift.

The Image of that Triune Gift is the temple. And that will be our central task in this volume: to set forth, to praise, and to interpret the metaphysical Holiness of God, as betokened in Israel's tabernacle and temple and brought to Its Consummation in the temple not made by hands. But here we begin with the foreshadowing, the hint and passing fragment of Trinity that can be found in metaphysics itself, in the pursuit of Being as a whole. This is the intellectual dignity of the Mystery of the Holy Trinity, that It sends forth Its Consummate Reality to the ends of the earth, even to the farthest reaches of the human intellect, the quest and thirst for Reality Itself. The search for the real is the trace of Trinity in human endeavor.

Notes

1. Jonathan Edwards, *A Treatise Concerning Religious Affections* (Philadelphia: James Crissy, 1821), 138.

2. Thomas Aquinas, *Summa Theologica*, trans. Fathers of the English Dominican Province (New York: Benziger Press, 1947), I, q. 12, art. 13, reply to obj. 1; vol. I, p. 111.

3. Barth, *Church Dogmatics*, I.1, The Doctrine of the Word of God, 295.

4. Barth, *Church Dogmatics*, I.1, The Doctrine of the Word of God, 348.

5. Barth, *Church Dogmatics*, I.1, The Doctrine of the Word of God, 301.

6. Barth, *Church Dogmatics*, I.1, The Doctrine of the Word of God, 301.

7. Barth, *Church Dogmatics*, I.1, The Doctrine of the Word of God, 296.

8. Barth, *Church Dogmatics*, I.1, The Doctrine of the Word of God, 298.

9. Barth, *Church Dogmatics*, I.1, The Doctrine of the Word of God, 303.

10. Barth, *Church Dogmatics*, I.1, The Doctrine of the Word of God, 303.

11. Barth, *Church Dogmatics*, I.1, The Doctrine of the Word of God, 306.

12. Aristotle, *Categories*, Cat. II, 1a20–1b9; W. V. Quine, "Main Trends in Recent Philosophy: Two Dogmas of Empiricism," *Philosophical Review* 60, no. 1 (1951): 20–43.

13. Saul Kripke, *Naming and Necessity* (Cambridge: Harvard University Press, 1980).

14. Barth, *Church Dogmatics*, I.1, The Doctrine of the Word of God, §8.1, 315, 316, 320.

15. Karl Barth, *Letters, 1961–1968*, trans. Geoffrey Bromley (Grand Rapids: Eerdmans, 1981), 294.

16. Barth, *Church Dogmatics*, I.1, The Doctrine of the Word of God, 296.

17. Barth, *Church Dogmatics*, I.1, The Doctrine of the Word of God, 299.

18. Barth, *Church Dogmatics*, I.1, xiii–xiv.

19. Rowan Williams, *On the Edge of Words: God and the Habits of Language* (London: Bloomsbury, 2014).

20. Paul Tillich, *Systematic Theology*, vol. 1 of *Reason and Revelation, Being and God* (Chicago: University of Chicago Press, 1951), 8.

21. See, for instance, Tillich's and Barth's 1923 exchange regarding theological dialectics. Translation found in *The Beginnings of Dialectic Theology*, ed. James M. Robinson (Richmond: John Knox Press, 1968), 133–58.

22. Tillich, *Systematic Theology*, 1:11.

23. Tillich, *Systematic Theology*, 1:63, 64.

24. As Freud has cautioned, "All this is exactly as we are bound to wish it to be."

25. Tillich, *Systematic Theology*, 1:251.

26. Paul Tillich, *Systematic Theology*, vol. 3 of *Life and the Spirit, History and the Kingdom of God* (Chicago: University of Chicago Press, 1963), 284.

27. Karl Popper, *Poverty of Historicism* (Abingdon: Routledge, 1957).

28. Alvin Plantinga, *God, Freedom, Evil* (Grand Rapids: Eerdmans, 1974).

29. Sallie McFague, *The Body of God: An Ecological Theology* (Minneapolis: Fortress Press, 1993).

30. Ludwig Wittgenstein, *Philosophical Investigations*, trans. G. E. M. Anscombe, 3rd ed. (Oxford: Blackwell, 1967), 31.

31. Wittgenstein, *Philosophical Investigations*, 32e.

32. Wittgenstein, *Philosophical Investigations*, 206e.

33. Augustine, *The Trinity*, IV.11, trans. Edmund Hill (Brooklyn: New City Press, 1991), 213.

34. Augustine, *Trinity*, IV.12.

35. Aquinas, *Summa Theologica*, I, q. 45, art. 7, responsio.

36. Aquinas, *Summa Theologica*, I, q. 45, art. 7, reply to obj. 3.

37. Aquinas, *Summa Theologica*, I, q. 32, art. 1, responsio.

38. Barth, *Church Dogmatics*, I.1, The Doctrine of the Word of God, 334.

39. Barth, *Church Dogmatics*, I.1, The Doctrine of the Word of God, 335.

40. Barth, *Church Dogmatics*, I.1, The Doctrine of the Word of God, 345.

§ 3. Realism as Trace of the Trinity

Realism, then, is the problem in the neighborhood. It may be of some help here to say a word or two about realism—though only a word or two! Like any large-scale philosophical term—rationalism, Platonism, materialism—realism is a vast army; it commands a vast terrain. One common definition of realism contrasts it with constructivism and idealism or, more tendentiously, with subjectivism: the real, under this heading, is the "mind-independent." Were there no minds, no beings with intellects, realism says that real objects would still exist and possess their proper powers. It's an attractive definition: it's sleek, rather commonsensical in its purview, and easy to apply. Yes, the tree makes a noise in the forest when it falls, even if no one is around to hear it. But I would rather not apply such a tight cordon around realism—I think many things, and many kinds of things, are real, including the "mind-dependent." All sorts of artifacts are real, I say: cars and rocket ships, paintings and bank statements, computers and board games, rituals of all kinds. These are real in their own properties and causal powers, not simply in virtue of their base metals, their natural woods or oils or chemicals, or the human actors who put them in play. *Realism*, as I use it, refers to anything that is *there* and can make itself felt. About realities, we can get things wrong: Karl

Popper's insistence on falsifiability pertains to the real, mind-independent or no. We can refer to the real; we can encounter it; we can learn more and correct our course. The real *resists* us; we stub our toes on it. Real objects work their effects on us, and we cannot simply think them away. We might even venture to extend realism to many elements thought to be "sub" or "super" real: to "accidents" or to social practices—a "social ontology"—should the hallmarks of "being there" and "making its effects felt" be satisfied, even in a rough and ready fashion. Perhaps a social practice, such as paying taxes, and a social organization, the Department of Revenue, have sufficient causal powers to make us speak of them as real. They most certainly cannot be thought away! But whatever we might say about extended cases, we want to affirm that for the spiritual and material realities, the sorts and kinds and types they exhibit are nearly unlimited. The real, I say, is a rich ocean, containing many kinds: not for me the "atoms and the void" or even "natural kinds and natural laws" only. No, the real is diverse, polymorphous, unimaginably fertile, and surprising. From an Infinitely Real and Fecund God pours forth such a torrent of realities, a rich cosmos, a feast. To think realism is to begin to think the Adventure who is God.

In this way, realism corresponds to St. Thomas's notion of the trace: realism is the sign that Someone is passing, though we do not know Who it is. It is the vestigium of the Holy Persons and Their Relation and order and unrepentant concreteness. It is a haunting of this bare earth. We might borrow St. Augustine's pregnant phrase here: metaphysical realism is a thing become sign. In this way the dogma of Trinity is the most rational of all doctrines. It is Ratio Itself. But we want to proceed carefully down this path. The light that Ludwig Wittgenstein has shone over our way illumines the main route we will pursue: the relation between secular speculative metaphysics and the doctrine of Holy Trinity will not be all of one kind or reduced to one comparison. We will not follow Paul Tillich's lead here, uncovering a method of correlation where a single *relatio* of question to answer, of human existence to Divine Ground, is recognized and established. Rather we will look for loose patterns, rules of thumb, or a commonsense awareness that we are in the same neighborhood, visiting the same streets. We are not aiming to conform to Karl Barth's strictures here, either. This is not a matter of "saying the same thing" or of solemnly declaring the single root of the dogma. Indeed, the point here is that the Mystery of Trinity is Self-Diffusing, Self-Giving, and It has communicated being in many and varied ways to the human intellect. We are not seeing many and varied *roots* of the dogma, but we are seeing the *echoes*, the resonance, the pattern, and family resemblance of Final Being in its finite and mortal beings.

Of course, this will ring the alarms of natural theology or the *Analogia Entis*, a special fear of Barth's in those early years. But we recall that the problem in the neighborhood is not a *fixed* relation and most certainly not a *causal* one. It does not follow the classic pattern of scholastic analogy, where likeness or proportion is recognized on the strength of a proper manifestation of a property to which everything else is related as cause or effect or sign of that proper expression. Nor does the commonsense relation we propose here follow on the Creative Power of God, who causes and brings about the creature. This is not a *single* joining together of being and Being, in which the dependent creature exhibits, as much as it is able, the Complete Being who just is God. Instead we have something like two complete systems, two "aspects" and entire modes of thought, two "ways of life," running on independent lines, that from time to time or over certain mountain passes or city trestles, draw near to one another, sound the same signal, and show signs of recognition or likeness.

But by and large, they run apart. Human beings, after all, can live in the creaturely realm of realism, in literature or in philosophy or in politics, undisturbed by Something passing by, majestically, humbly, far beyond our window sill; creatures can live there un-haunted and see only the figures and happenings and quarrels of the creaturely day. For the vision of the problem in the neighborhood, it is vital that this *relative* completeness be recognized. Creaturely reality enjoys its own integrity, its own finite autonomy. In metaphysical realism, we do not look for an incompleteness theorem, even should there be one in the physical or cultural realm lying beyond Kurt Gödel's mathematics. Unlike Tillich, or in different ways, unlike Karl Rahner, we are not thinking of the human realm as *open*, indeterminate, or a living query—however powerful that vision may be. Rather we are thinking of realism as an ordinary, full set of human convictions and topics—not closed in a final and irrefragable sense, not sealed or silent—but rather as a modestly autonomous field of human thought, following its own paths and toils. It might be possible to remain satisfied, perhaps completely so, by such human tasks. Our secular societies seem ready to enroll in such a modest, deflationary program. And we Christians should not assume there will be unshakeable obstacles to such small-scale satisfactions. This is not apologetics in the grand style! I do not have in mind here a *programmatic* relation of sign to Thing signified, a *structural* disturbance that would drive creaturely realism to find its Source and End. *That* is what correlation aims to do; and we should leave that task to others. Here we aim to look over the shoulders of cultural workers, those laborers in fields of realism, and to pick out the patterns as they emerge from an ordinary glance, a homespun comparison.

The metaphysical reality of Trinity, then, will be an Answer of an unsought sort. This is an odd relation, and it seems fitting for the idiosyncratic task we have taken to hand. For the problem in the neighborhood, the metaphysical realism that just is Trinity will remain a Mystery and a Hidden Good. This is a strange, piecemeal relation—but perhaps one that will strike a chord of remembrance all the same. We might think of this as the Solution we did not know to seek. It is the common experience of those who have been helped by others—by doctors or pastors or therapists or friends— that the aid they offer has not seemed to fit the need at all, at least at first, sometimes ever. The human state we call denial or the human affliction we call addiction is *constituted* by the delusive powers of the human heart and mind to find real help, indeed reality itself, unwanted and ill-suited to the world that sufferer has built. To be sure, creaturely realism is neither delusive nor enchained; it is rather a special kind of freedom in the human intellectual realm. But mutatis mutandis, the problem in the neighborhood will find Triune realism a Solution, a Confirmation, and a Consummation, only indirectly, only in a perfect but ill-fitting way. "So, this is what I was looking for!" such a realist might say. "I did not know it; I did not recognize that this was the Topic of my searching, the Answer to my investigations. They do not, indeed, seem like Answers; but rather Something Much More."

The Triune God is always Something More. We cannot say this too often; cannot praise it too highly; cannot stand, astonished, before it too long, amid the fire and thunder and ash of Almighty God. It is well to know the Lord and well to sing His praises, to recite and ponder and treasure His Powers and His Perfections; the knowledge of the Lord is the beginning of wisdom. But God is not simply, merely, plainly what we know. God is Something More. The Metaphysical Reality and Fullness that is the Triune Being is most certainly Mystery, a Hiddenness and Great Reserve. It dazzles. It opens out into Exceeding Darkness. But It is not just any Mystery. It is not Mystery per se. God is not a Puzzle Case, not even an Exalted and Holy Case. We do not affirm the consequent here: not every mystery, every riddle, every dark unknown is God. Almighty God, rather, is More. *That* is the Mystery. God is the Perfect Beyond, the Fullness, the Exemplar that outstrips, outfills every category, every ideal. He is Wisdom, Complete Ratio, Reason Itself—and More. He is the Good, the Perfect Good: the Reality that super-exceeds every good, the Superabundant Good, the Super-Celestial Bread. As Trinity God is Life, overpowering, fruitful beyond compare, a Wind from Beyond. This Ordered Wildness is God, the Triunity that cannot be contained. We praise, and we fall silent.

There is a relation between this Surpassing God and the realism we know on this earth, well beyond correspondence, well beyond the familiar patterns of promise and fulfillment or inauguration and completion; it is not linear or regular *in that sense*. "Eye hath not seen nor ear heard, neither have entered into the heart of man, the things which God hath prepared for them that love him" (1 Cor 2:9–10 AKJV). Indeed, they are not recognized but rather hidden: "We speak the wisdom of God in a mystery, even the hidden wisdom, which God ordained before the world unto our glory" (1 Cor 2:7 AKJV). The metaphysical realism that occupies some human authors shadows a Glory, a Weight and Saturation, that would startle, and unsettle, and undo the very thinkers who long for the real. Flesh and blood does not inherit the Kingdom, but rather, the mortal puts on immortality, and death puts on life, so the realism that drives our human longing for the substantial and credible must have dawning over it an Aspect suddenly new: the twinkling of an eye! We may in the end, or along the pathway, from time to time, spot this resemblance, see this pattern doubled and redoubled, our ears suddenly opened to the resonance, the mystic chord of memory, but we will exclaim: You are the One who Comes, and I knew it not! Realism is a Trinitarian trace in just this sense.

Now it is worth our while to think through carefully just why such a family resemblance is possible—probable—and permitted between divine and creaturely realisms. Just what is the Creator-creature relation that makes such a vision possible, likely, even compelling? It is just this: that the divine relatio to the creature is not uniform or simple or of one kind. It, too, is More. The relation of God to His creatures cannot be reduced to one and cannot be defined as one. This is a keen point and cuts all the way through theology to the fullness of the Divine Mysteries us-ward. The pull downward toward the base, the one thing, the one foundation or building block: this is among the strongest dynamics in human thought. "These are all that": reductive metaphysics from the time of Parmenides has longed to find the one, the one sort or kind, the one motion or cause, the one constituent that binds all and every. At the ground, all things are one—all material, all quarks and spin and charge, all sense impression, all clear and distinct idea, all construct. "All," we might say, is the antipode to the "More." The manifold is much more taxing to human thought than a simple nod to pluralism or diversity. Of course, we should give this nod! But to consider the world, itself and its kinds, not one thing but many, deep down, through and through, is an art that demands all our care. Christians have special reasons for pursuing the notion of metaphysical pluralism: they believe, as do Jews and Muslims, in the One God. Now this may startle, but the fundamental teaching of Israel, that the Lord our God is One, is not in truth and at the end a teaching about uniformity, reduction, and even less about a number, though it has from time to time been taken as so. In truth, it is the One God's Radical Unicity, His Utter Uniqueness and Trifold Unity that is Itself, in Its Superabundance, Beyond, always Beyond sameness. Triune monotheism is the Real Ground of diverse plurality.

We need not sort out here all that Augustine might mean by his maxim, that the "works of God toward us are one"; we can remain neutral for a time on this piece of Augustinia. What we do need to clarify in this place is the fundamental *schema*, the *pattern* that links God and cosmos, the form of linkage that joins Heaven and earth. I say: it is not one. When we affirm the radical declaration that "God is not in a genus," we affirm also that God's relation to creatures is not in a genus, not all of one kind. It is More than all that. Certainly, one does not *entail* the other; we do not find a systematic link here! Rather, we say that the Presence of the Triune Lord to His creatures follows the Infinite Life and Living Infinity who is God. The God-world relation is fruitful, many-sided, alive. It is too strong to say that this relatio is piecemeal or spontaneous or fragmentary: God is not the God of discord, of the arbitrary or scattershot; He is the God of Peace. And the God-world relation is not occasionalist. There *is* regularity, reliability, harmony, and intelligibility in this Divine Presence. In our world, there is the trace of Divine Order. But it is not all of one kind. We should not say, for example, that the Creator-creature relation is *causal*, or only so, though He is the world's Maker. Nor should we say that God relates to His world as Absolute Cause, though He victoriously brings things about. Nor should we say that everywhere, always, the Triune God relates as Sovereign or Victorious Power. Nor does He relate as Spirit, raising, elevating, drawing forward matter. God is not just Evolutionary Dynamism in His cosmos. He is not simply or only the Good, the Final Good, drawing the world to Himself as to its very own End. We do not seek or pick out a category or act to which all the Divine Relatio can be *reduced*.

Rather we say that the informal, crisscrossed, overlapping relations of the family resemblance shadow and remind and show forth the Elegantly Living, Free, and Self-Determining Presence of God to His creatures. To be sure, the Triune Lord brings about; He draws forward; He judges and stirs up; He hallows; He completes and consecrates and consummates: He the Lord does all these things. But He is not all Act or a single Act! And more, the Triune God comes to His cosmos in multiple relatio. He descends down through the categories of all being: He is the Transcendental One who communicates, in Free Incommunicability, His Perfections. He is the Incarnate Son, the God who is Sent. But He is not exhausted in Christology! He is the Holy Fire, the Searing Goodness that overspreads the world, enlivening, judging, hallowing. The Lord God is Present as Holy, Determining Himself over against all that is profane, Setting Himself apart, in the midst of Israel, in the midst of the temple. But He is not reduced to Spirit! And more, He is Present as Defiled, as the Offscouring of the world, as the Lost. He is Passed By, the Silent, the Forgotten and Invisible, Present as the Hidden One, the Being who is Unknown, Unheard. The Triune God is Abstract, Present to human thought as Idea, as Limit, as Absolute; He is Object, laid down in the religious ideation of human history. He is Present as Food and Drink, as Water from the Rock. The Triune God is all these; His relatio is just His Presence, His Infinite Life, shown around about us, always Rich, always Generative, always Good. In just this sense, God just *is* His own Relatio to the world.

But why should we say all this here? Is there not another time and place for all this rumination on the plural, odd-shaped, and diverse ways of God us-ward? Yes, indeed, there are many places! But these reflections belong here because they at ground and base are *Trinitarian*: they shadow the Threefold One. Not directly, certainly, or as a correspondence or uniform relation, but rather in a piecemeal, informal, and variegated way, this complex Presence of God in the world echoes the inner Reality of God. It is that astonishing! We are examining here the intellectual dignity of the dogma of Trinity. We are led to a form of realism that mirrors in a low-key and pluralistic way the metaphysical realism that just is God, His Real Relations and Infinite Life. And all this is not without resonance for the entire enterprise of theology itself! But the Divine Presence of God in the cosmos that He has made sets the pattern for all such focused and small-scale parables: He is the Eternally Rich God in His world, His Presence in the world. And He is such because He *is This*. He is Plural and Singular; He is Complex and Simple; He is Life, Generative and Proceeding; He is Sending and Sent; He is Difference as the One, the Utterly Unique, Utterly Formless Mystery. He is the Holy One. *This* is monotheism, Triune monotheism.

Let me borrow a leaf from the modern Thomists Ghislain Lafont and Gilles Emery. It is to these patient archivists of Thomas's treatise *De Deo Trino* that we owe the remarkable and incisive notion of redoublement, doubling or redoubling in the doctrine of Trinity. Emery writes:

> The study of God as principle is not determined by the aspect of unity or of Trinity, but rather is determined by the unique and entire reality of God (the three persons of one and the same essence) which is posed here in a theological synthesis resulting from the first two sections of the treatise. Regarding the first two sections, there is no question of a "one God" or of a "tri-God" but of God considered *under the aspect* of the essence and *under the aspect* of the distinction. [For that reason Emery hesitates to use the traditional names for the treatise of the *Prima Pars*, *De Deo Uno*, and *De Deo Trino*.] The nuance is important, because the structure set forth by Thomas poses simply the opportunity for a double consideration or a double approach to the God confessed by Christian faith. . . . In order to speak the Trinitarian mystery, it is

necessary always to employ two words, two formulas, in a reflection in two modes that joins here the substantial (essential) aspect and the distinction of persons (relative properties).[1]

The claim here is that the treatment of Trinity can only properly follow its course into the Mystery by speaking of Almighty God in two ways or patterns and with two vocabularies. The double treatises in Thomas's *Summa*, *De Deo Uno*, and *De Deo Trino*—should we label them such—far from atomizing or fragmenting the doctrine of God, follow the only path designated for a Triune Deity: redoubling. To quote Emery again: "Since the relations are really identical to the essence, the essence is not constituted by the relations: this totality (of our concepts), if one wishes to speak thus, would only be adequately expressed by the complex *redoublement* of our discourse joining the aspect of the divine substance and that of the relative property, this relative property being identical to the divine substance in the reality of God."[2] We might say that Emery echoes Barth's notion of interpretation: saying the Same Thing in other words. We retrace the Reality of God, each time using the insights, doctrine, and idiom proper to this Being, the Substance or Nature, on one hand, and the Persons or Modes, on the other. In both, we say the One God, but to say it fully, we say it twice. Perhaps reflection along these lines prompted the Reformed dogmatician Amandus Polanus to order his giant *Syntagma* along twofold lines, enunciating two polar attributes in order to say One. We want to consider carefully in this place why such twofold or divided speech might be required when speaking of God. Why this note of Complexity in the Utter Unique Simplicity of God?

Now we might be tempted to say that this is the limitation and frailty of human speech—and it may well be so that Polanus entertains such an approach. We could say that our Object, the Triune Lord, exceeds our idiom and tongue; *we* must use two, though our God is One. The tradition draws on this pattern heavily. We speak of "justice and mercy," and we conceive of them as two separate, perhaps competing traits; we affirm them both of the Good God, and we say that in Him "they are one." Or we might affirm that in our earthly life, temporality appears to rush by us as a stream, the future hurtling toward us, the past tumbling by and away. But in God, who is Eternal, all times are "open to His Eye," nothing is lost, all is One. Thomas himself defends Divine Simplicity, drawing on some of these traditional themes, but they are widespread indeed. And surely the elements of Holiness and Mystery that must attend all speech of Almighty God instruct us to respect the Infinite Distance that all human words must travel to reach and say and praise the Lofty One who dwells in the Full Sun of His own Unshadowed Being. But here we dare to say more.

We dare to say that there is a Resemblance, Something Like, Something More than redoublement in God Himself. *This* is realism in the doctrine of God. Here we see our first "family resemblance." We are not, then, finding an exact parallel—what the schoolmen would call a "univocal" predication—nor do we assume that *number* now belongs to God in a way that we identify with the real numbers or integers. We are not supposing that God is *Material* in this sense, as it seems do some Mormons or Spinozists. God, I believe, does not belong under the category "quantity," to borrow Thomas's language for the moment. We do not seek here a single point of comparison, a definite likeness, a common "point of contact." Just this is what we mean when we say that metaphysical realism is a commonsense, piecemeal parable of God's own Reality! Yet it is a *real* resemblance. But to what? Really, this is the question of all theological language, all longing for the True God. In this small space of that vast endeavor, we ask about doubling. To be sure, Trinity as a technical doctrine has elements we would in ordinary ways label double or twofold. We must take up in our turn the great themes of Procession and Mission, and they appear to be two. We count: Generation and Spiration; Incarnation and Outpouring of the Spirit—or, to echo Emery more closely, Essence and Subsisting Relations. Is this what we mean by doubling? Is this what we mean by resemblance in realism? To what do we refer when we speak of the Complex or the Double in the Awesome Mystery who is God?

We must speak here—we must dare this step—but we must not say too much. The Complex or the Double must be *there*; it must be Real. And we must know, confess, and adore it. But we must treat each in its proper order. There are many tidy things we can say at this frightening cliff that is realism in Christian dogma. We can draw on well-worn scholastic tools: We know, for example, that an Attribute is true; we do not know how it is true. Or we can say, we do not know what the Property is, but we know what it is not; we know its mode in our earthly realm, though we do not know the Divine Mode of the Utterly Simple God. These are trusty tools! We would not travel far in any theology, or not in much comfort, without them. But we will not find them of much use here. For our fundamental claim in this form of intellectual legitimacy is that the metaphysical realism we see as theology's kin cannot be applied or recognized in a tidy fashion. It is not one thing, not one mode, not one relatio. We here dare to say that the ordinary, commonsense realism of our intellectual life, and the theological realisms of the God-world relation, find their Source, and More than their Source, in God, the Triune Lord. The Real Relations in God, we dare to say, are not quite tidy; They are more Real than that. How do we properly speak, whisper but out loud, of such Unconstrained Life? Just what kind of realism do we imagine here?

Trinity, we say, is the confession that there is Difference or Diversity in God. Just this is the doctrine of the Divine Persons.

This is a Permanent, Vital, and Living Element of Him as Real. He *is* this Diversity; *this* is His Unique Oneness. We see something of this kind, glimpse some Aspect, in Holy Scripture, first and principally, that unique Book of the Acts and Being of Almighty God. It was the surface structure, the pattern, the large-scale form that led us to say that in this Book, we find God as its Author. So here we see in creaturely life, in the very notion of the Day, repeated yet new, the Eternity extended, the swarming and winged and fertile things springing forth from the Word, their diversity of kinds, their breadth and particularity, their concrete existence—in it all, we see a realism that echoes in its own small voice the Reality who is the Creator. There is the Living Pouring Forth, the Fertility, the Swarming Infinity that is God. There is the *Concreteness*, the hard Singularity that is the Relentless Realism of God, His own Mode, His Being. There is His Wisdom and Power, Invisible in the visible things that are made. As we catch a glimpse of the Divine Processions in the mighty Days of creation, the life and the Sabbath rest, so we seek a pattern of the Divine Doublement in the diversity of living things.

§3.1. Diversity in Creaturely Life

Let us begin by thinking more carefully about the reality of creaturely diversity or difference. Here is a fundamental problem in metaphysical realism, and it will not let us alone. For many reasons we would do well to turn aside and consider it with full attention. Why is there not just one kind of thing? Indeed, why is there not just one—one being, one organism, one thing at all? Note that we are asking now about the converse of the earlier worry about reductionism. The search of an underlying unity or sameness to which all things can be identified or returned is the underside of the question of pluralism and difference. There is a stubborn facticity to difference that will not allow it to be simplified or resolved without remainder. But can we *think* diversity? Can we understand the reality and integrity of objects in their particularity, their singularity? Can we know the individual? Can we know that one as different, as unique? This is a nest of conceptual problems in the constitution and knowledge of real objects that bears on the very notion of the *fundamental*. At the fundament, are there many things—or just one? At base, is reality plural? Is there rather only one kind, one order, one dynamism or law? What is the nature, at bottom and in the end, of the real?

Consider the very notion of the individual. Is there some element or some act that makes something or someone singular? The problem of individuation may be as many-sided and troubled as the very idea of substance; it is certainly a vast sea in the history of philosophy. A favorite candidate for individuation has been "matter": *this* flesh and *these* bones make me the individual human being I am. (But perhaps not the *person* I am!) This time-honored solution to our question has a pleasing symmetry about it. Natural kinds reproduce their kind, but the matter involved in replication determines the individual that emerges. It reminds us of the full battery of scholastic metaphysics: of form and matter; of prime matter; of kinds and artifacts; of potency and act; of causes and motion. We can be neutral here about such armature—we are not seeking to solve metaphysical dilemmas here. Indeed, we might hope to shelve all this apparatus in favor of a Scotist individuation by property, by "thisness" or "*haecceitas.*" But it is instructive in our dogmatic task to see that metaphysics in the West has been born along by a Tendenz for the class, the kind, the universal. The individual and its particularity has been assigned, by and large, to membership in these categories, and the diversity of singulars has been thought of less rational interest—perhaps irrational, unknowable!—and of less metaphysical salience. It does not take a philosopher of Søren Kierkegaard's stature to tell us that the individual and its difference appear unintelligible *in themselves*, however factual they may be. What, after all, do we conceive or think about the individual? How does the singular encounter us? Perhaps we think of a particular tree, a particular animal: we note its shape, color, or heft; a pattern of movement; a disfigurement. Perhaps we give it a name, perhaps as Saul Kripke famously noted, by some causal tie or association: the river Dart lending its name to the town Dartmouth, for example. (Names will do far more than this in Kripke's program, but here we think only of the origin and source.)[3] It seems, perhaps, that this individual name, perhaps with color and weight and trait trailing alongside, could give us knowledge of the particular—knowledge by acquaintance, even, as Russell would style this.[4] But we have reason to doubt this. For it seems that we encounter only kinds and forms and sorts—brown-ness, poundage, fan-shape, limb and coat—all determined and assigned by the indexical (*this* brown patch; *that* heavy coat) as though struggling to find words for the singular as it rises up before our eyes. Rahner revealed his idealist leanings when he argued that we could not know matter per se—not *as matter*, even less as *this* matter—but rather only the concept, the form and definition, the description under which it lies. These are only examples of epistemic problems that arise from a search for the individual in the midst of metaphysical realism—sketches and hints, only. We have not even begun to fight! Identity conditions, persistence conditions, problems of composition and constitution—the metaphysical struggle for the real is inexhaustibly complex.

But we cannot leave this area of reflection without considering the human individual, the place of difference among our kind. It would be a poor theology that did not recognize in the varying schools of secular realism a controversy central to all humane disciplines: the place and stature of diversity within humanity, the place and stature of individual difference. We might think here of the intense intellectual conflicts about the human individual and the movement often termed *individualism* in modern Western societies. Tillich's own structural reflections on the "ontological element of individuation and participation" pay tribute to the deep anxiety about the singular in a corporate, mass, and totalized culture.[5] Yet it would be difficult to pick up a current work of social criticism that did not name individualism as a hallmark, danger, and rot at the center of post-Enlightenment societies. It seems that the human individual does not rest easy within humanistic disciplines these days. The long flowering of individual distinctiveness, exalted from the Romantics to the personalists and existentialists, seems spent now, yet the demand and problem of difference remains. The deep longing, known with special keenness in our flattened world, to be known as distinctive, to be not a type or a class but an individual, *this very one*, abides in the midst of every call for the holistic, the organic, and the group. It is the ache at the bottom of every intimacy broken that the irreducible inwardness of each was not known, perhaps never known, but all was projection and wish and illusion, a portrait defaced and defiled or, worse, perhaps all too good. We might say that the modern epidemic of loneliness does not stem only from the atomized individual; it could never be that simple. The group, too, the family, the kind and class: Can these know the I? Or will "family resemblance" be all the comfort I can ever receive?

These intellectual and all-too-human personal quarrels over individual difference have found a special lodging in contemporary feminism. Just how does the feminist movement regard the individual; what is the place of the particular within a broad emancipatory cause? Naturally the elements of participation and resistance that mark all large-scale social movements touch the women's movement as well. A drive to incorporate, even submerge, individual difference within the aims and discipline of the group can be found in feminist activism as well as theory. There, too, the cult of personality is diagnosed as a dangerous temptation and the particular voice, the particular intellectual and organizer is welcomed by one hand while feared by the other. Solidarity, likeness, recognition of kinship, woman to woman: these have been mainstays of feminism's second wave, in Europe and in North America. Yet the neuralgic point Marxists have identified as the "question of leadership" troubles feminism as well. Early in the women's movement of the postwar era in North America individual leaders arose, and were made, who became immediately recognized in every newspaper and on countless TV screens: Angela Davis, Gloria Steinem, Betty Friedan, Kate Millett—who did not know their faces or remember famous lines they spoke, what controversies were sparked by their words, how criticism welled up against them on every side, both inside the movement and out? These individual women were admired, pushed forward, designated as spokeswomen, and castigated for their prominence. They had individual opinions that were unpredictable. But could an individual feminist break ranks? Was criticism or skepticism of central tenets possible or welcome? Such worry over the "leader" spread throughout the early days of the movement. Could consciousness-raising groups have leaders? Was hierarchy unacceptable, per se, and the individual the leading edge of unequal power, of domination? Should feminists play competitive sports and teach others how to excel in them? How should the history of humankind be rewritten and revolutionized by the passion and analysis of the women's movement? Should prominent women be remembered, honored, celebrated—the contributions of pioneers to what that generation called "herstory"? Or was this a symptom of the problem revolutionaries discovered in oppressive regimes: that the singular, the favored, the fortunate are allowed through, up into the bright light of fame and accomplishment, while the masses remain chained. Or worse, do not a privileged few become the ideal or definition of womanhood as a kind, portrayed and caricatured as elite, educated, and seamlessly bourgeois? Here the individual stands for the whole but stands in the way, too. Just where are the women of other classes, the proletarian women, the women of other ethnicities, women of color? Why are these women not the face of feminism? Feminism in European and North American cultures since the nineteenth century has shared with other emancipatory movements the conviction that the individual—her resistance and courage, her difference in the midst of conformity—was vital to a mass movement but dangerous, too.

We might consider, as well, the very notion of this class noun *woman* and its relation to the individuals who may exhibit, instantiate, represent it. Is there such a reality, such a woman? Is it a natural kind? Does it have essential properties? If so, are they biological, cultural, and mutable? What is the possibility of difference within the universal, womanhood? Does difference, variation, diversity belong to a defined common group, and if so, how? In the widely read and influential philosophical text *Inessential Woman*, Elizabeth Spelman offered a radical, analytic critique of universals in feminist theory. This is realist metaphysics with a literary flair and political passion. We might think of it as an early example of what we now call critical race theory, a pioneering feminist treatise on the complexity and urgency of *thinking difference*. Spelman opens with a lovely evocation of Iris Murdoch's *The Nice and the Good*. The Platonizing atmosphere of Murdoch's fiction serves Spelman well. She recalls Murdoch's literary character Uncle Theo as he sits ocean side:

> The beach is a source of acute discomfort to Uncle Theo. While the children's noise and exuberance bother him, what really seems to make him most anxious is the multiplicity of *things*. As if twinness [his twin niece and nephew, also at the shore] weren't already enough of an ontological disturbance, there are on the beach all those pebbles, each clamoring in its particularity, the totality of them threatening the intelligibility, the tractability, the manageability of the world. Theo is a man who can only negotiate the possibility of plurality if the many can be reduced to a few or, best of all, to one. The horror of the manyness of the pebbles could then be stilled by the awareness that they are all instances of a single thing, pebblehood.[6]

Discussing the conceptual anguish pluralism induces in Uncle Theo—and mutatis mutandis, feminist theory—Spelman introduces the delicious term *plethoraphobia* to describe Theo's deep unease over the different, the multiple. This phobic response to the individual, on one hand, and the multiple, on the other, is traced back to its Attic Greek roots: "What is the world *really* made of? Do we get closer to an answer to this question by noting the manyness of the pebbles, or by reflecting on that fact that though there are *many* pebbles, there is only *one* kind of thing, the kind of thing that they all are, namely a pebble? . . . According to Plato, this is what the true *philosopher* would say, even though the man in the street, and surely almost any woman anywhere, will most likely be drawn to the pebbles they can see and touch, and will think that what they can see and touch is what is most real."[7] Here Spelman anchors the problems of feminist theory directly into the complex of pluralism, reduction, and difference. At the edge of her discussion stand venerable dilemmas in epistemology: the knowledge of particulars, nominalism, and individuation. But the centerpiece of Spelman's work remains *woman, this* metaphysical term, its definition, yes, but even more the relation of this kind and abstract class with the women who live here among us, diverse and multiple creatures, of all sorts and conditions, and (though Spelman is silent on this point) images, too, of the Good God. Spelman sums up her worry about difference and unity as a form of "paradox":

> This leads us to the paradox at the heart of feminism: any attempt to talk about all women in terms of something we have in common undermines attempts to talk about the differences among us, and vice versa. . . . The focus on women "as women" has addressed only one group of women—namely, white middle-class women of Western industrialized countries. So the solution . . . has been to conflate the condition of one group of women with the condition of all and to treat the differences of white middle-class women from all other women as if they were not differences. . . . Paradoxically, in feminist theory it is a *refusal* to take differences among women seriously that lies at the heart of feminism's implicit politics of domination. . . . [There is] a cautionary tale for feminists who insist that underneath or beyond the differences among women there must be some shared identity—as if commonality were a metaphysical given, as if a shared viewpoint were not a difficult political achievement. . . . Thus the phrase "as a woman" is the Trojan horse of feminist ethnocentrism.[8]

Spelman gives us a rich and stylish reading of the complex interplay of kind and difference—though she is suspicious of that beloved term, *difference*—unfolding historical examples from the Western Attic tradition, from philosophers, misogynistic and (rarely) feminist, and from theorists of the women's movement and political activists at work in the combustion center of second-wave feminism. Her argument is complex and many-sided; we only touch the surface here. But in our investigation of realism, epistemic and above all metaphysical, we find the haunting significance of plurality and difference most keenly recognized and prized among feminist and critical race theorists; for them, our problem is also—in their own idiom—theirs.

Let me reflect on Spelman's work in my own idiom for a moment. I would ask: Is the universal category of being woman real? And not only whether it is, but what it is: Does *woman* have an essence and essential properties? What sort of individuation should theologians, should feminists, embrace in their realist theories; how can difference be thought under such political, moral, and conceptual conditions? Now, of course, we can seize on political elements directly: Can there be a woman's movement should we deny universals and classes altogether? It does not take the sophistication of *Gender Trouble* to see that the common and the unitary make political action far easier or perhaps possible altogether. And it is not clear, programmatically, that a universal term, such as *woman* or *African American*, would demand a definition, a conceptual filling out, in order to drive, organize, and unify a political movement. Now, we may suspect that the educated few who produce theory and analysis for social movements may quietly smuggle themselves into the universal definition; hence, the charge of "Trojan horse" for such innocent-looking concepts, standing quietly and well-behaved along the shoreline. Perhaps such suspicions are richly deserved—just this, as Spelman shrewdly notes, is what we mean by *privilege*. For our aims here, however, the problem in the neighborhood remains with the realist problem about diversity and difference. Can we "think difference" when we consider the female members of humankind, when we consider womanhood?

This is extraordinarily difficult to answer! In just this way, the problems of the abstract and the concrete, of the unitary and the individual, the one and the many reassert themselves in the secular field of political and feminist theory. In this many-sided attempt to find intellectual and cultural legitimacy for the Mystery of the Holy Trinity, we have landed firmly on the dilemmas of metaphysical realism and the common struggles such a conceptual program undergoes when it considers the stubborn pluralism of the world before us. It is not a part of the structure or agenda of the problem in the neighborhood to propose a clumsy solution to the feminist theory of difference by turning to Trinitarian dogma; I do not intend apologetics of that unsullied kind! Rather the aim here is to note how the very structures of intellectual realism show kinship, familiarity with the deep, rich contours of Trinitarian theology. And these structural conflicts are everywhere visible in Spelman's analysis of feminist theory.

It seems that realism, for feminism, requires a kind of redoublement all its own. The paradox of feminism, as Spelman sets it out, seems to require a twofold analysis: first, laying out the unity of "woman as woman" and then marking the diversity among women, the concrete, the different, the singular. It seems that feminist theory demands, as does critical race theory, a complete description of the reality of gender and race as a unity, a kind or universal, a living commonality, and a second complete description of gender and race as distinct, diverse, and particular. These may well be the "aspects" of being that Emery notes in his definition of redoublement, but that may be too anodyne. It seems that the lived reality of human beings, the metaphysical realism that is human creatures, requires a twofold *reality*; nothing less will do. Both must be real and have the unmistakable tang of the dynamic and the sturdy. We have something like the recursive account of Divine Being and Person or of Triune Person to Person: each is exhaustive, whole, complete, yet there must be more. It is not that woman or womanhood is not real simply because it is common. No, perhaps we should say that the unity among female human beings, the kind term that marks us as members of a family, exists, perdures, survives change, even revolutionary change. Perhaps it is possible, conceivable, that the category woman is itself immaterial, that is, wholly rational. Its realism may lie in what an earlier Kantian generation called its full "ideality." Were that so, we would not demand or expect that the discrimen of physical difference be exemplified there. Such difference, particularity, and singularity would belong to the second doubling, to womanhood as concrete. In this initial exemplification, its ideality, woman would be real as a form of being that expresses sexual dimorphism. It would be finite—in my terms, creaturely—and would gather together and set in contrast this form of humanity against the male. So it may be, as Augustine and Barth taught, that sexual difference will survive death and resurrection life.

That such a nature cannot be seen, that it is "being in general"; that it carries properties that seem at odds with one another, different yet somehow the same; that it is hidden though real: all this will not startle the feminist who is a Christian, for all this lies akin to the complex known as Trinity. Christians will think of the resemblance to the Unicity of God, the Perfect Unity, and this Deity's Predicates. It seems that such Perfect Oneness could not even receive Predicates: How can Being Itself be determined or particularized? It seems, too, that the complete Illocality of Divine Being, Its Immateriality and Universality, makes God less real, inert, insubstantial, invisible; Something far less than concrete being. But this is not so. The Oneness of God is the very marrow of Israel's Confession and, in just that way, the Ground and Grace of the church. God is Most Real Being; *Ens Realissimus.* The Divine Simplicity, Perfect Universality, and Unity of God does not impair but rather names the exceeding Reality of this One. Just so, we might consider the lesser reality of creaturely unity—womanhood— as no impairment to its facticity, nor impediment to its "predicates" and particular determinates. Unity does not exhaust the being of womanhood; it is fully and exhaustively real and exists as plural, diverse, particular.

We might wonder, too, about the sources for such abstract accounts of being and for the relation of these abstractions to the particular and diverse: How might feminist theory instruct us here, too, in rational problems in Trinitarian doctrine? Spelman teaches us to ask: Just what is the status of this kind term *woman*? How have we formulated such a grand, ideal concept? Have we taken the via of remotion here, removing from all living females the traits that individuate so that the remaining abstraction just is *womanhood*? Can this—should this—be done? All knowledge, Thomas is fond of reminding us, arises from our senses; feminist theory appears to be Aristotelian and empiricist in just this sense. We gather women together in schools, meeting rooms, playgrounds, and church parlors to discuss topics common to women's lives. This very common, ordinary, and everyday event remains a conceptual nightmare. In what way are these individual human beings women? Do we quietly, implicitly perform the intellectual act as old as Athens—to search for what is common to several individuals, distill that, and elevate it to a definition or essence? Would I, as a woman, belong to such a group because of some bodily trait—is that what "as a woman" means? Or is there a symbol system, a universe of practice and inhibition and duty that I inherit and perpetuate, that names me as a woman, qualifies me as a member of that set? Readers of *Huckleberry Finn* will remember the pivotal moment when Huck is unmasked as a boy, attempting to sew "as a girl." Or readers of classic feminist texts will remember the jarring insight of Iris Marion Young's essay "Throwing Like a Girl," a phrase at once bodily and searingly cultural. It is the rare adult who cannot summon up an occasion in which she was reminded or reprimanded that such behavior, attitude, or language is not "proper," not "ladylike"—what a term!—not "how a girl should act." And perhaps, too, we can recall the sweet moments when we seem to belong, to succeed in entering the mystical club called woman, to confidently walk through that door, to borrow an image from Spelman herself. How fragile this belonging! Yet how "natural," organic, and compulsive it seems, all the same! From these widespread, subtle, and all-too-familiar examples stem the notion of the "sex-gender distinction," an important element of Spelman's work and much modern feminist and gender theory.

Yet we in North America are learning and relearning gender as it appears to be at once more fluid and more malleable than earlier generations imagined as well as more stubborn, more burdensome, and more ill-suited than many of us recognized and some silently endured. Gender appears to echo Spelman's paradox: it is given, enforced, and "inscribed" yet also chosen, affirmed, and resisted. Hence arises the very odd conviction, also widespread and everyday, that some women are womanlier than others. It seems that membership in that universal is not given, stable, or determined but rather, in Simone de Beauvoir's famous words, "women are made, not born." It seems then that this universal, womanhood, is not abstracted from individual women, gathered together and compared, their traits drawn up and pruned to a common essence. Rather, it seems that *woman* is a *heuristic*, an ideal form, a prison house not of one's own making, a sentence—or a prize. If such is true—and the history of cultural anthropology might awaken us to this conviction—the unity of being that is woman-ness has never been realized. Rather, the women's movement, even in this postfeminist age, thrives from the recognition that individuals, the diverse and particular, do not form but rather are driven away from the universal that should be their natural home.

So, after all this reflection on real, natural kinds, it appears, then, that nominalism must be correct, epistemically, morally, and politically. If feminist theory has shown us anything, it must be—we seem driven to say—that only the concrete and particular are real. They alone are the Ens Realissimus, the most Real Being. We must have individuals, perhaps of female embodiment, who live out their life spans in relation to the means of production in a linguistic and ethnic culture or a way of life that is adapted, resisted, and adopted with companionship, with sickness and health, with the joy and sorrow that cross each life, and with an end that marks the finality of a singular, unrepeatable life. Spelman seems inclined to accept this verdict: she notes that commonality is a "political achievement" and may arise from careful, attentive, lifelong "apprenticeship" to the study and support of difference, to the indissoluble and radical singularity of each life, each community. We might think of this as an extension and sharpening of de Beauvoir's maxim: the unity of womanhood is made through moral and political alliance, not born. Perhaps the lesson Christians might spy in this nominalistic turn within feminist theory is this: Christians should begin, in effect, with the Concrete, the Persons and Their Relations. We move from there to the Processions and Nature, the Unity; but the primary reality remains the Personal. Political action springs from an encounter with the singular—with each pebble, one by one—and we learn, perhaps after long struggle, perhaps not at all, to recognize commonality as the singulars define them and set them out. "As a woman" is the end of all our travels, not the beginning. This may well be in feminist analysis and politics—but a Christian feminist, as I am, would hesitate before affirming such metaphysical austerities.

For the Mystery of Trinity runs in Its own Regal way, at times parallel to these political struggles, at times not, but always shining a generous light over this rocky terrain. As the doctrine of the

Triune God teaches that Deity is at once and both Concrete and Universal, Singular and Abstract, Differing and One, feminists and critical race theorists might take heart: realism can embrace, fully and exhaustively, both elements; instantiate and exemplify both. This is the metaphysical confidence the Christian faith might give to secular theory. But it is not all one way! For we Christians might take heart, too, from the recognition that the pattern of Triune Realism does not spring from theology alone. Rather that pattern— the search for the particular and the universal, the singular and the abstract—haunts secular reason as well. Just that is the problem in the neighborhood. To think deeply about the real, to encounter the objects in our midst, the lives displayed in their multiplicity on every side, is to be humbled by the mystery of the singular. It is not simply that human individuals we have known all our lives can startle and surprise us, and should, until the day we see them no longer. Of course, a human life is unpredictable, nonalgorithmic. It is rather that the singular within a complex cosmos—the organic and the inorganic, the very large and the very small, the many-celled and the single—each is conceptually strange, mesmerizing, itself a mystery. Its story, each by each, seems never spent, never fully told. And that those singulars seem at the same time to *belong*, by origin or nature, to some class or kind, and that those kinds can yield knowledge, even control or prediction: this, too, is the wonder of the real. For some metaphysicians, causal powers are a marker, perhaps *the* marker, of the real; I have endorsed it as one hallmark of the real, and kinds show themselves rich in causal powers. They teach us about our world; they define and exclude; they lead us to cures of disease, to causes of war, and to the rise of species; kinds and their definitions beget the orderly structure of reproduction and the theory of production. Just as with the singular, the natural and artificial kinds seem, in the end, to be all there is.

It is what we know and what there is to know. The singular and the multiple: both just are.

Now, this is what we mean by a problem in the neighborhood, by what we might term a *secular parable* of the Holy Trinity. Note the constraints here: we are not claiming that secular, political theory is Trinitarian or that feminism leads to aporiae that can yield only to Trinitarian metaphysics. No, there is nothing so direct, so straightforward, as all that at work here. We do not intend something more discrete and subtle, either. The aim is not to imply, artlessly, that all along realists of varying secular stripes are working away at the dogma of Trinity, avant là lettre, building up metaphysical structures that will be shown, in some magnificent dénouement, to be Nature and Person, Trifold Being in secular disguise. This is not secular question leading to theological answer. It is not a synthetic judgment, much less an analytic one. Rather, we say that those who think deeply about metaphysical realism will find themselves in the neighborhood, exhibiting family resemblances: they will discuss topics and structures, uncover problems, and search for schemas and solutions that will strike a chord with Christian realists. Theologians of the Trinity will feel at home there and see that the problems they face do not stand alone. And this comradeship will do theology good.

For we will see that the Mystery of Trinity does not demand a retreat behind the walls of seminary and convent and parish; this dogma need not receive its cultural legitimacy from Christian sources alone (though Holy Scripture remains final ground). Rather, the deep and controverted reflection on realism that takes place within secular systems of thought show striking kinship to problems in Trinitarian doctrine. This is not quite ad hoc apologetics, beloved by Barthians; really, it is more piecemeal than that. The rationality of this dogma will emerge in such comparisons and show the articulated structure of realism that awaits all who investigate the true and the real. And should this not be so? For Being Itself communicates Itself, the most Generous Giver, pouring Its own Reality down through the limitations and the pale light of our world and our kind, down, down to our darkness, breathing Life, even here, even among the dead. So, we would discover comradeship with all who search for the real amid the fraudulent and deceptive. In our longing to set forth proper Trinitarianism, we would join ranks with those who investigate the facts and depths of galaxies and protons; with those who refuse all sham or easy consolation; with those who seek the true and the real, though it cost them security or rank or approval; with all discoverers and explorers, all diagnosticians and analysts, all logicians and supremely, all metaphysicians; with novelists and poets of the real; with those who love the "counter, original, spare and strange"; with all those who with eagerness or grave reluctance hear and see what they would rather not: with all these realists, Christians are family and kin. And their moral and conceptual problems echo and illumine ours. We watch them at work; we look over their shoulders at the riddles they pursue. And we recognize them. We walk their streets, visit their neighborhoods; we are at home. They must wrestle with elements that stand not far from the Kingdom for they, too, are considering Being as such—though in idiom and aim, they live in a far country.

§3.2. The Rational Structure of Trinity

But now comes the reckoning. Have we now entered so fully into the *vestigia Trinitatis* that we have lost our way? Have we now fully rationalized the dogma of Trinity, such that it remains Mystery no longer and stands fully open to our mind's eye, asking for no revelation, no healing, no elevation of grace? Many more examples of the rational kinship of realists to Trinitarians might be adduced here. But we should pause before hurtling forward with these parallel examples—for a Christian doctrine that goes wrong at this intersection cannot be made right; it is wholly lost, however fine its surroundings. Has this common alternative in truth left us in danger of losing ties with Christian teachings on Divine Revelation, on grace, and on Truths exceeding human knowing? Have we in the end, and at grave risk, rationalized the dogma of Trinity? What is the proper place and rank of reason within Trinity? We must take care here.

What does it mean that God is Logos, Ratio? This, too, is what it means to think about the Triune Persons. That is where we must begin. Almighty God is not Being solely or simply Ens Realissimus, though, to be sure, He is these. He is *Rational Being*; He is the Inexhaustible Goodness of Rational Being. Now, we must think carefully what it means to affirm these truths. It might be possible—plausible, perhaps—to affirm all this as a collection of *predicates* or *properties* of the One God. We could say, that is, that the Gracious Lord has a Divine Nature and can be "known under a description" or under a list of defining categories: God is Rational, God is Wise and Good, God is Eternal. We might prescind from the "is of Identity" here and simply reflect on these as Names or Qualia, Characteristics of the Living God. It seems that as readers of Holy Writ, as faithful Christians—or, more properly, faithless and forgiven ones—we might seize on identifying traits, marks, or properties of the God who has graciously encountered us, in the books of Scripture and table. This is what God is like! we might exclaim. How He can surprise us, startle and judge, overwhelm and tenderly teach us, draw near in times of sorrow and terror, receive and shield us: *this* is our God; we have waited for Him. He is *this*

One and not another. The doctrine of God, that is, can be built up out of identifying descriptions, and we come to know this Gracious One through His meeting us, as Creator and Lord. Thomas Aquinas, it seems, has followed just this path when he leads us in the *Prima Pars* to know and love the One God, *De Deo Uno*. And when our fellow creatures awaken to this Reality, when the shock of earthly life and loss, its beauty or its cruelty, weighs heavy on them, or when its brutal foreshortening in a world of bare things threatens to empty existence of all purpose, then we will wish to speak of this God, to identify Him, to teach others His Ways and Nature. He is Rational; He is Good, the very Best; He is Love Itself. All this must be defended, warranted, welcomed! It is a cold, rationalizing heart that does not recognize the depth of faith, of longing, and of startled joy that springs from knowing the very Character of our Living God. But we have not penetrated to the deepest Mystery of this Lord or followed His teachings to the far reaches when we have said all this.

For God is not a Persona, a Character, or an Individual *in this sense*. He is not an Actor among many, not a Personality who waits to be drawn forward out of His deep reserve; He is not Limited, Finite, or Set Over Against or in Opposition. The Almighty Lord is not in a genus, does not belong to a kind or sort, even the singular; does not depend; does not need; does not come to an end. He is not a Particular. The True God is without form or likeness, without image in heaven or on earth; He is Radically Unique. He is the Holy One. Our task, our great permission and gift, is to think this thought.

If God is wholly Rational, Logos and Word, then it seems that the intellect probing this thought is fully licensed to make rational argument for the existence of this Benevolent Rationality, this Holy Trinity. It looks as though this dogma, far from being above or beyond reason, is the most rational doctrine of all, indeed the

Source and Exemplar of all logical thought. It appears that Trinity is the last doctrine to be investigated only by faith; rather, it seems to be the first and best candidate for a fully rational exposition and grounding. And, indeed, we can find some of this reasoning in the tradition. Thomas, for example, argues that God is the Most Rational Being, wholly Luminous and Intelligible in Himself. This he says in partial support of an Anselmian-like argument in the *Proslogion*. (I say "Anselmian-like" as I believe that had Thomas read the *Proslogion* directly, he would have registered more cogent and persuasive objections than the ones he did in the *Prima Pars*.)[9] St. Anselm in both the *Monologion* and *Proslogion* develops robust rational arguments for God's existence and Triunity, and unless we are willing to credit Barth's appeal to a revealed Name, we seem to stand here before a reasoned argument for a Rational God. Richard St. Victor's defense of Trinity based on an analysis of love or St. Bonaventure's on the exhaustive relations of divine mediation might be taken, too, as rational warrants for a Trifold God. Yet all this hardly amounts to a claim that the Holy Trinity can be known by unaided reason. *That* palm must be awarded to G. W. F. Hegel, who, it seems, held that thinking itself—its structure, logic, and motion—was Trinitarian. *Geist* is Trinity: this is both a deliverance of reason and the form of reason itself.

Now, what should we say about all this? On one hand, it seems that a doctrine of the fall should enter the lists here: perhaps only unfallen reason could think God as Trinity unaided by grace— and traditional Christians were offended by that presumption of Hegel's as much as anything else. But on the other hand, sin must not be allowed *positive* work in dogmatics; only realities, created and Increate, can serve this end. So, we remain face to face with this great question of Trinitarianism: Is the Rational God, the Holy Trinity, known by reason?

I believe that natural reason can glimpse elements or rational conceptual structures ingredient in Trinitarian dogma; it cannot see the Trinity as a living and integrated whole. The Divine Trinity can be known, in its living Unity, only by faith and through Scripture, because Trinity is a dogma of God's *Holiness*. The vestigia Trinitatis tell us, through traces, that Someone has passed by but not Who that One is. We can rationally grasp Identity and Difference, we can intellectually motivate a dialectic of the Abstract and the Concrete, and we can glimpse the far shore of Reality's Benevolence and Wisdom. But we do not arrive at, or ground rationally, the Living and Holy One, who is Self-Offered and Consummated in the Spirit, the Father of every Good and Perfect Gift. Sacrifice is *given* to Israel; the Divine Names are *given* in the Gospel. This is the Living One, Father, Son, and Holy Spirit, where all the foretastes, glimpses, and echoes receive their Infinite Resolution, Completion, and Rest. We know Holiness because He comes to us to stand before us, a Devouring Fire. This inexhaustible Life exceeds all our rational investigations because who God is, and what God is—Holy Triune Sacrifice—can only be *encountered*. It invades our world, commands our heart and mind and strength. Trinity is Event, the Thrice Holy God, who is Utterly Unique, His Own to give. His Reality—this "Being-There," and His mighty working—exist as Holy Life and He manifests that in us, in our intellect and spirit. *This* is our God; we have waited for Him. This is the existential moment in all dogma, and it is essential, unsurpassed.

We are set on this earth to contemplate this Reality, the Formless One, beyond all likeness, who is Truth and Goodness, the Living God. Just this is to think Holiness. It is to think Trinity. But where have we arrived in this utterly odd and unfamiliar pilgrimage of thought? What does it mean to affirm that God is Rational and Good *in this strange sense*? We are asked now to leave behind our home countries, our earthly goods and kinds, and travel to this far place, to ascend to it, where genera and class and property fall away, and Luminous Being shines forth, Infinite, Majestic, Utterly Strange. This is the Fire and Dark Light that Gregory of Nyssa finds at the end of Moses's ascent, the Cloud that covers and veils but discloses, too, the Unsearchable Being of God. It is to think through the grand narratives in Israel's history—the movement of prophets and kings and peoples, rising up and gathering at the seashore, traveling and camping by stages, those soldiers and midwives and sojourners, all alive under the Eye of Heaven, the One who keeps watch over Israel—to think through them and into them, to the Other Side, the *Jenseits*, that we discover the Being that is Beyond. We contemplate Israel's God but do not tarry at the narratives that portray that God as Actor in that history, Suzerain of that covenant, but rather press on to hear and to think the Referent who is Present there as the One beyond thought. We think through, apart from, or more deeply into *but do not deny* that two-story cosmos where creature and Creator belong together, the made and the Maker in one cosmic theater, moving from first light to consummation. We think, rather, of God Himself, His Triune Being; we contemplate this Reality, its Rationality and Goodness; we ascend there, to this Divine Majesty *A Se*, as much as is given us, as much as our weakness can bear. Can we do this, and moreover, should we? We are considering God as Rational, the Infinite Person of the Logos. Can this Divine Reason be known by human reason? Is this a lesson taught by Scripture? After all, we can hardly miss the Johannine resonance of this whole discussion. If we say that Trinity can be known only by faith, not by reason, we will want to know how to understand the scriptural teaching on Ratio and how it relates to the rational dignity of the dogma. Can Holy Scripture, should Holy Scripture, be read within the generous framework of the common alternative? How can such conceptual problems be explored within the living text of Scripture?

I have said that the problem in the neighborhood does not function as traditional apologetics; it is too loose-limbed a creature for that. Yet it does claim a foot in the world of secular, or "unaided," reason and seeks an echo there of the Infinite Mystery of the Triune God. It has examined secular parables to the One Nature and diverse Persons in some long-standing arguments in feminist theory; it has probed the problem of goodness in the real as echo of the Holy Spirit, the Good Gift; and it has considered the place of reason itself as resonance to the Eternal Son, the Wisdom and Logos, who is God. It would seem that a rational defense of the dogma, a full-throated one, must be now in the offing.

Yet I dare to say no. The problem in the neighborhood does not ask of these vestigia that they serve as proper argument or rational warrant. Only Holy Scripture, I say, can do this. Just so, you may say! But how can the Scriptures of the Old and New Testaments be read in this plummy philosophical fashion? Have I not solved my dilemma by turning Scripture inside out, making it, against all genre and form, into a treasure chest of Western concepts, a rational curio cabinet of the ancient Aegean? Such are the charges of hellenization of the Bible, and there is not world enough or time to recount how widespread is this charge among the moderns. Yet I persist! The rational dignity of the Trinity can be warranted and unfolded in Holy Scripture itself. Just this is what it means to say that the Logos of God is found there. Now I must say how. Just this is the turn from Prolegomena, as we have been considering it here, to dogmatic theology proper. As we open the pages of Holy Scripture, we are brought into the landscape, the structure, and the grounding of the dogma of the Holy Trinity itself. Contra mundum, I will say that the Holy Trinity is contained in Holy

Scripture, and more, in the glorious pages of the Old Testament. Vestiges we leave behind—we sail for home.

Notes

1. Gilles Emery, "Essentialism or Personalism in the Treatise on God in Saint Thomas Aquinas?" *Thomas* 64, no. 4 (October 2000): 532, 534.

2. Emery, "Essentialism or Personalism," 534.

3. Kripke, *Naming and Necessity*, 26.

4. Bertrand Russell, *The Problems of Philosophy* (Oxford: Oxford University Press, 1997), 46–55.

5. Paul Tillich, *Systematic Theology*, vol. 1 of *Reason and Revelation, Being and God* (Chicago: University of Chicago Press, 1951), 175.

6. Elizabeth Spelman, *Inessential Womanhood: Problems of Exclusion in Feminist Thought* (Boston: Beacon Press, 1988), 1.

7. Spelman, *Inessential Womanhood*, 1.

8. Spelman, *Inessential Womanhood*, x.

9. Aquinas, *Summa Theologica*, I, q. 2.

§ 4. Holy Scripture as Ground of Trinity

Central to our theological task is this metaphysical reading of Holy Scripture, the quiet conviction that the Bible can speak, too, of Being Itself, not as a distortion, not as a hellenizing of scriptural idiom, but as its very own speech, as its very own Mystery and Prize. This, too, is compatibilism in theological reasoning. We do not say here all that must be said about Holy Scripture, its inspiration and authorship; that will come another day. But here we say: the Bible is the final word in theology, in truth, not because it excludes, draws away, inhibits, or disperses the worldly thinking of the philosophers—precisely not that! It is final, consummate, unmatched authority just because it does not exclude, prohibit, and circumscribe but rather *includes*, encompasses, teaches, and points to the metaphysical Reality and Mystery that consumes and consummates all thought. In Holy Scripture, we stand before Realism at its Perfection, its Abstract Beauty and Goodness. In Holy Scripture we encounter Being as the Holy.

Now this conviction means that the most abstract, refined, and transcendent metaphysics can be ingredient—in a scriptural idiom!—within faithful scriptural reading and reasoning. We can discover and learn of, learn from, and feed on, the Triune Being of God in the Old and New Testaments. The Bible is universal and true and complete in just that sense. We do not leave the shores of the Red Sea for the Aegean when we talk about God as Rational, as Good, and as Infinite. We do not need to turn to philosophers to derive the rationality of the faith, though to be sure they bring many gifts to the church. Rather in the "mixed style" of the Bible—its sturdy, commonsense story and parable, and its very great depth and sophisticated conceptuality—we encounter the Holy God who is Beginning and End of thought. This is spiritual exegesis, certainly, but much more. It is the outworking of Scripture's Holiness, its Uniqueness as Book of God. It is Radiant with His Touch. We are given the God of the philosophers, the God of Georg Cantor and Albert Einstein, the God of the entire cosmos, in the little room that is Israel and Judah, the Sea of Galilee, and a lonely hill outside Jerusalem. Just that is proper confidence in Holy Scripture, the breadth of *sola scriptura*.

But we have not said, in all this, what we may and must say about God as Rational, as Triune Rationality. How does the magnificence of Holy Scripture bear on this troubled question of the place of speculative metaphysics within the dogma of Trinity? Of course it will follow from this exalted account of Holy Scripture that it will teach the Mystery of the Holy Trinity, and it follows that the technical elements of the dogma will have scriptural warrant, and beyond that, that the profound questions about the metaphysical Nature and Logical Structure of Almighty God will be taken up and chiseled there in the intellect of the world. But does all this exceeding boldness about Holy Scripture make Trinity rational or rationalized? Does Scripture give this Mystery to human thought in such a way that the common seizure of the rational and the real lay hold of the Holy God, the Triune, Himself? We must begin the exploration of these questions by a reflection on the stature and status of Holy Scripture itself as teacher of Trinity.

Just what kind of teacher do we encounter when we open the Holy Book? We will not travel far in the journey toward the rational and real should we fail to answer this prior question, for our journey begins, as it must end, in Holy Scripture. It has been the common conviction of biblical scholars and theologians, Catholic and Protestant, in the modern era that the Bible is not a philosophical text. There are few axioms held as firmly as this in our day about Scripture; it is in good measure just what we mean when we say that we read the Bible historically. Of course, that little word *historical* carries a big stick. Little is as controverted, and feared, as the critical assessment of the Bible as history—its accuracy, Tendenz, and religious aims. But another conviction lies prior to this critical question that has haunted modern exegesis: The Bible, it is said, is not a philosophical, conceptual, or argumentative text. It is rather a realist, social, and historical narrative of Israel's religious life, amid the nations of the Ancient Near East, and the gentiles of the Roman world, drawn into its orbit, circling now its Radiant Sun. The Bible is a *religious* text in just this sense. It contains the psalms and prayers of Israel, the teachings and aphorisms of its sages, the judgment of prophets, all collected into the vast narrative arc of a people born out of a flood, a dryland crossing, a moving through kingdom and empire and exile to the day its Eternal King is born, enthroned on a tree and entombed and risen to reign forever, on David's throne and Caesar's, too. The Bible is not philosophy; rather, it tells this God-ward story and preserves these devotional texts. It serves other aims and inculcates other virtues. It does not inquire into the knowledge and being of the cosmos, as do ancient philosophical texts, but rather confesses the origin and end of this cosmos under the Lordship of the One God. A moment spent poring over the *Categories* or the *Republic* will say much more than any analytic comparison of Bible and philosophy: the difference springs off the page. The Bible bends the knee of the heart or sharpens the dialectical sword, but the dialogue and treatise do not.

Now, all this is so transparently true, so obviously full of pith and insight and usefulness, that it is hard to know how we might ever set it aside or ever question its militant common sense. It lies behind the conviction that to read the Bible aright is to find the proper literary and historical genre it falls under and to honor that in our interpretation and application. The very distinction we ordinarily draw—it seems so self-evident!—between religion and philosophy echoes this fundamental casting of Holy Scripture as religious and historical text. The departmental structure of the modern university, with its philosophy department far down the hall from the religion or religious study office, rests not only on the modern attitude toward human inquiry, and on human religiosity, but also, perhaps principally, on the awakening sense, from the early modern era onward, that the Bible inhabits and erects a world all its own, an idiom and practice of the love of God, that stands apart from all profane questions and creeds. The Bible is religious, it is dogmatic, and it is a devotional text. The elaborate schemas in much modern theology, mostly Protestant but some Catholic, too (Blaise Pascal!), that set the God of Scripture over against the God of the philosophers in truth do not begin this great division of theology and philosophy but rather acknowledge it, a fact cemented in place, it is said, by the Bible itself. We read Holy Scripture to learn how Prophet and Sage teach about the Divine Will, to learn how to walk before the Lord in humility and righteousness, and to learn about the Divine Son, who walked in and out among us and remains with us to the end. Should we seek an analysis of this moral and catechetical task, an exposition of the conceptual work and argument that should guide this life of faith, we would turn to philosophy, the philosophy of religion or the first philosophy as it is useful to religion.

All this division by category was firmly in place by the time of the schoolmen—though with salient differences. St. Thomas himself marked out his *Summa* as worthwhile for students just because it offered analytic tools that belonged to nature as well as grace and showed profane philosophy as the handmaid to theology. But Thomas belongs to the premodern era in the reading of Holy Scripture. He did not consider the Bible a text deaf to the voice of philosophy or foreign to its analysis. For the Holy Scriptures of the Old and New Testaments were in the medieval and ancient world firmly planted on the side of theology—theology as a rigorous science, fully armed with argument, concept, and demonstration. The ancients knew the divisions we moderns observe—the theological and the philosophical, the natural and the gracious, the concrete and the speculative, the historical and the dogmatic. But for Thomas, for the premodern doctors of the church, the Bible belonged by divine right on the side of the doctrinal and conceptual. It was the unexcelled Source of dogma; it was dogma. The Bible taught scholastic theology, even in its idiom of metaphor, simile, and analogy.

Now, it is vital for our project here to see that a sea change has swept over this territory. The Bible, we moderns say, is now another kind of book, a Holy One, perhaps, even honored with properties unrecognized explicitly by the ancients, such as plenary or verbal inerrancy. The Bible is understood by its *style*, its language, its homeland—by what we have learned in our day to call its *Sitz im Leben*. Just this is what we mean by *genre*. We assign a Denkform to a distinctive genre, and we hold that the thought-world of such a text is comprised and constrained by this coherent, self-reinforcing milieu of language, idiom, style, and type. This is the world of lower criticism, and we have entered the European world of letters and historiography when we walk through these doors. It is often said that "historical consciousness," that prize of German modernism, discovered and elevated "historical difference," or "historicism." Certainly. But we could also say that to understand a text as an historical object is to *identify* its genre and its subject matter: it speaks of topics and realities as they come within the house of language, this particular language. Some things, we say in this school, cannot be said in a religious idiom or through that medium; another language, another genre, more conceptual, say, more abstract or didactic, must be found.

And we can see how very plausible and helpful all this is. It is not simply a matter of learning about a new expression or term— St. Augustine could write at some speculative length about this task in his works on Trinity and on Christian doctrine. No, this is something larger, more comprehensive and radical. We learn to listen here for a worldview, a universe that is expressed and contained by language. To say this is not to weigh in on the controverted matter of prelinguistic experience, should such there be; we can remain neutral here about the language-saturated nature of human inwardness. What we harken to here is the powerful identification of speech with thought and with referent: the meaning of a term, its use and range, its form and force of expression are caught up in the language style of the whole. And more: the *kind* of speech exhibited in a text or community is a *world*, an ordered cosmos that allows and prizes and seeks after certain things and leaves others aside. Indeed, it knows them not. *This* is what Karl Barth in his more modernist voice intends when he says, for example, that *truth* in Holy Scripture means "fidelity" or "just dealing" rather than any abstract, conceptual schema, such as a "correspondence theory of truth" or a Platonizing ideal of truth as eternal form. The patristic notion that Scripture is self-interpreting, that we compare unfamiliar phrases or terms in Holy Scripture with others, across the canon, to determine proper meaning and use, has undergone revolutionary change all its own. This patristic teaching, so well exemplified by Augustine, has, under the conditions of modernism, turned over into the radical conviction that language style *determines* referent and subject. Just this tells us as modern readers what we can expect to learn from a particular text and its school. It teaches us to listen to a distinctive voice, to peer into a distinct world.

And there is nothing to scorn here! Anyone who has read Sigmund Freud's marvelous case studies knows the intense concentration the analyst brings to the art of listening. An interpretation is built up from a thousand small details: of gesture and posture, those idioms of the body; of particular word choice, its resonance and association; the silences; the slips and forgotten things; the stray phrase that contains worlds, buried, repressed, disguised; the ring of truth or the odd note of evasion—all these are the universe of psychoanalytic reading. It is this art, the close attention to idiom and thought-world and genre, that gives us that matchless experience of *being heard*, that rare gift from intimate or counselor or pastor. It is not a matter of being *understood*. Many can hear and grasp the bare content of a discourse, can replicate and mirror its main themes—what we might call, in analytic idiom, the "manifest content." But this, we often say, is not what we seek; we are still not being heard for what is said, what is painfully left unsaid, the "hidden content." Erik Erikson records a lovely moment of this form of deep hearing, one ringed about by pathos, in his remarkable study of Martin Luther, *Young Man Luther*. He recovers a memory of his youth that, in Erikson's haunting phrase, had been "covered by the rubble of the cities and by the bleached bones of men of my kind in Europe." As a young artist, a troubadour loose in Europe, he sat with his friend and his friend's father, a Lutheran pastor, at the breakfast table, an intimate, homey scene, and he heard, as though for the first time, the Lord's Prayer in Luther's earthy and vibrant German: "Never having 'knowingly' heard it, I had the experience, as seldom before or after, of a wholeness captured in a few simple words, of poetry fusing the esthetic and the moral: those who have once suddenly 'heard' the Gettysburg Address will know what I mean."[1] This is the art of listening, the art of hearing and reading a text in its own genre and idiom, of the delicate and unfinished task of *receiving* what another wishes to say and recording that universe, that startling, fresh world, that has been extended to us in speech. We do not all say the same thing, even when we use the same words, perhaps especially then. It is the patient attending to another's speech, their whole communication, in every gesture and act and symbol, perhaps over many years, that allows us "suddenly to 'hear'" this book or this living text and to say, more deeply, more fully, I understand. This is the art of friendship, an interpretive act that outstrips all others. All this stems from identifying genre and subject matter, from reading texts as thought-worlds: it is a gift of the modern.

But it has exacted a cost in the reading and hearing of Holy Scripture. Our modern conviction that language shapes reality, giving it contour and definition, has led biblical interpreters to a radical foreshortening of Scripture, a narrowing of its reach. We have gestured toward that attenuation by noting the sharp rebuke modern exegetes give to perennial philosophy as proper instrument to read biblical texts. But we might be more precise. For it is the conviction of some modern dogmatic theologians—most prominently Barth, but also those in his train—that Holy Scripture *does* contain a form of metaphysics, certainly a realism, but not of a Hellenistic or Attic sort. The Bible, such dogmaticians say, is a *realist* text of a kind but not of a historical or modern philosophical school. It offers its own metaphysic, its own doctrine of God, its own theological realism. To say this, Barth argues, is to spring Scripture free of its Babylonian captivity to foreign conceptuality, argument, and gods. In its place is a joining of genre and subject matter, but this time as an autonomous, self-defined, and self-regulating revelation of the True God, of Israel's Lord. The traditional affirmations of Divine Predicates—God's Simplicity, Immutability, or Impassibility, say— are here thought to be relics of another genre and school: Athens rather than Jerusalem. The *arguments* advanced by the ancients for Divine Immutability, for example, are thought to rest on axioms alien to biblical thought, alien to biblical narrative and parable. The Divine Pathos of Jeremiah could never be reduced or properly thought through, these theologians say, under the categories of Western philosophy; these can only reduce, explain away, or muzzle the Fiery, Passionate Lord of Scripture. Only a patient unfolding of biblical imagery, a description of what is seen there, an attentive hearing of the distinctive idiom of Zion, can renovate and christen the categories and concepts of theology. These are familiar claims to students of modern dogmatics; we need not linger over examples here. But in this place we need to see more precisely the distinctive joining of genre and subject matter as it influences the course of modern theology. It is, in its own vocabulary and emphasis, a reflection on the teaching of speculative metaphysics, the particular realism and Rationality of Latin Trinitarianism.

For schools of philosophical debate are not, in truth, varying sorts of genera. So deep is our modern intuition that they are, and that they function in some way as do literary genres, that we often overlook the striking differences between them. Under Friedrich Nietzsche's broad influence, we have begun to speak in modern universities of philosophical schools as so many perspectives, so many self-enclosed and internally coherent styles of thought, languages, literary forms. To be sure, arguments emerge within these coherentist thought-worlds; these are not all claim and bare description. But they are sometimes thought to behave something like a non-Euclidean geometry, internally consistent, ramified on its axioms, tightly woven, but only on its own loom. The outsized relish for nonfoundationalism in present-day epistemology and the piecemeal or hybrid metaphysics of the postmodern strengthen the impression that philosophical schools behave like literary genres, cultural styles. Modern Protestant dogmatics is littered with such easy assumptions: this is a Platonizing point of view, that is an Aristotelian deity, here we see the strong influence of Spinoza, there is the idiom of Hegelian or Berkeleyan or absolute idealism.

But philosophers themselves do not speak this way. It is the mark of their plausibility as scholars in our culture that philosophers, especially of the Anglo-American school, consider their own field one of rational argument, of demonstration, of counterexample and defeaters. Theirs is a world of stout objectivity, and they take their task to set forth, defend, and clarify a claim or argument that appeals to, and rests on, human logic, rigor, and analysis. Just this ties together the centuries of philosophical debate. Analytic philosophers are often considered ahistorical in their reading and use of figures from past centuries—not for them the close language studies or the attentive care for cultural setting, comparative idiom. No, this is a resolute turning away of the assimilation of subject matter to genre. Past philosophers and theologians and rhetoricians are assumed to be setting forth argument and can be assessed, directly and firmly, on those grounds. Of course, there will be translation! Modern philosophers rely on classicists and philologists and historians to provide careful translations and commentaries on ancient texts. At times, even the most reductive and formalistic of present-day philosophers can pause in the work of disputation to study the word-use and semantic range of ancient terms. But this act of genre analysis does not spark the searching investigation of literary forms, idiomatic expression, and thought-world that characterize much modern biblical exegesis. We do not find a lengthy exposition on the Cartesian point of view or the Aristotelian form of expression; that is left to the historian of philosophy. The work of philosophers in contemporary Analytic Departments can be compared favorably with mathematicians for whom the great logicians of the past are fellow laborers in calculus or probability or geometry—right or wrong, respectable or passé, all on the basis of proof alone. We might say that in these fields the identity of genre and subject matter has passed them by. Do these archaizing— or futuristic?—fields shed light on the path ahead for proper biblical exegesis in theology?

I believe it can. And we begin this broad analysis and distinction of subject matter and genre by returning, now by another route, to the Barthian claim that Holy Scripture offers its own form of metaphysics, its own Divine Ontology. Just what kind of claim is this? Let me take a celebrated example from late in Barth's writings, from *Church Dogmatics*, IV.1, the remarkable treatment of the Deity of Christ, called (in English) "the Way of the Son of God into the Far Country." There Barth takes us through the various elements of the Divine Nature of the Son, the patristic and creedal developments, with special attention to the Kenoticists of the early modern era. Then, this astonishing passage:

> It is clear that once again, and this time in all seriousness, we are confronted with the mystery of the deity of Christ. Let us grant that this insight is right, that what the New Testament says about the obedience of Christ, on His way as a way of suffering, has its basis, even as a statement about the man Jesus, *in His divine nature and therefore in God Himself.* . . . We cannot conceal the fact that it is a difficult and even an elusive thing to speak of obedience which takes place in God Himself. Obedience implies an above and a below, a *prius*

and a *posterius*, a superior and a junior and subordinate. Obedience as a possibility and actuality in God Himself seems at once to compromise the unity and then logically the equality of the divine being. Can the one God command and obey? Can the one God be above and below, the superior and the subordinate? . . .

Granted that we do see and understand that [the proper being of the one true God is in Jesus Christ the Crucified], we cannot refuse to accept the humiliation and lowliness and supremely the obedience of Christ as the dominating moment in our conception of God. Therefore we must determine to seek and find the key to the whole difficult and heavily freighted concept of the "divine nature" at the point where it appears to be quite impossible—except for those whose thinking is orientated on Him in this matter—the fact that Jesus Christ was obedient unto death, even the death of the cross. . . . We have to reckon with such an event even in the being and life of God Himself. It cannot be explained away either as an event in some higher or supreme creaturely sphere or as a mere appearance of God. Therefore we have to state firmly that, far from preventing this possibility, His divine unity consists in the fact that in Himself He is both One who is obeyed and Another who obeys.[2]

After a spirited defense and exposition of the Divine Nature as encompassing obedience and command, super- and subordination, and in a special act of daring, assuring us that all this is a strong form of Personal "unity and equality," "without division or contradiction," Barth ends on a crescendo:

He is God only in these relationships [of the one to the other] and therefore not in a Godhead which does not take part in this history, in the relationships of its modes of being, which is neutral towards them. This neutral Godhead, this pure and empty Godhead, and its claim to be true divinity, is the illusion of an abstract "monotheism" which usually fools men most successfully at the high-water mark of the development of heathen religions and mythologies and philosophies. The true and living God is the One whose Godhead consists in this history, who is in these three modes of being the One God, the Eternal, the Almighty, the Holy, the Merciful, the One who loves in His freedom and is free in His love.[3]

Now there are many moving parts to this dramatic section in Barth's Trinitarian Christology, and I do not pretend to do justice to them here. But it is central and revealing for our task in the dogma of Trinity to see just how Barth understands Holy Scripture to teach and guide and ground the concept of Divine Nature and the Divine Sonship. This passage discloses, as does little else in Barth's corpus, the doctrine of revelation and the unique, scriptural metaphysics that governs the whole. The claim in shorthand is simply this: that Jesus Christ was obedient unto death, even death on a cross; therefore, His Deity is shown *in* His obedience, not apart from or over against it; therefore, Triune Reality and Equality *consist* in Super- and Subordination. This, Barth says, is *biblical* metaphysics, not the alien concepts and myths of high-water philosophers, the worldly metaphysicians of abstract monotheism. Well, all of this is very bracing! But can we, should we, follow such an exhilarating path?

I suppose that readers who have persevered this far know that I will hesitate before following Barth here, however much I stand indebted to him, his example, and his matchless dogmatic rigor. Barth is willing to assimilate rationality and ontology to the events, storyline, and idiom of Scripture in such a way that earthly argument is radically relativized, at times set aside entirely. What does it mean, after all, to say that obedience and subordination are forms of *equality*? What kind of conceptuality lies behind the claim that unity is preserved, best preserved, by One who commands and Another who obeys? What kind of argument can be set out for the conviction that a God who is measured and known and identified by historical events is the *Free God*, the Sovereign One? How has the doctrine of revelation been galvanized, transformed, by such moves? If we do not understand Barth's radicality here, we will see it nowhere else. Here is the fitting bookend to Barth's early insistence, found already in our sections from *Church Dogmatics*, I.1, that form and content may be distinct but must never be separated. The form of New Testament witness to Christ, His free obedience to the Way of the Cross, gives *in that very form* the content of the Divine Son, and in just that way, the Divine Persons and Nature.

Now, something has happened here to the notion of predication that is well worth our close attention. If I read him aright, Barth holds that our very *inability* to reason our way from subordination to equality, from command and obedience to unity and Oneness, just this is what we should intend by analogical predication—or at least by nonunivocal predication. The very complaint I would lodge here against Barth—that we must shun every hint of equivocation in our use of terms in the doctrine of God—is in Barth's hands the tool to defend this very practice. My incomprehension at the rational structure at work here shows, Barth tells me, that he is using the divine language, the idiom of revelation, that stands above all human reason and surpasses every tongue and every earthly mystery. *That* is what it means, Barth tells us here, that flesh and blood cannot reveal these things to us; only the Father in Heaven can. Revelation as the source of those truths beyond reason will carry a distinguishing mark—I think we can go this far—which is our deep, conceptual puzzlement over how such things can be and how they can be defended. Now I do not think that Barth is giving us here a modern version of Tertullian's maxim—if, indeed, he did utter this—that "I believe because it is absurd." Barth does not praise irrationality, here or anywhere. For him, God is supremely luminous, benevolent Light. But His Ways are strange! To think the thought of God is to be brought into a realm where our reason does not work properly; it is outstripped, overmastered. We "have to be shown," to be "told" how Divine Equality operates, just what it means to say that Father and Son are Equal and of One

Substance: "No other being, no created being, is one with itself as God is."[4] It is only limited, finite, creaturely reason that takes offense at subordination and obedience, considering them something "mean" and lowly, unworthy of God. But Scripture reveals to us that this Divine Command and Obedience is in truth, and startling truth, the Full Unity and Dignity of the Triune God. The Holy Spirit, Barth says in this section, "affirms" and "makes possible and maintains Fellowship" with Himself and the other Modes of Being of the Godhead, so all "division and contradiction is excluded"—a form of radical Augustinianism of the Third Person.[5]

But it is manifestly not clear how all this is supposed to work. And that seems to be Barth's point here and throughout this long paragraph. We are to say that our use of the predicates and properties is not governed by ordinary or common definitions; we are to say that Scripture overrules rational objections to an equality that is predicated on hierarchy; and we are to "fill out" the meaning of these terms, *unity* and *equality*, to specify and apply them, by the narrative we discover in the New Testament, the whole course of Christ's obedience. This I take to be the *force* of Barth's insistence that the dogmas of Trinity and Christology are *revealed*: they operate under the terms disclosed and enacted by the history of Jesus Christ. Barth is willing to nod toward justification or explication of his views. He says that only common and fallen reason takes offense at lowliness as a virtue or form of equality: to obey, it seems, could be to exercise equality if we simply shook off— grace shook off from us—our sinful pride. This is a quiet kind of apologia, though Barth does not make much of it. He is also willing to say that all is "elusive" and even "difficult," acknowledging in a delicate way that this will puzzle and trouble our rational faculties. He points to the Spirit as Source of Unity, a traditional locus of

Trinitarian dogmatics, and one designed perhaps to make us feel more at home. But Barth pointedly refused to *argue* for his position, or to give rational warrant, or overcome logical objections. We can, to be sure, call such a procedure "biblical metaphysics," but this violates the common definition and self-understanding of this conceptual discipline. The study of being, realism in its many forms, operates under the canons of general logic and argument; it persuades through appeal to these axioms, common definitions, and rational practice. But Barth treats metaphysics as a *genre*; it is a local language, bordered by the covers of the Bible. In his ontology, he simply states what he takes to be a biblical rule: this happened to Christ; He undertook it; He is the Divine Son; this must be true of God. This is regionalism in the defense of Trinity of a particular and radical kind.

Now it is just this form of Scriptural reasoning and revelation I want to resist. I hesitate to charge Barth with equivocation— that is an explosive weapon in theology or philosophy—but Barth places special strain on language and rationality throughout this paragraph of the *Dogmatics*. I can see that such positions flow from earlier Christological claims and follow the elevated pattern of the doctrine of revelation, laid out in earlier volumes. But Barth here asks us to hold that Holy Scripture teaches obedience in God, in the Divine Nature, and between the Persons, and that Super- and Subordination, Prior and Posterior, belong to the Full Deity and Dignity of the Divine Persons in their Relations. And this in virtue of Scripture's genre, its narrative, historical, and redemptive structure. It is in its own way a particular mixed genre, a frank univocity in the grounding of Christological events in the Divine Being, and a stubborn delight in drawing near to equivocation in the dogmatic conclusions that are thought to follow from these grounds. Scripture, it seems, is otherworldly in just this sense.

But are we, in truth, left with only these two choices, a full-throated worldliness and rationalism or a radical and defiant otherworldliness? Is Scripture as teacher confined to either a historical or a nonhistorical reading; to a particular, concrete genre or to a universal metaphysics; to a nonphilosophical or philosophical exposition; to suprarationalism or rationalism; revelation or reason? Are these in truth the choices we must face as we read and receive Holy Writ? Is this the forked road we face as we consider the place of reason and revelation in the Mystery of Trinity? I cannot believe this is so. I seek a way forward that does not plunge into either side of this divide yet does not deny them either. I seek a path in meditating on Holy Scripture and hearing its Word that cuts against this framework, resists this opposition and dualism. The rational stature of the doctrine of Trinity—the cultural legitimacy I have called the common alternative—rests on an interpretation of Holy Scripture that has broken free of these categories and turned over fresh ground. Our understanding of the Bible will exhibit the place of revelation in the Holy Mystery of Trinity *and* the place of common reason. The rational traces of Trinity, the "problems in the neighborhood," will be determined by the integration of metaphysical realism within biblical exegesis: the Bible, once again, will lead the way.

§4.1. The Eternal Generation of the Son: A Test Case

Let me take, as illustration, a text that was widely and commonly viewed as Trinitarian warrant in the Nicene era: Isaiah 53:8: "He was taken from prison and from judgment; and who shall declare his generation? for he was cut off out of the land of the living: for the transgression of my people was he stricken." For St. Gregory and St. Basil, as well as for Augustine, the whole anti-Eunomian party, this verse contained the scriptural ground for a Nicene understanding of the Eternal Generation of the Son. The Greek fathers would have relied on the Septuagint:

ἐν τῇ ταπεινώσει ἡ κρίσις αὐτοῦ ἤρθη· τὴν γενεὰν αὐτοῦ τίς διηγήσεται; ὅτι αἴρεται ἀπὸ τῆς γῆς ἡ ζωὴ αὐτοῦ, ἀπὸ τῶν ἀνομιῶν τοῦ λαοῦ μου ἤχθη εἰς θάνατον

The Latin Nicenes on the Old Latin or the newer Vulgate:

de angustia et de iudicio sublatus est generationem eius quis enarrabit quia abscisus est de terra viventium propter scelus populi mei percussit eum.

And for both, the "genean" or "generation" would be past telling, unknown, incalculable, and that means that the Divine Procession of the Son would be Mystery. Time and again this passage would be adduced as Scriptural teaching that the Arian or Eunomian worry about generation must be false. The Arians relied on an earthly and carnal account of begetting, the Nicenes charged; they imagined that subordination or, worse, a distinction of substance was implied by the very notion of generation. Not so, the Nicenes said. For the Holy Prophet Isaiah taught about the Servant: His generation was beyond all knowing; who can tell of it? It must be, they reasoned, that the Divine Processions did not mimic or parallel the creaturely—there was no "prior" and "posterior," no temporality, no dependence, and certainly no "subordination"—yet it was altogether proper to use the term *generation*, for so did Holy Writ speak of the Divine Son. If we put it so, anachronistically and atemporally, the Nicenes, when they took up Scripture, read a metaphysics directly contrary to Barth's: Christology and Trinitarian Processions taught them—unlike Barth—that the Son could never be subordinate or posterior to the Father. This prophetic verse from Isaiah taught the early church about the unique Generation, the timeless, immutable Procession of the Son, and not about the Way into the Far Country that must constitute the true Nature of the True God.

In this section, dedicated to an exposition and commentary on Isaiah 53, I want to *enact* a metaphysical and doctrinal reading of the prophetic text. My aim here is to examine, and learn from, this passage as a scriptural lesson on the Divine Generation of the Eternal Son. Isaiah 53 will be read, that is, as a prophetic unfolding of the Triune Procession of the Son: it will speak of the inner Life of God. Several dogmatic topics, seemingly foreign to the territory of the Suffering Servant, will now come into view: the nature of the Immanent Processions as Dynamic Uniqueness; the ethical character of Eternal Generation, its Holiness; the formal property of the Eternal Persons as Perfection or Telos; the Processional Life as Descent and as Gift, the Outpouring of the Spirit; and the Surpassing Mystery of the Eternal Son as the *Logos Asarkos*. This dogmatic and metaphysical reading of the Suffering Servant song will be defended through an experiment with the categories of the intelligible and the concrete, themselves Trinitarian concepts, and these, it is hoped, will not *erase* or *evade* the distinctive particularity of Israel but rather honor it as instructor and guide in the proper doctrine of God. Such is the form of metaphysical exegesis I aim to test here.

Now it is this very insistence on a well-tuned metaphysics in the Scriptures of Israel that make historians, schooled in the genre of critical history, the genre, too, of the covenant people, deeply uneasy. R. P. C. Hanson, the distinguished and stylish patristics scholar, speaks for many when he writes:

> The last word on the appeal to the Bible during this crucial period in the history of Christian doctrine [the fourth century AD], however, must be of the impression made on a student of the period that the

expounders of the text of the Bible are incompetent and ill-prepared to expound it. This applies as much to the wooden and unimaginative approach of the Arians as it does to the fixed determination of their opponents to read their doctrine into the Bible by hook or by crook. . . . But it is not so much the errors arising out of mistranslation that impeded a full understanding of the Bible by the theologians of the fourth century. It was much more the presuppositions with which they approached the Biblical text that clouded their perceptions, the tendency to treat the Bible in an "atomic" way as if each verse or set of verses was capable of giving direct information about Christian doctrine apart from its context, the "oracular" concept of the nature of the Bible, the incapacity with a few exceptions to take serious account of the background the circumstances and period of the writers.[6]

We might sum up Hanson's whole approach to patristic exegesis— his revulsion at it, in truth—by his ringing and rounded maxim: "The very reverence with which the [fathers] honoured the Bible as a sacred book stood in the way of their understanding it."[7] We can see that Hanson follows the path of modernist exegesis almost, we might say, by instinct: How atomized the reading of the fathers! How blind to context and genre; how ready to import their own doctrines and devotions into the text! How reverent it all is and how otiose! Hanson finds early exegesis littered with "perverse and some positively grotesque interpretation," principally because all sides to the early Nicene debates vainly sought to ground their doctrinal positions and idiom in Scripture itself:

> The pro-Nicenes are at their worst, their most grotesque, when they try to show that the new terms borrowed from the pagan philosophy of the day were really to be found in Scripture. The Greek speakers cannot pretend that *ousia* appears in either Septuagint or New Testament, but they rack the Bible to find examples of *hypostasis*, and when they find it do their best to make the context appear relevant. With one doubtful exception, Heb 1:3 where it means "substance," whereas they want to make it mean "person," this is an impossible task; but the impossibility does not deter them.[8]

To quote Hanson at length is nearly irresistible—he is so witty, so learned and so plainspoken, so stoutly modern in all his ways that it seems cheeseparing to slight the citations. That Hanson was a bishop of the Church of Ireland, an ecumenist, and a theologian can only deepen our conviction that the conflation of subject matter and genre, the modernist turn in the higher criticism of the Bible, has entered the main hallways of the church and has made itself right at home.

The point that Hanson makes so beautifully clear is that Isaiah 53:8, our cardinal text for the Generation of the Son, *cannot* in all good conscience be about the Divine Processions *because* the historical setting, genre, and semantic field of this verse is ancient Israelite prophecy, and in those years and out of that thought-world, no reflection on Eternal Begetting was conceivable or conceivably intended. Now Hanson takes no second to anyone in admiration for the ingenuity and inventiveness of patristic exegesis—page after page of *The Search for the Christian Doctrine of God* treats these texts with wonder—but it can hardly earn his respect. These early metaphysical readings can receive only a bemused shrug of the shoulders—who knew such a contraption could fly?—because the intellectual plausibility of present-day interpretation is guided, cemented down, by the conviction that historical form determines "what a text is about."

The referent for this passage in Isaiah must be the Suffering Servant, whoever and whatever this sometimes collective, sometimes singular figure might be, and the proper rendering of that phrase should follow ancient Hebrew diction: "Who could have imagined his future?" the New Revised Standard Version (NRSV) will say. To be sure, any modern interpreter who has scanned the current climate on objectivity, foundationalism, or realism will recognize immediately that the Bible could be "constructed" to say just about anything at all. A certain form of perspectivalism has gained currency in much modern and postmodern reading of texts; patristic exegesis can take its place among the thought-worlds on display, for study and for endorsement. But those in our time who hold to realism—and this theology rests on it—will find it nearly compulsory to anchor honest reading in generic and historical context: *this* is what the text says; after all the shouting dies down, *this* is the point, the semantic field, the meaning and referent of the text. Perhaps we may go further in our doctrinal or devotional use, perhaps we would make use of this prophetic passage in our Trinitarian reflection, perhaps we would enter more deeply, more speculatively on the mystery of the Son, but *this* is what it says.

It seems, then, that we are caught between two worlds. One world, realist by its own strictures, sees in the Holy Scriptures a universe coherent in its own inner workings, and proposing for our belief and our grateful obedience, a doctrine of God shaped only by these inner workings and justified only within its walls. We think of Barth here and his determined insistence that the Triune Nature of God must consist in Obedience and Command just because the Incarnate Son followed the way of obedience to its bitter end. The traditional metaphysical claims about Full Equality and Dignity, of Simplicity and Unicity, must conform to that biblical path; all must bend to this yoke. Another world, also realist in self-understanding and dignity, claims a rational, reasonable doctrine, wedded close to the norms of present-day academic life and the world of all cosmopolitan and self-respecting intellectuals. We think of Paul Tillich here or Bishop Hanson, where the self-evident claims of rationality—existential, historical, formal—structure and constrain the doctrine and exegesis of the church. These worlds collide in the Bible, but they also spring far apart. We have, on one hand, the regional account, where Scripture is governed by Christian norms alone: it is revelation, and it is self-interpreting. On the other, we have a secular, or for some theologians, an apologetic reading, where Scripture is interpreted under the hot lights of academic strictures, literary and archaeological findings, and critical norms of modern thought. The Bible speaks out of its time and place, and the church must make the best of it.

Now the aim of this theology is to *resist* this entire framework. We want to move behind this divide, this intellectual chasm, to unplowed fields, fresh ground, and look for the realism theology demands in a third use of Holy Writ. We seek a place for metaphysics, full-throated, speculative realism, *within* the domain of the Word, one that guides and grounds the rational dignity of the dogma of the Holy Trinity. But this is not an attack on the modern! Who wants to make war on the higher criticism? This is most certainly not the way forward; nothing is more filled with pathos than the spectacle of a long theological retreat before the invincible advance of historical criticism. It could not be possible to properly defend realism in theology without honoring intellectual integrity and honesty—this goes perhaps without saying. In our era, the "bar of honesty and of truth," so eloquently defended by Karl Rahner, includes and does not exclude or demean the historical, formal, and original setting of authors and actors, all under the full sun of the *Providentia Dei*. It may seem to more modernist-leaning readers—should such there be!—that I have no place for the careful, scholarly study of the Bible in its *Sitz im Leben*. But this is not so. The aim here is to understand what is *thinkable*, what is plausible and wins intellectual dignity, in the ways of God and the ways of God us-ward. The modern does not escape the Benevolent Guidance of God; it, too, is within His Love and His Judgment and is made proper and fitting for expression of the One Holy God. In our day we cannot think an author apart from his or her setting, the range of her vocabulary, the wide expanse of his unfolding material and moral experience. We have praised in course the mathematical and philosophical reading of past logicians and metaphysicians, their relative freedom from historicizing and irrealizing. But this is a move, laudable to be sure, *within* an intellectual realm bordered by the recognition of distinct culture, era, and event. Even the most daring logician and philosopher knows that Aristotle lived in another time, one quite different from our own; he is our contemporary *in a manner of speaking*. The most resolute presentist does not entertain doubts about whether the great Greek philosopher inhabited a world alien from ours; of course, we say, that is so. But it is a measure of the distance traveled in our time from the ancient that this concession is taken for a truism. Such metaphysicians or mathematicians aim to perform a second step on historical material: to receive a manuscript, a logion, or a proof and treat it, to elevate or excise it from its historical setting, so that it can stand among us as our contemporary. Always for a post-Enlightenment intellectual, human history is an element in rational understanding; it is a permanent marker of difference. So, the historical, critical reading of Holy Scripture—the realism that emerges from the encounter with the stubborn past—belongs and must remain ingredient in Christian systematic work. To resist a dilemma, to move *behind* it, is to acknowledge both alternatives, not to deny or fight them but to move resolutely beyond them both, all the same. How can this be done? Just what is a third via in the realist reading of Holy Scripture?

We seek a way of reading the Holy Scriptures of the Old and New Testaments, *both* covenants, in such a way that the metaphysical Perfections, Relations, and Life of the One God can be properly discerned and set forth, yet the Triune Lord does not dissolve into the rational dreams of arrogant creatures. We seek a theological realism that has conceptual rigor: real argument, real cogency and coherence, real symmetry, and, yes, systematic power. And we seek this *in* Holy Scripture: not above or beside it, not as hidden backdrop or solvent, not quiet authority over Holy Writ, but truly taught within and by Scripture itself. This, I say, is the path that cuts its own way through the varying schools of Trinitarian debate, the alternatives we have patiently explored in these last few sections. It will offer, we pray, a rational exposition of the dogma of Trinity that is proper to this Mystery, this Holy One, an intelligible defense, a plausible account—indeed, an account that walks the neighborhood of all realisms in human intellectual labor yet does not succumb to the ever-present temptation to say too much, to explain from first principles, to feel entirely at home in this divine address, this Exceeding Fire. It seeks to contemplate Heaven but in a rational worship. It seeks the Necessary Truth who is God, the Universal and Transcendent One, in the Concrete, the Singular Fire that is lit on this earth, that carries the well-pleasing savor Heaven-ward. It seeks the Intelligible Subject Matter, the Infinite One, in the structures of rationality itself, all this laid down in the clay, the rocky soil, and the verdant pastures of Holy Scripture. We aim here to find a path that vindicates our use of traditional, classical, and doctrinal metaphysics without losing the Reformation return to the Scriptures. We aim to find a path that vindicates the patristic and Reformation call to find and ground and honor all Christian teaching in the Bible without losing the intellectual rigor and dignity of a theology that is a rational science. Perhaps it is not too elliptical to say that a proper theological realism seeks to read Holy Scripture with Barth's passion and insight and rigor—to follow him at a great distance!—without finding ourselves compelled to accept his conclusions. Perhaps it will be best to *enact* this third way by returning to Holy Scripture—a way I will call "dogmatic reading"—to exemplify such a reading, to enter fresh ground in the interpretation of Isaiah 53.

One of the Suffering Servants Songs, this passage is manifestly concerned with the earthly life and sorrow of an Israelite, of Israel in the midst of hostile powers, and also, I say, of our Lord Jesus Christ in His solitary way to the Cross. It is manifestly so for the Christian reader—even in this figural reading, manifestly so. An element of the realism demanded and ingredient in Christian theology is the ready acknowledgment of the facts, standing stubbornly, plainly before us. Holy Scripture is unique, strongly so, but as we would expect with a form of reading that stands between two mountains, this uniqueness partakes in an odd way of both; it is also open to commonality. The general, the widely accepted, the defended and defensible: this, too, is incorporated in the dogmatic realism of scriptural exegesis. Dogmatic realism rests on the general assumption, widely shared by religious and secular interpreters, that the Bible is a collection of texts about God's will and ways with humankind: it is a book about the divine economy— though not only that! In time, we will see, it is a book also (and I say principally) about the Divine Immanence. It is not, as we saw earlier, a mystagogic text. It does not purport to tell in elaborate code the workings of an Inner Chamber, sealed to the uninitiate. We can share, then, the modernist concern for plain reading, for historical reading; we can acknowledge the Isaianic call to address the covenant people in its suffering, defilement, and exile and to hear the appeal to a transcendent meaning, even at this far reach of national existence. A dogmatic realism, that is, can see and harken to the subject matter *within* the genre: it, too, can fasten its eyes on the near distance, to focus on the immediate and the evident.

Such a realism can countenance, too, the present-day revival of the figural and the foreshadowed. It can see with the eyes of faith, as have Christians since earliest times, a distant shore, where Another stands, an Israelite, too, a Man of Sorrows, from whom we turned our faces and held of no account. A text can be *about*, can *refer*, in this larger, indirect, and structured fashion. Much has been written since the magisterial work of Hans Frei and Erich Auerbach on *figura*, and it need not be rehearsed here. Indeed, it belongs to other doctrines, other horizons. But sufficient for our work here is the recognition that dogmatic realism can expand from the most rigorous historical setting to the larger realm Christians have termed the history of salvation, the scope and architecture of a world, knit together by Divine Dispensation and Gracious Condescension. The Bible can be *about this*, too.

But the higher righteousness in dogmatic reading is the move from the economy to the Immanence of God, to truly *move* there. Notice how demanding this in truth has become for us in our day. We have learned in the poststructuralist climate of current literary exegesis to accept that Christian readers might ask: Is this a foreshadowing or a theophany of the Divine Son, His Preexistence and Manifestation in ancient Israel? Not among stern higher critics, to be sure, or among rabbinic exegetes, or among the orthodox secular, but among broad, literary, and religious readers such questions might be entertained. Does the Tri-Personed God visit His people before the Missions of Son and Spirit, before Incarnation and Pentecost? This is a kind of Christian reflection on the divine economy that may stretch but does not appear to break the common, figural reading that has been understood to mark the Western literary canon. So, too, in modern Christian theology, across the churches, we have learned to read a passage such as Isaiah 53 as teaching about the Incarnate Word and, even more, teaching that this economic Manifestation reveals to us the True God. In theological reading, that is, we have come to accept Isaiah 53 as a prophecy that reveals to us who God is *for us*: the God who saves, who makes his bed with sinners, who is cast out and cast off, who is of no account in a world come of age. This relationalism, too, has been countenanced in the main, modern readings of the Prophet Isaiah, indeed of Israel's Scriptures as a whole.

But this is not our aim. We do not seek to read the Holy Bible as a text principally and primarily—much less exhaustively!—as a book about Israel, the nations, and the Redeemer of the nations. This is not the proper scopus, or end, or referent of this Holy Book. We find *God* there, just that—not God for us, not the God of the economy, not the God prefigured and promised, not the God who in His Majesty is Identical or Analogous or Similar to His Manifestations, not these, first and principally! They are there; they need not be denied or lived down. Indeed, we give thanks for them. They inhabit these pages, and we can make common cause with those readers who find God turned toward the earth in grace and with patience and holy fire. But this is not the high purpose of Holy Writ. We cannot give way to the epistemic worries of the present day, such that historical, earthly, and altogether human ways and words lead only, ineluctably, to relationalism. The dignity and purpose and sacred power of Holy Scripture is this: that it teaches us about the High God, the Holy God in His Aseity, the Triune God *as such.*

Now I share the astonishment of most modernists at this claim. It does indeed seem lofty, overreaching, unforeseen, impossible under most epistemic canons. I, too, think the objection is that strong. I am not deaf to the pleas John Calvin and Calvinists raise against such speculation. Indeed, it is fearsome to imagine the Whole Goodness of the Lord God passing by, and it seems a pride as ancient as the Garden to wish—or worse!—to claim to see God face to face. Metaphysical realism of this sort, this high and lofty, muscular school, appears arrogant, at times ignorant, but scarcely plausible or rational. I would not live in this present age, or have sat in the classrooms of Enlightenment thought since John Locke and René Descartes and David Hume stood behind the lectern, if I did not feel startled by such outsized claims. How can such things be? It is the task of a contemporary doctrine of the Holy Trinity to attempt to answer such startled and baffled cries, to repent for the outrage, and this volume aims to be obedient to that calling. But a calling it must be. For there is no clearer starting point than the simple confession that I believe such things must be, all the same and against every objection. For this is the Bible, and God is its Author.

Now this means, at the very start, that the fathers must in truth be right about our passage. Isaiah 53 must at heart, in the depth and in the heights, be a passage about Heaven, about Almighty God in His Aseity. *This* must be what it says. But this must be so in such a way that the earthly Servant, the historical Israel, is not erased, forgotten, unheard, or the Man of Sorrows, the Lost One, passed by, rejected. This will not be done, however, by identifying the Immanence with the economy in such a way that the historical, formal elements of Holy Scripture become imported into the High Mystery of God's inner Life. That is Barth's path in *Church Dogmatics*, IV.1, and he is clear-eyed about the hazards and walks bravely toward them. But they are costs too high for a proper metaphysical doctrine of the Holy Trinity: the Lofty Inwardness of Almighty God is become too contingent, mutable, particular, and individual for a Unique, Formless, Necessary, and Tri-Personal God who is Utterly, Spiritually One. It cannot be, then, that Isaiah 53 becomes a dogmatically realist text by identifying the inner Life and Relations of Almighty God with oppression and rejection, with obedience and sin-bearing. The Preexistence of the Son, His proper Eternity, cannot mean this. But it is equally clear that the dogma of the Most Holy Trinity will not be properly set forth by prizing it free of such texts, placing it wholly and unrestrainedly in the logician's classroom, and resolving technical problems in technical vocabulary through puzzle cases, counterexamples, and exotic thought experiments. The metaphysical and intellectual dignity of the dogma cannot mean this, either! So, we must think afresh about the proper relation of Holy Scripture to its genres and to the doctrine it guides, supports, and judges.

§4.2. Dogmatic Reading: The Intelligible and the Concrete

We begin by considering in Holy Scripture the relation of the intelligible to the concrete. This is a relationship we confine to Holy Scripture alone. It is in these Holy Writings that we see metaphysics properly and fully joined to the concrete and the everyday. Holy Scripture, we might say, is a wholly redeemed creature—the only one, should we not include Mary, the God-bearer, here. (More must be said about this in the doctrine of the creatures.) The cosmos, we have said, bears *traces* of the Holy Trinity: the vestigia can be discerned wherever the real is sought. But the Holy Scriptures of the Old and New Testaments are not bearers of vestigia only. No, they enjoy the *sensus plenior*, the fullness of the metaphysical Mystery, laid down in the patterns, sinews, *verba*, and events of this text. The Bible is the fully healed instance of a creature, put in service to the Living God. For this reason, it is inexhaustible ground of the dogma of Trinity. For this reason, it is Holy Ground. For this reason, the Bible is the fullness of a creature's share in the Intelligible and the Concrete. It alone echoes fully, properly, the Triune Relations, the Concrete Persons in the Universal and Intelligible Nature—but also, more broadly, the Intelligible and Universal Meaning who is God, in the concrete material world that is creatures.

Certainly, the final relation of the Intelligible to the concrete, found in Holy Writ, must rest in God alone. For He just is the Universal Truth, the Perfect Intelligible who is also wholly Concrete, this *very One*. I have spoken of the Concrete Persons—Their Distinction, Relation, and Procession—in and as the Intelligible Nature, Truth Itself. But such concepts and pairings can never operate in a singular and wooden way in the Transcendent Mystery who is God. There are no *parts* in God! The Divine Persons are also wholly Intelligible, Luminous, and True; Deity Itself is Infinitely Concrete, like unto only Itself. Better: we should say that these Triune Realities indwell One Another. They are not separate Objects, so to say, in an Ocean of Deity but rather subsist perichoretically as Triune God. The relation of such a God to such a creature, even the unique reality of Holy Scripture, is never a simple, direct *mirroring*. God is Holy!

Naturally this whole schema of the Intelligible and the concrete does not sound promising when we consider the historicity, the particularity, and the humanity of Holy Scripture. But we are after something radical, and radically new here, a form of theological exegesis that does not force a choice between metaphysics and text, between the lofty and transcendent and the altogether earthly and, at times, earthy account of Israel and Israel's King. We need fresh terms and fresh frameworks to think this through carefully and dogmatically; our old dilemmas have served polemics far more ably than they have ecclesial dogmatics. So, we might hazard a reflection on the intelligible and the concrete, their relation, one to the other, and their status as pattern for proper, biblical dogmatic work. Note that we have selected a pair, which, though well-trodden in philosophical lecture halls, is not already deep within the annals of doctrine: we have set aside such worthy pairs, say, as substance and accident, or the necessary and contingent, or cause and effect, or even the celebrated modernist pair, speech and act, or more celebrated still, J. L. Austin's speech-act. Our pair is not itself doctrinal: not narrative and dogma, not economy and Immanence, not God for us and God in Himself, not time and Eternity, however long a shadow they cast over Barth's early wrestling with Holy Scripture in a post-Kantian world. We choose, rather, a pair that breathes an air of neutrality over this troubled landscape and permits us to consider with more indeterminate reflection on the proper path for dogmatic realism as it turns to the Holy Scriptures—so, the intelligible and the concrete.

We might immediately move these into the ontological or metaphysical realm: intelligible and concrete *objects*. The pair does not require us to do so; we could well take these as semantic terms and reflect on their grammatical relation, one to the other. But it is illuminating for us, I say, to import this pair immediately into the house of being, because it is *realism* that preoccupies us and, in the end (as in the beginning), Reality itself. Now it will become clear to anyone who reflects long on the intelligible and concrete object that these terms, too, carry the ambiguity, the hidden freight, and the astonishingly rich conceptual range of any of our more worthy pairs—perhaps even of substance and accident themselves! But this richness aids us, too, for we seek a pair that illumines a wide path and generates fruitful comparisons: their unsettled character will allow us more intellectual elbow room to weigh just how we are to read the prophetic texts, such as Isaiah 53. So consider Augustine's famous example, related in *Confessions*, book X, of learning a language through the display of an object named for a child by his elders—"an apple," Ludwig Wittgenstein later named it, in his discussion of this scene in the *Investigations*. This we might say is the exemplar of the concrete object. It is a thing, in Augustine's later idiom, and in the medieval reading of Holy Writ, the apple will be "thing become sign," a symbol of what is good for food and pleasant to the eyes and to be desired to make one wise. (But with "thing become sign" already we are in the midst of a radical account of the relation of Scripture to doctrine, too fully fleshed out for us to follow, at least at this early stage.)

Now an apple might be a concrete thing in this way: it takes up space, or in Cartesian terms, it has extension. An apple has borders: we know where it begins and ends; it is not a "vague object." It is enumerable; indeed, we might think of the integers as abstract or intelligible objects designed to tote up concrete things such as the five apples Wittgenstein hopes to buy from the grocers. An apple might be concrete in ever more specific ways: its weight and color, its species name, its individual markings and shape, its place next to the bananas or pears along the shelf, perhaps even its own history, from seedling to ripened and rounded fruit. In this way, we might imagine the categories Aristotle proposed for naming and defining and delimiting a concrete object. We might, that is, consider the individual, the particular as the hallmark of the concrete. Of course, we need not stop there. We could extend the concrete to events or processes: what becomes clear or definite when developed, hardened, arrested. We could consider collectivities concrete objects: the covenant people, the nation-state, the ball club, the classroom, the family. We could consider concreteness or concrete objects to be found in history, temporality, or finitude rather than in airy palaces or Xanadu or philosophers' studies. Concrete objects would be *there*: not simply extended matter but located in one place and not another, stable in just that way, that we could walk away and return to a spot to find it. It is "objective" in just this sense. For many of us in our age, it is also just what we mean when we say "real."

Now compare the intelligible or the abstract object with this rough-and-ready depiction of the concrete. We might at first think of it as the inverse or contrary of the concrete: not in space, not enumerable, not material or delimited or defined, without borders, without temporality, without specificity and specific name. It would be *abstract* in a rather literal sense, something removed or pulled away—extracted, we might say, from the world of time and of things. This would make the intelligible object *symmetrical* to the concrete, its polar opposite and shadow. We might say that we could arrive at such an account of the universal and intelligible through remotion or negation: it is what the concrete is not. This view is a certain form of relationalism, where concrete and abstract are unified as object and its shadow; they cannot exist apart, for the concrete thing when negated just is the spiritual, abstracted object. Were we to define the pair intelligible and concrete in this way, we might consider this a form of dialectical materialism. In this view, the intelligible object is utterly irreal. It has no place or stubborn identity, no objectivity or finitude, it cannot stand on its own or define its own geography but waits on another and is defined by its greater weight, the concrete object's obdurate thinghood. But of course, we need not see the abstract object in this light! There *are* other ways.

Indeed, it is a mark of earlier schools of realisms to countenance intelligibles as Real, even Most Real. We might consider an entire class of abstract objects—of kinds or classes; of numbers and ratios; of ideals, such as justice or fairness or hope—or perhaps we might countenance imaginary objects as did the philosopher Alexius Meinong, perhaps including characters in novels and plays, their utter definition by their authors yet their remarkable durability, persistence, and realism. Perhaps music, alluring from ancient times, might be held to be an intelligible object, notated certainly, but alive in realms far beyond the staff and quaver. Perhaps we might also call certain physical properties or regularities "natural laws" and assign to them a realism under several headings, yet in themselves—should we be able to speak this way!—abstract and universal and immaterial. Indeed, we might consider thought itself an intelligible object—its contents, certainly, but also thought itself, the act or state of thinking. This would be to countenance ideas or judgments as real in this distinctive sense. Surely Descartes and his particular form of dualism would herald and champion such a distinctive realism. (It is not so clear to me that Descartes should be ruled an idealist!)

Should we admit the reality of intelligibles in this more positive fashion, as do I, we would then enter another kind of metaphysical realm, a world or dimension of the immaterial or ideal. Here we would reckon with the problems Plato and his critics broached long ago: Just how does Justice exist without being any particular just act or state? How does treeness or goodness without any particular tree in view, any concrete good or excellence? Just what is a "human in general"? When we ascend from the world of earthly particulars to kinds and then forms and ideas, up, ever upward, toward the Intellectual Sun, the Idea of the Good, we seem to have left behind what is definite, bordered, weighty. Like Icarus we soar in dangerous realms. But just this is the radical world of theology, of spiritual thought. It inhabits a two-story universe. It is to point to but also to hold to, to believe and confess and defend, a realm that is not entirely seen, not principally material and concrete, not first or exhaustively delimited, defined, or manageable. It is this realm, the Heavenly Places, that has relation to earth, and we are to think carefully about how such things might be.

We might say, for one, that the concrete *participates* in the intelligible. We might say, then, in a rather bold Platonizing fashion, that the realm of the familiar and the concrete is *grounded* in an abstract and perfect realm and that each singular thing rests on, clings to, and receives definition and form from its abstract object, its idea. (Note here that this understanding of the intelligible ideal is a form of *realism*.) This, in rough form, is *methexis*, participation, and this relation, with all its elusiveness and mystery, has entered the bloodstream of Christian theology since late antiquity. We might go further. In this vein of metaphysics, we could say that the Heavenly Realm is Most Real, as did Plato in some dialogues. Our world of the earthbound and the concrete receives not simply its definition and kind, its form, from the Spiritual World but also its very being, its reality under the conditions of finitude. The concrete participates the intelligible as the dependent clings to and needs absolutely the independent and the self-existent. It is not a far step to Tillich's Ground of Being, and though he favors depth over ascent, we recognize the familiar terrain: the realm of the existent, the perishing, receives its life, its dynamism and form, from the Ground; in older idiom, it participates it. Mutatis mutandis, perhaps following this line of thought, we might say that Holy Scripture participates the metaphysical realm and receives its definition, goal, and breath of life from the Abstract, the Spiritual, and the Ideal. We might see something of this relatio in Gregory of Nyssa's theology of ascent, his reading of the life of Moses as a growth in virtue and wisdom that propels Moses into the Cloud and Fire of Sinai, the Luminous Darkness that covers him and draws him ever deeper, ever higher. Here Holy Scripture participates in the Luminous Realm, the heavenly, even as its heroes and moral exemplars ascend up the mountainside to the Dwelling Place of the Most Real, the Most Holy. Now this is a two-story universe knit together by participation, such that our realm is marked by contingency, by imperfection, by concreteness, hungering and thirsting for the Perfect, the True, the Eternal. Here is the inner emigration of the Christian, for such pilgrims belong to Another City, a heavenly one; for they that say such things declare plainly that they seek a country, a better country (that is, a heavenly one): wherefore God is not ashamed to be called their God: for he hath prepared for them a city.

Now in the end we will not follow this path, but it is well to consider its great strengths. We are told often that such Platonizing relation of the intelligible and the concrete suffers from a stability and a contemplative air that is altogether still, apolitical, and deeply reactionary. It appears to be the clearest form of that enemy of the social program in theology, the dualistic or the "otherworldly." How it seems to favor the quietism of a world well ordered and unchanging: Socrates stood still when he contemplated the verities. Our eyes here seem forever fixed on the far horizon, not in the world that is passing away but upward, beyond all becoming, to the Ocean Rest of the Ideal and timeless, of that which simply is. Perhaps such a fixed relation between objects, particular and ideal, could lead to world-forgetfulness, perhaps even world-denial. It is, some say, the very picture of the alienated soul, the rarefied spirit who seems to have forgotten the body in which it lives. But such a picture could scarcely depict the full measure, the complex, rich spiritual imagination that accompanies this relation of the concrete and the intelligible. For who has not felt the mystical longing of this ancient world? To capture, but for a moment, that song from another shore; to lift our eyes for a brief season from the recognized, present-day, angular, and heavy to a realm that beckons, just beyond: Is this not the hunger for a larger world, the hope and longing that we are not alone in this dark wood? It is not magic or atavism that touches us here but rather that subtle sense, bestowed from time to time, that there is More, a Perfection or Glory or Good that is not here but heard in some still moment, sensed in a realm above, apart. Its touch gilds the tired world. Perhaps a hymn to this participatory relatio seems only poetic, but it is far more.

For it is sufferers who speak this way. It is they who have tasted the bitterness of this earth, its oppressions and abandonments; it is they who know the lash of this world and long to be delivered from it. The one who suffers in this age sees, as do not the comfortable, that this world cannot give what it promises. It seems when we look out at the world through young eyes that the riches one hopes for—truly hopes for—love and work, Freud's great pair, or true democracy, or the courage of one's convictions: these the cultures and nations of the world could provide. But sufferers have old eyes. They see more clearly, more firmly what experience, age, great faith, or great literature should give us: that the goods of this earth cannot be won on this earth but point always beyond. Old eyes look beyond this land, this concrete realm, to one beyond. "I have been to the mountain top," Dr. King said the night before he died, "and I am not fearing any man tonight."⁹ It is that vision of an Intelligible Realm that carries the sufferer through this world. We might say that in this way participation is the *revolutionary* relation of concrete and intelligible; it dares to think beyond and above. The demand "not to understand the world but to change it" is propelled by a radical dissatisfaction with this world—but not by this alone. For Karl Marx knew, too, that suffering could lead to crushing endurance, a stubborn resistance to death, that knows no change, no hope, no relief, but endurance alone. Religion, he thought, was the medicine of that endurance, a heroic or dull resignation. But in truth it is worldliness, the sad conviction that we live only here, and only within the all-too-stark limits of this earth, its glittering shallowness, its seemingly bottomless taste for cruelty, that can give only hopelessness, iron resignation. But to glimpse Another City, to belong there, to participate in it, is to taste that Heavenly Freedom, the liberty of the children of God, and to receive from that Mountain Air the art of living like free people. No one can outstrip the revolutionary force of a clear-eyed, old-eyed sufferer who knows the Heavenly Realms and who clings to them.

In the end, however, we seek another form of this relation, another path that joins the intelligible and the concrete, doctrine to Scripture, the duality of Heaven to earth. This path, I believe, will lead to a proper use of Holy Scripture as ground of Trinity and instruction in the faith. We seek what I would call the explosive relation of intelligible to concrete: the relation where the Intelligible lives *in* the concrete. We will be careful in our handling of this explosive, because this relation of inwardness carries evident dangers. The student of the tradition will note immediately that I appear in grave danger of collapsing the Creator-creature distinction, and perhaps worse, of confusing them. The young Barth was fond of quoting Ecclesiastes 5:2: "God is in Heaven; and thou upon earth." The relation of Heavenly to the earthly, in those years at least, seemed well marked by diastasis and crisis, even participation and analogy, or some form of it, too rich for his blood. Whatever account we might give for this lively patrol of the borderlands between Creator and creature, Barth had good reason to be on his guard. The Creator-creature distinction and the bold metaphysics that supported the doctrine of a God in Heaven fell out of favor in much modernism; this-worldliness seemed far more compelling to European cultures that considered themselves Christian. It seems that joining the universal to the concrete such that the immaterial or doctrinal or Heavenly *indwells* the earthly and concrete runs the risk of repeating or strengthening the dangers of an earlier age—and this with full warning in our ears. Just how can the intelligible and doctrinal—the Intelligible, properly speaking— reside *in* the concrete without collapsing what must be distinct or without confusing what must be clear and bounded and kept Holy? This, in another key, is the problem of the *vestigium Trinitatis* that stood at the entrance to our reflections on Holy Scripture, a problem that Barth warned could lead only to a virulent form of natural theology, itself a corrosive attack on the proper distinction between Creator and creature. Much hangs on this little word *in*!

There is a world to explore here, but let me begin close to home: the relation of the intelligible object to the concrete. I propose that the intellectual object is in the concrete one, and the explosive relation between the two is not properly or principally participation but rather *indwelling*. How might that work? Return now to the example we used at the beginning: the apple held before a child's eye. Now here, note—and I think Wittgenstein was drawn to this fact—the child is taught by her elders to speak or pick out an object using *a universal and linguistic name*. What the parent teaches the child is the class name or species of that concrete particular: *apple* means that thing belongs to the universal or class apple. The child when hungry reaches for that very one, the concrete object, the fruit delightful to the eye, but he knows *language* when he uses universals, classes, groups, and kinds. He sees the concrete; he learns to *recognize* the kind, to speak the abstract. This relation of abstract language to concrete object deeply exercised Søren Kierkegaard and later Wittgenstein, but for our aims here, we can simply say that intelligible concept and concrete object join at the very heart of language.

Consider the powerful example of Helen Keller and her memory of learning language, learning, in truth, inwardness altogether. Keller remembers it as an emancipation, a spiritual deliverance into the realm of the human: "Thus I came up out of Egypt and stood before Sinai," Keller remembers of her teacher, Annie Sullivan, "and a power divine touched my spirit and gave it sight, so that I beheld many wonders. And from the sacred mountain I heard a voice which said, 'Knowledge is love and light and vision.'"[10] Many will know the moment Keller learned this "sacred knowledge," her encounter with water, splashing over her hand, while Sullivan spells the word, the mass noun, into her hand. Keller writes:

We walked down the path to the well-house, attracted by the fragrance of the honeysuckle with which it was covered. [The sensory elements in Keller's writing are striking.] Some one was drawing water and my teacher placed my hand under the spout. As the cool stream gushed over one hand she spelled into the other the word water, first slowly, then rapidly. I stood still, my whole attention fixed upon the motions of her fingers. Suddenly I felt a misty consciousness as of something forgotten—a thrill of returning thought [a theory of recollection?]; and somehow the mystery of language was revealed to me. I knew then that "w-a-t-e-r" meant the wonderful cool something that was flowing over my hand. That living word awakened my soul, gave it light, hope, joy, set it free! There were barriers still, it is true, but barriers that could in time be swept away.[11]

Keller remembers the liberative moment as a deeply moral one, the gift of a capacity for regret:

I left the well-house eager to learn. Everything had a name, and each name gave birth to a new thought. As we returned to the house every object which I touched seemed to quiver with life. That was because I saw everything with the strange, new sight that had come to me. On entering the door I remembered the doll I had broken. I felt my way to the hearth and picked up the pieces. I tried vainly to put them together. Then my eyes filled with tears; for I realized what I had done, and for the first time I felt repentance and sorrow.[12]

Now here we are seeing the birth of the intellectual, the generic and universal, *within* the concrete: what set Keller free, it seems, was the association of a class noun, a name, with a concrete sense impression, a natural kind with this very sensation, water with wetness. Keller's memoir is breathtaking, and there is much more to her and to her remarkable life than this early emancipatory encounter with language. But the deeply moral and human-making dimension of this linguistic disclosure—the spiritual and biblical language Keller uses is eloquent and unmistakable—places the child's acquisition of language in the proper theological and revolutionary setting. We might dare to say: in the encounter of the intelligible in the concrete, the mastering of that explosive relation, we are brought into the house of language but also, and more powerfully, into the House of Being. "Everything had a name."

The radical power of abstract naming, the inward corridor it bore into the young Keller's life, its moral roominess, arose not from encounter with a series of concrete objects, not even with learning to recognize commonalities or identifying traits or understanding a widening circle of groups of things, touching their similarity and difference. No, Keller seems to have been liberated, humanized, re-born inwardly by suddenly grasping—no, being illumined!—that this very one, this pool of cool wetness *was* water. We use the "is of identity" here properly, for Keller is stunned by the realization that this kind term, this name or mass noun, just *was* the refreshing stream spilling out from the pump house spigot. Now it seems to me that the remarkable spiritual richness of Keller's memoir tells us that we stand in a larger domain here than the narrower chamber of language acquisition. I do not doubt, certainly, that literacy or speech is emancipatory—a flood of freedom, fresh powers. But Keller's account suggests something richer still. She has encountered through this spiritual insight the knowledge *quid est*: she has known from earliest days the *quod est*, and her memoir reveals an intense attraction to the real, but she did not know *what it is* that she encountered. This moment of receiving the identity of an object, as well as its name, liberated thought, Keller reports, and a singularly human power to regard one's own actions with internal objectivity and contrition. The explosion of the intelligible in the concrete bestowed an understanding that gave birth to a form of self-consciousness, of inwardness, at once conceptual and moral but, far more than that, wonderfully free. Now I think we have every reason to consider Keller's experience an exemplar of Augustine's doctrine of illumination, and indeed Keller herself seems to reach for that Platonizing language in the midst of a broad, scriptural depiction of her transformation. Though Keller makes use of imagery and tone that suggests at that explosive moment she moved from animality to humanity, I think it might be closer to say that the key of universality and naming unlocked a door to selfhood, long imprisoned in a welter of sensation, passion, and desires. She came to live in a *world*, an ordered and structured place, and she inhabited it, both inwardly and outwardly, as a moral and free being.

An intelligible realm, then, indwells the concrete *as its meaning*. I intend this in a broad sense. The Abstract and Intelligible inhabit our realm of disparate, concrete objects in such a way that those random things become a *cosmos*, an integrated whole, a *Naturzusammenhang*, one with depth, with order, with moral and spiritual goodness, and with startling breadth. It is fit for human beings and humane acts but also for living things of all kinds, clean and unclean, for the glorious winged things and creeping things of all kinds, plants and rocky soil and the starry heavens above. We name these things, after the Genesis account, because the world of signs, the house of language, itself inhabits this universal realm. The Intelligible is *rational*, Ratio. And it is *Good*. It indwells this realm of ours at its fundament. *This* is realism, theological realism. We need not resist modern anthropological and evolutionary accounts of human consciousness or language acquisition; we are no more opposed to those central tenets of the modern than we are to the higher criticism of the Bible. Not opposition but rather a fresh start, a reframing of the whole: that is our aim. We need not take a specific position on competing forms of idealism or realism or dualism in our metaphysics, nor advocate for a particular account of meaning and referent. Rather, we seek to open a conceptual space in which many accounts of natural kinds and universal concepts and individuation can display their wares; where realism, in its many-sided vehicle, can be examined, studied, and corrected. The point of this reframing is to see that the Name, the Intellectual object, is *in* the concrete thing; it is to be discovered there. We are not in a senseless world. Christians can be bold about this claim! Human beings do not wander this earth surrounded by dead matter: this is not a chaotic or empty realm, bare and inert, lifeless. The human being is not *creator*; that is the moral force of this reframing. We do not bring through the haphazard oddity of language a skin of coherence and order, of value or meaning. No! The strong, the explosive and revolutionary claim of Christian thought—of biblical monotheisms—is that God saw everything that He had made, and behold, it was very good. The concrete has meaning; it is suffused with it, with depth and color and kind, of purpose and *qualia* and limit, of reproduction and growth, of form and identity and essence; "everything has a name."

Now, such bold realism can happily distinguish subject matter from genre. In this way, the Intelligible indwelling of the concrete aids and guides our reading of Isaiah 53. Distinguish, not separate: we distinguish the abstract from the concrete; we mark off the subject matter, the meaning and referent of a text, a passage, a sonnet or story or ode, from its concrete narrative, event, character, and content. We acknowledge that a particular story unfolds in graceful or terrible sequence, the characters within it a study in the specific differences of a life—its arts of cruelty and deception, but of kindness, too—but we need not say that this story's *meaning* is only its unfolding, that it happened this way and not another. To the doctrine of Holy Scripture belongs the full discussion of Frei's remarkable treatment of biblical narrative and his own complex account of subject matter and genre, meaning and content. But even here we must say that Frei held to a far closer binding of subject matter to genre than do I, an integration of meaning to narrative itself, such that the referent or meaning of a text, the identity of its characters, was the close fit between action and intention, the aim of the characters and their deeds. This, Frei said, is what any story is *about*.[13]

And we can see the deep roots of this notion in Karl Barth, one of Frei's exemplars in his justly celebrated *Eclipse of Biblical Narrative*. Barth himself affirmed, against all modernism, all Bultmann-inspired demythologization, and all Christological liberalism— really, against all takers at all—that form could not be separated from content: Christ not prized out of his historical Gospels, nor the church lifted far above the concrete world of Israel and Judah, the Prophets and Kings of ancient times, and the little Child who comes to break Satan's power. Famously, Barth wrote in the midst of his long, splendid doctrine of reconciliation that many sermons on the doctrine of atonement might be quietly refolded and placed back on the pulpit lectern, and in their place, the preacher might begin a reading, a simple, unadorned reading, of the Passion Narrative. The atonement, Barth often said, just *is* the history, the unfolding, of these events, the movement from the Gabbatha to Golgatha and to burial in a garden tomb. Like Frei, Barth had complex and impressive architecture built up around this identity of subject matter and genre, and we need not, cannot, settle all that here. But for both, the realm of the intelligible, of meaning and of Christian doctrine, cannot be extracted from the historical texts themselves; indeed, the meaning or subject matter just is the telling, perhaps in other terms, of these events, and the lives broken and broken open by them. Now the critical and conceptual apparatus that surrounds both these works is glorious—and no one is better able than these two theologians to say just why there is nothing like hearing the Bible stories, their matchless power, their revolution over human culture, human life; nothing can compare with them. Their realism, their "history-like" character, combines an authenticity of behavior and motivation with a proper dimension of mystery and the incalculable, the hallmarks of human agency. This "fit" between character and motivation is what Frei considered the meaning and the identity of biblical narrative.

But must we agree here, in order to agree on many other elements of this scriptural interpretation? I say no. For the meaning of a text is not to be reduced to its sequence, its unfolding in place and season: *War and Peace* is about the terrible Old Count, and the lovely Rostoff party, and Andrei on the borderland of life and death, and the Christ-like Maria, and the marvelous, mysterious ride through the winter night on a sleigh wrapped in furs and surrounded by great hounds and wolves. Yes, it is about all this. But the meaning of this great work—novel or not—is not *exhausted* by the retelling of these events. It is *in* those events; it illumines them from within. They *are* those meanings, but the intellectual concepts, freight, import of those events extend well beyond the characters and events themselves, extend into a world of intelligence and morality that is distinctive and integral. Leo Tolstoy himself seems to have held to a view something like this, as he appends two long conceptual chapters at the book's end to give a philosophy of history and the significance of leaders and their plans within the randomness of worldly events, of war and of peace. Now we might entertain some doubts about the depth and force of Tolstoy's historiography (I do, at any rate), but we see here an author's account of one *meaning* of the unfolding narrative, one abstract and rational analysis of the tableau that is Russia awaiting Napoleon and his great army. The subject matter of Tolstoy's great work can be distinguished from the concrete elements: that is the central point here. We need not find unanimity on complex hermeneutical and literary themes here to see that an intelligible realm inhabits a novel but spills out beyond its covers: the abstract is the intelligible, the ethical, within and beyond the concrete. It is truly *there*: the concrete bears its meaning, enacts it, but is also lit up from within by it; the concrete is understood by its indwelling spiritual concepts.

So, we must and can say that we are not faced with a world of brute facts, of bare particulars, senseless things, crowded together, in idle patterns and anarchic collisions; this nightmare is not our world. It is fashionable, perhaps, to think so in our day—a spasm of the reality principle, perhaps—but it is not, in truth, our world of living and inanimate things, not even deep down. Now it may be that a Cartesian, suffused with the radical light of a substance dualism, could regard the world of *res extensa* as the cold nightmare we have described. Perhaps such a notion, ringed with despair, seized Descartes and allowed him to cut into living animals as if dead and senseless, but Christians have every reason to repudiate such dark confusion. The distinction we draw between the intelligible and concrete rests not on separation but, in complete contrast, on indwelling. Indeed, it is the very immateriality, the spiritual and conceptual nature of the abstract object, that permits it to inhabit a material and concrete object, to illumine it, without competition, without destruction. The Intelligible in the concrete is theological compatibilism in the realm of persons and of things. It is realism in the realm of dogma.

§4.3. The Intelligible and Concrete in Isaiah 53

Mutatis mutandis: the *applicatio* of all this schematic to Isaiah 53. Isaiah 53, that is, must be an expression and echo of the Divine Son, the Holy Wisdom and Word, as Eternally Generated from the Father. Now I have ventured earlier that the fathers must be right in their reading of this text; it must tell us of the Eternal Generation of the Eternal Son. How can this be? Now, it will not be so by removing the eighth verse from the chapter and declaring it the secret meaning of the whole. R. C. P. Hanson is withering on such "atomizing," and one can sympathize with his distress. Long before the birth of the higher criticism, exegetes aimed to read passages as a whole, to comment on sections, not terms, and to forge *quaestiones* in the medieval classroom by a running commentary on an entire book or letter. To inwardly digest Holy Scripture in whole portions, not by letter: that is a proper goal of much—not all, but much—biblical interpretation. But our reasons for standing alongside Hanson here might surprise him. We are not in truth seeking to anchor Holy Scripture in its Sitz im Leben or bow before its genre and redaction. Rather a proper theological realism will see the Intellectual and the doctrinal *indwelling* the whole, each a side and a particular and an element within the Holy Book. We are looking here to reframe the whole, to cut a fresh pathway between patristic and modernist reading of Holy Scripture, to find realism in our interpretation that is rational *and* faithful to the teaching of the church. We have proposed a renewed interest in the Intelligible and the concrete, one in which the metaphysical Truth indwells the concrete object.

Now I want to be careful here. It would be easy to allow the schematic to overrun the text—this is Hanson's worry, in another idiom—and even easier to assimilate the Unique Text of Holy

Scripture to an overarching *relatio* and metaphysic. The Bible would then serve the schema, not the schema the Text. It will belong to the full doctrine of creation to unfold just how this renewed and explosive relation of Intelligible and concrete can countenance and support *pluralism* in an as yet unredeemed world, but this it must do. For the Presence of Almighty God to His world is not all one thing. It is not all of a kind or of a piece; it is not lifelessly uniform, not standard or regulated. Rather, the Indwelling of the Holy One with His earth is the Unique Reality of God Himself, in His Richness, His Life, His Majesty over all His ways. It is the Day, the Sabbath Rest of the Holy One, the Distinct yet the One. The Intelligible and the concrete are finally His, altogether His, and He will enter them, illumine them, and order them in His varying and various ways. He, in His Triune Life, will be Perfect Intellect, Perfect Concretion. And Holy Scripture, as creaturely exemplar of this Relatio, stands Unique among them.

Now in this Servant Song from the prophet Isaiah, we encounter the servant in the midst of his people, in the midst of the nations of this earth. He is making his way to his grave with the wicked, and it is a lonely way. He is despised and rejected; the nations laugh at this mangled one; he knows their icy contempt, whispered behind hands held up before one's face, turned away, turned toward a conspirator; they relish together their scorn of the weak. This is the tender plant that has no form or beauty. The servant is the offscouring of the busy world, the one of no account, the unseen, the thrown away. The prophet lays before our eyes what we never see: the nations that carry their burdens, endure them, year upon year, without notice from the great, busy with the technology that they say has changed everything, but still the servant nations live the *longue durée*, the changeless suffering of the poor. The prophet turns our faces away from the delicious conspiracy toward the human lives that become the furniture of our world: the still forms that stand at street corners, that fade into anonymity and colorless obscurity, on park benches and behind empty warehouses; the child unwanted, taunted, beaten; the passed over in every office and factory; the criminal, the immigrant, the bystander to our elegant life. The prophet shows us these things in all their searing concreteness. *This* is the Lord's servant, the one who disappears before our sightless eyes. Now this is denunciation, an exposure, of the world of the bare fact, the meaningless and forgotten. The prophet makes plain to us the life, collective and singular, of that which has been allowed to fall—has been crushed—into airless concreteness, into thinghood.

Now, the Mission of the Son, the Holy and Good Wisdom of God, is to enter this realm of the concrete, the forgotten. He is to put it on, to become *this*. He is not to *displace* it or supplant it, but to enter it, to clothe Himself with it. This, the faith tells us, is the *meaning* of this concrete life, this servant-become-thing. Unmistakable in the Septuagint is the language the apostle Paul will echo in the Carmen Christi for this Great Descent among us: the lowliness, *tapeinosis*, is the detention of this Prisoner, and His handing Himself over, *paradidomai*, to death is His Self-Offering that will exalt Him and number Him among the great. But we need not read this passage only in a straightforward and obdurate figural and Christological reading. Holy Scripture does not mean just one thing!

Rather we are to see meaning laid down in this prophetic text, laid down in the history of Israel, in the nation crushed by the rich empires on every side, lost in the narratives of great doings and great spoils. The prophet Isaiah speaks the Lord's word when he draws our eyes away from the glitter of Egypt and Babylon with its great cities and hanging gardens, its magnificent high relief work, its temples and grand arcades, away from all this to a nation pitiful in its exile and loss, a vulgar and little thing. The prophet pulls our eyes away from the *fascinans* of world history, not first and principally, as moral instruction: that we are to honor the poor and to welcome the stranger. Yes, this is Israel's law, Israel's prophets. But Isaiah 53 is not principally a teaching about the proper ethical response to the forgotten and downtrodden. Rather, it is to give us the *meaning* of these cataclysms in the life of individuals and of a people. That abstract meaning, that intelligible lesson in the midst of the unendurable is this: that this lost and little life is become the *Ebed Adonai*, the Servant of the Lord. And this Servant beyond all telling and all perception is suffering *for a purpose*: He is to bear the iniquity of us all. The humiliation of a prisoner, so broken that he cannot protest his own death; the scandal of the display and mocking of the helpless, in a savage and cultic exercise of nationalism; the cheap and contemptuous dismissal of a prisoner or exile among the transgressors—it really is all his fault!—and the cool acceptance of a miscarriage of justice by those whose sun is in the ascendance: all this, the prophet tells us, bears a moral and rational, a theological meaning. Isaiah says: it pleased the Lord to bruise him; he has put him to grief; and in these concrete events, in their very cruelty and seeming absurdity, God sees *the Righteous One*, His Servant, the One who makes many righteous. Israel is this nation, this people, this righteous servant. And from this nation will come the Servant who will make intercession for the transgressors of this sorry earth.

Now it will be our task to see just how all this searing depiction and stern interpretation of the Servant of the Lord is also and in truth the Generation of the Eternal Son. This is the patristic reading we aim to defend. But we must linger a moment longer on the level of the economy, on the concrete in its broadest sense. For the relation between the Intelligible and the concrete, the indwelling of meaning within the events and places of this earth, have raised conceptual and moral questions that must not be left behind in the sweep of this onrushing reframing. We have made a strong appeal to the intelligible within the material and visible and have pointed to its indwelling as well as its clear distinction from the concrete, the historical, and the physical. And we have enlisted all this in service of a traditional, but also novel, reading of the Servant Song in Isaiah 53. But have we in this way made the meaning, the intelligible and rational, the only real mechanism at work here? Has the abstract hollowed out the concrete such that a form of idealism, or perhaps dualism, has overcome and erased the concrete, the embodied, the material? There are many reasons to worry about such a result, to fend it off as best as possible—but chief among them here is the erasure of suffering, mindless, senseless suffering, in the welter of well-meant explanation and interpretation. Always this is a grave danger in the encounter with the concrete! The temptation of Christians, early and late, to *explain* pain, to justify it, or to sanction it in light of its meaning has proved nearly irresistible in spiritual and moral writing. Now, we can well see why. To name an illness, to diagnose a condition, to fit a random and terrible suffering to a pattern, to show its sense and its end: that is a great good, a relief and deliverance understood and sought by patients sitting, right now, this day, in hospitals and waiting rooms, across from doctors and therapists in their consulting rooms, and lying in their beds with their Bibles stretched open across their laps. Of course, the spiritual meaning of suffering cannot be denied as a religious quest or teaching. But it must be done in such a way that the suffering itself is not emptied or erased. This is vital, and remarkably demanding.

The concrete, physical, inert, and meaningless has special glory before God. God is Intellectual, Immaterial, and Spiritual, yes. But the Triune Holy Lord is also Concrete, searingly Concrete. And He has made good and very good the things of this earth, this vast universe. The mute, the stable, the perduring, the obdurate: these also are from the hand of Almighty God. We cannot see into concrete objects. We cannot penetrate them with our human intellects; we cannot master or comprehend them *as matter*. (Rahner is right on this score.) Of course, for us human creatures, matter nearly always bears meaning and carries deep within it the abstract kind and identity that give it the name, the *intelligibility*, that is the blessing of an ordered cosmos. (Just this, we may think, spurred on Gregory of Nyssa's lesson from his sister, Macrina.)[14] But the Creator sees otherwise. This One who is Being Itself, Most Real, the Source of all Abstraction and the Source of all Concreteness, this Triune Lord comprehends the concrete *as such*. It, too, is the child of His blessing. It is a central Christian teaching to recognize this! We are quick to see the kinds and families of living things, their identities as members of universal types, in their joyful and free life of blessing before the Lord. And we can see individuals taking up their place within these families of kinds, and of the natural realm gifting and nourishing and comforting these human lives in their pilgrimage from birth to death. But we are also to be quick in seeing the physical itself, the matter of this earth, and the uncatalogued, unsorted, unpatterned *thisness* of our reality as itself blessed and a blessing from God's hand. Note that blessing in this sense is not collapsed into the intelligible meaning; it is rather the inert *givenness*, the reality that is *there*, placed, located, anchored, and seen, that is itself a form of blessing. It, too, is *real*.

Pain is concrete in all these ways. It is the astonishing impenetrability of pain that is its unmistakable hallmark. We can of course grade and sort it; intelligibility indwells it, too. But pain itself outstrips description; words fall before it. We teach and praise empathy in others, compassion before suffering—and well we should do so!—but pain in concrete reality is beyond communication.

We do not share in it, and it is radically particular. When those who suffer intractable pain reflect on their suffering, they know, as we cannot, that they bear, in body and soul, some inertness, some burden and iron weight, that cannot be wholly illuminated; it is without genus or kind, without meaning in its material core, simply, brutally *there*. Sufferers stand before the incommunicable; they know the concrete in its utter facticity, its unrepentant reality, its random and blinding force. Above all this solidity of suffering must be honored. We know now, at great cost to others, that genocide and the Shoah must never be *dissolved* by explanation. The Holy God alone knows an explanation, a concept, that justly honors the slain, the dismembered dead. But for us there is, at deep ground, the horror, the surd that is such suffering. We fall silent before such pain, our hands over our mouths, like Job's friends before the urge to explain overcame them. This is an honoring of the concrete, the unrepeatable and unshareable that we owe, the least we owe, to those who suffer.

And the concrete must be honored in other ways as well, in itself and as such. We will reserve for the doctrine of creation a fuller accounting of the material and the historical. These are critical tasks for dogmatics in our day, quick as we have been to move to the spiritual, the intelligible, and the immaterial realms whenever theology truly got down to work. But here we should as foreshadow affirm our commitment to the matter of the cosmos and, most particular, the concrete objects of this globe, now surrounded and penetrated by humankind. How quick we are to attempt our abstract control over these things! We humans have of course used our intellect and the realm of meaning to reason toward the full appropriation of creaturely matter for our own ends: to make the concrete into a "resource." The tree become lumber; the mountain an ore deposit: this is the abstract indwelling the concrete in such a way that humankind—better, some human beings—thrive and the world of nature declines. Not in our creaturely realm is the healed and fully holy joining of the intelligible and the concrete! But this is not all one way! For we environmentalists defend the concrete in very high-toned spiritual abstractions. The notion of an ecosystem, the flourishing of creatures in their niches, the well-ordered harmonies of species and kinds and food chains: these are all biological and creaturely meanings of the natural realm, universals that make a world. And there are less lofty defenses as well: the frank appeal to human flourishing, dependent as it is on plants, on the oceans, on the ice caps and spring rains. We are not wrong to affirm our own neediness and frailty. We have in this way honored the material of our earth as it serves us, conserves us in our neediness, but we have not yet reached down and above to the concrete as such, nature in its *there-ness*. That something cannot be exhausted by our words; that it is incommunicable, inexplicable, reserved; that it inhabits a realm we cannot imagine but can only love; that it touches us and fills us with wonder: this is the natural beyond all saying. It shows itself. Perhaps Iris Murdoch expresses this best when she famously exclaimed, how difficult it is for us to acknowledge that anything else is *real!*[15] The dignity, the autonomy and objectivity of the concrete, its reality beyond meaning, is a savage fact and blessing of creation, of the Creator; it abides.

Just so dogmatics in the present day seeks a doctrine of the sacraments that also honors the concrete, the material. We foreshadow here, too, how a fuller account of sacramentality can parallel and enact the Truth indwelling the concrete, the Word become flesh. We need not, cannot, settle here all that devolves on a proper treatment of *Sacramentum et Res*, of sign and signified, of form and matter, word and species. But it is the common province of sacramental theologians to emphasize the materiality of the church's sacraments: the plain, unadorned water that will become sign of our deliverance; the bread and wine, common table food, visible and tangible even as it becomes or bears the Body of our Lord; and the oil that smears across foreheads in sickness, in blessing, in anointing for service and married life. These are concrete materials of the Presence of God in our midst, and they bear meaning, but are sovereignly indifferent to it, too. They, in themselves and as such, resist all that. Christians need not say that the *bread* remains after Consecration of the Elements; Roman Catholics must not, but many Lutherans and Anglicans may and do. But we might say, across the churches, that whatever we may affirm about *substance* need not carry over to the concrete or material itself. For it is at least an element of St. Thomas's account of transubstantiation that the taste and smell and "dimensive properties" of bread and wine—the accidents, in Aristotelian vocabulary—remain after Consecration, graciously inhering in the Substance of Christ's Glorified Flesh. In my idiom, the concrete remains. It may be bread; it may not. But the raw and stubborn materiality, the free-flowing liquid, the tang of bread or unleavened host: these the Lord God graciously conserves, and it, too, in its silence and impenetrability, comes from the Father of Lights.

So, we do well to honor the concrete in its broadest sense in the Prophetic text, Isaiah 53. But our aim here is to speak in the end of the Spiritual and Meaningful, to vindicate that doctrinal and conceptual and metaphysical dimension of the scriptural text. We seek here the Eternal Generation of the Son. We do not discard the economy. But we look within, deep within as well as above, for the Heavenly. Just what does it mean to speak of "generation"? This is our doctrinal question here. For the Hebrew and the Greek encompass multiple connotations of this word, as do the Latin and English. The Bible's first book, Genesis, demonstrates the richness of this word well: the generations of the heavens and the earth, their making. But also, the generations of the ancestors: their families, clans, their days and times. Generation can be a seen as the trace of a gerund of several kinds, of the act of making, seen from above as it were, as a whole, completed work, and of that which is made, its season and a day, as a group and a kin, facing their tasks together. It is a verb, an act, nominalized. The Generation of the Servant is our theme in this rich sense. In this precise sense, we consider and look within for the Eternal Processions, the Eternal Generation of the Word. Note, then, that we do not look at the historical and concrete Son, the economy in its narrower sense, and ask, how does the agency and especially the passion of this One Servant find its home or ground in the Eternal Generation? We do not look for the generation of Israel that spent its years in exile or for the origin of that people and its servant in some shadowy form in the Godhead. No. It is not from below to above that we seek here. And we do not hope to find the events of the One Sufferer *grounded* in the Deity. This is a form of direct grounding that never serves theology well. Indeed, it is this very move, from below to above, that Barth countenances; a direct and forceful grounding of the Obedient Son in the Divine Nature; an Echo and a Source, a Divine Form and Pattern we discern also in the Christomorphic Trinitarianism of Hans Urs von Balthasar and Sergius Bulgakov. But the concrete does not properly function in this way!

The concrete does not control or constitute the doctrine of God in its metaphysical Reality, however much we aim to honor the economy through training our sights there. It should not become foundation in this sense! Rather it is the Intelligible in the concrete, not the concrete in the Intelligible. We need not settle the epistemic matters here—the charge to think "oriented" from event of Jesus Christ, as Barth puts this—to affirm that doctrinally and objectively, the Realm of Truth enters into, controls, and bestows meaning on the concrete and earthly, and we are to search for that Immanent Realm of Lordly Aseity in the Holy Book of Scripture.

What we see in Isaiah 53, then, is this Verbal Form, the Act become Noun. This is the Generation that is narrated here, as doctrine: that a generation has entered exile, has been made a people far from home, of no account, and has been gathered up in a servant, a person and Israelite, who makes righteous what is broken and lost. Generation, then, is both a *Begetting* and a *Person*. And just this form of highly abstract and grammatical reading is fitting for the Generation of the Word, the deep structural Rationality of the Living God. Holy Scripture in just this way is the *Verba Trinitatis*. But we must say more. For such high abstractions do not capture the proper weight of the concrete, the proper honor of that which is not itself Immaterial and Doctrinal and Eternal. The scriptural text cannot be treated as a "resource"! It is not to be mined for useful concepts or relations; it cannot be erased in this way. Rather we must hear, in these very outpourings of the Suffering One, the Divine Life of the Eternal Son, Begotten, not made. He, the Eternal Son, has left His stamp on this text, has pressed His own Life deep down within it, and has touched it with His Eternity and Seal, and we must hearken to it. He is the Agent here; He the Maker of this text; He the Concrete Incommunicable Being who is Reason and Truth. He guides this text. He speaks His Word to us, Communicates it.

What we see in Isaiah 53, we must say, in the end, is the *Divine Procession of the Word*. This is the final and perfect Concreteness, pouring forth Eternally in the Perfect, Infinite, and Universal Nature. The Holy Scriptures of the Old and New Testaments exhibit the Divine Life, the Dynamism and Fire of the Intelligible in the Concrete, the Being, the Reality who is God as this Living

One gives rise to, generates and breathes the Wise Goodness of God, the Triune Lord. God is Love in this sense, too: the Infinite Outpouring of Goodness, the whole Goodness of the Lord passing by. The Bible bears the mark of the Divine Processions in just this way: it is the fiery record of Life, the Explosion who is God, roiling and breaking open, lighting up the night, burning at the very core. *This* is God, it says. For this reason, Thomas is right—dogmatically and exegetically right—to begin with Divine Processions. (We will have more to say on this critical point in time.) Far from a presumptuous speculation, an overreaching that abandons Revelation for vain human imaginings, Thomas follows the *Sache* of Holy Writ, its Subject Matter: the Divine Life. He distinguishes but does not separate subject matter from genre and treats it most properly as prime of place, the gateway into the Mystery of Holy Trinity. In time, we will follow this scriptural, Thomistic lead. But not without showing a concrete instance! Now all this is highly general, of course, and could properly, rightly, be affirmed of the Bible in all its passages and parts. But how can such a broad affirmation of the Divine Processions as scriptural guide our reading of this one text?

We begin with the search for the Generation of the Son, this Concrete Divine Relation. The first and principle thing we must say is that this *locus* is the object of a search, a quest, a pilgrimage. It does not lie right on the surface of the text; it is not manifest. We turn to Isaiah 53, confident that we will be taught about the Eternal Life of God; but we must wait there, expectant. We must bring to the passage our question: How are we to understand the Eternal Generation of the Son in this rejection and suffering of the Faithful Servant? What is to be learned here? This movement of the Ebed Adonai from collective to singular, from tender planting to mocking and contempt, from recognition to utter rejection and holding of no account, this pilgrimage to pain and sorrow, to lowliness: What can these events of terrible concreteness show us about the Divine, Eternal Generation of Wisdom? We must be able to affirm, that is, that the journey of the Suffering Servant is not *separated or divided* from Almighty God, or *contrary* to Him. True, it is not, *in itself,* God's own Life—just that is the affirmation of the Subject matter distinct from the genre, the Intelligible from the concrete, the Processions from the Missions. We do not have here a *univocal* or direct manifestation of the Inner Dynamism of God. Rather it is *indirect,* a lesson structural and spiritual, that is laid down here, deep within, its Meaning and its Goodness. But if it be *teaching* about the Living God, it must in some fashion be coordinate with or correspond to or, at the very least, not be repugnant to the Eternal Processions—that is the force of saying that Holy Scripture teaches the dogma of the Holy Trinity. This passage is the *shape, the movement* of the Divine and Glorious Generation as it enters the kingdom of the concrete, the earthly. But it will not be one lesson, one shape, one mark only. The proper exegesis of Holy Scripture in its act of faithfulness, is humble, fallible, corrigible. The pilgrimage that is Trinitarian reading of Holy Scripture covers many lands, honors many sacred places, sees diverse wonders, draws various lessons. The Bible is Inexhaustible, a Well springing up for every generation. So, we draw out one lesson.

This passage bears two formal characteristics: The Servant is Anonymous; and He makes many righteous. The Servant is hidden, without form, unseen and unmarked. He is Anonymous in this sense, too, that He may be the whole covenant people, but also the derelict soul, the least one among that people. He is Representative in this highly angular sense, that He is Unknown, Unseen, Unacknowledged, lost among the dead. He is of no account, an Anonymous, Unregistered member of an exiled people. So, it must be—we are permitted to say—that the Eternal Generation of the Son cannot be recognized by the peoples of this earth; it must be unheralded and misunderstood and unknown among us. It must exceed our understanding and powers of identification. Who can tell His Generation? This Anonymity tells us that the Divine Word exceeds the *Incarnate* Son: the Procession of the Wisdom of God is not exhausted or fully expressed in the Mission. There is something, Some Reality that is Unknown, Unrecognized, Unseen here—the Servant cannot be *placed*, named, mastered. There is Hidden Reserve to this Son, some element, some aim and determination, that cannot be seen or received by those around Him: we judged Him accursed, of no account. He bears a meaning that exceeds anything assigned to Him by earthly courts, but it is not just the Abstract, the meaning, that conveys an Excess to this Son. It is His very Life, His Presence among us, that cannot be fully or truly seen. He is without form or beauty: even His Concreteness, His *Thereness*, cannot be grasped; He seems to slip out from our view, a mangled and disturbed image. He is Stranger among us. This is the biblical expression of the dogmatic Sache of the *Extra Calvinisticum*, the Logos Asarkos. We must affirm in just this way that the Eternal Generation of the Son exceeds the Incarnation; the Procession, Eternally Fruitful and Expressive, gives rise to a Reason that is beyond the earthly Mission of the Son. Just this is the distinction of subject matter from genre! And we see the direction here, *from* Heaven *to* earth, from Meaning to suffering death. It is the Intelligible *in* the concrete: the concrete, yes, but the Universal, the Excess and Beyond, penetrating and illumining the concrete. That is the pattern here.

Now this lesson we have drawn from the prophet Isaiah cuts against much modern theology—it will surprise no student of theology to hear me say this. The Christological concentration of the Western church, especially since the Enlightenment, has brought the matter of Reformation debates—the *Extra Carnem* of the Reformed dogmaticians—into the broad current of constructive theology. The conviction that Revelation was a *Christological* Doctrine and that it at long last laid down a winning hand against the masterful play of Kantians and skeptics of all stripes: these two made the *identification* of the Eternal Son with the Incarnate Christ—Subject matter with genre—overwhelmingly attractive. We might say that modern Trinitarianism has taken its bearings from this identification, at times boldly asserting, as do Wolfhart Pannenberg and Robert Jenson, that the Son *just is* the earthly Christ or, in a more restrained fashion, that the life of the Incarnate Son reveals to us the Eternal Son, such that we know something *particular* about the Deity of the Son, as does Rahner. The modern animus against the scholastic teaching, that any of the Persons could have been Incarnate, stems, I believe, from this close binding of the Second Person of the Trinity to the Incarnate Christ. Indeed, it would be a monograph of its own to set out in full terms how Barth viewed the Son, the Logos, as *Jesus*, this very one. It seems that Barth was not ready to fully abandon the Logos Asarkos, but he could be very bold on this matter. The conviction that we know the Holy God through and because of Jesus Christ becomes a metaphysical claim that the Son just *is* the Revealer. "There is no God, no height or depth, where we do not find the face of Jesus Christ,"[16] Barth will often say, and it seems at times that this expansive claim dares to scale even the high wall between God's Eternity and the creature's historical time. Of course, these are the exceedingly dense thickets of the doctrine of the Incarnation and must return again to them when we set forth the Divine Missions to this earth. But even here we must say that the very *character* of the Incarnate Servant should warn us off from an earthly Christ who tells all and everything about the Eternal Word.

The Fifth Gospel—the Book of Isaiah—has brought us, through indirect means, to the heart of the doctrinal problem Barth called nominalism. This is not the nominalism familiar to historians of philosophy: the relation of individual substance to universal categories. In that historical tradition, nominalism then and now refers to a philosophical school that acknowledges only individuals as real; the classes or kinds to which they belong are human constructs, ideas, notions, or sets, without independent or sturdy reality. It is this historical and philosophical use of nominalism that hovers on the margins of Elizabeth Spelman's conceptual work. Barth, however, has something else in view. In his use of the term, Barth aims for something far broader: the question whether the Perfections or Properties of God are mere "names," *nomena*, a human word that applies we know not how to God, or perhaps cannot apply at all. The Divine Reality or Nature exceeds any name, in this nominalistic view; it is the great Unknown. We can reach only this Mystery's "energies" or "works," His relation toward us. We might say, in another idiom, that Barth here confronts the riddle of skepticism in the creaturely knowledge of God. Is there a "High God," an Excess, beyond Being, beyond Idea, that can move and reign and determine in utter Solitude, Unknown, Unthought? Barth considers nominalism—or, in scholastic terms, semi-nominalism— far more potent, more corrosive, than the medieval distinction of the Two Powers, the *Potentia Absoluta* and the *Potentia Ordinata*, fearsome enough to students of the *Via Moderna*.

The paralyzing fear of nominalism, Barth says, is the conviction and terror that God in truth and in metaphysical reality is Something or Someone *other than* the God and Father of our Lord Jesus Christ. There is some depth, some darkness, or some mysterious and terrible height that is not illumined or measured by Jesus Christ and could in some annihilating nightmare oppose or contradict the Good

News who is Emmanuel, God with us. This is Luther's agony, Barth tells us: The Holy God in his naked and terrible Power could be *against* us, not *for* us in Jesus Christ, could rise up out of this Mysterious Darkness an Enigmatic and Destructive Force, wholly Unknown, wholly Sovereign, Implacable, Remorseless. To say that the Divine Attributes apply to the economy or the Energies, the Works of God, or that they are true but cannot name the Mode of their truth: this is to plunge down a narrow passageway to an Unlit Prison, a Terror that observes no rules, no ratio. Barth holds that against such radical destruction, radical remedy must be applied. Only a Christology of a determinate and dominant kind can meet this threat: in Jesus Christ, the Incarnate One, we meet really and directly and fully the True God, the One who loves in freedom. There is no remainder. Just this is the denial of the Logos Asarkos, and it is strong medicine indeed.

Our security has been established now, Barth tells us, by our full confidence in what Jesus Christ has done for us—the "whole course of His obedience," as Calvin expresses this point. Barth is not so much struck by the historical *facts* or character of the Man Jesus; he does not propose that Jesus's physical traits reveal God, for example. Rather an "actualistic" account of Christ's manifestation of God secures our proper knowledge of the True God's Fidelity, Grace, Patience, and Mercy. It is just this move that underwrites Barth's daring appropriation of obedience and subordination to the Godhead and Divine Persons in relation. It takes only a little introspection to see the problems Barth courts, with eyes wide open: the threat that creation becomes necessary to God; the worry that our knowledge of God becomes univocal and altogether too confident, titanic; the danger that the Incarnation controls and constrains the entire Being and Act of God, such that His Freedom, vaunted and praised in word, is emptied and denied in deed. We might reply to all this, well, yes. These indeed are dangers in Christian doctrine, and Barth considers the risk sufficient to court them directly. I do not believe this is so, but the skeptical and moral problem Barth identifies cannot be so easily dismissed.

For just who is this Servant whose Anonymity and Surplus shocks us from the verses of Isaiah 53? Who is the Wise and Good God who exceeds and holds in reserve Concrete Deity beyond the Incarnate Son? Just who is, just who can be this Logos Asarkos? This Holy Mystery, the Triune Lord in the cloud and darkness and fire: Is He the One who works the alien work? Is He the great Irrational Force lying beyond all law, all pattern, all knowing? We speak here of the foundation of our faith, the foundation of reality itself. We have to see that, in truth, *this* is the experience— no, the anguished question—that is the Suffering Servant himself. This terrible question just *is* his life. We may style this, of course, the "problem of evil" or, more expansively, a "theodicy," and this indeed is the Sache, the subject matter of this song cycle. But we have to see that this is not in truth a *conceptual* problem. Barth's self-involving dogmatics, his "existential" impulse, wards off any danger in his great work of bare conceptual rationalism. But his *response* to this dilemma is strongly conceptual and dogmatic: the *Logos Ensarkos* will guarantee the successful predication of Names for God, and those Names will in the end speak just one, the lovely Name of Jesus Christ. But the *crisis* of the Suffering Servant—his detention, his imprisonment—just is the crushing silence of the concrete, his life in pain and grief, the overthrow of justice, his reduction to the deadness of a thing, the meaninglessness of the whole. This is Israel's life in the greedy clash of empires; the life of the covenant people of God at the hands of their enemies, then and today. We meet here the solemn uncertainty and ambiguity of this generation: Who can imagine its future? I think we have not penetrated to the searing realism of this text if we do not see that Luther's life struggle, to find a gracious God, is the life question and agony of this people, this Servant. The Servant's life is *meaningless* in its contours. Abused, forgotten, crushed by pain, left in a jail cell to rot: these are savageries familiar in our own day, cruelties that seem beyond all remedy. They are all *Logoi spermatikoi* in just this sense. We Christians can never forget the Servant who dies with the terrible cry from Psalm 22 on His lips. The plea that goes unanswered; the challenge that is met by no Whirlwind; the stark Silence, the scorn and pain; and darkness is His only companion. And we know that this One was not the only sufferer for He was numbered among the transgressors: legions have gone to their graves this way, unrelieved, inexplicable, unnoticed, unknown. Is this the terrible, strange Work of God? We have to consider carefully just what it means, after all, that Christ is *unsuccessful*, that He is the Man of Sorrows and acquainted with grief.

It is an extraordinarily deep contour of this One who dwells among us, this pattern of failure and rejection. I do not mean by that that the Redeeming Mission of the Son is a failure, that our salvation is incomplete or unfulfilled. No, but the victory cry that escapes from the dying lips of our Lord itself *conforms* to this anguished shape of sorrow and rejection. It is in this dying, this death of humiliation and scandal, the *stumbling block*, that Christ proclaims to us as His Telos, His Perfect Victory. Isaiah 53 served the early church as a prophetic text just because it followed that contour: the anonymity and rejection that *in a hidden way* is the intercession for, the making righteous, of the many. This Divine Shape, however, is all too easily explained away as the fallen rebellion of the creature, the sin of Jew and gentile. And of course, every form of sin is glaringly at work there! We could scarcely begin an exegesis of the Suffering Servant Songs, that genre, without a visceral catalogue of the cruelty and oppression that Israel and this one Israelite must endure. But we have not seen all that we are told to look upon if we halt our gaze here. The story of the suffering Israelite, of the Suffering Son, is not the unfolding of a success story turned tragically wrong. We are not to imagine that Jesus of Nazareth would have been a glorious Teacher of Righteousness, a popular Mystagogue, a well-regarded Shepherd King, who just happened to fall among thieves and be left for dead. No! The entire shape and force of the Old Testament witness to Christ—the Inconvenient One—and the unmistakable trajectory of the kingdom of Israel in the midst of ancient empire is of *descent*, of suffering, of failure and rejection.

All too eagerly we Christians have seized on the notion of sin and narrow-mindedness and materialism or legalism or some other form of projected folly to *explain and explain away* the history of Israel under the Caesars and the history of Jesus, the rejected Messiah. We Christians want to say, long to say, that the contour of the Eternal Son made flesh would have been delightful had sin not gotten in the way. Just this impulse guides the innumerable sermon illustrations in which Jesus's opponents are set forth as petty or insecure or craven before power or crowds; they long to be first, rather than serve; they fear change or conflict or uncertainty; they think they know best. It is a compassionate impulse that motivates these stories: of course, we can identify with all these follies! But embedded in such accounts of Jesus in His fateful ministry is the stubborn belief *that we* would welcome Him now, should He appear among us, and that those who have received the Gospel would follow Him in a far, far better fashion, toward a far, far better end. We Christians allow ourselves to imagine, that is, that the arc of the Incarnation is *success*. In itself, and apart from sin, the Word made flesh would be fully known, not anonymous, luminous, and fully attractive, a living Goodness that would radiate, powerfully, effortlessly, to every valley and peak, and draw all things to Himself. Such a Jesus would be something like an Enlightened *Bodhisattva*, a Pearl of great price, not hidden in a field, but displayed, gleaming and delightful, teaching and winning disciples, contagious with blessing. Of course, we imagine all that!

But the concrete contour of Israel and of Israel's Servant is not that, not at all. I do not think a serious reader of Holy Scripture can come away from this book with a cheery air of progress, of development, slow but steady, of God's Ways becoming level and plain, each day, better and better. The realism of the Bible interrupts such idle dreams; perhaps in this way, borrowing from Virginia Woolf, we could say this book is one of the few written for adults. The story of Israel is *agon*, wrestling. It is fidelity, yes, and covenant observant, yes, and broad and rich teaching on Almighty God, and joy in that teaching, too: we would have stony hearts not to see the glory of the people Israel in their ascent to the temple, their peace and joy in the Sabbath, their sweet succor of those in need. But all these, in fidelity and in infidelity, are caught up in this larger pattern, this brokenness and dispersion. The Incarnate Son is an Israelite in just this way. His life, from the throne of manger straw to the throne of grace on the Cross, is one of increasing conflict, of deepening rejection, of opposition even within, betrayal, and denial. The world does not know this One. It cannot escape the eye of a modern reader that history books are piled full of records and manuscripts, inscriptions and stelae, vast building programs and small jeweled cases, handled by the past, and not one of these is of Jesus of Nazareth or by Him. He is the Anonymous One.

In just this way, He is the prophet like Moses. It cannot strike us forcefully enough that Moses *had* to die on Mount Nebo, within sight of the Promised Land. Israel's greatest prophet, the law giver, the liberator, the people's first priest: he, this chosen one, is the *humblest* servant of the Lord, the lowly one who will die in an unmarked grave, grieved but without honors and rites, buried only by his Lord. Numbers and Exodus do indeed record acts of rebellion and pride on Moses's part; he is not without sin as is his descendant and representative. Yet Deuteronomy knows another meaning and explanation for Moses's rejection and death: "on account" of Israel and Israel's sins, Moses, too, must die. It is this Pattern, this Procession we are to see here. Moses, too, is anonymous; he, too, becomes unmarked, unknown in his death; in his downward path, he, too, takes up Israel and Israel's destiny as his own; and his greatness ends in failure and loss, a final plea to cross the Jordan refused, and he enters the grave with his generation, the rebels of the wilderness era. *This* is his generation. And Moses, too, conforms to this Divine Pattern of the Unknown, the Vicarious, and the Unsuccessful.

What have we been taught here about the Eternal Generation of the Son? We say: There is something deeply hidden about the Life of God, some profound Mystery here. It is not simply the Redoublement that accompanies all exposition of the Holy Trinity, though to be sure, we note that element here as well. But it is something more, something further, something far deeper than all that. This profound Humility that just is the Divine Power and Perfection is exemplified here, in the loss and suffering and grave of Israel and Israel's prophets that we must stand before, reverently and patiently. Who is this God, who discloses His Life in this way, through these descending ones? We see first that *revelation* as a broad and straightforward category—successful teaching—cannot be the principle purpose and telos of Holy Scripture. We are not being shown a history of progressive and effective instruction by which the covenant people and, later, the gentiles are informed about the True God and eagerly and docilely and faithfully receive that word. The Holy Scriptures are not that kind of book! We do not see disciples eagerly gathered around ancient teachers, imitating and extending and enriching the lessons the scribes and prophets bring to earth. No, it is striking, and unmistakable, that the law that is Perfect and enlightens the eyes, the Wisdom and Glory of the Lord that goes forth from there, the lessons and parables that issue from Israel's Redeemer: all these are met by puzzlement, or by eager acceptance and consent, only to have the cares of the day and the snares of wealth uproot them and wither them away; so very few seeds fall on good soil. It is not *complete* failure; the evil one does not snatch all away. But it cannot be overlooked that the teaching of Israel has been met by murmuring, inside the covenant and beyond it, too.

Skeptics of the faith often challenge us on this very neuralgic point: Why would God not write His Law and Divine Nature on the clouds *directly* so that all could read and obey? Why this embassy through human teachers; these lessons spoken by humble, often inarticulate messengers; these parables and sayings, hard to understand, hard to interpret; why entrust this to a small people in a small corner of the globe, when everything in heaven and on earth rests on it? Why not something and someone more successful? This objection to the faith and to Holy Scripture has been often treated as a shallow and unimpressive gibe—and to be sure it has been used in that way—but we need not dismiss it so cheaply. For there is indeed an oddity about the Pattern of Holy Writ, its status and stature as Intelligible Revelation of God, that is deeply unsettling, deeply puzzling. After his commissioning, the prophet Isaiah is told to "make the heart of this people fat, and make their ears heavy, and shut their eyes, until the cities be wasted without inhabitant, and the houses without man, and the lands be utterly desolate." It is this very counsel of failure that Jesus Christ takes as

His own, teaching only in parable so that people can hear and hear but not understand, see and see yet perceive nothing. The Gospel of John is no exception! For even there, in those luminous addresses, controversy, confusion, and polemic reign. And His Life is indeed one of misunderstanding, of distortion and opposition, ridicule and contempt—a Man of Sorrows and acquainted with grief. Why?

Learning about God, about His Life, must be, in truth, a very odd and startling event. I think we can scarcely exaggerate this unsettling truth. The revelation of God as Trinity, this Reality, Perfect in Intellection, Perfect in Concretion, cannot in truth be a kind of lesson or instruction that we recognize or welcome. It is not simply a resistance to teachings about sin or about judgment or even about death. We do indeed resist such austere lessons about our destiny and frame, but Holy Writ is not Word of God principally directed to these things. Indeed, we scarcely need a prophet to tell us the stark news that we will die and that all whom we love will go down to the dust. Even the body of the great Hector, breaker of horses, will be carried off the windy plains of Troy, itself broken and descended to the House of Death, its future to be reduced to ash. No, the Bible is about *God*, His Eternal Reality, and He is Author of these words, sender of these prophets, Teacher of these unwanted and unsuccessful truths. We must see that Almighty God seeks to teach us about His Life through *incompleteness*, through failure and anonymity. This does reflect the incompleteness of this world, its inadequacy as the final resting place for the human intellect or for the moral life. Yes, this Pattern of descent and anonymity does teach this form of world-denial and transcendence. But the Bible as this descent of Intelligible into the concrete must tell us more than that, more than the common instruction about the insufficiency of finite, temporal life for the insatiable hunger that is creaturely desire for God. The Bible is also in this Pattern of failure a *Teacher of the Divine Processions.* And the failure of revelation to completely disclose its Object, to exhaust or contain It, is the Mystery of the Divine Life, the *Eternal Generation* and *Spiration of God.*

We see that the Holy Trinity, its Eternal Life, must be Itself Mystery. We have here at long last the *scriptural* account for the relation of reason to the dogma of the Holy Trinity. Mystery not only surrounds but stands at the heart of Triunity, because, Holy Scripture tells us, the act of disclosure, of revelation, can never be complete, exhaustive, laid out fully to our sight. This does not make the doctrine *irrational!* The Mystery of Holy Trinity does not rest on paradox, or absurdity, or claims that cannot be *thought.* No! God is not Six Impossible Things before breakfast! We are commanded to know the Lord, to seek Him, to enter into His Gates, to love His Ways, to confess His Peace and Mercy, to learn what they mean. But this descent in the Pattern of God, this Anonymous Servant, tells us that our knowledge of God is always broken, incomplete, failed. It is not *wrong*; we do not stand before a blank wall, a Holy Negative, an Equivocity that spells only nonsense and irrationality. No, God is the Author of Holy Scripture; God comes to us in this earth, through the visible things He has made. But we see in those books a fragmentary Procession and Mission, a radical Descent that can never be wholly grasped, a Concreteness that cannot be wholly penetrated, a Light that can be seen only in dazzling glimpses, even when we do not turn our faces away. This is the Mystery *above* reason, not contrary to it, the inexhaustible Mystery who is the Triune Lord, the Fiery One. The Holy Trinity is a dogma of faith, not unaided reason, because the God displayed, laid down, in this text is the Intelligible Mystery who can never be mastered, never exhausted.

We will say more, we must say more, about the relation of faith and reason in Trinity, the place of mystery in this doctrine. But in our exegetical reflection here we must press on to a deeper reflection on the Divine Descent. We must now consider the *cost* of discipleship. That is the fiery lesson of the Logos Asarkos, the stark demand of the Suffering Servant. We walk by faith and not by sight: Isaiah 53 tells us that this is a costly truth. The Benevolence, the Sweet Love of God, is an Object of Faith; It is a Mode of the Triune Lord. And this Goodness is a Perfection of the Divine Nature, Radiant, Glorious, pouring out, pouring down on a weary world. But It is Invisible, Hidden! It is seen by the eyes of faith, indirectly, at remove and at a distance; such knowledge is the gift of Almighty God Himself. The Transcendental Perfections of God, His Truth and Goodness and Unicity, scale down the heights of Heaven us-ward, but the Reserve, the Excess, the Superabundance is the Lord's alone, His Mystery and Preserve. His Mode as Logos, as Reason and Meaning and Truth: these are His Sovereign Perfections, His alone. To see our world as it is—shimmering with beauty but with pain, too, and filled with the heroism of martyrs and saints as well as the unknown and unheralded, but with corruption and cruelty admixed, and with flourishing and gift and intimacy, the wild rose, the first spring scent of damp earth—all this and chaos and intractable pain and the unmarked mass grave: to see all of this and everything within it *and* to affirm the Benevolence and Truth of God—this is faith. Isaiah 53 tells us that the *meaning* of the Servant's suffering is that Almighty God *willed* it, inflicted pain on him, and laid on Him the iniquity of us all. In his Anonymity and silent descent, he enters the ground in order to make the many righteous: The Unseen One bears His own enemies' sins. Now, this is an Intelligible or Divine Meaning that is its own terrible truth. It does not *remove* faith to receive this conceptual explanation; indeed, it tries it. That the Eternal Son of God exceeds His earthly life is a Reason and Word that escapes all disclosure of Its Excess, is not *contrary* to this Meaning; rather, this fact confirms it. The Triune Mystery of God, His Holiness, can never be exhausted by Its bearers, even the Incarnate Life of our Lord. For this profound mystery of pain, its obdurate incommunicability, expresses the Alien Ways of our God, His Heights and Ways above all our ways, His Terrible Excess that is Deity. We trust in Him; we love this Lord; we follow His Ways. But they are costly, a descent, a loss. The Generation of the Son marks out a Derivation and Proceeding that will call forth and call on our faith. We receive this world, *all of it*, from His Hand. It will be the Pearl of Great Price, a Truth and Reason beyond all imagining, a Joy exceeding all others—but it will require our full treasure to purchase that field and to dwell in it.

What does faith, then, tell us about the Divine Logos, the Ratio, Eternal and Glorious, apart from and beyond the *sarx*, the flesh of the Redeemer? How does a faithful reading of Isaiah 53 tell us about *His* Generation? Just what is the doctrine of Holy Scripture in such telling? How does it reveal, teach, and disclose but also hide and reserve and guard? Just what kind of revelation can this be? Questions like spring lambs tumble out from this text!

We begin by saying, by confessing, that the Logos of God is Perfect, Complete, Consummate. This is the chief meaning—not the only, by any means, but the chief meaning—of the Pattern of Descent and Death that is the Suffering Servant of Israel. The Word of the Lord instructs us, in parable and riddle, that the Life of God descends, falls down from the Heights, pours down to the Concrete, the Perfect, the End. Be perfect, the Lord Christ commands us, as your Heavenly Father is Perfect. Perfection, Wholeness, Holiness is a Proper Attribute of God; indeed, all His Ways and Properties are Perfect, Perfections. But the Lord God, the Holy One, is not only Perfect in Nature, possessed of the fullness of Perfections, but this Lord is Perfect in His Life, His Dynamism and Fiery Generation.

The Triune God devolves, originates Perfection, the Perfect End. Most certainly this God is without limit or barrier, Infinite, Infinitely Beyond. Without measure He is Rich and Fruitful, Inexhaustible, Utterly One, Utterly Alive. God is Positively Infinite. All this is caught up in the notion of the Intellectual, the Immaterial, and the Ideal. God lives in His own Freedom, riding on the wings of the wind, expansive, unrestricted, Glorious. There is no end to His Greatness. All this is to be prized, cherished. Our love of God is our delight and devotion in the Divine Immensity, Measureless, Bottomless, the Ocean of Reality. But Isaiah shows us more. He shows us a Lord God whose *Life* is Perfection, drawing up and drawing down to an End, a Complete Sabbath Rest. *The Processions of God are this: the Descent to the Concrete, the Perfect*. Now it will be the task of the larger exposition of the Divine Processions to clarify, to develop, and to ground this definition in the whole corpus of Holy Writ. But even here we must say that the Life of God is no "play of concepts," no airy, technical Abstraction without the "labor of the negative," without Concreteness and Descent. No, this Triune Lord is Perfect Love, in Himself, in His Glorious Aseity, the *Definite* One.

Consider the semantic range of telos, in Greek and its cognates, of *tamim* and its kin in Hebrew, of Perfect and Complete in English. These are terms that are alive with movement, with direction toward an end, a goal and a conclusion; they are words rich with ripeness, maturity, fullness. They are the race that is run, the journey completed, the burden laid down—all consummated, all spent. Freud was a master of this rich sea of association.[17] Perfection is twin of death, he taught in his later years, an expression of Thanatos, the death drive. To master a task, to drive a point home, to secure and complete an argument, to bring to fullness, to give oneself over to rest and resolution, the darkened room: these all are little deaths, rehearsals and expressions of our own completion. These are acts of anger, Freud taught, of mastery and control, of destruction—but not simply these. For we come to love death, Freud says; it is the final, the perfect meeting of the twin drives of all human life, Eros and Thanatos; the entwining of love and death as the final resting place, the sweet release, the giving way. We need not follow Freud in all his remarkable and disturbing pathways, even these of his late period, to see that his analysis breaks open the biblical texts we have spread before us here. The Perfect is a Descent in this broad, psychoanalytic sense: it is a Fullness, a Delimiting, a Concrete End that *crystalizes*, distills, and defines what is Intelligible, Infinite Being. The Processions are not contrary to the Holiness of God, His Wrath and His Love, His Wrathful Love, but are indeed the Perfection of It, His Fire channeled and drawn to a Point, a Conclusion. The Divine Logos (Our God Logos, Freud admits in an unguarded moment!) is not enfleshed; He is not Death or Dying but rather Eternal, Eternal Life and Glorious Reason. But He is *Definite*, the very Structure of God, His Rationality, His Pure, Perfect Logical Form. He is the End of all God's Ways. But it is fitting and altogether proper that an earthly Servant, an Enfleshed One, should take the way of suffering and death, be lowered into the earth, descend to those in prison, and in His death make many righteous. It is fitting and altogether proper, a gift of astonishing grace, that this Eternal Perfect Reason should incarnate in One who will be *sacrifice*, a Lamb Perfect and Whole, without blemish or defilement. He is the Perfect Offering. Such atonement for sin will belong by rights to a full exposition of the Doctrine of Redemption, but even here we must say that it is not *contrary* to the Divine Life, the Eternal Generation of the Son, that Jesus of Nazareth be born to die, not a *thwarting* of the Divine Will but rather *an Expression of It*, a shadow and enactment of the Divine Procession as It descends to Its End.

Note here the Divine Readiness for Incarnation; this, too, is an element and dimension of the Perfect Generation of the Son. This is a moment for us to reflect more deeply on the God-world relation, the place and possibility of Holy Scripture as disclosure of the Divine Aseity in its Triune Structure. The architecture of the modern era in dogmatics has been built up around the conviction that Christology is the only, or the only Perfect place and topos where God can be known as the One He Is. The legacy of this building program is complex and need not detain us here; but it expresses and enacts a sturdy principle, that the Enfleshed Word is the Goal, the Telos of our faith and knowledge. The Finality, the Completion of human knowledge and trust of God is met in Jesus of Nazareth, His life and atoning death. This principle, natural though it be in a post-Kantian age, has brought in its train an odd flattening effect on the doctrine of God and of Holy Scripture as teacher of the One, Holy Lord. It has strengthened the ancient conviction, in an angular and overburdened way, that the Divine Essence cannot be known, certainly not seen in this life. In its place we have an unrelieved focus on the economy, the scriptural history of Israel and of Israel's Messiah, in such a way that we are urged not to look away from or above these things, not to speculate. At times this is given a moral turn of phrase: God is pleased to show me Himself in His Son; I will ask for no more. At others, we are asked to join this pronounced emphasis on the Incarnate One with a severe notion of the via negativa: The God *A Se* is *over against* or not-finite. God is paradoxically related to the world, it is sometimes said—Tillich resorts to this Schelling-like term frequently—because the Divine Reality is Eternal, not temporal, not mortal; Infinite, not finite, not local; Immaterial, Impassible, not worldly and passing away. All hail these Predicates! But—epistemically, this school says, we must acknowledge that we cannot know such a God, cannot *think*

Him, for He is the Utter Negation of the particular, the concrete, the diverse and frail being of the creature. He is the Noumenon. And metaphysically, this school says, we must confess that the relatio between such a God and such a creature is strictly speaking *impossible*; it overthrows any mortal relation we know or enjoy. Now such stern strictures on knowledge and creaturely stature before God can be overcome, if they be, by Divine Omnipotence alone, and that is the path of much modern theology. "God alone can make the impossible possible": that is the dogmatic affirmation of theologians for whom paradox and contradiction govern the God-world relation.

But the prophet Isaiah discloses to us a different lesson, a different relatio between Creator and creature. In his prophetic utterance on Israel's Servant, Isaiah teaches us about the Compatibility of the Perfect Generation of the Son with the Suffering One, lowly and rejected. Not the Identity! But rather the Compatibility or Readiness of the Triune God for the Incarnate appearance among us. This is the fittingness or beauty of the relation between the Concrete and the concrete, the earthly. Now note that this is a counterstroke against the strong Hegelian Tendenz of modern theology. The point here is not that the Creator-creature distinction is to be minimized or overridden, not at all! The framework we aim to set aside, the collapse of the subject matter into genre, leads in our day to a narrow dilemma: either God and the world are in some way Identical, perhaps the one enclosed in the Other, or they are not— they contradict one another. In his serpentine genius, G. W. F. Hegel sets out the modern path as a combination of the two: the world is the *negation*, the not-God, to which the Spirit must come, in order to become, through this Divine Agon and Diremption, Dispossession, the Divine Absolute. The Absolute Spirit receives the negative into Itself, becomes One with it, Identical in the midst of contradiction, and *this* is Spirit. But the dynamism of this whole program—a strongly energetic campaign—is built up from paradox and contradiction. The movement and life of God, Its Journey toward Absoluteness, compresses and then explodes the contradiction between the Deathless God and his solemn death in the center of history. The whole creation is the theater of this paradox, the rupture between Spirit and matter, Eternity and time, Infinite Life and finitude, suffering, loss. The event of the Incarnation is the Moment, the far extension of this negation, but even the act of Creation itself is a divine fashioning of its own contradiction. The world in this way is at once God-suffused and utterly godless. Now few modern thinkers, philosophers or theologians, read Holy Scripture as vigorously and well as does Hegel or, in other ways, the mythologist Friedrich Wilhelm Joseph von Schelling. The life, the urgency, the pathos of Holy Scripture does not fall flat in these thinkers, nor is it tidied up, made plain and ordered, inert on its ceremonial shelf. No, these Romantic idealists wind up the mainspring of the Bible, and it pulses and runs and wakes us up. No one, short of the remarkable Old Testament exegete Walter Brueggemann, can keep pace with these nineteenth-century system builders. We can only learn from their daring fidelity to the passion of Holy Scripture.

But in truth, the Bible does not tell this kind of story; it is not built up by these engine works. It is not an unfolding of the contradiction of the worldly. It is rather the disclosure—no, the *enactment*—of the Readiness of Almighty God for His creation, His Compatibility with it, and the creation's fittingness for its Maker. This is why the Bible can disclose and inscribe the Pattern of the Divine Processions in human words. It is why the Old and New Testaments can teach the Mystery of the Holy Trinity. It is why doctrine can be discovered and fittingly anchored in the pages of

Holy Writ. In the doctrine of the Divine Attributes, we have seen the astonishing Gift that is these Perfections, *communicated*, poured down to the thirsty earth, in a Transcendental Relation: The One, dazzling in Light and Goodness, plunged down into the knowledge and unity and goodness of the creature. This, too, is a relation of compatibility, theological compatibilism. But we can now be more specific, more delimited still: The Intelligible in the concrete, and these in the creaturely concreteness, is the Pattern of the Divine Life, bestowed on a dependent earth. This Descent into Specificity, into Determination, lays down the schema, the structure—the Ratio—of the Triune relation to the world: Perfect Meaning laid down in the ligaments of the cosmos.

But this Anonymous One, Israel's Suffering Servant, how can *he* be the compatible creature, the readiness and fittingness, described in such rich and exalted terms above? Surely, *contradiction* would be more proper here, would it not? *Hic Rhoda! Hic salta!* We have underscored his deep descent into pain and rejection; his failure and senseless suffering; the injustice he must endure, unheralded, uncorrected; the teaching and example that go nowhere, instruct no one; the brokenness that stands at the heart of it all. How is this brute fact, this brutality, a compatibilism of any sort at all? Here we must begin by a reflection on Holy Scripture itself and the gift of Prophecy. Just what is being placed in the mouth of the Holy Prophets? What are these words that become, in church and synagogue, the Word of the Lord? We will have occasion to think more fully, in the doctrine of creation, about the metaphysical likeness that we have termed here compatibilism. But in this exegetical work, we ask first about the words of the prophet: What status and stature do they enjoy? Once again, we see the great centripetal force of the economy in modern doctrine, how it appears to gather all to itself. We might think of the Law and Prophets, that is, as extended commentary on the Will and Instruction and Judgment of God on the creature, Israel. The Lord, it seems, gives the teachers of Israel, the teachers of the church, the word for the faithful: This is the Way; walk in it. And we can trace, once again, the desire to draw the High God down to His Acts us-ward: *this* is God, it seems, the One who is manifest among us, on our behalf and for our good. The Bible is made compatible, in its own fashion, by such sharp focus on the history of salvation, for it is, in truth and in whole, about us and for us. It is the imprint of the God for us. Or, perhaps, we might invert it in this way: God is the One who acts in these ways, who "raises Jesus of Nazareth from the dead," as Jenson famously expressed this point. The Suffering Servant of Israel discloses the Journey of the Son of God into the Far Country, to borrow Barth's powerful phrase; just this *is* the True and Good God.

Now the oddity of this entire move in modern dogmatics and dogmatic exegesis is that it seems to collapse, into a very narrow room, the entire field so vaunted in modern theology, that of revelation itself. Just what is being *revealed* here, we might ask. Is not all of this remarkably earth-bound, earth-scaled? Are we not hearing news, not from a Distant Land, not from a Heavenly Realm, but from one remarkably like our own, the world of human-infused actions and sufferings, remedies and judgments, and teachings of all kinds? Are we not drawing Divine Revelation into our sin and need and deliverance with so tight a joinery that we hear only of the God who knows only us? True, this is law and gospel; this is glorious good news; this is the heavenly chorus, and always we are to be grateful for this sweet song. But the *force* of a doctrine of revelation, I say, should be disclosure of the High God, the Aseity and Lordship of this Divine Reality, this Inexhaustible Light. Now I believe the doctrine of revelation has been asked to carry far too much of the burden of the day, imported far too much of the apparatus of epistemology into the precincts of dogmatics. Far better to constrain and overwrite it by the doctrine of compatibilism, a theological metaphysics, in which the Lord God is Manifested as Ready and Present in the creature's realm. Or, as we have delimited it here: the Divine Intelligible in the concrete, manifest and present to the creature in all its concreteness. Central to our task in the dogma of Trinity is to set the *direction* and *asymmetry* of the Relatio in proper order. Holy Scripture, in the Law and Prophets, bears the marks of God in Himself, the Sovereign and Unique One: the Aseity of God is the Object and Subject and, yes, Revealer of the Holy Bible. The direction moves properly from Above to below, not below to Above, and the Divine Character Present in the text is not the "economic" made One with "Immanent" but rather the "Immanent" hidden and indirect and exploding through the "economic." The Holy Scripture, as God's own Word, manifests an asymmetry that properly governs the whole. The Divine Processions, the Divine Life is the Controlling Reality; the Missions, and our response to those Missions, the dependent and subsequent. Just *this* is the proper relation and order between the "Ideal" and the "real" in Creator-creature relation—to express this in scholastic terms—or more indigenous to this theology, between the Intelligible Concreteness and the concrete world.

§4.4. The Canons of Lateran IV as Guide to Dogmatic Reading of the Divine Persons and Processions

Note, then, that we have now restated and expressed exegetically the justly famous maxim of the Fourth Lateran Council: "Be you perfect, as your heavenly Father is perfect, as if He would say more clearly: be perfect by the perfection of grace as your heavenly Father is perfect by the perfection of nature, namely, each in his own way, because between the Creator and the creature there cannot be a likeness (*similtudo*) so great that the unlikeness (*dissimiltudo*) is not greater."[18] According to the medievalist Fiona Robb, we see in this Canon the high medieval wariness of the direct and pithy earthy analogy. In accord with the more conceptual work of the university theologians, all analogy—unlikeness—must be governed by a greater unlikeness. "Analogy," that is, will be pushed closer to equivocation—a movement we see clearly registered in St. Thomas.[19] In our setting, we must be struck here by the joining of the dominical commandment to perfection with the relation of likeness, enclosed by an ever greater unlikeness. We have entered the realm, that is, of the Holy Trinity, the Perfection of God. Now, Lateran IV distinguishes the Creator and creature through *modes*: the Perfection of God is by Divine Nature; He is and possesses Perfection by His very Reality; but the creature strives for perfection by grace; it belongs to us not by right or by essential property but by Divine gift. This is not a relation of *participation*, though it is not hostile to it, but rather of *bestowal*: God is the Agent, the Source; the creature the needy recipient. Now this relation of grace is to govern the God-world connection: the movement from similarity to dissimilarity will follow the pattern of grace, from the Trinity who just is Perfection to the creature who is not but can receive it, by little and by little. The pair of likeness and unlikeness came to characterize some schools of the scholastic doctrine of analogy and lived on in the technical methodologies of Erich Przywara and Karl Barth. We might say, then, that were the *Analogia Entis* to be simply the name for this grouping of similarity and dissimilarity, of nature and grace, the quarrel between Vatican I Catholicism and Barth would quietly drop away. The Creator-creature distinction is maintained by a phrase at once traditional and restrained: there is something in common and much more that is uncommon. Ecclesiasticus and its evocation of the exceeding greatness of God above all His works, Irenaeus and his celebrated phrases about the Divine Light (it is Light but unlike any other light we know), and Augustine's haunting prayer in book X of the *Confessions* (What do I love when I love my God?) stand quietly in the background here. But this Canon, perhaps written by Innocent III himself, lends an air of authority to this scholastic movement from likeness to the Land of Unlikeness, as if any Christian, on a moment's reflection, would embrace this simple tie and separation between God and His creatures. Such is the air Conciliar documents breathe. But I believe in truth this is a complex, careful, and sophisticated canon on Trinitarian theology, especially as it touches on proper theological knowledge of God. With this canon in view, we can travel much further in doctrine, especially Trinitarian doctrine, and in dogmatic scriptural exegesis, than might first appear.

This is a Canon, after all, dedicated to Trinitarian controversies of the twelfth and thirteenth centuries in the Latin Church. They touch on the work of Peter Lombard, by those years a central teaching authority of the Christian schools. A prominent abbot, Joachim of Fiore, accused the Lombard of teaching—implicitly and unwittingly, of course—a Divine Quaternity rather than Trinity: a Divine Nature—that word carries resonances in this text!— and Three Divine Persons. (The complex history of the relation between the Trinity, as such, and the Processions prompted the Abbot's accusation. He held that the Lombard taught a Quaternity because, on the Lombard's account, one could properly speak of the Essence of the Holy Trinity that was not itself the Begetter, Begotten, and Proceeding, for were the Essence or Nature to beget, he said, it would generated itself, and such cannot be.) A charge of heresy was to be feared, always, and only more so after

Lateran IV, where temporal penalty and punishment was treated firmly and at length. What is remarkable and instructive for our ends here is the subtle way in which Holy Scripture is brought into the arena ruled over by Trinity and of the God-world relation. In the opening of Canon 2, the Conciliar author defends the Lombard by accusing Abbot Joachim of misusing the Johannine texts, which speak of the Unity of Persons in the Triune Godhead. The famous Johannine comma is adduced—no surprise there. But we might be surprised, and should indeed be instructed, by the form of Unity the Canon is said to propose, all on the basis of the Johannine Supper Discourses: "such a unity [as the Abbot proposes] is not a true and proper unity, but rather a collective one or one *by way of similitude* [the unchastened, "monastic" analogy] as many men are called one people and many faithful one Church, according to these words." Then are cited Acts 4:32, on the unity of believers, and Pauline texts, 1 Corinthians 6:17 and 3:8 and Romans 12:5, all stressing the oneness that is found among many. Then, central for our aims here: John 17:22–23: "To strengthen this teaching he [the abbot] cites that most important word which Christ spoke concerning the faithful in the Gospel: will, Father, that they may be one, as we also are one, that they may be made perfect in one," so that the faithful, he says, are one "in the sense that they constitute one Church by reason of the unity of the Catholic faith and one kingdom by reason of the union of indissoluble charity." Here we have a depiction of oneness, Divine and human, drawn from what Sarah Coakley has called the "Johannine dyad" of Father and Son[20] and a quiet assumption that both unities are formed through bonds of love—a "Communion" or "social" Trinitarianism that has dominated much present-day Trinitarian theology. This the Canon calls a "way of similitude," a likeness. Just this is now declared insufficient for Divine Trinitarian Unity. Already then in the exegetical and descriptive section of the

Canon, the crystalline conclusion of likeness in a sea of unlikeness is foreshadowed. Lateran IV sets forth its proper account of Unity, and of Johannine exegesis, with this crisp summary: "When therefore the Truth prays to the Father for the faithful, saying, Will that they be one in us, as we are one, this term, 'one' is understood first for the faithful, as implying a union of charity in grace, then the divine persons, as implying a unity of identity in nature." The controlling pair, then, of nature and grace announce themselves in this dogmatic exposition of John 17, the High Priestly Prayer for unity. The way we are to read Holy Scripture, this Canon tells us, is to draw a line, according to modus, between creatures and their *similitudo*, and the Creator and His Triune Unicity by Nature. Just this, the Canons assert, Abbot Joachim has failed to do. It seems that we are to acknowledge a certain likeness between Creator and creature, that they are one, but that in the midst of an even greater unlikeness, they are not both one by nature.

Now I believe that this rather straightforward conclusion can be pressed a bit further. Remember that the faithful are one in bonds of affection, and this is termed a "likeness." This cannot be the Unity enjoyed by the Divine Persons, the Conciliar author tells us, because the Father, Son, and Holy Ghost are *simul*, together and at once Three Persons and "Each One singly" that One Divine Essence or Substance or Nature, Incomprehensible and Ineffable, Supreme. We can say, then, that likeness itself is marked by this pattern of similarity and difference, and in all things Divine, likeness, or more properly Oneness, must be not only a Unity held in and by the Nature, but that this Perfection must be Unique, an Unlikeness to creatures and their commonalities. This suggests that the Canon's conclusion carries a radical extension: the likeness between God and creature is itself a mark of the Ineffable and Infinite Chasm fixed between the Lord and His cosmos. Holy Scripture, then, must be read to speak of God—as the High Priestly Prayer speaks of the Radical Oneness of the Divine Persons—but in such a way that the profound dissimilarity of God to any of these words is marked and laid on the heart.

We have good reason, then, to think of this remarkable Canon from Lateran IV as a high medieval exposition of the Trinitarian relations and Processions. Of course, this is true in a rather superficial sense: the document lauds Peter Lombard and censures Abbot Joachim for their Trinitarian views (but not, the Canon is careful to say, for the Abbot's personal devotion, obedience to the Apostolic See, nor for his community at Fiore). But more deeply and instructively, I believe we can say that this very relatio, of likeness and unlikeness, is an indirect pointer to and Pattern of the *Triune Processions themselves.* In God's own Ineffable Life, His own Mystery, we may say that the Dynamism between a Likeness and an Unlikeness is Generated by this relatio, Ever Greater. The Processions, we might say, follow this Pattern: They are the Ever-Greater Unlikeness in the midst of Likeness; or we might dare to say, *the Processions are the Mode and Dynamism of the Ever-Greater Unlikeness.* In time, we will say more about the Divine Processional Life. But even here we acknowledge and underscore that the Triune Life of God is the Fiery Explosion of God's Uniqueness, His Exceeding Mystery and Aseity.

Any student of medieval theology will recognize the move underway here. In the *Proslogion* St. Anselm famously uses a notion of the *maior*, the greater, to drive his proof to its conclusion: God is "That than which No Greater can be Conceived." It is greater to exist in reality as well as in the mind; therefore God exists in reality and in the mind. Later in the treatise, and in the *Monologion,* Anselm applies the dynamism of the greater—what philosophers these days call the "great-making principle"—to the Divine

Attributes. It may well be that such reliance on the idea of greatness as a mode and relation had reached Rome by the time of Lateran IV, or perhaps some common source animated them both. But the idea that a *relation* between two elements could be ordered not simply by *quality* or *quantity*—this is bigger or heavier than that—but by *modus*, a movement or way or mode of being, is a step toward an Act or Event of Being, a Dynamism that accompanies and drives any comparison between things. Canon 2 envisions a Perfection of God that is slipping away always from our insight or grasp. We might imagine the furthest reach of our sense of likeness to God, and at that limit, God continues to recede, His Majesty and Glory moving further out into the Infinite Light who is God. Just this is Mystery. As with Anselm's famous proof, we do not have a static and stable relation here, where perfection applies to both God and creature, but God's Perfection is greater. This is true, certainly! But this Canon shows us more. The mode of God's Perfection is His own Nature, His own Reality, and that constantly exceeds our approach to it. Not a steady proportion, not a predictable ratio that can be extrapolated or followed out, not a rule of that kind or, even less, an algorithm, but rather an Excess, an Ever Greater that moves beyond, out into the Mysterious Darkness, the Plenitude, that is the Divine Being. By approaching, and approaching truly, we stand further away. Just this, the Council tells us, governs the knowledge of creatures for their Triune Creator.

So, we might say, then, that this Mode of the Ever Greater belongs properly and by rights to the Trinity Itself. This is the *force* of saying that God needs no intermediary between Himself and the world but rather just *is* His own Relatio to the creature. In Himself, in His Divine Life, He is as He is Like yet more radically Unlike the creature. Or to express this in other terms: the proper predication of God, its likeness and greater unlikeness, conforms (in this Ever-

Greater Mode) to the Divine Persons and Relations, a Perfect Likeness and Unlikeness. For this reason, we say that the Divine Modes, the Persons, are *Incommunicable*: They are Radically Unlike. The distinctions among the Persons, their Unique *Proprium*, is ever greater than any distinction creatures could design or discover. Yet the Persons are One; They are of a Likeness far exceeding the similarity creatures find in bonds of love or closeness of any sort. They are One by Nature; They indwell One Another; They are of One Being and Substance. For this reason, we say the Divine Nature is *Communicable*, even as It retains its Majestic Incommunicability: the *Deitas* spreads abroad Its Goodness, Its Truth and Power, even Its Unity and Being, showering Reality and Likeness onto the earth. But even in this Transcendental Goodness, this astonishing Sharing of the Divine Being, God's Mode of Likeness is a Greater Unlikeness than anything we can say or imagine. Truly God was in this place, and I did not know it. For this reason, we say that the Holy One of Israel is Mystery; He, this very One, is *known* as Mystery. His drawing near, His intimacy to our thoughts and words, is *in this very way* His Great Height, and Majesty, and Glory. Ever Greater; our Lord is Ever Greater.

Now the methodological insights this Canon of Lateran IV sets forth arises out of its scriptural exegesis and commentary. We do not begin to feel the force of this great document if we do not see it as a careful and rich exposition of the Johannine and Matthean texts at the heart of Abbot Joachim's complaint and the Council's reply. Method follows doctrine! We are being shown here a rule for reading that guides our interpretation of Holy Scripture as well as the reach of its Revelatory power. In this Canon we see no hesitation about Holy Scripture as doctrinal teacher—that is the medieval confidence in the metaphysical scope of the covenants—but we also see no hesitation about the scriptural grounding of technical matters in the doctrine of the Holy Trinity. In this way, Lateran IV follows the pattern of Nicaea itself: a dogma that arises out of a particular exegesis—*pace* Hanson—and leads in turn to a rule for reading, a thoroughly exegetical, thoroughly doctrinal exposition. The first two Canons of this Council do not hesitate to speak of the Aseity of God and to make rulings about It; the remainder of the Canons can speak quite boldly about doctrinal and moral matters. But that, I believe, is grounded in the Ever Greater principle, the recognition that creaturely knowledge and, more, creaturely reality stand even in its likeness under the *crisis* of the Exceeding Divine Unlikeness.

Just so we must in this theology speak boldly of the Divine Aseity, to proclaim Him, to worship His Beauty and Holiness and Exceeding Light, to hearken to His Word, to bow before His Goodness: this is the joy of theology, its great task. This is taken up by a love of and loving attention to Holy Scripture: all the riches and wisdom are found there. But we echo a doctrinal theme as old as Irenaeus, as Augustine and Nyssa, when we say that the proclamation of the Divine Aseity, His very Life and Majesty, can be unfolded only in the Land of Unlikeness. Holy Scripture itself tells us that the One God is Utterly Unique, surpassing any form or measure; that His Ways are not ours; that He dwells in Light Inaccessible; that His Invisibility remains, even when seen in the visible things He has made. That cannot be simply a pious remark! The aim of Christian doctrine is not first and principally to teach Christian humility; though it should do so. Nor is it to posit a negative via in which we affirm only our own creaturehood and leave the Divine Mystery at the far edge of Being, in the Excess beyond utterance. No, doctrine is to speak boldly of God, not simply His Ways us-ward, not merely His Saving Grace, not just of the Divine Missions in Incarnation and Pentecost, though it must speak of these, and joyfully. But we must first and principally speak of the High God as He is. And this task must be governed by the principle of Greater Unlikeness. The inner Life of God is the Dynamic Procession of Ever-Greater Unlikeness. The Holy God is always More. Always Beyond and in Excess, in Unlikeness even in His Likeness, the Mode of Mystery that is fullness of Light and Fire and Reason Itself. *This* is the Divine Goodness, that He would come in His Incommunicable Mystery to us and lift us through His own Likeness to the cloud and thunder and great darkness to the Luminous Darkness that stretches out into the Infinite Fire. The Known Unknown: this is God.

Now this may strike us all as very lofty and fine—but is it not a rather pious account of equivocation? This fear, after all, is sounded in the Canon itself. If Holy Scripture gives us utterance, and we speak of God as He Acts and Is in Holy Writ, is our scriptural knowledge not surrounded and hedged in by this Greater Unlikeness, such that our words now drop out of our grasp, and we seem not to know their meaning at all? The Canon, after all, speaks not of Excess or Being Beyond but rather of Unlikeness, Dissimilarity; and this, it seems, is the very measure of equivocation. Just this is the fear that critics name when they warn against separating subject matter from genre: suddenly we are not at all sure what we are talking about. It is not simply the importing of foreign matter into the province of dogmatics, though of course this worries them, too. It's even more the fear that no common agreement, no likeness in the use of terms, governs our Christian speech, so that we might just as well say up as say down, say Glory as say Defilement and Shame. What could it mean, after all, to say that God is Light but unlike any light we know? Just how can we be confident in calling God Light or recognizing It as such if It be unlike all we know? How can we speak of Divine Concreteness shadowed in creaturely concreteness if that likeness is surmounted by a greater unlikeness? How could we proclaim the explosive power of the Intelligible in the concrete, the Spiritual in the creaturely concrete, if we know little, perhaps none, of the contours of this Intellection? This is the great puzzle of theological language, the great puzzle of transcendence. Now Thomas's doctrine of analogy, in one way, and Barth's doctrine of Christological revelation, in another, are meant to reassure us in the middle of this malaise: they are designed to show us what we can know, where we can speak with confidence, even in the midst of great Mystery and Majesty. But Lateran IV all the same speaks boldly, and it restrains boldly. Why is this?

Here I believe the Lateran Council instructs by silence: do not strive to say too much! It belongs more fully to the doctrine of faith to make account of this rather deflationary and reliabilist view of theological knowledge. But even here we can and must say that the reticence of the Canon seems exactly right. We do not aim here, or in later doctrines, to *explain* how creaturely predication of God is possible or successful. Much, much technical investigation in epistemology of varying schools seeks an explanation and mechanism for proper theological speech. All hail these methods! But a reader of the tradition can be excused for thinking that none of these methods can fully execute their aim: a confident grounding or warrant for creaturely language for God, not too much certainty, not too much doubt. Here it seems to me a light touch is all the more to be prized. It is the truth, acknowledged by all sides, that the Nature of this Object, this Unique Subject, makes proper knowledge without parallel and analogue; there simply is nothing like the knowledge and speech of God. Yet it exists and is commanded of us, our greatest treasure. For this reason, our statements about God are deliverances of faith, though they be entirely rational in character. We speak with proper confidence, we speak of God Himself, we worship this Holy One in our intellect and our speech. We do not aim to explain and justify all this; we are grateful, rather, for the gift of a tongue to praise Him. We should say, rather, that this scriptural teaching about the Divine Reality is *reliable*—just that. It is *enough*. We can go forward and trust these Holy Words. We can learn them, inscribe them on our lips and heart and in our down-sitting and our up-rising, as we walk along life's way; we can learn them from the saints, from the church's doctors, from the Book of Nature, from realisms of all sorts and kinds; we can bring all thoughts captive to Christ; we can inwardly feed on Holy Scripture and the liturgies of the church. We can do these things; we can be taught to do them. We can follow. The deep insight Barth gives to theology—that God is not *contrary* to the world but in Positive Relation to it—applies in theological speech as well. We do not stand in the realm of Hegel's negation, where the world is the Not-God, recognized and drawn into and made Identical to the Spirit who created it; the God-world relation is not diremption and agon. Rather, there is *likeness*, a radiant commonality, a share in the Divine Life, a Humility laid down in this earth. We can speak of such a God, use our small words, our earthen vessels, because the God of Light sheds His own Light into our realm: in His Light we see light. In just this way we can echo Gregory of Nyssa and Nicholas of Cusa who speak of God "without a contrary"; He is *Non Aliud*. His Holiness is Perfect, Sublime, such that It can draw near us and give us speech. It is not opposition, not contradiction, not visible and seen as over-against but rather Hidden, Radiant, Intimate. To speak of such a God, perhaps, is something of a skill, not a schematic, but again, we seek not to say too much. We believe in the church, and we rest with proper restraint, proper confidence, in the language of Zion that we hear there. The great Mystery who is God is encountered in His world and in His assemblies as the Likeness who is Unlikeness, the Near Transcendent One; He is Holy; He is Perfect.

Perhaps we might say that Christian speech is something like the manna gathered by the pilgrim people: enough for the journey, enough for the day, but not too much, not to be stored up, not to be controlled. However large or small the family, it is sufficient unto the day. But it is a strange and alien land these pilgrims cross! They will not live to journey's end, and they will be tested in every way. Nothing is as radical, as angular, to the familiar and the customary than is biblical religion; it is life before the Holy One. The seasons and the days, the seed times and harvests, the great pilgrimages and daily round: these will continue and give to all the faithful a sense of the ordinary, the tested and familiar. But this likeness, we must say, is governed by an Ever-Greater Unlikeness, by Holy Triune God who is Fire. Always disruptive, always New, Living: this Wise and Good God leaves nothing as it was before. To know *this* One, to think *these* thoughts, is to become a stranger in a strange land, all in the midst of the life and world and time we know so well. Such is the Crisis of Holiness.

This is the life and the mystery of the Suffering Servant. Now we see more clearly than before this great descent that is his pathway. We see the great downward movement to rejection, to suffering and failure, as a pilgrimage to the Land of Unlikeness. We cannot see Him, cannot speak of or regard Him, because He is the Alien One and His ways are strange. We can say that the Suffering Servant, in just this way, is not *contrary* to the Ways and Being of God. Rather, His odd unlikeness, His instability, between the collective and the individual, His meaningless pain and oppression, known as meaningful only to God, His hiddenness and anonymity, His fatal weakness: all this shows a proper *alignment* with the Holy God, a likeness in unlikeness. There is something Strange about Almighty God—that is, some Depth and Majesty that cannot be traced out. The Depth of Life in God, this Eternal

Movement that is Divine Plenitude and Stillness: this is Mystery and angular to all we know. But all this Divine Life, Isaiah tells us, is not merely Abyssmal, Unique Depth, though it is to be sure all this, too. It is even more an Astonishing Descent into Perfection. There is something in the marred face of the Servant that is to point us to this Divine Character of Descent. Shadowed in the lonely death of Moses, his unknown grave, his prohibited entry into Canaan, his earthly arrest by the River Jordan, is this Divine Descent into the Word, the Eternal Son. There is something in the marred and mangled deaths of the martyred faithful, the confessors, the resisters, and the liberators, something in the whole terrible, forgotten realm of the tortured that tells us of this Awe-Filled Downward Life. Haunting the life of the earthly Jesus, His Descent through David's royal line, His remorseless road to torment and death, is this Divine Descent, this Perfect and Dreadful Rest that is Unlikeness and Silence. What are we to see here, peering into these dark shadows, about the Holy God, the Lord of this Suffering Servant?

In the first and most innocent of these shadows, we see the Servant's *generation*, his lineal *descent* from Israel's covenant line. Divine Generation, we learn here, is in some way of Unlikeness, Like a familiar descent, a genealogy. As Genesis takes its name not only from the Generations of the heavens and the earth but also the generations of the ancestors, and the lineage of promise, from Sarah and Abraham, so, too, the Suffering Servant takes his place among the generations and household of Israel, allotted a portion with the great, and divided the spoils with the strong. Numbers and Chronicles, with their expansive lists of tribes, chieftains, and priests; the marking of towns and oases and fields by their families and by the generation of the ancestors who walked those grounds many seasons ago; the reciting of the great narratives of deliverance and trial, born by a generation already gathered to the ancestors: all this is just what one would expect in a Holy Book whose Author Descends into the Perfect Word. Just this expansive notion of Descent frames all the Gospels, giving lineage from Abraham and David, from Joseph, as is supposed, back to Adam (a descent of the descent), in a different manner, from John the Baptizer, and in still another, from God to God the Word. The Divine Generation is not simply an Ineffable Production, though it be that, or a Relation beyond saying in its Eternity and Changelessness, though it be those as well; it is also in its Unlikeness a kind of Lineal Descent, a Sonship from the Father of Lights. Because there is Divine Filiation, Divine Belonging, there are earthly generations, family resemblances. It is Eternal Generative Life, and from It springs Dependence, the Dependent who has Life in Himself. Every family on earth is named from this Lineal Descent, all children of this One God. All this we see in the generation of the Servant of God.

But we have not said enough when we have observed all this, not entered into the deep shadows that such a prophecy casts on our notion of the Divine Life. Descent and Generation are Downward in a more somber tone as well. This is the Depth of Holiness, this Descent. We are peering into the dense smoke that arises from altars and surrounds sanctuaries, the Holy Places that are reserved for only the High Priest, the hollow space between and above the cherubim, where only darkness and sweet savor ascend. We are reflecting with great reserve on the Suffering One who makes many righteous, who in the suffering descent to the grave pours forth holiness to sinners. We are thinking in reverent daring about Holiness that is not only Predicate, though It be that, but also Life, Procession. Our God is a Consuming Fire; that is His Dynamism. This Life is Holy: It burns and chastens; It sears and reduces to ash; It moves in constant Power, Descending from Flame to Flame, Unlike yet the

Same, without border or change; It sets apart and hallows; It guards Its own Proper Holiness with Zeal. This is the Fire burning in Jeremiah's bones, the unrelenting Urgency that will not let him rest, that will out, that will declare and speak, the Holiness that plunges down into the marrow, a Menacing Purity that comes down like a plumb line against the generations of Israel. The Holy Life of God is rigorous, demanding, unrepentant; It is Pure, Pure Fiery Light, plunging down into Perfection and Rest. Against sin, Holiness is Unrelenting, Wrathful. It will demarcate the profane; It will burn with Eternal Sanctity. It is Strange, an Alien Truth that is Its own. It stands apart. It begins all earthly sanctuary fires; It consecrates Its own altars; It defends Its own Holy Precincts and defines them. This is the earthly shadow of the Heavenly Sanctuary, the Holiness that just is Divine Descent.

But there are deeper shadows still. The Divine Life as It Generates and Pours out Holiness is akin, under the conditions of Ever Greater Unlikeness, to a kind of death, a kind of rupture and ending. This Holy Life is a kind of *Breaking*, a Holy Breaking, as it were. The Divine Processions are, yes, a declension to the Concrete and Perfect; the Generation of the Son as Eternal Line of Descent; the Breathing Forth as an Outpouring of Perfect Goodness. Yes, the Divine Life is this; principally this. But it is not merely this. The holy altar of Israel tells us this; the life of Moses tells us this; the prophets announce and live this somber truth; the costly death of the Suffering Son enacts this truth. There is a Rupture and a Breaking, Unlike all others, in the Divine Life of the Triune God— in the *inner Life!* We will have to carefully explore and delimit and constrain this dark notion; there can be no death and suffering and loss in God as we know these things in our mortality. There is no *grounding* in this sense! We do not seek to take the suffering of Israel's Servant up into the Godhead. No. We must carefully fence off this Transcendent, Divine Breaking from the economy, from this transitory life in our evil generations. Yet of it we must speak.

We must speak, first, of this Rupture as the establishment of the Holy God's Unlikeness. The Divine Processions are the life of the Holy God, and they measure, in their infinite soundings, the exceeding weight of Glory that is the Holy Life of God. But this Descent measures more. It measures out the Alien Character of God. The Processions *generate* this Strangeness: they set God—Nature and Life and Persons—*apart*. This is the *lesson* of Lateran IV. What we see in the Fiery Life of God is His own Alien Work, His own Self-Declaration of Remoteness and Reserve. He is no idol; He does not belong to any pantheon or table of the gods; He is not to be found among the spiritual powers of the cosmos. The Holy Triune God is utterly Unique. The Processions beget this Alien Distance. They guard the Inner Holiness, preserve and hide it. The Generation of the Son is the Breaking of all genus and family resemblance and likeness; it marks and keeps the utterly strange. We recall that the Canons of Lateran IV bespeak a *dynamic* unlikeness: every likeness is met by an ever-greater unlikeness. Though the Canons do not mention directly the Processions as engines of this Divine Pattern, they do note the Exceeding Mystery of the Unity of the Persons, the Ineffable and Unspeakable Unity of God Himself, Unlike any other unity. We may devoutly inquire about the source of this Dynamism, this startling Uniqueness. Holy Scripture tells of the Living God who is Holy Fire and of His Servant who is Unrecognizable, Alien in His suffering. In this prophetic text, we glimpse the depths of the Divine Life, the Power that does not simply receive Difference, does not quietly Stand Apart; though to be sure the Divine Nature exceeds and outstrips every likeness we apply. Rather we see here, and in this large Downward movement of Holy Scripture itself, the truth that God Himself is His own Distinction, His own Rupture from the world. He generates this Unlikeness, pours it out in Infinite Measure. He *consecrates* It.

It is sometimes thought that the distinction between the Holy Creator and the creature is most properly set forth through a denial of comparison, an incommensurability between God and the world. Of course, it is true that Creator and creature are infinitely unlike, even in the midst of the most intimate likeness and nearness! There is no need to *deny* this form of the God-world distinction. But it is not nearly radical enough. We do not begin to touch the Alien Uniqueness of God, the Crushing Concreteness and Unicity, by drawing a bright line between Creator and creature. Rather we must turn to the Lord God's own Aseity, not simply His Transcendence, His Mark as the Non Aliud. In God's inner Life we find the Source, the Fiery Explosion of God's own Strangeness. His utter Reserve. He sets Himself apart; He eternally breaks forth in this Self-Defined Reality, His own Living Wisdom. At every point, this Shocking God pours forth His own Perfections and scatters them like seed upon the rocky earth; yet even in the great Communication, the Holy God remains His own Incommunicate Mystery. He patrols that border; He provides His own Sanctuary. This is the Ever-Greater Unlikeness, the Divine Generation of Holiness.

We do not ourselves patrol that border. It is easy to misread the directive of Lateran IV, I believe, to teach principally a *method* of theological discourse. Perhaps as students of the tradition, we could even consider Irenaeus as a great architect of that method, as though he, too, showed many generations of theologians the path to walk in applying Divine Names and Predicates, likeness amid unlikeness. Now, of course there is truth in this directive; again, there is no need to deny this useful rule of thumb. But we have not plumbed the depths of the Divine Unlikeness were we to see it is a *creaturely* effort to preserve the One Lord from all rivals. No, we are not to think that principally and in the main, *theologians* think through the Mystery of the Divine Being and conclude from Its remarkable Strangeness that God is Unlike creature. No, the Agency here is *God's*. We creatures, we theologians, in truth, cannot ward off the great temptation to group God among the gods, the Holy One among the spiritual goods and powers of the earth. Our eyes are heavy, and we sleep the dream of idolatry, tying the Unique Lord to our good ends, the scaffolding of our own ideals. But God is Breaking, Rupture. The Flames of Sinai erupt against all these innocent and not-so-innocent dreams of ours. It is God Himself who establishes His Unlikeness, His Alien Nature. It is His Perfection, His Perfect Life. He sanctifies His own temple, He draws Himself apart, He sanctifies Himself. When we speak of the Descent of the Processions, Its Downward Movement, we mean in part that God in His own Fruitful Life, that it brings forth the Ever-Greater Strangeness, the Power of Self-Differentiating, the Power of Holiness. The Processions are the Greater Unlikeness.

And we mean more. By these Holy Processions we mean also the Infinite Depths of God. There is a form of the doctrine of Divine Simplicity that considers the Divine Nature to be Self-Same, through and through Deity, without admixture or interruption. And it is most certainly true that God has no parts! We will make no progress at all on the doctrine of the Holy Trinity if we do not see that it has nothing to do with mereology, the complex relation of wholes and parts. But Divine Simplicity, the Utter Unicity of the Triune God, cannot mean that the Divine Life, so to say, lies right on the surface, like a gleaming orb with its properties spread out on a metallic sheaf, flattened, so to say, to a shining, thin harmony. Deity is not Self-Same *in this sense*! Rather the Lord God is *Infinite Inwardness*. This is the Procession of the Holy Spirit, the Apostle tells us, to search even the Depths of God, to *know* them. This is what we mean when we speak of God as Personal or even, *a or the* Person. The modern era finds troubling the notion of Divine Personhood, especially those modernists under the tutelage of the absolute idealists. But we need not settle all these fears about the Personality of the Absolute God in order to say that Deity, just as it is Personal, must remain open to the expanse and descent of Depth. The Triune God's Ideality need not mean that the Divine Nature can have only a single, utterly identical Property or that the Divine Property can be only a series of repetitions of the fundamental Idea of God. This is a form of rationalism in the doctrine of God that will always be broken on the Living Dynamism of the Lord. Rather we must say that the salient element in the Personal is *Inwardness*. The very idea of a Living Being incorporates the spaciousness, the immensity not of Nature only or of Deity and Its Positive Infinity, true though they be, but of a Reserve, a Depth not exhausted in Agency or Perfections.

In our day we have every reason to prize the dimension of depth. Consider the relentless scouring that inwardness has received in our time. It is the startling power of Albert Camus's novel *The Stranger* that it can capture, with a numbing coldness, a life lived wholly on the surface, a being who must exist without depth. The chaos named in that book does not in the end rest on the seeming absurdity of the events or the troubled response of Mersault to the lives presented to him for affection or conflict. Rather, *The Stranger* draws its chilling power to unmake the reader from its utter *flatness*, its unrelieved aimlessness, a life in the shallows. Camus has depicted, narrated a life without depth, an impersonal human life, its chaos and absurdity. There is no argument here about personhood; no defiance or rebellion against the protocols of the personal; there is nothing programmatic here at all. Rather—and this is the searing flame of the book—Mersault simply stumbles through his days, from the scorching heat of an Algerian seaside to a night sky stretched out in cold indifference to his existence, his odd liberty in this coldness, this "benign indifference." Of course, the world has flattened still since Camus's days, and the inward narrowed and emptied yet further under the impress of a world bent on things, and electronic symbols of things. Only the distance of another era, another economy, will show us the real measure of this emptying, but even now we can say that the remorseless effort to make every public structure and space—the bus and the bus station; the open ceiling of a vaulted, old train station; a park bench; a shopping cart; a museum entrance—a commercial advertisement has driven the inward and the personal further away from everyday life, belittled and trivialized them. The element of likeness that is permitted us in the doctrine of God must reckon with this flattening of the human person, a hallmark of the global economy, a mark of its power and its decay. (Kathryn Tanner's searing indictment of finance capitalism, *Christianity and the New Spirit of Capitalism*, exposes the structure and pitilessness of this inner evacuation.)[21] But these elements, belonging by rights to the Doctrine of Creation, must be directed by the Ever-Greater Depth that is the Mystery of God's own Inwardness.

God is Personal in just this sense. Certainly, the use of "Person" in the dogma of Trinity has placed strain on the most proper Unicity of God, and we will have to guard this singular truth very carefully. But God as Person need not be held captive to this long-standing worry about technical vocabulary in the Mystery of Trinity. Instead we aim here to focus our prayerful attention on the Deep Descent that is Inwardness in the Life of God. The Rupture, the Breaking, that is Procession in God shows us that Divine Holiness is not only generated and guarded, marked off, by God Himself, but also that He possesses Depths that can be known only by God Himself.

The Incomprehensibility of God follows from these Hidden Reserves. This maxim of scholastic thought—that God exceeds our comprehension—rests not simply on Divine Infinity, though to be sure such Infinite Nature cannot be surrounded and surmounted by finite intellect and spirit. But Incomprehensibility rests also on the Divine Processions, the Radical Descent down into the Divine Being Itself. We might say, in an odd turn of phrase, that God is Solemn, or perhaps in a modernist nod, Sublime in just this way. He possesses and just is Infinite Reserve. This is central to the Scriptural portrait of Almighty God: His Holiness is sharply Personal. I, the Lord, am Holy: this is the leitmotif of the Holiness Code and the Prophets touched by the Holiness School, as are Ezekiel and Isaiah. This quality of Being, the Life Exodus brings before us so vividly, is no bare record of Divine Deeds or Mighty Works. Of course, the Triune God *acts*! Holy Scripture tells the tale of an Agent God. But it is not, in truth, the Acts, the "Energies" or Works, that hold center stage here, but rather the Subject who works, the Holy One who does these wonders on the earth. He is the One of Infinite Depth; His Hiddenness is His own most Holy Possession, His Sanctuary. This, too, is the Mystery of the Holy God. In just this way we aim to defend the rich legacy of Augustine's "psychological model"—hardly a felicitous phrase!—of the Holy Trinity. God is known, yes. He communicates His Perfections, yes, and there is likeness, even here, in the Life and Reserve of Personality. But He is Inward, Solemnly Inward. We should not properly consider this a matter of theological epistemology, though to be sure it touches on these preserves. But this element of the Divine Descent is more truly a matter of *Privacy*: He is the God in Secret, the Holy God who remains Private.

It may seem odd to speak of God in this way, as if this were a childish or all-too-human account of the Most Real Being. But this response, ready though it may be, should trouble us, we flattened, material beings. Our notion of privacy is so degraded that we can think of it most readily as a juvenile hiding behind bedroom doors, a turning away of the face or heart, and moody demand for a place, unpoliced, set apart. But privacy most fully, most truly is a *dignity*, the final reserve that is personal life. Not everything is told, not everything revealed, not every element of life open to others' eyes. It is the odd, distorting effect of a culture built on capital commerce that everything must be shared, everything undercut and ordered by price, everything for sale, everything subject to a "privacy policy" but in which nothing in truth is so honored, where everything is rather sold for commercial gain, everything treated as a commodity. In truth, however, nothing should be so prized, so personal, yes, so sacred as the dignity that belongs to the private reserve of a human life. Our shocking treatment of prisoners tells us that: their punishment is to live a completely flattened life, under surveillance, fully policed, without reserve, without privacy, without the humane unknown. The depths required for a human and humane life must be taught and guarded in a just society; it is no frill for elites. It is an inescapable dimension of the *imago Dei*. We can glimpse the dignity of privacy by its central, solemn place in the very Life of God. He, this Holy One, is Immeasurable, Private Depths.

In just this way, the Living God is the Free Lord. The Processions are the Sovereign Freedom of God. They are His Liberty. When we think of the Personal Inwardness of God, we consider His Living Freedom, His bursting forth, His Radiant Spaciousness. We do not mean here principally and primarily that God is Free in His Acts, though to be sure this is true, nor that God is Free to do otherwise, though the Divine Counterfactual must find a place in the doctrine of the Holy God as well. No, we mean more: the Generation and Outpouring of God is Substantial Freedom, His Life and His Being as Liberty. The Triune Lord is Private in just this sense: that He is the Freedom of His own inner Life. This need not mean, certainly, that there is no *necessity* in God. John Zizioulas appears to hold that Divine Being must be Free *absolutely*; His is a Freedom over against all necessity, including Divine Necessity.[22] But this opposition does not properly capture the radical nature of Processional Freedom. For it is not one property, one power over against another, nor is it *this* rather than *that*; the Life of God is Non Aliud, without Contrast or Consort of this kind. It is Freedom in just this sense, the Utter Transcendence and Singularity of Divine Selfhood. When the Apostle Paul tells the Corinthians that liberty can be found where the Spirit is (2 Cor 3:17), he binds the Glory of the Lord, the Spirit, and the gift of life close together. To be in the Spirit is to be caught up in this glorious Liberty, changed from glory to glory, brought into a Life that is Itself Free.

Now, this does not entail that the Lord God, in His Inner Freedom, is a *different* God from the One disclosed and living and present among us. Not so! This perpetual tremor of theologians before the Hidden Reserve of God is altogether natural, but in this place, we must say, unneeded and out of place. In the Divine Generation of God the Son, we do not see a formal analogue to the late medieval notion of the Two Powers or the semi-nominalism Barth feared among those who distinguished an Unknown Essence from a known effect or act of God. We are not faced with this kind of distinction here. Of course, there is a "problem in the neighborhood": the Inwardness of God may raise before our hearts and minds the image of a God who in Privacy contradicts the God Revealed, the God near us. But just this pattern is the playacting or hypocrisy our Lord Christ warns against in his very same teaching on the Father who is in Secret. The hypocrites receive their reward from the bystanders, impressed by their almsgiving, their long prayers, their public piety, but it shall not be so among disciples.

Those who follow this Master are to withdraw to their privacy, to pray and mourn in secret, to give so that the left does not know what the right hand is doing. Disciples are to liken themselves, in the midst of a Great Unlikeness, to the God who is in Secret, the Private God. Not God but sinful creatures are the deceivers and self-deceived; not the Holy God but the fallen creature who says, I will go, then does not enter the vineyard; not the God of Depths but the shallow creature who allows one's speech to be yes and no, to doublespeak, and to follow the father of lies. If ever there be a case of projection in Christian theology, this would be chief. The pronounced fear by wayward creatures before a God who does not reveal all, and everything, discloses the uneasy conscience of the two-minded creature, the one who fears and prizes secrecy as the work of the night. The Holy God just is His Holiness, His Wisdom and Goodness. This just is His Life, His Inwardness, His Liberty. He generates these Depths, and they are His, His alone. But they are the Reserve, the Infinite Private Domain, of the True God. They neither deceive nor contradict. Rather, the Depths are trustworthy; they hold true.

But they remain Depths, Holy Mystery. The Processions, that is, are *ethical* properties and relations within the Reality of God. It is easy, almost natural, in the dogma of Trinity to so fasten our eyes on the technical dimensions of this doctrine, its immense conceptual rigor, that we lose sight of the profound *moral* character of these elements. There is nothing in Almighty God that is *neutral*, nothing that is a "play of concepts," nothing that is Rational or Real but not Good. God is One. To "ethicize" the doctrine of Divine Processions is to see them as they must be: the Generation and Outpouring of Holiness, the Holy God.

Just this we see in the scriptural wrestling over the Mighty Depths of God. Our ancestors in the faith were broken on the

Reserve of God. We do not begin to understand the doctrine of the Divine Processions if we do not bow before the terrible struggle of the prophets and apostles with the Hidden Will of God. This is the enigmatic, the awe-filled character of the scriptural narratives Erich Auerbach taught us to see long ago: not everything is told, not everything motivated or explained. The lengthening shadows of the biblical events cover the figures in twilight. We can but think of the father of our faith, Abraham, and his three days' journey in primal silence to the mountain the Lord has shown him, the command, the knife, the fire, the innocent question, and the fathomless reply. Auerbach famously draws our eyes to this silent procession, its utter hiddenness and lack of motivation. Nothing here is explained; it is all dark testing. Of course, we Christians read the *Akida* in light of the sacrifice of the Son—but that does not *explain* or *reveal* the Private Will of Almighty God; rather, it deepens the mystery. Who cannot hear, echoing in our ears, the Servant Song: for it was the will of God to crush him with pain? Just this is the night-wrestling with the Ethical Hiddenness of God, His own Singular Life, His own Ever-Greater Unlikeness. What is not spoken out loud by Abraham or Abraham's Son is voiced in great anguish by Jeremiah, the passionate prophet of the Holy God. "Your words were found, and I ate them, and your words became to me a joy and the delight of my heart; for I am called by your name": so sings Jeremiah, the Lord's intimate. But set down, shoulder to shoulder with this tender hymn to the Divine Word, is this daring explosion: "Why is my pain unceasing, my wound incurable, refusing to be healed? Truly you are to me like a deceitful brook, like waters [*mayim* with echoes of *yam*, the primordial sea] that fail." Here the fever breaks out, the fire in the bones, that is the struggle with this Awe-Filled Freedom of God, His Private Life and Will. It is an ethical wrestling over the Benevolence of God, His Truth and Truthful Word, in the midst of Israel's sorrow and terror and exile. This is the terrible struggle of conscience Calvin famously records in his unrelenting doctrine of election:

> Whence does it happen that Adam's fall irremediably involved so many peoples, together with their infant offspring, in eternal death unless because it so pleased God? Here their tongues, otherwise so loquacious, must become mute. The decree is dreadful indeed, I confess. [the well-known *decretum horribile*] Yet no one can deny that God foreknew what end man was to have before he created him, [a note of the supralapsarian here?] and consequently foreknew because he so ordained by his decree. If anyone inveighs against God's foreknowledge at this point, he stumbles rashly and heedlessly.[23]

Calvin knew the Will of God as Abyss, as Fathomless Decree and Command, a Secret Counsel that could no more be properly examined and constrained than the potter by the pot, the master by the slave. To seek to stand in those Private Courts would be to enter the nightmarish "labyrinth," the tangle and pit that swallows those who defy the Secret Life of God. Like Augustine, his principle witness from the primal age of the church, Calvin will bow low before the majesty of God, this Infinite Reserve, but he will do so as one facing, directly and open-eyed, the profound moral struggle that is creaturely life before the Holy Life of God.

For this is what we reflect on here, at its deepest reach, when we consider the Downward Movement of the Inner Processions of God. The Law and the Prophets testify to this; the Suffering Servant goes down to the pit under its Mighty Hand. Nothing in the Divine Life, we must say again, is *simply* or *merely* Conceptual, a Concept of Origin or Mutual Relation. We must reserve until the Processions are unfolded systematically the proper examination of these terms of art, the Relation of Origin and the Relation of

Opposition. But even here we must ward off the quiet assumption that the highest terms of analysis and speculation in the dogma of Trinity can be weighed and considered apart from Holiness. There is nothing in God, in His Majestic Inwardness, that is not an expression of His Sublime Righteousness, His Singular Wisdom and Goodness. Deity is saturated Goodness, Substantial Living Holiness; there is no other. The Processions must be understood as a Living Stream welling up unto righteousness, an ethical Reality, or they cannot be understood at all. In this sense, and with a significant reserve, we can follow Rahner's lead in Trinity: not a Mystery of our salvation, but rather a Mystery of Living and Free Goodness; that is the doctrine of Triune Processions.

Just so we must enter our final meditation on the teaching of Isaiah 53 on the Generation of the Son and lift our eyes to the Immanent Processions of Son and Spirit. We must consider now the deepest reach of that Downward motion of the Divine Life, the Rupture that overspreads the whole of the prophetic office, the whole of Israel's pilgrim way. This is the Mysterious Life of Divine Outpouring, the Singular and Solitary Self-Bestowal of the One God. The Suffering Servant "hath poured out his soul unto death" and in just this way is accorded a portion with the great. In just this way, the Servant makes many righteous. The second major theme of this Isaianic song is now sounded: the meaning of this Suffering One is his life laid down for the sins of many, outpoured to make the many righteous. Here we encounter the manifest level of the text, its delicate reflection on the suffering of the One for the many: though the Anonymous One, the Servant, will take on the guilt and waywardness of others, and in his anguished death, intercede and make the many justified. This is the meaning of the text at the level of the economy, the narrative shape of Israel as Light to the nations.

These elements must guide any full doctrine of atonement, and we will turn to them when we move our attention, and praise, from the doctrine of Trinity to the doctrine of the Work of Christ. But here we have eyes only for the inner Life of the Holy Trinity, Its own Glorious Aseity and Life. This Subject Matter holds our attention before and above all else; for this is the First Commandment. And so here we reflect more deeply on the Outpouring, the Divine Life that is not only Generation but also Bestowal, Gift. The Divine Processions are not only Generation but also Spiration, not only Giving Rise to, but also Giving, not only Ratio but also Bonum, the Good of the Good God. In both, this Movement and Life will be Descent, the Motion of Almighty God to the Depths.

God outpours: that Procession of the Spirit is our focus now. This Divine Giving, too, is a Rupture, a Dying and a Breaking; it, too, will follow the great Downward arc of the One God in His Mystery and Reserve. The Life of God is *costly*. Now it is a delicate thing to speak properly of such cost—but speak of it we must. There is an old resistance to such language from the ancient times of the church: God is Impassible and Immutable, for He is without parts, without the composition and division of His creatures. God is His own Happiness, the schoolmen said; His Life is Perfect Serenity and Blessedness. Such a Divine Joy cannot suffer cost, cannot suffer. And there is a new resistance, born not of the Ideality and Simplicity of God but rather of His Fullness, His Perfect Generosity that yields only more Gift. As the sun gives warmth and light yet remains a fiery, molten star, so God gives without undergoing loss to Himself but rather is all the more the Generous One. God gives without suffering cost, Kathryn Tanner says, just because there can be no competition, no extraction and diminishment in Perfect Gift.[24] These are powerful objections to the very idea of the costly, to Rupture and Descent, objections rooted in profound doctrines of

God and of His very Nature as Luminous, Radiant Good. The very mark between Creator and creature is said to run right through this territory: God is Life, Eternal Life without shadow of turning; His creatures find there the deliverance, the joy that earth cannot yield. All these objections must have their day; their cause is the Transcendence and Unicity and Luminosity of the True God, and we, too, must join that cause. But the doctrine of God cannot be *programmatic* in its inmost structure. Rational, yes; argumentative and speculative, yes again; but it is not programmatic or closed off from the explosion that is Holy Scripture. And we have seen the Prophet Isaiah set forth a doctrine of the Divine Life that demands daring assent to the Infinite Depths of a Mysterious God. The prophet tells us: There is Height and Depth in the One God, in His Life and Self-Ordering; there is Light and Chiaroscuro in the Luminous Darkness of God, in His Life of Self-Giving; there is Perfection, Terminus, Definition in the Holy Lord. These are *costly* treasures.

The whole of Scripture tells us of this cost. Here is the Humble and Lowly Lord, the great Hidden One, the God whose ambassadors find rejection and obloquy and anguish their lot, the Near God who comes to us as the Rejected One, whose very ways are strange. The Spirit of this Lord conforms the witnesses to this mighty Down-Rushing Life, enduring hardship and loss, stoning and rod, smiling contempt and outrage. Discipleship of this Living God is costly. And how could it not, if God Himself lives this Descending Life? But just what sort of cost could this be?

We know ourselves how to count the cost of an earthly life, its frailties and pain, its sorrows or guilt. Our frame is for the dust. But the Lord of heaven and earth: What is the costly Outpouring for Him? It cannot be a cost that reduces God to creature, makes Him mortal, if only in concept, or frail, or vulnerable: the Omnipotent and Eternal God is the Revolutionary Overthrow of all that. Yet the line of Descent is clear, and if Holy Scripture is the guide to the Aseity of God—and everything does truly rest on that!—then the Outpouring of God must share in this costly Procession. It is a Downward March. In God Himself is this Metaphysical Disposition, this Readiness for the Mission of the Word, the dear Son come to die. Not a mirroring or reflection! Not an import of this death so the Living One enters the grave in His own Triune Life! No, the place of the economy is not primal in this fashion, not the engine nor the mirror of the Transcendent Life. Rather the Holy God, in His own Mystery, His own Deep Freedom, is the very Structure, the Ratio of the Temporal Missions, the Incarnate Son, the outpoured Spirit. This Triune Structure stands behind the altar, the holy place of Israel. The blood is spilled on the altar, poured out in basins, splashed against the horns of the altars, smeared and thrown and scattered in the holy precincts: the life is in the blood. Holiness costs the animal its life, the bird and the living grain their flourishing. The Holy God is sought out and imitated and followed by this likeness, the costly gift of blood, the life blood. But in a Greater Unlikeness! The Divine Processions set this Cost apart; it will be the Perfect Descent, the Perfect Gift. But a Lavish, Unstinting Pouring it will be. It will cost but in such a Mode that Eternal Life will be glimpsed there, a Descent that turns over into Victory.

Note that this costly Outpouring cannot be, if we read the Lord's Aseity aright, a terrible and sacrificial colloquy between Father and Son. We do not face here a retrojection of the Akida or Gethsemane into the Eternal Godhead. No! Holy Scripture is not univocal in this fashion. There are not "two wills," even less "three wills," "three personal centers," so to say, in the Triune Life of God, for our God is One. Nor do we see a "costly Divine Love" in which the Son offers and the Father grieves and the Spirit confirms such Divine sacrifice. The Holy Trinity is not a *pactum*, however honorable the scholastic tradition is that stands behind such a notion. We are not to imagine a royal audience or narrative of some kind in the Heavenly Realms; there is no exchange or deliberation or consent that "constitutes" the Triune Life, no drama in high places. To "actualize" the Being of God in this way—however many conceptual problems it may dissolve—cannot be the way forward from Sinai, from Israel's confession of the Shema, from the Pure Rationality of the very Idea of God. In my reading of Israel's covenant, the Transcendent Oneness of God cannot be so defended, nor can such pious Dialogue be reconciled, fully and coherently, with the Utter Unicity of the Lord, His Reality beyond image and kind, likeness and form. For this reason, among others, we must resist the idea that love, most especially Divine Love, requires an "Object," a Recipient or Beloved. All hail the Victorines—but Richard's contemplation of a Divine Love realized in the Beloved and made Perfect in the Spirit of Love (the *condilectio* of the Spirit) cannot properly defend the Simplest Unity of God, I say, however Augustinian the pedigree. The Canons of Lateran IV tell us that the unity of love found in the church or among creatures can never be compared or equal to the Utter Unicity of the God who is Love.

Rather, we must say that the Love which is God is the very Deity, the very Nature of the Lord; He is its Fullness, its Infinite Depths, its Radiant Light. He need not "enact" it or "give and receive" it in Divine exchange; He simply *is* it. Love, that is, most especially costly or sacrificial Love, cannot be located among the Divine Persons; we are not here considering a Society or Communion of Three distinct Persons. For that reason, the costly love that Moltmann or Balthasar, or in another idiom, Barth see in the Divine

Triunity cannot be the costly Processions taught in this theology. The Divine Outpouring and Descent cannot be rendered pictorial and agential in this way. Rather, the costly Holiness of God is His *Life*, His Generation and Spiration, not a Divine Act among the Persons. When we speak in this theology of the Rupture and Cost in the Divine Reality, another Downward Path must be found. We must seek a Divine Love that is the Procession, the Ever-Greater Unlikeness, that is the Exceeding Mystery of the Living God. *That* is the teaching, the disclosure and gift, of Isaiah 53 as exemplar of the Holy Trinity. So we must say that the Costly Descent of the Life of God leads to *sacrifice*, to the sacrificial cultus of Israel. We cannot take to heart the outpouring of the Suffering Servant—His afflicted life as ransom for the many—without turning to the temple as the home and scriptural outworking of costly love. It is common in much Protestant polemics to *contrast* the prophetic and the priestly; always the prophetic is to be preferred. But Holy Scripture, as instructor in doctrine, cannot be so read: always the Scriptures are a *whole*, always they integrate and balance and deepen one voice on another. It is the Intelligible laid down in the *whole* of Scripture. So, to follow more closely, more faithfully the instruction of Scripture, we must see the Divine Processions, evoked in Isaiah 53, joined to and furthered by the priestly and Holiness Schools. The answer to our urgent question—how are we to understand the costliness of the Spirit's outpouring Love?—can be found only where cost is fully counted: the sacrifice of Israel's altar. It is there that the Downward Dynamism of the Son and Spirit will be encountered in its fullness; there the Fiery Processions of God's inner Life will be displayed; there the Holy Trinity as costly Gift, offered and received, will be enacted for our instruction and our praise. To these books we now turn.

Notes

1. Erik Erikson, *Young Man Luther: A Study in Psychoanalysis and History* (New York: Norton, 1993), 10.

2. Barth, *Church Dogmatics*, IV.1, The Doctrine of Reconciliation, §59.1, 195, 199, 201. Emphasis added.

3. Barth, *Church Dogmatics*, IV.1, The Doctrine of Reconciliation, 203.

4. Barth, *Church Dogmatics*, IV.1, The Doctrine of Reconciliation, 202.

5. Barth, *Church Dogmatics*, IV.1, The Doctrine of Reconciliation, 203.

6. Hanson, *Search for the Christian Doctrine of God*, 848–49.

7. Hanson, *Search for the Christian Doctrine of God*, 849.

8. Hanson, *Search for the Christian Doctrine of God*, 846.

9. Martin Luther King Jr., "I've Been to the Mountaintop," in *A Call to Conscience: The Landmark Speeches of Dr. Martin Luther King, Jr.*, ed. Clayborn Carson and Kris Shepard (New York: Grand Central Publishing, 2001), 223.

10. Helen Keller, *The Story of My Life* (New York: Doubleday, 1904), 20.

11. Helen Keller, *Story of My Life*, 23–24.

12. Helen Keller, *Story of My Life*, 24.

13. Hans Frei, *The Eclipse of Biblical Narrative: A Study in Eighteenth and Nineteenth Century Hermeneutics* (New Haven, CT: Yale, 1974) and *The Identity of Jesus Christ: The Hermeneutical Bases of Dogmatic Theology* (Philadelphia: Fortress, 1975).

14. Gregory of Nyssa, *On the Soul and Resurrection*, trans. Catharine P. Roth (New York: St. Vladamir's, 2002).

15. Iris Murdoch, *Sovereignty of Good* (Abingdon: Routledge and Kegan Paul, 1970).

16. See Barth, *Church Dogmatics*, II.1 and IV.1.

17. Sigmund Freud, *Civilization and Its Discontents*, trans. James Strachey, introduction by Christopher Hitchens, repr. ed. (New York: W. W. Norton & Company, 2010).

18. Schroeder, *Disciplinary Decrees of the General Councils*, Canon 2, 241.

19. Fiona Robb, "The Fourth Lateran Council's Definition of Trinitarian Orthodoxy," *Journal of Ecclesiastical History* 48 (1997): 22–43.

20. Sarah Coakley, *God, Sexuality, and the Self* (Cambridge: Cambridge University Press, 2013), 101.

21. Kathryn Tanner, *Christianity and the New Spirit of Capitalism* (New Haven, CT: Yale University Press, 2019).

22. Zizioulas, *Being as Communion.*

23. J. Calvin, *Institutes of the Christian Religion*, trans. F. L. Battles (Philadelphia: Westminster, 1960), book III, chapter XXIII, 7.

24. Kathryn Tanner, *Christ the Key* (Cambridge: Cambridge University Press, 2010).

§ 5. Leviticus and the Holiness School: Trinity as Holy

Just why is Leviticus, the priestly and Holiness Schools, so foreign to the Christian imagination? Why the disdain, even revulsion for this book? Numbers, we saw, was a book without many champions, a seeming oddment of narrative and law and folk tale, hardly organized at all, it seemed, to many eyes—apart from the sharp-eyed Mary Douglas.[1] But still, Christian exegetes found a place for the narratives within Numbers: the stories of Moses, Miriam, and Aaron, of the daring and timid spies in the land of Canaan, the rebellion of Korah, and the healing seraphim lifted high on the staff, given burnished value in the Gospel of John, the humility of Moses and *his* rebellion, the odd and wonderful legends of Balaam and his shrewd donkey, all welcomed into Christian literature. But Leviticus appears to be orphaned—at least in modern Christian theology. We may well wonder why. It has been unshakably numbered in the Pentateuch from earliest days; it contains many prescriptions and instances of sacrifice, rich material for Christological and sacramental readings (as Ephraim Radner has shown in one of the few modern theological exegeses of the book);[2] and it rings with demands for justice to the land, the alien, the worker, and the neighbor, all treasured legacies for ethical monotheisms. Yet modern Christians continue to find Leviticus, its style and its teachings, rebarbative, inexplicable, alien. Why is this so?

Now, Douglas, one of the few modern-day defenders of the priestly writings, has an intriguing theory: Leviticus is an exalted species of "analogical or correlative" thinking, and the modern West, with its rational-analytic form of cognition, cannot make head or tail of it at all.[3] And surely the nonnarrative character of the whole, the seemingly unmotivated and arbitrary details of priestly duties, the apparent broken and interrupted treatment of distinct statutes, the unquenched search for proper food, proper clothing and eating, proper days and festivals and observances, the unrelieved fear of mold and skin disease, reaching out even to the houses Israel may dwell in: these seem alien and all too forgettable to the modern Christian mind. An air of the "sea of the Talmud" hovers over Leviticus; only the daring seem ready to make the plunge. Add to these perplexities the liberal Christian concern, a proper one, for equality between men and women, and for the honoring of same-sex unions, the Holiness Code—the closest thing to a favorite Christian text in Leviticus—soon becomes an unreliable ally, even an opponent. To all this we may say: well, yes. Leviticus *is* an ancient text, and it does not easily bend to our sway. But I believe there is more at work in the Christian distaste for Leviticus than a matter of style or some troubling ethical lapses, as it seems. There is a deep theological uneasiness about the book, its ornate priestly requirements, and its unrepentant celebration of sacrifice as reconciliation and as holiness. Why might this be? We can only speculate, but speculate we will.

There is something elemental about Divine Holiness that we modern Christians find deeply alien and unsettling. Some theorists in the modern era have attempted to explain, perhaps heighten, this unease about the Primal Absolute. Rudolf Otto gave us a memorable account of the *Tremendum*, the dangerous presence of the Holy, and Douglas the inextricable link between cosmology, forms of life, and the sense of Holiness in her pioneering works. And it may be Paul Tillich's lasting theological contribution to this theme to carve out conceptual room for the menacing Power of Being, its Depth and Numinous Charge. We need not endorse Otto's expansive taste for the irrational and uncategorical in the *Numen*: Holy Mystery is not contrary to reason, not alogical—or, less, amoral—but, as Otto helps us see, the *Holy* God is Fiery, a Living Explosion. Despite their aid, however, Christians in the modern era have found it difficult or unnecessary to incorporate these anthropological and conceptual insights into their life before God.

One reason, perhaps, lies close at hand. The deflationary impulse in modern liturgical worship is striking, and perhaps salient here. Liturgical leaders report that the laity first brought within the sanctuary to aid in worship will be filled with compunction about correct action: Do I know the proper names for these holy things? Have I handled them correctly, reverently? What will I do, what will happen, if I drop, if I spill, if I stumble over words, over furnishings? A living, perhaps unbearable sense of the Holy seems to animate the fresh recruit to worship leadership. Any seminary teacher can report similar anxieties by students first called to enter the sanctuary, to read or serve at the altar. Those of us from liturgical traditions might speculate why: rites with rubrics, we might say, seem to awaken a dread of the Holy. Do they not awaken a morbid obsession, we ask? Certain rituals kept with an unforgiving precision, for example, repeated in a compulsive and fearful style, and a relishing that is both precious and malicious: these traits can rouse a kind of malignant pleasure in the ritualist and a kind of horror in the observer, a repulsion at the perfect and, it may be, the magical. Sigmund Freud taught us to see the gnawing ambivalence at the root of the "compulsion to repeat"; he gave word and concept to the sickening fascination we experience in the ritual ceaselessly performed, each time more exacting, each time less forgiving, less effective. We might imagine that the liturgist or teacher faced with such scrupulosity might be led to give a theological précis on the nature of the Holy, the Righteous One *and* the Merciful, and the proper means to approach and live before this God. Perhaps this happens in sacristies and classrooms all over the church, hidden and unremarked! But in our era, I would hazard, the impulse of most priests, most faculty, most pastors is to *minimize* the dread, to soothe, to deny. We reassure, we aim to teach, yes, but also to deflate and contain: none of these things really matter, we say consolingly.

We may well wonder why we are so quick to salve anxiety in this way. There *are* proper worries about scrupulosity; no one in the grip of such intolerable conscientiousness should go unrelieved or unconsoled. The forms of liturgy and the forms of instruction should be designed to make confident and free the lay and ordained leaders of worship. But we should be properly hesitant to relieve the conscience-stricken through a minimizing of the Danger who is God. Leviticus tells us that the Presence of Holiness is something like lye or radium: it cleans and purifies; it contains fathomless energy; and it burns, cauterizes, scars. The laboratory procedures for handling acids and isotopes are the only form of safety. Following them exactly is the only practice that will make new scientists confident and free. The cultural legitimacy of science may aid us in theology to see how Holiness might better be encountered and served. Leviticus is something like a laboratory manual for entering the Presence of the Holy God.

The attempt in modern Protestant circles, especially—but not exclusively—to domesticate God, to find in Him only the kindly, only the friendly, the avuncular, is nearly proverbial. The young Karl Barth found this an irritating and symptomatic trait of *Kultur Protestantismus*. And despite his mighty labors to excise such smug domesticity, the one-sided, toothless God lives on. While the Goodness of God ought never be impugned, we might all agree that a Christianity that is only hospitable, only useful and edifying, has not taken the full measure of the Living God. He is Good, Goodness Itself, *and* He is Holy. Bending down in awe before Almighty God is the first act of proper piety. It is not simply that God is Incomprehensible, though it be true; nor that His Mystery cannot be dissolved, though that is also true; nor that His Transcendence makes every similarity collapse before the Incalculable Dissimilarity, though that is certainly true. It is even more that the Presence of the True God is *shocking*, an Undoing; there is no quiescence before the Revolution who is God. There is costly descent for us creatures, too! Certainly, Leviticus does not derive its laws from the experimental method or elaborate them through an exposition of causal or elemental properties—quite the opposite. The statutes and ordinances, the book is careful to underline, come from the Holy One Himself. They are the sympathetic vibrations of God's own Perfect Holiness. Torah is composed of positive law, grounded alone in the Majesty of God's own Righteous Life.

All this is fine, a critic might say, but you have not actually touched on the main reason for Leviticus's current disfavor, the inescapable rot of Leviticus; its disappearance from modern theology lies in its near-complete supersession—by Christians and by Jews. Why, such critics ask, then, have we ceased slaughtering animals, wringing the necks of birds, and elevating grain before this Holy God? Why, the critics help us ask, should we take the Holy as the "full measure" of the Living God if the book that teaches us this awe-filled dread has been so clearly abolished by Christians and Jews, each in their own way, each with their own scriptural rationale? It seems that the legal material in Leviticus has become otiose: like a long-dead article in the law code, it lives on as vestige and relic, without enforcement, penalty, or use. Surely the sacrificial rite in Leviticus can be no more than a hieratic memory of an archaic practice long past? Christians have faced from earliest days the task of categorizing and ranking the commandments of Israel, such that some are held to be uninterruptedly in force (the Decalogue is prime instance), while others are to be observed under new conditions and application (we might think of the Sabbath day, here, or the dimensions and design of the sanctuary) and others still to be overruled and considered no longer in force. The Reformers often spoke of these latter as the Ceremonial Law, which is abrogated, while the Moral Law remained unshaken and bedrock for every Christian. The dietary laws—*kashruth*—came under fire early: we can see remnants of those pitched battles in the Gospel of Mark, in the early chapters of Acts, and most prominently in the letters of the apostle Paul. If "all foods have been declared clean," have we not been given scriptural mandate to refashion, reorder, and revoke the ancient cultic laws of Israel?

We need not endorse the full program of F. C. Baur to see that the matter of Levitical law goes to the very heart of New Testament formation and the proclamation of the Gospel to the gentiles. We might follow the lead of the Federal theologians, for example, who turned to the notion of unfolding covenants to account for the temporary and unstable character of much of Israelite law. There could be a law code or covenant established with Adam and Eve, the covenant of creation; another with Noah, the Noachide commandments; the covenant of law, extended to Moses and ratified by all the people; and a covenant of grace, laid down and sealed in the blood of Christ, the law code for the children of light.

Or perhaps we could reach further back, to the *Treatise on Law*, promulgated by St. Thomas in his *Summa*. There we can see the high medieval art of distinctions in full play. The Eternal Law, never abrogated, never fully articulated, is simply God Himself, the Righteous Being of Almighty God; the law of Israel, given through Moses, in force for a season and a day; the positive laws of the many nations, announced by monarchs, drawn up by magistrates, adapted to local custom; and the law of Christ, the final and perfect law, preserving and grounding all that has gone before, elevating and perfecting the earlier code, abolishing all that is imperfect, superseded, and otiose.[4] On the strength of these rankings, Thomas dared to speak of the continued observance of Jewish law as *sinful*—but the logic of his position is not far from every Christian notion of Old Testament Law, developed across the churches. Of course, a careful exposition of covenantal nomism or Thomistic doctrine of law would require far more extensive and detailed commentary than these brief brush strokes could provide. But here, the broad architecture of Christian teachings about the law of Israel will serve us well. For the very idea that biblical law could come in *degrees*, that it could be divided into temporal categories of the lasting and the obsolete, that it could be schematized into (mere) ceremonial, ritual, liturgical decrees and into the (principally) moral, humane, and binding ordinances—this notion alone makes nearly the entire book of Leviticus an alien and unappealing fossil, perhaps immoral, of ancient jurisprudence. The dazzling centerpiece of Leviticus—the establishment of a Holy People before a Holy God—might dwindle to a flicker in a religious tradition that has learned to see such rites and such rules as the passing shadow of a Light now come into the world: and, behold, all things are become new.

The sacrificial cultus, set out in Leviticus with such precision and such self-evident reverence, could be considered, in this view, an arresting museum piece, perhaps, a vivid symbol, perhaps, of Someone yet to come, perhaps an artefact of rare oddity or beauty—but not, it seems, a book of living law that must find its place at the core of Christian teaching. It would be easy to speak of all this as so much vulgar anti-Judaism, anchored deep within Christian piety, and in this way make Leviticus a shining star of the proper attitude, the proper exegesis, the proper doctrine. But we would not have traveled far in the school of Christ were we to imagine that it could be all that easy. What the history of the Christian tradition, and the practice of Old Testament exegesis, has shown us is that the question raised by our critic cannot be answered with the wave of a hand. There is no recovery of Leviticus for dogmatic construction without a plain encounter with this deep, complex, and demanding legacy of scriptural law and its abolition.

Just what is the status of Levitical law within Christian theology? How should we Christians regard the sacrifices of the tabernacle and temple? How can the death of these animals, the smoky ash of these first fruits, cereals, and grain cakes, be instruction in the doctrine of God, the dogma of the Holy Trinity? Can Leviticus carry this stature, bear this weight, provide this direction? We will not understand much about the "Leviticus-forgetfulness" of this age if we do not answer these questions directly, thoughtfully, and unsparingly. As Brevard Childs notes, these questions are not new. The sacrificial cultus has been radically reinterpreted, spiritualized—superseded even—in the modern expression of both Judaism and Christianity.[5] Tellingly, Herod's temple, destroyed by the Romans in the year 70 CE, was never rebuilt. Even in the Orthodox circles that continue to study and teach the Levitical law of sacrifice, no steps have been advocated for "taking the kingdom by force," hastening the coming messiah by erecting a temple for him to enter and possess. No, waiting for the Divine

Eschaton is the religious prescription, even for those who look for the day when the full sacrificial cultus resumes. Rabbinic Judaism in Conservative and Reform schools have long taught that the Pharisees showed the way forward after the calamity of the temple's destruction: not slaughtered animals but rather prayer would be the covenant sacrifice, the prayer of thanksgiving and praise. The New Testament, Childs writes, refashioned sacrifice in another manner, seeing in Christ's own perfect obedience and death a sacrifice that puts an end to temple cultus—a supersession by and into a Temple not made by hands. Both Jews and Christians offered a fresh reading of the law of sacrifice through a reinterpretation of the Canon, Childs says, not prophet against law, not New Testament against Old, not Christian spiritualism against "carnal Israel," not shadow against fulfillment, not any of these old oppositions that ring the changes on Christian supersession of Israel. Rather, Childs argues, we see in these two biblical traditions, rabbinic Judaism and Christianity, a broad exegetical remastering of the central texts of Holy Scripture, one in which the temple sacrifices are shown to be sublated into the worshipping life of observant Christians and Jews. It seems then that the very practice of ritual sacrifice has made Christians and Jews uneasy, from the days of late antiquity forward. It appears that spiritualizing—rendering the bloody cult as bloodless sacrifice, in prayer or sacrament—exposes a troubled conscience about the entire notion of killing animals and birds as meal-offering to a Holy God. Even the psalmist seems troubled from time to time: "Do you think I eat the flesh of bulls or drink the blood of goats?" The worries about the Holy, the Law, and its Levitical rites pressed on us by modern pastors and analysts seem simply to echo an ancient moment in biblical religion: the putting away of primitive things for the higher religious ideal of intercession and anamnesis. What should a theology that aims to anchor the dogma of the Holy Trinity in Israel's sacrificial cultus say about all this?

The Levitical law of Holiness has not been put away: this is the first thing we must say. Now, this is not because we have found an acceptable spiritual translation of the sacrificial rite—however important that reinterpretation may become in the development of Christian and Jewish doctrine. Rather, it is the very *act* of sacrifice, the concrete event of altar roasting and feasting, waving and smearing and sprinkling, that is central to this doctrine of Trinity and has not been attenuated or sublated. We are looking at the gritty, bloody, smoky amalgam of ancient tabernacle and temple— these pungent, visceral, and terrible things—and discovering, laid down in their midst, the Mysterious Life of the Tri-Personed God. This is to say that the Mosaic code, and the events of the tent of meeting, have not entered into the past; they have not happened but rather are taking place, even now. They happen. The ordinances, statutes, and commandments of Leviticus have not passed away because they are unfolding, they are being enacted, *now*. I want to be careful here. I do not want to wash away the *history* of ancient Israel—precisely not that! The aim here is not to render Leviticus as a Platonizing text (though the temple may indeed be a Divine Idea), nor imbue it with a Sallust-like spirit, as though "like myth, they never happened but always are." The doctrine of Scripture that I am advancing here is not an attempt to *reify* the rites of Israel, to render them impenetrable to the acid of time, nor remove them from the sphere of motion and of change. Nor is it to say that some inner spark, some transliterated meaning, could be carried over from the old ways, peeling away the outer actions of Aaron and his sons as so many signs or foreshadowings of a spiritual ideal, now realized in its elevated essence in the present bloodless age. We need not head into a Hegelianizing path, either, categorizing the temple cultus as so much plastic representation, yielding up to the careful analyst, the very Idea of Sacrifice and Self-Giving. No, we are not attempting to handle the plain and the full sense of the biblical text in allegorizing or idealizing modes. Rather, we aim to underscore the strong *uniqueness* of Holy Scripture, its unmatched stature among the good creatures of God, which makes its history a living event before the Living God.

Perhaps certain parallels come to mind. We might consider the venerable notion of anamnesis in sacramental theology: the act of recollection that makes present what has happened, once and for all, in the history of the covenant people, for the good of the whole world. Not a fresh sacrifice, that is, a "bloodless one," say, not a repetition or new pleading of the original Self-Giving of Christ, but rather a *manifestation*, a showing of the death of Christ, once offered, now present among His people. This is, so to say, an "eternalizing" of a historical, unique event, the saving death of Jesus Christ. Of course, we need not reach for such exalted examples to call to mind a past event become present. A vivid recounting of a family story makes a long-dead ancestor present and vigorous among her descendants. An old letter, yellowed and folded up within the pages of a long-forgotten book, can suddenly materialize the correspondent from out of the past into the very different present of the addressee. The past speaks! Music conjures the past. Shakespeare lives in a vigorous production of *Macbeth* or *Julius Caesar*. The odd, recursive quality of time in literature and the arts makes an "eternal past" not so remote to us; indeed, it is just this ordinary, small-scale quality of the "present past" that enthralled Augustine, fascinating him by the simple act of memory. Despite such everyday and more polished examples, I should say that such eternalizing is a parallel to my exegetical aim here, but only a parallel, not an instance.

Or in a more rhetorical vein we might consider the literary significance of the perfect tense, an action inaugurated or begun in the past, completed there—it is "perfect"—yet continues into the present, making its effect known, disclosing its still vital power. Just this is ingredient in any full defense against supersessionism. I have studied the Bible; I have patented a new machine; I have joined a marching band: all idiomatic expressions of the perfect tense. Such literary analyses allow an event or figure from the past to populate the present as a real and causal force, demonstrating that the event begun sometime in the past is not locked up in times gone by, even when its *temporal* act is complete but rather continues, works, breathes here among us. In some such way, the Decalogue or the Sabbath, promulgated in ancient times, holds force today; the ripples from that old Explosion still spill over into our landscape now. Moses's inauguration of the tabernacle cultus; Jesus's institution of the Lord's Supper; the apostle Paul's promulgation of the mission to the gentiles: all these may be taken to illustrate a theological perfect tense, marking an event in the historical past that gives shape and life to the present day. This, too, is a parallel to the problem in the neighborhood, a shadow of Scripture's unique temporal character, not an instance of it.

And we might reflect, too, on the Lutheran *genus majestaticum*, a Christological parallel in which the human nature of Christ, on glorification and ascension, partakes in the Omnipresence of the Divine Perfections—now present, in His crucified and risen flesh, on a thousand altars, in every season and place. Here we can see something of the Divine Attributes being communicated to a mortal creature, such that the limitations thought to belong to creaturely nature are now superseded, or elevated, or glorified, and brought into the realm of the Lord's Perfect and Limitless Presence. Perhaps we might consider the historical reality of Christ's earthly life under this *genus* in a more general sense. His own past could be made present: He is Risen *as* the Crucified One. Thoughts along these lines may well have inspired Barth's remarkable treatment of Christ's earthly and Heavenly Lordship, "Jesus Christ, the Lord of Time."[6] In all these examples, we find a recognition of the *historical* nature of the event; it is not abraded or occluded. But the reality that belongs to the past also inhabits the present in an effective, living manner. They have been *completed, and* they live on. These illustrations might stock our theological imagination, so that the ever-present mode of the sacrificial cultus might take on plausible shape. But these all are secondary examples, not the main thing. Our *central* claim centers on the nature of Holy Scripture itself, its stature before and from God. Only from an acknowledgment of the Bible as unique creature of God can we properly glimpse and defend the notion that ancient Israel's sacrificial cultus lives on in Christian theology and guides and grounds the dogma of the Holy Trinity. Israel's temple sacrifices manifest and correspond to the Triune Lord's Self-Offering, His costly descent and ascent as Gift. The Levitical account of sacrifice reinscribes the Processional Life of God, the Holiness of the Trifold Lord. Only Holy Scripture can do this. To read Leviticus in this fashion is to receive that mysterious gift, the "dawning of an Aspect." The Spirit of Holiness opens our eyes, and we *see*.

This is not a plea, however, to begin once again the slaughter and roasting of animals on a consecrated altar. The Bible is not a *manual*: we do not turn to it to find out how to replicate in our sanctuaries the rites of ancient Israel. To see this, we have to consider the proper relation between text and referent in the realm of Holy Scripture. Students of hermeneutics will recognize that this is ground strewn by thistles and thorns: we will avoid these thickets as best we can! Our aim here is to speak not of the perfectly general problem of language and referent or of historical text and the events it seeks to depict. We need not even rehearse the pattern of genre and subject matter explored earlier. Rather, when we ask about the status of Leviticus and its rites of sacrifice, we ask about the scriptural writings and their *concomitant* historical referents, one brought along with the other. (Thomas makes fine use of concomitance in his Christology, but that is a story for another day.) Here we say that Leviticus brings in its wake the lived, historical enactment of its teachings. It *assumes* them quite properly into its own legal and narrative material. Just that is *realism* in the doctrine of Scripture. We are not making claims here about the nature of this scriptural realism, its completeness or inerrancy, its reliability or fallibility— these belong to another arena. Rather we here consider sufficient the claim that Holy Scripture is a *creature*, though a unique one, with creaturely properties, and that it realistically depicts the world and events that are assumed into its teaching, peoples and deeds. The past lives in its own textual present in this effortless way, hardly needing to be remarked on. But this is writing about a very odd past, a Unique Referent: the manifestation of God with His people Israel. Something very odd, very alien to human history is taking place among this small, ancient nation: the Transcendent and Holy God has drawn near to, descended to them. More than that: the One God, the Unique and Sole Deity, has created this people, freed and fed them, dwelt with them as Fire and Thunder and Cloud, and inaugurated their cultus with His own Fiery Glory, coming in these last days to tabernacle with them as flesh, as Spirit and Truth.

Now, what is the historical status of such a people, such a literature, such a turn of events? There can be, in the nature of the case, no parallel to such things. They—the text and the referent— are strongly unique. Perhaps something along these lines led Martin Buber to speak of the "abiding astonishment" of the Exodus, when all historical, material, and critical analyses have spent their power, and we have seen in them and through them to the Luminous Beyond. The historical events that have Almighty God as their source do not belong to history as do our mere mortal deeds. They are not simply acts that happen to have had God as One of their Actors; they are not Homeric. Leviticus is not a two-story universe of that Attic sort, in which in a dual vision we grasp the doings of mortals, overshadowed and determined by the doings of the immortals. No, for the True God to be at the center of this book is to *see* Mystery enacted. It is the Utterly Formless and Transcendent Aseity of God plunged down into the world of suffering and things and time, making them all possible, all suffused with Unapproachable Light. The book that speaks of these things carries the *Aspects*, the resonances, of this Revolution: the Life of God is in its sinews.

The law and history of such a book do not cease taking place. They do not *repeat*, an endless circuit, beginning again from the last vision of the Revelation to John. The biblical time is not circular in this way. It is dynamic; it unfolds. The historical dimension of ancient Israel, of Second Temple Judaism, of Jesus and His disciples, of His Risen Life, commissioning and sending forth apostles, to the edge of the known world: all these events unfurl and anchor themselves deep into the cultural, material, and religious life of the earth. They are not "salvation history," if by that term we mean a series of events that do not belong to universal time, to *chronos*, but rather belong only—and perhaps mystically—to a kairos time, lifted up out of the ambiguity and permanence of historical becoming. We are not seeking here a *sphere* in which sacred story can take place. Something universal is being disclosed and enacted in Holy Scripture and, as Erich Auerbach and Hans Frei said so well, the world is contained within it, not Scripture within the world. But what does this say about biblical temporality? In what sense can the sacrificial cultus of ancient Israel be codified, rehearsed, and taught, even to this very day?

Perhaps we might consider here the philosophy of time advanced by the English idealist J. M. E. McTaggart. In *The Nature of Existence*[7] he proposed that we consider time under two broad schemas: past, present, and future (later to be called the A Series) and earlier than and later than (later to be called the B Series). Famously, McTaggart distinguished these two series in order to demonstrate the *irreality* of time—an odd property, one might say, of such illuminating analyses of temporality. McTaggart was convinced, perhaps by fundamental intuition, that change demanded the A Series; no real movement in the world, no actual beginnings, transformations, or endings, could take place without the temporal sequence, past, present, and future. Yet, McTaggart argued, insoluble contradictions and infinite regressions stem from realism about these events in time. The conclusion is this: nothing exists in time. Now, as is the way with generative ideas, McTaggart's original aims in his essay have faded with time—an objection, perhaps, to his conclusion?—but his nomenclature lives on. McTaggart considered the B Series to have the property of "permanence": always an event—he used the death of Queen Anne—takes place before another: say, World War I, and always, World War I unfolds after the death of Queen Anne. Such a schema has been called block time, and it appeals to spatial rather than chronological structures of events. In fact, the B Series appears to dissolve time itself—certainly the intuitive conviction that an object or event comes toward us from the future, exists now with us in the present, and falls away into the past, where it remains. In place of this movement or flow, the B Series presents an unchanging structure: always this event before that, always that event later than this. All events seem eternal in this sense; they simply *are* in this asymmetrical relation, one to another.

The formal and structural qualities of this series carry an air of objectivity and stability; for just this reason, it is heralded as the scientific version of time. The physicalist and cosmological uses of the B Series, however, typically remain neutral on the metaphysical or realist implications of this schema, enough for theoretical work on the idea that time is spatialized, independent of its ontology. For theological reasons, however, we might think of the B Series in a more straightforward metaphysical fashion. It could serve as a possible analogue for the form of history Holy Scripture presents to us: in some sense, we might say, the persons, laws, and events of Israel take place eternally.

Their property as *historical*, we could say, has not been erased. Still Moses leads the slaves to liberty; still he ascends Mount Sinai in the thunder and thick darkness; still he carries tablets of the Law, which in fury he broke, and later delivers them again, the Ten Words written by the finger of God. The unfolding of events, the human-scale action of the figures within these events, their taking place at a particular time, their causal powers, if such they have, and their lasting effects on culture, and worship, and rite: all these belong to the B Series as much as they do to the A. But their metaphysical status, we might say, is no longer determined by their place within time. In the A Series, we assimilate ontology to temporality: the past is *over*; it no longer exists, apart from memory, say, or the perduring effects of a completed action. Just this is the haunting of time that the A Series expresses: the wind blows over our little days and cares, and the place will know it no more. Those days, those intimates, those lovely rooms or walkways: they are *gone*, shut up in the past. The present steals away from us into that dark room, a fleeting moment of *this* hour and day; we can only wait for the future and its ephemeral movement through our present into the past and the great army of the dead. Only temporality of this kind, the A

Series, can give us the "now," the event that takes place this minute, right now, present here with me. That is the power of the A Series, and the profound shock of loss, impermanence, and corruption of the present become past that convinced McTaggart that if the mobility and mutability of finite existence were to be defended or explained, only the A Series would do. (But he, of course, denied the consequent.)

Now, Holy Scripture itself speaks with great solemnity of seasons and days that exhibit the glory and plight of the past, present, and future. No theology that is built on Scripture could dispense with these fundamental categories of creaturely being. But we might still consider the B Series as offering us a glimpse of the startling and alien properties of biblical persons, teachings, and deeds: they are temporal yet permanent. Though partaking of history, they are eternal. Their structural relation exists, we might say, in an ordered and unchanging mode, bearing always the property of unfolding in a stable pattern with all other persons and deeds, a sturdy and fine-grained mesh of interconnection, by which the whole world of things and events is tied together, fixed, and rendered coherent. Perhaps such a notion, immiserated though it may be, could allow us to consider the ever-greater dissimilarity of a scriptural history, a sacrificial cultus, that does not fade away or volatilize but *remains*.

What kind of history is this? Barth was persuaded that we are immersed in a "mytho-poetic" world, in which the thought-form and idiom of the saga best capture the ineffable truth of God dwelling in the midst of creatures. Such exceeding wonder could never be recounted directly; words fail. But through the domains of poetry and legend, the full, concrete, and historical dimensions of this great covenant could be indirectly expressed, a refracted light from the dazzling Majesty of God's Presence with us. While wonderfully suggestive, Barth's proposal for scriptural genre does not carry us far enough into the metaphysical domain we require here. For in the end we can only advert to the doctrine of God to capture in some partial way the unique metaphysical status of Israel's history and cultus.

The *Mystery of the Holy Trinity itself*, in the end, is the only full, inexhaustible resource for grasping the unique ontology of Israel's covenant, its past and its vibrant present. The theophany of God to Israel, the entire *creatio ex nihilo* of this covenant people, is the manifestation of the Concrete Life of God, the Generative, Spiritual Life of the Tri-Personed God, visiting His people. In virtue of the Divine Processive Life, Israel's history, from tabernacle to Second Temple, is a record that *abides*, that never recedes into the barren and fixed past. It is eternally animated by the Divine Life. We can say it simply: It is *sanctified, consecrated*. There can be no supersession of this people and this covenant. The contagion that is Holiness does not dissipate, nor see corruption; it remains. Moreover, the Holy Spirit of God animates the life of the dead, sets them apart, raises them up. To say that the Holy Spirit speaks through the prophets is to say that the Holy God is compatible with human speech and, more, that the Holiness of God enlivens, directs, liberates, and *preserves* that speech, giving it life abundant. The indelible character of the Spirit's working, sealing and delivering, raising up and consecrating, inspiring and opening the eyes of the blind, transporting from the profane to the sacred, showing forth and exhibiting the Lord's Presence until He comes: these mighty workings of the Spirit are marks of the Divine Life that carry the eternal with them. They are a permanent hallowing. These are not the Mission of the Spirit or of the Son! We should not imagine that the history of Israel is a kind of Spiritual Impanation of the covenant people. No, instead we say that the Processional Life of God, His Perfect Life as the Spiritual Wisdom of God, burns, burnishes, sanctifies, purifies, and preserves the people, teaching, and rite that He inspires, guides, and creates. They are of old and are everlasting.

Now, this "eternalizing" of the covenant is a communicated Perfection of the Triune Life. It is not a created gift or property, though to be sure we borrow these idioms, nor is it an absorption of the created into the Creator, though under this Power, we can still speak of the creaturely reality transformed and illumined by Holiness. It is rather the correlate, in the doctrine of God, to the *election* of the people Israel. This law, this cultus, this people, this Moses, this Jesus, Mary's Son: they are the elect of God, the Spirit's own Lively Claim. The aim here is to distinguish—not separate—the Manifestation of the Living God in Israel from the Divine Workings *ad extra*. The beneficent acts of Creation and Providence, the Upholding of the world and its Blessing: these are the Good Gifts of God toward all finite reality, the expression of the Divine Nature, Its Unique Reality, toward the cosmos, worlds upon worlds. The relation of this One Lord to Israel is something more, something other than all that. The covenant people and its history is neither *contingent* nor happenstance. It does not just happen to be the case that this people stemmed from Abraham and Sarah or that it emerged from the mass of oppressed peoples under the thumb of mighty empires, when perhaps another might have broken free, might have worshipped its god in the wild places. No, Israel is not unique in an ordinary sense—not simply a particular group or nation among the many tribal confederations in the ancient Near East. It does not come to our attention simply as antecedent or propaedeutic to the Christian story or even in the slightly stronger sense of a particular people ingredient in our tradition and dear to our own hearts. It is not a *preference*, this intense focus on Israel! Rather, Israel, its teachings, leaders, and cultus are just what a creature looks like that has the Divine Life as its Intimate. The only proper partner, we should say, to Holy Scripture as correlate of the Holy God is Israel, the Beloved of God.

The language of marriage, never far from prophet or sage or psalm, gives us more than *metaphor* or symbol for the peculiar status of Israel and its history. Rather the singularity of Israel is *metaphysical*. It is the creaturely site of the Lord's Holiness; more: Its outworking. The Life that is the Fiery Glory of God fashions out of Its own Molten Love a partner out of the dust of the earth, stands it up on its feet, blesses and calls it, compacts with it, hallows it. Jesus tells His disciples on the night of His arrest that He, as does His Father, has Life in Himself: the Aseity of God's Processional Life is extended, in *creaturely mode*, to covenant Israel; It *generates* Israel, *ad extra*. This is why Israel is bride but also son, why it is covenant partner but also darling child. Israel has stature before God, certainly. But more so it has an ontological status without parallel: it has permanence, a historical eternity, under the conditions of an elect humanity. For this reason, it is *the* root, *the* source. The church receives many gifts from covenant Israel, but none more than the living enactment of the Divine Processions and Persons, laid down in the sacrifice that will not pass away.

So to properly investigate the Mystery of the Holy Trinity, we turn to Israel's history and cultus. We begin with the Levitical narrative, its recital of the wilderness campaign for the hosts of Israel.

§5.1. Levitical Sacrifice and Sin

The profound lessons of the Suffering Servant cannot stand alone; they rest on the foundation of Israel's covenant worship, on holy sacrifice. At the heart of Israel's life is the cultus; at the heart of Trinity is the *Divine Holiness*. The deep things of God—His Life of

Descent and Outpouring—constitute Holiness, and we catch sight of that Holy Life in Leviticus, Moses's instruction to the priests and people of Israel. Once again, we will read this text in a metaphysical, speculative, and dogmatic fashion. We will look for the Deep Pattern of the inner Life of God here. We will seek instruction on the Holy Life of God, His Fiery Procession, and the cost of such Perfect Love. We begin with a question Christian theology cannot help but ask: Why does Leviticus begin as it does?

Seven long chapters preface the inauguration of the tabernacle cultus, an opening excursus on the types and orders and settings for the sacrificial system of the covenant people. These appear to interrupt the narrative that ended with such solemnity in the final chapter of Exodus: the Lord God was with His people, in cloud and fire and glory, suffusing the tabernacle and illuminating the dark sky with Holy Fire (Exod 40). Modern readers may be forgiven the assumption that Leviticus would begin *there*, at the moment Moses had completed the ritual construction of the tabernacle and tent of meeting. But surprising and interrupting all narrative assumptions, Leviticus opens with a survey of the forms of Israel's sacrifice; the occasions on which they are offered; and the gestures, requirements, and ends that such rituals demand. Only after that catalogue may the narrative resume: Leviticus, chapter 8. In Leviticus, then, we see the first imprint of the relation between statute and narrative that will structure and animate Leviticus as it did of Numbers: blocks of ritual instruction or case law or registry, interspersed with powerful narrative of Moses, Aaron, and the people Israel in their journey through the wilderness. The balance is more austere in Leviticus. Unlike Numbers, Leviticus includes only three narrative sections— but they are telling. As Jacob Milgrom explains to us in his magisterial commentary,[8] these are the inner fulcrum of the whole, the pattern of obedience and rebellion that scars the very limbs of

Israel in its life at the base of Mount Sinai.[9] The narrative sections in Leviticus—chapters 8–10, then, in a salient but brief aside, chapter 16, and then a longer narrative in chapter 24 (in Milgrom's counting these constitute only two narratives)—recount another movement of obedience and rebellion, another echo of Exodus in the proper worship but also in the improper incursion, the idolatry, the blasphemy, brazenly carried out in the very moment of Almighty God's majestic Presence in and above the holy tabernacle. In the mystery of Israel's life before God, its profound election from the very heart of God, the joy of the covenant is mingled with the fever of sin, a rebellion against the Law they worship and obey and endorse. The pattern in Leviticus mirrors that in Exodus and yet more deeply engraves the crisis that is Israel's life—and therefore all human life—before a Holy God. In its formal chapter headings, Leviticus highlights the ready and willing ear for the Lord God but also the toxic elixir at the heart of its national life.

In the statutory sections, the teaching block in Leviticus begins solemnly, "The Lord spoke to Moses, saying." In the narrative, this rubric drops away altogether (chapters 9 and 10) or alters tellingly: "The Lord spoke to Moses after the death of the two sons of Aaron, when they drew near before the Lord and died" (chapter 16). Transitional sections can be found in chapters 8 and 24. There we see a hybrid form, a mixed genre, in which both forms of discourse, the legal and the narrative, are encompassed in a single chapter. Chapter 8, for example, in which the ordination ritual of Aaron and his sons are detailed, begins with the statutory rubric, "The Lord spoke to Moses, saying"; its content, however, is the joyful and ominous narrative that will follow. Chapter 24 extends this pattern: nine full verses about the priestly duties in the sanctuary are introduced with traditional legal formula: "The Lord spoke to Moses." But then, abruptly, in verse 10, the storyteller emerges: "A man whose mother was an Israelite and whose father was an Egyptian came out among the people of Israel." Quickly the short story unfolds, with mortal consequences: "and the Israelite woman's son and a certain Israelite began fighting in the camp." The remainder of this story will rehearse a violation of the sanctity of the Divine Name, a "cursing" or "reviling" that can lead only to death. (The theological exegesis of this chapter will find its proper place in the doctrine of faith, the calling on the Divine Name.) For its part, chapter 8 seems to follow the earlier, familiar pattern of law giving, specifying action and rite for Moses to undertake such that Aaron and his descendants may serve the Lord in His tabernacle. And the chapter closes with the repeated and reassuring refrain of the legal teaching chapters: "all the things that the Lord commanded by Moses were done." But chapter 8 in truth prepares us only for the startling change that plunges us into the narrative of chapter 9: "On the eighth day, Moses summoned Aaron and his sons and the elders of Israel." The rite of ordination is to begin, and it will be inaugurated by Moses, acting as elder and priest (pace Milgrom), preparing and clothing and sanctifying Aaron, his sons, and the people. By the next chapter the transition is complete: "Now Aaron's sons, Nadab and Abihu," a phrase speaking in full narrative voice. The history of Israel, the history of humankind, in its love for and also its tragic ignorance of, and rebellion against God, will now stride onto center stage.

It seems that Holy Scripture intends us to hear the somber movement, the descent, from obedience to rebellion, from Divine Presence in Cloud and Fire to the Consuming Flame of Holy Wrath, all through the formal movement from statute and commandment to concrete act and concrete, individual rejection of the Teaching of the Lord. As Milgrom carefully observes, law and narrative belong together: "law aris[es] synchronically from its

Sitz im Leben (its narrative) against the backdrop of the reality—socioeconomic, political, and religious—of its time. Law also develops diachronically, building on past precedents that form new realia for succeeding age. The law is incomprehensible without its framing narrative, which illustrates both the application and the limit of the law."[10] The notion that Holy Scripture could be *only* story or, perhaps more honestly, *should* be only story is a Christian, perhaps a Protestant, idle tale. Case law and rubric and absolute statute are the concrete structures of covenant life; they testify that life before God is not simply *event*, not contingent happening, but gives rise to, and in turn rests on, normative judgment. The Lord is a Righteous, Holy God; His own ways and works are ordered, good, and just. The Divine Nature, we say, in Trinitarian idiom, is both Life and Law, Procession and Person. A theology that can find no place or taste for law is one that has not reckoned with Structure, Integrity, Justice, as the Perfection of the Divine Life. Trinity is *Structured Infinity, Integral Justice*. As in the Servant Song of Isaiah 53, we see a framing of the intelligible and the concrete, a movement and relation between the general and the particular, the ordinance and statute of Israel, the Divine Purpose and Meaning, and the events of this earthly plane, so elusive and so saturated with the ambiguity and sorrow of the everyday, a movement and structure that in the end can speak to us only of the Eternal Life of God, the General and the Concrete, the Universal and the Particular, the Triune One, leaving His trace on the world He has made. Leviticus speaks to us of the Holy God, in His Transcendence and in His Nearness, and it speaks of this Triune Lord through the rupture, the relation, the movement, the *life*, of the law and the covenant history of the people of God. As in Exodus, as in Numbers, so Leviticus manifests and mediates the Holy One who is its Author and Source. The Holy Bible is the echo of the Holy God.

But we may wonder: How can this be so, in a pattern that includes not just worship and obedience but also sin and rebellion? How can such a pattern *echo* the Holy God? How can it be a resonance or correlate to the One without sin? We face here the heart of *sacrifice*. This act, for all its density and many-sidedness, is a *dealing with sin*, a response and cure to defilement and profanity. We could not read Levitical sacrifice as instruction of Trinity without including the rebellions and defilements and apostasies that surround its founding, for the cultus is inaugurated for just this end: to sanctify and cleanse the people and its temple from sin. Now, this does not make sin ingredient in or necessary to Trinity! The Triune economy and Immanence do not relate in such a fashion, from below to above. But the sin and defilement show us why the Divine Descent is sacrifice—is *costly*—because the Divine Fire is Holy; It hallows. The Holy Trinity is not grounded in texts of simple Divine Presence to creation. No! Trinity is not a doctrine of the Divine Nearness, merely. It is a dogma of Holiness, the Thrice Holy, and as such, in creaturely idiom, it must deal with sin. The Processional Life of God as *ethical*, as Goodness, is glimpsed in this Divine Act of deliverance. The Good Gift, the Divine Self-Offering, burns away the profane: the Eternal Generation of the Son is received in the Spirit, ascending up to the Father, the Origin and Source. This is the Pattern, the Structure, of Triune Holiness.

Once again, we are brought up short by the delicate, the complex, and the deeply mysterious relation between the Triune God and His creature Holy Scripture. It is not direct revelation! The *relatio* between such a God and such a creature is not one of direct information about the Divine Life or, even less, propositions about the Triune dogma. No! "Echo" does not mean "mirror." When we speak of the meaning of a text intermingling with the concrete and arbitrary, we do not intend that the doctrinal meaning can be *identified* with the events of narrative or statute. It is not *opposed* to it, on the other hand. The Divine Mystery is *laid down* in the sinews of the text, quietly and radically suffusing the whole, illuminating the whole with an alien Light, an astonishment and a Herald from afar. That is why there is something in the doctrine of God to learn from the stories of Israel's sin and rejection of the Law—and not simply moral object lessons. The indirect, contrastive, unexpected Manifestation of Divine Reality shimmers in every corner of Holy Scripture, even in the dark ones, graciously there. When we search the Scriptures for the Triune Lord, we examine the structure and pattern and vivid movement of Holy Writ to catch sight of this Living One: He is the Invisible made known in the visible, all the while remaining Invisible, the Hidden *Deitas* and Power. This is why the Bible is not principally *about* God, though, to be sure, it is also concerned with Him. It is not principally a set of Divine teachings, though, of course, it contains them. The Bible is not a series, not first and foremost a register of Divine Happenings in our creaturely midst, though graciously it narrates these. Rather, the *holiness* of the Bible—in the face and in the midst of—its sinful and wayward creatures, the whole army of the lost, is anchored in the Holy God's *Aspects*, the force of His Presence, His Path through the seas. We meet God in Holy Scripture because His Triune Majesty overspreads the whole, in daylight and rejoicing, and in the very dark night, setting down His Structured Life, His Measureless Concreteness in the people and the events and the world He has made. He will surprise us at the Jabbok and, in our struggles, bless us. We do not draw back, then, from searching for Almighty God in not only the commandments and statutes, where He dwells in Royal Dignity and Righteousness, but also in the sad revelers at the foot of the Holy Mountain, the proud rebels of Korah and his supporters— the molten censers of the fallen, holy by rebellion, crushed down to cover Israel's altar, as warning and as grace—the forward sons of Aaron, bringing alien fire, once again, to the sanctum of the tabernacle; in all these, we search for and are permitted to find the Living God.

So, we are right to interpret the *whole* of Leviticus—its obedience and disobedience, its narrative and its statutes, its welcome and unwelcome antiquity—in our search for the proper doctrine of the Holy Trinity. We are right, then, to begin our analysis—though it may seem odd—not with Leviticus, chapter 1, not with the sacrificial forms, but rather with chapter 8, the inauguration of the tabernacle sacrifice. We begin here because it is at this moment that the Lord God manifests His Presence in the sacrificial cultus; here that we see the One who is Maker of heaven and earth manifest His Glory in earthly cloud and fire; here that we encounter the majestic victory of this Holy One over all profanation and defilement; here we see in Triunity in Its Living Freedom over and with the creatures He loves and sets ablaze.

But we hasten to say that we properly begin here not *because* this is narrative rather than Law, not *in virtue* of its "telling a story" rather than giving a commandment—certainly not that! It is an old, a very old and pernicious Christian trait to regard Torah, law, as something transient, something inferior, something wooden and unfitting for the glorious liberty of the children of God. Part of this dangerous confusion about the status and stature of Israel's law is the opposition posed in some Reformation theologies between "Law and Gospel," as if the commandments, statutes, and ordinances of Israel were *as such* a trespass on the great Good News of Divine Pardon and Love for sinners. It is easy to give the name of Luther to this opposition, and in truth, he can speak this way, disturbingly so. But Luther was an exegete in a million; never could he rest easy with a simple opposition between Moses and Christ. Indeed, he knew full well that Christ, too, was a Lawgiver, the great Lawgiver, the Living Law, and Luther recognized that Christian life, too, was obedience and indenture to the neighbor. Luther knew as well that Moses could speak of Divine Pardon, of the Good and Gracious Lord, of the Everlasting Help that is Israel's God of Mercy. But the pattern was there to be built on, and theologians and exegetes did build.

The nineteenth-century struggle by Jewish and Christian exegetes over the legacy of the prophets and the Pharisees echoed this old opposition: prophecy must undermine law, Christians said, oppose it; covenant must ground and outlast commandment; grace must triumph over works. And Jews denied all that. It must be wondered whether the marked disinterest by Christians in Leviticus, and in the legal stretches of the Pentateuch, is not a modern chapter in this ancient story—the legend (or is it a fear?) that the Christian faith has broken free from law. But that cannot be! If Holy Scripture is the unique creature of God, the whole of it subject to the Distant and Ever Near Blaze of God, commandment must carry, too, its trace of the Living God. The aim is not to determine which statute of ancient Israel may be observed, which modified or excised—the Torah is not to be codified and ranked in this way—but rather to hear the *Vox Dei* in the command, to trace the Structure of the Divine Fire in its ligaments. That we must do; that the whole church must do. As Christians we may not distinguish Mystery and commandment quite in the way as did Leo Baeck, but these elements must surely undergird all Christian exegesis.[11] The Mystery, we would say, is *in* the commandment. So, a theological reading of Leviticus must contend with statute, but it may begin as well with narrative. Both echo the Sovereign Life of Almighty God. So, we begin with the cultus.

The whole people Israel gather before the tent of meeting for the consecration of the altar and the priests, Aaron, and his sons.

Moses, the friend of God, will be the earthly president of this rite; as commanded, he will slaughter and reduce to smoke the animals designated for this rite, administer blood to the altar and to limbs of the priests, wash and anoint and clothe them, and solemnly burn the ox—the bull that is a "wild and unruly thing"—its skin and flesh and bones, its defilement, outside the camp. He will instruct Aaron and his sons about the consecration and ordination: for seven days they are to remain within the sacred precincts, within the doors of the tent of meeting, not entering into the camp or the wilderness but feasting on the broiled meat and wheat cakes of the offerings, while the Lord God ordains them the whole week long. Aaron and his sons have been set apart for the holy work of sacrifice, and their consecration is something like a burnishing of a setting for gems, like a crown on their heads, and a mantle on their whole lives. This entire Mosaic rite of inauguration takes place before the covenant people, not in secret nor in hidden mystagogery but in plain view: a washing and anointing with blood, a sealing and a clothing all done before the eyes of Israel. It lasts a full week, from Sabbath to Sabbath, and we are invited to see this first consecration as a new creation, the beginning of the work of purification and hallowing, that is an inauguration of a whole, blessed cosmos, an exchange, mediated through Moses, between heaven and earth. The wholeness of the people; of the animals and bread; of the burning, within and without the camp; and of the week itself, tell us that this ordination rite is the creation, the good ordering, of Israel's world within the wilderness they now inhabit.

The sacrificial cult now begins. This is the Eighth Day, the Octave. It is at once the unfurling of the new week and the consummation of the old, the extension of the ordering of priests into the work of sacrificial communion with the Holy God. It is the first day after the Sabbath Rest, the Day of Resurrection. It, too, is the Day of Creation. In the eschatological day we enter into the Day that is Eternity, the Day in which Wisdom is begotten, the First Born. As the axis of death and life turns on this pivot from Sabbath burial to Eighth Day rising, so this setting forth and setting apart of Israel's new creation turns from consecration to sacrifice, from Moses's work of ordination to Aaron's work of divine exchange. We are ready for Israel's world to now unfold. On this Octave, Moses tells the new priests, the Lord will appear to you. He will be seen, manifest in this work that is set before you and all Israel. For Aaron and his sons, sacrifices of atonement, the sin offering, the wave offering, and a sacrifice of ordination had been carried out by Moses on their behalf. They had laid their hands on the heads of these creatures, and the animals were marked as theirs, their sin, their consecration. But now, on the Eighth Day, the full register of sacrificial rites will be carried out on behalf of the covenant people. The *olah*, the whole burnt offering, the sin and grain offering, the peace offering, the sacrifice of well-being, will be offered up on behalf of the people this day, and then the Lord Himself will appear. The ordering seems to be complete: all the rites specified in the opening chapters of Leviticus, and in Moses's instructions, appear to be followed, Aaron faithfully slaughtering and lifting up the animals, reducing to smoke and ash and bathing with blood everything as Moses had commanded. And his sons brought forward the blood. Carefully the narrator informs us that Aaron's sons were also consecrated, also fed and set apart during the sacrificial creation days, also shrouded by the blood they carried and had been their healing and atonement. For their life, too, was in the blood. Even as the sop of bread is given to all the twelve, to Judas, too—and especially to him—before he goes out into the night, so Aaron's sons are fully joined to this sacred action, fully disciples, fully called and anointed and set apart. Before Israel was all this done, done on their behalf and in their place. And in the end, after all the terrible work of killing and cutting and burning, those anointed hands are raised in blessing: Aaron gives the first priestly blessing over the people Israel. Perhaps the Aaronic blessing in Numbers 6 is a remembered echo of this great day, when altogether everything was blessed and found very good. Moses joins Aaron, emerging from the tent of meeting, giving again a blessing, from the original pair, the *adamah*, of Israel's liberation and consecration. Then, the *Kabod*, the Glory of the Lord manifested itself to all the people. The narrator solemnly intones: "Fire came out from the Lord and consumed the burnt offering and the fat on the altar; and when all the people saw it, they shouted and fell on their faces" (Lev 9:24). The Lord God Himself, His own Glory, has lit the altar fire with His own Combustible Life, the Explosion who is God.

The echo with Exodus is unmistakable here. The resonance has been plain throughout the narrative section: Moses is here carrying out the commandments and ordinances for consecration and sacrifice already stipulated in Exodus. But the notes sound more clearly here; they intensify. We are brought back first to the priestly Decalogue, written by the Finger of God. In that Divine Manifestation, the Lord God is Smoke and Cloud and Fire, His House the Mountain of Sinai, shrouded in thunder. This Fiery Lord first gathers to Himself Moses alone, who braves trumpet and thunder and makes out of these terrors a voice with which to speak to the Most High God. The people Israel are gathered below and observe the cordon stretched out around the Holy Mountain to keep them from Danger, to separate the Holy One from the creaturely, the common and the profane. Then the Lord commands the Adamic couple, Moses and Aaron, to ascend into the Holy Realm. But the people rightly fear the annihilating Fire of this Holy God and beg Moses alone to speak for them: "You speak to us, and we will listen; but do not let God speak to us, or we will die" (Exod 20:19). The Holy Mountain erupts and the earth trembles with the Nearness of the Commanding God. The people Israel are filled with the fear of the Lord, and they beg Moses to enter the cloud for them, and for their sake, for no one mortal looks on the Lord and lives.

Now Moses ascends, and as Gregory of Nyssa will explore with great mystical delicacy in the *Life of Moses*, he enters the Darkness, alone to encounter God. The first tablets of the Law are pronounced, and Moses delivers them to the people. They listen and, in that hour, obey: "All the words that the Lord has spoken we will obey," they say. The first sacrifice of the covenant will now be offered, Moses presiding over the building of the altar, the twelve tribes inscribed into this altar as its pillars, and over the bulls and oxen reduced to smoke and ash. Over the altar and, in unmistakable foreshadowing of that sacrifice outside the city walls, over the whole people, blood is poured: "Behold the blood of the covenant, which the Lord hath made with you concerning all these words," Moses intones.

Then there are further processions up Mount Sinai. In striking foreshadowing, the narrator tells us that Moses is now instructed to come up into the mountain with Aaron and his eldest sons, named Nadab and Abihu, with all the elders of the people, seventy of them. As the people gather at the foot of Sinai, Moses and the elders journey up into the cloud to eat and drink before the Lord; and in stunning vividness, they are said to "see the Lord." In early echoes of Ezekiel and the vision to St. John the Divine, we are told that in this Divine Presence there lay "under His feet as it were a pavement of sapphire stone, like the very heaven for clearness." Astonishingly in this Feast of the Last Days the elders of Israel are not slain but rather fed: "God did not lay His hand upon the chief men of the people of Israel; also *they beheld God*, and they ate and drank"

(Exod 24:11). Here we see once again the remarkable boldness of Holy Scripture about the Transcendence, the Nearness and Mystery of the Holy God: He cannot be imaged, cannot be seen, and cannot be borne by frail flesh, yet He, this very One, will bear them on eagles' wings, will manifest Himself to Moses, yes, but to Aaron and his sons, and the seventy elders, too, and will provide for them food enough, a Divine Feast and sacrifice of well-being. It is not, as proud Christians say, that only in our Gospels does the Lord God draw near with astonishing boldness. Everywhere in Israel's Scriptures, the Unrepentant Concreteness of God is expressed and comingled with the Brilliant Distance and Abstractness of the God who is Beyond. He slays and makes alive; He feeds from His own hand. To this first Eucharist the prophet, the priest, and the elders are called. But that is not the final visitation up Mount Sinai. Again, Moses is called to ascend. But this time, he is to bring Joshua, his assistant, or, in the greater felicity of the old translations, his minister. In taut lines, the narrator brings us to the threshold of Israel's apostasy: "To the elders Moses said, 'Wait here for us, until we come to you again; for Aaron and Hur are with you; whoever has a dispute may go to them.'" Forty days and nights will pass away as Moses entered deep into the Cloud of the Glory of God and deeper still into the Devouring Fire who is God, and the people Israel saw him disappear into that Glory.

"As for this Moses," the people now say, "the one who brought us up out of the land of Egypt, we do not know what has become of him." Thus begins the most famous rebellion of the liberated people, the golden calf forged out of the earrings of the people, melted down and molded by Aaron, the great high priest, as Scripture plainly tells us. "These are your gods, O Israel," the people famously intone over the graven image, and the sacrifices, the feasting, and the reveling began. In the vivid words of the old translation: "The people sat down to eat and to drink, and rose up to play." It is such a masterful narrative: the sharp exchange between the Liberator God and the liberating Moses over the people and their exodus from Egypt; the stunning intercession of the prophet for his people before the wrath of God; the ironic battle song of Joshua as the noise of revelry meets their ears; and then, the climax. After the careful description of Aaron's hand in all this menace, the text tells us that this great leader responds to Moses's angry questions, "So I said to them, 'Whoever has gold, take it off; so they gave it to me, and I threw it into the fire, and out came this calf!'" The passivity, the weak cunning, and the denial of the answer is matchless—never has Holy Scripture been more realistic in its portrayal of the great. But it would be easy to be captivated by this remarkable story in such a way that we lose sight of the larger structure in which it belongs.

The story of the golden calf belongs to the larger dynamic between the Torah instruction and narrative depiction of the exodus people. Once again, we see a narrative flow interrupted by sturdy blocks of legal prescripts—or, should we better say, the teaching is ruptured by the historical events, dislodging and breaking apart those laws? For the end of chapter 24 in Exodus is the clear prelude to Exodus 32, yet six long chapters of instruction about the sacred precincts, about the sanctuary and its fittings, about the clothing and hallowing of Aaron and his sons as priests, and the workers raised up to make the whole, and most tellingly, about the Sabbath rest as a sign of the Lord's sanctifying of the people—all this is laid down between the calling of Moses up into the Lord's Cloud and His sending him down in wrath to the camp once again. The rhythm between the Torah and the history, between, we may say, the everlasting and the temporal, or the general and the particular, the apodictic and the contingent, is the larger structure of the people Israel within the gracious Processional Life of God. The teaching blocks do not pertain to just any legal code here; rather, they set forth the Eternal Ordering of the sacrificial life of the people, urging it forward to the Sabbath rest, to the Eternal Day in which all is hallowed. This is the Realm, the Eternal Structure in which the covenant people is to come to its fullness, and it is spoken to Moses during those forty days and nights and written down with the Finger of God. Up above it is thus; but here below, the very people and Aaron, the holy priest, Moses's own second and voice, invert and subvert the Torah of Heavenly Counsel. Just this structure repeats in Leviticus—indeed forms the whole. The commandments and statutes and ordinances replicate and, in telling ways, alter that given in Exodus, and elaborate on it, with case law and illustration and careful application. The narrative material, so concentrated in Leviticus, enacts and then rebels against that very Teaching. In that structure we can now see more clearly the strange rebellion of the sons of Aaron, Nadab and Abihu.

These are the sons who entered into the Cloud, ascended the Holy Mountain, and ate and drank the food of angels. These are the sons who were washed and clothed and anointed by Moses, the sons who carried the blood of their own hallowing and that of their people. These are the sons who will fill their own censers—surely the possessive is significant here—and approach the Lord with alien fire, neither taught nor commanded by the Holy God. Everywhere, the Scriptures echo this struggle of fathers and sons, the betrayal and rebellion of father or son—of Abraham or Ishmael or Isaac; of Jacob and Samson (such a son and a father!)—and the obedience, at great cost, of the father to his prodigal, of David to his traitorous, beloved sons, or of the Only Son to the Father, who sent, and who welcomes home alive this Son who descended into the hellish grave that swallowed him up, the Egypt out of which the Father called His Son. In this Levitical rebellion, the Septuagint captures the fearful strangeness of the act by calling on the word for foreigner or alien to express the live coals brought by these sons to the sanctuary: alien fire. Once again, the Fire who is the Holy One explodes from the Divine Presence and consumes the creature, a whole burnt offering of the Divine Wrath. Aaron is speechless with the silence that expresses deepest horror and destruction, the utter stillness of grief. Like the revelers at the foot of Mount Sinai, these sons of Aaron will be killed by the Lord's hand, not plague this time but by His very own Glory. All Israel will mourn for the Divine Burning, but Aaron and his living sons must remain still and whole and undefiled within the doors of the tent of meeting, even grief being denied them. Their statutory work must continue, distinguishing the sacred from the profane, the clean and the defiled: that setting apart is their share in Divine Holiness.

But we are not through with the rebellion after the sanctification and law. For Aaron's younger sons—the ones spared the Consuming Flame and called to fresh duties before the Lord—take upon themselves to burn (with alien fire?) the sin offering for the people and apparently to eat it without ceremony. Like many human disputes, the details of this transgression seem confused and elusive. It seems the blood was not poured out in the sanctuary, that the sins of the people had not been atoned, and that the ritual eating within the precincts had somehow not been carried out properly or fully. But in another striking parallel with Exodus, this transgression, perhaps worse than the first, does not lead to annihilation and death but rather to a startling and odd pardon. Moses confronts Aaron, and Aaron's familiar excuses return. How could I eat on such a day? Didn't they do other things properly and by commandment? How could I bear such things as I have endured this day? And as he will with Miriam and Aaron later in the wilderness, so now Moses listens, he pardons, he intercedes. Again, we see this larger structure: the commandment, the rebellion, the Divine Wrath mingled with the astonishing Pardon and Mercy. How mysterious and deeply enigmatic the Judgment and Pardon of this Holy God! The small sins of Saul; the great rebellions of David: a kingship lost, a kingship righted, and extended over every generation. The Holiness of God, consecrating and pouring down on Moses, the most humble and hidden prophet, brings him, too, within this structure of the Living God, to anger and explosion, to grace and patience. The sins of Israel, the sins of humankind, are contained within this larger structure, this larger Holiness. The sacrificial cultus speaks of the Mysterious Largeness, the So Much More of the Holy One, the Triune Lord.

Into this Largeness are set the second narrative section of Leviticus, chapter 16, the proclamation and ordering of the Day of Atonement. Here the legal sections and the narrative are strongly compressed: only the first verse of this chapter may be considered plain narrative. It begins: "The Lord spoke to Moses after the death of the two sons of Aaron, when they drew near before the Lord and died." Perhaps we are to hear a more extensive narrative here, suppressed behind these clipped phrases. (Perhaps we should read Leviticus, chapter 24, in the same manner: a compressed narrative leading to law, the *lex talionis*.) Jacob Milgrom detects an original rite of purification for the tabernacle and sanctuary, defiled by rebellion and by the scorched corpses of Aaron's sons. Perhaps we are to see the remains, the scars of this primal uncleanness, and the terror that the Holy God would depart His throne room. Perhaps the very ritualizing of the event—a statute now forever, throughout your generations—is to speak a narrative whisper: this once was the only answer to a calamity at the very birth of the Holy. Yet even here, in this clear reference back to the alien fire of Nadab and Abihu, the legal formula hovers over the whole—"The Lord spoke to Moses, saying." We might reduce the narrative further, then, to the clauses that follow the priestly formula. And to ensure that the reader knows a block of cultic regulation is to follow, the formula is repeated in pure form: "The Lord said to Moses." The mysterious intertwining of sacrifice and exile will be laid out, regulated and given an everlasting stature: "This shall be a statute to you forever: In the seventh month, on the tenth day of the month, you shall deny yourselves, and shall do no work, neither the citizen for the alien who resides among you. For on this day atonement shall be made for you, to cleanse you; from your sins you shall be clean before the Lord. It is a sabbath of complete rest to you, and you shall deny yourselves; it is a statute forever" (Lev 16:29–31).

The rituals of atonement are twofold: a full exercise of the sacrificial cultus—burnt offerings, sin offerings, the linen vestments, the protective incense, the power of the blood, and the mysterious rite of the scapegoat, the atonement animal, chosen by lot and driven out into the wilderness, the territory perhaps of Azazel, with the sins pressed down on its head, to die in that barren and haunted place (pace Douglas) while its kin, the second atoning animal, is slaughtered on the altar of Israel. These rites, Leviticus tells us, make atonement for the sin of the high priest and his household, for the altar, for the sanctuary, for the tent of meeting, and for the whole assembly of Israel: the unclean shall be made clean on that day before the Lord. Against all rebellion, against all transgression, known and unknown, against everything that is wayward and disordered, thoughtless and cruel, sacrifice and atonement will be made. The path for the Holy God down into His resting place, His sanctuary, is now cleansed and hallowed. You shall be holy, for I, the Lord, am Holy.

Now it is plain that the rites of atonement extend far beyond the dogma of Trinity into the gracious realm of the Mission of the

Son, into His great atoning work. Until that doctrine, then, the full exposition of the Yom Kippur must be deferred; the richness of this Levitical account can only be given its full measure then. But even here we must say that this compressed narrative and its ritual teaching section must disclose to us, in its rich and hidden fashion, the Holiness of God who is Trinity. For in this final narrative moment of Leviticus we see once again the startling interplay of sanctity and sin, of the most holy and the rebellious, of the strictly ordered and the lavish pardon and exceptional grace—all of these in the Transcendence and Nearness of the Living God. Once again, the echoes of Exodus are manifest here, though to be sure, indirect and glancing. The intersection of the structure of Exodus and the structure of Leviticus, the narrative against the law, the narrative against another narrative, discloses the Surpassing Mystery who is Trinity. This is the large-scale Pattern of Holy Writ. Here we see a chiastic pattern that ties Leviticus ever more firmly to Exodus. For in the heart of the Levitical code is the narrative of the Octave, the ritual birth of the holy; and in the heart of Exodus, the movement by Moses up into the Luminous Darkness of the High God, the birth of the holy in the Ten Words. And conjoint with that pattern, the rebellions: the eating and drinking, not this time at the eschatological banquet on Sinai but in the great idolatrous feast of the golden calf, the bull of Israel's neighbor gods, the mighty image that will be made small, a mere beast of burden, bearing up the Lord's Great Sea in the temple of Solomon, and in Leviticus, that of the alien fire, and the refusal to eat the goat, sacrificed as a sin offering, or eat it properly—a feast denied. In just this way, we may now see this narrative, the cleansing of the tent of meeting and of the people Israel by sacrifice and by exile, as the final resonance with the great book of exile, Exodus. For this goat, driven out with sin on its head, set free to wander into the haunted desert: Do we not hear an echo of this exile in the liberation of Egypt's slaves, driven out, led out into the wilderness by Cloud and by Fire, purified to serve the God of Israel in the wasteland across the Red Sea? Is there not a journey here, a movement that is the great movement of Scripture, from defilement to atonement, from bondage to freedom, from sin to release and redemption? There can be no exact parallels here, of course. One is a sin offering, the other a liberation. But are not both a deliverance and a movement out into the wilderness? (Perhaps Douglas's reading of the scapegoat, not destined to die but rather set free into the wild as is the second bird of the purification rite, comes into its own here.)[12] Exodus and Leviticus belong together here, stitched on top and within one another, matching but also reworking everything received from the other. The heart of Exodus is the heart of Leviticus, and they join Word and sacrifice as they enter the Presence of the Holy. Exodus and Leviticus echo one another; they are paired. Together they bear down on one central point: the history of covenant and law belong together; sacrifice is the glowing pith of the people of God. Our task here is to think Trinity, to think the Generative and Holy Life of the One God, as it is exemplified, manifested, and taught under the act and idiom of sacrifice.

§5.2. Sacrifice as Triune Processions

Why is sacrifice the centerpiece of the Levitical law, indeed the heart of Israel's living worship of God? And why is it effective? We dare to say that these are the questions of Trinity, the scriptural expression of the quest for Reality Itself, the Ocean of Holiness. It is the Christian search for a proper and reverent and full exposition of the One who hallows on His altar, the One who is Lord, beyond all altars and all worlds.

Let me begin with the moving and frank depiction of the domestic world of the cultus, if we may put it so, by Jacob Milgrom in his shorter commentary for the *Continental Commentary Series*.[13] With disarming frankness, Milgrom describes the tent of meeting and the temple as household furnishings for the Lord God. In that place He has a resting chamber, a bedroom. In it is a table, an altar-table, we might say; there are loaves of bread nearby; a lamp to illumine the interior; water for washing; and a large exterior courtyard, segmented and shielded from any common or defiled use. Into this well-defined house food is brought, grain and meat, all reduced to roasted ash and an incensed smoke that, in rising upward, makes a pleasing aroma and savor to the Lord. Now Milgrom certainly does not end there! He demonstrates with great verve the transcendence of this homeyness by the Mosaic teaching about cultus and sacrifice. And he does not leave all that elevation and purification to the prophets or even to the later Holiness School. No, within Leviticus itself the priestly literature at once acknowledges and surpasses the plastic, vivid, and altogether earthy depiction of a sanctuary as a divine habitation. But Milgrom does not feel the need to deny this plain reading of an ancient temple, either. He shows little anxiety about the straightforward earthiness and materiality of these ancient rites, nor about the unmistakable domesticity of all the furnishings, the preparations, and the rites themselves.

In this way, Milgrom allows, ancient Israel took its place among the sacred peoples of the ancient Near East, each with their temple house and table altar, their guarded courtyards and domestic servants, their food offerings, slaughtered and roasted, gathered and elevated, eaten in solitude or in public with great pomp, heavily perfumed, smoky, and burnt. Throughout the Fertile Crescent, temples and tents of these kinds appeared and were tended; indeed, it seems a near universal that peoples and clans built houses for their gods and fed them there. Milgrom wants us to see that Israel belongs to that world, too. It will refine and reject and transcend its neighbors: it is the Precious Possession of the True and Living God, and its law and cultus will be hallowed, purified, and corrected by that election. But Divine election refines and purifies a practice that is the common possession of the peoples of the earth, of all gentile nations. For Israel, Divine election is not a *denial* of its membership in the league of nations, not a removal from all classes of comparison or common human practice. No, from the start, Israel's formation as God's own delight is at once distinctive—unique—*and* representative: Israel, too, is a universal religion and gathers together, in a higher union, the drives and longings of the human race. Israel's sacrificial cultus is the distillation and sanctifying of the religious impulse that is humankind's. For God has a House on this earth: there we may bring offerings and come within His courts.

In the first place, then, we can say with Milgrom that sacrifice simply is *offering*; it brings and relinquishes a creaturely life to the Divine. It is a meal, prepared by earthlings and savored by the gods. This root notion of offering will ground the doctrine of Trinity when we consider more closely the Mysterious Self-Giving of the Holy God. But here, in the foreground of that doctrine, we touch on the suspicion that "offering" may lead us into unpleasant neighborhoods. For example, the very idea that sacrifice is *propitiation*, an appeasing or entreaty of the Divine, can be traced back to the primal notion of a lavish meal, done to the death, we might say. (It is true, to be sure, that *propitiation* and *expiation* are kindred words, with common ancestors in etymologies and semantic fields, yet in dogmatic idiom, they are worlds apart.) Readers of Homer will know this universal sense of a sacrificial meal to placate the gods. The Iliad is washed over by the blood of pious sacrifices, elaborate and hasty, to prepare for battle, to give thanks for victory, to fulfill vows, perhaps uttered in the last struggle against horseman or spear, to honor the warriors of the past, to praise the gods and goddesses who make the plains of Ilium their affair. The piety of Agamemnon or Hector, or in later idiom, Aeneas, can be vouchsafed by their ready willingness to slaughter animals, to roast them in roaring bonfires, to pour out libations from fine wines, and to practice the ways of the ancients, to honor the rites of their clan. But always menace hangs over these feasts. It does not take the later tragedies of Aeschylus to tell us that for the ancients the divine forces are persecutory, hovering over the guilt and inexplicable sufferings of this age, pliable to entreaty and vow, yet vengeful, jealous, immeasurable, and unpredictable. To them is handed over the enigmas of this life, the human tragedies and icy cruelties, the ignorance and swirling passions that upend so many, the raw misery that the ancients learned to call fate. The sacrificial meal was an entreaty to such wild powers, a shield against their menace. That the gods were from everlasting made them the object of human envy but also of dread. For the resentments, the rivalries, the betrayals and alliances, and the memory of them were perpetual, ready in any generation to be visited on the impious, the unprotected. Sacrifice was knit deep into the fury and suffering of Homeric life.

And not just Homeric life—the modern Christian objections to sacrifice, most especially the sacrifice of Christ, seem to turn on this notion of the offering as appeasement and shield. The rebuke of what is taken to be an Anselmian account of the atonement—a strong misreading, I would say—rests on the proper horror Christians should take toward a god who would demand innocent blood as an appeasing meal, a propitiation of a Moloch. The early modern suspicion that sacrifice was only magic, dressed up in ritual, relies, too, on an idea that religious meals are means to satisfy a voracious, placable, and labile deity. The wiliness but also cravenness of a cultic religion that seeks to ward off Divine Wrath and Judgment through the manipulation of food and drink: this was deeply offensive to the ethical fine feelings of the early Enlightenment. A theology such as mine that seeks to place sacrifice in the center of Trinitarian worship and doctrine cannot overlook the primal connection made here, and in the many ancient societies of this earth, between a meal offered and a god appeased.

It seems, indeed, a deep human drive, this desire to please and protect through food. Sacrifice as a table offering reaches down into the very rich matrix of the human hearth, the primal melding of food and life, danger and reconciliation. The smallest household, the lactating mother and the hungry child, knows in its bones, in flesh and blood, the exchange of food and intimacy that is the human meal. These are the first gods, Freud reminds us, and we learn at the breast the longing to feed as sign and demonstration of divine good favor toward us. To feed others becomes the initial expression of a child's autonomy and resourcefulness: the first picnic lunch with stuffed animals arrayed around tiny tables; the meal prepared for cats or dogs or wild birds; the lunch exchange with schoolmates; the cooking lesson, in imagination or in the kitchen, fashioning a favorite dish for a beloved. These are the loving embrace of meals from infancy forward. But as primal matrix they, too, know sacrifice as menace and threat. To withhold, deny, or defile food is to strike at the very citadel of security in the world. Tiny children—the most holy gifts of the Good God— are abused, by their first gods and by the callous societies in which these holy gifts must live, by the scarcity, the meanness, and the foul indifference of the meals offered them by the ones who should protect and nurture them. It takes no social analysis to know that the common meal has become for developed nations the contested center of young adult lives, male and female, but mostly female. To see food as menace; to deprive oneself of nurture; to starve oneself, in defiance, perhaps, in primal suffering or fear; to eat in guilt or shame or anxiety: these are terrible afflictions, pressed down deep into the very idea of meal, offering, and sacrifice. Few elements of ordinary Western life are subjected to more panic, scrupulosity, and speculation, scientific or rule-of-thumb, than the table foods of everyday life. Certain foods are treated as little more than poisons, a risk to bodily health or mental function or psychic state; others become the dei ex machina of stamina, strength, longevity, brilliance. The visceral incorporation of a worldly element, a good creature of God, as means to sustain life has become overladen with the guilt, fear, and shame that receives the good as source of harm or, perhaps more deceptively still, as guarantee of a purified and perfect life. The obsession of a richly fed world about body weight, the nearly inexhaustible dream to control and improve and reduce it, the profound shame adults undergo when size and weight and body mass are not acceptable to their culture or their employment: these, too, are worldly instances of the meal as menace and the austere meal as penance and appeasement.

And as adults we, too, know the use of food as propitiation or as threat. Not just Jacob sends the herds and flocks ahead of him to placate a fearsome brother. The ritual meals at holidays, the special treat to soothe an injured pride, a rich dinner made as compensation or apology or concession, the small entreaty that is the house gift, after a visit that could not go well: these are the sacrificial meals of humankind that link food and appeasement firmly together. Food and longings are kin; they feed one another, in intimacy and peace, but also in cruelty and deprivation. The common vocabulary of food as ritual—varied in the world's cultures but present in some way in everyone we know—demonstrates the marriage between sociality and meal, intimacy and nurture. But it can be a troubled marriage indeed. That is sacrifice as propitiation.

It seems that Israel, too, knows sacrifice as danger and appeasement. The Annihilating Fire that comes out from the Lord after Aaron's sons bring illicit fire into the sanctuary, the cloud of incense that must be raised to protect the high priest from the Divine Presence, the repeated refrain within legal sections of the Pentateuch, that all must be done as the Lord commanded through Moses, the insistence that some animals and birds are unclean and that offering these as Divine Meal would profane and defile the sacrifice: all these appear to underscore the sacrificial offering as fearful exchange with an Unrelenting Power, an Invisible Danger. So, too, the phrase found amply within Exodus and in vestigial form within Leviticus, that the smoky and charred sacrifice was a pleasing odor and sweet savor to the Lord, appears to teach that the cultic meal offering placated a Deity who might, this day or another—who can tell?—send forth Fiery Wrath upon the earth. The full display of what analysts, following Freud, would call the ritual compulsions of neurotic fear seem to be unfurled in the sacrificial codes. Layers of protection—special and distinct clothing; physical distance or separation; kinship requirements; habitual washing; precise actions over the food, precisely selected and prepared; a wreath of incense— all seem designed to make manageable the utterly unpredictable and savage Holiness of the Lord God of Israel. As with any compulsion, these acts must be done exactly and repeatedly, yet in every act, we are brought closer and closer still to danger. This might be termed the ambivalence of sacrificial acts: the holiness that defiles. It seems that Israel's sacrificial cultus preserves primal elements of the near universal menace of food as intimate offering, placing it in the center of life with the Covenant God, and bathing the whole earth in the blood of dying animals. Can such acts teach the Mystery of the Holy Trinity? We cannot travel far in the doctrine of sacrifice without answering this disturbing question.

To begin an answer to this pungent question, we might start with the furthest reach of the practice of sacrifice: we could object to the very notion of sacrifice, whether propitiation or expiation or gift— a rejection of the idea altogether. Feminists have long objected to the seat of privilege given to the concept of sacrifice, as it seems perfectly designed to keep an oppressed group subservient, all under the ceremonial justification of self-oblation, perhaps to the very end. As Sarah Coakley, Caroline Bynum, and Janet Soskice have detailed with delicacy and power,[14] *sacrifice, dependence,* and *pardon* can become freighted terms for the powerless: for the dominant to sacrifice opens up a world that runs counter to their existence as elites—a religious form of freedom and gender transgression; for the underclass to sacrifice is to baptize the conditions of everyday life, to enshrine long hours, penury, and exploitation with a thin veneer of piety. Delores Williams galvanized a generation of womanist theologians with her searing indictment of sacrifice, a condition she termed "surrogacy." Not the Levitical or Holiness Codes but rather the Genesis narratives are her central texts. Hagar, Abraham's intimate, exemplifies the woman who must fight for survival— against other women, against her own partner, against the terrors of the wilderness, against exile, thirst, and despair. For the oppressed— for oppressed Black women, especially—the very notion and piety of sacrifice, Williams argues, can only deepen the inner emigration that is sacral life within the Christian church. Williams argues that the biblical figure of Hagar expresses, in compressed form, the constricted life Black women are forced to bear. They are assigned the role of substitute: the "surrogate." They must stand in for the white wife of the white husband, who will find his lusts satiated in a surrogate at once more exotic, as he imagines it, and more available.

The Black woman must serve as surrogate for the households of the oppressors, feeding and cleaning and nurturing and understanding: a mother for children not her own, while her own must scramble for their daily life. As surrogate the Black woman becomes the Mammy, the substitute figure of strength, warmth, shrewd insight and resilience, the one who will withstand and rise above, all for the ashen white culture, immiserated by its own cruel power. In Williams's words:

> Surrogacy has been a negative force in African-American women's lives. It has been used by both men and women of the ruling class, as well as by some black men, to keep black women in the service of other people's needs and goals. By appropriating the biblical Hagar stories, African-American people have kept the issue of surrogacy alive in the community's memory. Thus generations of African Americans can understand the struggle black women wage against the devaluation of their womanhood that social-role surrogacy supports.[15]

Of course, Williams is quick to note, rightly, that Black women are indeed strong, shrewd, and resilient: they *resist*. Williams makes no peace with idols of victimhood or passivity; she rejects with a kind of relish the shadow of noble suffering that lies across much of the praise of the Black Mammy. But surrogacy remains an oppression, a category and material power that is wielded by the powerful. In an extended meditation, Williams shows the way such surrogacy lives on in the central doctrines of the faith, most especially in doctrines of the atonement and the sacrifice they seem to endorse. Williams writes:

> One of the results of focusing upon African-American women's historic experience with surrogacy is that it raises serious questions about the way many Christians, including black women, have been taught to image redemption.... In this sense Jesus represents the ultimate surrogate figure; he stands in the place of someone else: sinful

humankind. Surrogacy, attached to this divine personage, thus takes on an aura of the sacred. . . . A major theological problem here is the place of the cross in any theology significantly informed by African-American women's experience with surrogacy. Even if one buys into the notion of the cross as the meeting place of the will of God to give up the Son (coerced surrogacy?) and the will of the Son to give up himself (voluntary surrogacy?) so that "the spirit of abandonment and self-giving love" proceeds from the cross "to raise up abandoned men" [Williams cites Jürgen Moltmann, here, *The Crucified God*], African-American women are still left with the question: Can there be salvific power for black women in Christian images of oppression (for example, Jesus on the cross) meant to teach something about redemption?[16]

Williams's trenchant criticisms of substitutionary atonement—a doctrine this theology endorses—will need to be taken up and addressed at the proper time. But here we must consider whether the very notion of sacrifice does not extend and repeat the surrogacy that has etched itself sharply into Black women's lives. Is not a sacrifice—the slaughtered animal, the harvested grain, the lifeless bird—not a surrogate of the purest and most terrible kind? The sacrificial animal dies; and I live, forgiven or cleansed or released. More poignant still, does not sacrifice provide food for human feasting, a surrogate for the meal for the Deity, while I, the creature, feed on its flesh? Sacrifice as practiced by the nations of this earth, and by ancient Israel, too, appears to reenact and reinforce that pattern of subjugation, of empty flattery, and of exploitation that constitutes surrogacy, the particular oppression of African American women.

Feminists might raise other objections as well. For women abused by violent men, sacrifice as Christian virtue seems only to teach an embrace of punishment and fear, a self-immolation to the anger and fear and aggression of the men who would claim to love and honor them. Of course, such a tragedy cannot be reduced to a platform: there is no direct and simple solution to the profound calls to love and cherish and honor, and also, to forgive, to bend low, to serve and to serve again. Iris Murdoch captures the tangled web of mercy and compassion, of terror and harm and injury, in the deeply troubled marriage of Mary Hartley Finch and Ben in *The Sea, The Sea*. The interested outsider, Charles Arrowby, of course knows the right path here: there is no enigmatic moral struggle for him! He considers himself in truth the proper insider, the one who loves and who knows. He imagines himself the selfless rescuer of the victimized Hartley, offering her at long last the perfect love only hinted at in their youthful romance. But things are not so plain to the insider, Hartley, the loving and traumatized wife. From her place in the marriage, from deep within the structure of violence, love, and abuse, Hartley's fidelity and loyalty and pardon take only richer, darker hues; we outsiders must witness this struggle with great reserve but with great compassion and respect, too. Sacrifice cannot be an easy task or concept for Christians. Feminists within the church need a ready ear for the moral life of women and men who have left all behind and travel into the wilderness where signposts have fallen away, and all appears to the pilgrim's eyes fearsome, strange.

A Christian theology that honors sacrifice, as does this one, must reckon closely with the dangerous alliance of violence and self-offering, of ritual killing and feasting. Exodus and Leviticus are all too plain in their recognition that this territory must be crossed, at times in danger and unaided, if sacrifice is to be treated as a biblical concept. The complex pattern we have traced between Divine Wrath and Divine Pardon, between obedience and punishment, between life cherished and received and set free, a life slaughtered and reduced to ash: these are the dark ribbons that run through the whole of the Holiness School. Sacrifice is awe-filled, terrible. It is life and it is death; it is blood and purity and fire; it is Holy. Sacrifice is not simple or clean. It was most certainly not either of these things in the days of ancient Israel, in the traveling tabernacle and in the great temple of Solomon or of Herod. Ancient sacrifice must have been something of solemnity and brutality; of hieratic, silent ceremony; and of the stench and roar of slaughtered animals, of small birds captured and wrenched apart, wrenched from life. Sacrifice does not need theology's honorifics: it is not a straightforward virtue or polite piety, nor does it seek such. We do not *idealize* sacrifice! Its place within the canon of Holy Scripture does not stem from a religious verdict that ritual offerings are to be valued above all other goods or held forth as model for human lives to emulate. No, sacrifice—the Heavenly and earthly sacrifice engraved into the heart of ancient Israel—is not a *recommendation* or *preference*. It is rather the molten core of the chosen people before the Holy God. It is realism in the life and worship of Israel. *This* exchange is ordered and wild, lawful and beyond any code or plan, deeply enmeshed in life and food and liberty, but saturated with bloody death, too. Sacrifice is the place where Israel meets the Holy God; it is holy fire, and an encounter that exceeds all telling. It is the Mystery of God, the Mystery of the Holy Trinity.

It is worth pausing for a moment over this point, for the centrality of holy sacrifice in the Mystery of Trinity must be honestly assessed and explicated in light of these widespread criticisms, early and late. Have I properly studied the logion "go learn what this means: I desire mercy, not sacrifice"?

It is hard to defend an intuition as deep as is this one, a theological instinct truly primitive to an entire conceptual program. I take it as brute fact, resting on no further analysis, that biblical Israel honored and enacted its covenant through the practice of ritual sacrifice. Properly basic to my reading of Holy Scripture is the conviction that Israel was called and fashioned by Almighty God to be His holy possession, to stand in the midst of the nations of the earth as a holy people, consecrated and set apart, the distinct sign of the Holy God. Be ye therefore holy as I am Holy: that I take to be the fundamental covenant claim of the One God on the child of His delight. If we may speak of *facts* in the world of biblical literature, this I take to be one, perhaps the primal one. The ligature between Exodus and Leviticus, between Leviticus and Ezekiel and Isaiah, between Leviticus and the sacrificial practice on the high places in Genesis, between the priestly and Holiness Schools and the defiled yet cultic death for others of the Eternal Son of God: these intimate bands join law and prophets, law and ancestors, sacrifice and the earthly Mission of the Son together in unshakeable marriage. We do not understand the Torah of Israel if we do not see the temple cultus at its heart. Sacrifice is not the *whole* of it, certainly not. The law of Israel is immeasurably rich, containing worlds of statute and ordinance, across common life and ethical practice. It is a *Holy* Instruction, so we can say: no sacrifice without mercy. The temple sermon of Jeremiah in this sense does not undermine but rather strengthens the tie between sacrifice and holiness: the two must be one. We should not read Jesus's "action against the Temple" as a prophetic denunciation of the temple itself or its cultus: that is a shopworn Christian trope, a theological pipedream. The Lord has come to His temple, we should rather say, as do Moses and Aaron—no, even more, as does the Divine Fire—and He purifies the sanctuary for heavenly use. The Torah of Israel places holiness at its center just because the tent of meeting will be a House of the Divine Presence. In just this way it assumes and rests on a legislation, an act, and a permission that allows a Fiery Holiness to dwell in their midst. The tabernacle with its ark of the covenant—at least in early days—is the Meeting Place of the Covenant God with His people. The encounter between such a God and such a people demanded a rite of cleansing and of thanksgiving, a costly offering that purified an earthy people for the Heavenly Courts. Sacrifice, like the categories of Trinity itself, must be "ethicized": it is a Holy Meal, made with mercy.

But for all this, we do not shy away from that little word *costly*! As impressive as have been the theologies of gift, and even more of noncompetitive giving,[17] the sacrificial cultus that stands at the very center of Israel's life is one of death and alienation, of expense and attrition, and not simply life and feasting. The "life that is in the blood" endorses the vitality and value of a living creature, certainly, but it is released, gathered, and spread about through the death of the animal: nothing less is imagined in Holy Writ. Sacrifice is food, yes, and a pleasing savor, yes again, but it is also slaughter and exile and handing over. It is *cauterizing fire*. That is the downward movement, the breaking, the exaction of sacrifice, the Pattern of the Divine Life. We cannot and need not *glorify* death and suffering; sacrifice is not a reveling in pain. Indeed, the rabbinic commentary on kashruth detailed the proper manner of humane slaughter. Animals must not be abused or tormented by their costly death on our behalf. But Holy Scripture is at its most realist here: unlike so much of bourgeois culture, it does not shy away from the harsh pain and renunciation that accompanies the joy of earthly life. The Presence of the God of Israel tabernacles, too, with this costly and abundant life: in it all, in its sorrows and griefs; its inexplicable suffering; the graves, honored and forgotten; the way not taken; the aching loss and defilement—in it all. Sacrifice is the scriptural name of this Omnipresent, Humble Lord, whose Way is near to life and pardon and festival, and to suffering and grief and death. He was stricken. That is what it means for the Holy God to be Present to His people. In the Processions, so in the Missions: the Descent into Self-Offering is costly.

Pastors know full well this amalgam of love, of gift, and of costly sacrifice in the creaturely realm. It is a piety of present-day obituaries to relate how the deceased met death, at home, surrounded by a loving family—but pastors know the cost of that piety. The person laid low by a fatal illness seeks to come home again, to be freed of hospital rules, alarms, and blood draws in the middle of that night: of course, the patient does! And in a loving family or friendship, the household wants the patient back with them, a beloved, soon to be lost, not a diagnosis, not a medical case. But this is an exacting decision! A bedroom must be moved or refashioned; bathrooms made ready for walkers or wheelchairs; schedules must be upended, perhaps day for night, or hour by hour; new and frightening drugs and dressings and tools make their appearance and must be put to use; trips are canceled, visits delayed, fresh visits begun. These are costs the family pays, the sacrifice they must make, for this good to be realized. It may be an offer from the heart, an offer consecrated by love—and pray God that it is!—but it may be shadowed by guilt, duty, or fear. Or perhaps it is better said that any death at home is a brutal mixture of all these things. And further, very few people in polite society know what death actually is, what dying is like, or what it costs. Hospitals remove this from our sight: the growing weakness, the last day the dying person dares to go downstairs, the day he does not leave the bed, the terrible day she no longer eats or does not drink, the curling inward of the muscles, the measured and then rasping breath, the loss of bodily control, the slow, lingering withdrawal of the cherished person from intimacy or any tether to the living. The family that accepts the dying request of their intimate to die at home faces all these brutal truths of bodily corruption: it is a shrivening and a costly sacrifice. The pastor who calls at the home, who listens to the bereaved, who brings Eucharist, compassion, or respite to a household—that minister of the Gospel knows that love is costly, even when eager—perhaps especially then.

Perhaps this is an example in extremis, a heightened coloration that distorts the day-to-day life of intimacy and family bond. We can hope this is so. But love asks much of the lovers: the small preferences overridden; the solidarity before critics when doubts lie close at hand; the habits and styles and aims of life, not always aligned with one's own; the sorrows of another that become one's own—these are not trivial elements of sacrifice in daily life, although they are often hidden from all but confessors. Of course, in any intimacy that is long-lasting and deeply satisfying, larger and more long-lasting costs will come in tow; one prays that Freud's lofty sublimation can perform its elixir here, too. But the small sacrifices of a gracious and generous and life-giving intimacy should give us pause, I believe, when we extol or insist on a good without cost. These examples are not *argument*, of course; they depict and do not defend. But if they express in some small measure the reality of our most intimate bonds, they will manifest to us the realism that stands at the heart of Scripture, the heart of Israel's sacrifice. It is life and it is death; it is healing and purification and pardon; and it is loss, cruel and permanent loss. All this is Holiness, the sacrifice of temple Holiness.

Now readers attentive to Childs's analysis of Leviticus, touched on earlier, will notice an odd feature of this discussion so far. Far from opposing Childs's account of the supersession of the temple cultus, it appears to confirm it. Everything I have spoken of thus far has been *metaphorical* or *spiritual* in character: the death of a beloved, the costs of intimacy, the sacrifices entailed in monogamous marriage and societies that claim to support it. What the pastor knows is not the death of animals, perhaps not even the loss of a harvest's first fruits, but rather the bending low of one human life, in love and in service to another. This seems to mirror the very spiritualizing the rabbis at Jahvneh, and the author of the Letter to the Hebrews, recommends. It seems we are all "heirs to the Pharisees," after all. After such a vivid defense of the gritty realism of the sacrificial cultus, it appears we could just as well anchor the Mystery of Trinity in the ideal of self-giving, or of lavish selflessness. These are costly, too!

But a systematic theology that aims to ground doctrine in Holy Scripture, one that holds that Scripture is both determinate and sufficient for dogmatic work, must be able to say more than a mild acquiescence in spiritualized exegesis. It must say something about the doctrine of God as manifested in the concrete life of Israel and the Coming King of this people. It must see the Intelligible laid down in the concrete, the Meaning of Reality, True, Necessary Reality bestowed on and integrated into the vital practice of ancient Israel. It must see Trinity in the costly sacrifice of altar and priest, the history of covenant Israel. It must see the Living Relation of the Divine Abstract to the Divine Concrete. Though of course this traces lineage back through the honorable notion of Scripture's *sensus plenior*, it is lineage only, not an instance of it. We are not now seeking a depth dimension not carried by the literal or plain sense—or even less, a spiritual sense that elevates and corrects the plain. No! We do not attempt to find a more palatable notion of bloody sacrifice in the ideals of spiritual worship or sacramental rite. We are not looking for a "useable past" or a modern equivalent to the forlorn past. This is a different act altogether. My aim is to listen intently for the Presence of the High God, the Transcendent and Lofty One, in the plain, historical record of Israel and Israel's Son. Sacrifice *contains* the Immanent Trinity, through His own gracious Nearness. Just this is theological compatibilism in the dogma of Trinity. It is the Lord's Mysterious Life to be Present as the Bounded Infinity, the Concrete True and Benevolent One. He is an Ever-Greater Dissimilarity to this earthly home in which He freely dwells; yet He, this very One, does dwell there. This is Holy Scripture as manifestation of the Holy God. It is the high mystery that is Scripture itself, that its things may become Signs; even more, that its record, in speech and actor and event, can exhibit not only or merely the economy but—astonishingly!—the inner Life of the Mysterious, Hidden, Humble Tripersonal God.

So, we now begin to unfold directly the manner by which Israel's sacrifice grounds Trinity. Leviticus tells us that the Holy Fire blazes forth from the tabernacle and consumes to ash the altar sacrifice: this is the Divine Life of the Transcendent God. The Mystery of Trinity begins with the remarkable admission that the Lord is a *Living* God. The Fiery Glory of this God is His Life, His Dynamic Vitality, His Consuming Flame. It roars out of its Hiding Place, it moves, it is Eternally Fertile. Just this the high theological tradition has termed the Divine Processions. The Holy Fire of God and Its Glory are the Old Testament expression of the Trinitarian Processions. This teaching etches a firm demarcation between the Holy God of Scripture and all purely ideal notions of Deity. The Lord God of Israel is not *inert*. Stable and Faithful, yes—even Intellectual—but this True God is not pure idea. He is not the *concept* of the Good, though He is the Good itself. He is not the *idea* of Transcendence, the Limit Concept against which an orderly world appears. He is not simply Depth, or the Immaterial, though, to be sure, He is all these things. He is Infinite Being, Absolute Infinity, yet not as a static reality, an unbounded set. He is not simply *Alive*, though of course He lives Eternally. We have not considered properly the Levitical theophany were we to say simply that this One who spoke with Moses and lit from His own House the fire of sacrifice is not inert but alive. Processional life is not a *contingent* truth about God. It does not emerge only from response to creation, nor does it exemplify only the *actions* of God toward the world. No, the Life of God, the fertile, generative, and moral Processions of God, are necessary to Him, *essential* to His Deity. The Nature of God is Descending, Holy Fire: there is no Deity or Essence that lies behind the Processions, though a conceptual distinction can always be drawn. Once again, we hear the echoes of Lateran IV, the furious worry between Abbot Joachim and Peter Lombard over Processions and Nature. Just this assertion is the biblical expression of *real relations* in God. The Processions do not belong only to the economy of salvation; rather, they structure and define Deity Itself, God's inner Life. The Lord God just *is* Holy Fire.

In his Trinitarian writings, St. Bonaventure spoke of God often as fertile; *fecund* is a favorite term. That is the *force* of saying the Processions are *generative* and *outpouring*. When Christians speak of the Immanent Processions of God, they do not simply mean that God lives, though of course that is true. They mean that this Life is *productive*—fecund—so that the Livingness of God is directed toward an *End*, a Perfection and Perfect Gift. This is important dogmatically, scripturally, because the inner Life of God, in all its Unlikeness, is not directionless, random, stochastic. We are not to think of God, in His own Reserve and Hiddenness, as simply "pulsing," so to say, an Energetic Bundle that merely radiates or diffuses. We do not stand before an Uncontained Explosion. Rather, Leviticus shows us a Lord who is Fire and Glory that is *directed*, purposeful, fertile. It moves toward Self-Offering, toward Perfect Gift: in Trinitarian idiom, toward the Persons. Indeed, the Fire just *is* the Persons in their Livingness, their Moving Fertility. We comprise all this doctrine in the dense and fecund image of the psalmist: with You is the Well of Life. (Here, as in Bonaventure, speaks a quiet and rich vein of female and erotic language for God.)

Bonaventure helps us see why the dispute between Joachim de Fiore and Peter Lombard is so urgent, so trenchant, that only a church council can settle it. Trinitarian dogma is not William James's "dry as dust" abstraction! The question between the two protagonists of Lateran IV has to do with this very affirmation about the Infinite Fertility who is the Living God. Is there, in the Lombard's sense, a *quaedam summa res* that is neither a Begetting nor a Begotten nor a Spirating? Could such a "certain concept of an Essence" be properly predicated of Almighty God? Now it is clear that worlds of discourse stand between the abbot and the schoolmen, so a proper meeting of minds was not to be expected. But the vital issue at stake is clear, and it is *our* question, too. Is God *fecund* in His very Life and Nature, as Bonaventure tells us? Is the Divine Life generative and purposeful, as we have claimed? Can Deity Itself be encountered and conceived as wholly and only *Abstract?* This is the question Trinitarian dogma raises about the Divine Nature and the Processions.

Peter Lombard claims that a Divine Nature or Essence that is Generative would necessarily beget Itself. Deity would be Self-Caused in a direct and paradoxical fashion. To ward off this Trinitarian incoherence, the Lombard advocates a conceptual or ideal notion, the Triune Nature, that is logical and ideally distinct from the Processions. For Joachim, such conceptual niceties cannot blind us to the real danger here: a Quaternity, composed of the Unbegetting Essence and three Divine Persons. As we have seen, the council sided with the Lombard here and advanced the cause of scholastic distinctions and conceptual analysis. Through an appeal to Bonaventure, I have favored the assimilation of Nature to Living Fecundity. Of course, in doing this, we are not forced to deny the Lombard's "conceptual distinction of Essence" nor the ruling of Lateran IV. Indeed, Bonaventure's own position can incorporate the full canons of the Council. But a strong endorsement of Deity as Essential Fecundity has raised to explicit concern the Lombard's dogmatic worry. Have I, as the Lombard feared, made God His own Origin?

Here we must think through carefully, as far as the Light will carry us, to the inner Life of God and His inexhaustible Reality. Is the Divine Nature the Source or Origin of the Processions? Does the Infinite Essence spontaneously and ineffably cause Itself, somewhat as David Hume thought the cosmos could do? (In the *Dialogues of Natural Religion*, Hume likened a spontaneous generation of the world to the human mind, seemingly uncaused in its own thought.) Should we consider the Divine Kabod, rushing forth from the Inner Sanctum, a kind of Divine "Roiling Sea," an Oceanic Fecundity that moves outward on its own Dynamic Tide? How should we think on these things?

Bonaventure leads us to speak of Divine Origin, the mystical Primacy of the First Principle, the Father. In time we will unfold more fully the doctrine of the Persons and their Relatio. But here we fix intently on *Origin*: the confession that the Processional Life in God has a *Terminus a Quo*, an Alpha as well as Omega, an Eternal Source of the Fiery Descent. We say, that is, that the *Person of the Father* is the Origin of the Fertile, Processional Life of God. Bonaventure held that Trinitarianism must teach a *redoublement* in the very idea of the Father, and Robert Jenson seems to have held to a parallel notion of the First Person in his "problem of the Father," his "Patrology." In their ambit, though not one voice with them, I would confess that the Divine Fire that explodes from the temple is *sent*: it was the will of Almighty God to hallow the temple by igniting its sacrificial offerings, His will to cleanse the temple by the whole burnt offering of the sons of Aaron. There is a Personal Subject that elects to act in this way. So, it must be, I say, that the

Origin of the Divine Fecundity is Subjective, Intellectual, Personal. We need not settle here the proper meaning of the word "Person," here, when used in Trinitarian dogma; that will come in time. But here we affirm that the Rupture and Descent, the Outpouring and the Offering that is the Processional Life of God, has an Origin—It is not a spontaneous Eruption—and this source is not the Nature Itself. It is the Majestic Reserve and Primacy of the Father.

Now this does not mean that the Father *causes* the Godhead! Almighty God is not a Self-Caused Cause or a Mystery and Paradox that both precedes and follows Itself. Rather we say that the Elements and Dynamisms of God are *equally* primordial and primitive. The Persons, the Processions, and the Nature just *are*, in the fundament and as the principle. That is the *force* of saying that God is Eternal; God is the Eternal. The Most Real Being is not caused—causal language does not belong to Necessary Being. So thoroughgoing is this exclusion that we should not say that the Father *causes* the Son, nor does the Prime Origin *cause* the Processional Life of Generation and Spiration. Indeed, the Nature Itself, were we to endorse this ordering, could not cause the Processions. Rather, we say that these equiprimordial Elements are *ordered*, One to Another, arranged in the Living Dynamism who is God. Certainly, these sequences are *Living*; they are not bare relations or priorities. The Primal Origin is *Father*, Agential and Living, as is the Fiery Descent of Generation and Donation, as are Son and Holy Spirit, the Self-Offering and the Return. *Exitus et Reditus* are *alive* in God, Eternally Alive.

Still, after all this, we are not done with Fecundity that is the Primacy of the Father. Bonaventure has more to say to us about the Divine Origin of Holy Fire. The schoolmen asked: Is it in virtue of being Father that the Son is generated? Or is it, rather, that in virtue of the Begotten Son that the Origin is Father? This delicate, technical question in the history of medieval Trinitarianism brings us more deeply into the redoublement of the Father, His Unique and Eternal Primacy. We are not about the act of devising puzzle cases here or to weigh scholastic distinctions as a source of hermetic delight. No, God is *Holy*; there is no complex and conceptual question in Trinitarian dogma that is not also *moral*, a plunging deep into the Good. Rather we ask this conceptual question to examine and meditate further on the fundamental Mystery of Agential Origin in the Triune Lord.

Should we say that the First Person just *is* God in a distinctive and primordial way that the Other Persons do not share? Is God the Father in a fundamental and singular fashion that is His alone? Is that why of the Old and New Testaments, the Prophets and the Incarnate Son, call God "Father"? Is it somehow truer to say of God that He is Father than that He is Son or Spirit? Is that why Christian liturgy begins with the Divine Father and addresses prayers first and principally to Him? We might think of some schools of Greek and Russian Orthodoxy as answering yes to all these questions. "God rules the world through His Two Hands, the Son and the Spirit": this maxim from Irenaeus is a mainstay of such Orthodoxy. We see the image here: the Agent, the full Subject and Actor, is the Father; *He* governs; *His* Hands are the Son and Spirit, sent by the Father into the world. The Processions are distinct from Each Other, and in virtue of these singular Hands—both Hands, equally so, each Distinct and Particular—the Persons of Son and Spirit are Distinct. Such is One account of "Relations of Origin" in which the Primacy of the Father grounds and directs the whole. Does the Levitical narration of the Holy Fire, sent out from the Holy of Holies, teach such a Primacy?

We must answer cautiously no, not exactly. As Bonaventure knew, there is a double sense to the word *Father* in the Triune Godhead. I might expand this Bonaventurian insight to say that in one movement within the Triune Life, the Son determines that the Origin is Father: without Son, no Paternity; without Offspring, no one is Parent. Just this is the scholastic and Augustinian notion of "relations of opposition," and we aim to endorse that view. The Father receives His Reality *as* Father from the Existence of the Son. This is the "recursive" concept of the Persons much favored by Sarah Coakley. Indeed, I would advance the full recursive reality of the Divine Persons: in virtue of the Spirit's Ascent and Return, the First and Second Persons receive Paternity and Filiation. Just this is what it means to say that the Son has Life in Himself and that the Lord is the Spirit: it is a manifestation of the full equality of the Persons. We will expand on these points as this exegesis continues. But here we want to underscore the Dignity, full Equality, and the Aseity of the Persons: They are Each and Altogether God in the full, primordial, and foundational sense. The "problem of the Unbegotten," as we might style the polemic of the fourth-century theologian Eunomius, can be resolved in the end, I say, by the Equiprimordial Equality of the Persons and Their recursive determination of One Another.

We can express this in sacrificial idiom. The Fire that consumes the offering on the first altar is a manifestation and correlate of the Holy God who is Self-Offering and Gift received. What is offered in the Holy Descent is the Divine *Self*, Eternally the Offered; the smoky ash returned in good pleasure to the Origin is the Gift, Consummated, Perfect, and Whole—Holy. The Spirit of Holiness is the Self as Gift Offered: the One God, descending down into Complete Self-Giving, ascending to Heaven as Gift Consummated. This is the Pattern, the Life of Holiness. The Divine Origin receives its Selfhood in virtue of the Offering: it really is God, fully and living, in this Self-Defined Self-Gift. The Divine Origin receives its Selfhood by the Consummation of the Offering, by its Self as Gift. The Gift received is the Telos, the Perfect Rest and Hallowing of the Offering, the Self-Offering that is the Sacrifice who is God. The Father is such in virtue of the Son; the Father and Son are such in virtue of the Spirit; They are Triune, the Holy Gift.

But all this, as Luminous and Perfect as it is, is not the only thing that can be said about Primacy. There *is* Origin in God, a Primal Source and Arche: from of old, thou art God, from everlasting to everlasting. This Absolute Alpha, the Ancient of Days, is the Father in the second sense of the Name. There is a First—"Firstness"—in God. This is the Subject, transcendent over His acts; this is the One who sends, the Self who is Offered, the Home to which the Gift returns. When we seek the Mystery of Beginnings, when we follow out the thought of all Life to its Absolute Origin, when we yearn to know the First Dawning and the Principle of all things, all concept and thought, we seek the Father. The Nicene Symbol appropriates Creation to the Father; this, too, is speaking of the Permanent Mystery of the First. (We will say more about Appropriations in the doctrine of creation and the God-world relation it entails.) But here we simply bow before the Mystery of the Source, the Father of Lights. This is the Portal of death, the Gate to the Absolute Beyond, the Prime and the Primal. All pours forth from this Portal, even the Fire that is the Down-Rush of the Divine Life. God is *Absolute*: that is Father as Origin.

So, we must conclude that in complex and glorious senses, the Life, the Procession of God, that Scripture teaches must be in some sense God Himself, His very Nature: there is no proper notion of the True God without Fire, without Divine Life. That is why the very idea of Being, to follow Holy Scriptures' guidance, must be "actualized," as Act of Being, as Thomas saw well. For as old as Parmenides is the ideality of a deity that is the stillness of Permanence, a perfect stasis of Pure Being that always *is*. Such ancient speculations are not to be scorned: they shimmer with the plenitude of Most Real Being. But they have not penetrated as fully into the Divine Cloud as has Moses, the friend of God. For the True God simply *is* Life.

§5.3. The Unicity of the Divine Processions

Now, Holy Scripture guides us in our proper speculation about these Processions; it does not leave us to imagine these Divine Motions all on our own, however rich and scholastic such metaphysical speculation be. The intimate joining of Exodus into Leviticus tells us that the Lord's Fiery Glory is both Flame and Light: the Pillar of Cloud during the day, the Pillar of Fire the whole night through. When Moses enters the Cloud resting on Sinai, resting on the tent of meeting, he moves within the Divine Interior: he is taken up into the Divine Glory, and his face is illuminated by that encounter. Just so is our Lord Christ illuminated and illuminating, rendered glorious and dazzling, by His Transfiguration within the Divine Cloud; rendered Ruler and Final Authority as He ascends upward into the Cloudy Glory of His own Origin. Fire is the Molten Core of God and, on that first day, the Origin of the entire sacrificial cultus. The Originary Day of the tabernacle rite is a *Manifestation*, a Theophany of the Aseity of God: we are shown His Fiery Procession. Of course, it is related in all the vocabulary and graphic imagery of *saga* or *legend*, as Barth used these terms. The Levitical narratives speak of the Otherside, the *Jenseits*, in the idiom of the Near Side, the *Hinseits*, the plasticity and temporality of the earthly world. But it *is* the *Jenseits*, the Divine Life *as such* that we see. The Ever-Greater Dissimilarity remains in the earthly Act of Manifestation: but it is the Lord in His Processions that acts in that way. The Fire and Cloud guide us, then, as we consider the very notion of Triune Procession.

We might ask, for example, whether we are right, in our speculative theology, to teach a twin procession. Are there in truth *two* processions in Almighty God? This does not seem to be a matter that can be easily settled. On one hand, we have ample testimony throughout Holy Writ of the Divine Life, a singular term, and there do not seem to be plain testimonies or patterns of a double life, or less, of Two Lives. Yet the Nicene tradition has spoken firmly of a twin procession, the Generation of the Eternal Son and the Procession or Spiration of the Eternal Spirit. And we have seen the significant theme of doubling in the doctrine of the Father and in the dogma as a whole. To defend the teaching of two distinct Processions, dogmaticians have adverted to the Persons, either in Theophanies or in Missions. In the history of salvation or the divine economy, we might reasonably count *two*, the Son and Spirit, or the Word and Gift of Almighty God. A short step leads from here to a doctrine of Trinity built up from the Missions or the Persons, the Incarnation and Outpouring of the Spirit on Pentecost. The central problematic of such a doctrine is how these two are *One*, the One God manifested to His people in these two modes or *prosopa*. Great subtlety has been demonstrated in the defense of just this claim, and I do not think this is effort wasted. By no means! Thinking carefully through the diverse Manifestations of the Lord to His creatures can only benefit a proper doctrine of God and, in the end, a proper doctrine of salvation. But it founders, I believe, on two principle shoals. Great care is exercised to demonstrate the *distinctiveness* of these Missions or Appearances: the Son is not the Spirit; indeed, the Spirit either *rests* on the Son, and the Child born is thus Holy, or the Spirit is *bestowed* by the Son, and the double Procession of the Spirit is thus thought to be confirmed. The time will come when these delicate matters of the Mission and Relation of the Persons must be discussed but in their own time. Here we simply note the pressure that is exerted on the Divine Unicity by the originary emphasis on *distinction*, separateness. On these two, after all, the very idea of distinct Processions rests. But this is in truth the lesser shoal, a kind of difference in the schools. The rock on which this programmatic falters, I say, is the deeper testimony of the Scriptures to the Divine Life.

In my view, the covenant literature of ancient Israel speaks plainly and fully of a Living God, of a Fiery Life that is the Divine Glory, a Surpassing Dynamism that brooks no rival. Nothing in the testimony of the Davidic Son or the Spirit raining down on Ezekiel, carrying him to high places and valleys strewn with bones, can compete with this central teaching. Our God is the Living One. To be sure, this One *acts*. The Speech and the Spiritual Presence of God manifest this Molten Energy who is God: He is Rational Light. These teachings must be honored! But they *follow*; they do not precede or ground. Once again, we will find a twofold sense but with a *Primacy*. One will lead, by Arche, the Other. We anchor the dogma of Trinity in the Divine Procession(s); they are our starting point. This is another way in which we gladly follow St. Thomas's lead—because this foundational claim, that God is the Living One, structures the whole of Israel's testimony. The New Testament rests on this foundation: the resurrection Life who is Jesus Christ is exemplified in the story of the burning bush, where before this God, all are alive. Of course, minority texts can control large sections of doctrine—consider the outsized influence of the Johannine prologue on the doctrines of Christology and Trinity. Scriptural exegesis for dogmatic construction is never a simple matter of *counting*; nothing as wooden as all that. But the *governing* motif, the *organizing* element in Christian doctrine, falls in the main on the principle structure, theme, and movement of Holy Writ.

That is why, at foundation and base, the Oneness of God must govern all other Christian doctrinal teaching.

So, we ask again: Should the dogma of Trinity teach a twofold Procession, an Eternal Generation and an Eternal Spiration? Here I believe we must take up with real earnestness the complex language of "doubling" and of "incorporation": Should Christian theology affirm *Two* Processions *in* One God? Immediately we can imagine objections. The modern reader thinks of mereology, the relation of part to whole. It seems inescapable in a fully rationalized system to avoid the impression that the Mystery of Trinity turns on a stark undermining of the Unicity or Simplicity of God: the dogma appears to teach that the One *contains* Two and that the inner Life of God is straightforwardly, eternally Complex. More troubling still: it seems that Trinity must teach Divine Parts, eternal distinctions that can never be unified and must be thought in some fashion to *constitute* the Triune Reality of God. The twin Processions of Son and Spirit from the Father seem to encapsulate all these dangers, to magnify them and enshrine them in dogma. Such considerations appear to have led some Latin theologians to eclipse the Processions in favor of an austere doctrine of origins alone: we should say, they argue, that the Son has the property of "Being from the Father," the Spirit the property of "Being from the Father and Son." We should not say more than this, they will argue. The Processional Life of God is best expressed, it is claimed, by speaking solely of Divine *Relations*: the Persons are relative predicates, distinguished simpliciter by Relations of Origin. We might think of Calvin as radical exemplar of this position and find in this radical insistence on Relations alone a movement within Reformed and Evangelical circles which have preferred not speaking of Eternal Generation or Spiration at all.[18] Famously,

Calvin's Trinitarian theology fell under a cloud of suspicion from its earliest days. He was thought to deny the Processions altogether and, in this way, threaten the *Homousion* of the Son, His full and equal Divine Nature—a charge Calvin vigorously denied. He held that "simple speaking" of Persons and Nature was sufficient for a biblical theology: no speculation, no prying into the heavens, no scholastic and alien philosophy. The assignment of possession and order, conveyed by the plain genitive *of* should eclipse and replace the complex notion of Procession, a Personal donation of Nature or Substance. Now, a theology such as mine, that begins all Trinitarian reflection on the Processional Life of God, can hardly adopt an austere school of the doctrine of origins. There is no eclipsing of the doctrine of Procession(s) through a sole affirmation of Relational Predication alone.

But its attractions can be plainly seen! No solution to the problems of the twofold Procession need be found—their Room is already bare—and the mortal danger of introducing Divine Parts into the Godhead sternly curtailed. The delicate conceptual problem of the relation of Personal Fecundity and Nature seems attenuated here: Person is related to Person by origin or order, taxis, and the Three possess (?), inhabit (?) simply are (?) One Nature. We leave metaphysically unspecified the Generativity that exists between Person and Person. In this school, we simply affirm that the Son is "of" the Father, the Spirit of the Father and the Son. The genitive here is not filled out metaphysically, and *relation* itself carries no particular divine property. Rather we might say it is treated as a name, a kind of rigid designator, that picks out the Persons as ordered One to Another. Divine Unicity seems well defended here, and the parsimony about metaphysical predicates seems to mirror well the spareness with which Holy Scripture speaks of the Missions of the Divine Persons. All good!

But can such an austerity speak with full-throated assurance of the Generative and Spiritual Nature of the Living God? Have we not stilled the scriptural voice that speaks of Divine Life, the Living Fire? Have we captured properly the Life that overspills, that begets, that swarms with Reality? Have we reckoned fully with the Holy Fire that is Glory and Fecundity and Light? Have we noted carefully and exactly the manner in which God Himself inexhaustibly wells up in Wisdom, pours forth Goodness? The Divine Life, so central to Scripture, is not *shapeless*. It is not simply another term for God, Deity, or Divine Nature. We are not speaking here of bare *synonyms*. Rather, to honor the Holy God of the Holy Bible is to catch sight of the Dynamism, the *Act* of God, which is not exhausted or first expressed in relation to creatures. God as Reality itself is Eternally Act, the Fiery Glory of an Unlimited, Wild, and Free Lord, the One who *is* Holy Life. Now, to say that this Lord has a *determined* Life, a concrete and specific Dynamism, is to speak of Procession(s), the Self-Generative Explosion and Gift who is God. The definitive character of the Living God means that we lay out the doctrine of the Divine Movement in specific, contoured, and dynamic terms. We do not leave it empty or anomalous. Rather, we turn to Holy Scripture, to the Holiness of the God of Israel, to properly fix the properties and dynamisms of this Active Lord.

Just so, but are they Two? We might think once again here of the Greek or Russian Orthodox predilection for Two Processions, each Singular and Definite, issuing in Two Persons from One Cause, One Source, One Principle: the Father as Principle Origin for the Persons of Son and Spirit, Each Divine by Nature, Each the Fiery Issue of the Father of Lights. The Divine Processional Life is well defended here, and it is clear that the Divine Persons share the One Nature *in virtue* of the Processions. The Son is generated; the Spirit spirated; Each from the Father with the concomitant

Divine Nature. Following Gilles Emery,[19] we might say that the Proceeding Persons are not generated from the Nature but rather by the Person of the Father; just this is His Primacy. But the Acts of Procession by which the Persons are Eternally issued just are the Dynamic Life, the Nature, of the Tri-Personed God. Now, such a Triune schematic immediately underscores the Eternal Distinctiveness of the Persons and, even more, proposes a *ground* for that Distinction: Two Processions ensure Two Definite Persons. The Father, in the primary sense, it seems, acts eternally in two specific manners: He begets and He breathes. Because His Acts can never be sterile or futile, Perfect Determinates must issue from these Acts. Never would the Movement of God be undefined or random; rather always it would be generative, useful, fruitful, and perfect. The proper and fitting Issue of the Divine Person's Life would be simply God: no creature could be the full measure of the Fertility who is God. (Bonaventure is one with the Orthodox here.) And there will be no confusion of the Persons under this schema. No ideational collapse of the Son and the Spirit, no reduction of the Proceeding Persons into the Origin. Two Persons are Dependent, and we know why. Three Persons are Distinct, and we are not left without rational conceptuality for these Determinates. Rather the twin Processions do this intellectual work of the faith. We need not rely on personal notions or properties to take on this task; something far stronger than property-distinction is in view here. Rather the double Acts of the Father ground the Personal Distinctions: His Reality is to pour forth His own Nature in Two Forms, Each God, All God. For the Orthodox (or those who defend this view), the mereological problem simply does not arise: they refuse the proposition that two Processions lead to two parts or elements with the One God. Rather, they stoutly affirm that the Father is the Arche, the Principle and Source of Unity, or, more daringly, the *Aitia*, the Uncaused Cause of the Godhead, and this suffices; for God is Mystery.

If the Personal is the Divine Ground in this fashion, we may wonder whether necessity can still be predicated of God. Indeed, some modern Orthodox are wary of arguments from necessity in the Trinity. John Zizioulas, for example, is very decided in his rejection of Divine Necessity. Not determined or entailed but rather *free*: these are the relations and acts that befit the God of liberty. No inert or "dead" hand of conceptual deduction, but rather the Living God of Freedom who overcomes determinism and death: this is the Triune God of Eternal Communion. For Bishop Zizioulas, the Latin worry over the proper distinction of the Persons reveals the weakness of the Western position—if there be a "Western position"!—on the Divine Processions. And it does seem that logical necessity *must* govern the Latin distinction of the Persons. "As the divine intelligence is the very supreme perfection of God," Thomas writes, "the divine Word is *of necessity* perfectly one with the source whence He proceeds, without any kind of diversity."[20] It must be, necessarily, that the Son's relatio to the Father in itself differs from the Father's relatio to the Spirit—the Begetter and Begotten are necessarily entailed; so, too, the twofold Giver and the Gift—for the Processions, Thomas says, are nothing but the Relations of Mutual Opposition, in some way and in the end, identical to the One Divine Nature. Conceptual necessity governs these Relations because the very Idea of God is Most Necessary Being, and the interconnection of relational properties— their mutual opposition—simply are the Persons: Son and Father opposed in generative relation; Son and Father equally opposed to Spirit in spirative relation. The modal property of necessity appears essential in order to clarify the relation of the Two and the One in Trinitarian dogma. The mutual entailments of the Subsistent

Relations constitute the sole distinction within the Godhead; all else is utterly, uniquely One, One Nature, One God. Yet even these Oppositions, the Subsistent Relations who are the Persons, can be seen as identical to the Nature, for They simply *are* the Living Principles of the Deity, the Nature of God in Act. So, in a Latin doctrine of Trinity, as is this one, necessity must govern the doctrine of Divine Processions.

So, again with great reserve, we might speak of this conceptual structure as finding an analogue in McTaggart's B Series: necessary, fixed, asymmetrical relations that are themselves eternal, immutable, and unchanging. For this reason, the relatio of the Persons can be spoken of by a general or class noun. In this narrow sense, the Two are One, two instances of one class, Procession. For this reason, Thomas begins *De Deo Trino* with a quaestio on Procession, simpliciter: whether there is Procession in God. In the *responsio* he elaborates: "since procession *always* supposes action, as there is an outward procession corresponding to the act tending to external matter, so there *must be* an inward procession corresponding to the act remaining within the intellect."[21] The necessity, the simplicity, and the conceptual interrelation of these elements makes the medieval Latin doctrine of Trinity unpalatable to the modern Orthodox.

The decided preference among such Orthodox is for the twin Processions: to properly express the Divine Life, we must speak of *two*. And these Two must express the Sovereign, Utterly Free will and desire of the Father: He gives Himself freely, *Personally*, and is oriented *ad Aliam*, toward Another. From this decided emphasis on Divine, Personal Freedom stem the Trinitarian doctrines of communion: we count Zizioulas, Catherine LaCugna, and Jürgen Moltmann in this school. Two Processions, and these of Loving Self-Gift—that is the heritage of some philo-Cappadocian and Orthodox dogmaticians. In sum, we have strong arguments from the modern East for two processions: they must be distinct and distinctive acts in order that a Trinity of Persons be established and, in their own idiom, be One. But the West, that is, the Augustinian-Thomistic tradition (the tradition in which I stand) locates the distinction not in the processions but rather in the opposition of the Persons— and in just that way, allows for a unitary category, Procession, to embrace two instances, the Internal Generation of the Son and the Internal Giving of the Spirit. How should such distinctions be read and ranked in light of Holy Scripture? Two or One?

Leviticus tells us that the Fire of the Divine Glory explodes out from the sanctuary and consumes the offerings: that is where we must begin. Manifestly, we have a Singular: the sole Fire reduces the slaughtered animals to ash, sparking a smoky cloud to rise up Heavenward. In Exodus, a singular Fire ignites the apex of Mount Sinai, roaring like thunder, sheathing the lower slopes in protective and holy cloud, ringing the upper regions by thick darkness. In the wilderness campaign the Divine Presence of the Covenant God was a singular Column, of Fire at night, of Cloud during the day, Each manifesting the Fiery Glory of God, shielded by the covering of mist and smoke and cloud. A singular Voice, the Vox Dei, speaks from this Glory, addressing Moses in the thornbush and the Fiery Throne of Sinai. In all these annals of the covenant, the Lord God issues forth as One, One Holy Life. We do not read of the Fire divided or the Life distinguished in two forms or measures; rather God's Holiness is Dynamic and Active in one concrete form: Fire. It seems, then, that we have not properly heard the idiom and witness of Holy Scripture if we insist on two distinct Processions, Each recognizable from the Other by a particular agency, begetting or spirating. The Processional Life of God, that is, cannot have Two Processions that are, *per se* and *as such*, different acts within the Godhead. Such pluralism belongs to the creaturely realm, to the economy: there we see the Triune God act in undivided manner but in distinct modes: Creation, Providence, Mission, Consummation. The proper and perfect works of God ad extra are not uniform or homogenous but rather pluriform, distinct, wonderfully rich. In this way, as in many others, the economy is not identical to the Immanence, the Missions to the Procession(s). The Unitary Life of God, His own Perfect Act, makes possible the multiplicity of His Acts toward the world and grounds the exceeding richness of the created realm. But this is a complexity rooted in a radical Unicity, for God, the Triune God, is One. The serious worry about mereology in the doctrine of God must be addressed directly in the Mystery of Trinity—nothing short of the inner Life of God can suffice to defend the Superabundant Oneness of God against any separation or partition. I believe that Christian doctrines of Trinity have not adequately defended the inner Life of God from charges of pluralism and complexity, states of Divine Reality that threaten to devolve into subdivisions and parts. In some Trinitarian doctrines, in truth, the pious refusal to consider the metaphysical salience of theology's concepts has left the faith open to the charge of an ill-formed or weak unity (such was the diagnosis of Lateran IV, we remember) or, worse, of tritheism, an apostasy of the Christian God. Here it is not sufficient, I believe, to advert to Divine Mystery, to stern apophatism, or to the antispeculative tradition in modern dogmatics. The cultural and conceptual legitimacy of the faith rests, I say, on a doctrine of the Triune Life that displays and relies on a conceptual battery of terms fully equipped to defend Israel's monotheism. We cannot simply *say* One; we must *think* it.

Now, this cannot be done, certainly, by a crude uprooting of Nicaea. For a theologian of the church, there is no "going behind" the fourth- and fifth-century Conciliar decisions: the Creedal

Symbol is bedrock for the faith. Equiprimordial is the conviction that the Conciliar decisions are themselves *scriptural*: they provide us a reading, interpretation, and narrative of Holy Scripture. Just this is under threat by the conviction of some Evangelical and Reformed theologians that the Eternal Generation or Spiration is not biblical and must therefore be excised from Trinitarian dogma. But this Protestant conviction will not persuade, unless the Creed is prized loose from Scripture and treated as a secondary, contingent, and conceptual deliverance of the early church. Oceans of argument and religious polemic lie under these bare affirmations; I do not pretend to do them justice here. But even in this narrow room, we must say that the affirmations of the Councils and the doctors of the church cannot be dissolved from our consideration by a simple charge that they are not biblical. Rather, a theologian of the church must look directly and open-eyed at the twofold demand: that Trinitarian dogma speak out of the Holy Scriptures *and* affirm the Eternal Begetting and Spiration of the One, Dynamic Life of God. How might the Oneness of the Divine Life be reconciled with the Two Inner Acts of God or, more, be understood as the Luminous Ground of these Acts?

Thomas shows us the way. In his deft analysis of the Divine Processions, he allows himself to speak of a single class, Procession, in which we are to discover two instances, the Eternal Begetting, and Spiration. Tellingly, Thomas prefers the scholastic term *Procession* for the Eternal Act of the Issuing of the Spirit: He *proceeds* from the Father and the Son. The full Johannine and creedal origins of this term are brought to the fore. We must speak, Thomas says, of the Spirit proceeding, the Son generated, and these two under the singular rubric of the Spirit, Procession. It seems that the class noun *Procession* belongs in some particular fashion to the Emergence of the Spirit, for the "procession which is not generation has remained without a special name."[22] Perhaps we might speak of this as a form of *redoublement*, where we acknowledge Generation and Spiration and, in a second manner, the One Procession, in which the begetting of the Son belongs as it were within the Spirit's own Donation. Indeed, Bonaventure's own experiment in doubling— the twofold Primacy of the Father, underscores the conviction that the Double, enclosed in the One, is necessary to proper Trinitarian dogma. Here is Thomas on this point: "We can name God only from creatures. As in creatures generation is the only principle of communication of nature, procession in God has no proper or special name, except that of generation."[23] Note here how sternly Christological Thomas is in his Trinitarian doctrine: it is *Generation* that holds center stage, the One Particular in the Act of God. It is *proper* to God as is nothing else, and the fulcrum of the Divine Life is forged from the Father begetting the Only Son. Yet the Holy Spirit serves the Unicity of the Godhead in a remarkably powerful manner. The insistence on the perfectly general or common character of the Internal Act of Procession frames the treatment of the Person of the Holy Spirit, the One without particular or proper Name: "While there are two processions in God, one of these, the procession of love, has no proper name of its own. Hence the relations also which follow from this procession are without a name: for which reason the Person proceeding in that manner has not a proper name."[24] Following Augustine, Thomas can say that the One proceeding is appropriately termed Holy Spirit "from the fact that the person who is called Holy Spirit has something in common with the other Persons. For as Augustine says, 'Because the Holy Spirit is common to both, He Himself is called that properly which both are called in common. For the Father also is a spirit, and the Son is a spirit; and the Father is holy, and the Son is holy.'"[25] We see here the larger pattern: the Holy Spirit and His Procession hold something in common for the Triune Persons. He is what They are; They are summed up, as it were, or represented by Him; His common or universal character is the larger concept in which the other Persons reside. There is, in Bonaventurian idiom, a doubling of the Mystery and Procession of the Spirit. In time this general movement of incorporation and representation will yield the prized relation of circuminsession, where Each is in Each, All in Each, All in All. But we glimpse that far shore of the Triune Mystery in this particular interplay of Procession as singular and as twofold, as *doubled*.

We might put this Mystery more strongly still. In Latin and Greek Trinitarianism together, we speak of Two Processions, Begetting and Spirating, and that twofold-ness must guide not only the material but also the *formal* elements of the dogma. This conceptual "two-ness" is the dogmatic expression and warrant for *redoublement*, for doubling in the doctrine of God. As God must be spoken in the Christian tongue twice over, in His Nature and Perfections and, then again, in His Persons and Procession, yet these Two are One, One God. So we may say that the Holy Life of God is Descent and Ascent, Generation and Donation, Exit and Return, Offering and Gift, yet these Two are One, One Living Fire. The lessons we draw from Bonaventure, from Thomas and Nicaea, are not "numerical"—not that God must "have" or "be" two—but rather *categorical* or *relational*. (It is, in philosophical idiom, the relation *pros ti*.) We do not *count two* "in" God (two acts or elements, still less, two substances); rather, we see that the Life of God is Doubling—Relatio—as One, One Life, One Procession, One God. The Generation and Spiration are the One Life of God expressed and poured out as Doubling. Or to speak in the language of the tradition: Relatio. These Two are One in the Relation of Identity.

Consider the Unitary Life of Almighty God as Holy Fire. Here we are shown in the sacrificial cultus a perfectly general property of the Holy One: He is altogether Fire, and His Life is an Exceeding Weight of Glory whose Inner Core is Molten Flame. Out of this Luminous Cloud, His Combustion pours forth. We must say that the Divine Persons, the Father of Lights, the Light that is come into the world, and the Flaming Spirit are all Fire, even as the Holy God is Himself Spirit, Utterly One. The doctors of the church spoke eagerly of Divine Fire when they considered the Holy Processions. Nicaea itself sums up the Divine Life: God from God, Light from Light. Fire, the light of the ancient world, does not possess clear, distinct, proper borders. It has origin and source in the fuel—the oil, the wood, the resin-soaked reed—but once ignited, it ranges free, without sharp edges or borders that contain and demarcate, utterly self-same and self-moving. In a more modern vein (though still not scientific), we might speak of it as ignited gas, combusted vapor. Fire is visible energy and in this way is analogue to the Omnipotence of God, what we might express as His Nature as *Living*, the Radiant Light of the Knowledge of God. Rowan Williams has written eloquently on the fittingness of fire as idiom for Trinitarian development: the flame passed from torch to torch, say, can extend itself without division or diminution; the second flame is fully fire yet distinctly its own light and heat.[26] Like water, like earth or air, fire is a mass noun, an element of the primal globe. It is self-same in each of its domains, yet without parts or components, it waxes and wanes on its own hidden schedule, it seems, and its far edge is known only by the burn scorched into the hand that draws near. It is dangerous. The mystery of fire, as of water, is deep in humanity's bones: it cauterizes and smelts, it destroys, it feeds and saves. Fire may be an "extended simple" in all these ways—metaphysically vague in its outer reaches yet utterly undivided.[27] Still, we may speak of a particular fire: it is *there* and not here; it can be counted in some larger fashion, from hearth to hearth, from lamp to lamp. In our earthly realm, such particularity seems tied to space. The material definition of the lamp or torch, and the distance between them, permit us to name distinct and separate fires. Certainly, this aspect of fire's mysterious constitution could not speak directly of the Divine Life, for God is Spirit, and God is Omnipresence. Yet we glimpse even here, in the midst of the Ever-Greater Unlikeness, the salience of *distinction* within a primal element without parts. More, earthly fire gives us creaturely analogues to the common and the distinct.

We might reflect, for example, on the *essential properties* of fire: heat and light. Once again we speak here of the Doubling of Qualia in the One Life. We may seize on one of these properties as the central, even sole attribute: for the chilled traveler, the hearth is *heat*; our intention is framed by this aspect, for we draw near only or principally to warm ourselves. We "see as." This is the Aspect that has dawned on us. But fire is primarily or solely light when we place the candle on the lampstand: it gives light to the whole house. Yet this is simply fire. We are not here, in this homespun analogy, considering something like the *inner workings* or *constituents* of fire. We are not "peering inside," as it were, to recognize elements that come to compose a living flame, much as the early naturalists examined the eye or the molten interior of the earth's crust. Even less are we considering fire as "folk name" for a scientific formula in Joules, say, or Ergs. No, we rather trade here on our ordinary experience, our ancient fascination and dependence on fire, stolen, it is said, from the gods. In fire's necessary properties, we discover something *essential* and *necessary*—no heat; no fire—yet this property may be taken also as an identity statement, a synonym or name. This is its doubling as a Relation of Identity. Fire *equals* light. Fire *equals* heat. The elements of God's good earth allow us to reflect more carefully on the general and the particular, the abstract and the concrete, the simple and the distinct.

Primal elements do not carry predicates in the same fashion as do ordinary "medium-size dry goods." Elements were considered the fundaments of the cosmos because they seemed closer to Being Itself in this regard: unlike everyday objects, they simply *were* their predicates. But they were not like "prime matter," the odd underlayment of earthly reality that existed in some undefined mode—it was close to nothing, Augustine memorably said—unceasing, it seemed, yet ready to receive all definitions, all forms. Elements, in contrast, possessed full reality in ancient thought; but they were strange. Fire could be seen under its aspects; they were "formally distinct," yet they could not be seen as accidents, strictly speaking, but rather as the *subject* of flame in a certain mode. For this reason, heat and light belonged essentially to fire yet remained one, simply one, with it. In a wonderful article, Ellen Charry has forcefully argued recently that Jewish critics of Trinitarian doctrine misunderstand the structure of the dogma when they assign it to a (false) doctrine of Divine Properties. Trinity, she says, does not derive from or elaborate on a notion of property but rather on the events of the economy.[28] Perhaps indeed we should say so for the ordo cognoscendi, or the order of discovery, but not so for the metaphysical doctrine itself. The centrality of fire in Holy Scripture and in Nicene Symbol and theology tell us that certain forms of properties and their relatio—essential ones, especially those that serve as names for the whole—offer rich analogues to the Processional Life of the Holy, Triune God. We dare to say: they are seals of the Living God.

With their aid, we return to the delicate question of the number of Divine Processions. The Divine Fiery Life of God must be

One: One Communicative Movement that terminates in the Perfect End, the Persons. Strictly speaking, we Christians must say not two Processions but One, yet One in its Doubling, Two identical elements of the Divine Life. Time and again we must underscore the Unicity of the whole of this Mystery, the Modes of this One God as the Living, Holy One. To affirm that Oneness is the governing Predicate and Mode of the doctrine of God does not entail affirming Unicity as a metaphysical category, existing apart from the Triune Nature of Three Persons in Relation. Not One Nature, Autonomous and Freestanding and *then* Processions and Persons. Rather Unicity as the fundamental credo of the doctrine of God, and the doctrine of Trinity, functions as do the Augustinian modes of "substance-wise" and "Relation-wise." Unicity as prime Mode of Almighty God speaks of the manner in which all is Reality in God: in Nature, in Procession, in Person, and in Relation, all distinction must be shown to be One, even in its Twofold-ness, One.

It is sometimes said that the proper defense against the danger of quaternity in the doctrine of God is to affirm strongly "Three in One" *and* "One in Three." But, as a conceptual or methodological maxim, I fear that is not strong enough. The aim of this maxim is to make the elements mutually indwelling or constituting: no Divine Nature without Persons; no Persons without Nature. We note in passing here the absence of the Processions. But some examples might clarify why such mutual coinherence does not protect adequately the Mystery of Trinity from the menace of quaternity. Consider a simple household example: four lengths of cloth in one jacket, one jacket in four lengths. In this material example, we can see that the symmetry of mutually constituting elements does not rule out *parts*—indeed this is a standard mereological sum—nor does it ward off a distinct and concrete nature (clothing or artifact) from the mutual relation of its elements. The little word *in* carries a heavy load here, and it is not transparent how we should interpret it. Parts subsist in wholes; a whole consists in its parts.

A theological analogue to this worry might be found in the apposite example of ecclesiology, treated in the great Constitution of Vatican II, *Lumen Gentium*. There the bishops in assembly proposed, in famous words, that the "One True Church of Jesus Christ *subsists in* the Roman Catholic Church." Here we have the symmetry and mutual indwelling the maxim suggests: a True Church in a visible, earthly Roman Catholic church, and the Roman Catholic Church indwelling the One True (Heavenly? Invisible?) Church of Christ. But once again, the weakness of the proposed safeguard shows itself: again we see a reality indwelling another, one in the other, but the ecclesial Nature, the True Church, is not *identified* simpliciter with or *exhausted* by the Roman Communion—indeed just this is the tantalizing draw of "subsistence"—but exists beyond it and serves as its telos and guide. (Of course, the ecclesiology of *Lumen Gentium* may invite sturdy Trinitarian reflection on other grounds; here we simply say that mutual indwelling cannot ward off a distinct and separate nature lying behind the symmetrical relation nor the hazard of parts within a greater whole.)

Consider, too, another example, drawn now from organic life. In a living subject, whose definition exceeds its shape or constituting materials, the symmetry of elements (four limbs in one torso, two essential properties in one human being) does not exhaust the concrete reality, the *existence* of the nature. But just this is what we seek to prohibit. We might think of this as the "interpretation problem" that has haunted Gregory of Nyssa's celebrated treatise, "To Ablabius," or "Not Three Gods." In the heart of that essay, Nyssa floats an ambiguous analogy for Persons and Divine Nature: Peter, James, and John as human. On one reading, it appears that

Gregory argues that a single nature, humanity, is shared or indwells three particulars, or instances; and the three individuals share in common and indwell humanity. But, critics charge, does this not make the nature exceed the individuals, "stand behind them"? More worrisome still, to these critics, is the anxious thought that Gregory has introduced three gods, each of whom possesses deitas. It seems that the Persons here are being enumerated, counted as distinct individuals. Indeed, just this is what nineteenth-century defenders of Latin Trinitarianism such as Theodore de Régnon fear: start with three Divine Persons, and the Unity of the Triune God cannot be won.[29] Now, Gregory of course does not intend to defend tritheism! His analogy seems, on second reading, to suggest that even in creaturely examples we can imagine three particulars not *dividing* a nature. But his analogy should make us properly wary of assuming that symmetrical relations can handle the conceptually demanding notion of the Divine Nature, Persons, and Processions in the Mode of Unity.

Let me finally suggest that the maxim, three in one and one in three, might be, in another respect, not too weak for this heavy lifting but in fact too strong. Consider now not material examples, as we have proposed so far. Rather, consider an ideational image: the triangle, say, or the rectangle. Here we have the maxim in what we might think of as a "definitional form." In an equilateral triangle, we find three sides in one triangle; one triangle in three equal sides. It seems that we have now thought away with full rigor the menace of an autonomous and freestanding nature, for a triangle just *is* three planar lines joined at an angle. There is no nature or essential property of "triangularity" that is not simply the relation of sides and angles, totaling 180 degrees. Now this, I say, is too strong! It seems that some social Trinitarians embrace just such a strong version of this maxim, for their aim, as I see it, is to *identify* the Divine Nature with the Persons in Their Orientation and Movement *ad Alias,* toward Others. Here we have hollowed out the metaphysical Reality of the Divine Nature; It has no other sense or referent than the Person as that which intends Another. But a full and proper Triunity, I say, must affirm the metaphysical Reality of each of the dogmatic terms: Nature, Person, Procession, Relation. God has a Nature, indeed, is a Nature!

Rather than relying on symmetrical relation to cure the dogma of Holy Trinity of the disease of quaternity, we should properly turn toward the Mode of Doubled Unicity, expressing and guiding the Fiery Descent and Ascent of the One Holy God. What we must aim for, in our metaphysical doctrine of Trinity, is a Unicity that just is the Act of Being of the Triune God, whose Nature is to Exist. The proper constraint on Trinitarian elements, that is, will not be found principally in a methodological maxim or an ordered set of relations (though to be sure these are helpful!) but rather in the full exposition of the metaphysical Reality and Modus of the Tri-Personed, Holy God.

The dogmatic aim we seek to satisfy here is to affirm the Deitas of God, Its own proper Nature, Substance, or Essence, *and* the Processional Life that is Its Act. Both must be "filled out" metaphysically, both true, both Doubled in Mode, both One God. Note that we are not quietly erecting a two-story doctrine of Trinity, one metaphysical, the other linguistic. No, the Mystery of Trinity cannot be a collection of grammatical or rhetorical rules! In my view the doctrine of God is not well served by second-order linguistic arrangements of affirmations, predications, and relations. Rather, the Holy Mystery who is the Tri-Personed God must be altogether *God*: all elements of the Mystery must be speculative metaphysics. The fundamental Perfection of Oneness is an Essential Modal Property: It is the manner in which the Holy God is Triune

Lord. When we speak of the Utter Purity and Simplicity of the Lord God, we enter the Solemn Mystery of this Lord's Holiness. His Mode of Dwelling—the Act of His Existence—is Superabundant Rest, Sabbath Peace, the Unicity beyond all image and form. As mortals given the exceeding gift of thinking this thought, we of course must reckon with the relation of our poor, finite words and cognition, to the Blinding Light who is God in His Mysterious Unity. But first we must simply set down the metaphysical realities of the Holy Trinity in their Mode of Distinction and their Greater Mode of Unicity; we *confess* this. Below we must consider more fully the relation of the Divine Perfections of the One Nature to the Triune Procession(s) and Persons. But here we must affirm directly that for Almighty God to be *Natura* is to be Holy Flame.

The Processional Life of the Divine Nature simply *is* that Nature under the description and Mode of Life. We do not retreat one step back from the Objectivity and Obdurate Reality of Almighty God: He is *there*, a Concrete Mystery in and beyond the cosmos He has made. But the Holiness of God teaches us to say that this Divine Object, this Deitas, lives and moves: The Nature *proceeds*. That is what it means to say that God is Fire. So, the dogma of Trinity is not advanced, I say, by considering "constituents," so to say, of the doctrine—the Processions, the Relations, the Properties or Notions, the Persons, the Nature—and, in some such way, ordering them and layering them, one on the other, or some subdivision artfully placed within the whole. In such a schema the fear of multiplying the metaphysical elements without constraint or purpose seems to hover over the whole. To this fear, parsimony lies close at hand. Why all these distinctions and sophisticated relations, we might ask when parsimony takes the upper hand, these seemingly baroque coordinates for the God who is One? Would not Occam's razor be better wielded here? So critics of this style of dogmatic construction might well say. The Mystery of the Holy Trinity, then, cannot be a bare exercise in conceptual refinement, each element coordinated with the next, the full constituents piled up into a single, Immeasurable, Articulated Whole. It is this path to the dogma that has lent the doctrine of the Trinity its air of refined impossibility, its conceptual splendor in the ruin of an implausible doctrinal edifice. All true. Yet we may stand back all the same to admire the metaphysical heavy lifting that is exercised in such doctrinal treatments. (One cannot help thinking of Bernard Lonergan's magnificent technical bravura in his volumes on speculative Trinitarianism.)[30] More worrisome to proper Trinitarian doctrine, I say, is our habitual reversion to lists. The traditional schematic, beloved of catechists across the church, of a Holy Triangle, with arrows drawn, labeled and directed, among the Persons, cannot in truth serve the Fiery Glory who is the Triune Lord. It serves a royal purpose as visual instruction in the terms, the taxis, the Names, and the relatio, in simple, geometric forms, but it can be little more than a formula, a second-order catalogue of the rubrics of this Mystery. Such linguistic rules, grammatical and visual, for dogmatic construction must yield to the splendor of biblical teaching. For Holy Scripture tells another story.

In Scripture, we see the Heavenly Fire consuming the offerings, a Sovereign Explosion that consumes sinner and sin-offering, in One dangerous Cataclysm. It is a Divine Holocaust. The dogma of Trinity must comport with this Combustion; it must elaborate and honor It. The Procession of this Living Holiness must be Unitary in its Doubling; It must be the Life of the Utterly Unique, Transcendent God. Yet we must also speak of the *intentionality*, the *purposefulness* of the Living God. He is not simply Alive, "sentient," so to say; He is not "random" Motion, not arbitrary or chaotic. He is the Utterly Rational Being; He is Ratio, Structure, Logos, Verbum.

The Processional Life of God ends, is defined, in the Person of the Son, the Word of God. The Heavenly Fire races out from the Most Holy Place for a purpose, a Telos: It is to begin the sacrificial cultus, to consume the slain in a single, incendiary Flame. Just so, this Fiery Glory consumes and slays the sons of Aaron, a Cauterizing and Wrathful Flame that will root out sin from the earth. We must speak of Procession, then, as directed toward an End, a Telos. Fire *generates* Heat. But It does so in the odd, analytic mode that is the Reality of the Exceeding Mystery of God: Fire just is Heat. Fire "contains" Heat, so to say, as Kant's analytic subject "contains" its predicate: we "look within" in order to find the same, the whole. (To be sure, we must remain wary of such Kantian forays, for we discovered earlier, the analytic distinction prompts its own riddles, its own delicate problems of necessity and distinction. Yet this Kantian notion shadows its Exceeding Dissimilarity, its Greater Unlikeness in Likeness, because the Fire that is Divine Glory "contains" as Its Identity the Heat that consumes the first fruits of the altar. This is an analytic doubling.) The inauguration of the tabernacle sacrifice manifests to us this inner Life of God, Its Dynamism that is a Fiery Heat, a Molten Flame. So, we learn from Holy Scripture that Fire is Heat, Living Heat. The Fire is the Living Nature of the Son. But we learn more. The Fire that issues forth from God and as God is Spirit, the Ascending Gift.

The Fire that escapes from the Holy of Holies is the Proceeding of the Spirit, for God is Spirit. In just this way the Spirit in the Upper Room rests on the assembly as tongues of Fire; in just this way, Elijah is lifted up into the Heavenly Places by the Fiery Chariot, the Spirit who ascends with the living, prophetic offering; in just this way, the Spirit's Utterance in Jeremiah is the Fire raging in his bones, tearing words from his mouth, reducing his silence to ash; in just this way, the Mysterious Flame of God and His Censer of

Smoke passes through the blood-red pieces of Abraham's sacrifice, sealing the covenant, covering the father of the faith in the Spiritual Darkness that is the Holy God in His Transcendent Nearness. The fearful and terrible judge Samson lives by the Fiery Spirit. It descends on him as a Rushing Force, impelling and compelling, reducing to ash the bonds that tied him as prisoner, a liberation for the one who waged war with fire. The Holy Spirit of the Lord, Isaiah tells us, entered deep into Moses and his people, marching with them as Fire and Cloud, through wilderness and the terrible depths; "His Presence saved them, He lifted them up and carried them all the days of old; the Spirit of the Lord gave them rest" (Is 63. 9–14). The Lord Christ baptizes with the Holy Spirit and with Fire, and with Unquenchable Fire will he burn our chaff, purifying us at great cost as are the sons of Levi. In the apocalyptic vision to St. John, the Spirit joins the seers to the Fiery visio Dei, the Lord as unspeakable glory, outstripping the jewels of His Throne, and from Him issue Lightning and Thunder, igniting the seven torches, the seven spirits of God (Rev 4. 2–5). The Fire that is the Processional Life of God is distinctly identified with the Spirit. It is His Mighty Rushing; His Free, Unbounded Wind; His Leaping Flames; His Procession.

So, we must say that the Movement, the Processional Life of God, proclaims the Realm of the Holy Spirit. His is the common, the unspecified, the utterly free Procession, the Divine Fire. It belongs with special dignity to Him. This is what it means to say that God Himself is Holy and Spiritual, the Holy Spirit. In this, Hegel is prescient: Spirit is the Name of God, His particular Character and Reality. And not just Hegel! God is Spirit, Christ tells us in the Gospel of John, the Ethereal and Utterly True Spirit, worshipped as earthly analogue in spirit and truth. But "analytically contained," enfolded within the One Procession is the Burning

Heat, who is Son of God. Here we may speak here more plainly, more traditionally, of perichoresis, the mutual Indwelling of the Processions of God. It is often said that the Triune Persons indwell One Another, a theme enunciated by Augustine and promoted as the source of unity by many modern Orthodox. But here we seek to intertwine or enclose the Procession of Generation within Inspiration, the Fire that rushes down like a Cascade from Mountain Springs. Not simply the Divine Termini, the Persons but also the Movement or Processional Life that issues in Them are related to One Another as an Indwelt Unity. It is Doubled. The radiant Heat that just is Fire exists within the Procession, the Light that is Spirit. The tabernacle Fire; the eternal flame that is never quenched in the temple; the Fire rained down from Heaven on the water-drenched sacrifice of Elijah; the Holy Fire the disciples plead to come down and consume the ungodly: all these *burn*. There is no sacrifice, no purifying judgment, no holocaust without the scorching Heat that proceeds from the Living God. What lesson in Trinitarian Mystery is Holy Scripture teaching here? How should we understand the One Procession that is, in another sense, twofold? Can we say something more than the analogies, commonsense and philosophical, that have so far been enlisted in the cause? How is Eternal Generation an Aspect or Mode of the Spirit's Radiant Procession?

We begin by taking up directly the question that surely haunts any Trinitarian doctrine such as this one, that is pressed full to the brim with talk of Unicity and Modes of Predication: Is this all Sabellian? We want to address directly the modalist threat that must hover over any treatment, such as is this one, where Unicity governs the doctrine of the Divine Procession(s), the whole of the doctrine of Trinity. We cannot overlook, also, the striking parallel of this Fire imagery to the analogy Epiphanius attributes to

Sabellius: the Father as the disk of the sun, the Son as its light, the Spirit as its warmth, all One God. (To be sure, the sun, its heat, and its rays as Trinitarian imagery are everywhere in the fathers.) More significant still is Sabellius's appeal to the Shema, the call to Divine Unity in Deuteronomy 6. Always he cites this text, Epiphanius complains; like this systematics, he seems to return time and again to the same well. According to the tantalizingly brief summary in the *Panarion*,[31] Sabellius taught a doctrine of God that tied the Persons of the Godhead to what scholastics would term the Missions—the economy of salvation, God come to us. The Persons and Processions do not belong to the inner Life of God; there are no real relations in the Godhead, to speak in later idiom. It is the One God, Sabellius seems to have taught, who appears in the history of salvation—now as Father, the Voice from Heaven, and the Lofty One; now as the Son, sent to redeem the sin-sick world; now as Spirit, to return the hearts of the children to their Parent. Such a doctrine of God appears to lean heavily—as does this theology—on the act of "seeing as." Indeed, it appears that Sabellius could use, too, the idiom of speaking: the Son is the Word of the Father, spoken into a silent and lost world. These are *Modes* of God, His passing Presence in the realm of things and time. In all this, God is Supremely One. When Jesus announces in the Fourth Gospel that He and the Father are One, Sabellius appears to have excavated the golden text. All the Persons, all the Missions, all the Nature are "simply One," One utterly Unique Lord.

Now, of course, this is drawn exclusively from one polemical source, Epiphanius, and belongs to a doctrinal era removed some century and a half from Sabellius's work and life. The *Panarion* rarely quotes Sabellius directly and at length; the whole treatise may fit more closely the genre of ancient handbook and heresiology than an analysis based on direct knowledge of sources. Everything else that Sabellius may have written is lost or destroyed. But he became the eponymous head of Monarchian modalism, a school of early Trinitarianism—or is it only early?—that grounded Divine Unity in the Father and expressed the saving significance of the Persons, their Guises of the Father, in their Modes of Presence in the economy. Oneness was All.

Under this description Sabellianism lived on as Trinitarian heresy for the schoolmen. Thomas sums up Sabellian modalism this way. In the *Prima Pars*, Thomas takes up directly the question before us, whether there are real relations in God. After raising objections from Boethius, he cites—rarely—an unvarnished dogmatic argument and definition for the *sed contra*: "The Father is denominated only from paternity; and the Son only from filiation. Therefore if no real paternity or filiation existed in God, it would follow that God is not really Father or Son, but only in our manner of understanding; and this is the Sabellian heresy."[32] Now here we find a definition of Sabellianism that rests on Procession. The issue at stake, Thomas thinks, is whether the Processional Relation, Father to Son, belongs to God realiter or, instead, exists only *in mentem*. Thomas is alive always to the distinction between linguistic and conceptual insight about God and the metaphysical reality of God's Property, Essence, and Persons. Might all this talk of Generation be simply that—talk of mere mortals about the Surpassing Mystery who is God? To secure Thomistic Trinitarianism against Sabellianism, the Processions and Real Relations are predicated directly, metaphysically, and properly of God Himself. Realism is the bulwark here against heresy. In this narrow sense, of course, any theology such as this one can evade the Sabellian heresy so long as real predication is affirmed and the Eternal Generation of the Son assigned to the inner Life of the God. Certainly, I affirm these things! But we may ask whether such a quick and superficial reply to Thomas's charge actually registers the *force* of his analysis. Is the deeper question of modalism properly addressed in this way? These questions are not easily answered.

On one hand, it may seem odd to even attempt to rebuke Sabellianism by citing the Latin doctors of the church. Augustine, and Thomas, his faithful disciple in these matters, stand accused by some Orthodox and some philo-Orthodox Westerners of promoting a doctrine of Trinity that is little more than modalism in creedal dress. Cardinal instances appear to be Karl Rahner—he speaks daringly of Modes of Subsistence (*Subsistenzweisen*)—and Karl Barth, at least in early form, who wrote frankly of *Seinsweisen*, Modes of God's own Reality or Being. And these were the "fathers of modern Trinitarian revival"! (Of course, their aims were entirely otherwise: to correct an unthinking and pious virtual unitarianism.) Consider, too, the outsized influence of Schleiermacher and his easy conscience in regard to Sabellius. The *Glaubenslehre*'s steady concentration on the economy appears primed for the "modes of mission" that Epiphanius assigns to Sabellius. We think, too, of Schleiermacher's late essay on Sabellius in contrast with the Trinitarianism of Athanasius. All these giants of the Latin tradition appear far advanced in the cause of Divine Oneness and on the scales weighting Transcendent Unity over distinction and difference. Or so the critics charge. Think, for example, of de Régnon (perhaps more supporter than critic,) or in more contemporary idiom, Jürgen Moltmann's or Catherine LaCugna's harsh indictment of the Latin tradition in Trinitarianism. To satisfy Augustine's or Thomas's standard for real relation in God may be to pass a very low bar indeed.

On the other hand, much of this discussion among many of the modern Western Trinitarians, and their critics, turns on the status and nomenclature for the Divine Persons; far less effort is expended on the Processions, Thomas's starting point in the entire treatise *De*

Deo Trino. We can remain neutral, for a time, on such controverted historical and conceptual problems in the doctrine of the Persons. Here, we must take up the Processional Life of God in a proper doctrine of the Holy Trinity. In my view, many conceptual and scriptural reasons buttress the scholastic starting point in the Divine Processions, and I am persuaded that Thomas is in the right here. So, a deeper reflection on the problem of Sabellian modalism in the Western teaching on the Processions is entirely fitting and, moreover, answers the larger task of gaining cultural legitimacy for the Trinitarian Mystery within this modern, intellectual world. In a deeper sense, then, we may ask: Just what is Sabellianism?

Could we not say that it is a conceptual inability to recognize the very idea of Procession? It is customary in surveys of Trinitarian doctrine to assign Sabellianism to a heterodox notion of the *Persons*: the Person of the Son, say, exists only as the Redeemer of the fallen world; He does not exist Eternally, just because He is the One God, now in the act of saving the lost. Sabellianism, in this view, constitutes a heresy not of Procession but rather of Person, the earthly Mission of the Divine Persons. The Deity of the Son or Spirit is never in doubt; indeed, Sabellius may be taken as an early advocate for the full Deity of these Persons. Yet this confession rests, it is thought, on a denial of their Immanent Reality: these Persons are simply earthly Modes of the Heavenly Father. But such an assessment does not grasp the deeper dimension of the Processions in the Eternal Act who is God. On my reading, Sabellianism fails to identify the proper locus for the Divine Life: it considers the Act of God as a work ad extra. The Processions are collapsed into a specific form of the works of God in creation. We can see something of this metaphysical retraction in so-called functional accounts of the Divine Perfections: we do not know, such theologians say, what God is in Himself but rather know only how God acts toward the world. To say that God is good is to affirm that God acts benevolently toward creatures. In the famous quaestio 13 of the *Summa*, Thomas assigns such a view to Maimonides, but it would belong, in a larger sense, to any Theist who held that God's inner Life could not be known—perhaps It is impenetrable darkness—but we can forge Divine Predicates out of actions perceived within and around us creatures. Sabellianism in the deeper sense is a movement within this larger school. We see God in the economy, His utter Generosity and Saving Grace; we rest our intellect there and construct our doctrine of God out of these remnants of Divine Liberality. It is antispeculative in a strong sense. The pronounced emphasis on the economy in the ante-Nicene era appears to meet its apogee in Sabellius. The disk of the Sun is turned toward us; we receive Its Light and Warmth, and we give thanks and ask for nothing more.

The impulse toward this form of Sabellianism is strong indeed in modern theology. Just this is relationalism in theology, the Divine Object known *only* in the creaturely subject, and known from Its effects, Its relatio to creatures. The *Critique of Pure Reason* taught us to consider relationalism the only possible critical form of theological knowledge, but the strong bent among Protestant divines toward a religion of the *benefici Christi* schooled us more strongly still in the current neuralgia toward transcendental metaphysics. We will not overcome this dogmatic austerity by a simple assent to Persons really "in God." In a very different setting, Calvin proposed something along these lines: we simply affirm three Persons in one Nature (perhaps, too, one Nature in three Persons) and guard zealously the border between piety and vain curiosity about those Divine things that must not be pried into. But I do not want to lump Calvin immediately in with a distinctly modern discussion. An ocean of revolution in thought and arms stand between the *Institutes* and our work today, so we would be wise to place Calvin's hesitancy about the Divine Processions in another camp from the modern preoccupation with the economy.

For us moderns, however, the Processions threaten to collapse into the *opera ad extra*—God is as He is with us—and the Persons of the Incarnate Lord and the Outpoured Spirit are the Means by which these Acts are distinguished from the Omnipresence of God and His works of Governance and Conservation. To large measure, the historical economy highlights the Divine Persons as the central concept in the dogma of Trinity. They are its matrix for development of the dogma and its centerpiece in preaching, exegesis, and catechesis. Technically, it is assumed that a bare notional assent to "Preexistence" or to the Eternal Reality of the Persons "in" God will suffice to stem Sabellianism. Such an assumption is a species of the "grounding problem," the notion that some visible, earthly reality has its origin or source (often noncausal) in another. (We witnessed its dangerous attractions in the doctrine of the Divine Perfections some time ago.) In Trinitarian theology, this assumption may take a transcendental form, in the Kantian sense, where the Eternal Persons are proposed as the "conditions for the possibility" of economic Missions. Here we do not metaphysically specify or "fill out" the Divine Posits; indeed, if we follow Kant faithfully, we cannot. But we say that, really, eternally, and in truth, God is in three Persons, and this is the only full and proper Ground of the Incarnation and gift of the Holy Spirit.

Out of inclinations of this kind, Christian teaching on the Mystery of the Trinity is often reduced to a bare affirmation of Person and Nature, three in one, one in three. An ordering often accompanies this affirmation, so that the Persons have an Internal Relation, it is thought, of Origin, and perhaps, more daringly, of Mutual Opposition. But just this is to lose sight of the crucial place of Procession in the Mystery of Trinity. Without Procession, the Divine Persons are left to take up residence, so to say, within the Reality or Nature or Substance of God or, in more radical forms of social Trinitarianism, to substitute for It. The "Personal inclination toward Another" does indeed give an ordering of One to Another, and a Relatio. But such mutual ordering does not ward off firmly the air of constituting parts in a Divine Whole; such a suspicion cannot but intrude on a doctrine of God in which Something resides.

Catholic critics of Calvin complained that his Trinitarianism denied the homoousion (of One Being or Substance) of the Son to the Father. But that criticism seems to me to aim wide of the mark. For Calvin and many Reformed theologians, indeed many modern Trinitarians, tout court, it is an article of faith that the Persons are Equal and without Subordination, One to the Other. The Persons, they would say, are Homoousia in every way that counts: fully God, fully and equally Personal, fully entwined or indwelling the Other. What cannot be said in such Reformed and modernist accounts is the *Life*, the Divine Act, that *communicates* the Divine Nature to and among the Persons. (Just that silence about the Divine Nature gave rise to Catholic criticism in the first place.) The Procession, the Divine Fire that just is God in Act, does not govern and animate the entire Relatio of the Divine Persons. The Fiery Descent of the Son, His Generation, which is Fire blazing forth from the Holy of Holies: this cannot be upheld in a Trinitarianism that speaks only of Persons and their Relations. The oversized importance of the economy in recent Trinitarian doctrine traces this Sabellian-like pattern—the Reality of God is known and can be known only by reflection on the *Opera Dei ad extra*, the history of God us-ward. Even the move made to unify the "economic" and "Immanent" Trinity, popular since Rahner and Barth, cannot in the end stem the Sabellian-like tide in the modern doctrine of God. For the *direction*, the impulse in these Trinitarian doctrines, is *from* the economy *to* the Immanence: as below, so above. That this imports much mischief into the doctrine of God is plain to the eye—but the key worry here is that the inner Life of God has been sharply attenuated, indeed eclipsed by the Works of redemption, which now inform and metaphysically fill out the Tri-Personal Life of God.

We might say that such moves in the doctrine of Trinity have impelled the collapse of the Immanent Trinity into the economy, elevating the concept for some and detemporalizing it for others. The Immanent Trinity *just is* the economic, expressed as "bare counterfactual" or Divine Ground or, stronger still, as Eternal refraction of the Acts of redemption. "We have to do with God," Calvin solemnly intones; but the God we moderns have traffic with seems to be a Being enclosed in the creation He has made. The very notion of Transcendence or Immanence in Trinity serves only as limit concept: It must stand behind what we see, but if it is to be more than a bare "I know not what," it can only mirror and be identified by the salvation we know. Trinity has become Christology in this very strong sense. It is little wonder that the counterpart to this modern Christocentric Trinity is a severe agnosticism about the metaphysics of Trinity altogether. These are twin movements, held together by a single maxim: about the High God we must not say too much—that it is, so to say, but not what it is.

In this way, the conceptual room needed to distinguish the providential works of God from His Saving Acts has been severely foreshortened, for the whole Christian knowledge of God takes place on the same level, the mundane record of God's Presence among us. But this is not simply a matter of weighting the Immanent Trinity over the economic, say! Rather, it is better said that the conceptual distinction between Procession and Mission has not been secured, for in these modern theologians, the Procession is but the bare Ground or Postulate of the earthly Mission. This carries the odd effect of rendering uniform all the works of God— *Opera Dei ad extra unum sunt*—because the Work, the Act, *as such* can be picked out only from the telos or effect: Governance differs from Incarnation only by its terminus, the course of nations, or the whole course of Christ's obedience. But the great work assigned to the Divine Procession is to set forth a unique Act of God, different in kind from all others, the Act that just is the Life of God Himself. The Procession(s) are the *Depth* of God, His Positive Infinity; nothing else is this or like it; it is the Greater Unlikeness, and it is Eternal in the Heavens. It is not enough to say that the Tongues of the Fiery Spirit are not the birth of the Messiah or that the Spirit of prophecy was given to a son of the covenant, to Jeremiah and not to the leaders of the nations, though it be the Assyrians or Ethiopians, both children of Providence. These worldly events are unique in a weak sense: they differ as do all temporal events by their particular character, purpose, and identity. What Procession properly means for dogmatic theology is that there exists an Act who is God, Utterly Unique, beyond kind and genre, Enacting the Mystery of Eternity. Anything that partakes of this Act, as do the Divine Missions, are *as such* distinct from all events on earth, even the Divine Work of God's Omnipotence and Wisdom. This is because the Perfections of God are communicated in a transcendental relation, the showering of the earth by the fertile Goodness of God's own Perfect Light. But the Acts of Mission differ radically from this Provident and universal Liberality; They are the Termini of the Unique Act who is God, the Fire of the Holy One. The Being of God, His inner Majesty, is the Reality, Ground, and Life of the Incarnation and Gift of the Spirit.

Now, the modern collapse of Procession into Mission—and the attendant confusion of Omnipresence, Incarnation, and Providence into the general Works of God—digs down the intellectual architecture that sets forth this inner Life of God. This is not Sabellianism in the classic sense; I do not mean to accuse modern Trinitarianism of major heresy! But there is a pattern at work here, an instinct toward the earthly and historical record of salvation that brings the larger wardrobe of Modalism into view. A full and resolute turn from Sabellianism requires an insistence on the proper direction in the Mystery of Trinity, *from* Above *to* below, and beyond that, to the Dynamism of the inner Life, the metaphysically Real and Living Processions of God. The Processional Life of God makes God *One*; It is God in Act, His own Modus of Unicity and Distinction and Holiness, that terminates in the Persons and whose Subsistence is the Perfection of Divine Procession. The Procession of the Spirit, the Consummation of the Divine Life, is the Finality of the Fiery Descent from Father to Son, the Hallowing and Perfection of the One Holy God. It is often said that heresy is the cause of the church's clarification of doctrine; it reveals and sums up what had been left inarticulate or confused in earlier teaching. Sabellianism serves just this purpose: it forces our hand on the Divine Processions.

The solution, however, will not spring from attempting to stir up drama in the Divine Inner Courts. It is not enough—or perhaps we should say, far too much—to aim to enliven the inner Reality of God by proposing a Divine Colloquy among the Persons. We will not uncover the Mysterious Holiness of God by importing into its Sanctuary a Divine Pactum, or a Love Exchange among Divine Persons. All hail the Victorines! But we cannot satisfy the demand for a Supercelestial Unity, an Absolute and Transcendent Unicity, that Lateran IV codifies, by proposing as divine analogy the conversation among intimates, or the willing and eager obedience of the perfect servant. In such schemas we simply lay down our arms; there is no defense here against a god of three wills, three acts, three minds. It is as though we took the worst reading of Gregory of Nyssa to heart and transported Peter, James, and John into the Eternal Godhead. Not so can we defend the One God of Israel! Certainly, we could tag all such objections as shopworn, Hellenistic thinking, hidebound and unwilling to consider fresh forms of metaphysics, scriptural ones. Such things, I believe, can be *said*; Oneness along these lines, I say, cannot be *thought*. We cannot in truth *execute* the thought of Unicity through the images of divine conversation or command: this indeed is the very thing that worries critics about Nyssa and, in converse, worried Sabellius about Christian confession of the Son and Spirit. Sabellius believed he could ward off the threat to proper Monotheism by moving the Divine Life and Persons to the economy: like a Divine Shooting Star, the One Comet would burst forth into distinct Streams and Sparks when it entered our atmosphere, our dark night. (Here perhaps the overworn analogy of the particle-wave theory of light might be best applied: for the "unity"—or, perhaps better, indeterminacy—of the nature of light is made distinct as particle or wave by the intervention of the "economy," the apparatus of the laboratory.)

Sabellius performed the great service of *seeing* the Divine Processions; but he did not see where They belonged. Sabellius understood that Processions were the key to Divine Unity; he grasped that central and inalienable truth, and that is his great merit. But he placed those Processions in the world of God's redeeming: the One God acting as Savior, as Hallower, in a history bound for Glory. Thomas, too, saw that Sabellianism concerned Processions, the Act of Paternity and Filiation. These, he said, must be in God *realiter*, in order that the Redeemer and Spirit be God, sent from God. In scholastic terms: the Life of God must be understood to consist in two forms, Procession and Mission, or better, One Procession with Eternal and temporal Ends. Within the Immanent Life of God, real relations exist, not simply a relation in mentem, in our thought of God, but Mutual Giving and Being Given, which just is the Personal Life of God.

In our day, the doctrine of Trinity needs a robust recovery of the Engine of Unity, the Divine Procession. The central task in the Mystery of the Holy Trinity, as I see it, is to worship, confess, and think through the Divine Act of God, His Holy Life. The sacrificial cultus of Israel just is the Processional Life, the Fire who is God, manifested before prophet, priest, and people. The Procession(s) communicate the Nature, yes. The scholastic terms *Generation* and *Spiration* convey this truth. But the central point is not the conveyance of Deitas, true though that be, but rather the Cascading Life of God that is Perfected, Terminated, Hallowed from Father, in Son, and Spirit. The *Divine Act* of sacrifice is the inner Life of God, made manifest on altar and in smoke. To think this thought is to reflect deeply on the Perfect and Infinite Life of God, the Triune monotheism of the Holy One of Israel. So, in the end, I believe we can say that a doctrine of the Holy Trinity that begins and focuses intently on the Divine Fire, the Mode of Unicity and Unlikeness, has learned from Sabellius, yes, and is grateful for his keen and penetrating view of the whole. But it parts decisively from him, for the Processional Life of God is not a matter of the economy, first and principally, but foundationally, wonderfully, transcendentally, it is a matter, *the Matter* of Deitas in Act, the Life of the Holy, Tri-Personed God.

So, we return to the Divine Act of Procession. The Fiery Act who is God is both Heat and Light but most consummately Light. The Processional Act is principally and most specifically Spirit; It also is Son, Son of the Father. This counts in the doctrine of

Trinity—it is no arcana—because the Fiery Act of God has *per Se*, a Movement, a Direction and Telos. No Dynamic Nature of God is random, inchoate. God's Nature is not simply *impulse*, a celestial scattering of Light. No! This is no more persuasive or proper than the notion, widely scorned in our era, that God is "static," "inert," a "lifeless identity," as Rahner charged, with Hegelian flourish. No, the Holy One moves from His own sanctuary to the altar and to the fragrant offering, ascending. Our God is a Consuming Flame, and His Act eternally rushes toward Consummation. It is the Perfect Act. Now, a Perfect Act leaves nothing behind: all the remnants are gathered up, twelve baskets full. The Origin of the Fiery Blaze is not lost or hidden, nor is the Scorching Blaze forgotten, the Heat that turns death into Offering, but All is gathered up in the Cloud of Light, the Sweet Savor of the Spirit, who ascends back up, into Heaven, the Infinite Light. This Heavenly Pattern of Exit and Return, *Exitus et Reditus*, just is the Processional Life of God. Because this is the Utterly Unique, the Utterly Simple One, the Likeness in the Greater Unlikeness, the Processional Moments are not distinct Events, nor do they steal away as the Spirit rushes onward, downward to Its Perfect End. Rather, this is *Eternal* Act. As we can say in the A Series of time, here below time is a creature passing away: the past is lost—that is why it is considered inalterable or necessary—and the present exists as a hair's breadth, fragile and windblown, all lost to us as the future bears down on us from a dark beyond. Not so is Eternity. It just *is* God, because it is the Act that does not pass away. Its Future, Its Perfect Consummation, just is the Permanence, the Hallowing, of the Entire Fiery Movement, from the Innermost Courts to the Heavenly Return. In famous words, Hegel spoke of this Consummation as the "Absolute Religion," when God becomes Absolute—that is, must be Eternally Absolute, Always and Everywhere. God is the Wonder, the Mystery where the Past, the Origin, is Eternally Present, Perfectly Held, in the Future Completion. God is Holy Spirit, because All are alive in Him.

§5.4. The Act of Sacrifice as Triune Holiness

The Holy Trinity is manifest in the sacrifice of the altar: that is the next step we must take. After clarifying the character and unity and distinction of the Divine Procession, we now turn to the core of the scriptural witness: Israel's covenant sacrifice, in tabernacle and temple. We have spoken of the Fire that surges out from the Most Holy Place, and Its Heat and Light that descends, purifies, chars, and ascends; now we take up the practice of sacrifice itself. In the mystery of sacrifice, we find enacted the Heavenly Life of God as Tri-Personed Being. Our invitation and task now is to explore just that cultus and its teaching for our worship of the Most Holy God.

We return to Milgrom's central conviction: that sacrifice is an offering to Deity. We noted above the theme, sometimes elaborate, sometimes homespun, of ancient temple cultus as food, set forth before a god, in a palace, complete with dining room and resting place. Making offering to a Deity brings gift to the worshipper but also cost. *Sacrifice*—making holy—gathers up these ritual acts into a single term: it is heavenly food, choice and costly, offered in the heavenly precincts, that in smoke and ash pleases and placates the gods. As Milgrom deftly explains, ancient Israel is not afraid to join its neighbors in this near-universal cultus of divine feeding. It takes the lingua franca of ancient culture and elevates it to Torah, the Command and Grace of the Living God. And we say more: in that ancient act, the Mighty Lord of Israel enacts His own Life, His own Triune Self-Offering that is the Eternal Flame, the Eternal Sabbath who is God. We turn our intellectual worship to face that altar now.

The first thing we must say is that in the inauguration of the cultus, God Himself makes the Offering. This is the distinctive, the decisive element in the Levitical institution of the cult. God Himself provides the animals for the burnt offerings; and He Himself lights and constitutes the first Fire. "Here is the fire and the wood; but where is the ram for the whole burnt offering?" Isaac asks his father, Abraham, in the terrible, long approach to Mount Moriah, the place of sacrifice. "The Lord Himself will provide the animal for the holocaust, my son," Abraham replies. The searing power of the Akida sums up, as can nothing else, the terror and grace of Holy Sacrifice. Barth relied on this remarkable verse in Genesis 22 to head up his treatment of providence, and indeed, the Lord here is provident for He Himself provides the substitute for an annihilating death. But even more than providence we hear, in this searing narrative, foundational to Genesis, the properties of *sacrifice*: The Lord Himself will make the offering and make it holy. For its part, Leviticus makes clear that the animals acceptable for offering to God must be from the herd or the flock—wild animals may not be used for the rite of sacrifice. Instead the cattle, sheep, and goats that sustain Israel's life will become the slaughtered offering, reduced by fire to an ascending cloud of fragrant smoke, lifted up to Heaven. These animals, Holy Scripture tells us, are given to humanity by God: He gave them to the children of Noah as food, when the floodwaters receded at last from the earth. All the birds of the air and the cattle in their thousands are mine, says the Lord; He is the Creator of all living flesh, including the animals that will become the domestic wealth of Israel. Out of shepherds and herdsmen the Covenant Lord forges Israel. Its kings will be taken from the flock or the herd; its matriarchs will draw water and pasture the sheep. Certainly, the Creator has made every living thing, and from each of the natural kinds, the clean and unclean, a pair were saved: that is the Lord God's gracious love for every creature that has within it the breath of life. But the cattle, sheep, and goat are particular possessions of the Lord God. He considers them "clean." Paradigmatically, these three parts, the hoof and chew the cud: we might say that they fully exemplify the animal that walks upon the earth. Indeed, the Hebrew word translated as "cattle" in most of the Old Testament could also be translated simply as "animal" or "beast." Cattle for Israel are the paradigmatic animal. They are given to Israel as the perfect sacrifice: the bull, first and lavishly, but also the unblemished kid or lamb, the herd animal without fault or injury. They become the prized possession of Israel, itself the prized possession of the Covenant God, because they make possible, they hallow, the worship of the people Israel. They place sacrifice in the center of Israel's life, a blazing core of sanctity in the midst of a pastoral nation. Leviticus shows us that Israel and the sacrificial cultus go hand in hand: sacrifice makes Israel, forges it by fire; Israel makes sacrifice by covenant law, offering the divine gift of the flock and herd, to the One who created and gave them, gave them up.

All this we see in condensed form in a psalm of the Holiness School, Psalm 50, a psalm of Asaph, Levite, and musician before the ark of the covenant. Here the Lord of Fiery Glory presents Himself: "Before Him is a devouring Fire, and a mighty tempest all around Him." As in the Prophets, the Psalmist recounts the Lord God bringing His people into the dock: "Hear, O my people, and I will speak, O Israel, I will testify against you." Shadows from the apostasy in the wilderness fall over this psalm, too: "You hate discipline; you cast My words behind your back; you make friends with evil; you slander your own mother's child." The Divine rebuke: "What right have you to recite my statutes or take my covenant on your lips?" For, the Holy One says, "you did these things and I remained silent, and you thought that I was like you."

Here, in the idiom of the psalmist, is the metaphysical claim of the Lord God's Utter Uniqueness, His surpassing and ever-greater Unlikeness, and, even more, of His Obdurate Holiness. The Fiery Surface of God is burnished with justice; He holds in contempt of court the pious who violate the righteous covenant under cloak of darkness. It is in this brutal clash between the Justice of God and Israel's sin that sacrifice takes center stage. The sacrificial cultus exists in the midst of a chosen and sinful nation to hallow ground for the Indwelling of the Holy God. The Domestic Quarters, Courtyard, and Holy Places stand exactly in the middle and midst of Israel so that a space may be conserved and opened up for Holiness, the Radiant Fire who is God. The Covenant Lord does not reject sacrifice—this is not the prophetic animus—and in fact confirms it: I do not reject your sacrifices or rebuke you for them, He tells His people. Rather, the Holy One demands the cultus be *enacted* in the people's Holiness. As the Holiness School underscores: "Be ye therefore holy, as I, the Lord, am Holy." Then, the decisive instruction about sacrifice, food, and offering: "I take no bull from your stalls, nor goats from your folds, for every wild animal of the forest is mine, the cattle on a thousand hills. I know all the birds of the air, and all that moves in the field is mine." Here the psalmist underscores the religious *reality* of sacrifice: The people Israel do not bring offerings to God; He possesses all; He gives all Israel has, so that sacrifice may be made. The psalmist ridicules the older, vulgar notion of sacrifice as literal feeding: "Do you think I eat the flesh of bulls or drink the blood of goats? If I were hungry, I would not tell you, for the whole world and all that is in it is mine." Rather, sacrifice is the worship of covenant fidelity—"paying vows to the Most High"—and the act of thanksgiving. For the sacrifice of well-being, the thank offering, *feeds Israel*; the people themselves feast that day on the flesh they have slaughtered and laid on the altar of the tabernacle. As manna is God's own gift to a rebellious and starving people, and the bread and fish food enough for the desperate crowds, who longed for the bread that would last, so the sacrifice that is taught in covenant law comes from God. It is Most Holy.

Psalm 50 tells us the nature of sacrifice: it is God's own Life as Gift. Our task now is to reflect on that Sacrificial Life as Trinity, as the Mystery of the Dark Depths of God and His Eternal Divine Self-Giving. Sacrifice is the Structure of the Infinite God, His consummate and absolute Self-Act. Unlike the father of the faith, the Lord God brings both the Fire and the Ram; He provides the creaturely gifts and the consuming Flame. But this Divine Self-Gift is not done outside the covenant or the covenant people. Holy sacrifice *constitutes* Israel. So, we must examine Israel's own place in this act in order to glimpse its divine contours. The people are to *tithe*. They are to bring the first fruits and the offerings of thanksgiving; they are to lay down before God the choice parts of the whole, the food and livestock that sustain them. But sacrifice is not all feeding, not all thanksgiving and hurrahing in the harvest. Sacrifice, as Leviticus shows us, concerns *sin* and the remedy for sin. It comes in the midst of a rebellious house, a people wandered far away from the worship of the True God, in the very center of a tabernacle attended by priests who bring alien fire, who cannot bring "that Moses" back to mind, but offer up instead a molten bull, a calf and god of their own invention. In just this way, Leviticus relates the human story. It tells the grimy episode of the fall in cultic idiom; all human beings belong to this wayward and lost congregation. Our remedy comes from the Lord Himself. He will provide the law, the animal and grain, and emerge Himself as the Fire to make Sweet Savor before His Face. In His generosity, He permits us to bring offerings and come into His Courts. He allows us a share in this sacrificial work. His Gift becomes our offering, and we sinners meet Him there.

Now, we might well ask: Why does this work? Why is sacrifice the sure remedy for sin, known and unknown, intended and unintended? Why is it not simply a *gesture*, an act of contrition, or of self-denial? Why is it, in truth and in reality, *pleasing* to the Lord God? The entire controversy over cultic worship, indeed over prayer itself, is caught up in this simple question: Is there in truth a *transaction*, an event of *meeting*, in sacrifice that makes it not "magical" or, even less, hollow or "ceremonial," but on earth as in Heaven, a *deliverance*, a help, a cure in the blood? This, in cultic idiom, is the question of the Holy Trinity.

Sacrifice is prescribed, and a healing ordinance, just because it *encounters* and *echoes* the very Triune Life of God. Israel's sacrificial cultus is the sacred center point of the cosmos, the Beth-El, the holy axis on which the universe turns. The real work of the cosmos is being done there, as it is done on a thousand altars, in season and out, the work that has been given us creatures to do, to make offerings to God that are *conformed* to the very Being of God. We do not see this action aright if we imagine only under the categories of gift or tithe or self-denial: sacrifice is not primary and first, a work *we* do before the Holy One. To be sure, it carries the outer form of Milgrom's maxim: it is an offering to a god. It is creaturely and common, in just this proper sense. But Israel's cultus is an *exchange*, a *rescue*, just because it follows and imitates the Holy Life of God: the life of the sinner and the Divine Life of the Holy God meet on the altar of Israel. The sinner rests his or her hand on the animal to be slaughtered and burned: the offering becomes the sinner who brings the gift. Sacrifice becomes self-offering in just this gracious sense, that sinners need not be slaughtered and charred before God but may be given a redeemer, a helper who stands in their place and goes the dark way to death, bearing on its head the crown of the transgressor. But the Divine Life, which meets the animal in its death, the gift that is at once the sinner's and the Holy God, does not hold back in this way, nor receive the help of a substitute. God is Himself the *Go'el*, the Giver and the Gift. The Fiery Procession that is God moves out from the Dark Origin, the Unfathomable Depth of God, and descends down through Infinite Space, into the Offering that is God's own Life, His own Holy Gift. He lays down His Life. God is the Most Generous Giver in an absolute sense. He does not simply share and communicate His Perfections with creatures, though, to be sure, He does this. He does not simply permit an offering, or a creaturely working, of a petition to come before Him, though, again, He does this. But in Trinitarian Sacrifice, Almighty God gives *Himself*, His Life as the Distillate, the Concretion, of Deity. He is Molten Gift. The costly Breaking, the Plunging Down, the Life that is Blood: that is the Divine Generation, the Hiddenness poured out and made Manifest.

And wonderfully, that astonishing Self-Gift is not the *Goal*, the *Terminus*, of the Divine Life. Rather, Sacrifice, as Divine Act, is the Ascension of the Whole Burnt Offering back to the Origin, the Well of Life. God is Breaking, yes, and Self-Giving and Offering, yes again. And God is the Annihilating Fire that burns all the way down, all the way through. But that is not the very End of God! The sacrificial cultus that we are enjoined to see and enter into does not find its completion in the creature burned to ash or even in the blood smeared on altar and priest and sanctuary. No, the effective exchange, the peace forged between heaven and earth, comes to its fulfillment in the Rising Smoke, the Offering that is Savor, a Fragrance, the Heavenly Ascension. That is the Consummation of the Perfect Gift, that it receives this Fiery Self-Gift as its own Life and carries that Offering up into the Vast Reaches of the Infinite

God. The sacrificial cultus is perfected in the sweet savor that rises Heavenward—that is why the great and small of Israel turn their faces upward and watch the smoke, the chariot, the cloud and the Lord ascend. It is to Heaven that these go, and the sight of all is trained on that Heavenly calling. The Procession of the Spirit is the gathering up of the Offering, joining with It and raising It up, completing and returning It to the Giver of every good and perfect Gift. The Self-Offering that is God is turned from Ash to Glory, to the Superabundant Light that rises. Sacrifice as the Triune Life is Complete and Absolute in this return. It is Fire's Consummation and Glory. From all Eternity the Divine Procession moves out and down through Infinite Light, always Giving, always Pouring down in Heavenly Descent; always Gathering together, always Rising, returning Home. That is the Infinite Life of the Holy God.

The Triune Life is thus a single, complex act of the One God. The Processions of Generation and Procession are not distinct acts, issuing from diverse Actors. No! We are not asked to imagine that in the inner reaches of the Godhead, there are Three who "move" or "bend" or "love" One Another into reality. There are no more three agents in God than there are three wills. The Life of God is just that: His own Eternal and Infinite Self-Act. Just this is the Primal Mystery of the Father. We do not have a doctrine of God in which the Father acts in one way, the Son reacts or initiates action in another, and the Spirit in some such way receives or constitutes and initiates an act in a third. They do not "interact"! The conceptual problem of the number of Divine Processions is only deepened and rendered more obscure by a dogma that teaches in some fashion three distinct, enumerable acts that must be affirmed, in turn, as the One Divine Nature. It will be always a threat to the Exceeding Oneness of God to use a plural nominative pronoun—They—for the Divine Subject. Most certainly we must speak in this dogma about three Names, three Persons, and these terms must be shown in living, eternal relation. But there cannot be Three Divine Subjects, even in greatest intimacy: this, too, we have been taught by Lateran IV. We begin this doctrine, instead, with the Processional Life rather than the Persons to underscore just this axiom, that Almighty God is not a Community, not an Interplay among Divine Realities, and most certainly not an exchange among Transcendent Subjects. The Procession of God from the Primal Origin gives rise to the Persons; the Persons do not collectively execute and initiate acts Themselves. It is One Life.

Now, this has been a neuralgic point in many Trinitarian controversies. It seems that any dogma of Trinity that begins with the Persons courts the danger of three distinct and agential Subjects who must in some exceedingly demanding way become One. I say, a danger only, not a consequent. Were tritheism to be *entailed* by a priority given to the Divine Persons, it would have to be seen as a heretical starting point in dogma, a doctrinal disorder that contravenes scriptural teaching. But the Councils and tradition have not spoken this way, and I believe we should follow that lead. This is a conflict of the schools but an exacting one. The danger is *conceptual*, for there are constraints and connotations that we human subjects find exceedingly difficult to deny or see past. The intellectual dignity of the dogma rests, I believe, on our searching attempt to render coherent and persuasive the central tenets and arguments of the faith. It seems, for example, that our metaphysical conceptions rest on the priority of a subject or substance or agent over its acts or reception of another's action: hence, the Mysterious Primacy of the Father—the very idea of relation—rests on this priority of Subject over relation. It is for this very reason that Thomas's *equation* of Person with Subsistent Relation is profoundly taxing on the theological intellect. Schleiermacher's remarkable dialectical system is built out of the priority and interplay of subjects in their relations. It has been thought in some circles that a firm insistence that the Divine Persons are "inclined toward One Another" or "essentially related," One to the Other, would seal off the danger of a frank tritheism in the doctrine of God. And it is indeed of the first rank to seal off such a threat! But such schemas leave open the conceptual field to the primordial place of the subject over its act, the entity over its relata. We can affirm, to be sure, that such Subjects are never without their Relata or even that the Subjects are essentially related, but I believe that will never be strong enough to exclude a set of Three who generate or receive a Divine Nature. For just that is the conceptual residue of the notion of Person. Were Person to be identical and exhausted by Relation, we would not have achieved the aim of the dogma: we would have the Transcendent Ideal of Relation, but Person would serve merely as synonym for those Relata. It is this danger that theologians hope to avert, perhaps at times almost by instinct, by beginning with the Divine Three who then are intimately, internally, and eternally related by origin and impulse.

There are, certainly, troubles in the neighborhood here, and it may well be that Trinity is Mystery in this sense also, that the conceptual riddles will never be smoothed or dissolved; always this Sublime Idea recedes into the far horizon of our thought. And it may well be, too, that a dogmatic account of the Trinity might begin with the Persons in such a way that these conceptual dangers and obscurities are put away, and the Triune God made to shine forth brightly. But Three Eternal and Living Subjects will always militate against the idea of the One. So, the *order* of our concepts here remains vital. Logical priority must be given to those notions that indicate and express the Sovereign Unicity and Uniqueness of our God, for from these flow the Persons, the Perfections of the Divine Life. At the Transcendent Limit of Infinite Life is the Principle or Perfection of that Act: The Life of God distills into that Absolute End. Holy Scripture opens our eyes to see the Living God; and we must begin there.

To anchor the Processional Life in sacrifice is to see with fresh eyes that all the Ways of the Lord are Good. The Processional Life of God is Itself *moral*; It is Holy. The Triune Processions are not merely Structures of the Lord's Infinite Life, though they be that; they are *ethicized*. There is no topic or act or structure, no proper dogma or doctrine of Trinity, that is not in itself and as such Holiness. We do not enter fully into the Glory that is Trinity should we regard it principally as architectonic for Eternal Generation and Spiration. The fundamental axiom of the doctrine of God, His Simple Perfection, is Unicity, but the mode and tone and exceeding wonder of God's Processional Life is Goodness. Sacrificial Holiness discloses Trinity as the Gift of Goodness in motion, in Self-Giving Act. Much of the technical apparatus of the dogma speaks as if we write only of *concepts*, inert and stationary ideas that must be knit together in correct fashion, to harmonize today's teaching with the Nicene tradition. Of course, there are glorious technical matters to explore! But the Metaphysics of God is always and everywhere Life; and a Life that is Holy. Trinity is a Mystery of Goodness as Molten Lava, as the Movement of Giving as a moral act. To know this is to know the Trinitarian revival as lavish Feast. Sacrifice is the motion of Goodness, not as Form or Ideal or Nature only, but as Enacted Life. We learn from this central cultic act that the Good is not only Transcendental, though it is this. The Good is not only the very Nature of God, though inescapably, necessarily, it is this. The Good, we confess in the Mystery of Trinity, is also *Actus Purus*. It has a movement and direction, an exile and a return. Like Israel in its pilgrimage, Goodness moves out, moves away and downward, down into Egypt-land, down into the foreign captivity of Babylon, out into the region of the gentiles, to the edges of the earth, but Goodness is even more the movement home, the rejoicing in return, the new life, snatched from death, the feast and festival, the welcome and the peace that breaks out over the troubled earth. The Good who is Triune lives Eternally this Life, the Cosmic Shape of Goodness. The Lord is Sacrifice, descent and ascent, the Offering that is Well Pleasing, the Great Amen. This is the Living Form of Love.

Now, it may appear at first glance that we have simply unfolded Trinity as the Mission of God, the Life of the Triune One with His covenant creatures—an economic account, after all. For what, after all, might we mean by "offering" were there no recipient, even in anticipation, of the self-gift? Does it make any sense to speak of a Sacrificial Offering in a Divine Aseity without cosmos and without creatures? I have made this question acute because already I have advocated starting the dogma of Trinity with the Processions and not with the Persons. As Barth has shown us, the freedom of the Lord God over His creation can be buttressed easily by an appeal to the Eternal Persons: They love, They offer, and They receive, and this is Perfect Repletion. But we have insisted that love is not as such relational, and even more, we have dared to begin a dogma of Trinity, not with the economy, not with the Persons in relation, but with the Procession(s). Can we find some coherent and intellectually persuasive notion of offering that does not *in itself* imply a subject and object of that act? Can we think Trinity without creation? Mutatis mutandis, this is the dilemma of relationalism brought into the species of sacrifice.

As sacrifice is a gift and offering to the gods, it may seem as if I would break the apparent ligature between Trinity and creation by affirming that God is Himself simply the Giver and the Recipient.

But in truth I do not believe that Holy Writ teaches us that God offers Gifts to Himself. Leviticus does not pry open a door into Heaven, I say, through which we creatures glimpse God exchanging Gifts to Another, offering His own Self from One Person to Another, not a Divine Pactum, not even over a Holy Gift. No! The Son does not give Himself to the Father, say, or the Father receive that Filial Self-Gift in the Spirit. Nor, in more baroque fashion, do we propose that the Father gives Himself as the Offering that the Son returns in the Spirit. All these Heavenly dramas can only trade on the notion of Three Heavenly Wills, Three Persons in Sacred Harmony, Three Gifts, exchanged, in perfect harmony and love. But just this is what Triune monotheism rules out. For just this reason, we may think, Thomas assimilated the Eternal Son and Spirit to the Divine Intellect and Will: One Subject, in Augustinian distinctions. So we must ask intently: Has any other pathway opened up to think through the notion of Self-Giving, or have we imported a term, *offering*, and an act, *sacrifice*, that can but drive this theology to a destination unwelcomed, alien, and unsought? A proper ordering of the Aseity to the economy—the Processions to the Missions—and a proper ordering of the Processional Life to the Persons lies at stake here.

Holiness itself must begin to supply our answer. We have to reckon here with a remarkable turn of phrase, common to the Holiness School and clearly resonant in the Supper Discourses in John: that the God of Israel *sanctifies Himself*. Of course, Holy Scripture prepares us in many and various ways for other objects, other people and acts, to be sanctified—set apart, consecrated, purified, and hallowed. Much of Holy Scripture, and not simply that of the Holiness School, is devoted to this act of spiritual consecration. But here we stand before a deeper mystery: that God Himself can be sanctified; dedicated, set apart, hallowed. And, remarkably, that such sanctifying is God's own Self-Act: He hallows Himself.

In the apocalyptic chapters toward the close of the book of Ezekiel, chapters 38 and 39, we read that the Lord God will set His face against Gog, Israel's cosmic enemy, and in the divine overthrow of the armies from Magog, the Holy One shall manifest Himself: before the eyes of the nations, He will sanctify Himself, and they shall know that I am the Lord (Ezek 38:23). Just this is Christ's own testimony to His disciples on this night of His betrayal: He sanctifies Himself in the truth (John 17:19). Clearly, we see here a form of Self-Distinction, a Self-Proclamation that sets the Lord God apart from all creatures, all pretended deities, all rebellion and rejection. He is the Lord. When Jesus in the Fourth Gospel designates Himself by that resonant scriptural phrase "I am," we are to hear this Ezekielist Self-Declaration: He is the Lord, before the eyes of all nations. It is His Deity that speaks. In this sense, we hear in these passages echoes of Wolfhart Pannenberg's delicate and complex notion of the Son of God as Self-Distinction from the Father, and Barth's own insistence that God attests and affirms Himself, against all human error and folly. Hegel's primal conviction that God is Spirit reflects his exegesis of these texts: God is Self-Differentiated Reality, the Deity whose Self-Knowledge is explicit and objective but also claimed and endorsed as His very own Life. It is Holiness, as such, in and for itself. All these elements of distinction and affirmation belong properly to the biblical testimony to God's Self-Sanctification. But we can peer deeper still into this startling turn of phrase, to the doctrine of God that it intimates.

Holiness as Eternal Substance is Infinite Act. It is also a qualia, a property and Perfection of God: God is His Predicate, Holiness. But it is not first a qualia and then an act, as if Holiness determined the Deitas of God, which then was put in act by the Divine Will and Election. Rather, God's Perfect Holiness, His Perfection and

Property, devolves from the Lord's own Self-Act. Eternally, His Life is the Hallowing, in freedom and distinction, of the Infinite Reality that is Being itself. Now such daring language must be handled with care. At first glance, it may seem scandalously Hegelian, a notion of God in act that renders the Divine Being temporal, sequential, and evolutionary—a god who becomes absolute in his own odd pilgrimage toward sanctity. Worse, it might evoke the truly scandalous language of Jungian depth psychology in which the "God of the Old Testament" shows his primal rage and jealousy, only to grow more self-contained and integrated in the "God of the New." God in His Self-Act cannot mean any of these things! We must insist that there is no nature prior to act, no "substance" or "form" that is then temporally or even sequentially thrown into movement, a divine stasis now energized and explosively alive. No, the Lord God *is* Life, the Living One. His Structure, His Infinite Nature, is Movement, this Eternal Outpouring and Return; He just *is* this, Identical to His Life. Like a Clifford torus, the Infinite Circle that is Divine Being can enfold and dynamically unfold yet be nothing more or else than this Structure in Act. Yet Infinite Being is not simply mathematical, an Abstract and Bounded Infinite, though it be that, as well. The Infinite Movement that rings Eternity is even more Sanctification, Goodness in Act.

When Holy Scripture teaches us that God sanctifies Himself, we see what holiness is. It is the Pouring Out, the Cascading Down of the whole Self, the Descent of Life as Free Gift. The Treasure Chest is open, and the Gold pours out. The Triune Lord generates Holiness; this is the Self-Sanctification of God. As the Word that the Lord God speaks into Eternity—welcome and the world comes to be—so the Self-Offering of God is jussive: let the Offering issue forth. But the *direction*, the dynamism is reversed. In the communication of God's Perfections, the creature is welcomed *into* the House of

Being; in the Eternal Procession, God gives forth, pours *out* Infinite Being. One is creative reception, the Other creative Gift. It is the consecration, the hallowing of Being Itself.

We might think, in our modern skepticism and blindness, that being or—more deflationarily—existence is itself neutral: bare fact. In our era, we can imagine that goodness or value is our gift to the brutal chemical and physical cosmos: we sentient creatures add surplus value, our preferences or desires, to the heartless world. Freud famously considered this a species of the reality principle. As mature adults, we recognize the cold and relentless, the impersonal dynamism that is the natural world; we see its icy face turned away from all our small desires and plans. But to this world we might bring our drives, our passions, our elevated ideals. These are the sublimated and rationalized drives of our dreaming youth, now translated as gifts to a senseless world. It is the primal conviction of many in our day to see this world much as did Freud a half century ago. William James gave voice to much modern intuition, that we conscious beings bring value to a hard world of fact. So we see the world or fear it so.

At night the eerie image of a bloodless world steals over us, a moonscape of forces and odd social laws and predation that remain utterly foreign to us and our kind: we do not belong here. It seems we must shelter within a human skin and view the environment as a world built up out of our own vital interiors. The warm pulse of the human and the humane must be imposed, constructed, above all defended against a vast cosmos indifferent, hostile, to our goods, our little prospects, our kind. This nightmare can be given anodyne names: the Humean "fact-value distinction"; the ever-present "social construction" of reality; or Rorty's "linguistic turn." But it remains a *retreat*. We mortals concede the terrain we live in; we depopulate it and leave it bare. Small tags of culture, or ghosts of aqueducts or theaters or grand archways, linger in this sterile natural world; but we know now we never should have called it home.

The Mystery of the Holy Trinity is the firm no to all this retreat. The dogma of Trinity just is the intellectual affirmation that Being *is* Holy; there is none that is neutral, indifferent, void. Such a claim is far more radical than often imagined. This is not simply an affirmation that the creation is good. It *is* that, certainly, but it is also far more. Goodness can be naturalized in many moral systems. We might well think that value has objective stature, that it inheres in material reality beyond our preferences and dreams, or that goodness is ingredient in the natural forces and dynamisms laid out in the sciences, whether spotted by them or no. Christians have particular reasons for naturalizing goodness: the doctrine of creation teaches us to do so. But this is but a first step in the recognition of Holiness in reality itself. The *force* of the dogma of Trinity is to exhibit how and why we confess that Being itself is Good, is Holiness itself. When the Lord God declares that He sanctifies Himself, we are to hear, in the Heavenly chorus, the Thrice Holy praise of the seraphim: God enacts His Holiness. Our metaphysical doctrines conform to this seraphic call and explicate it. The very nature, identity, and fabric of being *is* a particular form of goodness, the form and act of holiness. This does not exclude but rather explicitly includes the majestic and terrible. The Holy Fire that issues from the temple sanctuary is awesome in its destructive power: it reduces the offering and, more, the offender to ash. Blaise Pascal's infinite silent spaces properly fill that philosopher with solemn dread: the measureless galaxies, silently circling their suns; the great novae born millennia ago, reduced to ash before their light reaches our distant globe; the mysterious dark matter and its terrible gravitational darkness; the frightful dynamisms of disorder and entropy in the very fabric of our cosmos: these are majestic workings of creaturely being. Certainly, the natural realm inspires and graces us but also strikes fear in our hearts—its menacing illnesses and predation; its remorseless stretches of drought and fire and flood; its animal life that undergoes cruel suffering, even apart from humankind, the great menace to all life on our earth. These are the depth dimensions of natural goodness, the majesty that speaks of a *Holy* Good, a Sacrifice laid down in the heart of Being. But all this wonder and awe that belongs by right to the doctrine of creation can here be only an overture to the Mystery of Trinity, the Holy Goodness who is God.

The Holy God rides on the wings of the wind; He is devouring Fire; He speaks and the world passes away. This is Goodness that has the Dynamism of Processional Life at its very core. The whole earth stands in silence before this Lord when He comes to His temple. It is the apocalyptic silence for a time and two times when the seal is broken, and the Lamb slain before the foundation of the world is known as Victor. Goodness that is Being is not a bare Perfection, neither inert nor beheld without reverence. Triune Goodness is *worshipped*. It demands personal holiness to enter into the Structure that is Trinity; only confession and prayer can guide us, finally, in the exposition and knowledge of this Mystery. The Holy God must break us open, must hallow us, so that we can take even the first step in confession of this True Name. The Unspeakable Majesty of God is His Self-Act of Holiness; He is the Eternal Sacrifice that encompasses Reality in Its explosive danger and astonishing life. In Heaven, too, the Life is in the Blood.

So, the Self-Offering of God enacts the Transcendent and inner Being of the Lord. He is Perfect Holiness, Perfect Infinite Being. In all Eternity, God is enacting the Structure of Being. He is exemplifying and affirming the Truth that Being Itself is neither shapeless nor amorphous, neither chaotic nor defiled. It is rather the Perfection of this Infinite, a Vast, Imperious Ordered Reality, a Bounded Royalty. The Self-Offering that composes Eternity is this Self-Definition, the Limit that does not impede but rather exhibits, manifests, the Perfect Reality who is God. God moves toward this Telos, this Perfect End, to be the Gift that is the far reach of Deity. Trinity means: I, the Lord, sanctify Myself.

Holiness is also Sacrificial Love: this is the next lesson Leviticus teaches us. We are being shown, in this cultic instruction, and in the narrative moments of sin, destruction, and pardon, the Reality of God as Costly Self-Giving, not to us, only, but in Himself. Just this is what it means for God to be Love. His Nature is Love; and His Fiery Procession is Love in Act. Notice, now, that we do not insist on a doctrine of the Divine Persons in mutual operation and relation here in order to speak fully and richly of Divine Love. God *is* Tri-Personal, certainly; but His Life as Loving as not predicated first and exhaustively on the Holy Persons but rather on the Processions, on the Light that is Burning Heat. *This* Life is Love. The Aseity of God, His utter Transcendent Sovereignty, is this Eternal Movement, out from the very Arche of God, the Primal Origin and Father, down Infinite Reaches, as Self-Giving, and taking it up, back into the Utter Depths, who is God. Love has this animate shape. Even as the structure of God is Holiness, and we glimpse Absolute Holiness in this Living Structure, so we discern, through the Spirit's grace, the Structured Life that is Love. That is the proper direction of Trinitarian reflection: Holy Scripture as the teacher of Divine Immanence; then, the astonishing Gift of that Holy Love, come down to the stony earth. The Mystery of the Holy Trinity teaches us that first and principally, love and goodness are *movements*, structured acts that flow from the depths out and down, covering the old wounds, returning in sweet savor to the love that gives yet more.

It is tempting in Christian ethics to focus our intent and analytic gaze on the *content* of moral decisions, the distinct good that is named and sought and realized in the moral life. What things are to be prized; what scorned or discarded? What virtues embraced and learned? What does a flourishing life look like; what is loveable within it? What are Holy Gifts; what is defiled? Such questions belong, certainly, to ethical reasoning. We would not travel far in the pilgrimage to a holy life did we not examine the good, the holy, and the defiled. But the Mystery of God's own Perfect Life tells us that these reflections are not the first, the prime matters, of a Christian treatise on the good. Rather, as with the Triune Life Itself, the royal road to holiness is a Living Shape, a Procession. The good takes this living shape: it is self-giving, the pouring out of a life as gift, and it is receiving, welcoming, taking up, and taking home the offering as one's own very life. Love looks like that.

We can say more. Often, we imagine that love is *relational*. It must consist—perhaps, it is thought, for Trinitarian reasons—of persons bound to one another, intimates or neighbors or enemies, now open and expressive, true and compassionate to one another. Love is taken to be a desire for another, the classic Eros of much Hellenistic literature, or perhaps love is thought to be a recognition of another individual, of her traits and achievements, her intellect and passion, the *philia* of classical friendship. Or in more exalted tones, the utter selfless love of the unworthy, the abiding charity toward the ungrateful or mean-spirited, the kindness to those who know only contempt and only that they show—the *agape* of the New Testament, and the hero of Anders Nygren's classic study. (But on these themes, Pope Benedict's early encyclical, *Deus Caritas Est*, warns caution; things are surely not so neat as all that.)[33] Such categories invite us to consider love a state between two persons, or many, a drawing together in passion or tenderness or loyalty and joy. Certainly, these are marks and gifts of love! And the Canon of Lateran IV recognizes them as such. Yet we need not deny these cherished prizes of the humane life in order to see that they are not the principle, the origin, but rather the dependent, the consequent of holy love. For the dogma of Trinity teaches us that love, real goodness, is first a living shape, a movement within the self, a structure of each life, each heart, that is built on the altar and fiery smoke of sacrifice. To live in correspondence, as resonance of the Good God, is to *offer* oneself—just that. It is not first reciprocal, not first the prizing of the beloved, not first the pardon and help and welcome that we extend with a gracious hand. No, love that is shaped by Almighty God, the trace of that Life, is simply giving, pouring out, whether another receives or rejects, whether another stands nearby or not. It is a state of the whole person, each life in its own interior movement, its own just cause. It stands ready. It has made the "movement of Eternity," the sacrifice laid down and received, the descent and breaking, breaking open, and the return, carrying the sheaves. The Holy Trinity is this Perfect, Eternal Motion, the swelling, full Tide of Holiness, that breaks out and recedes, pours down and turns again home. The Procession of God is Living Depth, welling forth, the Fecundity of Love, cascading down, burning, blazing, and rising up, always upward to Infinite Light, as Infinite Light.

The structure of Triune Love we see manifest in the sacrifice foretold and enacted in the Last Supper. The sacrifice of the altar, and the sacrificial meal, are not left behind when the Old Testament turns toward the New but are rather underscored, heightened, and consummated in the life and death of the Incarnate Son. As the fiery Wisdom of God, come to earth, the Incarnate Son enters into and takes upon Him the life of the people Israel, its history and law, its temple worship, festivals, and sacrifice. The Evangelist Luke is careful to place Jesus from earliest days in the temple; His relatives are priests and devout pilgrims. The fourth Evangelist knows Jesus in His flesh as temple, the One not made by hands. His "action against the Temple," recorded in all the Gospels, announces the Holy Lord come into His temple, purifying and cleansing a people for the Divine Indwelling. And the Epistle to the Hebrew gathers these themes together in a powerful evocation of Jesus as High Priest, the sacrificial Offering, given and poured out at His own hand: the Perfect Self-Offering.

The sacrifice of the Holy Son culminates and bears down on the Passion, the solemn days from the noisy entry into Jerusalem to the silence on Golgotha, the place of the skull. Sacrifice is costly; sacrifice is love: the Passions shows us this. The death of the Beloved Son will occupy us properly in the doctrine of redemption, taken up in the Divine Missions of the Triune God. But here we lift up the sacrificial Meal itself, the Passover Meal of the Passion. John the Evangelist knows Jesus as the Lamb of God and the Passover Lamb: the Son is slaughtered as the sun descends on the Day of Preparation for the Passover, the Festal Day when the lambs are slaughtered for the great Pesach, the Mysterious night passing of the Lord through Egypt. The synoptists know the Passover tradition in another form: the disciples gather around their Lord on the Passover for their solemn farewell meal. But in all the Gospels, Passover and sacrifice are combined, indeed, identified. We must say that Passover and sacrifice are *doublets*, a relation of identity. Christ, our Passover, is sacrificed for us. The meal over which Christ presides evokes His death, breaking, and descent. "This is My Body, which is given for you," Jesus intones in Luke. "This My Blood of the Covenant, which is poured out for many," Jesus says in Mark, a bold echo of the Passion predication of the Life, given as ransom for the many. The blood poured out will be remission of sins, Jesus promises the disciples in Matthew: the sacrifice of *this* Life is a sealing of the covenant and so a remedy for sin. It is Most Holy. The Meal of this sacrifice is a sharing in the Holiness plunged down into the weary and rebellious earth.

When we examine this sacrificial Meal from the majestic heights of the Trinity, we catch sight of this same Triune Pattern. The Fire descends from the inner Sanctum and terminates in Utter Self-Gift, burned to ash on the hard wood of the Cross. The Meal that is lavishly spread at the cost of a life is a proclamation of that death until the Son comes again. As we eat that Bread and drink that Cup, we share in that death, clothing ourselves with that sacrifice, drawing near at risk and fear to that Holiness who is Love, placing our hands on the Head of the Perfect Sacrifice, receiving on those same hands the Gift that is Ransom and Health—that Covenant Meal is thanksgiving, and it is sacrifice. There is real *exchange* here. The Processional Fire enacts Its Infinite Movement as Descending Son, Eternally Begotten from the Holy of Holies, broken on the Altar of Perfect Self-Offering—but then—wonderful joy!—ascending, rising in the Spirit, the Gift consummated and utterly free in the Highest Heaven. The Eucharistic Meal is also this Heavenly Banquet, spread forth on Mount Sinai, the Holy Meal before the Lord in which Moses and Aaron and the Elders, but also Nadab and Abihu and Judas Ben Iscariot, are wonderfully fed from the Lord's own hand. This is the Structure of Holiness, the Movement of Love. It is the inner Life of God, the Most Holy and Blessed Trinity. The Triune Lord has sanctified Himself.

Notes

1. Mary Douglas, *In the Wilderness: The Doctrine of Defilement in the Book of Numbers*, rev. ed. (Oxford: Oxford University Press, 1993; revised edition, 2001).

2. Ephraim Radner, *Leviticus* (Grand Rapids, MI: Brazos, 2008).

3. Mary Douglas, *Leviticus as Literature* (Oxford: Oxford University Press, 2000).

4. Aquinas, *Summa Theologica*, Ia IIae, Qq 90–108.

5. Brevard Childs, introduction to *The Old Testament as Scripture* (Philadelphia: Fortress, 1979).

6. Barth, *Church Dogmatics*, III.2, The Doctrine of Creation, §47.

7. J. M. E. McTaggart, *The Nature of Existence*, vol. 1 (Cambridge: Cambridge University Press, 1921).

8. Jacob Milgrom, *Leviticus*, 3 vols., Anchor Yale Bible Commentary (New Haven: Yale University Press, 1998–2001).

9. Milgrom, *Leviticus*, vols. 1 and 2.

10. Milgrom, *Leviticus*, 3:2, 103.

11. Baeck, "Mystery and Commandment," in *Judaism and Christianity*.

12. Mary Douglas, *Leviticus as Literature* (Oxford: Oxford University Press, 1999), 247–51.

13. Milgrom, *Leviticus*, Continental Commentary Series (Minneapolis: Augsburg Fortress Press, 2004).

14. Sarah Coakley, *Powers and Submissions: Spirituality, Philosophy, and Gender* (Oxford: Blackwell, 2002); Caroline Walker Bynum, *Holy Feast and Holy Fast: The Religious Significance of Food to Medieval Women* (Oakland: University of California Press, 1988); Janet Martin Soskice, *The Kindness of God: Metaphor, Gender, and Religious Language* (Oxford: Oxford University Press, 2007).

15. Dolores Williams, *Sisters in the Wilderness: The Challenge of Womanist God-Talk* (Maryknoll, NY: Orbis, 2013), 58.

16. Williams, *Sisters*, 143–44.

17. See, for example, John Milbank, *Being Reconciled: Ontology and Pardon* (London: Routledge, 2003); Kathryn Tanner, *Economies of Grace* (Minneapolis: Fortress Press, 2005).

18. Fred Sanders and Scott Swain, eds., *Retrieving Eternal Generation* (Grand Rapids, MI: Zondervan, 2017).

19. Gilles Emery, *The Trinitarian Theology of St. Thomas Aquinas*, trans. Francesca Aran Murphy (Oxford: Oxford University Press, 2007).

20. Aquinas, *Summa Theologica*, I, q. 27, art. 1, ad obj. 2.

21. Aquinas, *Summa Theologica*, I, q. 27, art. 1. Emphasis mine.

22. Aquinas, *Summa Theologica*, I, q. 27, art. 4, ad obj. 3.

23. Aquinas, *Summa Theologica*, I, q. 27, art. 4, ad obj. 3.

24. Aquinas, *Summa Theologica*, I, q. 37, a. 1, responsio.

25. Aquinas, *Summa Theologica*, I, q. 37, a. 1, responsio, citing *De Trinitate*, book 15, chapter 17; book 5, chapter 11.

26. Rowan Williams, *Tokens of Trust* (Louisville, KY: Westminster John Knox, 2007), 68–72.

27. Pickup, "The Trinity and Extended Simples."

28. Ellen Charry, "The Doctrine of God in Jewish-Christian Dialogue," in *The Oxford Handbook of the Trinity*, ed. Gilles Emery and Matthew Levering (Oxford: Oxford University Press, 2011), 559–72.

29. Théodore de Régnon, *Etudes de Theologie Positive sur La Sainte Trinitite* (Paris: Victor Retaux, 1898).

30. Bernard Lonergan, *The Triune God: Doctrines*, Collected Works, vol. 11 (Toronto: University of Toronto Press, 2009); *The Triune God: Systematics*, Collected Works, vol. 12 (Toronto: University of Toronto Press, 2009).

31. Epiphanius, *Panarian*, trans. Frank Williams, books II and III (New York: Brill, 1994), chapter 69, section V.

32. Aquinas, *Summa Theologica*, I, q. 28, a. 1, sed contra.

33. Benedict, *Encyclical letter Deus caritas est of the Supreme Pontiff Benedict XVI to the bishops, priests and deacons, men and women religious and all the lay faithful on Christian love* (Ottawa: Canadian Conference of Catholic Bishops, 2006).

§ 6. Holy Trinity as Being Itself

We note first, then, that Triune Holiness tells us that Being Itself is in truth not the most general or, in this sense, the least informed or least definite category. For Aristotle, Being was the ultimate category in that it contained none of the specific markers that belonged to finite reality. It was beyond genus; as Thomas also knew, beyond the most primal differentia of genus and species; beyond definition by class or kind or motion. Indeed, it seemed beyond predication itself. Like prime matter, Being exceeded all form; it seemed perfectly universal, perfectly empty. For that reason, "existence was not a predicate" because Being did not define or form or specify an object but rather simply ushered an object into cosmic reality. For Aristotelians, Being was certainly more metaphysically stout than the modern "existential quantifier," but all the same "Being" seemed to mark out only "that which is"; it added nothing to the concept. Such a metaphysical framework gives Reality itself an odd character: shapeless, barely recognizable as real, conceptually—metaphysically?—vague, necessary as underlayment but colorless and dull compared with the vibrant, pulsing world of things and their doings. Just this framework seems draped over modern skepticism about Being as a category of thought. Certainly, Immanuel Kant sped this skepticism along with his sustained attack on the ontological proof, as he termed it: necessary existence or necessary Being could not serve as a property of God, because "being" or "existence" is no kind of "predicate." In Kant's celebrated example, existence makes all the difference to the wallet of the bearer of one hundred thalers but adds nothing to the notion of a thaler. We know nothing more about German currency when it exists than before, when it was only a dream *in mentem*. Whatever we may think about this version of a theistic proof, and Kant's analysis of it, we may say confidently that it does not touch the *Proslogion* or the conceptual dynamism that is "that than which no greater can be conceived." But our focus here is not on the proof, Anselmian or no, or on Kant's witty rebuke of it, but rather on the deeper conviction about Being that such criticism employs. Being Itself, the Transcendent and Absolute Noumenon, may exist—it may be "filled out" metaphysically. But for some Kant scholars, it may not. That a philosopher of Kant's stature could remain neutral about the primal metaphysical category, Being, is a marker of how the mighty have fallen. Even the greatest of conceptual notions, "that which is," can be sheared off as sawdust from ancient academic workshops, now long abandoned.

Modern analytic philosophy is famously neuralgic about broad metaphysical categories such as Being; some have even hazarded the hope that the big questions in philosophy could simply dry up and wither away.[1] This is a problem in the neighborhood unlike all others: it touches all things. The "wonder about Being," once considered the birth pangs of philosophy, now seems to provoke only indifference or, perhaps at best, the ripple of a mild antiquarian interest. Of course, philosophers and social theorists speak best about their fields, and there is much, much about grand ideas, master narratives, ontotheology, and foundationalism of every kind that would belong in a full discussion of the problem of Being. But from the prospect of theology we can say that the anodyne concept of Being, the bland generality of this notion—and the otiose place it seems to hold in a world of the gritty, the empirical, and the particular—all appear to make this primal idea, Being Itself, a tired formula that a modern wind blew mercilessly away.

This weary form of the "forgetfulness of being" makes the dogma of Trinity an intellectual provocateur, an agitator, in the search for a true philosophy. The entire endeavor to see in Being a *question*, *the* question for the knowing intellect, is a *vestigium Trinitatis*. Christian reflection on the Structure of Deity offers metaphysicians a vision and an argument about the nature of Being Itself—a vibrant opposition to a Reality that quietly melts away.

For Being Itself is not shapeless or amorphous or vague, certainly not! The interplay of the Abstract, the Intelligible, the Concrete, the Universal and the Particular, the Infinite and the Formed: all these are ingredient in the Structure that is Trinity. Just this is what we mean when we say that God is Infinite Being. Now, to speak of Form in God, and Procession, is to address one of the primal questions in theology: How is the Lord, royally set forth in Holy Scripture, to be understood in light of the very idea of Being? Large tracts of Christian writing have assumed or loudly proclaimed that they have nothing to do with one another: Athens has nothing to do with Jerusalem. It has been thought, early and late, that God as shown forth in Holy Writ is an elevated Person—a Member of the Dramatis Personae, as Robert Jenson styled this—and an Actor who penetrated the world of persons and things and claimed them for His own. This is the Lord God, walking in the cool of the evening, eating and drinking with Moses and the elders, majestically enthroned on a sapphire throne, wreathed in incense and royal robes, conversing with Abraham and Sarah, with Moses and Hannah, and rumbling out in Fiery Speech from the holy mountains of Israel. This Lord has a mighty and outstretched arm, and He parts the heavens and comes down. It is not the Incarnation that is shocking to such a biblical portrait of God—in truth taking human flesh as His own seems all too natural to a Personal God of this kind—but rather the entire conception of Deity as Limitless, as Necessary and beyond recognition. To bring the language of biblical Personalism and rational, Transcendent Being together as one: *that* is the offense to reason. The manifold methods of exegesis, in the ancient church and the modern, aimed to reduce the offense: metaphor, counseled by St. Thomas as well as Sallie McFague; allegory and spiritual senses, availed of by Maimonides and Bernard of Clairvaux; narrative or historical Denkform or mythos, critical to modern interpretation—all were attempts to find rational resolution to the thorn in the flesh that is Bible as Revelation. The very idea that Scripture concerned itself with *individuals*, human persons or nations, seemed contrary to the canons of intellectual science, which knew only general concepts, forms, and types. Indeed, this conflict made the knowledge of particulars a lasting problem in scholastic thought, medieval and modern, and much effort was expended to defend its rationality and probity. Still, despite these advanced exertions at reconciliation, it seems that there is no reasoned pathway from the biblical God to the intellectual quest for Being Itself; indeed, they seem hopelessly, heartlessly opposed.

Mutatis mutandis, this is the riddle Karl Barth posed as the nineteenth-century struggle over personality and absoluteness, an insoluble dialectic that drove theology between Scripture and philosophy, without rest and without reconciliation.[2] The Primal Being, the Necessary One, must exist as the Limitless, Unconditioned, and Transcendent One; it must be Being that is Perfect and Absolute in Itself. Yet Personality appears to require demarcation, definition, and limitation: *this* God and not another.

That Being Itself could have an Identity, that it could be *this very One*, seemed destined for shipwreck on the harsh terrain of the Unconditioned. Absolute idealism aimed to resolve this dialectic, but at the terrible cost of the contradictory or paradoxical. Christians who read their Bibles in order to learn who God is seemed destined for disappointment. How could the Lord God of Israel be the Identity or Truth of this unsearchable Idea, the Absolute? Heirs of the Reformation have struggled with this divide and with the rational obligations of the faith: metaphysics and dogmatics have a stormy marriage, perhaps a tragic one.

The dogma of the Holy Trinity is the church's proud answer to this painful and troubled dispute. It is itself the rehearsal and praise of the Lord God who is Infinite *and* Conditioned; Absolute *and* Personal; Necessary *and* Transcendent and beyond thought and this very One, the Holy Sacrifice, in Heaven and on the earth. He is this because Trinity teaches us that Being itself is Bounded Infinity. This is another form of Triune *Redoublement*.

We turn, then, to one last question in our exploration of the Divine Processional Life: Its Immensity or Perfect Infinity. To say that God is without parts, that his Life has no end and no temporality, is to affirm, perhaps tacitly, that Deitas is Unbounded, Limitless. Indeed, for those who read the Bible philosophically— as I do—the Concreteness and Specificity of the "scriptural God" (hardly a welcome phrase!) seems hard to square with a Lord who is Infinite Being Itself. Yet Nicene Christianity is the confession of the One God who is the Life of Father, Son, and Spirit, the Generation and Donation of Holiness. Such delimitation and definition appear irreconcilable with Divine Infinity and Immateriality. Indeed, many Jews and Muslims join with metaphysicians in declaring the enterprise doomed in its initial voyage. The intellectual dignity of Trinity, in the early church, rested on various, often tortuous, attempts to combine the Boundless One with Subordinates or Emanations or Mythic Figures of many kinds. But Nicene Trinitarianism refuses such cold comfort. The Persons must be Equal; Their Life the Whole and Entire Godhead; Their Substance the orderly Generation and Spiration from Father to Son and Spirit. Infinity and Concreteness must be integrated and reconciled. How this is so demands our attention now.

§6.1. Trinity as Structured Infinity

Thomas begins our exploration of Divine Infinity, for it is he who has given voice to the proper astonishment at this Mode of Divine Reality. In quaestio 7 of the *Prima Pars*, Thomas lays out in four concise articles a notion of infinity that will take us by the hand, as it were, from Duns Scotus to Georg Cantor and the Nicene explosion of Holy Trinity. For Thomas, infinity is a Name of God. No creature is Absolutely Infinite; only relative or negative infinity can be realized by finite created things. But Thomas, in his remarkable fashion, quietly notes the problems with this neat dichotomy. For it may be, after all, that infinity is not a Perfection. This, in Hellenic and medieval idiom, is the problem of the amorphous and perfectly general character of being as rational notion. Thomas notes in quaestio 7, article 1, that Aristotle and many of the ancients considered infinity an imperfection as it had no form, and the form was the source of rational perfection. Indeed, infinity seemed to them to be a property of matter, for only matter could be "in potency" to an infinite number of forms: wood, that is, could be shaped into limitless wooden objects. This was only heightened in the enigmatic primal matter, as it subserved anything at all that exists: pure potency that yet belongs in some way to Being, prime matter appeared the essence of imperfect infinity. Moreover, creaturely being seems infinite even in its created intellect. This was a greater good than the primal, indeterminate infinity while being creaturely, all the same. Human beings can know limitless truths; the intellect is not narrowed to certain facts or species of things but rather moves out restlessly to everything that can be thought. For Karl Rahner, this is our constitution as transcendental beings, a finite dynamism that ceaselessly drives outward to the infinite, the very horizon of intellect. So it seems that infinity in all its ways is a form of creaturely being, perhaps most especially of matter— or "quantity," as Aristotle termed this category of predication. Infinity seems to be a limitless sea of things, in stability or in flux, in substance or in becoming, the tidal wave of objects, rising up from matter or energy and returning again to the deeps. God could be none of these; for God is Perfect, Bodiless Reality. So, it appears that infinity should only exist among creatures and at that, at least in matter, as an imperfection.

Thomas with a firm hand overturns the entire ancient scaffolding of the infinite. He has learned from the Damascene (and he from Gregory Nyssa) that "God is infinite and eternal, and boundless."[3] Infinity is now to be understood as a *Perfection*, God's Perfection and, in truth, His alone. The revolution turns on God's immateriality. The infinity that the ancients knew, Thomas explains, attempted to interpret the vast outpouring of material things from a material first cause, an "infinite body as the first principle of all things."[4] This was an imperfect understanding, because the Immaterial, Spiritual God, not matter—not even a singularity—is the First Principle. His Infinity will be a radical reversal of the very idea of the Limitless. Thomas invites us to consider God as Self-Subsistent Being; He alone has no cause. As such, He will be Perfect Form, utterly without dependence, perfectly prior or fundamental, and in Essence and Aseity, contrary to what is finite. Such a One will be Infinite *as such,* incommensurate with the world of limitless potencies and things. He will not partake in quantity; rather, He will be *this very One* and not another—that is, not creaturely, not finite. His Identity, His *This-ness* as what is not creaturely, not finite, just is His Infinity. Thomas terms this "essential" or "absolute Infinity," and it is God's alone. Note already how Thomas has taken specificity in hand.

The burden of quaestio 7 is to demonstrate that creaturely being cannot be infinite as is the Divine Infinity—it follows from Thomas's definition of the Absolute Infinite as noncreaturely. But, of course, the schoolmen knew the fascination of the created infinite as a dimension, a magnitude. Mathematicians, ancient and modern, considered numbers to be limitless, as would be a line, the infinite extension of the point. Division invited a notion of infinity: matter perhaps could be infinitely divided, prescinding material simples; lines could be infinitely divided, by halves or quarters, say—the source of Zeno's riddle about motion. The medieval Arabists considered it possible that creaturely being could be "accidentally infinite" and that under the category of "multitude." The example Thomas uses is the charming one of a carpenter with a limitless task: nailing shut a board, say, with an indeterminate and inexhaustible number of hammers, each breaking, one after another, so that an infinite number is required for the infinite, Sisyphean task. All these Thomas will rule out as candidates for a true, realized, or actual creaturely infinity. Numbers are successive and not present all at once; hence, they are not an actual infinity but only relative, or "in potency." This, too, undermines the infinity of the afflicted carpenter and any purveyor of serial multitudes. And more generally, creaturely being is defined by form, a specificity that distinguishes it from other beings. Even number, immaterial as it is, is specified as a "multitude measured by one." None of these has being from itself, including the angelic species, and the harmonious movement of spheres and circles, the perfect motion without beginning or end. All these Thomas will relegate to a "relative infinity," the kind of absorbing puzzles that belong to creaturely being that cannot be numbered by finite intellects and that stretch out before us as enigmatically and indeterminately boundless, deep, and measureless. But God is none of these.

Divine Infinity is left undefined in this question; indeed, it exceeds all definition. Just this is an instance of Thomas's firm rule that the essence of God cannot be known in this life. It is set forth in the question as a negative attribute: Absolute Infinity is the name of *the distinction* between Creator and creature. But in keeping with Thomas's later appeals to positive predication in the famous questions 12 and 13, he regards Essential Infinity as a *Perfection*. It simply is God; His Perfect Deity. Here is a powerful exemplar of the delicate relation between the incommensurate and the analogous in Thomas's whole conception of the God-world relation. We might consider the relative and absolute infinities in analogous relation, the relative taking a share in the Infinite Being who is God, communicating as the creature can receive it, His own Perfect Unboundedness. But such analogies do not capture the radical disjunction Thomas also affirms between God and everything He has made. Thomas, too, understands all similarities to be surrounded by an ever-greater dissimilarity. Self-Subsistent Being is *as such* Infinite, and this is unimaginable to us and outstrips any divisible or illimitable reality we can conceive. Such Divine Infinity is not magnitude or multiple, it is not self-extension or repetition, it is not motion, it is not property. It is the surpassing and inconceivable Distinction God Himself *is*, in relation to the cosmos. Yet it is more, always more. Apart from the creature, God is Infinite; He is Necessary and of Himself. But such positivity exceeds our intellect, constrains and breaks it, so that we speak of it only in its negation—but in just this way indicate its superabundant Perfection. The One Lord's Infinity is the Incommunicable Being, communicated in finite, divisible, and successive finite infinities.

In this sense, we should not draw too firm a line between Thomas and Scotus. Their accounts of the Divine Infinite shadow one another. The controverted notion of the "univocity of being" that Scotus affirms does not count against analogous relation, as the distinguished Scotus scholar Allan Wolter argues.[5] We may take Infinity as cardinal instance of this refined form of "communicated Incommunicability." Students of Scotus will know that for many complex reasons, Scotus held that "being as a category" could be notionally understood apart from its metaphysical instantiation: we can think "being" apart from affirming that there is such. (The parallel with the *Proslogion* was not lost on Scotus; indeed, the *Ordinatio* is an extended and relentless analysis of Anselm, at times disapprovingly, but at others, in a refashioned form that wins his assent.) The *reality* or actualism of Being is brought about by its modus: Being is either Infinite or finite mode. Infinitude or finitude is in this way the fundamental trait of Being; it *realizes* it. Nothing is, nothing can be, apart from belonging to one side of the great chasm between Infinity and finitude. Thus, analogy and incommensurability are joined. Scotus argues—persuasively, I say—that analogy rests on univocity: like relative identity, an analogy is comparison against one thing, *pros hen*. This it has in common, even if only in mentem; the distinction is built on the differing relations, the proportions, to this one common measure. Being is analogous in just this sense. Absolute Infinity and the creature both stand in reality. They both *are*. But they differ in their mode, as the Infinite or the finite. But here analogy presses up against incommensurability, for the Essentially Infinite is worlds apart from the finite, even in creaturely, relative infinite modes. Thus, the share in Being that creatures possess enacts a form of Being that differs radically from the Lord God's: our reality is not His. Scotus expresses it this way: "Infinite" we understand by means of finite (the analogy). I explain "infinite" in a popular definition as follows: "The infinite is that which exceeds the finite, not exactly by reason of any finite measure, but in excess of any measure that could be assigned" (the disanalogy).[6] Of course, Scotus's interpretation, especially on this matter, is a controverted art form, and I do not pretend to canvas the literature here on the sharp disagreements in the schools about Scotus, analogy, and Being. But I do hope to bring out here the remarkable quality of intellect and depth Scotus exhibits in his teaching on Divine Infinity. It is unlike any other.

In the *Ordinatio*, Scotus joins together the notions of Infinity and contradiction in illuminating fashion. His fundamental instinct is that Being has a "drive to exist": what is possible to exist, will. We can miss the radicality of this instinct. It envisions a reality that simply will exist, save contradiction barring the way. Being Itself, then, simply will exist, for there is nothing self-contradictory in the very notion of Being—a wonderful and fertile idea! The Transcendent Being, however, is Infinity in essence. Indeed, this is Its *primary* Perfection. As there is nothing self-contradictory in Infinite Being, It, too, will exist—but exist in the mode of necessity, Necessary Being. The modal property of necessity does not hold pride of place as it does in Thomas, yet it serves the higher purpose in Scotus of denoting the utter Uniqueness of God, His Aseity.

Now, the role of contradiction in Scotus's thought is extensive, occupying nearly every scene in the play. The finite, as concept, is not contradictory to Being: we can conceive finite beings; they exist. Yet finitude does not *exhaust* the notion of Being; they are not coextensive or identical. For we also can conceive of infinity, though to be sure only in its imperfect or relative sense (it is defined in terms of the finite), and it, too, is not repugnant to being. Infinite Being exists, but It also does not exhaust the very idea of being. It must be, then, that Being has compossible modes or properties; it can be understood as compatible with finitude and with infinity. So—at certain seasons and in certain texts of Scotus's comet-burst of a career—we must say that Being is indifferent to infinity or finitude. Contradiction does not rule out either mode or make it self-contradictory to say that there is a being who is not finite or not infinite. We say, then, that in reality these two exist: the Infinite God and the finite creature. Infinity has now become the Name of the Real Being. Indeed, by Scotus's day, the classical distaste for the unbounded has been stood on its head: "The infinite seems to be the most perfect thing we can know."[7] Being, then, contains in its concept the indeterminate, imperfect elements once assigned to infinity: it is the idea of reality that is perfectly general, unlimited, and underdefined, compossible with either finitude or infinitude. It is a translation of prime matter into the house of Being. But the *existence* or *act* of Being is altogether different: it is defined and exclusive. Either finite or Infinite, and these are contradictories. The Act of Being who is God just is Infinity in Act, Positive Perfection. Finite being, creaturehood, is limited, dependent, contingent on God, the Infinite. Such a Being, that than which none greater can be conceived, is without contradiction, for infinity is not repugnant to Being, and it is greater for Infinite, Perfect Being to exist in act than merely in thought; thus, God exists, and Anselm is vindicated. Or, as Scotus expresses this at the end of question 3, the long exploration of the existence of an Infinite Being: "In the realm of beings there actually exists a being which has a triple primacy [that is, of efficient causality, of finality, and of preeminence], and this being is infinite. Therefore, some infinite being actually exists.

This notion of God as an infinite being is the most perfect absolute concept we can have of him. . . . Consequently, we prove that God, conceived under the most perfect aspect possible to us, actually exists."[8]

Now, how has Scotus advanced our understanding of the Lord God who is Structured Infinity? We can trace the history of medieval reflection on infinity in Scotus's treatment: it has clearly advanced over early misgivings about infinity as imperfect and lack. It has blossomed as a clear Perfection, an ideal. (It seems the early pre-Socratic philosophers have won out over Plato and Aristotle here.) And we can see Scotus's firmer grasp on the relation between infinity and immateriality, which stood in some obscurity in Thomas's treatment. Thomas saw that ancient worries over infinity stemmed from its association with matter, and he could incisively distinguish Divine Infinity from differing forms of material unboundedness. But this led him to affirm rather quickly in the first article of question 7 that God's immateriality—His Reality as Bodilessness—was the root of His Perfect Infinity. Scotus, after a generation of reflection on these questions, knows now that such a connection is inadequate to the Uniqueness of Divine Infinity. In some complex reasoning within question 3, on Divine Existence, Scotus shows that immaterial intelligences, such as angels, could be considered infinite, were bodilessness the central differential between finite and infinite Being. Now, immateriality is not the whole of Thomas's account, not by a good measure! He is careful to say that infinity is not simply the opposite of finitude but rather that God's Infinity just is His Aseity, His Self-Subsistence, and in just that way, His Freedom and Distinction over all creatures. But Scotus has now a full armature to set forth this Aseity and Sovereignty without appeal to causality, subsistence, or contingency. He has shown us how infinity is a *mode*, not a predicate, not a property.

This step forward is predicated on his careful and controversial use of contradiction and univocity—the indifference of Being toward either finitude or infinity. Scotus's greater appeal to conceptual reasoning, and a semantic expression of fundamental categories, allows him to investigate Being as a notion apart from any metaphysical realization.

The heavy lifting in this operation is performed by means of the contradiction we noted earlier: Is it possible to conceive of a concept without falling into contradiction or incoherence? We might think here of celebrated examples of analytic judgments: a bachelor as an unmarried man, say or, in Scotus's example, the human being as rational animal. To attempt to conceive of a married bachelor is to enter into self-contradiction; so, too, Scotus says, to attempt to think of an irrational human being. Notice that we do not need any ontological affirmations here—we are not considering human beings as they exist, married or no, rational or no. Nor need we understand much about the concept we examine. We do not have to know about the unmarried state, about its causes or remedies, should such it need; the traits of any individual bachelor; or even the history of the concept. We examine only whether the notion under study gives rise to a contradiction when the two terms are joined. In this sense, Scotus follows closely the pattern of the *Proslogion*: the *Ordinatio*, too, is a reductio. Being is the most exalted, the most general category, under which contradiction can be examined. We need not have a full account of Being, what it is, its origin and end, or even its quiddity, its "such-ness," to explore the relation of compatibility or contradiction. We need only know that it is conceivable, possible, coherent to bring together the notion of Being and the notion of finitude, without absurdity, to know that "being" is compossible with "finitude." In fact, Scotus permits us to know even less than this. We could simply know that "being" is not *synonymous* with finitude to achieve the same results. When we examine what we do know about the concept Being, we discover that finitude or infinity is not contained there. (The Kantian language is nearly irresistible here.) In that sense we can say that the concept is *indifferent* to the predicates and, in this way, not contradictory. This is all we need to affirm that being could be either finite or infinite.

Infinity, then, must be something other, even in concept, than Being. In Scotus's conceptual universe, we do not have two forms of Being, an infinite sort—a singular—and a finite sort, the multitude. We do not have before us the task of relating or joining or rendering incompatible two realities, One beyond genus, the other the vast sea of genera and kinds. Finitude and infinity are not predicates of Being, Scotus tells us, and Being does not bear them as a property or quality. Rather, finitude and infinity are ways—modes—in which being enters reality. The contraries now are substantiated: Infinite Being is contrary in mode to finite. But ways of being do not contradict one another as do properties. These are not direct contradictories: we cannot define one directly in opposition to the other. For Scotus to affirm that the Infinite is "not finite," we now see, is not to say they mutually define one another through opposition or contradiction. No, as *Seinsweisen*, they stand in a comparative relation that is without measure. Just this is the delicate relation of an incomparable comparison, an incommensurate likeness. Here we catch a glimpse of the range and power of Infinity as a principle Perfection of God. Scotus begins his treatment of this mode through comparison with finite creatures, for he agrees with Thomas that our knowledge springs from earthly experience. But he does not fill out the notion of infinity as does Thomas: it is not Self-Subsistence or Cause *sine causa*. It is not the Inoriginate of Nyssa and his later descendants. Rather

Infinity, Divine Infinity, is simply *excess*. It exceeds the finite by an excess measure. Scotus even in this popular definition shows great care in his terms: the Infinite does not simply exceed the finite by any measure we can name; it *exceeds* any measure we name. For this reason, the relation between the finite and Infinite cannot be measured; we can say only that God is beyond any measure. Scotus's language allows us to speak of Infinity as something related to finitude: he still holds to Thomas's claim that Infinity is defined in terms of the finite, as its negation, yet it is free over it, too. For we cannot name the measure or proportion between the two. The Infinite simply exceeds the finite, by every degree and magnitude, and in this way, God Himself simply outrides the cosmos and its creatures beyond comparison. It is the Greater Unlikeness in the ocean of likeness. The mode by which God is Absolute Being, His Infinite Reality, instantiates His Unique distinction from all created goods.

Infinity as modus begins to pry the notion of the infinite up out of the ideas of measure, magnitude, and multitude. In Scotus, we catch sight of an idea of Infinity that slips off these mortal tethers; it is no longer bound to earthly concepts of space, number, amount, and mass. The Lord God has ordered all things by measure, number, and weight, but God Himself in His own Infinite Act is beyond all these. Infinity, then, cannot be fully or simply the Unbounded or Limitless: it will not be a *negative* Perfection in a Scotist world.

To illustrate, let me turn to the primordial matrix of modern investigations of infinity, René Descartes's *Meditations III*. Here in the justly famous Third Meditation, Descartes directs his mind to the notion of infinity. Already he has anticipated Georg Cantor's move to distinguish the "transfinite" from the Absolute Infinite; indeed, just this is the framework for the entire Third Meditation. Descartes holds that we have a "clear and distinct idea" of Infinity:

The idea of this Being who is absolutely perfect and infinite is entirely true; for although, perhaps, we can imagine that such a Being does not exist, we cannot nevertheless imagine that His idea represents nothing real to me, as I have said of the idea of cold. This idea [of God] is also very clear and distinct; since all that I conceive clearly and distinctly of the real and the true, and of what conveys some perfection, is in its entirety contained in this idea. And this does not cease to be true although I do not comprehend the infinite, or though in God there is an infinitude of things which I cannot comprehend, nor possibly even reach in any way by thought; for it is of the nature of the infinite that my nature, which is finite and limited, should not comprehend it; and it is sufficient that I should understand this, and that I should judge that all things which I clearly perceive and in which I know that there is some perfection, and possibly likewise an infinitude of properties of which I am ignorant, are in God formally or eminently, so that the idea which I have of Him may become the most true, most clear, and most distinct of all the ideas that are in my mind.[9]

In this celebrated section from *Meditation III*, we have Descartes's full conceptual armory: formal, objective, and eminent ideas; clarity and distinction; reality in mind; containment. (The last does not belong by rights to Kant!) Descartes does not set out just what we should mean by clarity and distinction—this is a well-known *crux interpretationem* in the *Meditations*. But he does use a *via negativa* that allows us some purchase on this central phrase. The contrast between cold and heat, he says, shows that both magnitudes are a mixed and confused notion. "By their means I cannot tell whether cold is merely a privation of heat, or heat a privation of cold, or whether both are real qualities, or are not such."[10] They seem to be qualia that depend on one another to guide our use in everyday life, but we cannot clarify for ourselves just what is foundational in the pair or, indeed, if either one is but appearance or even illusion. It seems then that a clear and distinct idea presents itself—shows itself—in our awareness; we cannot but recognize the power of such an idea. And it has markers all its own: we can contrast it firmly from all others that seem to rival it; it is a separate notion, all its own; it possesses an objective reality that we cannot deny.

In fact, it seems that Descartes holds that a clear and distinct idea of God is inescapably *representational* or, in his idiom, "objective." We may deny the extra-mental existence of God, he claims, but we cannot deny that this idea, in its clarity and force, is concerned with something real. This is a delicate and important claim, and one difficult to capture expressively. Descartes says that the obscure and mixed notions of heat and cold show us that we can exercise the method of doubt on them: we can entertain the notion that temperature—under the description of "heat" and "cold"—does not belong to external reality but is merely sensation or appearance to us. Perhaps one of them is real; the other its absence. Perhaps they are only gradations of some third element that has gone unnamed, unrecognized. This moment of irrealism in the idea of temperature does not pertain to a clear and distinct idea: a true idea carries the tang of reality. We might wonder here about the "hippogriffs" Descartes loves to adduce or, in more modern parlance, a Meinongian object, both imaginative and conceptual, that does its work in the mind alone.[11] Can we have a clear and distinct idea about hippogriffs, about unicorns, about Sherlock Holmes? Is the idea of an Infinite God like this? (Those philosophers who consider the *Proslogion* a form of argument about Meinongian objects will recognize the force of such a question.) It seems that Descartes holds that at least some clear and distinct ideas strike us directly and immediately as intending real objects *extra nos*. We say this is *about* something *in re*; it concerns reality. This is not quite the same as saying it has real effects—though I think such crystalline notions will bring about attitudes or actions on the part of the thinker, if nowhere else. (Just this is Meinong's fascination with ideas that "subsist" in us, such as beloved or fearsome literary characters.) Descartes, rather, seems to believe that clear and distinct ideas "contain" or convict us of their substantiality, their ontological seriousness, if we may put it so. They are not fanciful or obviously pasted together from congeries of natural wonders or emotionally charged with wish and longing. Proper and full ideas strike us as *encounter*, as a concept that touches something deep in the realm of the real. Now, as Descartes is careful to say, this does not immediately entail *existence* in the reality outside the mind. Clarity and distinction do not imply "mind independence." (Of course, we may not want to divide up reality in this way, but existence apart from mental thought is one of the great axes on which the *Meditations* turn.) But we are not mistaken about their aim: such an idea intends the real.

But not all ideas carry the same force of objectivity: this is Descartes's claim about "degrees of reality." Some ideas are simply more real than others, in this very rich and odd sense. It is not that some objects possess greater reality than others, though that may also be true. It is rather that some *ideas* rank above others; they have a nobility all their own. This is an interesting claim and a far-reaching one! Descartes holds that certain clear and distinct ideas have a foundational place in our mental universe; they occupy and exercise the mind as cogito, the thinking thing, in its fullest and deepest mode; they concern that which will abide—as concept, if nothing else. We have here something like the "first principles" of the mind, the axioms on which thinking is built. It may well be that Descartes has a mathematical or geometric model in mind; these are clearly basic elements in a Cartesian landscape of thought. But I think Descartes is also preoccupied here by the remarkable relation of "objectivity" to "mode" in our realm of ideas. For Descartes, an idea is a mode of thought: it is the manner in which the cogito exists. I might have a clear and distinct idea of a triangle, say, and in that thought, my mind, which is not extended or material, assumes the mode of triangularity: I think in triangular shape. Indeed, we may well wonder in Descartes if the "I think that accompanies all our thoughts," as Kant would have this, has not been subsumed by the fully proper idea in its objective force and internal reality. Thoughts along this line have led some interpreters of Descartes to say that he has established "thinking thing" but not the crucial cogito, the I who thinks, because the human subject is given over to thought in its mode as idea. (This again is an enduring puzzle about Being, its abstraction and its concretion, its generality and individuality—all rich puzzles and vestigia.) We may remain neutral here about that question of interpretation but remain focused on the dignity of these all-absorbing true ideas.

The idea of God, the Infinite One, holds pride of place. It is the crown of all ideas in eminence, in clarity, in objective reality. God is the greatest idea a mind can think. Indeed, as mode, the mind enters the manner of Deity: in thinking God it becomes what Thomas names "Deiform." That modus is the clear and distinct idea of Infinity. As finite, we think Infinite: thus the "transfinite" and the "Absolute" exist avant là lettre in Descartes. But all this simply brings us to the threshold of the unstated relatio in Cantor: just what is the relation between our finite thought of the infinite and the Divine Infinite, between the transfinite and the Omega, the Absolute? This is the central question for Descartes as it is, mutatis mutandis, for Anselm. Note how Descartes waves away, in a few clauses, what Thomas and other schoolmen would suggest as answers to this question. Descartes does not think we have something like a relative or negative notion of infinity in the clear idea that occupies our mind with such distinct power. He writes: "Nor should I imagine that I do not perceive the infinite by a true idea, but only by the negation of the finite, just as I perceive repose and darkness by the negative of movement and of light." Here we see Descartes's quiet refusal of definitions as old as Thomas and Scotus that derive infinity from contrast or opposition to the finite. He continues: "For, on the contrary, I see that there is manifestly more reality in infinite substance than in finite, and therefore that in some way I have in me the notion of the infinite earlier than the finite—to wit, the notion of God *before that of myself.*"[12] What he takes away with the left hand, he returns, however, with the right, for he notes the presence of desire, of lack and need, and a conviction of his own imperfection that contrasts with the Perfect Substance—but in just this way must precede his own self-knowledge as the Infinite Standard by which he manifestly falls short. Indeed, we may say that Descartes's entire aim in this Third Meditation has been driven by the distinction between the Perfect Idea of the Infinite and the imperfect mind that contemplates it. "If the objective reality of any one of my ideas is of such a nature as clearly to make me recognize that it is not *in me* either formally or eminently, and that consequently I cannot myself be the cause of it, it follows of necessity that I am not alone in the world, but there is another being which exists, or which is the cause of this idea."[13]

Descartes then undertakes to show that the clear and distinct of Infinity cannot derive from the human mind, "formally or eminently." Descartes is alive to the suspicion that all our representations of reality extra nos are in fact a distorted mirror of our own inwardness: we can externalize ourselves to populate an entire world so that it expresses our nature under the fiction of an outside world. We can understand ourselves as substance, for example, so that a stone, Descartes says, can be nothing more than our self-concept—I am a thinking substance—expressed in a partial and limited way, as a hard, perduring object, extended over time.

The rational self can make a world, that is. Social constructivists have nothing on Descartes in this matter! He argues that the cogito can be the eminent cause of all corporeal substance—its extension, duration, outline, and place—as an inferior reflection of the mind, which conceives of substance in this way and can very well manufacture the idea that such objects exist in their own right. I see myself in nature just because I am nature, externalized. And this is not to even countenance the indistinct and mixed notions that I entertain about the world—its relative properties, such as hot and cold, north and south, heavy and light—and its fanciful creatures I can stitch together out of my idea of the corporeal and the animal. The idea of God, the clear and distinct Infinite, is the only bulwark against a terrifying loneliness in which I alone exist, with my fantasies of material companions projected into an empty cosmos. The urgent task of the *Meditations* is to test whether the idea of God can withstand the method of doubt, the corrosion of irrealism, and the charge of projection. Can Infinity be our own invention? Descartes firmly answers no.

The very concept of God, Descartes says, is of a most real Being, whether we hold such an idea exists in external reality or no. We do not attribute to the notion of Deity those elements we readily recognize as spurious or confused: we do not think of color, say, as a central aspect to the idea of God. Those who doubt the existence of God share with believers the conviction that the very concept of Deity is of perfection or completion or measurelessness. Descartes's aim here is to argue from the completeness and perfection of the Idea of the Infinite to its reality outside our mind. This he does through the axiom of efficient cause: by the "natural light of reason," he claims, we see that there must be as much, or more, efficient and "total" reality in the cause as in the effect. "It is manifest by the natural light that there must be at least as much reality in the efficient and total cause as in its effect. For, pray, whence can the effect derive its reality, if not from its cause?"[14] The Perfect God who has placed this Idea in our minds—all other sources have been discounted—must possess as much reality as our idea, indeed, infinitely more. The Infinite, Perfect God, then, exists and exists necessarily.

Descartes's *Meditation III* inexhaustibly fascinates us because it sets out the conviction that we know God truly—we think the proper and substantial Reality of God—yet this does not make our minds divine. It is customary in many modern circles (and not only they!) to assume that our Ideas of God are incomplete, partial, obscured, and confused; we see only in part. When the complete comes, we will see in fullness—but only then. But Descartes dares to say that we have a perfect and perfectly clear Idea of God—we know in truth what it means to speak the word *God*—and in just this way, we know we are not God, that our minds are not this Infinite Thought or extensions of It, and that we do not inhabit this thought as we do our other clear and distinct ideas, by executing them fully, from their principles, as a Thomist would say. This is so because the Idea of God is not material or an element in res extensa. It does not occupy Cartesian space, nor does it possess the character of body. It is rather Thought Itself—Self-Thinking Thought. God as the Simply Perfect, Absolute Infinite just is the concept of Pure, Living Intellect, the Perfection of Immeasurable Reason. As creaturely cogito, we think this Thought as singing is to Song: God is the Whole, the Enacted Infinite, of which we are the dependent, the image. (To apply the analogy properly, we must conceive the Song as the cause of the singing.) But we are nonextended substance, one thinking the Other, the Other sustaining the thinker. (We might suspect here a strong Scotist element in Descartes's thought, perhaps inherited from his quiet study of Francisco Suárez.)[15] We think the Omega as the transfinite. That is the God-world relation in Cartesian and Cantorian idiom.

Now, the task for any Cartesian is to see how this meditation can be secured from the danger of pantheism or a particular form of psychologism. It appears, from all that has been said, that Descartes falls prey to a univocal form of predication, between the human and the divine cogito. Indeed, more serious still, the Third Meditation appears to assimilate the human nature to the Divine: both are intellectual substance. This is the Scotist "univocity of being" in a pronounced and flattened metaphysical form. Barth considered Cartesianism the central and fatal error in all modernism: to say "God," the modernist says, is to say "human being in a very loud voice." The God-world relation has collapsed into identity or, perhaps at best, a continuum. God becomes the Supreme Instance of human, intellectual nature. The Likeness has swallowed up the Unlikeness; it indeed is the "Greater." Now, this is not to impugn all forms of the ontological argument. Barth championed Anselm in his book on the *Proslogion, Fides Quaerens Intellectum*, but this was a reading of the text that drew a sharp border between Anselm and all other pretenders to this form of demonstration. (Barth would have found my quiet marriage of Anselm to Descartes, mentioned earlier, appalling.) Barth in his relentless diagnosis of theological disease has placed his finger on the neuralgic point: Can the notion of infinity, as innate concept, express the God who is not world, not creature, but Lord? Can the Creator-creature distinction be honored and preserved in a Cartesian Infinity? Can the Holy God of Holy Scripture be discovered in the conceptual world of modern infinity, the transfinite and the Absolute?

Descartes appears to have no doubts on this score. He concludes the Third Meditation in an Augustinian voice, turning aside to address the wonders of the true God.

It seems to me right to pause for a while in order to contemplate God Himself, to ponder at leisure His marvellous attributes, to consider, and admire, and adore, the beauty of this light so resplendent, at least as far as the strength of my mind, which is in some measure dazzled by the sight, will allow me to do so. For just as faith teaches us that the supreme felicity of the other life consists only in this contemplation of the Divine Majesty, so we continue to learn by experience that a similar meditation, though incomparably less perfect, causes us to enjoy the greatest satisfaction of which we are capable in this life.[16]

For Descartes, the Absolute and the Personal join: to think the One is to worship the Other. Though the eye of the mind is dazzled by the Divine Light, yet the Cartesian can rest confident that the God who is clearly and distinctly thought as Infinite is indeed the One who will be contemplated, in beatific vision, in the next perfect and eternal life. But can *we* be so sure in this confident alliance? We have set before us two entire programmatic questions, in metaphysics and in epistemology. Can the God of the Infinite, this very One, be thought? Can His Nature be distinguished from ours all the while being thought by us? Can the Lord God of Israel, the God of temple and cultus, the God and Father of our Lord Jesus Christ, be thought as the Omega? Can His Being be identified with the Absolute Perfect Infinity we have explored through this *vestigium Trinitatis*? And if so, can it be properly distinguished from the human nature that thinks this Thought?

We must answer a confident yes to all these queries. Thought and Being must be ultimately One: just this is what we mean when we say the Living One is Personal. And we must say more. The Lord God of Israel is the Lord of the entire cosmos, of all that is, visible and invisible. God is not *regional*. There is no domain in which He lives, as if isolated from all others; no private space or refuge where He belongs, as if He does not command every place; no concept or land or event in which He is not the Creator and Sustainer, the

Telos of the entire landscape of being. This is what we mean by the intellectual dignity of the dogma of Trinity, just that. We should not imagine that the realm of Holy Scripture is one in which God makes an appearance for the first time in the history of culture, as if He is withdrawn from all other creatures, all other thought. We do not turn to Holy Writ to discover the only place where the true God is worshipped, against all idols, though, to be sure, idolatry is diagnosed and cauterized there. We do not find in Christian teaching a Reality that now can be thought or encountered, as if utterly new, though, again, Scripture contains much fresh divine teaching. The One Lord is not confined but utterly Unbound and Free. For this reason, God can be *thought*. Indeed, we must say that the telos of all thought is the Idea of God: He it is who is discovered at the end of all our ways. Christian theology must have the confidence to proclaim its Sovereign Lord as the Source of all being, as Being Itself.

In another form we have now encountered theological compatibilism once again: that the Lord God, *as such*, in His Aseity, is known in the concepts, words, and names of His poor creatures. We have not adopted the central axiom of cause into this relation, so it does not have the force of a *demonstration* that occupies so many of our epistemic and metaphysical ventures into Divine Existence. We say rather that it has pleased the Gracious Lord to be known in this way, to be present to thought under these creaturely means. But theological compatibilism shares a *formal* relation with the Cartesian idea: that the idea, the "effect," represents the Cause, the Perfect Source and Being, and more powerful still, it knows the Lord under the conditions of unknowing. Just this is Descartes's genius: he speaks confidently of this Divine Idea; he prizes it for its modes of chiseled clarity. He discovers it can have no creaturely source; it is the Thought of God, but it remains Mystery. For it names what is incomprehensible and infinitely Rich. Descartes dares to claim that we can *know*, can *think*, truly and fully, what we cannot specify, enumerate, explain, or master. Just this is the Idea of God. Descartes shows us how we can guard against human arrogance and titanism in the knowledge of God without adverting to radical agnosticism or incompleteness. We do not protect the Sovereignty of God by reducing creaturely knowledge to ashes and fragments. Rather we boldly claim *knowledge*, the very Aseity of God, which includes—no, *entails*—that God, the Triune Lord, is Mystery, Infinite Glory. This is theological compatibilism in the dogma of Trinity.

It is a small step from here to the modern notions of Infinity set out by the great nineteenth-century mathematicians Bernard Bolzano, Richard Dedekind, and Georg Cantor. We need not explore the complete range of modern analyses of infinity—their operations, paradoxes, and geometric expressions—to see that the very idea of the infinite has here undergone a significant change. The revolutionary concept that now drives this expansion of the idea of infinity is the set: set theory radically remakes infinity. Cantor especially opens the doorway to a positive conception of the infinite: it is the set of whole numbers, say, or the set of all natural or real numbers. The set allows us to put aside the worries of a bare negative or potential infinity, in which we simply begin a series of numbers, say, and through an ellipsis indicate we cannot finish the sum. No longer is infinity caught between the act of division or between the act of interminable addition; the problem of the infinitesimal in calculus need no longer occupy the investigation of the infinite. Instead, we may now focus on the *complete*, the whole of an infinite series, by viewing it, so to say, *sub species aeternitatis*. (Surely, a significant phrase from Cantor!) "From above" we see the whole set of numbers, though the last be unknown or unspecified; the whole set of fractions between the integers of 1 and

2, though not exactly counted; the entire set of hammers, broken, set aside, and launched afresh in the endless hammerings of our tireless carpenter—these, too, can be seen as a whole, a set of frail and replaceable ball peens. Now, Cantor held that such sets were transfinite: they concerned finite objects or concepts—numbers—but in their infinite collections and series. These sets could be manipulated in wonderful ways: they can be organized (be "well-ordered"); they can be enumerated (be assigned a "cardinal"); they can be measured in their ordering (treated as an "ordinal" set). And in all these ways, they permit themselves to be handled much as are natural or real numbers in standard arithmetic fashion.

The very notion of a "set" is theoretically and theologically salient. A set is not like a type—of which there are instances or, in modern parlance, "tokens"—nor is it a kind of universal or class: there is nothing "higher" or more general about a set. We do not have a definition of a "kind" here, as we do in the kind mammal or shellfish, into which we now include individuals, and undertake the complex task of accounting for individuation. Sets have no metaphysical status aside from their members. They are simply the gathering of those members together. Just this is the solvent to the menace of Russell's paradox. In some such way, the infinite set teaches us a parable of the Triune Realities: Persons, Processions, Relations. These do not belong to a higher class or concept or universal; they are not instances of a higher Divine Type. We do not have parts in Trinity, even in concept! Rather, the Persons, as Perfections of the Divine Processional Life, are simply gathered together as a quasi-set. They are Three, and their distinctiveness, a quasi-ordinal, is complete; however, They mutually indwell One Another. Perhaps we might say in Their own vast Dissimilarity, They are similar to infinite sets that share the same cardinality.

Now, little about set theory is without controversy; even now it is not settled territory. The question of the metaphysical status of these transfinite sets—do they exist?—gave rise to some remarkable puzzles. Bertrand Russell discovered a celebrated paradox in a "realized" set theory, the eponymous paradox, and led Cantor to describe the complete set of sets as an "inconsistent totality" or, more puckishly, a "misbehaving set." Readers of modern mathematics will recognize the parallel between these paradoxes and Kurt Gödel's well-known incompleteness theorem, in which he demonstrated the impossibility of deriving and grounding all mathematical principles from within their own axioms. Even the central continuity axiom of set theory—that numbers are "dense," abutting one another, such that the natural numbers are directly succeeded by the real—seems unprovable from within its own resources, that is, by formal set theory.

Such enticing problems in the very notion of infinity tell us that we have stumbled across another problem in the neighborhood. In the development of modern set theory, we have the secular parable, the *vestigium Trinitatis*, of the Mystery of the Holy Trinity. It is another beachhead from which the intellectual dignity and defense of the dogma can be launched; we search for the Real together. Indeed, if we hold that God is Rational, Intellectual in complete fullness, then the elements of pure thought, logic, and mathematics, the combatants of Russell's and Alfred North Whitehead's early *Principia*, should echo the Structure of Reality Itself. In some such way, Augustine puzzled over the dazzling properties of truth and Truth Itself and Descartes, over the clear and distinct idea of the Infinite, objectively complete in my mind and Formally Perfect as "total and efficient Cause" of my idea. Consider, too, the wonderful oddity of sets in combination: for any two cardinal sets, k and l, if at least one is infinite, and the cardinal k is equal to or greater than one, we can affirm: $k + 1 = 1 + k = k \times 1 = 1 \times k = k$.[17] Here we have the size of the infinite sets added and multiplied, with full symmetry, yet the sum of them is the original cardinal, k. In some such way, we might imagine the Infinite Being of God, proceeding to its Termini, the Persons, each of whom is Infinite, the sum (or even multiple) of whom is simply One, the One Infinite Being of God. We almost touch the hem of the Garment here, and many modern mathematicians have felt the enchantment of the infinite pulling them into a sphere of the Spirit. Think of David Hilbert's famous cri de coeur: "The infinite! No other question has ever moved so profoundly the spirit of man; no other idea has so fruitfully stimulated his intellect; yet no other concept stands in greater need of clarification than that of the infinite."[18] Or perhaps more eloquently put still, a silent mixture of pathos and hope, is the mute testimony chiseled into David Hilbert's gravestone: "We must know! We will know!" We carry that burning desire to *know* with them into the exalted air of the Most Holy Trinity.

For the Divine Triunity is a Structured Infinity. Here the language and astonishing power of modern work on infinity allows us to take one more turn in our reflections on the Absolute Infinite: Infinity is not *necessarily* and *per se* Unbounded. We need no longer conceive of the Infinite as that which is Unlimited or Undefined; rather, we may acknowledge its final Perfection, its Totality as a Bounded, Defined Infinity. We hasten to say that modern set theory has not grounded or given warrant for such a teaching; indeed, the claim that God is Structured Infinity is simply a restatement of the Nicene Symbol, I say, in modern idiom. What we have searched for is the proper intellectual measure for stating the Holy Sacrifice of the Triune God; the glittering notion of the infinite has opened the door, and set theory allowed us to walk further in this scriptural pathway. We might say, in truth, that set theory allows us to take up the Scotist question about univocal being in a fresh and productive manner. We might say, that is, that the concept Being, before it is defined and realized in mode, is something like—mutatis mutandis—the transfinite numbers, prescinding from existential quantifiers. But it is God Almighty, the Absolute Infinity, who in truth and reality exists: He just is the metaphysical fullness of Absolute Being; the Intelligible and the Concrete; the Universal and the Particular; the Free, Sovereign, and Unconstrained Fire of Being who is Processional Life, Heat and Light, the Unconditioned, the Living Structure of the One God, Father, Son, and Holy Spirit. The Holy Trinity is the Realized and Perfect Infinite, Bounded by the very Structure of His Life, His Telos and Dynamism, His Endless Life that has, too, its End, Its Perfect Movement, Perfect and Complete Sacrifice. Holy Scripture speaks of Him; scholastic, mathematical analysis speaks of Him, too, likeness enclosed in Greater Unlikeness, and these idioms join in the dogma of the Holy Trinity.

In just this way, we should affirm that the Holy Triune God is both Personal and Absolute. Should we affirm the Positive Infinity of God, we need no longer choose between the scriptural God—His distinct, recognizable Authority and Identity; His characteristic movements and invasions; His teachings, precepts, and ordinances—and the God of the philosophers, the Pure Act of Being, Being Itself, and the analogous Source of all that is.

Just so, Almighty God is the Personal Absolute. As God is the Infinite, so is He Personal. The dogma of Trinity begins with Procession, but it must end in the Persons, the *Teloi* of the Divine Life. These are the Eternal Ends of the inner Ways of God. We cannot begin with these Realities, but we must end with them. The Persons are the culmination of the Glory of God, the Full Reception of the Living, Pouring Forth and Generating anew the Life of the

Living God. The Holy Fire descends and burns and ascends anew: this Completed Mystery we now explore.

Notes

1. Philip Kitcher, *Life after Faith: The Case for Secular Humanism* (New Haven, CT: Yale University Press, 2014).

2. Barth, *Church Dogmatics*, II.1, The Doctrine of God.

3. Aquinas, *Summa Theologica*, I, q. 7, a. 7, sed contra.

4. Aquinas, *Summa Theologica*, I, q. 7, a. 7.

5. William Frank and Allan Wolter, *Duns Scotus, Metaphysician* (Purdue, IN: Purdue University Press, 1995).

6. Duns Scotus, *Philosophical Writings*, trans. Allan Wolter (Indianapolis: Hackett, 1987), 72.

7. Scotus, *Philosophical Writings*, 72.

8. Scotus, *Philosophical Writings*, 77.

9. René Descartes, *The Philosophical Works of Descartes*, trans. Elizabeth Haldane and G. R. T. Ross, vol. 1 (New York: Dover, 1955), 166.

10. Descartes, *Philosophical Works*, 164.

11. Alexis Meinong, *Untersuchungen zur Gegenstandstheorie und Psychologie* (Leipzig: Von Johann Ambrosine Barth, 1904), published in English as "The Theory of Objects," in *Realism and the Background of Phenomenology*, ed. R. Chisholm (New York: Free Press, 1960).

12. Descartes, *Philosophical Works*, 166.

13. Descartes, *Philosophical Works*, 163.

14. Descartes, *Philosophical Works*, 162.

15. Francisco Suárez, *Disputationes metaphysicae* (1597), in *Opera omnia*, ed. D. M. André, vols. 25–26 (Paris: Vivés, 1866); *On Beings of Reason*, ed. and trans. J. P. Doyle (Milwaukee: Marquette University Press, 1995); and extensive translations into English of the *Metaphysics* by Sydney Penner.

16. Descartes, *Philosophical Works*, 171.

17. This way of framing Cantor's theory is adapted from Jonathan Bain's lecture on ordinal and cardinal numbers in his fall 2006 course on conceptual mathematics at Polytechnic University, now part of New York University. http://faculty.poly.edu/~jbain/Cat/lectures/07.OrdsandCards.pdf.

18. David Hilbert, "Über das Unendliche," address to *der Westfälischen Mathematischen Gesellschaft* in *Mathematische Annalen* 95 (1926): 161–90.

§ 7. The Divine Persons

And the LORD descended in the cloud, and stood with Moses there, and proclaimed the name, "The Lord." And the Lord passed by before him and proclaimed, "The LORD, The LORD, a God merciful and gracious, slow to anger, and abounding in steadfast love and faithfulness, keeping steadfast love for the thousandth generation, forgiving iniquity and transgression and sin, yet by no means clearing the guilty, but visiting the iniquity of the parents upon the children and the children's children, to the third and fourth generation." (Exod 34:6–7)

We now come to the end, the telos, and the completion: the Divine Persons in Their Relations. They are the End, the Completion of the Life of God, yet in turning now to the Divine Persons, in one sense, we must say that we say nothing new. Indeed, the doctrine of the Divine Persons can only repeat, confirm, and secure what has been said about the Divine Life, the Processions of God. *In one way,* then, the doctrine of the Triune Persons has nothing to add to Triune doctrine. The Persons, too, exist in the category of Relation, the Doubling in the Relation of Identity. They are not the real subject matter of the dogma, as if it had a centerpiece like this, and They are even less the reflection of the revealed economy up into the Eternal Godhead. They re-say—double—the doctrine of the Procession(s) in the language of the Whole, the Absolute.

The intensive concentration on the doctrine of the Persons sparked by the explosive debates in the early church about the Missions—Their full equality, Their Deity without subordination, Their "Preexistence"—this rich matrix of argument, conceptual clarification, and, yes, puzzle cases does not properly concern us here. The Divine Persons do not emerge from the economy! The *Missio Dei* will afford full scope for the complex and sublime reflections on time and Eternity, the proper notes and properties of the Sent Ones, the Divine Life that is Eternal yet now creaturely—but these are not the material of the eternal dogma of the Holy Trinity. Here we must say that the Persons in their Relations simply and properly sum and complete and rehearse all that is the Divine Life in Its Self-Offering and Consummation. Yet this doctrine is not less for all that. It is the end, the *final* word, and, in just this way, the telos of the entire Mystery. The Triune Persons just are the Lord God *as Name*, as the Life who is God as Subject, as Agent, as the Lord who does wonders and remains faithful to the thousandth generation, forgiving iniquity and sin, yet not clearing the guilty, unto the third and fourth generation. Here in the renewal of the covenant, the Lord discloses, proclaims, *Himself*: He is the I AM, who is Loving and Just, who is Covenant and Mercy, Word and Pardon. In His very Being He utters Himself, giving His Name again and again, revealing to Moses His Character as *moral* and *rational*, His Properties of *Hesed* and Mercy, Blessing and Grace and Covenant. The One who stands before Moses has already disclosed His entire Goodness, passing before the friend of God, in His Hidden Majesty: the Lord God is entirely and wholly Commandment and Goodness, the Eternal Ratio and Law. Before this One we bow down in adoration; at this Name we fold ourselves down, close to the earth from which we spring, acknowledging the Glory who is God and adoring His Mercy. After the great apostasy of the golden calf, the

Lord God does not leave us to our pitiful dissolution but binds us again to Himself; we become His, in this servant over all His house, lowering ourselves before this One who exalts us, carrying us on eagles' wings to Himself.

The doctrine of the Divine Persons, for us mortals, is the joining of proclamation and worship, the expression of Leviticus and Exodus. In the Divine Processions, we read Leviticus in light of Exodus; in the Divine Persons, we read Exodus, the Proclaiming God, in light of Leviticus, the Living and Holy Fire. In both we seek the full meaning of sacrifice, the Complete Holiness of the Living God. In both we stand humbled before the God who is the Fiery Glory of Israel, the Merciful Law of the Eternal. Certainly, we acknowledge and draw our life from this Lord who draws near us, but here we raise our sights above, to the Lord in His own Proclamation, His own Self-Demonstration and Self-Sanctification. We consider, in our own poor words, the Aseity of the Thrice Holy God. He stands before us as He Who Is, the Living Lord, the Merciful Word.

We do not *add onto* God and His Life. The Divine Persons must not be considered Someone or Something Apart from the Processional Life: They are not additional elements or dimensions within the Living God. The Divine Persons, rather, are the Processions taken as a whole, as Absolute. They stand in the Relation of Identity, as Doubles. They are the Reprise, the Confirmation of the Life of God. They speak of the Infinite Life of God as a Set, as a Consummation of the entire series, seen sub species aeternitate. They are not now the Life, the Generation and Spiration, the Descent and Ascent in the Majestic House of God, but are rather the Rational Goodness of the Whole, the Names of the Agential Mercy of God, wholly One, wholly Distinct, utterly Holy. The Persons *consummate* the Mystery of Trinity. They are the Living God in His Absoluteness, His Infinite Perfection. His Divine Action is the pattern of sacrifice, the Fire that proceeds and consumes, lifting the Offering to Himself. But His Divine Name is the Lord, Merciful and Just, Commandment and Pardon, Word and Loving-Kindness. He calls Himself this One; He enacts Himself in His Name; His unutterable Majesty stands before us in this Proclamation. The Heat and Light of the Divine Fire are shown to have Absolute and Intellectual *Names*: not mute powers, not inert forces but Intelligent Agency, Rational and Commanding Goodness. In the doctrine of the Triune Names, we encounter and think in our small concepts the Living Being who is Sovereign, who strikes the earth with the Rod of His Mouth, who is Alpha and Omega, Commandment and Mystery. We sum up our doctrine of God in these Divine Names.

Now, notice the force of saying, in one sense, "there is nothing new here." This is the Relation of Identity. We cut against a long tradition in Trinitarian theology that has treated the doctrine of the Persons as a separate treatise, with dogmatic vocabulary all its own. This is the rich Augustinian and scholastic reflection on Persons and Relations, those of Origin and of Mutual Opposition. This nomenclature is designed to bring us into greater clarity about the interconnections of the Persons and Their Ordering in the Godhead. Indeed, in much Trinitarianism, early and late, the gracious task of the dogma of Trinity *begins* with Persons and Their Relations. The Divine Processions are seen under the governance of Persons: the Father *generates* the Son; He or They *spirate* the Spirit, or in an Augustinian inflection, the Spirit Personally enacts and hallows the Love between the Two.

Yet there are glimpses, even within this Person-centric tradition, of a Naming that is a verbal echo of the old. For St. Augustine, for example, the treatise on the Persons takes on a grammatical and rhetorical form through his analysis of "relative predication": in Christian speech we recognize predication that is "Substance-wise" and that which is "Relation-wise," Substantial and Relative in category, we might say. Here the already legendary influence of Aristotle's *Categories* gives voice to how a Christian properly reads the *Carmen Christi* and Paul's First Letter to Corinth. We see the Son, now lower than the angels, a Son of Man, and now exalted and glorified once again in the Form of God. The profound reflection on the Son leads Augustine through the complex terrain of Triune Relations—and they in turn to the Missions, especially of Incarnation—with an anxious eye alert always to the Spirit and His Relative Nature as Love. Some of the most complex writing of *De Trinitate* is given over to the proper taxis of Son and Spirit and the deep puzzlement over the distinction between the Two—why the Godhead does not generate Two Sons; yet the Spirit remains a Person, a distinct *Nomen*, not a Force only. Of course, much of this fascinating book is devoted to an intense investigation of the Pauline corpus and the Gospel of John, but the Old Testament is hardly ignored. Indeed, the central distinction, canonized under Augustine's influence, between a theophany and a Divine Mission can be traced to Augustine's deep meditations on the Descent of God to His people under the Old Dispensation. But once again, the prominent note that is sounded is that of *Person*: Is it the Son who walks among the people Israel? Does the Spirit descend to prophet and priest? Does the Father dwell in the midst of His people, in law and temple? The economy of our salvation leads Augustine again and again to the inner Life of God, the Aseity; he dares to read the Scriptures as the book of the Immanent Trinity, a vital and life-giving venture. (We can only hope to follow his lead here.) But Augustine's fundamental instinct is not only grammatical but also the conviction that the Persons are the *Agents* of the Divine Triunity, the Ones giving rise to the Other and communicating the Nature through particular acts of Generation and Procession.

We might say that for Augustinianism in general, the Processions are ordered to the Persons: They give rise to One Another through the Life-Giving Acts. (And here we do not follow Augustine in this inversion.)

Springing from this focus on the Divine Person as Agent is the close attention paid by Augustine to the Aristotelian category of *relation*: we predicate the Persons in their relatio, One to the Other. Augustine gives us a Trinitarian rule (one echoed and developed by the Cappadocians): we speak of the Persons as mutually entailed. The Father, Son, and Spirit, as Names, give the Christian the impression that we must worship *Three*; the air of autonomy or separation among the Persons seems implied by these distinct titles and names. But Augustine in a stroke undermines this threat. He discovers in these Names a *relation*, a necessary implicature of the titles themselves. Father *entails* Offspring: Son. Son necessarily implies Parent: Father. We cannot have One without the Other. Later scholastic tradition will refer to this implicature as the "relations of opposition": Father requires but is not the Son; the Son depends utterly on the Father and is not the Parent. In this narrow sense, They *oppose* One Another. This is a relatio in which Two are necessary, but They are not identical, not analytic. Rather, They stand on opposite ends of a relation: the Father begets the Son; the Son is the Only-Begotten of the Father. Augustine makes this plain through his use of relative predication. The Begetter begets the Begotten; the Only-Begotten is begotten by the Begetter. We might think of this as a categorical reflection on the very notion of Begetting. The idea of Generation or Begetting rests on a Generator, a Parent, an Agent of the fruitful relation. But it entails also the fruit of this Act, the Offspring, the Begotten, not made. "This Day have I begotten Thee": this verse from Psalm 2, cited at the Son's baptism by John, anchors the entire investigation over the relation among the Divine Persons. Augustine considers this divine relation as mutually defined: Begetter known by the Begotten; the very sense of Begotten in the idea of the Begetter, the Generator.

Perhaps it is reflection along these lines that leads St. Thomas to the complex and obscure notion of a "subsistent relation." The Generator-Generated might be considered a single Complex, a Relatio with Two Teloi, the Origin and the Terminus. What exists, Thomas suggests, is not a Person, with an external or accidental relation to Another, but rather the Relation, Generation, with Its mutually entailed, mutually defined Poles, Father and Son. Just this Relation in its Complexity, its Twofold-ness, is the Divine Persons. Perhaps this is how we should read the Augustinian legacy in the Thomistic teaching of Subsistent Relation.

Readers will be quick to note—as Augustine knew all too well—that very little has been said here about the Procession and Person of the Holy Spirit. This troubled Augustine deeply, as it has students of the Latin tradition from the earliest days. We might think of Sarah Coakley's analysis of the Father-Son dyad in *God, Sexuality, and the Self* as the last in this distinguished line.[1] The problem leaps to the eye. It seems rather natural, though perhaps odd, to speak of the Father and Son as two Ends of a mutually defining relation; though these are familial Names, They contain, not too far below their smooth surfaces, the notion of Agency and Passion, a Paternity and Filiation. The mutual dependence of the One on the Other—true for the Father as it is for the Son—seems caught up in the very idea of "family" or "ancestry," the "generations" of patriarchs in Genesis, the "genealogy" in the Gospels. It is as though in this family relation we spy the shadow of "event metaphysics": the "substances" or "things" just *are* the event of reproduction, taken as a Subsistent or Name. But language and life do not seem so ready to help in the matter of the Holy Spirit and His Procession. Just where is the "natural" implicature between Father and Spirit, or more pressingly, between Father, Son, and Spirit? We do not seem to discover a Relatio that entails the Two (or Three), and we do not seem invited to meditate deeply on an Act, even Procession, that leads us to distinguish and relate the Spirit to the Father or Son.

Augustine is at pains to acknowledge this very problem; he is convinced that what is true for the Father and Son must be true for the Spirit in His origin and mutual relation. The Christological form, tied back to the Philippians hymn, *must* also apply to the Procession and Person of the Spirit: this, too, must be a matter of relative predication, of a "relation of opposition." Just this Christological conformation, we may think, troubles Coakley from the start. Her "Spirit-impelled" doctrine of Trinity suggests an inversion of the Augustinian pattern. Now the Son and Father will be conformed to the desiring impulsion of the Spirit. But Augustine cannot rest content with such reversals. The Spirit, too, must be an Internal Relation within the Godhead. (Much about the primal "starting points" in theology and the axial definition of Holy Scripture can be seen here, in the pressure Augustine's Christology exerts on his doctrine of Trinity.)

Augustine reaches for the notion of Gift. The Letter of James stands ready at hand: "Every good and perfect gift comes down from above, from the Father of Lights, in whom there is no variation or shadow due to change" (Jas 1:17). A small step joins this verse to the ample New Testament witness to the Spirit as Gift: poured out on all flesh, given by the Son in His Ascension, resting on Mary as Blessing and Life and on the apostles like flame, radiating out from their commission and fearless proclamation of the Risen One. Augustine proposes that we consider Procession a form of *donation*, Giver and Gift. To be sure, this is not all that Augustine says; *De Trinitate* is a tireless unfolding of fresh ways to conceive the Spirit in the intimacy of the Generation of Father and Son. But he comes to rest on Gift as the most familiar, most readily recognized Relation that entails an Agent and a Passion, an Origin and a Goal. No Giver without Gift; no Gift without the Giver. This is a relation of opposition, a mutually defined relatio in the Spirit's Presence within the Triune Life. We know from Romans 5 that the Gift given is Love, poured into our hearts by the Spirit, the final fruit of a hope that cannot wither, cannot run dry. As below, so Above: the Spirit just is that Gift, that Love, donated by Father and Son in their utter dependence and fruitfulness, One to the Other. The Persons, for Augustine, cannot be but mutually entwined, Each in All, All in Each, just because the intimacy of Love emerges from, hallows, and fructifies the mutual dependence of the Father and Son: They give and are given in turn.

Now this is a lovely vision! It would be a stony heart that did not see Augustine's intellect ablaze with the Love that animates the spheres. But it is a vision born of a difficulty, a solution forged from a worrying inconsistency. Of course, Augustine felt this! He was more alive to the riddles and constraints of this dogma than any of his readers—his greatness can be measured by his restless intellect, searching for answers, never yielding, never complete. He faced squarely the dynamic but caustic power of a governing idea in the Mystery of the Triune God. "Relation" is this governing idea; its ground is the Mystery of the Incarnation. We reflect deeply, recursively, on the Generation of the Son; we recognize His Deity and seek His proper place within the Godhead. From this intense devotion to the Divine Son is born the celebrated trios of De Trinitate: Lover, Beloved, Love; Mind, Intellect, Will; Memory, Word, Love. Within the severe constraints of creaturely analogues, Augustine sets before us an intricate chain of images, each proposing a lively relation among the three, each showing the agency of the nouns, acting and receiving the whole of the other. But hovering over the whole is the relation of generation: the Father's begetting of the Son is the governing pattern of the Triune Relations.

For this reason, the Spirit must be found to conform to this Generation, yet in such a manner that the Spirit is not Son. Giver and Gift conform to the pattern of relative predication; it mirrors formally the Father's generation of the Son; it follows and does not lead in the ordering of Divine Relations. The Holy Spirit is the Fruit of the Son's loving generation. All of this is good, even very good. But the constraints are evident here and pull against the whole. We have to find—discover—the pattern for the Spirit that conforms in this way and follows this taxis. Indeed, we might say that the very idea of taxis just is this complex: the Father's generation of the Son as Ground and Priority of the Procession of the Spirit. This is the reason Augustine will not stop his search for proper Divine Names at the biblical word *Spirit*. Of course, he acknowledges that Name, but he must press on to find another word that expresses a relation of opposition, one that mirrors the Son's dependence on the Father, the Father's entailment of the Offspring. Perhaps, we must say, that this simply is the limit of creaturely striving: all our doctrines carry the air of contrivance, of invention. Perhaps creatures can do no better than this, and Augustine's is the best of our kind. Just this confession makes the intellectual defense of the Mystery of Trinity vexing, perhaps even illusory, and turns the adventurer in this dogma into the safe harbor of traditionalism. I do not want to take this lightly, as if this volume alone could shrug off constraints and human frailty and stare deep into the open Mystery of God. No, the Holiness of the Triune Lord cannot be so breached, for He is a Consuming Fire. But we must say that the priority given to Persons in relation, to Mutual Opposition, and to Personal Acts exerts special pressures on the dogma of Trinity. Just so the very notion of Person carries particular weight in the dogmatic work of the Immanent Trinity.

Now, Augustine is famous for denying the probity of the entire question about the character or nature of a Divine Person: "What is a Person? Why do we say Three Persons? So that we can answer the question, Three what?"[2] We will have to take up this question in turn. Indeed, Augustine's very tentativeness in wading into the already controverted matter of the Divine Person brings to the fore the Relation of Opposition between Father and Son. If we cannot define a Divine Person, we can at least affirm that the Two spring from the event of generation, Father acting on the Son. Perhaps the accented place of Agency in Augustine's investigation of the Generation of the Son inspired later Augustinians to seek once again a proper definition of the Divine Person. Boethius's celebrated definition—an individual substance of a rational nature[3]—found its way into most later Augustinian treatises on the Trinity, including Thomas's *De Deo Trino*. The stern intellectualism of Augustine's analogies makes the rationality of the Person a natural correlate. Of course, a Divine Person is a Rational Substance! But the modern worry over the nomenclature of "Person"—a worry catalogued by Karl Barth and Karl Rahner in full cry—can be detected already in Augustine's measured hesitation before the definition of the central term *person*.

The worry is straightforward and serious indeed: Do we not have Three Substances, Three Individuals, Three Agents here? Is that not Tritheism? How can *person*, defined as did Boethius or as moderns do—an individual center of consciousness, say—be deprived of a distinct will, a distinct agential power, an autonomy, if only in definition? Gregory of Nyssa's fateful analogy in "On not Three Gods" seems primed to raise the fears of Tritheism: in some way, as we argued earlier, we are to imagine God as three human individuals, three men, instantiating a single human nature. Of course, Nyssa had no dreams of smuggling three gods into the Heavenly City under the cloak of darkness! His analogy must have been intended in another way—perhaps, as suggested earlier, as illuminating how natures are not divided by the distinction of individuals. But of course, the specter is now in full view! John Zizioulas or Catherine LaCugna aim to ward off this profound rupture within monotheism by pointing to the definition of the Person as *ad Aliam*, toward Another. A Divine Person "tends" toward the Other, loving and sustaining and endorsing the Other, or stronger still, finding His own Reality in the Other. But this intimacy of the wills cannot but summon up the memory of Lateran IV, the ruling that such unity of sociality is not the Transcendent Oneness of the Triune God. Yet the attempt to confine the damage by refusing a definition does not stem the tide, for we have before us still the Agents in Relation and, above all, the governing pattern of the Father begetting the Son. A Person of some distinctive dignity, One who acts, and who intends His action, who *loves* it, *loves Him*, seems all but defined as Individual of a Rational Nature but by words. We need not rehearse the wearying tale of modern attempts to make such Trifocal doctrines palatable or even delectable to Christians; this is the social Trinitarianism that guides the humane practice of communitarianism and intimate, equal regard. All hail these aims! But Three who consent, who love, who elect and dirempt the Self, who give without counting cost, who suffer and obey, who give of their own to fund Another's life—remain simply Three, by any *counting*, at least.

I think we can insist that these Three are One in some radical, unconventional fashion, perhaps considered scriptural or nonmetaphysical or perhaps, in an Augustinian nod, beyond definition—but this is a Oneness that defies thought. We may have other reasons for demurring from social Trinitarianism—perhaps on grounds of the radical Creator-creature distinction—but here we must ask whether the intense focus on *Persons*, Their acts and relata, have not made the Unicity of God a distant country. It is the *novelty* of the Persons and Their technical architectonic, in subsistence but also even in concept, that weighs heavily on the Mystery of Trinity, breaking our attention and worship of the One God to fix on the Agent who gives rise to the Son, who breathes forth His Spirit. I cannot think that our fealty to this One Lord of Heaven and earth has been properly deepened and straitened by the novelty of focus on Persons in Relation and Their priority in Trinitarianism; indeed, I fear much the worse.

And yet. Has not Augustine—and his disciples, early and late— put his finger on just the neuralgic center of all Christian discourse? Has he not drawn the final line between the Old and the New, between Theophany and Mission, between the Days of Promise and the Days of Fulfillment? Has he not spoken rightly of the Divine Son? Can this Divine *Hapax* be nothing to dogma—to the final Mystery of Trinity? Is not the doctrine of the Persons just this, a proper notice and reverence and intellectual confession of this One *Novelty*, the Eternal Son, made *manifest*? We stand here before the axial question of the divine economy, the Incarnate Son, the heartbeat of scriptural life. We do not ask here about the warrant or starting point of the Mystery. That is a deep matter of theological method we have aimed to treat in our opening reflections on the Old Testament as ground of the Triune Mystery. Here we ask after something more urgent, more tantalizing than any methodological query about the economy. Our brief excursus into the depths of Augustine has led us to a proper, *the* proper, *dogmatic* question: Does the very idea of the Divine Person demand from us a confession that something *new* of the Eternal is enacted in creation? Has the delicate relation of time to Eternity not now inserted itself into the dogma of Trinity? Or to put this in more familiar epistemic idiom: Have we indeed said nothing new when we speak now of the Eternal Persons of the One Holy God? Is this in truth a Relation of Identity, an Echo or Doubling? Is it not rather a Divine *Novum*? This is not, strictly speaking, a puzzle over the "Preexistence of the Son," an oddly formed worry all its own. Rather we ask whether, in the dogma of Trinity, the Divine Persons in Relation are fully, properly, and exactly captured in the Fiery Procession(s) of the Holy God of Israel's temple. If in Holy Scripture we encounter God—we find Him there—then the novelty we quietly affirm in the phrase *New Testament* now becomes the skandalon of event in the One God: the Word becomes flesh. In this Divine *Missio*, are we to see something we had not seen before? Is the language of Person and Relation now the idiom of the canon itself?

This is a nest of problems, at once epistemological and metaphysical, that can but haunt a theology grounded in Israel's Scriptures as is this one. If we begin with the Processional Life of the Living God, must we end with the Personal Acts, Their relations and oppositions, the Old now taken up and redefined by the New? Is this just what we must mean when we see that of old God spoke in many and various ways, but now He speaks through the Son? Has Augustine, in his profound meditation on the Son's Eternal Generation, not said just what remains to be said and said it truly? Is the Gospel not the *epoche*, the rupture of the Mystery of God in the center point of time: the disclosure of the Living God as the Father and Son, joined intimately in Divine Love? It is cheap for us moderns to say that Marcion was wrong; of course, the Old Testament, we say breezily, must be part of Christian Scripture! But have we actually wrestled with the problem Marcionites, early and late, have pressed on us? Have we reckoned with full seriousness, reckoned *dogmatically*, with the Disclosure of the Son? We must ask especially here: Is this not saying something new, because *something new*, *Someone* new has appeared?

Now, one easy way of dissolving this knot is to press down firmly on the epistemic lever in this whole complex. We could say, after all, that there is, there can be, nothing new *in God*; rather, our form of speech only and our concepts evolve. Not God but we change. This is an attractive solution, certainly, and a natural one. We develop the dogma of Trinity as a species of the qua problem, outlined earlier: the Living God of the holy temple is now known *as* the Triune Relation of Persons, Father, Son, Spirit. The same God now known as another Name. We apply a linguistic solvent here—fresh idiom for an Eternal Reality—and we affirm the traditional Changelessness of God. This is a form of propositionalism in theology: in the new covenant, God gives us new information, new language, for an old Truth. There is truth in this solution: certainly, the Mystery who is God will remain One, the Self-Same, as our knowledge and worship and chastening deepen and expand and grow. Indeed, this is one semantic way of interpreting the phrase, "We say nothing new here."

But a theology built on theological compatibilism, as is this one, cannot rest easy with a full-throated epistemic solution. All this is not merely *verbal*. Our words cannot be so cleanly distinguished from their Referent, nor can the new Names represent but a semantic change, a kind of empty synonym for an older Title. No, if God in His Aseity makes Himself known in our poor words and praises, the elements of Trinitarian dogma that hit our ear in novel fashion must themselves *refer*, pick out something New. Just this is realism in theological discourse. Luke the Evangelist calls this moment the "fulfilled time," the kairos, when the Son is disclosed on earth. Under the Providence and Mercy of God, the Divine

Person *as such* is manifested. We speak of this as the Divine Mission, and the Mystery of this Gift and Sending must be explored properly in its own place. But even here we must reflect on the place of the concept *person* within the Eternal, Unchanging Immanence of God. How should we define and use this Trinitarian term of art? How does the Old stand in relation to the New? How is the Gospel of Jesus Christ tied and related to Israel's covenant, the Eternal, Old Dispensation? In Trinitarian dogma, we stand before the mystery of the canon of Scripture itself. Trinitarian theology comprises, in its inner core, the neuralgic problem of supersessionism in Christian doctrine.

Jesus said: "Do not think that I have come to abolish the law or the prophets; I have come not to abolish but to fulfill [*pleroo*]. For truly I tell you, until heaven and earth pass away, not one letter, not one stroke of a letter, will pass from the law until all is accomplished [*ginomai*]" (Matt 5:17–18). Here in our Lord's teaching from the Sermon on the Mount is the instruction we are to lay to heart. Just what is this fullness, this pleroma and consummation, that Christ brings to the Law and Prophets? How is the iota, the stroke, come to its fullness, in the work accomplished, brought to pass, in Jesus Christ? To answer these questions is to answer the mystery of Scripture's canon, the mystery of the New in the Old. Here we find our instruction about the Triune Person and His relata within the Fiery Holiness of the One God. Here we find the proper Referent and use of the word *person* in the Mystery of God. Here is the balance, the proper relation we seek, between Old and New, Eternal and Temporal, the Everlasting and the Taking Place, within the Mystery of the Triune God. In His teaching from the mountain— the "new Sinai"—our Lord tells us that He, the Messiah, comes not to annul the Law, not to strip it away from even its smallest ornament, but rather to *complete* it, to perfect and stabilize it, to confirm it till

Heaven and earth pass away: to render it Eternal. For this reason, the fullness spoken of by Christ here rings the changes on the Heavenly fullness, the pleroma, that is the Replete Presence of God in His own Realm, the Highest Heaven. It is the completion of every last thing, the full measure, the rounded existence, the Eternal rest that is the haunting silence of Divine Fullness. It is this sphere, this perfection, that Christ brings to the Law and Prophets, His Mission for which He came. All must be accomplished, everything completed and laid down, all fragments gathered up, all the broken mended, all made whole when the Law can live without its jot and tittle. The whole outpouring of figure and event and uprising and calamity we call the Gospel narrative must be made whole, come to pass, in order that the work of Christ may be accomplished: this is the fullness of the Law and the Prophets. Here is laid the foundation, the security, and firmness of Israel's treasure; here the complete and perfect rest from exile and loss, from decay and abrogation, from striking down and rooting out, has been accomplished. The Old has become the Perfect, the Consummate, and though heaven and earth pass away, the word shall stand forever. Here we see the Alpha become the Omega, the Perfect realizing and filling to the brim the Origin, the Primacy of all things. This is the proper relation between the covenants, the proper tie between Moses and Christ, the true pattern and eventful movement between Prophet and Fulfillment. From this teaching we learn the proper place of the Divine Person, the Ratio, Donum et Lex, within the Living Holiness of the Eternal God. We learn here, from our Lord, just how to say the New, that is the fullness of the Old—just how, in the Mystery who is God, to say, in a new way, in *Redoublement*, nothing new. The Twofold Identity of the Processions guide us here, too.

The Divine Persons in Their Relations are the *Fullness* of the Sacrificial Fire. This is what it means to say that the dogma of the Holy Trinity is found and warranted and taught in Israel's Scriptures. It is not to deny the significance of these New Names, nor to ignore as though insubstantial the covenant forged in the holy blood of Christ, nor to treat as an empty repetition the Scripture poured forth by the witness of the Risen One. Rather, it is to see even in these small frail human words of doctrine, these stabs at the Exceeding Darkness who is the *Lux Mundi*, these icons and terms and technical burrowings that compose the church's dogma, to see even here the relation of *consummation*, of *Perfection*, who is the Personal God. Notice that we do not mean here something that is now filled up, as though it were once empty; something that is made complete, as though it were but half finished; something made right, as though it were once wrong. No! This is not the pattern of *Consummation*. Were we to see this completion, perfection as the emending of the wrong, the amending of the unfinished, we would happily shear off the jot and tittle; indeed, we would be wrong not to annul, not to set aside, not to correct and begin again. Just so are we to renounce idolatry, to break down walls that separate, to reject the false teachings that make our ears itch, to throw down all the high places and high necks, raised against the Lord's Heaven. Israel is shown the narrow way; it is taught the life it should choose, the death it should abhor; it is chastened, corrected, instructed in the path it should go. These proper, narrow ways are *replacements*, abolitions, rejections of idolatry and defilement. Not everything is of the Lord; not everything is acceptable and clean and right. But not so are we to receive the Law and the Prophets. They are not half-truths, waiting for a Clearer Light. They are not a partial step, even less a false one, waiting the Correction. Jesus Christ is the new Moses in just this providential and dogmatic sense of novelty: He *confirms*; He establishes; He renders perfect, complete, and whole the Law of Moses as the Divine Will of the One God. Nothing is lost, but all is gathered up. This is the New as the Absolute, the Consummation of the Old. It says, with authority, and with fresh command: nothing new. As the Holy Eucharist does not make fresh sacrifice but re-presents the one, perfect, and complete sacrifice of the cross, so the instruction of Christ does not promulgate new law but presents with complete authority the old as the eternal law, given by the prophet Moses. Just so, the Divine Persons of the Holy Trinity say nothing new to us in the doctrine of God but fulfill, perfect, and consummate the Holy Fire who is the Living God. A Divine Person, we can now say, is *the Consummation of the Divine Life*. It is the Spiritual Life, the Consummate Spirit, who is God.

Now, just what can this mean? We are attempting to think through carefully here, faithfully and exegetically, what it can mean to say that our Lord is a *Living* God. Of course, the long exploration of the Divine Procession(s) began this conceptual work. We unfolded there, through a meditation and investigation of Holy Scripture, the form and progress of the Living Agency of God with His people, its depths and heights, its chastening Fire and Wrath, its kindled Love and Mercy, even to those who dwell on His Holy Mountain, feasting in His Presence, its costly Self-Offering and Sanctity. This is the Fire who is the Holy Lord, the Life of descent and ascent that is God's own Offering in His own temple. But this scriptural language can dull our ears to the *conceptual* explosion that is the metaphysical claim to a Living God. It is, certainly, an easier path—a royal road, really—to Divinity to set aside the notion of Divine Life altogether, to consider Deity an Abstract Noun: the Idea of the Good, say, or Transcendent Truth, or Reality Itself. These are not false! We could never honor the proper Objectivity of God were we to cast away the Perfect Stasis of God as the Right or the Good. And it is not quite sufficient, on the other hand, simply to insist that God is Subject as well as Object, though, to be sure, that is true. We have not fully penetrated the Mystery of Divine Life by affirming that God is Agent or Subject or Eternal I AM in the midst of His own Nature, though we gratefully confess these truths. The task before us is to take up this *conceptual* work, to consider within the doctrine of God what life, Divine Life, can mean for our understanding and worship of the True Lord. How can we *think* the familiar biblical confession: the Lord lives?

"The Lord lives" must include a vitality—a synonym, really—and a *movement*: it must double within identity. Even a sessile creature possesses the motility of its own internal production and reproduction. To say that our God lives is to affirm that there is animated motion, concourse, that is the interior Reality of God. Just this we see figured in Holy Writ in the searing image of Fire. At once diffuse and centered, at once without borders yet possessed of an inner core, dynamic, explosive, ranging and withdrawing, illumining and charring: Holiness as Life. We are to consider Almighty God as Living Holiness in this way, a Self-Movement that is the danger of True Goodness. It must be, then, that Deity as Immaterial Life exhibits and enacts a Movement that is Its very own Nature. The conceptual material for such a claim is not easy to find. It seems far simpler, more cogent, to claim that movement, as such, is the province of the material. Just this, we may think, undergirds René Descartes's massive reconceptualization of all material bodies as res extensa. Movement appears to require a notion of *space*: from here to there we move and take up a new position, a new coordinate. Yet Descartes stands, too, in a long line of Augustinians for whom *thought* itself is immaterial motion. Aristotle's "self-moving Thought" captures the conceptual affirmation of cognition as a form of "inner movement"—a phrase put to wonderful use in Thomas's *De Deo Trino*. (We may well wonder whether the anxious worry in contemporary philosophy of mind about the supervenience of thought to brain may reflect this unease about immaterial movement.) Holy Scripture, however, does not easily revert to the concept of God as Living Thought.

This is not the problem of anthropomorphism that seems to bedevil philosophical theism. We do not have to worry, or worry away, the scriptural comfort with divine arms or hands or figure, moving majestically through the garden in the cool of the evening. Not these as obstacles to conceptual work but, rather, the confident conviction, in the Bible, that we encounter a Lord who is beyond form and likeness yet lives and moves. It seems that the sages and prophets, kings and midwives, forlorn widows and sojourners, all turn toward and invoke the Name of the God who is somehow "whole," more than thought, more than a motile cogito, yet Living Invisibility. Israel's Scriptures insist on a God who can pass a creature by in His Full Goodness; who can sit on something like a sapphire throne; who can forge ordinances and precepts and write them with a divine finger, molten with righteousness; who dwells in light inaccessible; who cannot be seen but in death. Almighty God does not comport well with a "floating head," or, in more philosophical parlance, a "brain in a vat." Again and again, Holy Writ tells us, in parable and prophecy and theophany, that the Lord God is not a "part" of an agent, even an elevated and exalted one; the True God is a "whole," a complete spiritual Being. Just this we glimpse when we watch Scripture boldly affirm that the Lord is Being Itself, Life and Source, yet this very One: He Who Is. The Individual and the Universal belong first and properly to this Holy Being. In every aspect of scriptural depiction, the God of Israel exhibits and is the whole of Personal Reality, the Complete Presence, joining Particularity and Universal Jurisdiction, locality and utter transcendence, Mystery and Commandment. This in scriptural genre is the subject matter of a Living God, Immaterial yet Mobile, Personal, Whole, Dynamic, yet Beyond and First and Above all things.

Of course, it would be conceptually smooth, the wide and easy path, to conceive of God as an exalted creature—the Man Upstairs, as we colloquially say, in a revealing turn of phrase—and think of the Bible as an ancient text enamored of plastic and volatile deities. This would be a primitive notion, soon to be replaced by the sleek and supremely refined Divine Cogito or Dunamis. But Holy Scripture refuses to bifurcate the Divine Life in this crude way. Israel worships a God who is Personal, Bounded, and Concrete *and* who is Invisible, Imageless, and Holy Immaterial. The task of a dogma of the Holy Trinity is to attempt to think *this* thought, the Bounded Infinite Living One.

We are not to consider the Lord God first as a Nature and then affirm It moves, as do most creatures. We are not to borrow Aristotle's notion of an organism as self-moved and, through remotion, apply it, elevated and purified, to the heavenly throne room. No, God is not a human subject who upon consideration and election moves to its desired end—or wards off a threat to such delicious self-will. Rather God just *is* Life; He does not simply possess or exercise it. God's very Reality is Alive, an Eternal Movement, a Supercelestial Flame, directed to His own End, Its Consummation.

Now it has puzzled seekers after God since Pythagoras how a Being so defined—transcendent, immaterial, eternal—could live, could possess its own Self-Motion. Naturally mathematical analogues entice: the rational generation from a principle, the algorithmic procession of sums, the logical deduction from premises—all seem to possess a certain form or shadow of movement, a beginning and end, without embodiment and, in some cases, without temporality. The wonderful complexities of the transfinite must surely fall within this school! But the ancient seekers after God knew also the

Benevolence and Intellect of the Most Real Being; God was not "Number" in an exhaustive sense. The confession of the people Israel traveled over the same ground. This worship and praise knew, too, that the Lord God moved, lived, and, more, was Life! Yet this Lord was beyond form and image, could not be seen with the creaturely eye, burned with Holy Fire, and inhabited Eternity. Such a mobile Nature must be both Dynamism and Purpose: God must be the Event of His own Substance. Just this Thomas aims to capture in his crystalline phrase "the Pure Act of Being."

Now such an Eternal Life has a Novelty that is Ever-Old, Ever-True. A Living God just is the Happening, the Explosion that is Eternity. Platonists have strained to express this Event as the Eternal Now, the *Nunc Stans*. But we need not express this metaphysic in temporal terms; indeed, it is better, richer, to speak in Substantial idiom, for it is the Divine Reality we seek here. There must be a Going Out and a Coming In, an Origin and End, a Movement from Above to Below, a Procession and Return, an Exile and Welcome, that just is God. This is the Life who is God, beyond thought and imagining, yet Sublime, Intimate. It transfixes our gaze, this Living One; It is our highest thought. There is no emptiness, no collapse, no finitude in this God; He is the Infinite One, Endless Life. Yet He is *this very One*. He is set off, set apart, *definite*. He is not a diffused force, not an irregular being or property, not spent, not weary, not utterly general or random or chaotic, but Ever Fresh, Springing Forth, Glorious and True; He is *this* God and not another. This is the Bounded Infinite, the Holy God.

Into this Eternal Mystery, we elevate the idea and Name of Person: the Consummation and Perfection of this Everlasting Life. There is Novelty here; that is the first thing we must affirm. It is not an empty gesture that we see in the proclamation to the shepherds from the Angelic chorus: *this* Day a Son is given. We do not now train our sights on the Divine Mission, the Incarnation of the Word. That will find its proper, its glorious place. But we dare to think here about the Reality of the High God we are to discern in the events in Bethlehem. We learn about the Triune Mystery here as the shepherds gaze up into the Highest Heavens, watching the Silent Music take wing to its home. The Liveliness of the Immanent Trinity is being taught here in the manifestation of the Child of Bethlehem. What we are being shown in this great, glad tiding is the *Name* of the Son; the *Name* of the Spirit in whom this Son is born, Holy and Great; the *Name* of the Father in Heaven, extolling His Beloved in the waters of repentance: this Day the Son is begotten of the Father in the descent of the Spirit. Even as the Son *ascends* in the Spirit on Resurrection Day, so the Spirit *descends* on the Son's baptism: the Two movements indwell and are One. These Names are the integuments of the New Testament, the Divine Structure of the Gospel. They are new, but as a fresh expression and doubling of the old. For Israel, too, knows a Name theology: the Lord God makes His Name to dwell in Zion, and to this temple, Israel brings its whole burnt offerings and its praise. Deuteronomy glorifies the Divine Name, dwelling in the midst of Israel, and Psalm 89, a covenant psalm, dares to make the Name known. Not simply the Lord, but David will cry out to Him, You are my Father, my God, and the Rock of my salvation! The Personal Names that dominate and structure the New Testament *enact* the Name theology of the Old; they are novel as the confirmation, completion, and exaltation of the old. But they are not Names only! We are not to imagine that we have simply added an address to the God known as Lord; it is not simply a *description* we are given here—though certainly, it is that. We are being shown, in the humble heart of David's city, what the *Divine Event*, the Divine Life, means. We stand before the Terminus of the Divine Movement, the Goal and Perfection of this

Life. We stand transfixed before the Unfolding and Consummation of the Divine Act who is God. Bethlehem, the House of Bread, exhibits the Perfection of the Eternal God.

This is Old, of ancient times. The Novelty of the Divine Person is the firm Constellation of the Eternal Life who is God. Something *happens* in David's Royal City; we do not shrink back from the Angel's proclamation. We dare to say that it happens *in* God, in His Transcendent, Glorious Life. Our doctrine of Holy Scripture demands that we encounter Almighty God in these books, these parables and wise sayings, these healings and teachings, these ordinances and statutes, these fiery, smoky offerings. The axe head floating upward, the rains drenching down on a sin-sick earth, the fire ascending up from water-soaked altars: in all these, in every dark corner and luminous passage, we find the One, Eternal, Triune God. His Aseity haunts these pages, and we are to hunger after It, to seek this Star and come with our treasure chests, to learn of Him there. For this reason we must come to understand that the New Covenant proclaimed and established in Israel, under Caesar's rule, takes place *in God*. We must dare to say this. But it takes place not as do events on this earth, not in creaturely time, not under the old enemy, death, that robs and empties and scatters. No, the New takes place *as the Old*, like the Processions themselves; it twins what was and always shall be. For the Lord God is the One who was, who is, and who is to come.

What we strive to think here is the Absolute as Tri-Personal Life. G. W. F. Hegel has given us the marvelous idea of an Absolute that *becomes*, a Dynamism that moves out from "Lifeless Identity," the "play of concepts," to plunge down into the world of suffering and change, to put on Immortality, to achieve Absoluteness, the Consummate Idea. Of course, Hegel thinks nothing but Christ and Him crucified: this is conceptual work forged from the death of

God, the Passion of the Beloved Son. But we do not follow Hegel in *this* way; this is not a theology of the Cross or an extended reflection on the Incarnation as central axis of the doctrine of God. Yet we receive thankfully from Hegel the bravura claim that Becoming and Absoluteness can be thought together, a contradiction that expresses truth. In the lectures on the Consummate Religion, Hegel can dare to argue that the Divine Idea can journey through history, be clad in it, and emerge from its radical diremption, its land of unlikeness, into an Absoluteness that always was. Perhaps this can only appear to us, outside Hegel's system, as sleight of hand: borrowing, it seems, from the definition of Absoluteness, Hegel insists that what is Absolute was always so, yet it becomes this. We might think of this as a backtracking counterfactual of a supreme sort, an Event that outdoes itself. We gladly see in him a Christian philosopher who aims to render scriptural event in *concept*: Hegel thinks the Living, and the Dying, God. Just so, in the Mystery of the Holy Trinity, we aim to think the Eternal Event of the Divine Person, the Ancient Novelty of the Triune Name.

It seems that Holy Writ demands that we consider deeply a form of expression and conceptual work that verges on equivocation, even contradiction. Everything in Trinitarian—and Christological— speech appears to skirt the very edge of the unintelligible, the contradictory, the irrational and paradoxical. At times Christian thinkers seem to revel in it: where are Søren Kierkegaard or Paul Tillich without the paradox of Christ? But others seem drawn to bitter waters, yet drink they must. Think of St. Cyril: the Lord Christ who suffers death impassibly; or the Cappadocians, for whom the Lord of heaven and earth descends into the small chamber of a room in Bethlehem; or perhaps we may dare to say, the apostle to the gentiles, for whom the One who possesses the form of God as His birthrite becomes slave, becomes empty with humility and scorn.

The events of Incarnation and Passion seem hell-bent. They take on the radical dissolution of thought in the journey of the Living God to the dark caverns beneath the earth. Hans Urs von Balthasar's *Mysterium Pascale* rings the changes on this self-contradiction of faithful thought—and not just that of Christology. The doctrine of God brings the Christian to the lonely territory of a Subject who is Object, a Unicity that is Trifold, an Immateriality that Eternally Elects to become flesh in time, an Ancient One that becomes Ever New. This is biblical thinking in the realm of concept. It is likeness in the Ocean of the Ever-Greater Unlikeness.

But all this, we dare to say, is *not* contradiction! We are not readying here, at the close of a long discourse on Trinity, an apologia for paradox or contradiction. No! God is not a Divine Impossible, an Eternal Self-Annihilation, in which what must not, cannot be, is. Such caustic disintegration of thought, Barth tells us, belongs only to Nothingness, the supreme opposition to God; the primal chaos the Good God abhors and rejects.[4] This Good God cannot be an exalted form of conceptual evacuation: He is the Truth, the Light, the Tri-Personal, the One. Yet we cannot ignore these contrary statements and their power. They are not simply apophatic. We do not aim to make use of opposing concepts as a Dionysian trajectory into the Ineffable. These Names, the Ancient Novelty, are not simply the sign and springboard of a conceptual idiom which cannot refer, cannot denote, its Unspeakable Reality. Nor are we seeking a form of Kantian resolution through a transcendental maneuver: we do not take these Names, nor the Christological contraries, as signs of irresoluble conflict—antinomies, paralogisms, amphibolies—that force us to reconsider the very task of philosophical reasoning. (I take Tillich's doctrine of symbols to rely on a Kantian-style claim about the proper use of theological language and referent.) This is not a covert transcendental move.

Rather, we aim to follow Amandus Polanus in his conviction that in Divine Things in order to "say one" we must "say two."[5] This is the lesson Bonaventure teaches in the Mystery of the Father; it is the lesson of the Processions, Two that are One. This is not strictly speaking a form of apophasis or an appeal to a discourse beyond direct referent but rather an affirmation that two predicates must be applied to the Most Holy God, both meaningful and proper, both true, and their form of application to be a Mystical Repetition of the Nature of God Himself. To say "God," the One, is to say these "two things," knowing that they are One in the same fashion that God exists. We say His Reality when we say that "Two are One": He is Ever More Unlike, He is Distinct from creatures, He is Mystery and Lord. I say that these contrary pairs denote the *Mode* of the One Holy God: we refer in this way to *how* He is God. Readers of the apophatic school of Thomism will recognize some parallels here to Thomas's claim, in the famous quaestio 13 of the *Prima Pars*, that positive predication of God is possible, necessary, and proper, though we do not know *how* such predicates, multiple, distinct, and definite, are utterly One in God. Such claims have often been viewed as a form of ineffability—nominalism, Barth called it[6]— where distinct Names and Attributes of God were emptied of (ordinary?) meaning by the insistence that in the Simplicity of God all particular predicates are in truth Identical and One. But I think we need not apply Thomas's dictum in such a straitened fashion. We might take Duns Scotus to have developed and codified a Thomistic position: "formal distinction"—Scotus's term for a proper, multiple, and distinct predication of the One God—might capture, in truth, the force of Thomas's original claim. We say "two" and we know it means "one," and we affirm the two, in their proper semantic force— God truly is Just and Merciful, Justice and Mercy, is Generation and Spiration, is Alpha and Omega, Son and Spirit from the Father—and we acknowledge that to ask how this is so is to simply say God, to say His Glorious and Transcendent Being and Nature, that which Is and Is Beyond. This is not to affirm contradiction, I say, but rather to affirm that God, the Utterly Unique and Holy One, *is*.

His mode of Being is His own, the Incommunicable, the Sublime: He does not conform to our creaturely being or idiom. In considering the subtlety and complexity of divine predication, we simply are placed before the exceedingly difficult task of conceiving that Something Other than the cosmos and its finite beings exists and is Real. To think *this* thought, that the cosmos is not the full reach of reality, is to conceive of a Form of Being, fully Real, Distinct, Definite, that is not creature and does not conform to creaturely structures and idioms. It is not irrational, not the kenosis of reason, to borrow a bon mot from Christology. The Modus of the Triune God is the Luminous Reason of Deity Itself, Its Holy Ratio. The Lord may and has communicated with that which is not God—the Incommunicable is Communicable—but retains Its own Majesty, Its own Peculiar Being in the midst of Its Self-Giving. All this we aim to catch up in the idiom of contrary predicates, the Novel Eternal, the Ancient New, the "One" that is said as "two." Just so do we say that the Divine Names are the Novelty of Ancient Times, the Event of the One past all shadow of change.

So, we must press on to render conceptual, as much as is fitting and proper to us and our frailties, how the Event of the Gospel is the Consummation of the Name given to Israel. How is it that sacrifice, the temple fire that consumes and consummates Its own Self-Offering, is that Divine Life and those Divine Names made Perfect in the Event we call the New Testament? It must be that we are granted permission to stand in the place of shepherds and magi, of a young woman of great sanctity and her husband, a righteous man, in the midst of the animals of the stall and field, to gaze with them on This Reality that has taken place, the Event of the Eternal God. We are seeing the birth of the Names, Father, Son, and Spirit, as the Ancient Names, made new, made Perfect. This is the birth of the Absolute. It must be, then, that in the inner Life of God, the Processional Life of Heat and Light, of Holy Fire in Its Full Burning, we catch sight, in our own creaturely twofold-ness, of the Dynamism who is God, Pouring Forth and Coming to Sabbath Rest in the Trifold Name. This must be an Eternal Event that breaks forth into our realm, our time. It sears the earth. But It belongs to Heaven. To say that God is Life, the Living One, is to affirm that God "takes place" as the Procession turns over into Person. At Bethlehem the heavens are torn open and mere creatures glimpse in our human way the Energy that is the Mystery of Trinity, the Divine Impulsion that lights up Eternity, moving and descending and ascending through ranks of angels and the heavenly host, triumphantly coming to Its Rest, Its Perfect End. This Procession terminates in the Persons, and They are the Consummation of the Divine Life, Its Eternal, Unchanging Perfection.

Now, we might consider a creaturely analogy for the Divine Persons and Their Life: the bounded infinite of the transfinite number. Of course, this is a finite analogy, a "speaking two." But it is a proper analogy because God is the Measure, the Order of the cosmos, the Perfect Law, and possesses what Thomas finely calls a transcendental number. (This is a number that does not "count"; it is not an enumerator.) We take the notion of the transfinite number from the doctrine of the Divine Processions and now apply it to the Doctrine of the Persons, the Consummation of the Divine Life. Georg Cantor's controversial innovation, we remember, was to take the classic mathematics of the infinite, grounded in geometry and figure, and move it into the realm of the formal and logical, the province of pure thought. In his exuberant essay of 1905, Bertrand

Russell crows about the utter collapse of old school mathematics under the iron fist of the formal infinite.[7] Logic is the basis of mathematics, Russell asserts in his vivid apodictic style, because it is the very structure of reason, and the infinite set is its trophy. As we noted earlier, Cantor proposed that we can simply take an infinite string of numbers, integers or irrationals, and consider them *as a whole*: an assembly or set. A set, we said, is not anything beyond its members; it simply gathers them together as a whole. We need not import the complex problems of class nouns and individuals or of universal natures and their instantiations. Importantly, sets do not represent a separate conceptual category: they are a deflationary term, indicating only the elements, gathered together. (Think of a set of dining room chairs: nothing more than the chairs themselves, considered as a group.) We can measure them through an ingenious method of "correlation," or "bijection." The natural numbers, as a whole, can be placed in one-to-one correspondence with the odd numbers, for example; they have the same number of members, share the same "cardinality." Yet not all infinite sets are the same "size, or order." The transfinite number can be expanded on, giving it a fresh "ordinal," an unimaginably huge series of infinites. We perform mathematical operations on these sets—rather odd ones, it turns out—but recognizable from the world of natural numbers and shop-counter arithmetic. This confirms what Cantor imagined: that the infinite could have finite properties without losing its identity as infinite. (Just this is expressed by the neologism, transfinite number.)

Cantor was reaching for the *theological* significance of the infinite set and dedicated much of his late work to this theme—along with an ill-fated journey into Shakespearian authorship. Cantor knew that God must be the Absolute Infinite, the "Omega," as he styled it, not the creaturely infinite, the transfinite set. Yet, like Descartes,

Cantor saw the analogy: he thought the idea of infinity and found it twofold, creaturely and divine. Certainly, this way of expressing the God-world relation posed dangers. Critics were quick to seize on the Spinoza-like assimilation of Divine Infinity to the rational and logical infinite. But Cantor would not be drawn. A devout Lutheran, he remained firm in his conviction that the notion of infinity opened windows onto the Godhead; he was dazzled by the sight.[8]

For our part, we catch sight, at great distance, of the Triune Persons when we contemplate the notion of the infinite set. If we do not lean too heavily on this distinction, we could say that as in the Processions, we focused upon the *Infinite* Set, so here, in the Persons, we set our eyes upon the Infinite *Set*. (We say nothing new here.) Here we are offered the chance to think about the whole, the boundedness of the unrestricted, and the nature of that completion. Consider that brief example of the set, parenthetically mentioned above: the set of dining room chairs. Now I claimed above that this set was "nothing more" than its members—the chairs themselves. We know this commonplace use from the retail convention of selling objects "as a set." This does not mean that we acquire six dining room chairs, say, and then heap into our shopping cart an additional item, the set. No, it means something else: we buy these chairs altogether, not à la carte, and we may even consent to this because we, too, think they "belong together." But in truth, anything could be a set. We could round up oddments in our apartment and declare them a set—perhaps of "present-day furnishings." But we need not supply a category at all; no class noun is required by the notion of a set. We round them up, we point to that grouping, we say: here is a set! Notice what we are doing here conceptually.

The notion of a set allows us to consider as a whole a random assortment of objects, nouns, ideas, even events, without discovering or assigning a genus or universal to which they belong. A set is a way of indicating *completion*; it belongs wholly to the members, and adds nothing to them, and constrains or defines them in no way. A set simply announces the members have assembled together. In one deft move, set theorists have offered us an escape route from the conflict sparked by Gregory of Nyssa's treatise *On Not Three Gods*. Sets do not form "upper-level" categories, such as "natures" or "kinds" or "universals." We need not worry that we now discover, ranged before us, four "things": the three disciples, Peter, James, and John, and their human nature, a "fourth," on some more Platonizing readings. (This threat of infinite regress worried Aristotle and led him to affirm the inseparability of form and matter.) On some accounts, the universal "furniture" might be "something else" in addition to the dining room chairs: an ideal, perhaps; a measuring rod and definition; an existing Idea or Form; a kind of artifact. But sets achieve nothing in return for their labor. They simply signal that the gathering together has ceased, and a whole has been brought to mind. Infinite numbers of objects, infinite numbers of integers, rational and irrational numbers, can be made complete in this fashion—or so Cantor claims. We cannot think the whole set—we do not know the last number in the series of integers, we cannot— yet we can declare them whole, a set, and denote it through the convention of the ellipsis ({1,2,3 . . . }—the set of infinite integers). Two insights emerge: the insubstantiality of the set itself, and its compatibility with some forms of ignorance, even great ignorance.

Mutatis mutandis: the Divine Personal Life as Infinite Set. When we speak of the Divine Persons, we say nothing new: *this* is the manner in which we say this phrase. The Divine Life just is the Lord's own Fire, His Nature as Living Sacrifice, that is both Blazing Heat and Light, the Generation and Descent of the Divine Glory, and Its Ascent Heavenward. When we speak of the

Triune Person, we say nothing new: we speak rather of this Life as *Complete*, as Consummate Whole. The Person, we might dare to say, is Infinite Life "as a Set": It is nothing above or in addition to its "members." And this we can confess despite our utter worship of the Divine Mystery, the Infinite and Holy God who in His Greater Unlikeness cannot be measured and comprehended by our poor and sinful intellects. We bow before this Mystery. It may be "clear and distinct," were we Cartesians, but only in this sense— we think Infinity under a condition of Completion, a Whole and Absolute. This is the Boundedness of Infinity, the Definitiveness and Concreteness of God. Almighty God is *this* Name, *this* Father, Son, and Spirit, One Holy God. These are not Divine Individuals, were there such; or "Parts" in some Divine Manifold, were such possible; or distinct Faculties, were the One God to have "compartments" in the Divine Life. No, this is not three wills, not three separate agents, not three parts, and, most certainly, not three gods. What this analogy permits us to think is a *mode* whereby the Processional Life, in its Primal Origin, Its Self-Giving as Begotten and Consummation in the Spirit is One God. This Living Energy is a Set, a Completion as the Divine Persons, and as Infinite Sets, added together, They are but One, One Cardinal, Ordered Infinite. What is new in this *applicatio* is the recognition that there are "boundaries," definite structures that signal a Whole Gathering, a Set. Nothing scattered, nothing diffuse or disordered, but rather a Perfection, a Gathering to a Greatness: that is the Novelty enacted in the Telos of the Divine Name, the Persons.

We need not and we cannot describe the Divine Persons. They do not possess "character traits" or properties of distinctive "personalities"—not ones that are given to us mortals, at any rate. In its own place, we will explore the scholastic notion of appropriation, whereby the distinctive roles and properties of the Divine Missions are "appropriated," assigned by fittingness and need, to the Eternal Persons, without laying claim to knowledge of the Persons *A Se*. This is a central task in the discussion of the temporal and relational properties acquired in the Act of Creation and the Sending of the Persons. The Nicene Creed is a compendium of those Appropriations, composed as a litany of the Triune economy. Indeed, it is just this notion that distinguishes the Missions from the Eternal Processions: their determination, by sovereign grace, by the exigencies and demands of creaturely time. But even in this place we can say that the Divine Person, as such, does not possess a "Separate Existence," a "quasi-substantial" Identity that stands over against or beyond the Divine Life It consummates. We resist here the idea, advanced with great brio by Robert Jenson in his *Systematic Theology*, that Divine Persons are "Identities," Dramatis Personae, disclosed in the Event of the Resurrection of the Crucified Son. "God is He who raised Jesus Christ from the dead," Jenson writes in an epigraphic maxim.[9] Of course this is the natural move to be made by those theologians for whom the economy is root and foundation of all theological knowledge. But we have done our best to ward off such a foundation and gladly "appropriate" the "speculative" dimensions of a confident scholastic tradition, Protestant and Catholic. Just this is signaled by the prominence given to the Divine Procession(s) and by the continual search for the Divine Aseity in the midst of scriptural knowledge and worldly vestigia.

Augustine is right, then, to resist a definition of *person in this sense*: there is no separate Res, no distinct Object or Enumerable Nature that *is* Divine Person. A Divine Person is not a "Thing," so to say, that could be defined or characterized or studied—or counted even—apart from the Life that It perfects. Rather, we see the Divine Fire *as a Whole*, a Perfection, and as an Infinite Life we do not know It exhaustively or completely. We know, rather, that It is Completed, an Absolute. Note the passive construction here. We cannot specify the Reality of this Perfection or articulate the "entire membership" of the Infinite Life; we do not know the Personal Processions "from the inside," as it were, from Its own Principles, as Thomas would style this. This is the Greater Unlikeness. We know and confess and adore Its Being Completed, the Persons' Consummation and Sabbath Rest. From the creaturely view we behold the Whole Life in Its Integrity, Its Termini, and we receive the New Name, ever Ancient, of Father, Son, and Spirit, all Holy, Thrice Holy.

How can we cease praising this Divine Sabbath Rest? Six days the Lord has labored and fashioned all that is, and on the Seventh Day He rested and declared It Holy. The Glory of Almighty God is the Movement that does not rush onward frantically or ceaselessly, an Impulsion that knows no rest, no Stopping Place, no Abiding Place when evening has come and the day is past. Almighty God is not a Verb *in this sense*: He is not a perpetual Gerund, ever busy, ever producing or expanding or striving. *His* is not the "Spirit of capitalism." He is the God of Peace, the Eternal Sabbath, sweet and full of rest. We creatures go forth to our labor until the evening; we till the fields of thorn and thistles; we bear our children in pain; we search and strive and find no rest. This is the poverty of the children of Eve. The poor of this earth know what it is to work without ceasing; only they are denied any "useless hour"; only they know the cruelty of life that is only labor, seeking more work, more "odd jobs," more miles from wearied bones, from broken-down cars and long-delayed city buses; only the poor must endure the cold fact that their children's school play or schoolwork or illness must go on without them—for they must work, work only, and seek work. On hard-scrabble farms, in small shops and hidden factories, in polluted and defiled places where none but the poor will work: these are the hellish places on our earth where rest is never known.[10]

But the Living God *is* Rest, Holy Rest. He it is who is Life; who lives and in his Personal Will welcomes into being His creatures; who never dies, never grows faint or weary, yet comes to a close, marks the morning and the evening, gathers to a Completion, and blesses that Rest. Peace is the very Life of God. *This* is the Meaning laid down in the Divine Event that is the Lord's Fiery Life. In the end we may say that *this* is what we mean when we speak of God as Holy, the Hallowed One. The Lord sanctifies Himself in just this way: He gathers the Divine Life to its Rest. The blessed dead enter into the Peace who is God when they fully rest from their labors, when they fly away from the life that is labor and sorrow. For us creatures, the end of striving is cessation, death, the last breath; for Almighty God it is the Personal End, the Consummate Life. In just this way we can hallow our deaths in this small measure: we can glimpse in this rounding off of our lives the creaturely expression, the mortal analogue of the Sabbath Rest who is God, and we pray in our death to be gathered to Him in this small likeness, both ended, both at rest. As the Days of Creation are One yet several; as they swarm with life yet draw to a conclusion; as they are ranked and ordered, yet blessed and altogether very good, so Almighty God, the Triune Lord, is Eternal Life that marks and determines its End. To worship this Holy God is to reverence a Perfect Life, an Eternal Movement that has entered into Its Absolute Silence. This is the Peace that passes all understanding.

It seems as if we must now be ourselves at an end in the setting forth of the Mystery of the Holy Trinity. Is this not already the consummation of doctrine, to speak of the Divine Absoluteness and Sabbath Rest? Yet the dogma of the Holy Trinity speaks of Three Persons, and They in Eternal Generation and Spiration, in

One Nature, One God. Have we spoken properly of this Triune Mystery? Have we spoken of Three? Has the "twofold-ness" of Processional Fire, of Exit and Return, of Universal and Concrete, of Eternity and Novelty captured, or even intimated, the Eternal Giving and Begetting that always was and never comes to an end? What can we say about the Divine Relations, of Origin and Opposition, and their relation to the Divine Nature? Is the Spirit the Fruit of the Father and the Son, an Eternal Procession as from a Single Principle? How can these Persons indwell One Another, Distinct and Inseparable and One? The consummation of this dogma consists in these doctrinal questions and the technical distinctions they enjoy and demand. What must we say; what can our theological affirmations permit us to say, about these necessary and holy matters?

We must say first that the canon of Holy Scripture teaches us that Divine Persons forge and follow the order and direction in the Divine Life. The Novelty that is the Event of the Triune Names confirms the Personal Motion of the Holy God as He explodes forth from the temple. There is now a Name to this Explosion, an Origin who is a Divine Person. This Origin, this Primal Beginning, is the Father in His Primal Mystery, the One whom David knows as his own Father and Lord. This Absolute Origin takes David as His king; Benjamin as His Son, close to His heart; Israel as His child, sent down into Egypt for shelter and nurture, called out from there as the Lord's own son. The pouring forth of the Fiery Glory of God from the temple sanctum is now Named: the Origin of this Holy Fire is the Father in His doubled Mystery as joined eternally to the Son. The whole people Israel, sustained, enslaved, delivered, is as creature, the Father's son, as is the great king, David, the shadowing forth of the Name of the Son. The Father's Self-Offering, the fiery descent onto the altar table, the Complete Breaking Open and

Giving of the Father's own Life just is the Son, as the Self, Offered, the only Name given under Heaven for health and salvation. The Dynamic Life that drives prophets and seers, that animates speech and law, that knits parched bones into life: that is the Name of the Spirit, the fruit of the Self-Offered, ascending as the Eternal Holiness of God.

But this Name, though now given, is saying in its own sense nothing new. For the Name is but the Eternal Life, the Procession(s), considered *as a whole*. Like a set, a Divine Name is nothing over or beyond the "members," the Processions. We do not have an additional "Reality," a Novelty that is "quasi-substantial" or an "innovation" in the Being of God. No! The Name is the Complete Holiness of God, His own Fiery Life taken as a whole, as Perfection. For this reason, the Name uttered in the Heavens over Bethlehem's fields is in truth the re-presentation, the Summing Up and Consummation of the God declared to Israel. For just this reason, Christian doctrine can never supersede, replace Israel's teaching. The Divine Persons just are the One Holy God, taken in His Absoluteness, His Totality. They add nothing new; they are no Addition or "Happening" in the Life of God; the Lord God does not "become" Triune. Rather, the Set that is the Divine Procession(s) has an odd, a unique relation to time—as is proper for the relation of the Lord God to His creature, time. This Eternal Movement out from the Sanctum and Its Return is Perfect Motion, a Complete and Absolute Life. It does not take place in time, and it is not enacted or "spread out" over any era, even that of Holy Israel. Rather, Trinity simply *is*. Just this is what we mean by "Eternal Generation," "Eternal Spiration." But this Structure is Eternal in a Divine sense: It *lives*. The Names given as Gospel confirm that the Lord God is Eternally *thus*; they secure and confirm what has been burned into the memory of people Israel. The Donation of the Divine Names is backward-looking. It elevates and takes up the Whole of God's inner Life, manifested in temple and ark, sacrifice and Spirit of prophecy, and declares Its Name as Perfected Whole. The past is *canonized*. Even in the Novelty of the Divine Names, we say nothing new but rather double, echo the old.

The Sacrifice welcomed Home, the Complete Welcome and Sweet Savor, the Ascent and Utter Rest: this is the Ancient Novelty of the Name Holy Spirit. The Sacrifice of Israel now culminates in the Personal Names, and They in order: the Father is Personal Origin of Life; the Son, the Complete Personal Oblation of that Life; the Spirit, the Consummation of the Whole, the Perfection of the Full Divine Life. The Personal Names trace the Eternal Movement from Alpha to Omega, the ordo and taxis by which the Life of God is to be praised and prayer offered in His Name, the Completion by which the Fire who is God is Consummated, rendered Holy, rendered Absolute.

This taxis Eternally takes place. The Event of God's Bounded Life, bursting forth, drawing to its Perfection, inhabits Eternity. Yet it is Motion, Movement, Direction, and Life. The history of the scriptural canon unfolds *within* this Explosive Life. It is not quite right to say that in the covenant with Israel, blazed on stone at Sinai, and fulfilled in a stable in Bethlehem, worshippers of the True God now know an additional truth—the Personal Names of the Divine Life. Of course, this cannot be *wrong*; the acts of God us-ward are filled with Meaning, and they convey Truths as well as great Joy. But it is more proper, truer to the metaphysics of Holy Scripture, to say that the Eternal Motion of God, rendered Consummate in the Persons, forms the structure, the ark, of the canon. From the Sanctum to the Empty Tomb, the Fire who is God rushes forth to its Perfect Rest. These events that compose covenant and Gospel— the Law, Prophets, and Apostles—take place within this Eternal

Movement and find their definition there. Just this is what we mean by *canon*. The Complex that is the Holy Trinity of the One God breaks out over this small people, poised within mighty empire, and finds its closure in the witnesses to the Resurrection who speed on to the ends of the earth. They inhabit Eternity as do no other people, and no other worldly events.

We do not mean that Hegel is right—that God is a Temporal Event who takes up and creates history within His own Dynamic Idea. No! This is not a proper way to speak of the God-world relation, nor of Eternity and time. But Hegel was a sublime reader of Holy Scripture. Head and shoulders above the rationalizers of his day, Hegel caught sight of the riches, the depth, and mysterious power that are the Holy Bible; he knew that it *took place*. But he took away from that insight a conclusion that would shape his entire program: that the mysterious depths he saw unfolding in Scripture took place *within* God; indeed, it *was* God. He understood that Almighty God was Self-Moving Idea—a genius insight—but he believed it entailed a movement through contradiction and struggle in the land of time and things, issuing forth in Absoluteness on the other side of the Divine Son's Passion. The economy, we might say in modern idiom, is taken up into the Immanent God, and in diremption God unfolds as creature, rendered Absolute in the Divine Recognition of Its own Life as Other. This, we must say, even in admiration, is not the proper direction for a dogmatic doctrine of Trinity. Not from economy to Immanence but rather from Eternal Procession to Mission: this is the proper measure of God's relatio to creature.

We must argue for a doctrine of inspiration in the entire canon of Holy Scripture that conforms itself to the Event of the Triune Persons. Holy Scripture is strongly unique in just this sense: it, and the creaturely figures and events it paints, stands as something like the *sensorium Dei* Newton described long ago. (Of course, *only* "something like"—Holy Scripture remains strongly unique.) We meet God there because this Eternal Generation and Procession shelters and defines the people Israel. Israel takes place "within" the Divine Life in this sense: what is Eternal, what always was, overshadows the covenant people as It did the maid Miriam, and the Child of the Covenant, Israel and its King, are holy. This is a Bounded Infinite. The Boundary of the Infinite Life is the Movement from Father to Son and Spirit, the Set that simply is the Completion and Peace of the whole Divine Life. Holy Scripture, its onrush from Canaan to a hill outside Jerusalem, is Word of God in just this sense: it *takes place* as the creaturely corollary to the Generation of the Gift, received Home in the Spirit. Certainly, this is seen only by the eyes of faith. To its contemporaries, Israel was but the unhappy crossroads of empire, a sometimes useful, often troublesome backwater that belonged to the mere edges of the world. But to the faithful, Israel is the creaturely correlate of the Event of God, the People and Land that is molded by the Personal taxis who is God. When Almighty God determines that His Holiness receive an echo, a Redoublement, in creaturely form, Israel is born. Some kind of Sovereign "compression" has taken place here, whereby we see the long series of Israel's days *as a whole*, a set, and this creaturely set is unified before the timeless and Eternal Event of God's Personal Life.[11]

To be sure, we hardly know how to say any of this! I stand on the very edge of my conceptual arsenal here and can only hope to stretch what I have been given to see, to gesture toward this hapax that is the covenant life of Israel. This much, perhaps, we can say. We must affirm that the Triune Life of God is timeless: God is not a historical Being but an Eternal One: there never was a time when the Son was not. (On these grounds, Hegel might be considered a wonderfully sophisticated form of Arianism.) The people Israel is however fully historical and temporal, a full creature of the Living God. But it has been granted to see and live among the Dynamism who is God; it shelters there. (Perhaps just this is what we should consider the *force* of Thomas's teaching that Jesus came to teach the people the doctrine of the Trinity.) So, what is New is also and more properly Old; what takes place, also and more properly what always was. But this One Lord relates to Israel as to no other, making Its Personal Boundedness the contours of this people. It is a treasure unto the Lord. What is Transcendent impresses Itself on this people and its book: It communicates the Incommunicable and seals what is Eternal to the very structure of this creaturely history. That is Israel's holy life as echo of the Holy Trinity.

Now, this meditation on the divine taxis, as it breaks out over Israel, leaves still unanswered the question that haunted the doctrine of the Divine Procession(s): Are there Three Persons in God or One? Or in my refashioned language from Cantor: a Single Bounded Infinite Set or a Set of Sets, an Ordinal of the Divine Infinity? The Relations among the Persons, Their Origins and Oppositions, and the Perfection and Order of the Spirit must be clarified in any full dogma of Trinity; we turn to them now.

Augustine has given us the language of relative predication: the Divine Persons just are the Passive–Active Pair that constitute Their Relations. But how should this profound expression of the Divine Unicity be extended from Pairs to a Triad? This structural question troubled Augustine, and his anxiety is the whole church's worried care over the place and stature of the Holy Spirit within the Triune Godhead. Perhaps we might say that the neuralgic fever of the apocalyptic and the unconstrained outpouring of the charismata is the imprint of this dogmatic *aporia* in the lives of the faithful. Time and again, it seems, the church needs awakening to the Spirit, needs to excavate conceptual room for the Holiness of the Spirit within the Holy Life of God—not just the bourgeois historians of the gloriously immanent kingdom of God need the shock of the eschatological. The entire apparatus of Triune Personal Relations limps badly from a structural focus on the Pair of Father and Son in Relation, the Mutuality of Relative Predicates, the dominance in the Christian imagination of the Generation of the Son.

For manifold reasons, the first volume of this doctrine of God insisted in a rather brassy maxim that "not all is Christology!" But the weight of that maxim delivers its full force in the Trinitarian Mystery. The Personal Relations of the Holy God cannot be properly cast as a Central Pair—Coakley's Father-Son dyad—that can turn over in some fashion into a Second Pair, the Father-Spirit or, for the Latin Church, the FatherSon-Spirit. The Doubling, critical to any proper account of the Processions, and to the Mystery of the Father's Primacy, cannot be allowed to exhaust the whole of Trinitarian relations and structure. The history of the dogma in its early years must not become the Eternal Structure of the Triunity. Rather, the Spirit's late appearance, among the doctors of the fourth century, cannot be properly elevated into dogma, such that the Spirit is Third, not in *taxis* but rather in *stature*, in conceptual power. The full Deity of the Spirit, championed by the Cappadocians, by Coakley and many Orthodox and Pentecostal theologians, must be brought into the integuments of Latin Trinitarianism. The wonderfully subtle notion of relative predication needs expansion here: the Divine Persons in relatio must be a Structure *among* Persons, a fully Triadic integument. We must find voice to express the biblical insight, granted in some obscurity to the philosopher Hegel, that God is *Spirit*: He is the Consummation of the Consummation, the Absoluteness of the Divine Persons. He is Nothing New, nothing Subordinate or Discretionary; He is the

Eternal Perfection of the Godhead. The Sacrifice as It is welcomed Home is Complete: It is Hallowed, the Self-Sanctification of God.

So, the Relata among the Persons must be something like this. The Persons must execute, follow, and perfect the Processional Life of God, from Alpha to Omega, from *Exitus* to *Reditus*. They are Mutually Defining—Relations of Opposition—in that the Holy Sacrifice who is God is *Self*-Offering: the Father pours forth His Life which is the Son, the Perfection of the Father's Life, which just is the Spirit of Holiness, Perfecting and Rendering Complete that Fiery Love. (Students of *De Trinitate* will recognize the Augustinian imprint here.) In this way, the Relations of Origin and the Relations of Opposition join together, the Origin giving rise to the Mutual Definition, the Reception of Holiness that simply is Almighty God. The Spirit must Proceed from the FatherSon, just because these Divine Names are the Doubled Unity of the Fiery Life, descending and terminating in the Perfection that is Sacrifice, Self-Offering. The Filioque Clause in the Latin Creed should not be taken as a willful incursion and innovation to the Nicene Symbol; it is rather the proper expression of the Finality of God, His own Reality as Omega, that is the Seal of the Father's descent as the Perfect, as the Son. The Spirit is the Name of the Absoluteness, the Perfect Consummation of that Gift. It is *recursive* on Deity as a Whole. If we think of the Infinite Life of God, Eternally descending and illuminating the Divine Realm, we think of it as a Gathering, a Totality: that is Spirit. The Spirit names the Fiery Outbreak of Holiness, the Dunamis that animates prophet and seer, the Contagion that over-sweeps the encamped pilgrim Israel, the Sweet Savor that is the Well-Being of God. It is God as Absolute, Living Rest.

So, we do not attempt to find in the Names themselves the key to the mutual relata: we do not need pairs that define One Another *in this sense*. Of course, all students of relations of opposition have felt the odd conventionality of this task—such Divine Mysteries cannot be a "linguistic" or "grammatical" predication in an arbitrary and verbal manner. We are not simply looking for ways ordinary language can express relative predication! Once again, we recognize the importance of metaphysical over grammatical claims in Trinitarianism. At its best, the doctrine of relative predication aimed to find interlocking Names that relieve the pressure on Divine Unicity and showed how Three Names indicate One God. But odd elements have emerged from such familiar and devout aims. Trinitarian speculation has attached quasi-substantial descriptions to the Names, seeking some greater insight into the Divine Mystery by examining a father's love for his son or the pattern of likeness between generations. The scriptural declarations that "this Day the Father has begotten the Son" seems to impel theologians to "fill out" the Divine Persons with Agency and Drives all Their own. From the Victorines to modernists such as Barth, Jürgen Moltmann, and LaCugna, the "personal character" of the Father and Son, Their Love for One Another, the Obedience of the Son, has awakened in many minds the conviction that the Divine Persons have "personal centers of consciousness," aims and desires and sources of action. It has underscored a notion of Divine Person as Rational Individual. But there are not three such! The language of divine kingship or of Command and Obedience should not be elevated in such univocal fashion into the Godhead. Rather, the Divine Persons are simply Names of Infinite Sets, the Deity taken as a Whole.

We must see, rather, that the doctrine of Divine Persons invites us to contemplate Each as expression of the Whole: the Persons Altogether and Each name the Perfect Holiness of God, His Totality. This is the doctrine of Perichoresis that must govern the Divine Relata and keep watch over the Radical Unicity of God. The dogma of the Holy Trinity demands that we speak of Three,

Three Perfect Totalities that manifest the Whole God. And in just this way, They are One. The Lord God is One Acting Subject, not Three. Just this, we may think, animates Augustine's relentless excavation of the Pauline phrase: "Christ, the wisdom and power of God" (1 Cor 1:24). The Eternal Son must be Wisdom, he initially claims, and surely that must be true and a proper Trinitarian reading of 1 Corinthians. Yet it must not be the case, Augustine reflects, that the Father is wise through the Son's Wisdom—as though, in my idiom, the Persons represented "parts" or "aspects" or "faculties" of the One God. The Father must not be unwise in Himself, Augustine concludes, for the Father just is God. Therefore, the Father must *in Se* be Wise; the Son, Wise; the Spirit, Wise. The Persons in this sense are simply One: One Wisdom.[12]

The Incommunicable Existence of Each Person is Its Consummation, Its Telos, and Its Arche, of the Processional Life of God; yet Each just is the Whole. Just so, Each of these Names must denote and manifest the One God, the Whole, not "parts," were there such, or "Agencies," were we to grasp such singularities. This exacting lesson we must learn, and learn again, from Scripture's steady insistence on speaking of the Son and Spirit as "of the Father." Not "two hands," not "two emanations" or "instruments," but One God, in the Trifold Completion of His Perfect Rest. We must speak of the Divine Persons in the white-hot light of Unicity: the Origin, the Fiery Charring, the Reception and Welcome, Each must be God, Complete and Whole. To speak of God is to indicate and praise the One who is Fire. His Glory, given to no other, is a Burning. The Holy God is Utter Origin, none other. He is Holiness, a Consuming Flame. The Father of Lights is altogether Luminous, the Whole Light. The Son is the Perfect Burnt Offering, the Whole Luminous and Rational Gift. The Spirit is the Consummate Holiness, the Omega, who is God, the Complete Sacrifice and

Sanctity that is the Lord. The doctrine of mutual relations does not mean, cannot mean, that there is "less God" in the Son, the Spirit, or Father alone. No, these Names as *recursive* on the Whole means that Each says God, just this—not three agents, not three virtues or powers, not communion of wills but One God, One Agent, One Triune Lord. But it also means that they are not a bare "list." We do not have in the Divine Persons a congeries of titles, an ensemble of Names, carved out and collected from the scriptural witness. No, the doctrine of the Persons is nothing as externally related as all that. Rather, the Divine Names are recursive and consummative on One Another: Each contains All. This is the Mutual Indwelling of the Persons: the Totality that is the Person must contain the Whole, the Persons, Procession(s), and Nature. To say Spirit is to speak the Perfect Consummation of Self-Offering, Giver and Gift. To say Father is to acknowledge the Spiritual Completion of the Self-Giving who is God. The Son names the blindingly vulnerable Perfection of Self-Offering, a Descent from the Absolute Origin, in a Spirit most Perfect, most Holy.

But in the end, we must confess that the Spirit is the End who just is God. The Divine Life in Each and All terminates in the Persons: All are the End who is God. But the Spirit *names* this Absolute Holiness. He is the Holy Spirit. It is the Omega, the Reception of the Holocaust, the Perfect Peace that breaks out from Eternity. Sacrifice is the Name of God, but It is not imperfect or incomplete or a tearing and charring only. Sacrifice is Propitious, Effective, an Offering of Well-Being, of Sweet Savor. The Name of the Spirit speaks of the Gathering Together of the whole Act who is God: the End mutually defines the Beginning as well as Offered. The Spirit of God sweeps back over the entire Godhead, as over the primal depths. The Spirit is the Gift given by the Ascending Christ, the Holocaust who returns to the Father, to return again to His earth in the Last Day: the Spirit is the Last Thing. The taxis of the Persons remains in Their Circuminsession: the Spirit perfects the Origin who Offers Himself. So we can speak still of Event, Movement, Life in God, an Impulsion and Explosion, that moves from here to there, that unfolds as This and returns to Rest, yet this Life is the Eternal Act of the One who gives Himself, the One Perfected and Holy God in this Gift. The Spirit confirms and secures and re-presents the Whole Triunity: He is the Holy One.

The Lord is in His Holy Temple; let all the earth keep silent before Him.

Notes

1. See Coakley, *God, Sexuality, and the Self*, chapter 5 and pages 58, 101, 327, 330.

2. Augustine, *The Trinity*, trans. Edmund Hill (Hyde Park, NY: New City Press, 1991), book 7, chapter 3.

3. Boethius, "Treatise against Eutyches and Nestorius," in *The Theological Tractates: The Consolation of Philosophy*, trans. H. F. Stewart, E. K. Rand, and S. J. Tester (Cambridge: Harvard University Press, 1973), 84.

4. Barth, *Church Dogmatics*, III.3.

5. Amandus Polanus, *Syntagma theologiae Christianae, juxta leges ordinis methodici conformatum, atque in libros decem digestum* (Hanau: Wechel, 1609–10).

6. Barth, *Church Dogmatics*, II.1,

7. Bertrand Russell, "My Mental Development," in *The World of Mathematics*, ed. J. R. Newman, vol. 1 (New York: Simon & Schuster, 1956), 381–401.

8. On infinity and transfinite numbers see Cantor, "Foundations of a General Theory of Manifolds: A Mathematico-Philosophical Investigation into the Theory of the Infinite," trans. W. B. Ewald, in *From Kant to Hilbert: A Source Book in the Foundations of Mathematics*, ed. W. B. Ewald (New York: Oxford University Press, 1996), 2:878–920. Originally published as

"Grundlagen einer allgemeinen Mannigfaltigkeitslehre: Ein mathematisch-philosophischer Versuch in der Lehre des Unendlichen" in 1883. Also see "Beiträge zur Begründung der transfiniten Mengenlehre," in *Contributions to the Founding of the Theory of Transfinite Numbers*, trans. Philip E. B. Jourdain (Chicago: Open Court, 1915).

9. Jenson, *Systematic Theology*, 1:63.

10. Kathryn Tanner, *Christianity and the New Spirit of Capitalism* (New Haven, CT: Yale University Press, 2019). See especially Tanner's reflections on the compression and distortion of time, chapters 2 and 4.

11. Paul Griffiths, *Decreation: The Last Things of All Creatures* (Waco, TX: Baylor Press, 2014), part III, Timespace, esp. paragraph 16.

12. See Augustine, *The Trinity*, book 1.

Index